Essentials of the Legal Environment of Business

Version 2.0

Don Mayer, Daniel M. Warner, George J. Siedel, and
Jethro K. Lieberman

978-1-4533-8672-9

Essentials of the Legal Environment of Business
Version 2.0

Don Mayer, Daniel M. Warner, George J. Siedel, and Jethro K. Lieberman

Published by:

FlatWorld
175 Portland Street
Boston, MA 02114

Gen: 20190723

Brief Contents

Contents

About the Authors

Don Mayer

Don Mayer teaches law, ethics, public policy, and sustainability at Daniels College of Business, University of Denver, where he is Professor of the Practice of Business Ethics and Legal Studies. His research focuses on the role of business in creating a more just, sustainable, and productive world. With James O'Toole, Professor Mayer has co-edited and contributed content to *Good Business: Exercising Effective and Ethical Leadership* (Routledge, 2010). He is also coauthor of *International Business Law: Cases and Materials*, in its sixth edition with Pearson Publishing Company. He has taught business ethics at St. Mary's College of California, the University of Michigan, Manchester Global Business School, the University of Iowa, and Oakland University (Michigan).

After earning a philosophy degree from Kenyon College and a law degree from Duke University Law School, Professor Mayer served as a Judge Advocate General's (JAG) Corps officer in the United States Air Force during the Vietnam conflict and later went into private practice in North Carolina. In 1985, he earned his LL.M. in international and comparative law at the Georgetown University Law Center. Later that year, he began his academic career at Western Carolina University and became a full professor at Oakland University in Rochester, Michigan, where he taught for many years before moving to the University of Denver.

Professor Mayer has won numerous awards from the Academy of Legal Studies in Business, including the Hoeber Award for best article in the *American Business Law Journal*, the Maurer Award for best article on business ethics (twice), and the Ralph Bunche Award for best article on international business law (three times). His work has been published in many journals and law reviews but most often in *American Business Law Journal*, the *Journal of Business Ethics*, and *Business Ethics Quarterly*.

Daniel M. Warner

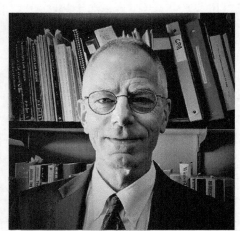

Photo courtesy of Western Washington University College of Business

Daniel M. Warner is a magna cum laude graduate of the University of Washington, where—following military service—he also attended law school. In 1978, after several years of criminal and then civil practice, he joined the faculty of the College of Business and Economics at Western Washington University, where he is now a professor of business legal studies in the Accounting Department. He has published extensively, exploring the intersection of popular culture and the law, and has received the College of Business Dean's Research Award six times for "distinguished contributions in published research."

Professor Warner served on the Whatcom County Council for eight years (two years as its chair). He has served on the Faculty Senate and on various university and college committees, including as chairman of the University Master Plan Committee. Professor Warner has also been active in state bar association committee work and in local politics, where he has served on numerous boards and commissions for over thirty years. He is a past president of his local water association.

George J. Siedel

George J. Siedel completed graduate studies at the University of Michigan and Cambridge University. Following graduation from law school, he worked as an attorney in a professional corporation before joining the faculty of the University of Michigan. Professor Siedel has been admitted to practice before the United States Supreme Court and in Michigan, Ohio, and Florida. He has also served on several boards of directors and as Associate Dean of the Ross School of Business at the University of Michigan.

Professor Siedel was a Visiting Professor at Stanford University and Harvard University, a Visiting Scholar at Berkeley, and a Parsons Fellow at the University of Sydney. He has been elected a Visiting Fellow at Cambridge University's Wolfson College and a Life Fellow of the Michigan State Bar Foundation. As a Fulbright Scholar in Eastern Europe, he held a Distinguished Chair in the Humanities and Social Sciences.

The author of numerous books and articles, Professor Siedel is the recipient of research awards from the University of Michigan (the Faculty Recognition Award) and the Academy of Legal Studies in Business (the Hoeber Award, the Ralph Bunche Award, and the Maurer Award). The Center for International Business Education and Research selected a case written by Professor Siedel for its annual International Case Writing Award. He has also received many teaching awards, including the 2014 Executive Program Professor of the Year Award from a consortium of thirty-six leading universities committed to international education.

Jethro K. Lieberman

Jethro K. Lieberman is Martin Professor of Law Emeritus at New York Law School, where for many years he served as dean for academic affairs. He taught at NYLS and at Fordham University School of Law for 33 years. Before that, he was vice president at what is now the International Institute for Conflict Prevention and Resolution (CPR) in New York. For nearly ten years, he was legal affairs editor of *Business Week* magazine. He practiced antitrust and trade regulation law at a large Washington law firm and was on active duty as a member of the Navy's Judge Advocate General's (JAG) Corps during the Vietnam era. He earned his BA in politics and economics from Yale University, his JD from Harvard Law School, and his PhD in political science from Columbia University. He is the author of *The Litigious Society* (Basic Books), winner of the American Bar Association's top literary prize, the Silver Gavel. Among his many other books are *Liberalism Undressed* (Oxford University Press) and *A Practical Companion to the Constitution: How the Supreme Court Has Ruled on Issues from Abortion to Zoning* (University of California Press).

He is a long-time letterpress printer and proprietor of The Press at James Pond, a private press, and owner of the historic Kelmscott/Goudy Press, an Albion handpress that was used to print the Kelmscott Press edition of Geoffrey Chaucer's *Canterbury Tales* in the 1890s. For a complete bibliography, see www. jethrolieberman.com.

Acknowledgments

The authors would like to thank the following colleagues who have reviewed the text and provided comprehensive feedback and suggestions for improving the material:

- Jennifer Barger Johnson, University of Central Oklahoma
- Dawn M. Bradanini, Lincoln College
- Larry Bumgardner, Pepperdine University
- Michael Edward Chaplin, California State University–Northridge
- Nigel Cohen, University of Texas–Pan American
- Mark Edison, North Central College
- Gideon Mark, University of Maryland
- Henry J. Hastings, Eastern Michigan University
- Henry Lowenstein, Coastal Carolina University
- Tanya Marcum, Bradley University
- Harry McCracken, California Lutheran University
- Robert Miller, Dominican University
- Leo Moersen, George Washington University
- Tonia Hap Murphy, University of Notre Dame
- Bart Pachino, California State University–Northridge
- Kimber J. Palmer, Texas A&M University–International
- Lawrence Price, Saint Mary's University of Minnesota
- Kurt Saunders, California State University–Northridge
- Ron Washburn, Bryant University
- Ruth Weatherly, Simpson College
- Eric Yordy, Northern Arizona University

The authors would also like to thank Vicki Brentnall of FlatWorld, without whose patience and graceful prodding this version would not be published. Thanks also go out to Nikki Ross of FlatWorld for her work on the PowerPoints and to Sean Wakely of FlatWorld for his guidance.

Dedication

Don Mayer

Dedicated to the students and faculty at Daniels College of Business, and to a very special man, Daniel Patrick Mayer.

Preface

Our goal is to provide students with a legal environment textbook, with cases, one that is engaging, up to date, appropriately comprehensive in its coverage of legal and regulatory issues, and organized to permit instructors to tailor the materials to their particular approach.

Here we give you cases, in the courts' own words, edited for brevity. The cases illustrate legal issues and principles, judicial reasoning and vocabulary, all of which provide a richer student experience than "thumbnail" descriptions of what issues the judges were faced with, and how they reasoned. We remain convinced that students should be exposed to the actual language of the courts. In addition, monetary denominations are regularly noted both as stated in the cases and in current U.S. dollars (for example, a contract made in 1960 for $500 doesn't seem worth much litigation until you realize that would be about $4,300 in current dollars).

The book is up to date: while we retain some favorite older cases, classics like Palsgraf v. Long Island Railroad, we have included new ones that satisfy our criteria for currency and importance. And too, the cases must be engaging and accessible. Non-case law is not static, either: we address salient statutory and regulatory law and—throughout the book—the social forces that affect lawmaking.

Students are likely to become more engaged if they recognize that law relates to everyday events with which they are already familiar (or with which they are becoming familiar in other business courses), if they understand some of the social and historical context for the law, and if the text is presented clearly, concisely, and with a readable style. (An earlier business law text by authors Lieberman and Siedel was hailed as "the best written text in a very crowded field.") We think this text does that.

The book is appropriately comprehensive. It provides context and essential concepts that graduates from American colleges and universities should know, and it satisfies AACSB standards.

If you conscientiously teach an academic subject for many years (over 100 years of combined teaching and textbook writing inform this text) you come to understand how to present complex, interrelated material smoothly with an eye toward the students' pedagogic success. We do want them to learn this stuff!

As to pedagogy, we think that good organization of the extensive subject matter in the legal environment of business is key. For clarity and student understanding, this new text is rigorously organized in three main sections:

(1) An **Introduction to Law** section, which—as the chapter titles suggest—introduces students to main concepts of the legal environment of business.

(2) A **Black-Letter Law** section takes up the business law fundamentals of tort, contract, property, agency, and business organization.

(3) A **Government Regulation** section, dealing with various aspects of government regulation of business, including (something we think is unique here) regulation for a social safety net.

And, reflecting further concern for clear organization, the basic organizing structure of government is shown to play out over and over throughout the text. Law is always and everywhere made, and constrained, by five main entities: legislative, executive, judicial, administrative agencies, and—sometimes—direct democracy. All governments have some division of authority like this, though the division may not be explicit, and the power allowed to each authority differs. We find that the reiteration of these five law-making entities across a range of issues is very useful pedagogically. Similarly, in discussion of contract, as such, or in the context of agency, business organization, employment, consumer law (among others) this pattern plays out: any contractual relationship is entered expressly, impliedly, or apparently.

We have spent considerable time and effort on the Instructor's Manual. Cases appear in the text in the courts' words; the cases are briefed in the IM the "old fashioned way": facts, procedure, issue, holding, reason. We hope this makes it easier for instructors to read the briefs themselves. And the Manual also includes some tips for teaching the material garnered from the authors' years of experience: where do students have problems? What is useful to mention in Chapter 8, for example, that students will encounter again in Chapter 15? PowerPoint slides have also been updated and improved, as have the test file questions.

Students can buy electronic versions of the text, or they can order color hard-copy versions. For students, every chapter contains overviews that include the organization and coverage, a list of key terms, chapter summaries, and self-test questions in multiple-choice format (along with answers) that are followed by additional short-answer problems with answers available in the Instructors' Manual. Students also have access to electronic flash cards based on key terms.

Moreover, the price for students to buy the text is very reasonable—that's a real benefit to Flat-World's publishing format.

The FlatWorld publishing format has a further benefit for instructors who want to customize the text. Perhaps you don't have time to take up—say—the philosophical underpinnings of business ethics. You can rearrange chapters or parts of chapters, delete material or move it, and the text maintains its integrity by automatically changing internal references.

Writing a textbook is no short-term project. We authors are sincerely pleased to present to students and to our colleagues this excellent text.

CHAPTER 1
Introduction to Law and the Legal Process

Chapter Learning Objectives

After reading this chapter, you should be able to:

1. Distinguish different philosophies of law—schools of legal thought—and explain their relevance.
2. Identify the various aims that a functioning legal system can serve.
3. Explain how politics, law, and business are related.
4. Identify the sources of law and which laws have priority over other laws.
5. Understand some basic differences between the U.S. legal system and other legal systems.

Philosophers have considered issues of justice and law for centuries, and several different approaches, or schools of legal thought, have emerged. In this chapter, we will look at those different meanings and approaches and will consider how social and political dynamics interact with the ideas that animate the various schools of legal thought. We will examine the connections between "the rule of law" and how the rule of law can create a positive, stable environment for business activities. We will also look at typical sources of "positive law" in the United States and how some of those sources have priority over others, and we will set out some basic differences between the U.S. legal system and other legal systems.

1.1 What Is Law?

Learning Objectives

1. State a definition of *law* that you find to be useful.
2. List and describe the various functions of the law.
3. Explain the relationship between law, business activities, and politics.

Law is a word that can mean many different things. *Black's Law Dictionary* says that law is "a body of rules of action or conduct prescribed by controlling authority, and having binding legal force. That which must be obeyed and followed by citizens subject to sanctions or legal consequence is a law."[1] A simpler and more hopeful definition might be this: "Law is a system of social control designed to achieve a good society."

Law: Its Functions

In a nation, the law can serve the following purposes:

- keep the peace ("public safety");
- maintain the status quo;
- preserve individual rights;
- protect minorities against majorities;
- promote social justice;
- provide for orderly social change.

Some legal systems do some, but not all, of these functions. Although a nation ruled by an authoritarian government may keep the peace and maintain the status quo, it may also oppress minorities or political opponents (e.g., Russia, China, Zimbabwe, or Syria under Bashar al-Assad). Under colonialism, European nations often imposed peace in countries whose borders were somewhat arbitrarily created by those same European nations. Over several centuries prior to the twentieth century, empires were built by Spain, Portugal, Britain, Holland, France, Germany, Belgium, and Italy. In the late 19th and early 20th century the United States assembled an empire, too, at times possessing (and in some cases still retaining) Hawaii, Puerto Rico, Panama Canal Zone, Cuba, U.S. Virgin Islands, American Samoa, the Philippines, and various other Pacific Ocean and Caribbean islands (including Guam and Midway Islands).[2] With regard to the functions of the law, each empire may have kept the peace—largely with force—but it changed the status quo and seldom promoted the native peoples' rights or social justice within the colonized nation.

Unfortunately, tribal and ethnic factions worldwide (often exacerbated by a history of colonialism) can make it difficult for nation-states to adopt enforceable laws and promote justice. In Rwanda, for example, power struggles between Hutus and Tutsis resulted in genocide of the Tutsi minority.[3] In nations of the former Soviet Union, the withdrawal of a central power structure created power vacuums that were exploited by ethnic leaders. When Yugoslavia broke up, the different ethnic groups—Croats, Bosnians, and Serbians—fought bitterly for territorial control rather than share power. A more recent example is Iraq, where Sunni and Shiite sectarian differences have proven to be a major barrier to maintaining a united government.

Law: The Moral Minimum in a Democratic Society

The law does not correct (or claim to correct) every wrong that occurs in society. At a minimum, it aims to curb the worst kinds of wrongs, the kinds of wrongs that violate what might be called the "moral minimums" that a community demands of its members. These include not only violations of criminal law but also torts (see Chapter 7) and contracts (the law regarding broken promises). Thus, it may be wrong to refuse to return a phone call from a friend, but that wrong will not result in a viable lawsuit against you. But if a phone (or the Internet) is used to libel or slander someone, a tort has been committed, and the law may allow the defamed person to be compensated.

There is a strong association between what we generally think of as ethical behavior and what the laws require and provide. For example, we may harm others by breaking our promises; contract law upholds society's sense that promises—in general—should be kept. Promise-breaking is generally seen as unethical, except for some situations where a broken promise seems permissible. For example, in breach of contract cases, some excuses are accepted when it would be reasonable to do so, such as when the promisor is intoxicated, feeble-minded, or not yet 18 years of age.

The connection between law and ethics is also strong for **tort** law (see Chapter 7); harming others is usually considered unethical. If people are not restrained by law from harming one another, orderly society would be undone, leading to lawlessness and warlordism. Tort law provides for compensation when adequately serious injuries or harms occur. As for property law issues, we generally believe that private ownership of property is socially useful and generally desirable, and it is generally protected (with some exceptions) by laws. You can't throw a party at my house without my permission, but my right to do whatever I want on my own property may be limited by law; I can't, without the public's permission, operate an incinerator on my property and burn heavy metals, as toxic ash may be deposited throughout the neighborhood.

tort

Harm caused to others in some way that is not a breach of promise.

Law, Business, and Politics

In the United States, legislators, governors and presidents, judges, administrative agencies, and—in some states—the people themselves via initiatives or referendums make law, with substantial input from corporations, lobbyists, and a diverse group of nongovernmental organizations (NGOs) such as the American Petroleum Institute, the Sierra Club, and the National Rifle Association. In the states, judges are often appointed by governors or elected by the people. The process of electing state judges has become more and more politicized in the past fifteen years, with growing campaign contributions from those who would seek to seat judges with partisan leanings.

Some businesses have increasingly espoused political positions, such as the Koch Brothers sponsorship of the American Legislative Exchange Council (ALEC), with a primarily "libertarian" viewpoint for limited government regulation and an emphasis on state rather than federal power. Other business leaders have intervened politically to oppose unlimited gun sales or state laws that discriminate against LGBT citizens. Along with 40 plus years of increased lobbying by business interests in Washington, DC and in state capitals, the influx of corporate and NGO money into state and federal campaigns—both legislative and judicial—has increased the influence of business in shaping "the rules of the game" for economic activities in the United States.

In some countries—which we will usually refer to as "**nation-states**," the legal term for countries in international law—the connection between business influence and politics is so strong that the word "corruption" is often used. In many nation-states, major government policies and contracts can be directly influenced by secret bribes to public officials. For example, Odebrecht is a Brazilian construction company that became an international giant through years of using bribery and corruption to secure around 100 projects in 12 nation-states, generating ill-gotten gains of about $3.3 billion. Governments in Brazil, Peru, and other nation-states have been shaken by scandal, and the U.S. government is investigating Odebrecht for bribery payments in the U.S. as well under the Foreign Corrupt Practices Act (1977).[4]

nation-states

The basic entities that comprise the international legal system. Countries, states, and nations are all roughly synonymous. The word "state" can also be used to designate the basic units of federally united states, such as in the United States of America, which is a nation-state.

Among nation-states, the U.S. has been known as a bastion for "judicial independence." That is, the state and federal courts have a role as part of the "checks and balances" in our Constitutional system, and are not under the direct control of the federal legislature or executive branch (in most nation-states, that means the presidency or its equivalent.) Where a nation's leader can ignore conclusions and orders by the highest court in the land—or fire judges he or she doesn't like—judicial independence is entirely missing. (See Chapter 3) Yet, the World Economic Forum lists the U.S. as only 26th in its ranking of nation-states where the judiciary is largely free of political influence from other parts of the government, from individuals, and from companies.[5]

In most nation-states, knowing who has power to make and enforce the laws is a matter of knowing who has political power; in many places, the people or groups that have military power can also command political power to make and enforce the laws. Revolutions are difficult and contentious, but each year around the world you will read about protests and revolts against existing political-legal authority. Those who hold power are loathe to yield it, despite aspirations for democratic rule, or greater "rights" for citizens. These are recurring theme in politics and law globally, as is the repression of those rights by elites in power, and the resentments that can build toward legal change. While "business" typically prefers stable, democratic governance, companies must also operate in a variety of legal environments, some of which reflect entrenched centers of power and some of which are ethically corrupt.[6]

Key Takeaway

Law is the result of political activity, and the legal-political rules for people and business firms differ vastly from nation to nation. Unstable, corrupt, and authoritarian governments often fail to serve many of the principal functions of law that citizens and businesses desire.

Exercises

1. Consider North Korea. What political rights do you have that the average North Korean citizen does not?
2. What is a nongovernmental organization, and what does it have to do with government? Do you contribute to (or are you active in) a nongovernmental organization? What kind of rights do they espouse, what kind of laws do they support, and what kind of laws do they oppose?
3. Contrast the political advocacy of the Brady Campaign Against Gun Violence with the political advocacy of the National Rifle Association. Which has been more effective in shaping state and federal policies regarding the sale of semi-automatic weapons used in mass shootings in the U.S.?

1.2 Schools of Legal Thought

Learning Objectives

1. Distinguish different philosophies of law—schools of legal thought—and explain their relevance.
2. Explain why natural law relates to the rights that the founders of the U.S. political-legal system found important.
3. Describe legal positivism and explain how it differs from natural law.
4. Compare and contrast "critical legal studies" and "ecofeminist legal perspectives" with both natural law and legal positivist perspectives.

There are different schools (or philosophies) concerning what law is all about. Philosophy of law is also called **jurisprudence**, and the two main schools are **legal positivism** and **natural law**. Although there are others (see Section 2), these two are the most influential in how people think about the law.

Legal Positivism: Law as Sovereign Command

Legal positivism is law posited (set down—as in the word "deposit") by authority. As legal philosopher John Austin concisely put it, "Law is the command of a sovereign." Law is only law, in other words, if it comes from a recognized authority and can be enforced by that authority, or **sovereign**—such as a king, a president, or a dictator—who has power within a defined area or territory. In the U.S., sovereign authority would include the president, the Congress, and the federal courts and, on the state level, the same three branches of government.

The positive-law school of legal thought would recognize the lawmaker's command as legitimate; questions about the law's morality or immorality would not be important. In contrast, the natural-law school of legal thought would refuse to recognize the legitimacy of laws that did not conform to natural, universal, or divine law. If a lawmaker issued a command that was in violation of natural law, a citizen would be morally justified in demonstrating civil disobedience. For example, in refusing to give up her seat to a white person, Rosa Parks believed that she was refusing to obey an unjust law. Mohandas Ghandi led a movement in colonial India to free itself from British rule, and the movement, like Nelson Mandela's in South Africa, was guided by the same principles that animated the movement for civil rights for African Americans in the 1960s. Yet not all civil disobedience is peaceful; opponents of Bashar al-Assad took up arms, and became "terrorists," and have been unsuccessful in resisting al-Assad's authoritarian ways.

Natural Law

The **natural-law school** of thought emphasizes that law should be based on a universal moral order. Natural law was "discovered" by humans through the use of reason and by choosing between that which is good and that which is evil. Here is the definition of natural law according to the *Cambridge Dictionary of Philosophy*: "Natural law, also called the law of nature in moral and political philosophy, is an objective norm or set of objective norms governing human behavior, similar to the positive laws of a human ruler, but binding on all people alike and usually understood as involving a superhuman legislator."[7]

Both the U.S. Constitution and the United Nations (UN) Charter have an affinity for the natural-law outlook, as it emphasizes certain objective norms and rights of individuals and nations. The U.S. Declaration of Independence embodies a natural-law philosophy. The following short extract should provide some sense of the deep beliefs in natural law held by those who signed the document.

> **The Unanimous Declaration of the Thirteen United States of America**
>
> **July 4, 1776**

jurisprudence

The philosophy of law. There are many philosophies of law and thus many different jurisprudential views.

legal positivism

A jurisprudence that focuses on the law as it is—the command of the sovereign.

natural law

A jurisprudence that emphasizes a law that transcends positive laws (human laws) and points to a set of principles that are universal in application.

sovereign

The authority within any nation-state. Sovereignty is what sovereigns exercise. This usually means the power to make and enforce laws within the nation-state.

natural-law school

The legal philosophy that there are certain universal rules recognized by everyone, and that the law should be based on those universal principles.

> *When in the Course of human events, it becomes necessary for one people to dissolve the political bands which have connected them with another, and to assume among the powers of the earth, the separate and equal station to which the Laws of Nature and of Nature's God entitle them, a decent respect to the opinions of mankind requires that they should declare the causes which impel them to the separation.*
>
> *We hold these truths to be self-evident, that all men are created equal, that they are endowed by their Creator with certain unalienable Rights, that among these are Life, Liberty and the Pursuit of Happiness. That to secure these rights, Governments are instituted among Men, deriving their just powers from the consent of the governed....*

The natural-law school has been very influential in American legal thinking. The idea that certain rights, for example, are "unalienable" (as expressed in the Declaration of Independence and in the writings of John Locke) is consistent with this view of the law. Individuals may have "God-given" or "natural" rights that government cannot legitimately take away. Government only by consent of the governed is a natural outgrowth of this view.

Civil disobedience—in the tradition of Henry Thoreau, Mahatma Gandhi, or Martin Luther King Jr.—becomes a matter of morality over "unnatural" law. For example, in his "Letter from Birmingham Jail," Martin Luther King Jr. claimed that obeying an unjust law is not moral and that deliberately disobeying an unjust law is, in fact, a moral act that expresses "the highest respect for law": "An individual who breaks a law that conscience tells him is unjust, and who willingly accepts the penalty of imprisonment in order to arouse the conscience of the community over its injustice, is in reality expressing the highest respect for law. ... One who breaks an unjust law must do so openly, lovingly, and with a willingness to accept the penalty."[8]

Other Schools of Legal Thought

The **historical school of law** believes that societies should base their legal decisions today on the examples of the past. Precedent would be more important than moral arguments.

The **legal realist school** flourished in the 1920s and 1930s as a reaction to the historical school. Legal realists pointed out that because life and society are constantly changing, certain laws and doctrines have to be altered or modernized in order to remain current. The social context of law was more important to legal realists than the formal application of precedent to current or future legal disputes. Rather than suppose that judges inevitably acted objectively in applying an existing rule to a set of facts, legal realists observed that judges had their own beliefs, operated in a social context, and would give legal decisions based on their beliefs and their own social context.

historical school of law

The legal philosophy that societies should base their legal decisions today on the examples of the past. Precedent would be more important than moral arguments.

legal realism

Laws and doctrines change over time to remain currently relevant.

The legal realist view influenced the emergence of the **critical legal studies (CLS) school of thought**. The "Crits" believe that the social order (and the law) is dominated by those with power, wealth, and influence. Some Crits are clearly influenced by the economist Karl Marx and also by distributive justice theory (see Chapter 2). The CLS school believes the wealthy have historically oppressed or exploited those with less wealth and have maintained social control through law. In so doing, the wealthy have perpetuated an unjust distribution of both rights and goods in society. Law is politics and is thus not neutral or value-free. The CLS movement would use the law to overturn the hierarchical structures of domination in modern society.

Related to the CLS school, yet different, is the **ecofeminist school of legal thought**. This school emphasizes—and would modify—the long-standing domination of men over both women and the rest of the natural world. Ecofeminists would say that the same social mentality that leads to exploitation of women is at the root of man's exploitation and degradation of the natural environment. They would say that male ownership of land has led to a "dominator culture," in which man is not so much a steward of the existing environment or those "subordinate" to him but is charged with making all that he controls economically "productive." Wives, children, land, and animals are valued as economic resources, and legal systems (until the nineteenth century) largely conferred rights only to men with land. Ecofeminists would say that even with increasing civil and political rights for women (such as the right to vote) and with some nations' recognizing the rights of children and animals and caring for the environment, the legacy of the past for most nations still confirms the preeminence of "man" and his dominance of both nature and women.

critical legal studies (CLS) school of thought

Jurisprudential school that believes the wealthy have historically oppressed or exploited those with less wealth and have maintained social control through law.

ecofeminist school of legal thought

The jurisprudence observing that the same social mentality that leads to domination and exploitation of women is at the root of man's exploitation and degradation of the natural environment.

Key Takeaway

Each of the various schools of legal thought has a particular view of what a legal system is or what it should be. The natural-law theorists emphasize the rights and duties of both government and the governed. Positive law takes as a given that law is simply the command of a sovereign, the political power that those governed will obey. Recent writings in the various legal schools of thought emphasize long-standing patterns of domination of the wealthy over others (the CLS school) and of men over women (ecofeminist legal theory).

Exercises

1. Vandana Shiva draws a picture of a stream in a forest. She says that in our society the stream is seen as unproductive if it is merely there, fulfilling the need for water of women's families and communities, until engineers come along and tinker with it, perhaps damming it and using it for generating hydropower. The same is true for a forest, unless it is replaced with a monoculture plantation of a commercial species. A forest may very well be productive—protecting groundwater; creating oxygen; providing fruit, fuel, and craft materials for nearby inhabitants; and creating a habitat for animals that are also a valuable resource. She criticizes the view that if there is no monetary amount that can contribute to gross domestic product, neither the forest nor the river can be seen as a productive resource. Which school of legal thought does her criticism reflect?

2. Anatole France said, "The law, in its majesty, forbids rich and poor alike from sleeping under bridges." Which school of legal thought is represented by this quote?

3. Adolf Eichmann was a loyal member of the National Socialist Party in the Third Reich and worked hard under Hitler's government during World War II to round up Jewish people for incarceration—and eventual extermination—at labor camps like Auschwitz and Buchenwald. After an Israeli "extraction team" took him from Argentina to Israel, he was put on trial for "crimes against humanity." His defense was that he was "just following orders." Explain why Eichmann was not an adherent of the natural-law school of legal thought.

1.3 Basic Classifications of U.S. Law

Learning Objectives

1. Differentiate between civil law and criminal law.
2. Differentiate between substantive law and procedural law.
3. Differentiate between common law and statutory law.
4. Differentiate between public law and private law.
5. Differentiate between law and equity.

Law may be classified in various ways and may be helpfully understood when presented in opposing pairs.

Civil Law versus Criminal Law

criminal case

Proscribes conduct perceived as threatening, harmful, or otherwise endangering to the property, health, safety, and moral welfare of the public; the plaintiff is always the government.

civil law

In contrast to criminal law, the law that governs noncriminal disputes, such as in lawsuits (as opposed to prosecutions) over contract disputes and tort claims. In contrast to common law, civil law is part of the continental European tradition dating back to Roman law.

criminal law

That body of law in any nation-state that defines offenses against society as a whole, punishable by fines, forfeitures, or imprisonment.

Most of the cases we will look at in this textbook are civil cases. Criminal cases are certainly of interest to business, especially as companies may break criminal laws. A **criminal case** involves a governmental decision—whether state or federal—to prosecute someone (named as a defendant) for violating society's laws. The law establishes a moral minimum and does so especially in the area of criminal laws; if you break a criminal law, you can lose your freedom (in jail) or your life (if you are convicted of a capital offense). In a civil action, you would not be sent to prison; in the worst case, you can lose property (usually money or other assets), such as when Ford Motor Company lost a personal injury case and the judge awarded $295 million to the plaintiffs, or when Pennzoil won a $10.54 billion verdict against Texaco (see Chapter 7).

Some of the basic differences between **civil law** and **criminal law** cases are illustrated in Table 1.1.

TABLE 1.1 Differences between Civil and Criminal Cases

	Civil Cases	Criminal Cases
Parties	Plaintiff brings case; defendant must answer or lose by default	Prosecutor brings case; defendant may remain silent
Proof	Preponderance of evidence	Beyond a reasonable doubt
Reason	To settle disputes peacefully, usually between private parties	To maintain order in society
		To punish the most blameworthy
		To deter serious wrongdoing
Remedies	Money damages (legal remedy)	Fines, jail, and forfeitures
	Injunctions (equitable remedy)	
	Specific performance (equity)	

sovereign immunity

The doctrine that the government cannot be sued without its consent.

Regarding plaintiffs and prosecutors, you can often tell a civil case from a criminal case by looking at the caption of a case going to trial. If the government appears first in the caption of the case (e.g., *U.S. v. Lieberman*), it is likely that the United States is prosecuting on behalf of the people. The same is true of cases prosecuted by state district attorneys (e.g., *State v. Siedel*). But this is not a foolproof formula. Governments will also bring civil actions to collect debts from, or settle disputes with individuals, corporations, or other governments. Thus *U.S. v. Mayer* might be a collection action for unpaid taxes, or *U.S. v. Canada* might be a boundary dispute in the International Court of Justice. Governments can be sued, as well; people occasionally sue their state or federal government, but they can only get a trial if the government waives its **sovereign immunity** and allows such suits. *Warner v. U.S.*, for example, could be a claim for a tax refund wrongfully withheld or for damage caused to the Warner residence by a sonic boom from a U.S. Air Force jet flying overhead.

Substantive Law versus Procedural Law

Substantive Law

Many rules and regulations in law are **substantive**, and others are procedural. We are used to seeing laws as substantive; that is, there is some rule of conduct or behavior that is called for or some action that is proscribed (prohibited). The substantive rules tell us how to act with one another and with the government. For example, all of the following are substantive rules of law and provide a kind of command or direction to citizens:

- Drive not more than fifty-five miles per hour where that speed limit is posted.
- Do not conspire to fix prices with competitors in the U.S. market.
- Do not falsely represent the curative effects of your over-the-counter herbal remedy.
- Do not drive your motor vehicle through an intersection while a red traffic signal faces the direction you are coming from.
- Do not discriminate against job applicants or employees on the basis of their race, sex, religion, or national origin.
- Do not discharge certain pollutants into the river without first getting a discharge permit.

substantive law

Those laws that define appropriate behavior, or that define and forbit inappropriate behavior.

Procedural Law

In contrast, **procedural laws** are the rules of courts and administrative agencies. They tell us how to proceed if there is a substantive-law problem.

For example, if you drive fifty-three miles per hour in a forty mile-per-hour zone on Main Street on a Saturday night and get a ticket, you have broken a substantive rule of law (the posted speed limit). Just how and what gets decided in court is a matter of procedural law. Is the police officer's word final, or do you get your say before a judge? If so, who goes first, you or the officer? Do you have the right to be represented by legal counsel? Does the hearing or trial have to take place within a certain time period? A week? A month? How long can the state take to bring its case? What kinds of evidence will be relevant? Radar? (Does it matter what kind of training the officer has had on the radar device? Whether the radar device had been tested adequately?) The officer's personal observation? (What kind of training has he had, how is he qualified to judge the speed of a car, and other questions arise.) What if you unwisely bragged to a friend at a party recently that you went a hundred miles an hour on Main Street five years ago at half past three on a Tuesday morning? (If the prosecutor knows of this and the "friend" is willing to testify, is it relevant to the charge of fifty-three in a forty-mile-per-hour zone?)

In the United States, all state procedural laws must be fair, since the due process clause of the Fourteenth Amendment directs that no state shall deprive any citizen of "life, liberty, or property," without due process of law. A state court's criminal fine of $200 plus court costs is designed to deprive you of property (in the form of money) if you violate the speed limit. Federal laws must also

procedural laws

The rules that the court, lawyers, and parties must follow to properly try a case; procedural laws deal with dates, times, numbers, and other procedural aspects of a case that must be met in order for the case to proceed according to the law.

be fair, because the Fifth Amendment to the U.S. Constitution has the same due process language as the Fourteenth Amendment. This suggests that some laws are more powerful or important than others, which is true. The next section looks at various types of positive law and their relative importance.

Common Law versus Statutory Law

Common Law

precedent

A prior judicial decision that is either binding or persuasive, and as such, provides a rule useful in making a decision in the case at hand.

stare decisis

Latin, "precedent governs," the rule of law articulated in one case will be used to decide future cases based on the same facts; it is the basis of the common law.

Even before legislatures met to make rules for society, disputes happened and judges decided them. In England, judges began writing down the facts of a case and the reasons for their decision. They often resorted to deciding cases on the basis of prior written decisions. In relying on those prior decisions, the judge would reason that since a current case was pretty much like a prior case, it ought to be decided the same way. This is essentially reasoning by analogy. Thus the use of **precedent** in common-law cases came into being, and a doctrine of **stare decisis** (pronounced STAR-ay-de-SIGH-sus) became accepted in English courts. *Stare decisis* means, in Latin, "let the decision stand."

Most judicial decisions (those that don't interpret legislation) are common law and involve these three areas of law:

- Property law. Property law deals with the rights and duties of those who can legally own land (real property), how that ownership can be legally confirmed and protected, how property can be bought and sold, what the rights of tenants (renters) are, and what the various kinds of "estates" in land are (e.g., fee simple, life estate, future interest, easements, or rights of way). Property law applies contract and tort law as those affect people's "quiet enjoyment" of their real estate, however it may be owned.

- Contract law. Contract law deals with what kinds of promises courts should enforce. For example, should courts enforce a contract where one of the parties was intoxicated, underage, or insane? Should courts enforce a contract where one of the parties seemed to have an unfair advantage? What kind of contracts would have to be in writing to be enforced by courts?

- Tort law. Tort law deals with the types of cases that involve some kind of harm and/or injury between the plaintiff and the defendant when no contract exists. Thus if you are libeled or a competitor lies about your product, your remedy would be in tort, not contract.

Without laws enforcing property rights, promises, and providing protection against uninvited harm (torts, that is), doing business in a national or global economy would be almost impossible. You could not trust your counter-party's word unless you knew them personally, and if the transaction "went south" you would have only the voluntary willingness of the counter-party to do what is right and fair. Your competitors could trash talk your business on social media and elsewhere, and you would be powerless to fight back (except on social media, which would not provide you with any monetary remedies or injunctions against your lying competitors). The stability that businesses prize is largely possible through the common law of property, torts, and contracts, along with legislation at the state and federal levels.

In England and in the laws of the original thirteen states, common-law decisions defined crimes such as arson, burglary, homicide, and robbery. As time went on, U.S. state legislatures either adopted or modified common-law definitions of most crimes by putting them in the form of codes or statutes. This legislative ability—to modify or change common law into judicial law—points to an important phenomenon: the priority of statutory law over common law. As we will see in the next section, constitutional law will have priority over statutory law.

Statutory Law

Statutory law is law made by a legislature, whether state or federal. We take up statutory law in greater detail in Chapter 4 Section 1.

Public Law versus Private Law

Public law is concerned with regulating the relations of individuals with the government and the organization and conduct of the government itself.

    Private law is concerned with private persons, property, and relationships.

public law

Concerns the relations of individuals with the government and the organization and conduct of the government itself.

private law

The law governing private persons, property, and relationships.

Law versus Equity

After the Norman Conquest in 1066, English law evolved into two distinct systems: law and equity.

Law

"Law" referred to the legal system headed by the Crown—the common law. By the 15th century this law was highly developed, but ossified. It required that plaintiffs fit their complaints into special types (called "writs") and the only relief available was monetary damages. Because of this formality (or formalism) litigants were not infrequently frustrated in their attempt to get justice.

Equity

If the plaintiff's problem didn't fit into the writs or was not solvable by money, the only thing to do was appeal to the Crown for special relief—for "equity" or "fairness," based not on precedent as with the common law, but on natural justice and moral rights (the alternative would be to fight it out in the streets). The Crown assigned these cases to a minister, called the Minister (or Chancellor) of Equity. Plaintiffs found the courts of equity attractive: relief was often faster and more appropriate than in law. For example, if the defendant's cows were trespassing on the plaintiff's property, the plaintiff didn't want money so much as to have the defendant keep his darn cows on his property. Courts of law couldn't order that, but courts of **equity** could.

equity

The body of law that addresses concerns that fall outside the jurisdiction of common law.

    By the 1450s the Chancellor's courts of equity had become a separate and parallel system that had wide discretion to grant relief in the form of new remedies, like specific performance and injunctions. The two systems operated out of separate courthouses, and chancellors (judges) in equity did not rely on precedent as in the common-law system; their decisions were guided by equitable maxims (a "maxim" is a handy little saying). Here are some equitable maxims:

- Equity is fairness, and will not enforce unfair agreements.
- Equity is equality.
- Equity suffers no wrong without providing a remedy.
- He who seeks equity must himself have behaved equitably.
- Equity considers substance, not formalities.
- Delay resulting in prejudicial change defeats equity.

Also, in equity there was—and is—no jury, and the technical rules of evidence don't necessarily apply.

Equity is alive and well in the United States (and in Britain and Commonwealth countries) today, though equitable and legal issues are heard in the same courtroom by the same judge. If the plaintiff wants non-monetary relief, she must ask for equitable relief. A judge hearing a case in equity is said to be "sitting in equity." The following older case, *Campbell Soup Co. v. Wentz*, is a classic case explaining the role of equity in the U.S. legal system.

Case

Equity in Contracts

Campbell Soup Co. v. Wentz

Federal Circuit Court case, 1948, analyzing whether a set of facts presents a case of law or of equity.

Campbell Soup Co. v. Wentz

172 F. 2d 80 (3rd Cir. Federal Ct.,[9] 1948)

Goodrich, J.

On June 21, 1947, Campbell Soup Company (Campbell), a New Jersey corporation, entered into a written contract with George B. Wentz and Harry T. Wentz, who are Pennsylvania farmers, for delivery by the Wentzes to Campbell of all the Chantenay red cored carrots to be grown on fifteen acres of the Wentz farm during the 1947 season. Where the contract was entered into does not appear. The contract provides, however, for delivery of the carrots at the Campbell plant in Camden, New Jersey. The prices specified in the contract ranged from $23 to $30 per ton according to the time of delivery. The contract price for January, 1948 was $30 a ton [about $315 in 2019 dollars].

The Wentzes harvested approximately 100 tons of carrots from the fifteen acres covered by the contract. Early in January, 1948, they told a Campbell representative that they would not deliver their carrots at the contract price. The market price at that time was at least $90 per ton, and Chantenay red cored carrots were virtually unobtainable. The Wentzes then sold approximately 62 tons of their carrots to the defendant Lojeski, a neighboring farmer. Lojeski resold about 58 tons on the open market, approximately half to Campbell and the balance to other purchasers.

On January 9, 1948, Campbell, suspecting that Lojeski was selling it "its contract carrots," refused to purchase any more, and instituted these suits in equity against the Wentz brothers and Lojeski to enjoin further sale of the contract carrots to others, and to compel specific performance[10] of the contract. The trial court denied equitable relief. We agree with the result reached, but on a different ground from that relied upon by the District Court.

[The trial court held that Campbell's case was not in equity, but in law, because there was adequate legal relief available to Campbell's—it could sue the Wentzes for money damages. The trial court dismissed the case, and Campbell's appealed.]

A party may have specific performance of a contract for the sale of chattels if the legal remedy is inadequate. Inadequacy of the legal remedy is necessarily a matter to be determined by an examination of the facts in each particular instance.

We think that on the question of adequacy of the legal remedy the case is one appropriate for specific performance. It was expressly found that at the time of the trial it was "virtually impossible to obtain Chantenay carrots in the open market." This Chantenay carrot is one which the plaintiff uses in large quantities, furnishing the seed to the growers with whom it makes contracts. It was not claimed that in nutritive value it is any better than other types of carrots. Its blunt shape makes it easier to handle in processing, and its color and texture differ from other varieties. The color is brighter than other carrots. It also appeared that Campbell's uses these Chantenay carrots diced in some of its soups and that the appearance is uniform. The preservation of uniformity in appearance in a food article marketed throughout the country and sold under the manufacturer's name is a matter of considerable commercial significance and one which is properly considered in determining whether a substitute ingredient is just as good as the original.

Here the goods of the special type contracted for were unavailable on the open market, the plaintiff had contracted for them long ahead in anticipation of its needs, and had built up a general reputation for its products as part of which reputation uniform appearance was important. We think if this were all that was involved in the case specific performance should have been granted.

The reason that we shall affirm instead of reversing with an order for specific performance is found in the contract itself. We think it is too hard a bargain and too one-sided an agreement to entitle the plaintiff to relief in a court of conscience. For each individual grower the agreement is made by filling in names, quantity, and price on a printed form furnished by the buyer. This form has quite obviously been drawn by skillful draftsmen with the buyer's interests in mind. Paragraph 2 provides for the manner of delivery. Carrots are to have their stalks cut off and be in clean sanitary bags or other containers approved by Campbell. This paragraph concludes with a statement that Campbell's determination of conformance with specifications shall be conclusive.

The next paragraph allows Campbell to refuse carrots in excess of twelve tons to the acre. The next contains a covenant by the grower that he will not sell carrots to anyone else except the carrots rejected by Campbell nor will he permit anyone else to grow carrots on his land. Paragraph 10 provides liquidated damages [damages the defendant has to pay for breaching the contract as set out in the contract] to the extent of $50 per acre for any breach by the grower. There is no provision for liquidated or any other damages for breach of contract by Campbell.

The provision of the contract which we think is the hardest is paragraph 9. It will be noted that Campbell is excused from accepting carrots under certain circumstances. But even under such circumstances the grower, while he cannot say Campbell is liable for failure to take the carrots, is not permitted to sell them elsewhere unless Campbell agrees. This is the kind of provision which the late Francis H. Bohlen would call "carrying a good joke too far." What the grower may do with his product under the circumstances set out is not clear. He has covenanted not to store it anywhere except on his own farm and also not to sell to anybody else.

We are not suggesting that the contract is illegal. Nor are we suggesting any excuse for the grower in this case who has deliberately broken an agreement entered into with Campbell. We do think, however, that a party who has offered and succeeded in getting an agreement as tough as this one is, should not come to a chancellor and ask court help in the enforcement of its terms. That equity does not enforce unconscionable bargains is too well established to require elaborate citation.

The judgments will be affirmed.

Case Questions

1. What relief did the plaintiff (Campbell's) want from the lower court?
2. Why did the lower court refuse to give Campbell's that relief?
3. The court on appeal came to the same result as the lower court, but for a completely different reason. What was that reason?

Exercises

1. Jenna gets a ticket for careless driving after the police come to investigate a car accident she had with Jason on Hanover Boulevard. Jason's car is badly damaged through no fault of his own. Is Jenna likely to face criminal charges, civil charges, or both?
2. Jenna's ticket says that she has thirty days in which to respond to the charges against her. The thirty days conforms to a state law that sets this time limit. Is the thirty-day limit procedural law or substantive law?
3. Why is it generally thought that the *first* responsibility of a government is to ensure public safety? How does tort law and contract law contribute to keeping the public safe?
4. What are the major differences between law and equity?
5. Raul has a piece of garden artistry in his front yard; vandals trash it and Raul wants to sue. Is this private law or public law?
6. Would it be correct to say that equity is no longer part of the U.S. legal system?

1.4 Sources of Law and Their Priority

Learning Objectives

1. Recognize the different sources of law in the U.S. legal system and the principal institutions that create those laws.
2. Explain in what way a statute is like a treaty, and vice versa.
3. Explain why the Constitution is "prior" and has priority over the legislative acts of a majority, whether in the U.S. Congress or in a state legislature.

Overview of the Sources of Law

In the United States today, there are five sources of law. Or six, if you count the Constitution as a source of law; perhaps the Constitutions (state and federal) could better be considered the framework within which the sources of law operate.

1. The legislature makes law, called **statutes** (at the federal and state level) or **ordinances** (at the local level—city and county councils and the like).

2. The executive makes law. She or he can issue **executive order**s that have the effect of law affecting internal governmental operations, and can veto or threaten to veto legislation, which can affect the law.

3. The judiciary—judges—make law by judicial review, judicial interpretation of legislation (judges have to say what the law means if that's in dispute), and by development (or "discovery") of the common law.

4. The administrative agencies effectively make law (but it's not called "law" because the makers are not the legislature—not elected): like the federal or state Health Department requiring certain sanitation protocols for food-stuff handlers.

5. The people themselves can make law in those states that allow the initiative and referendum.

In international legal systems, sources of law include treaties (agreements between nation-states—contracts, really) and what is known as customary international law (usually consisting of judicial decisions from national court systems where parties from two or more nations are in a dispute—kind of an international common law).

As you might expect, these laws sometimes conflict: a state law may conflict with a federal law, or a federal law might be contrary to an international obligation. One nation's law may provide one substantive rule, while another nation's law may provide a different, somewhat contrary rule to apply. To understand which laws have priority, it is essential to understand the relationships between the various kinds of law.

Constitutions

Constitutions, whether at the state or federal level, are the foundation for all other laws. The Constitution will provide the state or nation's legislative, executive, and judicial framework. Among the nations of the world, the United States has the oldest constitution still in use. It is difficult to amend, which is why there have only been seventeen amendments following the first ten in 1789; two-thirds of the House and Senate must pass amendments, and three-fourths of the states must approve them.

American states also have constitutions. Along with providing for legislative, executive, and judicial functions, state constitutions prescribe various rights of citizens. These rights may be different from, and in addition to, rights granted by the U.S. Constitution.

Law by the Legislature

The primary law-making entity in the United States is the legislature. Local governments, states, and the federal government have legislatures.

State legislatures (sometimes called "assemblies") are usually made up of both a senate and a house of representatives. Like the federal government, houses of the state legislature will agree on the provisions of a bill, which is then sent to the governor (acting like the president for that state) for signature. Like the president, governors usually have a veto power. The process of creating and amending, or changing, laws is filled with political negotiation and compromise.[11]

On the local level, counties and municipal corporations or townships have legislatures too. They are usually authorized under a state's constitution to create or adopt ordinances. Examples of ordinances include local building codes, zoning laws, and misdemeanors or infractions such as littering or jaywalking.

statute

A law adopted by the legislature at the federal or state level.

ordinance

A law adopted by the legislature (county commission, city council) at the local level.

executive order

A directive from the executive branch of government (president, governor, mayor) to employees of the branch describing how the executive wants the branch to operate (the boss gives instructions to workers).

constitutions

The founding documents of any nation-state's legal system.

Congress

The legislative body of the United States.

House of Representatives

One of the two branches of the United States Congress (and many states use the same term); House members are all elected every two years.

Senate

One of the two branches of the U.S. Congress (and also a term used in many state legislatures); senators are elected for six-year terms.

treaty

A "contract" between or among nations by which each agrees to behave in a certain way.

convention

An agreement between nation-states for regulation of matters affecting all of them; a treaty.

In Washington, DC, the federal legislature is **Congress** and has both a **House of Representatives** and a **Senate**. The House is composed of representatives elected every two years from various districts in each state. These districts are established by Congress according to population as determined every ten years by the census, a process required by the Constitution. Each state has at least one district; the most populous state (California) has fifty-two districts. In the Senate, there are two senators from each state, regardless of the state's population. Thus Delaware has two senators and California has two senators, even though California has far more people. Effectively, less than 20 percent of the nation's population can send fifty senators to Washington. The House of Representatives, on the other hand, is directly proportioned by population, though no state can have fewer than one representative.

A **treaty** or **convention** is considered of equal standing to a statute. Thus, when Congress ratified the North American Free Trade Agreement (NAFTA), any judicial decisions or previous statutes that were inconsistent—such as quotas or limitations on imports from Mexico that were opposite to NAFTA commitments—would no longer be valid. Similarly, U.S. treaty obligations under the General Agreement on Tariffs and Trade (GATT) and obligations made later through the World Trade Organization (WTO) would override previous federal or state statutes.[12]

The process by which legislation is made is taken up in Chapter 4 Section 1.

Law by the Executive

As we'll see in more detail in Chapter 4, the executive (president, governor, mayor, county executive) effectively has law-making power by executive orders and vetos of legislation, among others.

Law by the Judiciary

In the U.S. the judiciary—judges—have three law-making powers:

- Judicial review. Judges can declare acts of the legislature unconstitutional—invalid.
- Judicial interpretation of legislation. If it is disputed, judges decide what the legislature meant when it adopted a statute.
- Judicial adoption (or "discovery") of the common law. Common law is judge-made law; the American common-law tradition was inherited from England. Confronted with a legitimate dispute to decide, courts must, with a few exceptions, decide it (or else people will tend to decide disputes on their own, violently). So, if there is no state statute, the court will have to make up a rule (a "case of first impression"). A new common-law rule will be acceptable if it is reasonably agreeable to the sensibilities of the general population; that is, if it is not out of line with customary practices and tradition. The defining characteristic of common law is that lower courts must follow the precedent decided by the highest court of their jurisdiction. The common law is found in the published decisions (cases) of judges; it is also referred to as case law (and sometimes "judge-made law").

Because judges do not always agree on first principles (i.e., they subscribe to different schools of legal thought), there are many divided opinions in appellate opinions and in each U.S. Supreme Court term. [13]

Law by the judiciary is examined more closely in Chapter 4 Section 1.

Delegating Legislative Powers: Rules by Administrative Agencies

The state and federal legislatures have found it necessary and useful to create government agencies to which they delegate authority to administer various laws (see Chapter 4 Section 2). The Constitution does not expressly provide for administrative agencies, but the U.S. Supreme Court has upheld the delegation of power to create federal agencies. Agencies adopt regulations which have the force of law. Each state publishes the regulations of its administrative agencies (in Washington State, for example, the regulations are in the Washington Administrative Code); formally adopted Federal regs are published in the Code of Federal Regulations (CFR). Here you can find information about the CFR: https://www.govinfo.gov/help/cfr .

Examples of administrative agencies would include the Occupational Safety and Health Administration (OSHA), the Environmental Protection Agency (EPA), and the Federal Trade Commission (FTC).

Law by Direct Democracy

In 26 states the people themselves can make law directly by the initiative and referendum process. This is discussed in Chapter 4 Section 2.

Priority of Laws

By its "Supremacy Clause" the U.S. Constitution takes precedence over all statutes and judicial decisions that are inconsistent. For example, if Michigan were to decide legislatively that students cannot speak ill of professors in state-sponsored universities, that law would be void, since it is inconsistent with the state's obligation under the First Amendment to protect free speech. Or, if the Michigan courts were to allow a professor to bring a lawsuit against a student who had said something about him that was derogatory but not defamatory, the state's judicial system would not be acting according to the First Amendment. (As we will see in Chapter 7, free speech has its limits; defamation was a cause of action at the time the First Amendment was added to the Constitution, and the Supreme Court understands that the free speech rights in the First Amendment are not so absolute as to negate existing common law in 1789, when the Bill of Rights was ratified by the states.)

Statutes generally have priority over case law (judicial decisions). For example, under common-law judicial decisions, employers could hire young children for difficult work, offer any wage they wanted, and not pay overtime work at a higher rate, but various statutes changed that. For example, the federal Fair Labor Standards Act (1938) forbade the use of oppressive child labor and established a minimum pay wage and overtime pay rules.

Key Takeaway

There are different sources of law in the U.S. legal system. The U.S. Constitution is foundational; U.S. statutory and common law cannot be inconsistent with its provisions. States have constitutions, too. State legislatures and Congress create statutory law (with the signature of the executive), and courts will interpret constitutional law and statutory law. Where there is neither constitutional law nor statutory law, the courts function in the realm of common law.

Both the federal government and the states have created administrative agencies. An agency only has the power that the legislature gives it. Within the scope of that power, an agency will often create regulations, which have the same force and effect as statutes. Treaties are never negotiated and concluded by states, as the federal government has exclusive authority over relations with other nation-states. A treaty, once ratified by the Senate, has the same force and effect as a statute passed by Congress and signed into law by the president.

Exercises

1. Give one example where common law was overridden by the passage of a federal statute.
2. How does common law change or evolve without any action on the part of a legislature?
3. Lindsey Paradise is not selected for her sorority of choice at the University of Kansas. She has spent all her time rushing that particular sorority, which chooses some of her friends but not her. She is disappointed and angry and wants to sue the sorority. What are her prospects of recovery in the legal system? Explain.

1.5 Legal and Political Systems of the World

Learning Objective

1. Describe how the common-law system differs from the civil-law system.

Some nation-states have legal and political systems very different from the U.S. system, which came from English common-law traditions and the Framers of the U.S. Constitution. Our legal and political traditions are different, both in what kinds of laws we make and honor, and in how disputes are resolved in court.

Common-Law Systems

The common-law tradition is unique to England, the United States, and former colonies of the British Empire. Although there are differences among common-law systems (e.g., most nations do not permit their judiciaries to declare legislative acts unconstitutional; some nations use the jury less frequently), all of them recognize the use of precedent in judicial cases, and none of them relies on the comprehensive, legislative codes that are prevalent in civil-law systems.

Civil-Law Systems

The main alternative to the common-law legal system was developed in Europe and is based on Roman and Napoleonic law. A **civil-law** or code-law system is one where all the legal rules are in one or more comprehensive legislative enactments. During Napoleon's reign, a comprehensive book of laws—a code—was developed for all of France. The code covered criminal law, criminal procedure, noncriminal law and procedure, and commercial law. The rules of the code are still used today in France and in other continental European legal systems.

The **code** is used to resolve particular cases, usually by judges without a jury. Moreover, the judges are not required to follow the decisions of other courts in similar cases. As George Cameron, Emeritus Professor at the University of Michigan business school puts it, "The law is in the code, not in the cases." He goes on to note, "Where several cases all have interpreted a provision in a particular way, the French courts may feel bound to reach the same result in future cases, under the doctrine of *jurisprudence constante*. The major agency for growth and change, however, is the legislature, not the courts."

Civil-law systems are used throughout Europe as well as in Central and South America. Some nations in Asia and Africa have also adopted codes based on European civil law. Germany, Holland, Spain, France, and Portugal all had colonies outside of Europe, and many of these colonies adopted the legal practices that were imposed on them by colonial rule, much like the original thirteen states of the United States, which adopted English common-law practices.

There are also legal systems that differ significantly from the common-law and civil-law systems. The communist legal systems that remain (e.g., in China and North Korea) operate on very different assumptions than those of either English common law or European civil law. Islamic and other religion-based systems of law bring different values and assumptions to social and commercial relations. There is fear in some parts of the United States that, somehow, Sharia (the strict Islamic Law championed by the Taliban or ISIS) will supplant our own legal traditions. [14]

civil law

A legal system in which core principles are adopted by statute into a referable system which serves as the primary source of law (as compared to the common-law system, in which judge-made law—not statute—plays a large role).

code

A systematic and comprehensive written statement of statutory law addressing a certain legal topic (like the Traffic Code).

Key Takeaway

Legal systems vary widely in their aims and in the way they process civil and criminal cases. Common-law systems use juries, have one judge, and adhere to precedent. Civil-law systems decide cases without a jury, often use three judges, and often render shorter opinions without reference to previously decided cases.

Exercises

1. Use the Internet to identify some of the better-known nations with civil-law systems. Which Asian nations came to adopt all or part of civil-law traditions, and why?
2. You may have heard of the Uniform Plumbing Code, or the Uniform Electrical Code; your state has probably adopted the Uniform Traffic Code (here is California's: http://www.dot.ca.gov/trafficops/camutcd/traffic-manual.html). How is California's "code"different from the uniform plumbing code or electrical code?
3. How likely is it that Islamic law will supplant U.S. legal traditions?

1.6 A Sample Case

We have already looked at one case, *Campbell Soup Co. v. Wentz*. This text has (edited) cases; here we examine a sample case for more careful analysis.

Our sample concerns federal law as adopted by Congress, Title VII of the Civil Rights Act of 1964. It is a federal statute that applies to all employers whose workforce exceeds fifteen people. The text of Title VII provides:

> *(a) it shall be an unlawful employment practice for an employer—*
>
> *(1) to fail or refuse to hire or to discharge any individual, or otherwise to discriminate against any individual with respect to his compensation, terms, conditions, or privileges of employment, because of such individual's race, color, religion, sex, or national origin.*

employment at will

The common-law doctrine that allows employers to discharge an employee at any time and for any reason. Courts have created exceptions for "bad reasons."

In common law—where judges decide cases without reference to statutory guidance—employers were generally free to hire and fire on any basis they might choose, and employees were generally free to work for an employer or quit an employer on any basis they might choose (unless the employer and the employee had a contract). This rule is called "**employment at will**." State and federal statutes that prohibit discrimination on any basis (such as the prohibitions on discrimination because of race, color, religion, sex, or national origin in Title VII) are essentially legislative exceptions (or intrusions) to the common-law employment-at-will rule.

sexual harassment

Sexual harassment is bullying or coercion in a sexual context, the unwelcome or inappropriate promise of rewards in exchange for sexual favors.

In the 1970s, many female employees began to claim a certain kind of sex discrimination: **sexual harassment** (and the claim has, in more recent years, brought down some influential men in politics, industry, and entertainment—the "me-too movement"). Some women were being asked to give sexual favors in exchange for continued employment or promotion (*quid pro quo* sexual harassment) or found themselves in a working environment that put their chances for continued employment or promotion at risk. This form of sexual discrimination came to be called "hostile working environment" sexual harassment.

Notice that the statute itself says nothing about sexual harassment but speaks only in broad terms about discrimination "because of" sex (and four other factors). Having set the broad policy, Congress left it to employees, employers, and the courts to fashion more specific rules through the process of civil litigation.

federal district court

Trial court in the federal judicial system.

writ of certiorari

An order by a higher court, directing a lower court to deliver its record in a case so that the higher court may review it.

The following is a case from the U.S. federal court system; there was trial or hearing in the **federal district court**, an appeal to the Sixth Circuit Court of Appeals, and a final appeal to the U.S. Supreme Court. Teresa Harris was the plaintiff (she had the complaint), having lost at both the district court and the Sixth Circuit Court of Appeals, petitioned for a **writ of certiorari** (asking the Supreme Court to issue an order to bring the case to the Court). Petitions for certiorari are granted less than 2% of the time. The Supreme Court chooses its cases very carefully. Here, the court wanted to resolve a difference of opinion among the various circuit courts of appeal as to whether or not a plaintiff in a hostile-working-environment claim could recover damages without showing "severe psychological injury."

Note that the Supreme Court makes use of precedent: it refers to previously-decided cases (some of which it accepts as good, and some of which it rejects). In doing so it gives the citation where a person could actually look up the case, like this: "Rabidue v. Osceola Refining Co., 805 F.2d 611, 620 (CA6 1986), cert. denied, 481 U.S. 1041, 95 L. Ed. 2d 823, 107 S. Ct. 1983 (1987). After the first few representations of such citations, we (the authors) usually will in this text replace them with [Citation]. That means the court gives the citation(s) all right, but we authors don't want to take up a lot of real estate on the page with what will probably not be useful to most students.[15]

Harris v. Forklift Systems

Supreme Court, interpreting the Civil Rights Act of 1964 as to the meaning of discrimination on account of sex.

Harris v. Forklift Systems

510 U.S. 17 (U.S. Supreme Court, 1992)

O'Conner, J.

In this case we consider the definition of a discriminatorily "abusive work environment" (also known as a "hostile work environment") under Title VII of the Civil Rights Act of 1964, 78 Stat. 253, as amended, 42 U.S.C. § 2000e et seq. (1988 ed., Supp. III).

Teresa Harris worked as a manager at Forklift Systems, Inc., an equipment rental company, from April 1985 until October 1987. Charles Hardy was Forklift's president.

The Magistrate [lower court judge] found that, throughout Harris' time at Forklift, Hardy often insulted her because of her gender and often made her the target of unwanted sexual innuendoes. Hardy told Harris on several occasions, in the presence of other employees, "You're a woman, what do you know" and "We need a man as the rental manager"; at least once, he told her she was "a dumbass woman." Again in front of others, he suggested that the two of them "go to the Holiday Inn to negotiate [Harris's] raise." Hardy occasionally asked Harris and other female employees to get coins from his front pants pocket. He threw objects on the ground in front of Harris and other women, and asked them to pick the objects up. He made sexual innuendoes about Harris' and other women's clothing.

In mid-August 1987, Harris complained to Hardy about his conduct. Hardy said he was surprised that Harris was offended, claimed he was only joking, and apologized. He also promised he would stop, and based on this assurance Harris stayed on the job. But in early September, Hardy began anew. While Harris was arranging a deal with one of Forklift's customers, he asked her, again in front of other employees, "What did you do, promise the guy . . . some [sex] Saturday night?" On October 1, Harris collected her paycheck and quit.

Harris then sued Forklift, claiming that Hardy's conduct had created an abusive work environment for her because of her gender. The United States District Court for the Middle District of Tennessee, adopting the report and recommendation of the Magistrate, found this to be "a close case," but held that Hardy's conduct did not create an abusive environment. The court found that some of Hardy's comments "offended [Harris], and would offend the reasonable woman," but that they were not "so severe as to be expected to seriously affect [Harris's] psychological well-being. A reasonable woman manager under like circumstances would have been offended by Hardy, but his conduct would not have risen to the level of interfering with that person's work performance.

"Neither do I believe that [Harris] was subjectively so offended that she suffered injury. . . . Although Hardy may at times have genuinely offended [Harris], I do not believe that he created a working environment so poisoned as to be intimidating or abusive to [Harris]."

In focusing on the employee's psychological well-being, the District Court was following Circuit precedent. See *Rabidue v. Osceola Refining Co.*, 805 F.2d 611, 620 (CA6 1986), cert. denied, 481 U.S. 1041, 95 L. Ed. 2d 823, 107 S. Ct. 1983 (1987). The United States Court of Appeals for the Sixth Circuit affirmed in a brief unpublished decision * * * reported at 976 F.2d 733 (1992).

We granted certiorari, 507 U.S. 959 (1993), to resolve a conflict among the Circuits on whether conduct, to be actionable as "abusive work environment" harassment (no quid pro quo harassment issue is present here), must "seriously affect [an employee's] psychological well-being" or lead the plaintiff to "suffer injury." Compare *Rabidue* (requiring serious effect on psychological well-being); *Vance v. Southern Bell Telephone & Telegraph Co.*, 863 F.2d 1503, 1510 (CA11 1989) (same); and *Downes*

v. *FAA*, 775 F.2d 288, 292 (CA Fed. 1985) (same), with *Ellison v. Brady*, 924 F.2d 872, 877–878 (CA9 1991) (rejecting such a requirement).

Title VII of the Civil Rights Act of 1964 makes it "an unlawful employment practice for an employer…to discriminate against any individual with respect to his compensation, terms, conditions, or privileges of employment, because of such individual's race, color, religion, sex, or national origin." [Citation]. As we made clear in *Meritor Savings Bank, FSB v. Vinson*, [Citation] (1986), this language "is not limited to 'economic' or 'tangible' discrimination. The phrase 'terms, conditions, or privileges of employment' evinces a congressional intent 'to strike at the entire spectrum of disparate treatment of men and women' in employment," which includes requiring people to work in a discriminatorily hostile or abusive environment. [Citation]. When the workplace is permeated with "discriminatory intimidation, ridicule, and insult," that is "sufficiently severe or pervasive to alter the conditions of the victim's employment and create an abusive working environment," Title VII is violated.

This standard, which we reaffirm today, takes a middle path between making actionable any conduct that is merely offensive and requiring the conduct to cause a tangible psychological injury. As we pointed out in *Meritor*, "mere utterance of an . . . epithet which engenders offensive feelings in an employee," does not sufficiently affect the conditions of employment to implicate Title VII. Conduct that is not severe or pervasive enough to create an objectively hostile or abusive work environment—an environment that a reasonable person would find hostile or abusive—is beyond Title VII's purview. Likewise, if the victim does not subjectively perceive the environment to be abusive, the conduct has not actually altered the conditions of the victim's employment, and there is no Title VII violation.

But Title VII comes into play before the harassing conduct leads to a nervous breakdown. A discriminatorily abusive work environment, even one that does not seriously affect employees' psychological well-being, can and often will detract from employees' job performance, discourage employees from remaining on the job, or keep them from advancing in their careers. Moreover, even without regard to these tangible effects, the very fact that the discriminatory conduct was so severe or pervasive that it created a work environment abusive to employees because of their race, gender, religion, or national origin offends Title VII's broad rule of workplace equality. The appalling conduct alleged in *Meritor*, and the reference in that case to environments "'so heavily polluted with discrimination as to destroy completely the emotional and psychological stability of minority group workers,'" [Citation] (1972)], merely present some especially egregious examples of harassment. They do not mark the boundary of what is actionable.

We therefore believe the District Court erred in relying on whether the conduct "seriously affected plaintiff's psychological well-being" or led her to "suffer injury." Such an inquiry may needlessly focus the factfinder's attention on concrete psychological harm, an element Title VII does not require. Certainly Title VII bars conduct that would seriously affect a reasonable person's psychological well-being, but the statute is not limited to such conduct. So long as the environment would reasonably be perceived, and is perceived, as hostile or abusive, *Meritor*, [citation], there is no need for it also to be psychologically injurious.

This is not, and by its nature cannot be, a mathematically precise test. We need not answer today all the potential questions it raises, nor specifically address the Equal Employment Opportunity Commission's new regulations on this subject, see [Citation] (1993). But we can say that whether an environment is "hostile" or "abusive" can be determined only by looking at all the circumstances. These may include the frequency of the discriminatory conduct; its severity; whether it is physically threatening or humiliating, or a mere offensive utterance; and whether it unreasonably interferes with an employee's work performance. The effect on the employee's psychological well-being is, of course, relevant to determining whether the plaintiff actually found the environment abusive. But while psychological harm, like any other relevant factor, may be taken into account, no single factor is required.

Forklift, while conceding that a requirement that the conduct seriously affect psychological well-being is unfounded, argues that the District Court nonetheless correctly applied the *Meritor* standard. We disagree. Though the District Court did conclude that the work environment was not "intimidating or abusive to [Harris]," it did so only after finding that the conduct was not "so severe as to be expected to seriously affect plaintiff's psychological well-being," and that Harris was not "subjectively so offended that she suffered injury," ibid. The District Court's application of these incorrect standards may well have influenced its ultimate conclusion, especially given that the court found this to be a "close case."

We therefore reverse the judgment of the Court of Appeals, and remand the case for further proceedings consistent with this opinion.

So ordered.

Note to Students

This was only the second time that the Supreme Court had decided a sexual harassment case. Many feminist legal studies scholars feared that the court would raise the bar and make hostile-working-environment claims under Title VII more difficult to win. That did not happen. When the question to be decided is combined with the court's decision, we get the holding of the case. Here, the question that the court poses, plus its answer, yields a holding that "An employee need not prove severe psychological injury in order to win a Title VII sexual harassment claim." This holding will be true until such time as the court revisits a similar question and answers it differently. This does not happen often.

Case Questions

1. Is this a criminal case or a civil-law case? How can you tell?
2. Is the court concerned with making a procedural rule here, or is the court making a statement about the substantive law?
3. Is this a case where the court is interpreting the Constitution, a federal statute, a state statute, or the common law?
4. In *Harris v. Forklift*, what if the trial judge does not personally agree that women should have any special right not to be subjected to this offensive but—alas—not uncommon treatment in the workplace? Why shouldn't that judge dismiss the case even before trial? Or should the judge dismiss the case after giving the female plaintiff her day in court?
5. What was the employer's argument in this case? Do you agree or disagree with it? What if those who legislated Title VII gave no thought to the question of seriousness of injury at all?

1.7 Summary and Exercises

Summary

There are differing conceptions of what law is and of what law should be. Laws and legal systems differ worldwide. The legal system in the United States is founded on the U.S. Constitution, which is itself inspired by natural-law theory and the idea that people have rights that cannot be taken by government but only protected by government. The various functions of the law are done well or poorly depending on which nation-state you look at. Some do very well in terms of keeping order, while others do a better job of allowing civil and political freedoms. Social and political movements within each nation greatly affect the nature and quality of the legal system within that nation.

This chapter has familiarized you with a few of the basic schools of legal thought, such as natural law, positive law, legal realism, and critical legal studies. It has also given you a brief background in common law, including contracts, torts, and criminal law. The differences between civil and criminal cases, substance and procedure, and the various sources of law have also been reviewed. Each source has a different level of authority, starting with constitutions, which are primary and will negate any lower-court laws that are not consistent with its principles and provisions. The basic differences between the common law and civil law (continental, or European) systems of law have also been discussed.

Exercises

1. What is common law? Where do the courts get the authority to interpret it and to change it?
2. After World War II ended in 1945, there was an international tribunal at Nuremberg that prosecuted various officials in Germany's Third Reich who had committed "crimes against humanity." Many of them claim that they were simply "following orders" of Adolf Hitler and his chief lieutenants. What law, if any, have they violated?
3. What does *stare decisis* mean, and why is it so basic to common-law legal tradition?
4. In the following situations, which source of law takes priority, and why?
   a. The state statute conflicts with the common law of that state.
   b. A federal statute conflicts with the U.S. Constitution.
   c. A common-law decision in one state conflicts with the U.S. Constitution.
   d. A federal statute conflicts with a state constitution.

Self-Test Questions

1. The source of law that is foundational in the U.S. legal system is:
   a. common law
   b. statutory law
   c. constitutional law
   d. administrative law
2. "Law is the command of a sovereign" represents what school of legal thought?
   a. civil law
   b. constitutional law
   c. natural law
   d. ecofeminist law
   e. positive law
3. Which of the following kinds of law are most often found in state law rather than federal law?
   a. torts and contracts
   b. bankruptcy
   c. maritime law
   d. international law
4. Where was natural law discovered?
   a. in nature
   b. in constitutions and statutes
   c. in the exercise of human reason
   d. in the *Wall Street Journal*

5. Wolfe is a state court judge in California. In the case of *Riddick v. Clouse*, which involves a contract dispute, Wolfe must follow precedent. She establishes a logical relationship between the *Riddick* case and a case decided by the California Supreme Court, *Zhu v. Patel Enterprises, Inc.* She compares the facts of *Riddick* to the facts in *Zhu* and to the extent the facts are similar, applies the same rule to reach her decision. This is:

   a. deductive reasoning

   b. faulty reasoning

   c. linear reasoning

   d. reasoning by analogy

6. Moore is a state court judge in Colorado. In the case of *Cassidy v. Seawell*, also a contract dispute, there is no Colorado Supreme Court or court of appeals decision that sets forth a rule that could be applied. However, the California case of *Zhu v. Patel Enterprises, Inc.* is "very close" on the facts and sets forth a rule of law that could be applied to the Cassidy case. What process must Moore follow in considering whether to use the *Zhu* case as precedent?

   a. Moore is free to decide the case any way he wants, but he may not look at decisions and reasons in similar cases from other states.

   b. Moore must wait for the Colorado legislature and the governor to pass a law that addresses the issues raised in the *Cassidy* case.

   c. Moore must follow the California case if that is the best precedent.

   d. Moore may follow the California case if he believes that it offers the best reasoning for a similar case.

Self-Test Answers

1. c
2. e
3. a
4. c
5. d
6. d

Endnotes

1. *Black's Law Dictionary*, 6th ed., s.v. "law."

2. The United States has nearly 800 military bases in more than 70 countries and territories abroad, costing an estimated $85–100 billion a year (not including bases and troops in war zones). David Vine, "Where in the World is the U.S. Military?" *Politico Magazine,* July/August 2015. https://www.politico.com/magazine/story/2015/06/us-military-bases-around-the-world-119321

3. Genocide is the deliberate and systematic killing or displacement of one group of people by another group. In 1948, the international community, through the United Nations, formally condemned the crime of genocide. The euphemistic term is "ethnic cleansing."

4. Linette Lopez, One company has thrown politics in the Western Hemisphere completely off-kilter *Business Insider,* May 30, 2017. https://www.google.com/search?q=Linette+Lopez,+One+company+has+thrown+politics+in+the+Western+Hemisphere+completely+off-kilter+Business+Insider,+May+30,+2017.&ie=utf-8&oe=utf-8&client=firefox-b-1

5. Judicial Independence, World Economic Forum, http://reports.weforum.org/pdf/gci-2017-2018-scorecard/WEF_GCI_2017_2018_Scorecard_EOSQ144.pdf

6. https://hbr.org/2017/03/being-an-ethical-business-in-a-corrupt-environment

7. *Cambridge Dictionary of Philosophy*, s.v. "natural law."

8. Martin Luther King Jr., "Letter from Birmingham Jail."

9. The Third Circuit Federal Court of Appeals is headquartered in Philadelphia; it serves Pennsylvania, New Jersey, and the U.S. Virgin Islands. https://www.ca3.uscourts.gov/

10. "Specific performance" is an order directing a person to sell to a contract buyer the unique, otherwise not (readily) obtainable thing the buyer contracted for because money won't provide a remedy (again, because the thing is not available on the market except from this seller).

11. State legislation primarily involves the following topics—Contracts, including sales, commercial paper, letters of credit, and secured transactions—Torts—Property, including real property, bailments of personal property (such as when you check your coat at a theater or leave your clothes with a dry cleaner), trademarks, copyrights, and the estates of decedents (dead people)—Corporations—Partnerships—Domestic matters, including marriage, divorce, custody, adoption, and visitation—Securities law (the law governing the sale of stocks)—Environmental law—Agency law, governing the relationship between principals and their agents—Banking—Insurance

12. One example of treaty obligations overriding, or taking priority over, federal statutes was the tuna-dolphin dispute between the United States and Mexico. The Marine Mammal Protection Act amendments in 1988 spelled out certain protections for dolphins in the Eastern Tropical Pacific, and the United States began refusing to allow the importation of tuna that were caught using "dolphin-unfriendly" methods (such as purse seining). This was challenged at a GATT dispute panel in Switzerland, and the United States lost. In short, by agreeing to dispute resolution at the GATT (and subsequently, the WTO), a U.S. environmental statute can be ruled contrary to prior U.S. treaty obligations.

13. One example of that is the doctrine of "originalism," often espoused by the late Justice Antonin Scalia. He insisted that the words and phrases in the Constitution be interpreted in accordance with what the Framers would have understood those words to mean. His views might well correspond to both the historical school and, to some extent, the natural-law school, given the Framers' admiration for "unalienable rights."

14. https://www.cbsnews.com/news/fears-of-sharia-law-in-america-grow-among-conservatives/

15. Here's a tip: when you see the word "[Citation]" in this text, it means that just before that word or just after is a statement of law where the judge who's writing the opinion you're reading refers to the law of another case (precedent). You want to pay attention to the statements of law, and see whether the court in this case accepts or rejects that precedent.

CHAPTER 2
Introduction to Business Ethics

A great society is a society in which [leaders] of business think greatly about their functions.
— *Alfred North Whitehead*

Chapter Learning Objectives

After reading this chapter, you should be able to:

1. Define ethics and explain the importance of good ethics for businesspeople and business organizations.
2. Understand the principal philosophies of ethics, including utilitarianism, duty-based ethics, and virtue ethics.
3. Distinguish between the ethical merits of various choices by using an ethical decision model.
4. Explain the difference between shareholder and stakeholder models of ethical corporate governance.
5. Explain why it is difficult to establish and maintain an ethical corporate culture in a business organization.

Few subjects are more contentious or important as the role of business in society; particularly, whether corporations have social responsibilities that are distinct from maximizing shareholder value. While the phrase "business ethics" is not oxymoronic (i.e., a contradiction in terms), there is abundant evidence that many businesspeople and firms seek profit only for themselves, and do not care much about others, or society generally. But business organizations ignore the ethical and social expectations of consumers, employees, the media, nongovernmental organizations (NGOs), government officials, and socially responsible investors at their peril. Legal compliance alone has probably never served the long-term interests of any companies, and given world-wide population growth and environmental degradation, enlightened businesspeople find that sustainable profitability requires thinking about people and the planet as well as profits.

This chapter has a fairly modest aim: to introduce potential businesspeople to the differences between legal compliance and ethical excellence by reviewing some of the philosophical perspectives that apply to business, businesspeople, and the role of business organizations in society.

2.1 What Is Ethics?

Learning Objectives

1. Explain how not only individuals, but also companies and institutions, can be seen as more or less ethical.
2. Explain how law and ethics are different, and why a good reputation can be more important to business firms than legal compliance.

Most of those who write about ethics do not make a clear distinction between ethics and morality. The question of what is "right" or "morally correct" or "ethically correct" or "morally desirable" is variously phrased, but all of the words and phrases are after the same thing: what act is "better" in a moral or ethical sense than some other act? In this text, *ethics* and *morality* will be used as equivalent terms.

People often make judgments about the ethics of individuals, but will also make judgments about the ethics of corporations and nations. There are clearly differences between people, corporations, and nations; we tend to see individuals as having a soul, or at least a conscience, but there is no general agreement that nations or corporations have either. Still, our ordinary use of language does point to something significant: if we say that some nations are "evil" and others are "corrupt," then we make moral judgments about the quality of actions undertaken by the governments or people of that nation. For example, North Korea was characterized by President George W. Bush as part of an "axis of evil," or we might read in Transparency International's annual report that Nigeria is one of the most "corrupt" nations in the world. We could also conclude that Volkswagen acted "unethically" in creating software that defeated emissions testing, thereby misrepresenting to the public and to the government their diesel cars' emissions performance. In short, people often make moral judgments about other people (you!), a business firm where there has been a "scandal," or even a nation-state.

A word such as *good* can embrace ethical or moral values but also non-ethical values. If I like Daniel and try to convince you what a "good guy" he is, you may ask all sorts of questions: Is he really smart? Well-off? Fun to be with? Humorous? Athletic? I could answer all of those questions with a yes, but you would still not know any of his moral qualities. But if I said that he was honest, caring, forthright, and diligent, volunteered in local soup kitchens, or tithed to the church, many people would see Daniel as having certain ethical qualities. If I said that he keeps the Golden Rule as well as anyone I know, you might conclude that he is an ethical person. But if I said that he is "always in control" or "always at the top of his game," you would probably not make inferences or assumptions about his character or ethics.

There are three key points here:

1. Although morals and ethics are not precisely measurable, people generally have similar reactions about what actions or conduct can rightly be called ethical or moral.
2. As humans, we need and value ethical people and want to be around them.
3. Saying that someone or some organization is law-abiding does not mean the same as saying a person or company is ethical.

Here is a cautionary note: for individuals, it is not easy to recognize an ethical problem, have a clear and usable decision-making process to deal with it, and then have the moral courage to do what's right. All of that is even more difficult within a business organization, where corporate employees vary in their motivations, loyalties, commitments, and character. There is no universally accepted way for developing an organization where employees feel valued, respected, and free to openly disagree; where the actions of top management are crystal clear; and where all the employees feel loyal and accountable to one another.

Before talking about how ethics relates to law, we can now define ethics as the study of morality—"right" and "wrong"—in the context of everyday life, organizational behaviors, and even how society operates and is governed. Though again, we will use the terms "ethical" and "moral" interchangeably.

How Do Law and Ethics Differ?

There is a difference between legal compliance and moral excellence. Few would choose a professional service, healthcare or otherwise, because the provider had a record of perfect *legal* compliance, or always following the letter of the *law*. There are many professional ethics codes, primarily because people realize that law prescribes only a *minimum* of morality and does not provide purpose or goals that can mean excellent service to customers, clients, or patients.

Business ethicists have talked for years about the intersection of law and ethics. Simply put, what is legal is not necessarily ethical ("the law allows much that honor fobids"). Conversely, what is ethical is not necessarily legal. There are lots of legal maneuvers that are not all that ethical; the well-used phrase "legal loophole" suggests as much.

Here are two propositions about business and ethics. Consider whether they strike you as true or whether you would need to know more in order to make a judgment.

- Individuals and organizations have reputations. (For an individual, moral reputation is most often tied to others' perceptions of his or her character—is the individual honest, diligent, reliable, fair, and caring? The reputation of an organization is built on the good will that suppliers, customers, the community, and employees feel toward it. Although an organization is not a person in the usual sense, the good will that people feel about the organization is based on their perception of its better qualities by a variety of stakeholders—customers or clients, suppliers, investors, employees, government officials).

- The good will of an organization is to a great extent based on the actions it takes and on whether the actions are favorably viewed. (This good will is usually accounted for in the sale of a business as one of the assets that the buyer pays for. While it is difficult to place a monetary value on good will, a firm's good reputation will generally call for a higher evaluation in the final accounting before the sale. Legal troubles often follow unethical decisions, and a reputation for having legal troubles will lessen the price for a business and will even lessen the value of the company's stock as bad legal news comes to the public's attention.)

Another reason to think about ethics in connection with law is that the laws themselves are meant to express some moral view. If there are legal prohibitions against cheating the Medicare program, it is because people (through their legislators) have collectively decided that cheating Medicare is wrong. If there are legal prohibitions against assisting someone to commit suicide, it is because there has been a societal decision that, on balance, assisting suicides is wrong. Thus the law provides some important cues as to what society regards as right or wrong, even as society reconsiders its past judgments about right and wrong.

Finally, important policy issues that face society are often resolved politically through law, but it is important to understand the moral perspectives that underlie public debate—as, for example, in the continuing controversies over immigration, LGBTQ rights, stem-cell research, welfare (individual or corporate), gun control, medical use of marijuana, and abortion. Some ethical perspectives focus on rights, some on social utility, some on virtue or character, and some on social justice. People consciously (or, more often, unconsciously) adopt one or more of these perspectives, and even if they completely agree with an opponent on the facts, they will not change their views. Fundamentally, the difference comes down to incompatible moral perspectives, a clash of basic values. These are hot-button issues because society is divided, not so much over facts, but over basic values.

Understanding the varied ethical perspectives that drive people's opinions in these public policy debates is a worthwhile skill to have as a business leader, as business becomes increasingly active in social and political issues.

Why Should an Individual or a Business Entity Be Ethical?

The usual answer is that good ethics is good business. In the long run, businesses that pay attention to ethics as well as law do better; they are viewed more favorably by customers and other stakeholders. But this is a difficult claim to measure scientifically, because "the long run" is an indistinct period of time and because there are as yet no generally-accepted criteria by which ethical excellence can be measured. In addition, life is still lived in the short run, and there are many occasions when something short of perfect conduct is a lot more profitable.

Some years ago, Royal Dutch Shell (one of the world's largest companies) found that it was in deep trouble with the public for its apparent carelessness with the environment and human rights. Consumers were boycotting and investors were getting frightened, so the company took a long, hard look at its ethic of short-term profit maximization. Since then, changes have been made. The CEO told one group of business ethicists that the uproar had taken them by surprise; they thought they had done everything right, but it seemed there was a "ghost in the machine." That ghost was consumers, NGOs, and the media, all of whom objected to the company's seeming lack of moral sensitivity.[1]

The market does respond to unethical behavior. In Section 3, you will read about the Sears Auto Centers case. The loss of good will toward Sears Auto Centers was real, even though the total amount of money lost cannot be clearly accounted for. People are somewhat distrustful of auto mechanics in general, but many years later, some people who remember the "scandal" will not go near a Sears Auto Center; the customers who lost trust in the company will never return, and some of their children avoid Sears Auto Centers as well.[2]

The Arthur Andersen story is even more dramatic. A major accounting firm, Andersen worked closely with Enron in hiding its various losses through creative accounting measures. Suspiciously, Andersen's Houston (Texas) office also did some shredding around the clock, appearing to cover up what it was doing for Enron. A criminal case based on this shredding resulted in a conviction, later overturned by the Supreme Court. But it was too late. Even before the conviction, many clients had found other accounting firms that were not under suspicion, and the Supreme Court's reversal came too late to save the company. Even without the conviction, Andersen would have lost significant market share.

The irony of Andersen as a poster child for overly-aggressive accounting practices is that the man who founded the firm built it on integrity and straightforward practices. "Think straight, talk straight" was the company's motto for many years. Andersen established the company's reputation for integrity over a hundred years ago by refusing to play numbers games for a potentially lucrative client. But corporate cultures change, even an ethical culture started by Arthur Andersen that prevailed until the 1990s. Barbara Ley Toffler, who was partner-in-charge of the firm's Ethics & Responsible Business Practices, noted in her book *Final Accounting: Ambition, Greed, and the Fall of Arthur Andersen*, that by the 1990s the firm had come to have a culture of putting the firm's revenues ahead of the client's needs and honest certifications to the public.

Maximizing profits while being legally compliant is not a very inspiring goal for a business. People in an organization need some quality or excellence to strive for. By pushing the edge of what is legal, by looking for loopholes in the law that would help create short-term financial gain, companies have often learned that in the long term they are not actually satisfying the market, the shareholders, the suppliers, or the community generally.

Key Takeaway

Legal compliance is not the same as acting ethically. Your reputation, individually or corporately, depends on how others regard your actions. Good will is hard to measure or quantify, but it is real nonetheless and can best be protected by acting ethically.

Exercises

1. Think of a person who did something morally wrong, at least to your way of thinking. What was it? Explain to a friend of yours—or a classmate—why you think it was wrong. Does your friend agree? Why or why not? What is the basic principle that forms the basis for your judgment that it was wrong?

2. Think of a person who did something morally right, at least to your way of thinking. (This is not a matter of finding something they did well, like efficiently changing a tire, but something good.) What was it? Explain to a friend of yours—or a classmate—why you think it was right. Does your friend agree? Why or why not? What is the basic principle that forms the basis for your judgment that it was right?

3. Think of an action by a business organization (sole proprietor, partnership, or corporation) that was legal but still strikes you as wrong. What was it? Why do you think it was wrong?

4. Is it morally wrong to drive on the left-hand side of the road for a short while if there were no oncoming traffic? Many would say not, but it is still legally wrong. How does this make sense?

2.2 Major Ethical Perspectives

Learning Objectives

1. Describe the various major theories about ethics in human decision making.
2. Begin considering how the major theories about ethics apply to difficult choices in life and business.

There are several well-respected ways of looking at ethical issues. Some of them have been around for centuries. It is important to know that many who think a lot about business and ethics have deeply-held beliefs about which perspective is best. Others would recommend considering ethical problems from a variety of different perspectives. Here, we take a brief look at (1) utilitarianism, (2) deontology, (3) social justice and social contract theory, and (4) virtue theory. We are leaving out some important perspectives, such as a thorough discussion of "rights," Carol Gilligan's ethics of caring, Kohlberg's theories on moral development, and feminist thought about ethics and patriarchy. We also leave out an increasingly important aspect of business ethics—the growing influence of behavioral psychology, a field which has revealed significant gaps in our ability as individuals and business firms to make rational decisions.[3]

Utilitarianism

utilitarianism

The theory that the "right" moral act is the one that produces the greatest good for society.

Utilitarianism is a prominent perspective on ethics, one that is well aligned with economics and the free-market outlook that has come to dominate much current thinking about business, management, and economics. Jeremy Bentham (1748–1832) is often considered the founder of utilitarianism, though John Stuart Mill (1806-1873—he wrote *On Liberty* and *Utilitarianism*) and others promoted it as a guide to what is good. Utilitarianism emphasizes not rules but results. An action (or set of actions) is generally deemed good or right if it maximizes happiness or pleasure throughout society. Originally intended as a guide for legislators charged with seeking the greatest good for society, the utilitarian outlook may also be practiced individually and by corporations.

Bentham believed that the most promising way to obtain agreement on the best policies for a society would be to look at the various policies a legislature could pass and compare the good and bad consequences of each. The right course of action from an ethical point of view would be to choose the policy that would produce the greatest amount of utility, or usefulness. In brief, the utilitarian principle holds that an action is right if, and only if, the sum of utilities produced by that action is greater than the sum of utilities from any other possible act.

Notice that the emphasis is on finding the best possible results, and depends on the assumption that we can measure the utilities involved. (This turns out to be more difficult that you might think.) Notice also that "the sum total of utilities" clearly implies that in doing utilitarian analysis, we cannot be satisfied if an act or set of acts provides the greatest utility to us as individuals or to a particular corporation; the test is whether it provides the greatest utility to society as a whole. Notice that the theory does not tell us what kinds of utilities may be better than others—whether witnessing a performance of Mozart's Requiem or watching The Simpsons for 90 minutes—delivers more "good," or how much better a good today is compared with the same or similar good a year from today.[4]

Whatever its difficulties, utilitarian thinking is alive and well in U.S. law and business. It is found in such diverse places as cost-benefit analysis in administrative and regulatory rules and calculations, environmental impact studies, the majority vote, product comparisons for consumer information, marketing studies, tax laws, and strategic planning. In management, people will often employ a form of utility reasoning by projecting costs and benefits for plan X versus plan Y. But this is not the same as a true utilitarian approach: many cost-benefit analyses are (1) put exclusively in terms of money, recognizing no other values or goods, and (2) directed to the benefit of the person or organization doing the analysis, not to the greatest good for society as a whole.

An individual or a company that consistently uses the test "What's the greatest good for me or the company?" is not following the utilitarian test of the greatest good overall. Another common failing is to see only one or two options that seem reasonable. The following are some frequent mistakes that people make in applying what they think are utilitarian principles in justifying their chosen course of action:

1. Assuming that the greatest good for you or your company is in fact the greatest good for all—that is, looking at situations subjectively or primarily with your own interests in mind.

2. Underestimating the costs of a certain decision to you or your company. The now-classic Ford Pinto case demonstrates how Ford Motor Company executives greatly underestimated the legal costs of not correcting a feature on their Pinto models that they knew could cause death or injury. General Motors learned a similar lesson in its failure to fix an ignition switch that sometimes shut off cars moving along roads and highways, leading to significant injuries to drivers and occupants.

3. Underestimating the cost or harm of a certain decision to someone else or some other group of people.

4. Favoring short-term benefits, even though the long-term costs are greater.

5. Assuming that all values can be reduced to money. In comparing the risks to human health or safety against, say, the risks of job or profit losses, cost-benefit analyses will often try to compare "apples to oranges" and put arbitrary numerical values on human health and safety.

The most common objections to utilitarian thinking are that we simply can't reliably predict the future consequences of an act that seems justified under utilitarian thinking. The second objection is that the autonomy, dignity, and rights of individuals are not taken into account. Consider the famous case of *The Queen v. Dudley and Stephens* to see both of these objections in stark relief.

Case

The Utilitarian Ethics of Murder and Cannibalism

> ### The Queen v. Dudley and Stephens
> 14 Queens Bench Division 273 (1884)

The Queen v. Dudley and Stephens

An 1884 case from the high court of Britain examining whether murder and cannibalism could ever be legally excused.

Huddleston, J.

On July 5, 1884, the prisoners, Thomas Dudley and Edward Stephens, with one Brooks, all able-bodied English seamen, and the deceased also an English boy, between seventeen and eighteen years of age, the crew of an English yacht, were cast away in a storm on the high seas 1,600 miles from the Cape of Good Hope, and were compelled to put into an open boat belonging to the said yacht. That in this boat they had no supply of water and no supply of food, except two 1 lb. tins of turnips, and for three days they had nothing else to subsist upon. That on the fourth day they caught a small turtle, upon which they subsisted for a few days, and this was the only food they had up to the twentieth day when the act now in question was committed.

That on the twelfth day the turtle were entirely consumed, and for the next eight days they had nothing to eat. That they had no fresh water, except such rain as they from time to time caught in their oilskin capes. That the boat was drifting on the ocean, and was probably more than 1,000 miles away from land. That on the eighteenth day, when they had been seven days without food and five without water, the prisoners spoke to Brooks as to what should be done if no rescue came, and suggested that some one should be sacrificed to save the rest, but Brooks dissented, and the boy, to whom they were understood to refer, was not consulted. That on the 24th of July, the day before the act now in question, the prisoner Dudley proposed to Stephens and Brooks that lots should be cast who should be put to death to save the rest, but Brooks refused consent, and it was not put to the boy, and in point of fact there was no drawing of lots.

That on that day the prisoners spoke of their having families, and suggested it would be better to kill the boy that their lives should be saved, and Dudley proposed that if there was no vessel in sight by the morrow morning the boy should be killed. That next day, the 25th of July, no vessel appearing, Dudley told Brooks that he had better go and have a sleep, and made signs to Stephens and Brooks that the boy had better be killed. The prisoner Stephens agreed to the act, but Brooks dissented from it. That the boy was then lying at the bottom of the boat quite helpless, and extremely weakened by famine and by drinking sea water, and unable to make any resistance, nor did he ever assent to his being killed. The prisoner Dudley offered a prayer asking forgiveness for them all if either of them should be tempted to commit a rash act, and that their souls might be saved. That Dudley, with the assent of Stephens, went to the boy, and telling him that his time was come, put a knife into his throat and killed him then and there; that the three men fed upon the body and blood of the boy for four days; that on the fourth day after the act had been committed the boat was picked up by a passing vessel, and the prisoners were rescued, still alive, but in the lowest state of prostration.

That they were carried to the port of Falmouth, and committed for trial at Exeter. That if the men had not fed upon the body of the boy they would probably not have survived to be so picked up and rescued, but would within the four days have died of famine. That the boy, being in a much weaker condition, was likely to have died before them. That at the time of the act in question there was no sail in sight, nor any reasonable prospect of relief. That under these circumstances there appeared to the prisoners every probability that unless they then fed or very soon fed upon the boy or one of themselves they would die of starvation. That there was no appreciable chance of saving life except by killing some one for the others to eat. * * * There remains to be considered the real question in the case—whether killing under the circumstances set forth in the verdict be or be not murder. The contention that it could be anything else was, to the minds of us all, both new and strange.

First it is said that it follows from various definitions of murder in books of authority, which definitions imply, if they do not state, the doctrine, that in order to save your own life you may lawfully take away the life of another, when that other is neither attempting nor threatening yours, nor is guilty of any illegal act whatever towards you or any one else. But if these definitions be looked at they will not be found to sustain this contention. * * * Now, except for the purpose of testing how far the conservation of a man's own life is in all cases and under all circumstances an absolute, unqualified, and paramount duty, we exclude from our consideration all the incidents of war. We are dealing with a case of private homicide, not one imposed upon men in the service of their Sovereign and in the defence of their country.

Now it is admitted that the deliberate killing of this unoffending and unresisting boy was clearly murder, unless the killing can be justified by some well-recognised excuse admitted by the law. It is further admitted that there was in this case no such excuse, unless the killing was justified by what has been called "necessity." But the temptation to the act which existed here was not what the law has ever called necessity. Nor is this to be regretted. Though law and morality are not the same, and many things may be immoral which are not necessarily illegal, yet the absolute divorce of law from morality would be of fatal consequence; and such divorce would follow if the temptation to murder in this case were to be held by law an absolute defence of it. It is not so. To preserve one's life is generally speaking a duty, but it may be the plainest and the highest duty to sacrifice it. War is full of instances in which it is a man's duty not to live, but to die. The duty, in case of shipwreck, of a captain to his crew, of the crew to the passengers, of soldiers to women and children, as in the noble case of the Birkenhead; these duties impose on men the moral necessity, not of the preservations but of the sacrifice of their lives for others, from which in no country, least of all, it is to be hoped, in England, will men ever shrink as indeed, they have not shrunk. It is not correct, therefore, to say that there is any absolute or unqualified necessity to preserve one's life.

It would be a very easy and cheap display of commonplace learning to quote from Greek and Latin authors, from Horace, from Juvenal, from Cicero, from Euripides, passage after passage, in which the duty of dying for others has been laid down in glowing and emphatic language as resulting from the principles of heathen ethics; it is enough in a Christian country to remind ourselves of the Great Example whom we profess to follow. It is not needful to point out the awful danger of admitting the principle which has been contended for. Who is to be the judge of this sort of necessity? By what measure is the comparative value of lives to be measured? Is it to be strength, or intellect, or what? It is plain that the principle leaves to him who is to profit by it to determine the necessity which will justify him in deliberately taking another's life to save his own. In this case the weakest, the youngest, the most unresisting, was chosen. Was it more necessary to kill him than one of the grown men? The answer must be "No." * * *

It is not suggested that in this particular case the deeds were devilish, but it is quite plain that such a principle once admitted might be made the legal cloak for unbridled passion and atrocious crime. There is no safe path for judges to tread but to ascertain the law to the best of their ability and to declare it according to their judgment; and if in any case the law appears to be too severe on individuals, to leave it to the Sovereign to exercise that prerogative of mercy which the Constitution has entrusted to the hands fittest to dispense it. It must not be supposed that in refusing to admit temptation to be an excuse for crime it is forgotten how terrible the temptation was; how awful the suffering; how hard in such trials to keep the judgment straight and the conduct pure. We are often compelled to set up standards we cannot reach ourselves, and to lay down rules which we could not ourselves satisfy. But a man has no right to declare temptation to be an excuse, though he might himself have yielded to it, nor allow compassion for the criminal to change or weaken in any manner the legal definition of the crime. It is therefore our duty to declare that the prisoners' act in this case was wilful murder, that the facts as stated in the verdict are no legal justification of the homicide; and to say that in our unanimous opinion the prisoners are upon this special verdict guilty, of murder.

[The court then sentenced both prisoners to death.]

Case Follow-Up. This was not the first time that English sailors stranded at sea resorted to desperate measures to survive. This was the first prosecution in England for cannibalism, and it is noteworthy that Tom Dudley, as captain of the ship, wrote a full account of what had happened upon his return to England. But he returned to a Victorian England that had notions of "high morality," and the ruling class regarded itself as the pinnacle of civilization. England's agents (some of them corporations like the East India Company) were out conquering India and large parts of Africa in the name of the Queen. Cannibalism was something that "savages" did, and to the upper class, cannibalism under any circumstances was unthinkable. The leaders of Victorian England saw themselves as stewards of "the rule of law," and Dudley and Stephens returned to this moral climate in 1884. By contrast, in the seagoing communities of England, there was an immediate outcry; the popular sentiment in these communities was that it was clearly unfair to prosecute Dudley and Stephens. The discontent after their sentence was imposed did not die down. Finally, the establishment relented as William Harcourt, the Home Secretary in Queen Victoria's government, recommended that the death penalty be commuted by the queen. She agreed and set the punishment at six months imprisonment.

Case Questions

1. Can you recommend a morally better option that they "should" have pursued instead of killing the cabin boy? Explain why the option you recommend was morally "better."

2. If you are not convinced that utilitarianism justifies their act, explain why not. Perhaps you think that Richard Parker's (the cabin boy's) "rights" were violated, since he did not consent? Would it have been "better" if he were conscious enough to have told Dudley and Stevens, "I know I'm a goner. Kill me mercifully and try to survive."? Even so, would you still have reservations about Parker's permission and his companions' acceptance of his offer?

3. Speaking of "rights," would Parker have the unquestionable "right" to decide to die and have his body used by others to survive? (Kant, as you will see, would claim that he does not have that right.)

4. So, why is a case about cannibalism in a business school textbook? Sometimes, a business will deliberately sell a product that it knows could kill people. Consider the Ford Motor Company's decision to bring the Pinto to market knowing that a certain number of people would die or be seriously injured if the car were rear-ended by another vehicle going more than 20 mph. Is there a utilitarian way to morally justify that decision? Does it make a difference that the executives at Ford would not know the victims personally? What if they had accurately estimated that serious burns or death would only occur once for every 500 million miles that Pintos were driven? (that is, assume that only one Pinto in 5,000 would be likely to be involved in a rear-end collision that would cause serious injury or death).

Rules and Duty: Deontology

In contrast to the utilitarian perspective, the duty-based view presented in the writings of Immanuel Kant purports that having a moral intent and following the right rules is a better path to ethical conduct than achieving any particular result that seems "good." A deontologist or duty-based thinker like Kant holds that ethical action arises from doing one's duty, and only those duties that are defined by rational thought. Duties, according to Kant, are not just owed to particular kinds of human beings, but are owed to all human beings. Kant considers all humans as equal, not in the physical, social, or economic sense, but equal before God, the Creator, or the wider universe (to take a more secular approach).

deontology

A theory that judges the morality of choices not by results (or "goods") but by adherence to duty discerned by rational thought. The duty to act in accord with these norms is one that bears no relation to the expected consequences of the action.

For Kantian thinkers, this basic principle of equality means that we should be able to universalize any particular law or action to determine whether it is ethical. **Deontology** requires that we put duty first, act rationally, and give moral weight to the inherent equality of all human beings. Kant has two notable formulations of his "Supreme Principle of Morality," or two versions of "the categorical imperative." The first one is: Act only so that you would be satisfied if your action should become a universal law.

The second version of the categorical imperative is: Act in such a way that you treat humanity, whether in your own person or in the person of any other, never merely as a means to an end, but always at the same time as an end.

There is considerable scholarly discussion on whether these two formulations amount to the same basic duty. For the sake of brevity, and the enjoyment of application, let's consider each one in turn.

Say you are thinking about misrepresenting yourself on a resume for a job you really wanted, as you are convinced that doing so would get you that job, and since this is your "dream job," you might be very tempted to do so. ("What harm would it be?" you might very well ask yourself. "When I have the job, I can prove that I am perfect for it, and no one is hurt, so both the employer and I are clearly better off as a result!") The behavioral psychologist would likely say that you have a "self-serving bias" (as most people do) and are obviously biased in your calculations, and Kantian ethicists propose the antidote: the essential character of your chosen course of action should follow a rule that can be a universal one—a rule of action that would be good for all persons at all times.

Using Kant's first categorical imperative, there are two requirements for a rule of action to be universal: consistency and reversibility. Consider reversibility: reversibility requires you to actively imagine both that you were the employer in this situation and that you were another well-qualified applicant who lost the job because someone else padded his resume with false accomplishments. If the consequences of this exercise in moral imagination are not appealing to you, your action is probably not ethical.

The second requirement for an action to be universal is the search for consistency. This is more abstract. A deontologist would say that since you know you are telling a lie, you must be willing to say that lying, as a general, universal phenomenon, is acceptable. But if everyone lied, then there would be no point to lying, since no one would believe anyone. It is only because honesty works well for society as a whole and is generally practiced that lying even becomes useful to the liar! That is, lying cannot be universalized, for it depends on the preexistence of honesty.

Taking the same example and looking at Kant's second formulation of the categorical imperative, we can see that you would be treating others (the employer and other applicants, among others) as mere means to your own ends. Full respect for the humanity of those others would urge honesty, so that others might choose wisely and well.

By recognizing the inherent worth of all human beings, Kant sets the stage for general recognition of human rights, and thus resists even the possibility that the majority can benefit from the suffering of a small minority whose right not to be treated as a means to others' ends is overcome by "the greatest good." But his approach has been criticized as confounding where duties are in conflict, such as where promise-keeping (universalizable) and truth-telling (also universalizable) come into conflict. Suppose the Gestapo asks the owner of the house where Anne Frank lives if he knows where she is. The homeowner who lies violates a duty to be honest, yet may well have promised Anne Frank and her family not to reveal her whereabouts. Kant tries to finesse this by allowing the homeowner to say something truthful but misleading. (For example, "I saw her at the market two hours ago.") When President Clinton testified under oath that he "did not have sexual relations with that woman, Monica Lewinsky" he was speaking a sort of truth, but a misleading one. Whether Kant would approve of that misdirection or not has been discussed by ethics professors.[5] But the discussion is not entirely academic; must CEOs and other managers in a company tell all of the truth all of the time, or does Kant's approach to truth-telling allow for some creative but misleading statements?

Social Justice Theory and Social Contract Theory

Social justice theorists worry about "distributive justice"—that is, what is the fair way to distribute goods among a group of people? Marxist thought emphasizes that members of society should be given goods according to their needs. But this redistribution would require a governing power to decide who gets what and when. Capitalist thought takes a different approach, rejecting any giving that is not voluntary. Certain economists, such as the late Milton Friedman (see the sidebar in Section 3) also reject the notion that a corporation has a duty to give to unmet needs in society, believing that the government should play that role. Even the most dedicated free-market capitalist will often admit the need for some government and some forms of welfare—Social Security, Medicare, assistance to flood-stricken areas, help for AIDs patients—along with some public goods (such as defense, education, highways, parks, and support of key industries affecting national security).

People who do not see the need for **public goods** (including laws, court systems, and the government goods and services just cited) often question why there needs to be a government at all. One response might be, "Without government, there would be no corporations." Thomas Hobbes believed that people in a "state of nature" would rationally choose to have some form of government. He called this the **social contract**, where people give up certain rights to government in exchange for security and common benefits. In your own lives and in this course, you will see an ongoing balancing act between human desires for freedom and human desires for order; it is an ancient tension. Some commentators also see a kind of social contract between corporations and society; in exchange for perpetual duration and limited liability, the corporation has some corresponding duties toward society. Also, if a corporation is legally a "person," as the Supreme Court reaffirmed in 2010, then some would argue that if this corporate person commits three felonies, it should be locked up for life and its corporate charter revoked!

Modern social contract theorists, such as Thomas Donaldson and Thomas Dunfee (*Ties that Bind*, 1999), observe that various communities, not just nations, make rules for the common good. Your college or school is a community, and there are communities within the school (fraternities, sororities, the folks behind the counter at the circulation desk, the people who work together at the university radio station, the sports teams, the faculty, the students generally, the gay and lesbian alliance, etc.) that have rules, norms, or standards that people can buy into or not. If not, they can exit from that community, just as we are free (though not without cost) to reject U.S. citizenship and take up residence in another country. The fate of Syrian refugees in 2015 demonstrates just how fragile national communities can be and how difficult a right of exit can become.

Donaldson and Dunfee's integrative social contracts theory stresses the importance of studying the rules of smaller communities along with the larger social contracts made in states (such as

public goods

Goods that are useful to society (parks, education, national defense, highways) that would ordinarily not be produced by private enterprise. Public goods require public revenues (taxes) and political support to be adequately maintained.

social contract

The idea that people in a civil society have voluntarily given up some of their freedoms to have ordered liberty with the assistance of a government that will support that liberty. Hobbes and Locke are generally regarded as the preeminent social contract theorists.

Colorado or California) and nation-states (such as the United States or Germany). Our Constitution can be seen as a fundamental social contract.

It is important to realize that a social contract can be changed by the participants in a community, just as the U.S. Constitution can be amended. Social contract theory is thus dynamic—it allows for structural and organic changes. Ideally, the social contract struck by citizens and the government allows for certain fundamental rights such as those we enjoy in the United States, but it need not. People can give up freedom-oriented rights (such as the right of free speech or the right to be free of unreasonable searches and seizures) to secure order (freedom from fear, freedom from terrorism). For example, many citizens in Russia now miss the days when the Kremlin was all powerful; there was less crime and more equality and predictability to life in the Soviet Union, even if there was less freedom.

Thus, the rights that people have—in positive law—come from whatever social contract exists in the society. This view differs from that of the deontologists and that of the natural-law thinkers such as Gandhi, Jesus, or Martin Luther King Jr., who believed that rights come from God or, in less religious terms, from some transcendent moral order.

John Rawls and Robert Nozick on Social Justice

Donaldson and Dunfee draw on a long tradition of social contract thinkers. Thomas Hobbes, Jean Jacques Rousseau, and John Locke all had ideas about the rightful roles of the governed and their government. Locke was especially influential with the Framers of the U.S. Constitution, believing that there were "unalienable rights" that government could never rightfully take away from the people. Free speech (the First Amendment) and the "right to bear arms" (the Second Amendment) are often mentioned by those wary of government over-reach. In creating Integrative Social Contracts Theory (ISCT), Donaldson and Dunfee pay special attention to a modern social contract theorist, John Rawls.

Rawls believed that "justice" was the first principle for creating the good society. All too briefly put, we can do a "thought experiment" and imagine that your class in the legal environment can discuss at length what basic principles would govern the social-political rules of society. Rawls would insist that in doing so, none of the class could know what kind of genetic, economic, or social attributes they would have in this "good society." You would not know if you were born to a wealthy family, had a serious mental or physical handicap, were endowed with great intelligence, or had any particular ethnic or racial background. That is, you could emerge into this good society fairly well-endowed (money, social status, majority race, great intelligence and athletic ability) or poorly endowed (poor, low-caste, of a minority race or religion, handicapped in one or more ways in the struggle for power, wealth, and position). Behind this "veil of ignorance," Rawls believed that the fairest possible principles would be chosen. This reaches the question of "distributive justice," or how goods are allocated in a given society. Who has power, wealth, and employment are perennial political issues, and differing views depend on whether Rawls makes more sense to you than his colleague at Harvard, Robert Nozick.

Robert Nozick makes a philosophical defense of libertarian principles, challenging Rawls' ideas of distributive justice. He believes individuals have rights that are so strong that they raise the question of what, if anything, the state may do. His answer is that only a minimal state, one that enforces property rights and contracts and protects people against force, theft, or fraud, is morally justified. "Any more extensive state violates person's rights not to be forced to do certain things, and it is unjustified."[6]

Nozick believes that government should not force anyone to help other people. Thus, taxing the rich to help the poor is coercion and violates people's right to do what they want with the things that they own. Nozick would not be troubled by executive compensation in the U.S. that would be regarded as excessive in other countries. He rejects the idea that there should or could be any government-led "just distribution" of goods in society. What really matters is how the distribution came about: was there justice in the initial acquisition of your holdings and was there justice in transfer of those holdings? If the resources you use to make your money were legally yours in the first place, they continue to be yours. And if you made your money through free exchanges in the market or from gifts bestowed upon you by others, you are entitled to what you have and the state may not take it without your consent. Provided that no one starts out with ill-gotten gains, the distributions that result from free-market transactions are just, however equal or unequal that would make different strata in society.

Since property is the basis of most wealth, critics have asked whether the "legality" test is sufficient. If genocide or marginalization of Native Americans was necessary to create the United States, and if slavery was foundational to a profitable economy in the American colonies and post-Revolutionary states, doesn't a test for just distribution based on "legal ownership" ignore some serious moral harms? "Might makes right" and "the winners write the history books" seem apropos here.

That critique aside, Nozick would say that the moral crux of the libertarian claim is that each of us owns ourselves. Owning ourselves we must also own our labor. But if we own our labor we must be entitled to the fruits of that labor. Thus, taxing billionaires to give money to the poor takes days or months of earnings and essentially forces the billionaire to work for someone else, which is a kind of slavery, and denies that I truly own myself. (There is of course some irony in Nozick's appealing to the notion of slavery here to make his point.)

The libertarian position is only partly agreeable to traditional conservatives, who prefer small government, limited taxation, and fewer public goods. Libertarianism can offend social conservatives, as the concept of "owning ourselves" with no governmental interference would also allows us to sell our kidneys, become surrogate mothers for the right price, sell ourselves in prostitution, have an abortion (because you, and not the government, are the rightful owner of all that is inside of you), allow ourselves to be cannibalized (recall Robert Parker in Dudley and Stephens' case), retire at age 35 to an opium den, or drink ourselves into an early grave.

On Rights and Duties

The relationship between rights and duties—in both law and ethics—calls for some explanations:

1. If you have a right of free expression, the government has a duty to respect that right but can put reasonable limits on it. For example, you can legally say whatever you want about the U.S. president, but you can't get away with threatening the president's life. Even if your criticisms are strong and insistent, you have the right (and our government has the duty to protect your right) to speak freely. In Singapore during the 1990s, even indirect criticisms—mere hints—of the political leadership were enough to land you in jail or at least silence you with a libel suit.

2. Rights and duties exist not only between people and their governments but also between individuals. Your right to be free from physical assault is protected by the law in most states, and when someone walks up to you and punches you in the nose, your rights—as set forth in the positive law of your state—have been violated. Thus, other people have a duty to respect your rights and to not punch you in the nose.

3. Your right in legal terms is only as good as your society's willingness to provide legal remedies through the courts and political institutions of society.

A distinction between basic rights and nonbasic rights may also be important. Basic rights may include such fundamental elements as food, water, shelter, and physical safety. Nonbasic rights might be other desirable rights that go beyond being needed for survival, such as education. Another distinction is between positive rights (the right to bear arms, the right to vote, the right of privacy) and negative rights (the right to be free from government seizure of your property, to be free from unreasonable searches and seizures, the right to be free from cruel or unusual punishments). Yet another distinction is between economic or social rights (adequate food, work, and environment) and political or civic rights (the right to vote, the right to equal protection of the laws, the right to due process). The 1948 Universal Declaration of Human Rights lists all kinds of rights, but those rights can only be manifested through the positive law of various nation-states or by agreement among nation-states.

Aristotle and Virtue Theory

virtue ethics

Aristotle's perspective on finding happiness through the application of reason in human affairs advises continual practice to develop habits of virtuous moral character. In a modern setting, deliberating on core values and their application to individual and corporate ethical dilemmas and adhering to the recommendations of core values analysis would provide similar practice.

Virtue theory or **virtue ethics**, has received increasing attention over the past forty years, particularly in contrast to utilitarian and deontological approaches to ethics. Virtue theory emphasizes the value of virtuous qualities rather than formal rules or useful results. Aristotle is often recognized as the first philosopher to advocate the ethical value of certain qualities, or virtues, in a person's character. As LaRue Hosmer has noted, Aristotle (384–322 BC) saw the goal of human existence as the active, rational search for excellence, and excellence requires the personal virtues of honesty, truthfulness, courage, temperance, generosity, and high-mindedness. This pursuit is also termed "knowledge of the good" in Greek philosophy.[7]

Aristotle believed that all activity was aimed at some goal or perceived good and that there must be some ranking that we do among those goals or goods. Happiness may be our ultimate goal, but what does that mean, exactly? Aristotle rejected wealth, pleasure, and fame and embraced reason as the distinguishing feature of humans, as opposed to other species. And since a human is a reasoning animal, happiness must be associated with reason. Thus, happiness is living according to the active (rather than passive) use of reason. The use of reason leads to excellence, and so happiness can be defined as the active, rational pursuit of personal excellence, or virtue.

Aristotle named fourteen virtues: (1) courage, particularly in battle; (2) temperance, or moderation in eating and drinking; (3) liberality, or spending money well; (4) magnificence, or living well; (5) pride, or taking pleasure in accomplishments and stature; (6) high-mindedness, or concern with the noble rather than the petty; (7) unnamed virtue, which is halfway between ambition and total lack of effort; (8) gentleness, or concern for others; (9) truthfulness; (10) wit, or pleasure in group discussions; (11) friendliness, or pleasure in personal conduct; (12) modesty, or pleasure in personal conduct; (13) righteous indignation, or getting angry at the right things and in the right amounts; and (14) justice.

From a modern perspective, some of these virtues seem old-fashioned or even odd. Magnificence, for example, is not something we commonly speak of. Three questions emerge: (1) How do we know what a virtue is these days? (2) How useful is a list of agreed-upon virtues anyway? (3) What do virtues have to do with companies, particularly large ones where various groups and individuals may have little or no contact with other parts of the organization?

As to the third question, whether corporations can "have" virtues or values is a matter of lively debate. A corporation is obviously not the same as an individual. But there seems to be growing agreement that organizations do differ in their practices and that these practices are value driven. If all a company cares about is the bottom line, other values will diminish or disappear. Quite a few books have been written in the past twenty years that emphasize the need for businesses to define their values in order to be competitive in today's global economy.[8]

As to the first two questions regarding virtues, a look at Michael Josephson's core values may prove helpful.

Josephson's Core Values Analysis and Decision Process

Michael Josephson, a noted American ethicist, believes that a current set of *core values* has been identified and that the values can be meaningfully applied to a variety of personal and corporate decisions.

To simplify, let's say that there are ethical and nonethical qualities among people in the United States. When you ask people what kinds of qualities they admire in others or in themselves, they may say wealth, power, fitness, sense of humor, good looks, intelligence, musical ability, or some other quality. They may also value honesty, caring, fairness, courage, perseverance, diligence, trustworthiness, or integrity. The qualities on the second list have something in common—they are distinctively ethical characteristics. That is, they are commonly seen as moral or ethical qualities, unlike the qualities on the first list. You can be, like the Athenian Alcibiades, brilliant but unprincipled, or, like some political leaders today, powerful but dishonest, or wealthy but uncaring. You can, in short, have a number of admirable qualities (brilliance, power, wealth) that are not per se virtuous. Just because Harold is rich or good-looking or has a good sense of humor does not mean that he is ethical. But if Harold is honest and caring (whether he is rich or poor, humorous or humorless), people are likely to see him as ethical.

Among the virtues, are any especially important? Studies from the Josephson Institute of Ethics in Marina del Rey, California, have identified six **core values** in our society, values that almost everyone agrees are important to them. When asked what values people hold dear, what values they wish to be known by, and what values they wish others would exhibit in their actions, six values consistently turn up: (1) trustworthiness, (2) respect, (3) responsibility, (4) fairness, (5) caring, and (6) citizenship.

Note that these values are distinctly ethical. While many of us may value wealth, good looks, and intelligence, having wealth, good looks, and intelligence does not automatically make us virtuous in our character and habits. But being more trustworthy (by being honest and by keeping promises) does make us more virtuous, as does staying true to the other five core values.

Notice also that these six core values share something in common with other ethical values that are less universally agreed upon. Many values taught in the family or in places of worship are not generally agreed on, practiced, or admired by all. Some families and individuals believe strongly in the virtue of saving money or in abstaining from alcohol or sex prior to marriage. Others clearly do not, or at least don't act on their beliefs. Moreover, it is possible to have and practice core ethical values even if you take on heavy debt, knock down several drinks a night, or have frequent premarital sex. Some would dispute this, saying that you can't really lead a virtuous life if you get into debt, drink heavily, or engage in premarital sex. But the point here is that since people do disagree in these areas, the ethical traits of thrift, temperance, and sexual abstinence do not have the unanimity of approval that the six core values do.

The importance of an individual's having these consistent qualities of character is well known. Often we remember the last bad thing someone did far more than any or all previous good acts. For example, Eliot Spitzer and Bill Clinton are more readily remembered by people for their last, worst acts than for any good they accomplished as public servants. As for a company, its good reputation also has an incalculable value that, when lost, takes a great deal of time and work to recover. Volkswagen, Wells Fargo, Facebook, Shell, Nike, and other companies have discovered that there is a market for morality, however difficult to measure, and that not paying attention to ethical concerns often comes at a serious price.

In the past fifteen years, the ethics and compliance officer career has emerged, partly as a result of criminal proceedings against companies, but also because major companies have found that reputations cannot be recovered retroactively but must be pursued proactively. For individuals, Aristotle emphasized the practice of virtue to the point where virtue becomes a habit.

core values

Values that are generally recognized as positive ethical characteristics of an individual or a business organization. People may have strong views about other kinds of ethical values, but core values are more widely accepted.

Companies are gradually learning the same lesson; a good "corporate culture" can reward ethical behavior and punish poor behavior. Just as people can cultivate virtuous habits, as in Josephson's core values, organizations can take care to habitually live their values as well as proclaim them.[9]

Key Takeaway

Throughout history, people have pondered what it means "to do what is right." Some of the main answers have come from the differing perspectives of utilitarian thought; duty-based, or deontological, thought; social contract theory; and virtue ethics. Business organizations, with the assumption that profits are all that matters, can easily misuse utilitarian thought, overlook the value of their reputations, and should bear in mind that they are created and maintained by a larger economic/political/social system as part of an evolving "social contract" among people, firms, and the governments that set the rules for economic activity.

Exercises

XYZ Motor Corporation begins to get customer complaints about two models of its automobiles. Customers have had near-death experiences from sudden acceleration; they would be driving along a highway at normal speed when suddenly the car would begin to accelerate, and efforts to stop the acceleration by braking fail to work. Drivers could turn off the ignition and come to a safe stop, but XYZ does not instruct buyers of its cars to do so, nor is this a common reaction among drivers who experience sudden acceleration.

Internal investigations of half a dozen accidents in U.S. locations come to the conclusion that the accidents are not being caused by drivers who mistake the gas pedal for the brake pedal. In fact, there appears to be a possible flaw in both models, perhaps in a semiconductor chip, that makes sudden acceleration happen. Interference by floor mats and poorly designed gas pedals does not seem to be the problem.

It is voluntary to report these incidents to the National Highway Traffic Safety Administration (NHTSA), but the company decides that it will wait a while and see if there are more complaints. Recalling the two models so that local dealers and their mechanics could examine them is also an option, but it would be extremely costly. Company executives are aware that quarterly and annual profit-and-loss statements, on which their bonuses depend, could be decisively worse with a recall. They decide that on a cost-benefit basis, it makes more sense to wait until there are more accidents and more data. After a hundred or more accidents and nearly fifteen fatalities, the company institutes a selective recall, still not notifying NHTSA, which has its own experts and the authority to order XYZ to do a full recall of all affected models.

Experts have advised XYZ that standard failure-analysis methodology requires that the company obtain absolutely every XYZ vehicle that has experienced sudden acceleration, using microscopic analysis of all critical components of the electronic system. The company does not wish to take that advice, as it would be—as one top executive put it—"too time-consuming and expensive."

1. Can XYZ's approach to this problem be justified under utilitarian theory? If so, how? If not, why not?
2. What would Kant advise XYZ to do? Explain.
3. What would the "virtuous" approach be for XYZ in this situation?
4. Why didn't the Ford Motor Company disclose to its customers the risks it knew about from safety testing the Pinto? If it told customers there was a 1 in 5,000 chance that their Pinto would be rear-ended, causing an explosion of the car's gas tank that would endanger passengers, would they lose much business? Would they have to sell the car for less? By how much, do you suppose?
5. In a free-market economy, voluntary consent of both buyer and seller creates a dynamic of wealth creation and innovation, and the celebrated "invisible hand" of Adam Smith that needs no government oversight. Does Ford's failure to voluntarily disclose the truth about the Pinto's safety tests mean that the marketing of Pinto vehicles was marred by lack of

true consent between buyer and seller? Did the customers of Volkswagen—who bought diesel cars in the U.S., relying on the company's statements about those vehicles' pollution standards—voluntarily consent to drive vehicles that did not meet VW's stated emissions standards?

2.3 Ethical Problems with Corporations and Corporate Governance

Learning Objectives

1. Recognize that serious ethical problems frequently arise given the basic structure of the typical corporation (the shareholders elect the directors, who hire the manager to run the company).
2. Understand how the shareholder profit-maximization model is different from stakeholder theory.
3. Discern and describe the ethical challenges for corporate cultures.
4. Explain what conscious capitalism is and how it differs from stakeholder theory.

The Legal Organization of the Corporation Creates an Environment Rife with Ethical Problems

Figure 2.1, though somewhat oversimplified, shows the basic legal structure of a corporation under Delaware law and the laws of most other states in the United States. Shareholders elect directors, who then hire officers to manage the company (discussed in more detail in Chapter 10). From this structure, some serious ethical issues can arise.

FIGURE 2.1 Corporate Legal Structure

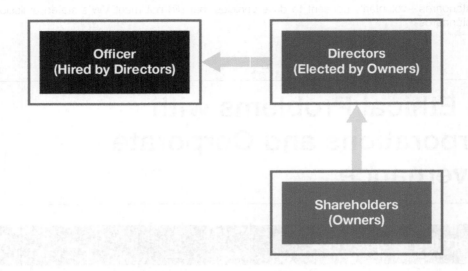

Because the directors of a corporation do not meet very often, it's possible for the officers hired (top management, or the "C-suite") to give selective information to the directors; directors are not always ready and able to provide the oversight that the shareholders would like. Nor does the law require officers to be shareholders, so that officers' motivations may not align with the best interests of the company.

This is the "agency problem" often discussed in corporate governance—how to get officers and other top management to align their own interests with those of the shareholders. For example, a CEO might trade insider information to the detriment of the company's shareholders. Even board members are susceptible to misalignment of interests; for example, board members might resist hostile takeover bids because they would likely lose their perks (short for *perquisites*) as directors, even though the tender offer would benefit stockholders. Among other attempted realignments, the use of stock options was an attempt to make managers more attentive to the value of company stock, but the law of unintended consequences was in full force; managers tweaked and managed earnings in the bubble of the 1990s bull market, and "managing by numbers" became an epidemic in corporations organized under U.S. corporate law. The rights of shareholders can be bolstered by changes in state and federal law, and there have been some attempts to do that since the late 1990s. Ultimately, shareholders do have the power to replace nonperforming or underperforming directors, which usually results in changes at the C-suite level as well.

Shareholders and Stakeholders

There are two main views about what the corporation's duties are. The first view—maximizing profits, the shareholder theory—is a long-prevailing view among business managers and in business schools. The second view—the stakeholder theory—is that the corporation has a broader duty to society.

Shareholder Theory, Maximizing Profits: Milton Friedman

Nobel Laureate economist **Milton Friedman** (1912–2006) is often quoted as having said that the only moral duty a corporation has is to make the most possible money, or to maximize profits, for its stockholders. Friedman's beliefs are noted at length (see sidebar on Friedman's article from the *New York Times*). As he asserted in that now-famous article, in a free society, "there is one and only one social responsibility of business: to use its resources and engage in activities designed to increase its profits as long as it stays within the rules of the game, which is to say, engages in open and free competition without deception and fraud." [10]What follows is a portion of what Friedman had to say in 1970.

> ### "The Social Responsibility of Business Is to Increase Its Profits"
>
> Milton Friedman, *New York Times Magazine*, September 13, 1970
>
> *What does it mean to say that "business" has responsibilities? Only people can have responsibilities. A corporation is an artificial person and in this sense may have artificial responsibilities, but "business" as a whole cannot be said to have responsibilities, even in this vague sense....*
>
> *Presumably, the individuals who are to be responsible are businessmen, which means individual proprietors or corporate executives....In a free enterprise, private-property system, a corporate executive is an employee of the owners of the business. He has direct responsibility to his employers. That responsibility is to conduct the business in accordance with their desires, which generally will be to make as much money as possible while conforming to the basic rules of the society, both those embodied in law and those embodied in ethical custom....*
>
> *...[T]he manager is that agent of the individuals who own the corporation or establish the eleemosynary institution, and his primary responsibility is to them...*
>
> *What does it mean to say that the corporate executive has a "social responsibility" in his capacity as businessman? If this statement is not pure rhetoric, it must mean that he has to act in some way that is not in the interest of his employers. For example, that he is to refrain from increasing the price of the product in order to contribute to the social objective of preventing inflation, even though a price increase would be in the best interests of the corporation. Or that he is to make expenditures on reducing pollution beyond the amount that is in the best interests of the corporation or that is required by law in order to contribute to the social objective of improving the environment. . .*
>
> *. . . the imposition of taxes and the expenditure of tax proceeds are governmental functions. We have established elaborate constitutional, parliamentary, and judicial provisions to control these functions, to assure that taxes are imposed so far as possible in accordance with the preferences and desires of the public....*

Milton Friedman

Milton Friedman (1912–2006) was an influential American economist and textbook author, primarily associated with the University of Chicago. His political philosophy (and that of "the Chicago School") extolled the virtues of a free-market economic system with minimal government intervention, and he had a significant influence on 1980s political economics (Ronald Reagan and Margaret Thatcher).

Friedman assumes here that there is a viable, operative set of political institutions that will collect taxes and use them to benefit society; that assumption seems less viable in 2019. Friedman's basic claim here is that any expenditure not made for the benefit of the "owners" (the shareholders) is essentially an unfair tax on the shareholders.

Stakeholder Theory: Consider a Broader Range of Interests

Stakeholders of a corporation include its employees, suppliers, customers, and the community. Stakeholder theory advocates emphasize that corporations have obligations that extend beyond the bottom-line aim of maximizing profits. A stakeholder is anyone who most would agree is significantly affected (positively or negatively) by the decision of another moral agent.

There is one vital fact about corporations—the corporation is a creation of the law. Without law (and government), corporations would have no existence. The key concept for corporations is the legal fact of limited liability. The benefit of limited liability for shareholders of a corporation means that larger pools of capital could be aggregated for larger enterprises; shareholders could only lose their investments should the venture fail in any way, and there would be no personal liability and thus no potential loss of personal assets other than the value of the corporate stock. Before New Jersey and Delaware competed to make incorporation as easy as possible and beneficial to the incorporators and founders, those who wanted the benefits of incorporation had to go to legislatures—usually among the states—to show a public purpose that the company would serve.

In the late 1800s, New Jersey and Delaware changed their laws to make incorporating relatively easy. These two states allowed incorporation "for any legal purpose," rather than requiring some public purpose. Thus, it is government (and its laws) that makes limited liability happen through the corporate form. That is, only through the consent of the state and armed with the charter granted by the state can a corporation's shareholders have limited liability. This is a right granted by the state, a right granted for good and practical reasons for encouraging capital and innovation. But with this right comes a related duty, not clearly stated at law, but assumed when a charter is granted by the state—that the corporate form of doing business is legal because the government feels that it is socially useful to make it so.

Implicitly, then, there is a social contract between governments and corporations—as long as corporations are considered socially useful, they can exist. But do they have explicit social responsibilities? Milton Friedman's position suggests that having gone along with legal duties, the corporation can ignore any other social obligations. But advocates of **stakeholder theory** would say that a corporation's social responsibilities go beyond just staying within the law and go beyond the corporation's shareholders to include a number of other important stakeholders, those whose lives can be affected by corporate decisions.

According to stakeholder theorists, corporations (and other business organizations) must pay attention not only to the bottom line but also to their overall effect on the community. Public perception of a company's unfairness, uncaring, disrespect, or lack of trustworthiness often leads to long-term failure, whatever the short-term successes or profits may be. A socially responsible corporation is likely to consider the impact of its decisions on a wide range of stakeholders, not just shareholders. As Table 2.1 indicates, stakeholders have very different kinds of interests ("stakes") in the actions of a corporation.

stakeholder theory

The view that all stakeholders to a corporate decision deserve some kind of moral consideration and that corporations that keep all stakeholders in mind will, over the long term, deliver superior results to shareholders.

TABLE 2.1 The Stakes of Various Stakeholders

Ownership	The value of the organization has a direct impact on the wealth of these stakeholders.	Managers
		Directors who own stock
		Shareholders
Economic Dependence	Stakeholders can be economically dependent without having ownership. Each of these stakeholders relies on the corporation in some way for financial well-being.	Salaried managers
		Creditors
		Suppliers
		Employees
		Local communities
Social Interests	These stakeholders are not directly linked to the organization but have an interest in making sure the organization acts in a socially responsible manner.	Communities
		Government
		Media

The Corporate Manager as Fiduciary for the Company

In a 2017 article in the *Harvard Business Review*,[11] Joseph Bower and Lynn Paine argued against the Friedman view that the only obligation of a corporate manager is to maximize shareholder value. The crux of their argument is that shareholders are not "owners" in the usual meaning of that word. Shareholders, unlike owners, do not have any duty to protect the company or its future, as they are shielded by the law of limited liability that applies to shareholders of corporations incorporated anywhere in the U.S. (Limited shareholder liability is true for most non-U.S. corporations as well.) Thus, these "owners" are shielded from any liability for corporate debts or wrongful acts. Shareholders may buy and sell shares without restriction, and can own shares without revealing their identity. They can even "short" a corporation whose shares they already own, effectively betting against its stock rising in the short term. They are distant, often physically, but also psychologically and in terms of knowledge of, and participation in, the corporation's activities. When you and I think of "ownership," we ordinarily understand that with ownership comes responsibility. Yet shareholders have accountability only to the limit of their investment in a company's shares.

Even from a legal standpoint, the ownership metaphor is misleading. Shareholders are beneficiaries of a company's success in the market, but they do not have "dominion" over a piece of property. They don't have access to corporate premises or use of the corporation's assets. They do have rights and privileges under state corporation laws, such as voting for directors, amendments to the corporate charter, and the sale of corporate assets. Within Delaware corporate law (and every other state in the U.S.), shareholders' election of directors means that management is vested in the Board and in the managers hired by the Board.

As we will see in Agency Law (Chapter 10), corporate managers and Board members do not take orders—as agents would—from shareholders. If shareholders "owned" the company, they would be principals and the managers would be agents instructed to stay within the confines of the principals' directions. But there are so many different motives and interests of shareholders (most of whom are institutions rather than individuals) that carrying out "the shareholder's wishes" is far more complex than it sounds. Shareholders have differing investment objectives, differing attitudes toward risk, and differing time horizons. Pension funds may prefer current income, while some endowments may seek long-term growth. Shareholder resolutions seldom get unanimous agreement.

Instead of seeing Board members and managers as agents, Bower and Paine argue that they are actually (legally) "fiduciaries" for the shareholders and for the corporation in general. Fiduciaries make discretionary decisions, agents do not. Finally, to maximize current shareholder value, some shareholders might (secretly, or even openly) wish that the company would bend or break the law in order to maximize profits, but such wishes are not consistent with state corporate law or many federal laws.[12] Focusing only on maximizing shareholder value has also created long-term problems for some companies. Where shareholder activists push for a reduction of expenditures on research and development, the long-term interests of the company itself may be poorly served. Selling off parts of the company to generate short-term cash returns (and dividends for shareholders) may be a transfer of wealth rather than an increase in the long-term value of the company. Implicit in their argument is the stakeholder view—if companies pay close attention to all stakeholders, and give moral consideration to each, they are far more likely to sustain themselves in the long term. Indeed, Bower and Paine make the argument that managers violate their fiduciary duties if they are too driven by quarterly earnings reports and the demands of activist investors, and thereby fail to reinvest in the company's future.

Corporate Culture and Codes of Ethics

A corporation is a "person" capable of suing, being sued, and having rights and duties in our legal system. (It is a legal or juridical person, not a natural person, according to our Supreme Court.) Moreover, many corporations have distinct cultures and beliefs that are lived and breathed by its members. Often, the culture of a corporation is the best defense against individuals within that firm who may be tempted to break the law or commit serious ethical misdeeds.

What follows are a series of observations about corporations, ethics, and corporate culture.

Ethical Leadership Is Top-Down

People in an organization tend to watch closely what the top managers do and say. Regardless of managers' talk about ethics, employees quickly learn what speech or actions are, in fact, rewarded. If the CEO is firm about acting ethically, others in the organization will take their cues from him or her. People at the top tend to set the target, the climate, the beliefs, and the expectations that fuel behavior.

Accountability Is Often Weak

Clever managers can learn to shift blame to others, take credit for others' work, and move on before "funny numbers" or other earnings management tricks come to light.[13] Again, we see that the manager is often an agent for himself or herself and will often act more in his or her own self-interest than for the corporate interest.

Killing the Messenger

Where organizations no longer function, inevitably some employees are unhappy. If they call attention to problems that are being covered up by coworkers or supervisors, they bring bad news.

Managers like to hear good news and discourage bad news. Intentionally or not, those who told on others, or blew the whistle, have rocked the boat and become unpopular with those whose misdeeds they report, or with managers who don't really want to hear the bad news. In many organizations, "killing the messenger" solves the problem. Consider James Alexander at Enron Corporation, who was deliberately shut out after bringing problems to CEO Ken Lay's attention.[14] When Sherron Watkins sent Ken Lay a letter warning him about Enron's accounting practices, CFO Andrew Fastow tried to fire her.[15]

Ethics Codes

Without strong leadership and a willingness to listen to bad news as well as good news, managers do not have the feedback necessary to keep the organization healthy. Ethics codes have been put in place—partly in response to federal sentencing guidelines and partly to encourage feedback loops to top management. The best ethics codes are aspirational, or having an ideal to be pursued, not legalistic or compliance driven. The Johnson & Johnson ethics code predated the Tylenol scare and the company's oft-celebrated corporate response.[16] The corporate response was consistent with that code, which was lived and modeled by the top of the organization.

It's often noted that a code of ethics is only as important as top management is willing to make it. If the code is just a document that goes into a drawer or onto a shelf, it will not effectively encourage good conduct within the corporation. The same is true of any kind of training that the company undertakes, whether it be in racial sensitivity or sexual harassment. If the message is not continuously reinforced, or (worse yet) if the message is undermined by management's actions, the real message to employees is that violations of the ethics code will not be taken seriously, or that efforts to stop racial discrimination or sexual harassment are merely token efforts, and that the important things are profits and performance. The ethics code at Enron seems to have been one of those "3-P" codes that wind up sitting on shelves—"Print, Post, and Pray." Worse, the Enron board twice suspended the code in 1999 to allow outside partnerships to be led by a top Enron executive who stood to gain financially from them.[17]

Ethics Hotlines and Federal Sentencing Guidelines

The federal sentencing guidelines were enacted in 1991. The original idea behind these guidelines was for Congress to correct the lenient treatment often given to white-collar, or corporate, criminals. The guidelines require judges to consider "aggravating and mitigating" factors in determining sentences and fines. While corporations cannot go to jail, its officers and managers certainly can, and the corporation itself can be fined. Many companies will claim that it is one or more "bad apples" that have caused the problem; the guidelines invite these companies to show that they are in fact tending their orchard well. They can show this by providing evidence that they have (1) a viable, active code of ethics; (2) a way for employees to report violations of law or the ethics code; and (3) an ethics ombudsman, or someone who oversees the code.

In short, if a company can show that it has an ongoing process to root out wrongdoing at all levels of the company, the judge is allowed to consider this as a major mitigating factor in the fines the company will pay. Most Fortune 500 companies have ethics hotlines and processes in place to find legal and ethical problems within the company.

Managing by the Numbers

If you manage by the numbers, there is a temptation to lie about those numbers, based on the need to get stock price ever higher. At Enron, "15 percent a year or better earnings growth" was the mantra. Jeffrey Pfeffer, professor of organizational behavior at Stanford University, observes how the belief that "stock price is all that matters" has been hardwired into the corporate psyche. It dictates not only how people judge the worth of their company but also how they feel about themselves and the work that they are doing. And, over time, it has clouded judgments about what is acceptable corporate behavior.[18]

Managing by Numbers: The Sears Auto Center Story

If winning is the most important thing in your life, then you must be prepared to do anything to win.

—Michael Josephson

Most people want to be winners or associate with winners. As humans, our desire to associate with those who have status provides plenty of incentive to glorify winners and ignore losers. But if an individual, a team, or a company does whatever it takes to win, then all other values are thrown out in the goal to win at all costs. The desire of some people within Sears, Roebuck and Company's auto repair division to win by gaining higher profits resulted in the situation portrayed here.

Sears, Roebuck and Company was a fixture in American retailing throughout the twentieth century. At one time, people in rural America could order virtually anything (including a house) from Sears. Not without some accuracy, the company billed itself as "the place where Americans shop." But in 1992, Sears was charged by California authorities with gross and deliberate fraud in many of its auto centers.

The authorities were alerted by a 50 percent increase in consumer complaints over a three-year period. New Jersey's division of consumer affairs also investigated Sears Auto Centers and found that all six visited by investigators had recommended unnecessary repairs. California's department of consumer affairs found that Sears had systematically overcharged by an average of $223 for repairs and routinely billed for work that was not done. Sears Auto Centers were the largest providers of auto repair services in the state.

The scam was a variant on the old bait-and-switch routine. Customers received coupons in the mail inviting them to take advantage of hefty discounts on brake jobs. When customers came in to redeem their coupons, sales staffers would convince them to authorize additional repairs. As a management tool, Sears had also established quotas for each of their sales representatives to meet.

Ultimately, California got Sears to settle a large number of lawsuits against it by threatening to revoke Sears' auto repair license. Sears agreed to distribute $50 coupons to nearly a million customers nationwide who had obtained certain services between August 1, 1990, and January 31, 1992. Sears also agreed to pay $3.5 million to cover the costs of various government investigations and to contribute $1.5 million annually to conduct auto mechanic training programs. It also agreed to abandon its repair service quotas. The entire settlement cost Sears $30 million. Sears Auto Center sales also dropped about 15 to 20 percent after news of the scandal broke.

Note that in boosting sales by performing unnecessary services, Sears suffered very bad publicity and losses were incalculable. The short-term gains were easy to measure; long-term consequences seldom are. This case illustrates a number of important lessons:

- People generally choose short-term gains over potential long-term losses.

- People often justify the harm to others as being minimal or "necessary" to achieve the desired sales quota or financial goal.

- In working as a group, we often form an "us versus them" mentality. In the Sears case, it is likely that Sears "insiders" looked at customers as "outsiders," effectively treating them (in Kantian terms) as means rather than ends in themselves. In short, outsiders were used for the benefit of insiders.

- The long-term losses to Sears are difficult to quantify, while the short-term gains were easy to measure and (at least for a brief while) quite satisfying financially.

- Sears' ongoing rip-offs were possible only because individual consumers lacked the relevant information about the service being offered. This lack of information is a market failure, since many consumers were demanding more of Sears Auto Center services than they would have (and at a higher price) if relevant information had been available to them earlier. Sears, like other sellers of goods and services, took advantage of a market system, which, in its ideal form, would not permit such information distortions.

- People in the organization probably thought that the actions they took were necessary.

Noting this last point, we can assume that these key people were motivated by maximizing profits and had lost sight of other goals for the organization.

The emphasis on doing whatever is necessary to win is entirely understandable, but it is not ethical. The temptation will always exist—for individuals, companies, and nations—to dominate or to win and to write the history of their actions in a way that justifies or overlooks the harm that has been done. In a way, this fits with the notion that "might makes right," or that power is the ultimate measure of right and wrong.

Conscious Capitalism

One effort to integrate the two viewpoints of stakeholder theory and shareholder primacy is the conscious capitalism movement. Companies that practice **conscious capitalism** embrace the idea that profit and prosperity can and must go hand in hand with social justice and environmental stewardship—they operate with a holistic or systems view. This means that they understand that all stakeholders are connected and interdependent. They reject false trade-offs between stakeholder interests and strive for creative ways to achieve win-win-win outcomes for all.[19]

> **conscious capitalism**
>
> Companies that practice conscious capitalism embrace the idea that profit and prosperity can and must go hand in hand with social justice and environmental stewardship.

The "conscious business" has a purpose that goes beyond maximizing profits. It is designed to maximize profits but is focused more on its higher purpose and does not fixate solely on the bottom line. To do so, it focuses on delivering value to all its stakeholders, harmonizing as best it can the interests of consumers, partners, investors, the community, and the environment. This requires that company managers take a "servant leadership" role, serving as stewards to the company's deeper purpose and to the company's stakeholders.

Conscious business leaders serve as such stewards, focusing on fulfilling the company's purpose, delivering value to its stakeholders, and facilitating a harmony of interests, rather than on personal gain and self-aggrandizement. Why is this refocusing needed? Within the standard profit-maximizing model, corporations have long had to deal with the "agency problem." Actions by top-level managers—acting on behalf of the company—should align with the shareholders, but in a culture all about winning and money, managers sometimes act in ways that are self-aggrandizing and that do not serve the interests of shareholders. Laws exist to limit such self-aggrandizing, but the remedies are often too little and too late and often catch only the most egregious overreaching.

Having a culture of servant leadership is a much better way to see that a company's top management works to ensure a harmony of interests.

Key Takeaway

The corporation sits at the center of a variety of stakeholders, all of whom require managerial attention to different degrees. Thinking ethically as a corporate manager means giving due deliberation to long-term reputation and legal risks.

Exercise

1. Think of a corporation that has recently had legal or regulatory problems that resulted in lawsuits, government fines, and/or loss of reputation. Do some in-depth reading on that company and list the ways in which its corporate governance for ethics was lacking.

2.4 Business Ethics Globally

Learning Objectives

1. Understand that local and national culture affects what is considered ethical behavior worldwide.
2. Understand that a business person from one nation-state working in another may find its cultural or ethical standards offensive.
3. Recognize the role that multinational corporations can play in addressing business ethical issues and promoting (or not) responsible global business practices.
4. Understand why bribery—aside from being illegal—is a bad way to conduct business.

As challenging as doing ethical business is domestically, the challenges are even greater globally. Legal regimes run the gamut from democratic capitalism to state-led economies (like China's) to authoritarian family-ruled nation-states, to corrupt regimes and even failing states, where warlords and insurrectionist groups hold significant territory and could affect stable business operations. Cultural and legal differences can also complicate business strategy, where nepotism, bribery, child labor, discrimination against women and minorities, and desperately bad working conditions can challenge the most ethically-minded business firm. In this section, we will consider some of these challenges.

When in Rome: When Foreign Cultural Norms Matter

What is regarded as unethical in one country may be perfectly acceptable in another. For many years, both the law and the culture of Saudi Arabia prevented women from working or driving cars. Following the old injunction, "When in Rome, do as the Romans do," a company like FedEx would not dream of opening a branch in Riyadh with women drivers. Partly this is the law and partly this is the culture. Even when there are no clear legal restrictions, there may nonetheless be customs and norms for companies to consider. For example, nepotism is customary in India. If there are job openings at Tata Motors, the customary process would not be a merit-based, interview-all-comers approach; rather, the company would first look to family and relatives of current employees. The company's failure to do so would be a breach of local custom.

In a similar way, host country standards might allow for a lot more gift-giving in China or Japan than is customary in the U.S. What looks like a "bribe" in the U.S. is regarded quite differently elsewhere. Standards of employee safety may also differ, so that the "value of human life" may be regarded much differently by businesses in other nations. Tom Donaldson and Tom Dunfee pointed out in *Ties That Bind*, their landmark book on global business ethics, that in South Korea, a macho culture among construction workers made it "wrong" for a U.S. company to insist that workers wear safety helmets. A U.S. company operating there must decide whether its own core safety values would require push back against such a custom, at the risk of offending some local workers as a breach of customary standards.

Some years ago, along with Diana Robertson, Tom Dunfee wrote "Foreign Assignment," describing how a young woman banker from the U.S. named Sarah Strong faced discrimination at her branch bank posting in Mexico City. Her superior ordered Sarah, a single woman, to "dress sexy" and flirt with the customers, and although she was highly qualified (with three years of solid banking experience in the U.S. and an honors MBA grad from a prestigious business school), she was not allowed by her manager to deal directly with the clients, who didn't want to see women making decisions involving their money. She became discouraged and complained to her superior, who told her to be patient, "play along" and please the customers.

The case raises a number of interesting questions, including whether the U.S. bank should have placed her there in the first place, whether she was wise to take on the assignment, whether she was adequately briefed about having to be somewhat sidelined there, and whether the bank gave her an alternative path for her career advancement. But the main point of interest for global business ethics is whether the bank was actually confronting an entrenched local business norm that made it reasonable for them to "do in Mexico City as the Mexicans do." This is, was it really necessary to treat Sarah as a means to the end of "successfully doing business" with well-funded Mexican men? (Kant would remind us that treating others as a means to our own ends is morally impermissible.) The Mexico City branch of the U.S. bank might have been mistaken about their perceived "necessity" here. People (and firms) may have a tendency to see what they want to see, or believe what they want to believe,[20] or in many cases rely on less than fully informed sources about what the cultural norms really are.

There are lots of ethical landmines for corporate reputation when it comes to working conditions abroad. The sweatshop controversies that have affected Nike, the Gap, and many other U.S. companies highlight the lack of good wages and working conditions in many emerging economies. Even where the U.S. company is not legally responsible, a supplier's poor working conditions can give companies a tarnished reputation. Foxconn, a Taiwanese company, has long manufactured Apple's iPads and iPhones in the People's Republic of China (PRC), and Foxconn also supplies Dell and Hewlett-Packard (HP). The working conditions at Foxconn were so strict and the hours so long that some young employees were committing suicide by jumping out of factory windows on upper-level floors.[21] Foxconn's solution was to erect large nets above the ground to prevent such suicides. Despite the working conditions, there are many who seek employment there. Given the brand loyalty among customers of Dell, HP, and especially Apple, these conditions may not affect sales and profits, though some legal risks remain. In some cases, suppliers have been known to violate local law in order to meet the demands of U.S. tech firms.

Suicides in a Chinese Factory

CNN's John Vause takes us to a Chinese factory that's dealing with a series of suicides among workers. (2011)

View the video online at: http://www.youtube.com/embed/H0aZWWZnXDA?rel=0

Multinationals and Human Rights

While a multinational company (MNC) should certainly consider differing cultural norms, there may be some standards that even the most profit-minded company should not violate. In 1989, Tom Donaldson suggested that there were 10 minimum standards that a MNC must observe.[22] They were:

- The right to freedom of movement
- The right to property
- The right not to be tortured
- The right to a fair trial
- The right not to be discriminated against, e.g. on the basis of race or gender
- The right to physical safety
- The right to freedom of speech and association
- The right to basic education
- The right to political participation
- The right to a minimal level of existence

A lot has changed since 1989, though. There are some rights in the above list that come from a distinctly Western and democratic perspective. Many people assumed that capitalism and democracy would go hand in hand after the end of the USSR and the end of the "Iron Curtain" in Eastern Europe. Few experts could have foreseen popular resentment against "globalization" and the rise of authoritarianism (as in Turkey, Egypt, Russia, Poland, and Hungary) along with the rise of Chinese "state capitalism" as a viable model for emerging economies. The right to freedom of speech and association seems especially vulnerable in places like the PRC, where major technology firms (Facebook, Google) would like to have a greater foothold. But doing business in China comes at the cost of complying with a legal regime that suppresses opposition parties, freedom of speech, and freedom of movement as well.

But because MNCs are such a considerable force, economically and politically, academics, civil society, and international institutions continue to voice concern that MNCs need to observe fundamental human rights, even in host countries where the sovereign does not recognize or affirm those rights in practice.

In 2005, the United Nations appointed John Gerard Ruggie to the task of clarifying how business could support human rights. Within six years, he and his team developed "Guiding Principles on Business and Human Rights," meant to provide a roadmap for ensuring responsible global corporate practices. The principles were unanimously endorsed by the UN and embraced and implemented by other international bodies, businesses, governments, workers' organizations, and human rights groups.

 The UN's Take on Business and Human Rights

Ruggie's Guiding Principles for MNCs and Human Rights

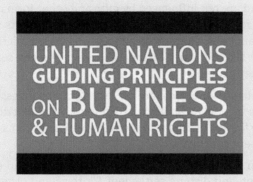

View the video online at: http://www.youtube.com/embed/BCoL6JVZHrA?rel=0

Paying attention to human rights in host countries is not just a matter of acting ethically; there can be legal consequences as well. Unocal, a California oil company, joined with a French oil company (Total) to work with the government of Myanmar (also known historically as Burma) to build a pipeline through Myanmar to Thailand. The "Yadana Field" was a natural gas field in the Andaman Sea in Myanmar's territorial waters estimated to have over 5 trillion cubic feet of natural gas, enough to continue in production for 30 years. The government stood to net an estimated $200–$400 million a year for the life of the project. As a relatively poor nation, such an income to the government could be used to benefit the greater society, so whatever the cost to people in the way of the pipeline could be justified by utilitarian thinking. While Total and its partner companies would actually construct the project, the government agreed to "assist by providing security protection and rights of way and easements as may be requested by" the companies.

Yet Myanmar was a military dictatorship accused of violating the human rights of its citizens. In 1988, after crushing pro-democracy demonstrations and killing thousands of people throughout the country, Myanmar's military seized power. It created the State Law and Order Restoration Council (SLORC) to govern. The SLORC, made up of 19 senior military officers, then imposed martial law on the country. In its 1991 report on Myanmar's human rights practices, the U.S. State Department wrote that the SLORC maintained order through "arrests, harassment, and torture of political activists. . . . Torture, arbitrary detentions, and compulsory labor persisted. . . . Freedom of speech, the press, assembly, and association remain practically nonexistent." In its 1995 report, the Department of State wrote: "The Government's unacceptable record on human rights changed little in 1994. . . . The military forced hundreds of thousands of ordinary Burmese (including women and children) to "contribute" their labor, often under harsh working conditions, to construction projects throughout the country. The forced resettlement of civilians also continued."

A group of Myanmar residents filed a lawsuit against Unocal in U.S. Federal court in 1996. The plaintiffs alleged they had suffered human rights abuses such as forced labour, murder, rape and torture at the hands of the Myanmar military during construction of a gas pipeline, and that Unocal was complicit in these abuses. The parties reached an out-of-court settlement in which Unocal agreed to compensate the plaintiffs and provide funds for programs in Myanmar to improve living conditions and protect the rights of people from the pipeline region (the exact terms of the settlement are confidential). This settlement was accepted by the court, and the case was closed on 13 April 2005.

Bribery and Corruption, at Home and Abroad

Within the U.S., companies that do a lot of purchasing make sure that their agents get the best quality at the best price, and are not influenced by gifts and other forms of bribery from potential suppliers. General Motors, for example, has imposed strict rules for its purchasing agents not to accept anything of significant value from those offering goods or services to GM. In the 1990s, "significant" was anything over $30.00 (clearly excluding those prized box seats at the Joe Louis arena for Detroit Red Wings hockey games).

Abroad, however, the rules of the game are far less strict, regardless of what "the law" says in writing (see the case in this section, *Kirkpatrick v. Tectonics*). Abroad, bribery allows inferior goods and services to "win" where foreign officials are secretly given large sums of money in exchange for granting lucrative government contracts.

Free market capitalism requires a legal system that supports and enforces private property rights, contract enforcement, and dispute settlement for torts and other harms. The competitive market, in economic terms, features many buyers and sellers and lots of competition, and limits spillover effects ("negative externalities") where economic activities negatively affect people who aren't involved in the transaction and who don't consent to paying for these effects. For example, the production of cement and its subsequent sale results in contracts between the manufacturer, the distributors, the retailers, and the ultimate purchasers. The property owners adjacent to the cement factory will likely incur costs from the factory's discharges of soot, pollutants, and its noise and vibration—the neighbors may need to paint their house more frequently, dry their clothes inside instead of hanging them on the line, or may even contract emphysema, requiring medical care or lost time at work.

The neighbors may also lose property value as the neighborhood becomes less desirable. If the factory is going "24/7" they may even lose some sound sleep from the noise and vibration. These costs, which economists term "social costs," are not reflected in the price of the product. Such losses must be adjusted in civil lawsuits, but often third parties find the legal process costly and difficult as well. In short, the legal system does a poor job of making the cost of a product take care of these spillover effects on non-consenting parties.

Democratic free-market capitalism—in theory—also discourages monopolies and oligopolies and government subsidies. (A government subsidy can be a tax break, a low-interest loan, or an outright grant to certain companies or industries.) But monopolies and oligopolies are not regulated very well, and subsidies for favored industries are fairly common. (See Tim Wu, *The Curse of Bigness: Antitrust in the New Gilded Age*, 2018).

But what about bribery? Could it possibly be consistent with the underlying values of free-market capitalism?

Free market principles and Milton Friedman would certainly frown on secret deals and unfair competition. May the best product or service win in a competitive marketplace! A company that bribes to get business, whether at home or abroad, is also not following Kantian advice. If all firms who sought contracts offered bribes, offering bribes would be pointless—the whole reason to bribe is to offer the right official or purchasing agent the best payoff for that person or group of people, while other potential contract winners make their best offer without bribing. If everyone submitted "winning bribes," bribing would gain no specific advantage over other bidders, which is the whole point of making the bribe.

Kant would object to bribery because it represents a lie or often involves a series of lies. In the case below, *Kirkpatrick v. Tectonics.* Kirkpatrick represents that it is going to do the job for a certain amount, but it is actually doing the construction job for less, because part of the contract price is going to certain government officials "under the table." Or, the contract price is accurate, but they are also making side payments to those key officials. The public officials no doubt represent that they have secured the services of a reputable U.S. company to do the construction at the Air Force base for a publicly announced price, but that is a lie, as well. They are not telling their citizens that part of the price includes money to certain government insiders. When Kirkpatrick makes its public accounting statements, it will typically "bury" the payment in a hard-to-find line item that will not identify it as a bribe.

A bribe, being secret, does not represent honest business behavior. It also disrespects free-market capitalism under the rule of law where arguably the bribe is a government subsidy to the bribing company. It disrespects the economists' views (such as Friedman's) that open and free competition is the socially responsible way for companies to operate.

The U.S. Foreign Corrupt Practices Act (1976) forbids the bribing of foreign public officials. Under international law, the United States is free to prescribe and enforce rules for U.S. citizens, not only within the U.S., but also for actions of a citizen abroad. Corporations are considered citizens (See Chapter 3), so the U.S. Attorney could bring this action against the U.S. companies that bribe foreign officials.

After 1977, U.S. companies doing business abroad complained that they felt hobbled by the FCPA, and often asked legislators to repeal it. Eventually, some exceptions were made for "expediting payments" where a firm's goods were being held up by low-paid foreign customs workers, who routinely asked for bribes as "grease payments," whether or not such payments were legal under that nation's laws. But the bribing of high-level public officials who have the authority to conclude major contracts has been illegal for U.S. firms since 1977. Other nations have gradually joined the U.S. in making the bribery of public officials illegal.

In 1997, 29 nations signed on to the OECD's anti-bribery and corruption convention, bringing European and Japanese companies into line with the U.S. law. Yet compliance is still lagging, meaning that many nations are still not policing firms headquartered there that do significant business abroad. Part of the problem is the undeniable force of the common corporate complaint that "everyone else is doing it." No firm wants to lose profits in a game where the playing field is not level. This is exactly like the problem of the Tragedy of the Commons, where "everyone else doing it" with no effective legal sanctions means that it's "every man for himself"—mutual cooperation gives way to personal (or corporate) aggrandizement at the expense of others, or the gradual extinction of the common resource.

The following video illustrates how firms competing with each other for scarce resources are likely to take more than a fair or sustainable share of available goods. This is depicted in terms of the fishing industry, but the same principles apply to scarce resources such as government contracts.

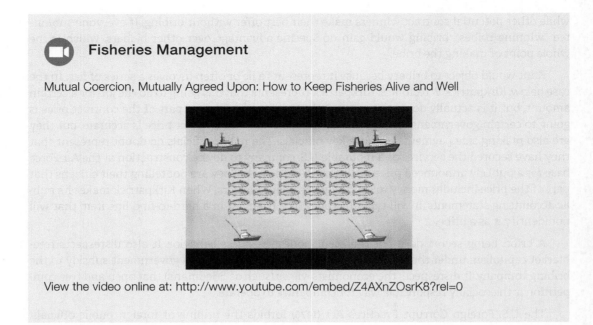

Fisheries Management

Mutual Coercion, Mutually Agreed Upon: How to Keep Fisheries Alive and Well

View the video online at: http://www.youtube.com/embed/Z4AXnZOsrK8?rel=0

Case

Bribery of Foreign Agents and the Enforceability of U.S. Business Ethics Standards

Kirkpatrick v. Environmental Tectonics

U.S. Supreme Court case, 1990, applying the act of state doctrine to the bribery of a Nigerian public official.

Kirkpatrick v. Environmental Tectonics
493 U.S. 400 (1990)[23]

Scalia, J.

In 1981, Harry Carpenter, who was then chairman of the board and chief executive officer of petitioner W. S. Kirkpatrick & Co., Inc. (Kirkpatrick) learned that the Republic of Nigeria was interested in contracting for the construction and equipment of an aeromedical center at Kaduna Air Force Base in Nigeria. He made arrangements with Benson "Tunde" Akindele, a Nigerian citizen, whereby Akindele would endeavor to secure the contract for Kirkpatrick. It was agreed that in the event the contract was awarded to Kirkpatrick, Kirkpatrick would pay to two Panamanian entities controlled by Akindele an amount equal to 20% of the contract price, which would in turn be given as a bribe to officials of the Nigerian government. In accordance with this plan, the contract was awarded to Kirkpatrick; Kirkpatrick paid the promised "commission" to the appointed Panamanian entities; and those funds were disbursed as bribes. All parties agree that Nigerian law prohibits both the payment and the receipt of bribes in connection with the award of a government contract.

Respondent Environmental Tectonics Corporation, International, an unsuccessful bidder for the Kaduna contract, learned of the 20% "commission" and brought the matter to the attention of the Nigerian Air Force and the United States Embassy in Lagos. Following an investigation by the Federal Bureau of Investigation, the United States Attorney for the District of New Jersey brought charges against both Kirkpatrick and Carpenter for violations of the Foreign Corrupt Practices Act of 1977 and both pleaded guilty.

Respondent then brought this civil action in the United States District Court of the District of New Jersey against Carpenter, Akindele, petitioners, and others, seeking damages under the Racketeer Influenced and Corrupt Organizations Act, the Robinson-Patman Act, and the New Jersey Anti-Racketeering Act. The defendants moved to dismiss the complaint under Rule 12(b)(6) of the Federal Rules of Civil Procedure on the ground that the action was barred by the **act of state doctrine**. [That every nation-state is bound to respect the independence of every other nation-state, and the courts will not sit in judgment of another government's acts done within its own territory.]

> **act of state doctrine**
>
> That every sovereign state is bound to respect the independence of every other sovereign state, and the courts will not sit in judgment of another government's acts done within its own territory.

The District Court concluded that the act of state doctrine applies "if the inquiry presented for judicial determination includes the motivation of a sovereign act which would result in embarrassment to the sovereign or constitute interference in the conduct of foreign policy of the United States." Applying that principle to the facts at hand, the court held that respondents' suit had to be dismissed because to prevail respondents would have to show that "the defendants intended to wrongfully influence the decision to award the Nigerian contract by payment of a bribe, that the government of Nigeria, its officials or other representatives, knew of the bribe offer, that the bribe was actually received or anticipated and that but for the payment or anticipation of the payment of the bribe defendants would not have been awarded the Nigerian contract."

The Court of Appeals for the Third Circuit reversed [holding that on the facts here the doctrine did not apply because no embarrassment of the Executive Branch in its conduct of foreign affairs was evident.]

This Court's description of the jurisprudential foundation for the act of state doctrine has undergone some evolution over the years. We once viewed the doctrine as an expression of international law, resting upon "the highest considerations of international comity and expediency" [Citation, 1918]. We have more recently described it, however, as a consequence of domestic separation of powers, reflecting "the strong sense of the Judicial Branch that its engagement in the task of passing on the validity of foreign acts of state may hinder" the conduct of foreign affairs [Citation, 1964]. Some Justices have suggested possible exceptions to application of the doctrine, where one or both of the foregoing policies would seemingly not be served: an exception, for example, for acts of state that consist of commercial transactions, since neither modern international comity nor the current position of our Executive Branch accorded sovereign immunity to such acts, or an exception for cases in which the executive branch has represented that it has no objection to denying validity to the foreign sovereign act, since then the court should be impeding no foreign-policy goals.

We find it unnecessary, however, to pursue those inquiries, since the factual predicate for application of the act of state doctrine does not exist. Nothing in the present suit requires the court to declare invalid, and thus ineffective as "a rule of decision for the courts of this country," the official act of a foreign sovereign.

[Decision of court of appeals affirmed.]

Note: The Supreme Court determined that the secret arrangements between Kirkpatrick and Mr. Akindele that paid off unspecified Nigerian "officials" was not an official act of a foreign sovereign that required U.S. courts to refuse jurisdiction on foreign policy or separation of powers grounds. (See Chapter 3).

Case Questions

1. Why would a U.S. company knowingly bribe a public official when doing so was against both Nigerian and U.S. law?

2. If the Nigerian law was not being enforced, what "school of thought" would view the Nigerian law as "not really the law"?

3. How much would you sympathize with Kirkpatrick & Co. if there were fierce competition for the contract, and the company badly needed to establish a business presence in Nigeria? Would Milton Friedman's version of corporate social responsibility justify what they did? What about utilitarianism?

Key Takeaway

Doing business globally presents novel ethical challenges. Cultural differences may be pronounced enough that a multinational would be wise to follow host country norms, even where those norms are not written into law. Not all foreign countries have laws coming from democratic political-economic systems; multinational companies must often find a way to do business in places where the rule of law is less established, and where authoritarian and/or corrupt rulers have the power to make or break a company's efforts to do business there. Bribing for business in such countries may be tempting, but ethically and legally short-sighted. Some emerging economies have low or nonexistent labor and environmental standards, but minimal compliance with the standards may tarnish corporate reputations among customers in the U.S.

Many countries have pledged to do more to secure human rights, and many businesses have pledged to uphold those rights. But voluntary progress remains slow, and which rights are most deserving of state and corporate protection is far from clear. The Unocal case illustrates that where there are gross violations of human rights (torture, forced labor), there may be legal consequences as well as negative impacts on corporate reputations.

Exercises

1. If businessmen in, say, Thailand, find dealing with professional women (instead of men) unsettling, should a U.S. firm set up shop in Thailand with women executives, or not?

2. Why is bribery as common as it is? Aside from American squeamishness about the practice, what's wrong with bribery if it gets business done in nation-states where it is common?

3. What is the problem, if any, with nepotism?

4. If behavior that would be considered unethical in the U.S. (child labor, for example) is practiced by foreign firms associated with American ones, is the American firm likely to suffer adverse consequences in the foreign country? In the U.S.?

2.5 Summary and Exercises

Summary

Doing good business requires attention to ethics as well as law. Understanding the long-standing perspectives on ethics—utilitarianism, deontology, social contract, and virtue ethics—can be helpful in sorting out the ethical issues that face us as individuals and businesses. Each business needs to create or maintain a culture of ethical excellence, where there is ongoing dialogue not only about the best technical practices but also about the company's ethical challenges and practices. A firm that has purpose and passion beyond maximizing shareholder value in the short term is best poised to meet the needs of diverse stakeholders, and can best position itself for long-term, sustainable success for the firm. The ethical challenges facing companies operating in the U.S. are magnified when doing business abroad. Firms doing business abroad face cultural and legal differences in host countries, and honoring basic human rights globally can poses challenges to a profit-driven organization where the rights are not supported by the host country's positive law.

Exercises

1. Consider again Milton Friedman's article ""The Social Responsibility of Business Is to Increase Its Profits""

   a. What does Friedman mean by "ethical custom"?

   b. If the laws of the society are limiting the company's profitability, would the company be within its rights to disobey the law?

   c. What if the law is "on the books," but the company could count on a lack of enforcement from state officials who were overworked and underpaid? Should the company limit its profits? Suppose that it could save money by discharging a pollutant into a nearby river, adversely affecting fish and, potentially, drinking water supplies for downstream municipalities. In polluting against laws that aren't enforced, is it still acting "within the rules of the game"? What if almost all other companies in the industry were saving money by doing similar acts?

2. Consider again the *Harris v. Forklift* case at Chapter 1 Section 6. The Supreme Court ruled that Ms. Harris was entitled to be heard again by the federal district court, which means that there would be a trial on her claim that Mr. Hardy, owner of Forklift Systems, had created a "hostile working environment" for Ms. Harris. Apart from the legal aspects, did he really do anything unethical? How can you tell?

   a. Which of his actions, if any, were contrary to utilitarian thinking?

   b. If Kant were his second-in-command and advising him on ethical matters, would he have approved of Mr. Hardy's behavior? Why or why not?

3. Consider the behaviors alleged by Ms. Harris and assume for a moment that they are all true. In terms of core values, which of these behaviors are not consistent with the core values Josephson points to? Be specific.

4. Assume that Forklift Systems is a large public corporation and that the CEO engages in these kinds of behaviors. Assume also that the board of directors knows about it. What action should the board take, and why?

5. Assume that the year is 1963, prior to the passage of the Civil Rights Act of 1964 and the Title VII provisions regarding equal employment opportunity that prohibit discrimination based on sex. So, Mr. Hardy's actions are not illegal, fraudulent, or deceitful. Assume also that he heads a large public company and that there is a large amount of turnover and unhappiness among the women who work for the company. No one can sue him for being sexist or lecherous, but are his actions consistent with maximizing shareholder returns? Should the board be concerned?

   Notice that this question is really a stand-in for any situation faced by a company today regarding its CEO, where the actions are not illegal but are ethically questionable. What would conscious capitalism tell a CEO or a board to do where a group of its employees are regularly harassed or disadvantaged by top management?

6. It is obvious that wealth is a status-assignor in the U.S. (and pretty much everywhere, for that matter). If people want status, if it is important to them that others look up to them, they will try to get rich. What does this obvious observation have to do with business ethics?

   1. 6.If an American CEO—a married man—lied about his resume, had a history of bankruptcy and of shady deals; if he, by his own admission, groped women; if he paid off high-priced "call girls" to buy their silence; if he insulted his subordinates and insisted it was "my way or the highway"; if he gave important assignments to people whose only apparent qualification was loyalty to him—what should the corporate board of directors do?

Self-Test Questions

1. Milton Friedman would have been most likely to agree to which of the following statements?

    a. The purpose of the corporation is to find a path to sustainable corporate profits by paying careful attention to key stakeholders.

    b. The business of business is business.

    c. The CEO and the board should have a single-minded focus on delivering maximum value to shareholders of the business.

    d. All is fair in love, war, and business.

2. Milton Friedman meant (using the material quoted in this chapter) that companies should:

    a. Find a path to sustainable profits by looking at the interconnected needs and desires of all the stakeholders.

    b. Always remember that the business of business is business.

    c. Remind the CEO that he or she has one duty: to maximize shareholder wealth by any means possible.

    d. Maximize shareholder wealth by engaging in open competition without fraud or deceit.

3. What are some key drawbacks to utilitarian thinking at the corporate level?

    a. The corporation may do a cost-benefit analysis that puts the greatest good of the firm above all other considerations.

    b. It is difficult to predict future consequences; decision makers in for-profit organizations will tend to overestimate the upside of certain decisions and underestimate the downside.

    c. Short-term interests will often be favored over long-term consequences.

    d. all of the above

    e. a and b only

4. Which ethical perspective would allow that under certain circumstances, it might be ethical to lie to a liar?

    a. deontology

    b. virtue ethics

    c. utilitarianism

    d. all of the above

5. Under conscious capitalism,

    a. Virtue ethics is ignored.

    b. Shareholders, whether they be traders or long-term investors, are always the first and last consideration for the CEO and the board.

    c. Maximizing profits comes from a focus on higher purposes and harmonizing the interests of various stakeholders.

    d. Kantian duties take precedence over cost-benefit analyses.

Self-Test Answers

1. c
2. d
3. d
4. c
5. c

Endnotes

1. See Shell's 1998 sustainability report, which reflects a re-thinking of its relations to various stakeholders. https://go.shell.com/2SQZXLj

2. Another example reflects what happened to the venerable Wells Fargo Bank as a result of its various scandals: https://www.fool.com/investing/2017/09/06/chart-the-cost-of-wells-fargos-sales-scandal.aspx

3. See Drumwright, M., Prentice, R. and Biasucci, C. (2015), Behavioral Ethics and Teaching Ethical Decision Making. *Decision Sciences Journal of Innovative Education*, 13: 431–458. doi: 10.1111/dsji.12071

4. See Alex Berenson and Mark Cuban, The Number: How the Drive for Quarterly Earnings Corrupted Wall Street and Corporate America. (2003)

5. Michael Sandel, Justice: What is the Right Thing to Do (2009). Chapter 5, pp. 134–138.

6. Robert Nozick, Anarchy, State, and Utopia (1974), p. ix.

7. LaRue Tone Hosmer, *Moral Leadership in Business* (Chicago: Irwin Professional Publishing, 1994), 72.

8. James O'Toole and Don Mayer, eds., *Good Business: Exercising Effective and Ethical Leadership* (London: Routledge, 2010).

9. For a good example, see Charles Duhigg, The Power of Habit: Why We DO What We do in Life and Business (2012), especially Chapter 4, "Keystone Habits, or the Ballad of Paul O'Neill," discussing how O'Neill's leadership on making safety a habit in a global company, Alcoa, transformed the corporate culture and delivered greater profits as well.

10. Milton Friedman, New York Times Magazine, September 13, 1970, Milton Friedman, New York Times Magazine, September 13, 1970.

11. The Error at the Heart of Corporate Leadership, Joseph Bower and Lynn Paine, *Harvard Business Review*, May/June 2017.

12. Don Mayer, Legal Loopholes: A Reply to Professor Ostas, *American Business Law Journal*, 2011).

13. See Robert Jackall, *Moral Mazes: The World of Corporate Managers* (New York: Oxford University Press, 1988).

14. John Schwartz, "An Enron Unit Chief Warned, and Was Rebuffed," *New York Times*, February 20, 2002.

15. Warren Bennis, "A Corporate Fear of Too Much Truth," *New York Times*, February 17, 2002.

16. University of Oklahoma Department of Defense Joint Course in Communication, *Case Study: The Johnson & Johnson Tylenol Crisis*, accessed April 5, 2011.

17. FindLaw, *Report of Investigation by the Special Investigative Committee of the Board of Directors of Enron Corp.*, February 1, 2002, accessed April 5, 2011, http://news.findlaw.com/wsj/docs/enron/sicreport.

18. Steven Pearlstein, "Debating the Enron Effect," *Washington Post*, February 17, 2002.

19. Milton Friedman, John Mackey, and T. J. Rodgers, "Rethinking the Social Responsibility of Business," Reason.com, October 2005, http://reason.com/archives/2005/10/01/rethinking-the-social-responsi.

20. See generally the work of Daniel Kahnemann and Amos Tversky.

21. Inside Apple's Chinese 'sweatshop' factory where workers are paid just £1.12 per hour to produce iPhones and iPads for the West http://www.dailymail.co.uk/news/article-2103798/Revealed-Inside-Apples-Chinese-sweatshop-factory-workers-paid-just-1-12-hour.html

22. Thomas Donaldson (1989) Moral Minimums for Multinationals. *Ethics & International Affairs*, 3, 163–182. http://dx.doi.org/10.1111/j.1747-7093.1989.tb00217

23. This case also appears in Chapter 6, International Law.

CHAPTER 3
Introduction to Constitutional Law and Commerce

Chapter Learning Objectives

After reading this chapter, you should be able to:

1. Explain the historical importance and basic structure of the U.S. Constitution.
2. Know what judicial review is and what it represents in terms of the separation of powers between the executive, legislative, and judicial branches of government.
3. Locate the source of congressional power to regulate the economy under the Constitution, and explain what limitations there are to the reach of congressional power over interstate commerce.
4. Describe the different phases of congressional power over commerce, as adjudged by the U.S. Supreme Court over time.
5. Explain what power the states retain over commerce, and how the Supreme Court may sometimes limit that power.
6. Describe how the Supreme Court, under the supremacy clause of the Constitution, balances state and federal laws that may be wholly or partly in conflict.
7. Explain how the Bill of Rights relates to business activities in the United States.

The U.S. Constitution is the framework for all of U.S. law. Business and commerce are directly affected by the words, meanings, and interpretations of the Constitution. Because it speaks in general terms, its provisions raise many issues for scholars, lawyers, judges, politicians, and commentators. For example, arguments still rage over the nature and meaning of "federalism," the concept that there is shared governance between the states and the federal government. The U.S. Supreme Court is the ultimate arbiter of these disputes, and as such it has a unique role in the legal system. It has assumed the power of **judicial review**, unique among federal systems globally, through which it can strike down federal or state statutes that it believes violate the Constitution and can even void the president's executive orders if they are contrary to the Constitution's language. No knowledgeable citizen or businessperson can afford to be ignorant of its basic provisions.

judicial review

The power the Supreme Court has to say what the U.S. Constitution means. Because the Constitution speaks in broad terms, the interpretations of the Supreme Court as to the meaning of its provisions define what the Constitution means. The Constitution can only be changed by amendment or by further interpretation by the Supreme Court.

3.1 Basic Aspects of the United States Constitution

Learning Objectives

1. Describe the American values that are reflected in the U.S. Constitution.

2. Know what federalism means; what separation of powers means.
3. Explain the process of amending the Constitution and why judicial review is particularly significant.

The Constitution as Reflecting Traditional American Values

Constitution

The United States Constitution, adopted as the supreme law of the nation in 1788.

In the U.S., the one document to which all public officials, federal, state, and local, and military personnel pledge their allegiance is the **Constitution**. If you serve, you take a solemn pledge; the Constitution provides:

> *The senators and representatives before mentioned, and the members of the several state legislatures, and all executive and judicial officers, both of the United States and of the several states, shall be bound by oath or affirmation to support this Constitution.*[1]

As you look at the Constitution and how it affects the legal environment of business, please consider what basic values it may impart to us and what makes it uniquely American and worth defending "against all enemies, foreign and domestic."[2]

In Article I, the Constitution places the legislature first and prescribes the ways in which representatives are elected to public office. Article I balances influence in the federal legislature between large states and small states by creating a Senate in which the smaller states (by population) as well as the larger states have two votes. In Article II, the Constitution sets forth the powers and responsibilities of the branch—the presidency—and makes it clear that the president should be the commander in chief of the armed forces. Article II also gives states (through the so-called Electoral College) rather than individuals, a role in the election process. Article III creates the federal judiciary, and the Bill of Rights, adopted in 1791, posits that certain individual rights must be preserved against activities of the federal government. In general, the concept of "unalienable" rights—rights that cannot be waived or sacrificed to government—is particularly strong.

The Constitution itself speaks of rights in fairly general terms, and the judicial interpretation of various rights has been in flux. The "right" of a person to own another person was notably affirmed by the Supreme Court in the *Dred Scott* decision in 1857.[3] The "right" of a child to freely contract for long, tedious hours of work was upheld by the court in *Hammer v. Dagenhart* in 1918. Both decisions were later repudiated, just as the decision that a woman has a "right" to an abortion in the first trimester of pregnancy could be repudiated if *Roe v. Wade* is overturned by the Supreme Court.[4]

General Structure of the Constitution

Look at the Constitution (go ahead—do it! http://constitutionus.com/). Notice that there are seven articles, starting with Article I (legislative powers), Article II (executive branch), and Article III (judiciary). Notice that there is no separate article for administrative agencies, sometimes erroneously referred to as "the Fourth Branch" of government. The Constitution also declares that it is "the supreme Law of the Land" (Article VI). Article VII allowed for ratification by 9 of the 13 states under the Articles of Confederation. Following Article VII are the ten amendments adopted in 1791 that are referred to as the Bill of Rights. Notice also that in 1868, a new amendment, the Fourteenth, was adopted, requiring states to provide "due process" and "equal protection of the laws" to *persons* (not just citizens) within the jurisdiction of the U.S.

Federalism

The partnership created in the Constitution between the states and the federal government is called **federalism**. The Constitution is a document created by the states in which certain powers are delegated to the national government, and other powers are reserved to the states. This is made explicit in the Tenth Amendment. The states created the federal government, not the other way around!

Separation of Powers and Judicial Review

Because the Framers wanted to ensure that no single branch of the government, especially the executive branch, would be ascendant over the others, they created various checks and balances to guarantee that each of the three principal branches had ways to limit or modify the power of the others. This is known as the **separation of powers**. Thus the president retains veto power, but the House of Representatives is entrusted with the power to initiate spending bills.

Power sharing was evident in the basic design of Congress, the federal legislative branch. The basic power imbalance was between the large states (with greater population) and the smaller ones (such as Delaware). The smaller states feared a loss of sovereignty if they could be outvoted by the larger states, so the federal legislature was constructed to guarantee two Senate seats for every state, no matter how small. The Senate was also given great responsibility in ratifying treaties and judicial nominations. The net effect of this today is that senators from a very small number of states can block treaties and other important legislation. The power of small states is also magnified by the Senate's cloture rule, which currently requires sixty out of one hundred senators to vote to bring a bill to the floor for an up-or-down vote. The cloture rule is often referred to in the context of a "filibuster."[5]

Because the Constitution often speaks in general terms (with broad phrases such as "due process" and "equal protection"), reasonable people have disagreed as to how those terms apply in specific cases. The United States is unique among industrialized democracies in having a Supreme Court that reserves for itself an exclusive power to interpret what the Constitution means. The famous case of **Marbury v. Madison** began that tradition in 1803, when the Supreme Court had marginal importance in the new republic. The decision in *Bush v. Gore*, decided in December of 2000, illustrates the power of the court to shape our destiny as a nation. In that case, the court overturned—by one Justice (it was a 5–4 ruling)—a decision by the Florida Supreme Court on how to recount the Florida vote for the presidency. The court's ruling was purportedly based on the "equal protection of the laws" provision in the Fourteenth Amendment, and it essentially declared George W. Bush the winner in Florida's electoral college votes, assuring him the Presidency over his opponent, Albert Gore.

From *Marbury* to the present day, the Supreme Court has made clear that the U.S. Constitution sets the framework for all other U.S. laws, whether created by legislation or judicial decisions. Thus, any statute (or portion thereof) or legal ruling (judicial or administrative) in conflict with the Constitution is not enforceable.[6] And as the *Bush v. Gore* decision illustrates, the states are not entirely free to do what they might choose; their own sovereignty is limited by the Constitution's provisions,

federalism

The idea, built into the structure of the Constitution, that states and the federal government have concurrent powers. In effect, federalism is the concept of shared governance between the states and the federal government.

separation of powers

In the original design of the Constitution, the executive, legislative, and judicial branches were all given powers that could modify or limit the powers of the other branches of government. For example, the president wields a veto power over congressional legislation.

Marbury v. Madison

U.S. Supreme Court case, 1803, establishing the power of judicial review: that the Court could declare acts of Congress unconstitutional.

such as the equal protection clause, the Supremacy Clause, the "commerce clause" in Article I, and other constitutional provisions.

If the Supreme Court makes a "bad" decision as to what the Constitution means or how it may apply to important federal or state legislation, it is not easily overturned. Either the court must change its mind (which it sometimes does) or two-thirds of Congress and three-fourths of the states must make an amendment (Article V). In recent years, constitutional challenges to the Affordable Care Act (also known as "Obamacare") have been numerous, but the Court has (by the thinnest of margins) upheld the constitutionality of the legislation thus far.

Because the Supreme Court has this power of judicial review, there have been many arguments about how it should be exercised and what kind of "philosophy" a Supreme Court justice should have. President Richard Nixon often said that a Supreme Court justice should "strictly construe" the Constitution and not add to its language. For Nixon, finding "new law" in the Constitution was "judicial activism" rather than "judicial restraint." Republican presidents since Nixon have announced their intention to only appoint Supreme Court justices who are "strict construction-ists." The general philosophy behind the call for "strict constructionist" justices is that legislatures make laws in accord with the wishes of the majority, and so unelected judges should not make law according to their own views and values. Nixon had in mind the 1960s Warren court, which "found" rights in the Constitution that were not specifically mentioned—the right of privacy, for example. *Roe v. Wade* (1973) is often pointed to as a prime example of judicial activism for creating a "right of privacy" to announce a woman's right to make determinations about abortion in the first trimester without undue government interference.

In later years, critics of the Rehnquist and Roberts courts would charge that conservative Justices have also created newly-found rights that were not specifically mentioned in the Constitu-tion, such as the right of states to be free from federal anti-discrimination laws. Another example of Supreme Court judicial activism from the Roberts court is *Citizens United v. Federal Election Commission* in Section 5, which held that corporations are "persons" with "free speech rights" that include spending unlimited amounts of money in campaign donations and political advocacy.[7]

Because ***Roe v. Wade*** has been very controversial, this chapter includes a seminal case on "the right of privacy," *Griswold v. Connecticut* (below). Was the court correct in recognizing a "right of privacy" in Griswold? This may not seem like a "business case," but consider—the manufacture and distribution of birth control devices is a highly profitable (and legal) business in every U.S. state. Without the *Griswold* decision, selling or owning contraceptives could today be a punishable mis-demeanor offense in Connecticut or other states with similar laws. Moreover, *Griswold* illustrates another important and much-debated concept in U.S. constitutional law—substantive due process (see Section 5). The problem of judicial review and its proper scope is brought into sharp focus in the abortion controversy. Abortion became a lucrative service business after *Roe v. Wade* was decided in 1973. That has gradually changed, with state laws that have limited rather than overruled *Roe v. Wade*, and with persistent anti-abortion protests, killings of abortion doctors, and efforts to publicize the human nature of the fetuses being aborted. The key here is to understand that there is no *explicit* mention in the Constitution of any right of privacy. As Justice Harry Blackmun argued in his majority opinion in *Roe v. Wade*,

Roe v. Wade

A 1976 Supreme Court decision declaring that governments cannot unduly restrict a woman's access to abortion in the first trimester of a pregnancy.

The Constitution does not explicitly mention any right of privacy. In a line of decisions, however, the Court has recognized that a right of personal privacy or a guarantee of cer-tain areas or zones of privacy, does exist under the Constitution....[T]hey also make it clear that the right has some extension to activities relating to marriage...procreation...contra-ception...family relationships...and child rearing and education....The right of privacy...is broad enough to encompass a woman's decision whether or not to terminate her preg-nancy.

In short, U.S. Supreme Court justices, appointed not elected, wield enormous power through judicial review. In deciding that the right of privacy applied to a woman's decision to abort in the first trimester, the Supreme Court did not act on the basis of a popular mandate or clear and unequivocal language in the Constitution, and it made illegal any state or federal legislative or executive action contrary to its interpretation. Only a constitutional amendment or the court's repudiation of *Roe v. Wade* as a precedent could change that interpretation, a repudiation that many anti-abortion activists have long sought.

Case

The Constitutional Right to Privacy

Griswold v. Connecticut
381 U.S. 479 (U.S. Supreme Court, 1965)

Griswold v. Connecticut

A 1965 Supreme Court case addressing constitutional privacy rights.

[A nineteenth-century Connecticut law made the use, possession, or distribution of birth control devices illegal. The law also prohibited anyone from giving information about such devices. The executive director and medical director of a planned parenthood association were found guilty of giving out such information to a married couple that wished to delay having children for a few years. The directors were fined $100 each [about $820 in 2019 dollars.

They appealed throughout the Connecticut state court system, arguing that the state law violated (infringed) a basic or fundamental right of privacy of a married couple: to live together and have sex together without the restraining power of the state to tell them they may legally have intercourse but not if they use condoms or other birth control devices. At each level (trial court, court of appeals, and Connecticut Supreme Court), the Connecticut courts upheld the constitutionality of the convictions.]

Douglas, J.[8]

We do not sit as a super legislature to determine the wisdom, need, and propriety of laws that touch economic problems, business affairs, or social conditions. The [Connecticut] law, however, operates directly on intimate relation of husband and wife and their physician's role in one aspect of that relation.

[Previous] cases suggest that specific guarantees in the Bill of Rights have penumbras, formed by emanations from those guarantees that help give them life and substance. Various guarantees create zones of privacy. The right of association contained in the penumbra of the First Amendment is one. * * * The Third Amendment in its prohibition against the quartering of soldiers "in any house" in time of peace without the consent of the owner is another facet of that privacy. The Fourth Amendment explicitly affirms the "right of the people to be secure in their persons, houses, papers and effects, against unreasonable searches and seizures." The Fifth Amendment in its Self-Incrimination Clause enables the citizen to create a zone of privacy which the government may not force him to surrender to his detriment. The Ninth Amendment provides: "The enumeration in the Constitution, of certain rights, shall not be construed to deny or disparage others retained by the people."

The Fourth and Fifth Amendments were described as protection against all governmental invasions "of the sanctity of a man's home and the privacies of life." We recently referred in *Mapp v. Ohio* to the Fourth Amendment as creating a "right to privacy, no less important than any other right carefully and particularly reserved to the people."

[The law in question here], in forbidding the *use* of contraceptives rather than regulating their manufacture or sale, seeks to achieve its goals by having a maximum destructive impact on [the marital] relationship. Such a law cannot stand. * * * Would we allow the police to search the sacred precincts of marital bedrooms for telltale signs of the use of contraceptives? The very idea is repulsive to the notions of privacy surrounding the marital relationship.

We deal with a right of privacy older than the Bill of Rights—older than our political parties, older than our school system. Marriage is a coming together for better or for worse, hopefully enduring, and intimate to the degree of being sacred. It is an association that promotes a way of life, not causes; a harmony in living, not political faiths; a bilateral loyalty, not commercial or social projects. Yet it is an association for as noble a purpose as any involved in our prior decisions.

Mr. Justice Stewart, whom Mr. Justice Black joins, dissenting.

Since 1879 Connecticut has had on its books a law which forbids the use of contraceptives by anyone. I think this is an uncommonly silly law. As a practical matter, the law is obviously unenforceable, except in the oblique context of the present case. As a philosophical matter, I believe the use of contraceptives in the relationship of marriage should be left to personal and private choice, based upon each individual's moral, ethical, and religious beliefs. As a matter of social policy, I think professional counsel about methods of birth control should be available to all, so that each individual's choice can be meaningfully made. But we are not asked in this case to say whether we think this law is unwise, or even asinine. We are asked to hold that it violates the United States Constitution. And that I cannot do.

In the course of its opinion the Court refers to no less than six Amendments to the Constitution: the First, the Third, the Fourth, the Fifth, the Ninth, and the Fourteenth. But the Court does not say which of these Amendments, if any, it thinks is infringed by this Connecticut law. * * *

As to the First, Third, Fourth, and Fifth Amendments, I can find nothing in any of them to invalidate this Connecticut law, even assuming that all those Amendments are fully applicable against the States. It has not even been argued that this is a law "respecting an establishment of religion, or prohibiting the free exercise thereof." And surely, unless the solemn process of constitutional adjudication is to descend to the level of a play on words, there is not involved here any abridgment of "the freedom of speech, or of the press; or the right of the people peaceably to assemble, and to petition the Government for a redress of grievances." No soldier has been quartered in any house. There has been no search, and no seizure. Nobody has been compelled to be a witness against himself.

The Court also quotes the Ninth Amendment, and my Brother Goldberg's concurring opinion relies heavily upon it. But to say that the Ninth Amendment has anything to do with this case is to turn somersaults with history. The Ninth Amendment, like its companion the Tenth, which this Court held "states but a truism that all is retained which has not been surrendered," *United States v. Darby*, 312 U.S. 100, 124, was framed by James Madison and adopted by the States simply to make clear that the adoption of the Bill of Rights did not alter the plan that the *Federal* Government was to be a government of express and limited powers, and that all rights and powers not delegated to it were retained by the people and the individual States. Until today no member of this Court has ever suggested that the Ninth Amendment meant anything else, and the idea that a federal court could ever use the Ninth Amendment to annul a law passed by the elected representatives of the people of the State of Connecticut would have caused James Madison no little wonder.

What provision of the Constitution, then, does make this state law invalid? The Court says it is the right of privacy "created by several fundamental constitutional guarantees." With all deference, I can find no such general right of privacy in the Bill of Rights, in any other part of the Constitution, or in any case ever before decided by this Court.

At the oral argument in this case we were told that the Connecticut law does not "conform to current community standards." But it is not the function of this Court to decide cases on the basis of community standards. We are here to decide cases "agreeably to the Constitution and laws of the United States." It is the essence of judicial duty to subordinate our own personal views, our own ideas of what legislation is wise and what is not. If, as I should surely hope, the law before us does not reflect the standards of the people of Connecticut, the people of Connecticut can freely exercise their true Ninth and Tenth Amendment rights to persuade their elected representatives to repeal it. That is the constitutional way to take this law off the books.

Case Questions

1. Which opinion is the strict constructionist opinion here—Justice Douglas's or that of Justices Stewart and Black?

2. What would have happened if the Supreme Court had allowed the Connecticut Supreme Court decision to stand and followed Justice Black's reasoning? Is it likely that the citizens of Connecticut would have persuaded their elected representatives to repeal the law challenged here?

3. As this is written, there is much discussion about whether a solid five-member conservative U.S. Supreme Court (it could well last thirty years) might change its mind on the right to an abortion. What arguments could make it do so? (Hint: look again at the dissent above.)

4. Why would a state legislature, in 1873 or today, declare the dissemination or use of birth control devices illegal? What state interest does such a prohibition protect?

Key Takeaway

The Constitution gives voice to the idea that people have basic rights and that a civilian president is also the commander in chief of the armed forces. It gives instructions as to how the various branches of government must share power and also tries to balance power between the states and the federal government. It does not expressly allow for judicial review, but the Supreme Court's ability to declare what laws are (or are not) constitutional has given the judicial branch a kind of power not seen in other industrialized democracies.

Exercises

1. Suppose the Supreme Court declares that Congress and the president cannot authorize the indefinite detention of terrorist suspects without a trial of some sort, whether military or civilian. Suppose also that the people of the United States favor such indefinite detention and that Congress wants to pass a law rebuking the court's decision. What kind of law would have to be passed, by what institutions, and by what voting percentages?

2. When does a prior decision of the Supreme Court deserve overturning? Name one decision of the Supreme Court that you think is no longer "good law." Does the court have to wait one hundred years to overturn its prior case precedents?

3. The Constitution provides that government officials "shall be bound by oath or affirmation" to support the Constitution. What is the difference between and "oath" and an "affirmation" and why would the Framers phrase the loyalty requirement that way?

4. Public officials and armed services members are required to pledge loyalty to the U.S. Constitution. At the same time, the Constitution provides that "no religious test shall ever be required as a qualification" for public service in the U.S. What is a "religious test" and why does the Constitution forbid it?

5. Today it is claimed by some that the Republican U.S. Senate "stole" a Supreme Court nominee from the Democrats. Justice Scalia died unexpectedly in February, 2016. President Obama, in accordance with law and tradition, nominated a replacement. The Senate, under its Republican majority leader, refused to take up any replacement nomination until after the

2016 election—in January, 2017—after which President Trump's nominee was approved by the Senate. Why is it not a good idea for the public to perceive the courts as partisan?

3.2 The Commerce Clause

Learning Objectives

1. Name the specific clause through which Congress has the power to regulate commerce. What, specifically, does this clause say?
2. Explain how early decisions of the Supreme Court interpreted the scope of the commerce clause and how that impacted the legislative proposals and programs of Franklin Delano Roosevelt during the Great Depression.
3. Describe both the wider use of the commerce clause from World War II through the 1990s and the limitations the Supreme Court imposed in *Lopez* and other cases.

commerce clause

Article I, Section 8, of the U.S. Constitution is generally regarded as the legal authority by which the federal government can make law that governs commerce among the states and with foreign nations.

Article I, Section 8, the **commerce clause** gives Congress power to make laws relating to foreign trade, Indian-tribe commerce, and to commerce among the various states. Most of the federally created legal environment springs from this one clause—if Congress is not authorized in the Constitution to make certain laws, its actions may be ruled unconstitutional by the Supreme Court. Over the past 30 years, the Supreme Court has been more active in ruling that certain acts of Congress are unconstitutional than it has been since the early 20th century.

Basic Provisions of the Commerce Clause

Here are the first five parts of Article I, Section 8, which sets forth the powers of the federal legislature (Congress). The commerce clause is short, but, again, most federal legislation affecting business depends on this very clause:

Section 8

[Clause 1] The Congress shall have Power To lay and collect Taxes, Duties, Imposts and Excises, to pay the Debts and provide for the common Defence and general Welfare of the United States; but all Duties, Imposts and Excises shall be uniform throughout the United States;

[Clause 2] To borrow Money on the credit of the United States;

[Clause 3] To regulate Commerce with foreign Nations, and among the several States, and with the Indian Tribes;[9]

[Clause 4] To establish a uniform Rule of Naturalization, and uniform Laws on the subject of Bankruptcies throughout the United States;

[Clause 5] To coin Money, regulate the Value thereof, and of foreign Coin, and fix the Standard of Weights and Measures;

Early Commerce Clause Cases

For many years, the Supreme Court was very strict in applying the commerce clause—Congress could only use it to regulate by legislation aspects of the movement of goods from one state to another. Anything else was deemed local rather than national. For example, In *Hammer v. Dagenhart*, decided in 1918, a 1916 federal statute had barred transportation in interstate commerce of goods produced in mines or factories employing children under fourteen or employing children fourteen and above for more than eight hours a day. A complaint was filed in the U.S. District Court for the Western District of North Carolina by a father in his own behalf and on behalf of his two minor sons, one under the age of fourteen years and the other between fourteen and sixteen years, who were employees in a cotton mill in Charlotte, North Carolina. The father's lawsuit asked the court to enjoin (block) the enforcement of the act of Congress intended to prevent interstate commerce in the products of child labor.

The Supreme Court saw the issue as whether Congress had the power under the commerce clause to control interstate shipment of goods made by children under the age of fourteen. The Court found that Congress did not.

In previous cases, the Supreme Court had affirmed legislation that struck down harmful practices (importing contaminated foodstuffs, transporting women across state lines to engage in prostitution); it justified its decision by observing that, "[T]he use of interstate transportation was necessary to the accomplishment of harmful results." In other words, although the power over interstate transportation was to regulate commerce, that could only be accomplished by prohibiting the use of the *facilities* of interstate commerce to effect the evil intended. But in *Hammer v. Dagenhart*, that essential element was lacking. The law passed by Congress aimed to standardize among all the states the ages at which children could be employed in mining and manufacturing, while the goods themselves are harmless. Once the labor is done and the articles have left the factory, the "labor of their production is over, and the mere fact that they were intended for interstate commerce transportation does not make their production subject to federal control under the commerce power."

In short, the early use of the commerce clause was limited to the movement of physical goods (or people) between states. Just because something might enter the channels of interstate commerce later on does not make it a fit subject for national regulation. The production of articles intended for interstate commerce is a matter of local regulation. The court therefore upheld the result from the district and circuit court of appeals; the application of the federal law was enjoined. Goods produced by children under the age of fourteen could be shipped anywhere in the United States without violating the federal law.

From the New Deal to World War II

During the global depression of the 1930s, the U.S. economy saw jobless rates of a third of all workers, and President Roosevelt's (1882–1945) **New Deal** program required more active federal legislation. Included in the New Deal program was the recognition of a right to form labor unions without undue interference from employers. Congress created the National Labor Relations Board (NLRB) in 1935 to investigate and to enjoin employer practices that violated this right.

New Deal

The name given to President Franklin Roosevelt's programs to redress economic inequality and provide employment during the Great Depression.

NLRB v. Jones & Laughlin Steel Corporation

A U.S. Supreme Court case, 1937, validating the National Labor Relations Act and effectively opening the door to acceptance of major New Deal legislation.

In **NLRB v. Jones & Laughlin Steel Corporation**, 1937, a union dispute with management at a large steel-producing facility near Pittsburgh, Pennsylvania led to litigation. In this case, the NLRB had charged the Jones & Laughlin Steel Corporation with discriminating against employees who were union members. The company's position was that the law authorizing the NLRB was unconstitutional, exceeding Congress's powers. The Court held that the act was narrowly constructed so as to regulate industrial activities that had the potential to restrict interstate commerce. The earlier decisions under the commerce clause to the effect that labor relations had only an indirect effect on commerce were effectively reversed. Since the ability of employees to engage in collective bargaining (one activity protected by the act) is "an essential condition of industrial peace," the national government was justified in penalizing corporations engaging in interstate commerce that "refuse to confer and negotiate" with their workers. This was, however, a close decision, and the switch of one Justice made this ruling possible. Without this switch, the New Deal agenda would have been effectively derailed.[10]

The "Substantial Effects Doctrine": World War II to the 1990s

Subsequent to *NLRB v. Jones & Laughlin Steel Corporation*, Congress and the courts generally accepted that even modest impacts on interstate commerce were "reachable" by federal legislation. For example, the case of *Wickard v. Filburn*, from 1942, represents a fairly long reach for Congress in regulating what appear to be very local economic decisions (see Case following, Section 2).

Ollie McClung's barbeque place in Birmingham, Alabama, allowed "colored" people to buy takeout at the back of the restaurant but not to sit down with "white" people inside. The U.S. attorney sought a court order to require Ollie to serve all races and colors, but Ollie resisted on commerce clause grounds—the federal government had no business regulating a purely local establishment. Indeed, Ollie did not advertise nationally, or even regionally, and had customers only from the local area. But the court found that some 42 percent of the supplies for Ollie's restaurant had moved in the channels of interstate commerce. This was enough to sustain federal regulation based on the commerce clause.[11]

For nearly thirty years following, it was widely assumed that Congress could almost always find some interstate commerce connection for any law it might pass. It thus came as surprise to many in 1995 when the Rehnquist court decided *U.S. v. Lopez*.[12] Lopez had been convicted under a federal law that prohibited possession of firearms within 1,000 feet of a school. The law was part of a twenty-year trend (roughly 1970 to 1990) for senators and congressmen to pass laws that were "tough on crime." Lopez's lawyer admitted that Lopez had had a gun within 1,000 feet of a San Antonio schoolyard but challenged the law itself, arguing that Congress exceeded its authority under the commerce clause in passing this legislation. The U.S. government's Solicitor General argued on behalf of the Department of Justice to the Supreme Court that Congress was within its constitutional rights under the commerce clause because education of the future workforce was the foundation for a sound economy and because guns at or near schoolyards detracted from students' education. The court rejected this analysis, noting that with the government's analysis, an interstate commerce connection could be conjured from almost anything. Lopez could not be convicted under a federal criminal statute that lacked constitutional basis under the commerce clause.

Congress made no attempt to pass similar legislation after the case was decided. But in passing subsequent legislation, Congress was often careful to make a record as to why it believed it was addressing a problem that related to interstate commerce. In 1994, Congress passed the Violence Against Women Act (VAWA), but only after holding hearings to establish why violence against women on a local level would impair interstate commerce.[13] In finding VAWA unconstitutional, the Supreme Court held that Congress lacked the authority to enact a statute under the commerce clause or the Fourteenth Amendment because the object of the statute's concern (violence against women) did *not* substantially affect interstate commerce. Chief Justice William Rehnquist wrote for the court that "under our federal system that remedy must be provided by the Commonwealth of Virginia, and not by the United States." Dissenting, Justice Stephen G. Breyer argued that the majority opinion "illustrates the difficulty of finding a workable judicial commerce clause touchstone." Justice David H. Souter, dissenting, noted that VAWA contained a "mountain of data assembled by Congress...showing the effects of violence against women on interstate commerce."

The absence of a workable judicial commerce clause touchstone remains. In 1996, California voters passed the Compassionate Use Act, legalizing marijuana for medical use. California's law conflicted with the federal Controlled Substances Act (CSA), which banned possession of marijuana. After the Drug Enforcement Administration (DEA) seized doctor-prescribed marijuana from a patient's home, a group of medical marijuana users sued the DEA and U.S. Attorney General John Ashcroft in federal district court.

The medical marijuana users argued that the CSA—which Congress passed using its constitutional power to regulate interstate commerce—exceeded Congress's commerce clause power. The district court ruled against the group, but the Ninth Circuit Court of Appeals reversed and ruled the CSA unconstitutional because it applied to medical marijuana use solely within one state. In doing so, the Ninth Circuit relied on *U.S. v. Lopez* (1995) and *U.S. v. Morrison* (2000) to say that using medical marijuana did not "substantially affect" interstate commerce and therefore could not be regulated by Congress.

But by a 6–3 majority in *Gonzales v. Raich* (2005), the Supreme Court held that the commerce clause gave Congress authority to prohibit the local cultivation and use of marijuana, despite state law to the contrary. Justice John Paul Stevens argued that the court's precedents established Congress's commerce clause power to regulate purely local activities that are part of a "class of activities" with a substantial effect on interstate commerce. The majority argued that Congress could ban local marijuana use because it was part of such a class of activities—the national marijuana market. Local use affected supply and demand in the national marijuana market, making the regulation of intrastate use "essential" to regulating the drug's national market.

Notice how similar this reasoning is to the court's earlier reasoning in *Wickard v. Filburn*. In contrast, the court's conservative wing was adamant that federal power had been exceeded. Justice Clarence Thomas's dissent in *Gonzales v. Raich* stated that Raich's local cultivation and consumption of marijuana was not "Commerce...among the several States." Representing the "originalist" view that the Constitution should mostly mean what the Founders meant it to mean, he also said that in the early days of the republic, it would have been unthinkable that Congress could prohibit the local cultivation, possession, and consumption of marijuana.

Case

Testing the Reach of Congress's Commerce-Clause Power

Wickard v. Filburn

317 U.S. 111 (U.S. Supreme Court, 1942)

Wickard v. Filburn

U.S. Supreme Court decision, 1942, analyzing the scope of Congress's power to regulate "interstate commerce" under the commerce clause.

Jackson, J.

Mr. Filburn for many years past has owned and operated a small farm in Montgomery County, Ohio, maintaining a herd of dairy cattle, selling milk, raising poultry, and selling poultry and eggs. It has been his practice to raise a small acreage of winter wheat, sown in the Fall and harvested in the following July; to sell a portion of the crop; to feed part to poultry and livestock on the farm, some of which is sold; to use some in making flour for home consumption; and to keep the rest for the following seeding.

His 1941 wheat acreage allotment was 11.1 acres and a normal yield of 20.1 bushels of wheat an acre. He sowed, however, 23 acres, and harvested from his 11.9 acres of excess acreage 239 bushels, which under the terms of the Act as amended on May 26, 1941, constituted farm marketing excess, subject to a penalty of 49 cents a bushel, or $117.11 [about $2,000 in 2018 dollars] in all.

The general scheme of the Agricultural Adjustment Act of 1938 as related to wheat is to control the volume moving in interstate and foreign commerce in order to avoid surpluses and shortages and the consequent abnormally low or high wheat prices and obstructions to commerce. The Secretary of Agriculture is directed to ascertain and proclaim each year a national acreage allotment for the next crop of wheat, which is then apportioned to the states and their counties, and is eventually broken up into allotments for individual farms.

It is urged that under the Commerce Clause of the Constitution, Article I, § 8, clause 3, Congress does not possess the power it has in this instance sought to exercise [because it is an activity of local character only].[14] * * *

But even if appellee's activity be local and though it may not be regarded as commerce, it may still, whatever its nature, be reached by Congress if it exerts a substantial economic effect on interstate commerce and this irrespective of whether such effect is what might at some earlier time have been defined as "direct" or "indirect."

The effect of consumption of homegrown wheat on interstate commerce is due to the fact that it constitutes the most variable factor in the disappearance of the wheat crop. Consumption on the farm where grown appears to vary in an amount greater than 20 percent of average production. The total amount of wheat consumed as food varies but relatively little, and use as seed is relatively constant.

The maintenance by government regulation of a price for wheat undoubtedly can be accomplished as effectively by sustaining or increasing the demand as by limiting the supply. The effect of the statute before us is to restrict the amount which may be produced for market and the extent as well to which one may forestall resort to the market by producing to meet his own needs. That appellee's own contribution to the demand for wheat may be trivial by itself is not enough to remove him from the scope of federal regulation where, as here, his contribution, taken together with that of many others similarly situated, is far from trivial.

Case Questions

1. Why would Congress want to regulate the price and supply of wheat? Why did it not let the free market decide?
2. If Congress can control what a person can grow and consume on his or her own land, are there any limits to the power of the federal government?
3. How could it be said that Wickard's consumption on his own farm of wheat grown on his own farm could affect interstate commerce?

Key Takeaway

The commerce clause is the basis on which the federal government regulates most interstate economic activity. The phrase "interstate commerce" has been subject to differing interpretations by the Supreme Court over the past one hundred years. There are certain matters that are essentially local or intrastate, but the range of federal involvement in local matters is still considerable.

Exercises

1. Why would Congress have power under the Civil Rights Act of 1964 to require privately-owned restaurants and hotels to not discriminate against interstate travelers on the basis of race, color, sex, religion, or national origin? Suppose the Holiday Restaurant near I-80 in Des Moines, Iowa, has a sign that says, "We reserve the right to refuse service to any Muslim or person of Middle Eastern descent." Suppose also that the restaurant is very popular locally and that only 40 percent of its patrons are travelers on I-80. Are the owners of the Holiday Restaurant in violation of the Civil Rights Act of 1964? What would happen if the owners resisted enforcement by claiming that Title II of the act (relating to "public accommodations" such as hotels, motels, and restaurants) was unconstitutional?

2. If the Supreme Court were to go back to the days of *Hammer v. Dagenhart* and rule that only goods and services involving interstate movement could be subject to federal law, what kinds of federal programs might be lacking a sound basis in the commerce clause? "Obamacare"? Medicare? Homeland Security? Social Security?

3.3 The Dormant Commerce Clause

Learning Objectives

1. Understand that when Congress does not exercise its *positive* powers under the commerce clause, the Supreme Court may still limit or strike down state legislation (it may exercise the *negative* power of the commerce clause) that discriminates against or places an undue burden on interstate commerce.

2. Distinguish between "discrimination" dormant-commerce-clause cases and "undue burden" dormant-commerce-clause cases.

Under the Commerce Clause, the federal government has two types of power: a positive power to make law (like the minimum wage), and a negative power to strike down state laws that run afoul of the commerce clause's purpose

Positive Power of the Commerce Clause

As we have seen, Congress has the power to legislate under the commerce clause and often does legislate—this is the *positive* power of the commerce clause. For example, Congress might say that trucks moving on interstate highways must not be more than seventy feet in length. But if Congress does not exercise its powers and regulate in certain areas (such as the size and length of trucks on interstate highways), states may make their own rules. States may do so under the historic police powers of states that were never yielded up to the federal government.

The "Negative" Power of Commerce Clause (Dormant Commerce Clause)

dormant commerce clause

Even when the federal government does not act to make rules to govern matters of interstate commerce, the states may (using their police powers); but they may not do so in ways that unduly burden or discriminate against interstate commerce.

These police powers can be broadly exercised by states for purposes of health, education, welfare, safety, morals, and the environment. But the Supreme Court has reserved for itself the power to determine when state action is excessive, even when Congress has not used the commerce clause to regulate. This power—the power to strike down "offensive" state laws is the *negative* power of the commerce clause; more formally it is claimed to exist in the **dormant commerce clause**.

There are two ways that a state may violate the dormant commerce clause. If a state passes a law that is (1) an "undue burden" on interstate commerce or (2) that "discriminates" against interstate commerce, it will be struck down. *Kassel v. Consolidated Freightways* (in Cases, at Section 3) is an example of a case where Iowa's prohibition of double trailers on highway trucks was declared void by the Supreme Court as an undue burden on interstate commerce.[15]

State-imposed undue burdens on interstate commerce interfere with the federal purpose of a national free-trade zone, so does state-imposed discrimination against interstate commerce. The court has been fairly inflexible here—if one state discriminates in its treatment of any article of commerce based on its state of origin, the court will strike down the law. For example, in *Oregon Waste Systems v. Department of Environmental Quality*, the state wanted to place a slightly higher charge on waste coming from out of state.[16] The state's reasoning was that in-state residents had already contributed to roads and other infrastructure and that tipping fees at waste facilities should reflect the prior contributions of in-state companies and residents. Out-of-state waste handlers who wanted to use Oregon landfills objected and won their dormant commerce clause claim that Oregon's law discriminated "on its face" against interstate commerce. Under the Supreme Court's rulings, anything that moves in channels of interstate commerce is "commerce," even if someone is paying to get rid of something instead of buying something.

Thus, the states are bound by Supreme Court decisions under the dormant commerce clause to do nothing that differentiates between articles of commerce that originate from within the state from those that originate elsewhere. If Michigan were to let counties decide for themselves whether to take garbage from outside of the county or not, this could also be discrimination based on a place of origin outside the state. (Suppose, for instance, each county were to decide not to take waste from outside the county; then all Michigan counties would effectively be excluding waste from outside of Michigan, which is discriminatory.)[17]

The Supreme Court probably would uphold any solid waste requirements that did not differentiate on the basis of origin. If, for example, all waste had to be inspected for specific hazards, then the law would apply equally to in-state and out-of-state garbage. Because this is the dormant commerce clause, Congress could still act (i.e., it could use its broad commerce clause powers) to say that states are free to keep out-of-state waste from coming into their own borders. But Congress has declined to do so. What follows the *Kassel* case below is a 2003 statement from one of the U.S. senators from Michigan, Carl Levin, regarding the significant amounts of waste that were coming into Michigan from Toronto, Canada.

Case

What Is an "Undue Burden" Under the Commerce Clause

Kassel v. Consolidated Freightways Corp.

450 U.S. 662 (1981)

Kassel v. Consolidated Freightways Corp.

U.S. Supreme Court opinion (1981) addressing the extent to which state laws may be said to "unduly burden" interstate commerce.

Powell, J.

The question is whether an Iowa statute that prohibits the use of certain large trucks within the State unconstitutionally burdens interstate commerce.

Appellee [plaintiff at the lower court level] Consolidated Freightways Corporation of Delaware (Consolidated) is one of the largest common carriers in the country: it offers service in 48 States under a certificate of public convenience and necessity issued by the Interstate Commerce Commission. Among other routes, Consolidated carries commodities through Iowa on Interstate 80, the principal east-west route linking New York, Chicago, and the west coast, and on Interstate 35, a major north-south route.

Consolidated mainly uses two kinds of trucks. One consists of a three-axle tractor pulling a 40-foot two-axle trailer. This unit, commonly called a single, or"semi," is 55 feet in length overall. Such trucks have long been used on the nation's highways. Consolidated also uses a two-axle tractor pulling a single-axle trailer which, in turn, pulls a single-axle dolly and a second single-axle trailer. This combination, known as a double, or twin, is 65 feet long overall. Many trucking companies, including Consolidated, increasingly prefer to use doubles to ship certain kinds of commodities. Doubles have larger capacities, and the trailers can be detached and routed separately if necessary. Consolidated would like to use 65-foot doubles on many of its trips through Iowa. The State of Iowa, however, by statute, restricts the length of vehicles that may use its highways. Unlike all other States in the West and Midwest, Iowa generally prohibits the use of 65-foot doubles within its borders.

Because of Iowa's statutory scheme, Consolidated cannot use its 65-foot doubles to move commodities through the State. Instead, the company must do one of four things: (1) use 55-foot singles; (2) use 60-foot doubles; (3) detach the trailers of a 65-foot double and shuttle each through the State separately; or (4) divert 65-foot doubles around Iowa. Dissatisfied with these options, Consolidated filed this suit in the District Court averring [claiming] that Iowa's statutory scheme unconstitutionally burdens interstate commerce.

It is unnecessary to review in detail the evolution of the principles of Commerce Clause adjudication. The Clause is both a "prolific source of national power and an equally prolific source of conflict with legislation of the state[s]" [Citation, 1949]. The Clause permits Congress to legislate when it perceives that the national welfare is not furthered by the independent actions of the States. It is now well established, also, that the Clause itself is "a limitation upon state power even without congressional implementation." *Hunt v. Washington Apple Advertising Comm'n*, [Citation, 1977.] The Clause requires that some aspects of trade generally must remain free from interference by the States. When a State ventures excessively into the regulation of these aspects of commerce, it "trespasses upon national interests" [Citation, 1976], and the courts will hold the state regulation invalid under the Clause alone. The Commerce Clause does not, of course, invalidate all state restrictions on commerce. It has long been recognized that,"in the absence of conflicting legislation by Congress, there is a residuum of power in the state to make laws governing matters of local concern which nevertheless in some measure affect interstate commerce or even, to some extent, regulate it." [Citation, 1945.] The extent of permissible state regulation is not always easy to measure.

Applying these general principles, we conclude that the Iowa truck length limitations unconstitutionally burden interstate commerce.

In *Raymond Motor Transportation, Inc. v. Rice* [Citation], the Court held that a Wisconsin statute that precluded the use of 65-foot doubles violated the Commerce Clause. This case is *Raymond* revisited. Here, as in *Raymond*, the State failed to present any persuasive evidence that 65-foot doubles are less safe than 55-foot singles. Moreover, Iowa's law is now out of step with the laws of all other Midwestern and Western States. Iowa thus substantially burdens the interstate flow of goods by truck. In the absence of congressional action to set uniform standards, some burdens associated with state safety regulations must be tolerated. But where, as here, the State's safety interest has been found to be illusory, and its regulations impair significantly the federal interest in efficient and safe interstate transportation, the state law cannot be harmonized with the Commerce Clause.

Consolidated * * * demonstrated that Iowa's law substantially burdens interstate commerce. Trucking companies that wish to continue to use 65-foot doubles must route them around Iowa or detach the trailers of the doubles and ship them through separately. Alternatively, trucking companies must use the smaller 55-foot singles or 65-foot doubles permitted under Iowa law. Each of these options engenders inefficiency and added expense. The record shows that Iowa's law added about $12.6 million each year to the costs of trucking companies.

Consolidated alone incurred about $2 million per year in increased costs.

In addition to increasing the costs of the trucking companies (and, indirectly, of the service to consumers), Iowa's law may aggravate, rather than, ameliorate, the problem of highway accidents. Fifty-five-foot singles carry less freight than 65-foot doubles. Either more small trucks must be used to carry the same quantity of goods through Iowa or the same number of larger trucks must drive longer distances to bypass Iowa. In either case, as the District Court noted, the restriction requires more highway miles to be driven to transport the same quantity of goods. Other things being equal, accidents are proportional to distance traveled. Thus, if 65-foot doubles are as safe as 55-foot singles, Iowa's law tends to increase the number of accidents and to shift the incidence of them from Iowa to other States.

In sum, the statutory exemptions, their history, and the arguments Iowa has advanced in support of its law in this litigation all suggest that the deference traditionally accorded a State's safety judgment is not warranted. See *Raymond* [Citation]. The controlling factors thus are the findings of the District Court, accepted by the Court of Appeals, with respect to the relative safety of the types of trucks at issue, and the substantiality of the burden on interstate commerce.

Because Iowa has imposed this burden without any significant countervailing safety interest, its statute violates the Commerce Clause. The judgment of the Court of Appeals is affirmed.

Case Questions

1. Under the Constitution, what gives Iowa the right to make any rules regarding the size or configuration of trucks on the state highways?
2. When is it appropriate for a state to adopt legislation that "burdens" interstate commerce? What is the difference between a "burden" and an "undue burden"?
3. Constitutionally, what was wrong with Iowa's truck-length limitation? What would the practical effect be if the law stood as acceptable?

Dealing with Unwelcome Waste

Senator Carl Levin, January 2003, Letter to Constituents

Michigan is facing an intolerable situation with regard to the importation of waste from other states and Canada.

Canada is the largest source of waste imports to Michigan. Approximately 65 truckloads of waste come in to Michigan per day from Toronto alone, and an estimated 110–130 trucks come in from Canada each day.

This problem isn't going to get any better. Ontario's waste shipments are growing as the Toronto area signs new contracts for waste disposal here and closes its two remaining landfills. At the beginning of 1999, the Toronto area was generating about 2.8 million tons of waste annually, about 700,000 tons of which were shipped to Michigan. By early this year, barring unforeseen developments, the entire 2.8 million tons will be shipped to Michigan for disposal.

Why can't Canada dispose of its trash in Canada? They say that after 20 years of searching they have not been able to find a suitable Ontario site for Toronto's garbage. Ontario has about 345,000 square miles compared to Michigan's 57,000 square miles. With six times the land mass, that argument is laughable.

The Michigan Department of Environmental Quality estimates that, for every five years of disposal of Canadian waste at the current usage volume, Michigan is losing a full year of landfill capacity. The environmental impacts on landfills, including groundwater contamination, noise pollution and foul odors, are exacerbated by the significant increase in the use of our landfills from sources outside of Michigan.

I have teamed up with Senator Stabenow and Congressman Dingell to introduce legislation that would strengthen our ability to stop shipments of waste from Canada.

We have protections contained in a 17-year-old international agreement between the U.S. and Canada called the Agreement Concerning the Transboundary Movement of Hazardous Waste. The U.S. and Canada entered into this agreement in 1986 to allow the shipment of hazardous waste across the U.S./Canadian border for treatment, storage or disposal. In 1992, the two countries decided to add municipal solid waste to the agreement. To protect both countries, the agreement requires notification of shipments to the importing country and it also provides that the importing country may withdraw consent for shipments. Both reasons are evidence that these shipments were intended to be limited. However, the agreement's provisions have not been enforced by the United States.

Canada could not export waste to Michigan without the 1986 agreement, but the U.S. has not implemented the provisions that are designed to protect the people of Michigan. Although those of us that introduced this legislation believe that the Environmental Protection Agency has the authority to enforce this agreement, they have not done so. Our bill would require the EPA [Environmental Protection Agency] to enforce the agreement.

In order to protect the health and welfare of the citizens of Michigan and our environment, we must consider the impact of the importation of trash on state and local recycling efforts, landfill capacity, air emissions, road deterioration resulting from increased vehicular traffic and public health and the environment.

Our bill would require the EPA to consider these factors in determining whether to accept imports of trash from Canada. It is my strong view that such a review should lead the EPA to say "no" to the status quo of trash imports.

Question: Why doesn't the state of Michigan just prohibit out-of-state trash from being dumped in its landfills?

Key Takeaway

Where Congress does not act pursuant to its commerce clause powers, the states are free to legislate on matters of commerce under their historic police powers. However, the Supreme Court has set limits on such powers—states may not impose undue burdens on interstate commerce, may not discriminate against articles in interstate commerce, and may not adopt laws or regulations in direct conflict with federal law.

Exercises

1. Suppose that the state of New Jersey wishes to limit the amount of hazardous waste that enters into its landfills. The general assembly in New Jersey passes a law that specifically forbids any hazardous waste from entering into the state. All landfills are subject to tight regulations that will allow certain kinds of hazardous wastes originating in New Jersey to be put in New Jersey landfills but that impose significant criminal fines on landfill operators that accept out-of-state hazardous waste. The Baldessari Brothers Landfill in Linden, New Jersey, is fined for taking hazardous waste from a New York State transporter and appeals that ruling on the basis that New Jersey's law is unconstitutional. What is the result?

2. The state of Arizona determines through its legislature that trains passing through the state cannot be longer than seventy cars. There is some evidence that in eastern U.S. states longer trains pose some safety hazards. There is less evidence that long trains are a problem in western states. Several major railroads find the Arizona legislation costly and burdensome and challenge the legislation after applied-for permits for longer trains are denied. What kind of dormant commerce clause challenge is this, and what would it take for the challenge to be successful?

3. North Carolina's Board of Agriculture adopted a regulation in 1972 requiring all apples shipped into the state in closed containers to display the United States Department of Agriculture's grade or nothing at all. Washington state growers had adopted a different grading standard, which would show Washington State's "Extra Fancy" apples as a higher grade than the highest federal labeling standard, "U.S. Extra Fancy." In effect, the N.C. rule downgraded Washington's best apples to the federal best-apple standard. N.C. asserted its regulation was a valid exercise of police power to create "uniformity" and to protect its citizens from "fraud and deception." Two points of relevance: North Carolina was attempting to promote is apple industry, and there was no evidence of any "consumer deception" because of the use of Washington apple-grading standards. Did the N.C. regulation violate the commerce clause by either discriminating against interstate commerce or by unreasonably burdening interstate commerce?[18]

3.4 Preemption: The Supremacy Clause

Learning Objectives

1. Understand the role of the supremacy clause in the balance between state and federal power.
2. Give examples of cases where state legislation is preempted by federal law and cases where state legislation is not preempted by federal law.

Preemption in General

The **preemption doctrine** derives from the **supremacy clause** of the Constitution, set out below. This means that *any* federal law—even a regulation of a federal agency—would take control over *any* conflicting state law. (Similarly, a state statute is superior to a conflicting county or city ordinance.)

The Supremacy Clause

Article VI

preemption doctrine

In U.S. federalism, federal law is superior to state law. In general, the law of a jurisdiction's highest authority is superior to any lower-level jurisdiction's law-making authority.

supremacy clause

A clause in the U.S. Constitution providing that federal law and treaties are superior to any conflicting state or local law.

This Constitution, and the Laws of the United States which shall be made in Pursuance thereof; and all Treaties made, or which shall be made, under the Authority of the United States, shall be the supreme Law of the Land; and the Judges in every State shall be bound thereby, any Thing in the Constitution or Laws of any State to the Contrary notwithstanding.

Express Preemption: No State Action Allowed

federal preemption

The doctrine that—under the Constitution's Supremacy Clause—federal law or regulation is superior to any conflicting state or local law, rendering the state regulation void.

When Congress does use its power under the commerce clause, it can expressly state that it wishes to have exclusive regulatory authority. For example, when Congress determined in the 1950s to promote nuclear power ("atoms for peace"), it set up the Nuclear Regulatory Commission (the NRC) and provided a limitation of liability for nuclear power plants in case of a nuclear accident. The states were expressly told to stay out of the business of regulating nuclear power or the movement of nuclear materials. Thus, Rochester, Minnesota, or Berkeley, California, could declare themselves nuclear-free zones, but the federal government's NRC legislation would have preempted any such legislation in the event of an actual case or controversy. If Michigan wished to set safety standards at Detroit Edison's Fermi II nuclear reactor that were more stringent than the federal Nuclear Regulatory Commission's standards, for example, Michigan's standards would be subject to **federal preemption** and thus be void. (To "pre-empt" means to take over in advance: your favorite TV show has been preempted by a special news documentary.)

Cipollone v. Liggett Group (1992) was a closely-watched case concerning the extent of an express preemption provision in two cigarette labeling laws of the 1960s. The case was a wrongful death action brought against tobacco companies on behalf of Rose Cipollone, a lung cancer victim who had started smoking cigarettes in the 1940s. The court considered the preemptive effect on state law of a provision in the federal labeling law that stated, "No requirement based on smoking and health shall be imposed under state law with respect to the advertising and promotion of cigarettes." The court concluded that several types of state tort actions were preempted by the provision but allowed other types to go forward.[19]

In recent years, several states have passed laws for medical and recreational marijuana that are inconsistent with the federal Controlled Substances Act. In 1970, Congress (at the urging of President Nixon as part of his "law and order" agenda) enacted the federal Controlled Substances Act (CSA) and placed the plant cannabis, referred to in the CSA as *marihuana*, into Schedule I—the most restrictive schedule. Schedule I substances are the most tightly controlled of the CSA's five classifications. Schedule I substances are said to have "a high potential for abuse," "no currently accepted medical use in treatment in the United States," and "lack accepted safety for use under medical supervision." Both medical marijuana and recreational marijuana are treated by this federal law as criminal. As noted above, in *Gonzales v. Raich*,[20] the Supreme Court affirmed the primacy of federal law over California state law, even where the federal law was allegedly violated by wholly intrastate cultivation and possession of a few marijuana plants prescribed for medical use. The advent of legal recreational marijuana in eight states as of July 2018 may test the inherent federal-state tensions here; during the Obama administration (2008–2016), the Department of Justice did not press the conflict, but the Trump administration might.[21]

Large industries and companies actually prefer regulation at the national level (that is, they prefer federal preemption). It is easier for a large company or industry association to lobby in Washington, DC, than to lobby in fifty different states. Accordingly, industry often asks Congress to put preemptive language into its statutes. The tobacco industry is a case in point.

No Express Preemption: State Action May Be Allowed

Congress can allow what might appear to be inconsistencies; the existence of federal statutory standards does not always mean that local and state standards cannot be more stringent. If California wants cleaner air or water than other states, it can set stricter standards—nothing in the Clean Water Act or Clean Air Act forbids the state from setting stricter pollution standards, because there is a legitimate state interest in promoting local health. As the auto industry well knows, California has set stricter standards for auto emissions. Since the 1980s, most automakers have made both a federal car and a California car, because federal Clean Air Act emissions restrictions do not preempt more rigorous state standards.

Implied Preemption

Implied preemption presents more difficult issues than express preemption. The court has to look beyond the express language of federal statutes to determine whether Congress has "occupied the field" in which the state is attempting to regulate, or whether a state law directly conflicts with federal law, or whether enforcement of the state law might frustrate federal purposes.

Federal "occupation of the field" occurs, according to the court in *Pennsylvania v. Nelson* (1956), when there is "no room" left for state regulation. Courts are to look to the pervasiveness of the federal scheme of regulation, the federal interest at stake, and the danger of frustration of federal goals in making the determination as to whether a challenged state law can stand.

In *Silkwood v. Kerr-McGee* (1984), the court, voting 5–4, found that a $10 million punitive damages award against a nuclear power plant was not impliedly preempted by federal law. Even though the court had recently held that state regulation of the safety aspects of a federally-licensed nuclear power plant was preempted, the court drew a different conclusion with respect to Congress's desire to displace state tort law—even though the tort actions might be premised on a violation of federal safety regulations.

Key Takeaway

In cases of conflicts between state and federal law, federal law will preempt (or control) state law because of the supremacy clause. Preemption can be express or implied. In cases where preemption is implied, the court usually finds that compliance with both state and federal law is not possible or that a federal regulatory scheme is comprehensive (i.e., "occupies the field") and should not be modified by state actions.

Exercises

1. For many years, the United States engaged in discussions with friendly nations as to the reciprocal use of ports and harbors. These discussions led to various multilateral agreements between the nations as to the configuration of oceangoing vessels and how they would be

    piloted. At the same time, concern over oil spills in Puget Sound led the state of Washington to impose fairly strict standards on oil tankers and requirements for the training of oil tanker pilots. In addition, Washington's state law imposed many other requirements that went above and beyond agreed-upon requirements in the international agreements negotiated by the federal government. Are the Washington state requirements preempted by federal law?

2. The Federal Arbitration Act of 1925 requires that all contracts for arbitration be treated as any other contract at common law. Suppose that the state of Alabama wishes to protect its citizens from a variety of arbitration provisions that they might enter into unknowingly. Thus, the legislation provides that all pre-dispute arbitration clauses be in bold print, that they be in twelve-point font or larger, that they be clearly placed within the first two pages of any contract, and that they have a separate signature line where the customer, client, or patient acknowledges having read, understood, and signed the arbitration clause in addition to any other signatures required on the contract. Is the Alabama law preempted by the Federal Arbitration Act?

3. The State of Calhio (fictional U.S. state) banned smoking in all public buildings. The County Council in Freedom County, Calhio passed an ordinance allowing smoking in the county employee lounges or rest rooms. Is the County ordinance valid?

3.5 Business and the Bill of Rights

Learning Objectives

1. Understand and describe which articles in the Bill of Rights apply to business activities and how they apply.
2. Explain the application of the Fourteenth Amendment—including the due process clause and the equal protection clause—to various rights enumerated in the original Bill of Rights.

The Bill of Rights

Bill of Rights

The first ten amendments to the U.S. Constitution.

After the Constitution was drafted there was concern that the new federal government should be prohibited from infringing upon (violating) individual rights. It was agreed that after ratification, the new Constitution would immediately be amended to specifically prohibit certain actions by the federal government. These amendments are the **Bill of Rights**,[22] originally meant to apply to federal actions only. During the twentieth century, the Court began to apply selected rights to state actions as well; that is, the Court began to "incorporate the Bill of Rights against the states". So, for example, federal agents were prohibited from using evidence seized in violation of the Fourth Amendment (the "exclusionary rule"), but state agents were not, until *Mapp v. Ohio* (1961), when the Court applied the guarantees (rights) of the Fourth Amendment to state action, as well. In this and similar cases, the Fourteenth Amendment's due process clause was the basis for the court's action. The due process clause commanded that *states*, not just the federal government, provide due process in cases affecting the life, liberty, or property of persons (not necessarily citizens) in the U.S., and the court saw in this command certain "fundamental guarantees" that states would have to observe. Over the years, most of the important guarantees in the Bill of Rights came to apply to state as well as federal actions. The court refers to this process as "selective incorporation."

    Note the following:

1. The guarantees of the Bill of Rights apply *only* to state and federal government action. They do not limit what a company or person in the private sector may do. For example, states may not impose censorship on the media or limit free speech in a way that offends the First Amendment, but your boss (in the private sector) may order you not to talk to the media. (Can the NFL prohibit football players from "taking the knee," kneeling, during pre-game national anthem sessions to make a political point? Yes: the NFL is not the government, it is a private entity.)

2. In some cases, a private company may be regarded as participating in "state action." For example, a private defense contractor that gets 90 percent of its business from the federal government has been held to be public for purposes of enforcing the constitutional right to free speech (the company had a rule barring its employees from speaking out in public against its corporate position). It has even been argued that public regulation of private activity is sufficient to convert the private into public activity, thus subjecting it to the requirements of due process. But the Supreme Court rejected this extreme view in 1974 when it refused to require private power companies, regulated by the state, to give customers a hearing before cutting off electricity for failure to pay the bill.[23]

3. States have rights, too. While "states rights" was a battle cry of Southern states before the Civil War, the question of what balance to strike between state sovereignty and federal union has never been simple. In *Kimel v. Florida*, for example, the Supreme Court found in the words of the Eleventh Amendment a basis for declaring that states may not have to obey certain federal statutes.

First Amendment: Freedom of Speech

In part, the **First Amendment** states that "Congress shall make no law . . . abridging the freedom of speech, or of the press." The Founding Fathers believed that democracy would work best if people (and the press) could talk or write freely, without governmental interference. But the First Amendment was also not intended to be as absolute as it sounds. Oliver Wendell Holmes's famous dictum that the First Amendment does not permit a person to shout "Fire!" in a crowded theater, where there is no fire, has seldom been answered with the question, "Why not?" And no one in 1789 thought that defamation laws (tort actions for slander and libel) had been made unconstitutional.

Because the apparent purpose of the First Amendment was to make sure that the nation had a continuing, vigorous debate over matters political, political speech has been given the highest level of protection over such other forms of speech such as (1) commercial speech, (2) speech that can and should be limited by reasonable "time, place, and manner" restrictions, or (3) obscene speech. These may be more readily regulated than political speech.

Because of its higher level of protection, political speech can be false, malicious, mean-spirited, or even damned lies. (You may even have noticed this in election campaigns, past and present!) In any defamation action, truth is a defense, but in a defamation action brought by a public figure or public official she or he must prove that the defendant not only had the facts wrong but also publicly, *maliciously* lied or acted with reckless disregard for the truth.[24] Celebrities have the same burden to go forward with a defamation action. It is for this reason that the *National Enquirer* writes exclusively about public figures (like Bill and Hillary Clinton), public officials, and celebrities; it is possible to say many outrageous and eye-catching things that aren't completely true and still have the protection of the First Amendment.

Political speech is so highly protected that the court has recognized the right of people to support political candidates through campaign contributions and thus promote the particular viewpoints and speech of those candidates. Fearing the influence of money on politics, Congress has from time to time placed limitations on corporate contributions to political campaigns. But the Supreme Court has had mixed reactions over time. Initially, the court recognized the First Amendment right of a corporation to donate money, subject to certain limits.[25] Yet in another case, *Austin*

First Amendment

That part of the Constitution restricting government from abridging freedom of religion, press, or the right of assembly.

v. Michigan Chamber of Commerce (1990), the Michigan Campaign Finance Act prohibited corporations from using its own general funds money to support or oppose candidates in elections for state offices. But a corporation could make such expenditures if it set up an independent fund designated solely for political purposes. The Michigan law had been passed on the assumption that "the unique legal and economic characteristics of corporations necessitate some regulation of their political expenditures to avoid corruption or the appearance of corruption."

But as you will see in *Citizens United v. Federal Election Commission*, below, *Austin* was overruled; corporations are recognized as "persons" with First Amendment political speech rights that cannot be impaired by Congress or the states without some compelling governmental interest, and restrictions on those rights must be "narrowly tailored." Our politics is now thoroughly awash with money.[26]

Note also the First Amendment has—in addition to its guarantee that the government should not restrict freedom of speech or press—two other very important provisions. The first is freedom of religion, and that is in two pieces: the government will not establish a religion nor interfere in the free exercise of religion. The second is the right of the people to assemble peaceably and petition the government for a redress of grievances.

Along with *Citizens United*, below, you will see a First Amendment case where California attempted to limit the sale of graphic, violent video games to minors (*Brown v. Entertainment Merchants Association*). The dissenting opinion by Justice Thomas captures the approach of "originalism" championed by Justice Scalia, and Justice Breyer's dissent points out the irony of the majority's position.

Fourth Amendment

Fourth Amendment

The Constitutional amendment (1791) granting protection against unreasonable searches and seizures.

The **Fourth Amendment** says, "all persons shall be secure in their persons, houses, papers, and effects from unreasonable searches and seizures, and no warrants shall issue, but upon probable cause, before a magistrate and upon Oath, specifically describing the persons to be searched and places to be seized."

The Court has read the Fourth Amendment to prohibit only those government searches or seizures that are "unreasonable." Because of this, businesses that are in an industry that is "closely regulated" can be searched more frequently and can be searched without a warrant. In one case, an auto parts dealer at a junkyard was charged with receiving stolen auto parts. Part of his defense was to claim that the search that found incriminating evidence was unconstitutional. But the court found the search reasonable, because the dealer was in a "closely regulated industry."[27]

In the 1980s, Dow Chemical objected to an overflight by the U.S. Environmental Protection Agency (EPA). The EPA had rented an airplane to fly over the Midland, Michigan, Dow plant, using an aerial mapping camera to photograph various pipes, ponds, and machinery that were not covered by a roof. Because the court's precedents allowed governmental intrusions into "open fields," the EPA search was ruled constitutional. Because the literal language of the Fourth Amendment protected "persons, houses, papers, and effects," anything searched by the government in "open fields" was reasonable. (The court's opinion suggested that if Dow had really wanted privacy from governmental intrusion, it could have covered the pipes and machinery that were otherwise outside and in open fields.)

The Supreme Court justified the EPA's search at least partially on the basis that the EPA had used a commercial technology available to anyone. That is, anyone could have rented a private plane and used an expensive (but available) aerial mapping camera to look at Dow's Midland facility. In *Kyllo v. United States*, 533 U.S. 27 (2001), however, the use of a thermal imaging device from a public vantage point to monitor the amount of heat radiation was deemed a search that required a prior warrant. The object of the authorities' search was an indoor marijuana operation. But the

Court was divided, 5–4, and the decision hinged at least partly on the thermal imaging device being not commercially available to the public.

Note again that constitutional guarantees like the Fourth Amendment only apply to governmental action. Your employer or any private enterprise is not bound by constitutional limits. For example, if drug testing of all employees every week is done by a government agency, the employees may have a cause of action to object based on the Fourth Amendment. However, if a private employer begins the same kind of routine drug testing, employees have no constitutional arguments to make; they can simply leave that employer, or they may pursue whatever statutory or common law remedies are available.

Fifth Amendment

The **Fifth Amendment** states (in part), "No person shall be . . . deprived of life, liberty, or property, without due process of law; nor shall private property be taken for public use, without just compensation." The Fifth Amendment thus has two principal parts as relates to U.S. commerce (it has other vitally important parts, like the privilege against self-incrimination): (1) due process (which has two parts, substantive and procedural), and (2) the takings clause.

Procedural due process. In criminal cases, the Fifth Amendment prevents government from arbitrarily depriving a criminal defendant of life, liberty or property. In civil lawsuits, it is also constitutionally essential that the proceedings be fair. This is why, for example, the defendant in *Burger King v. Rudzewicz* had a legitimate constitutional argument, even though he lost. (See the case in Chapter 5).

Substantive due process. The Fifth Amendment is also the source of what is called **substantive due process**. During the first third of the twentieth century, the Supreme Court often nullified state and federal laws using substantive due process. In 1905, for example, in *Lochner v. New York*, the Supreme Court voided a New York statute that limited the number of hours that bakers could work in a single week. New York had passed the law to protect the health of employees, but the court found that this law interfered with the basic constitutional right of private parties to freely contract with one another. Over the next thirty years, dozens of state and federal laws were struck down that aimed to improve working conditions, secure social welfare, or establish the rights of unions. However, in 1934, during the Great Depression, the court reversed itself and began upholding the kinds of laws it had struck down earlier.

Since then, the court has employed a two-tiered analysis of substantive due process claims. Under the first tier, legislation on economic matters, employment relations, and other business affairs is subject to minimal judicial scrutiny. This means that a law will be overturned only if it serves no rational government purpose. Under the second tier, legislation concerning *fundamental liberties* is subject to "heightened judicial scrutiny," meaning that a law will be invalidated unless it is "narrowly tailored to serve a significant government purpose."

- The first category includes most of the liberties *expressly* enumerated in the Bill of Rights. Through a process known as selective incorporation, the court has interpreted the due process clause of the Fourteenth Amendment to bar states from denying their residents the most important freedoms guaranteed in the first ten amendments to the federal Constitution. Only the Third Amendment right (against involuntary quartering of soldiers) and the Fifth Amendment right to be indicted by a grand jury have not been made applicable to the states. Because these rights are still not applicable to state governments, the Supreme Court is often said to have "selectively incorporated" the Bill of Rights into the due process clause of the Fourteenth Amendment.

- The second category of fundamental liberties includes those liberties that are *not* expressly stated in the Bill of Rights but that can be seen as essential to the concepts of freedom and equality in a democratic society. These unstated liberties come from Supreme Court prece-

Fifth Amendment

That part of the U.S. Constitution addressing (1) the requirement of a grand jury, (2) double jeopardy, (3) the privilege against self-incrimination, (4) the right of due process, and (5) eminent domain.

substantive due process

The judicial doctrine that a law or regulation itself takes property from someone, as opposed to having property taken (as with a fine, say) after a trial; the substance of the law violates due process (as opposed to the procedural application of the law).

dents, common law, moral philosophy, and deeply-rooted traditions of U.S. legal history. The Supreme Court has stressed that the word liberty cannot be defined by a definitive list of rights; rather, it must be viewed as a rational continuum of freedom through which every aspect of human behavior is protected from arbitrary impositions and random restraints. In this regard, as the Supreme Court has observed, the due process clause protects abstract liberty interests, including the right to personal autonomy, bodily integrity, self-dignity, marriage, and self-determination. As noted in Chapter 15, however, the elevation of "freedom" in so-called "substantive due process" cases created serious social and political tensions in the first few decades of the 20th Century. The tension was resolved in cases such as *West Coast Hotel v. Parrish* (validating a state minimum-wage law).

These liberty interests often are grouped to form a general right to privacy, which was first recognized in *Griswold v. Connecticut* (in 3.1 earlier in this chapter), where the Supreme Court struck down a state statute forbidding married adults from using, possessing, or distributing contraceptives. Four members of the Court found that the law violated the sanctity of the marital relationship. According to Justice Douglas's plurality opinion, this penumbra of privacy, though not expressly mentioned in the Bill of Rights, must be protected to establish a buffer zone or breathing space for those freedoms that are constitutionally enumerated.

The **Takings Clause** of the Fifth Amendment ensures that the government does not take private property without just compensation. In the international setting, governments that take private property engage in what is called expropriation. The standard under customary international law is that when governments do that, they must provide prompt, adequate, and effective compensation. This does not always happen, especially where foreign owners' property is being expropriated. The guarantees of the Fifth Amendment (incorporated against state action by the Fourteenth Amendment) are available to property owners where state, county, or municipal government uses the power of eminent domain to take private property for public purposes. Just what is a "public purpose" is a matter of some debate. For example, if a city were to condemn economically viable businesses or neighborhoods to construct a baseball stadium with public money to entice a private enterprise (the baseball team) to stay, is a public purpose being served?

Consider **Kelo v. New London**, where Mrs. Kelo and other homeowners fought the city of New London in its attempt to use powers of eminent domain to create an industrial park and recreation area that would have Pfizer & Co. as a principal tenant.[28] The city argued that increasing its tax base was a sufficient public purpose. In a very close decision, the Supreme Court determined that New London's actions did not violate the takings clause. However, political reactions in various states resulted in a great deal of new state legislation that would limit the scope of public purpose in eminent domain takings and provide additional compensation to property owners in many cases.

Fourteenth Amendment: Due Process and Equal Protection Guarantees

The **Fourteenth Amendment** (1868) provides "No state shall deny any person of life, liberty, or property, without due process of law" (again, the Fifth Amendment imposes that requirement on the *federal* government). This can be either an issue of *procedural* due process (as in *Burger King v. Rudzewicz*) or an issue of *substantive* due process. For substantive due process, consider what happened in an Alabama court in the 1990s[29] (and note that the 14th Amendment protection applies to any *person*, not just any citizen).

In *BMW v. Gore*, Dr. Ira Gore was unhappy about a "brand new" BMW he had purchased from an Alabama car dealer for $40,000 [about $77,000 in 2019 dollars]. He later discovered that the vehicle's exterior had been slightly damaged in transit from Europe and had been repainted by the North American distributor prior to delivery to his dealer. Because it was not in fact "brand new," the vehicle was, by best estimates, worth about 10 percent less than he paid for it. The distributor, BMW of North America, had routinely sold slightly damaged cars as brand new if the damage could be fixed for less than 3 percent of the cost of the car. In the trial, Dr. Gore sought $4,000 in compensatory damages and also punitive damages. The Alabama trial jury considered that BMW was engaging in a fraudulent practice and wanted to punish the defendant for a number of frauds it estimated at somewhere around a thousand nationwide. The jury awarded not only the $4,000 in compensatory damages but also $4 million in punitive damages (about $7.7 million in 2019 dollars!), which was later reduced to $2 million by the Alabama Supreme Court. On appeal to the U.S. Supreme Court, the court found that punitive damages may not be "grossly excessive." If they are, then they violate substantive due process. Whatever damages a state awards must be limited to what is reasonably necessary to vindicate the state's legitimate interest in punishment and deterrence.

In addition to its due process clause, the 14th Amendment provides that no state shall "deny to any person within its jurisdiction the equal protection of the laws." "Equal protection" means that, generally speaking, governments must treat people equally when it dispenses its protections. "Protections" means, for example, protections against ignorance (why we have government-run schools), or protection against the consequences of unsanitary drinking water, or against the consequences of unemployment. (A more easily understood expression would probably be "equal benefits of the laws.") Classifications that differentiate among people or corporations unfairly will not be permitted. A well-known example of unfair classification would be race discrimination—requiring white children and black children to attend different public schools or requiring "separate but equal" public services, such as water fountains or restrooms. Yet, despite the clear intent of the 1868 amendment, "separate but equal" was the law of the land until *Brown v. Board of Education* (1954).[30]

Governments make classifications every day, so not all classifications can be illegal under the equal protection clause. People with more income generally pay a greater percentage of their income in taxes. People with proper medical training are licensed to become doctors; people without that training cannot be licensed and commit a criminal offense if they do practice medicine. To know what classifications are permissible under the Fourteenth Amendment, we need to know what is being classified. The court has created three classifications, and the outcome of any equal protection case can usually be predicted by knowing how the court is likely to classify the case:

- Minimal scrutiny: economic and social regulations. Government actions are usually upheld if there is a rational basis for them.
- Intermediate scrutiny: gender. Government classifications are sometimes upheld.
- Strict scrutiny: race, ethnicity, and fundamental rights. Classifications based on any of these are almost never upheld.

Under minimal scrutiny for economic and social regulation, laws that regulate economic or social issues are presumed valid and will be upheld if they are rationally related to legitimate goals of government. So, for example, if the city of New Orleans limits the number of street vendors to some rational number (more than one but fewer than the total number that could possibly fit on the sidewalks), the local ordinance would not be overturned as a violation of equal protection.

Under intermediate scrutiny, the city of New Orleans might limit the number of street vendors who are men. For example, suppose that the city council decreed that all street vendors must be women, thinking that would attract even more tourism. A classification like this, based on sex, will have to meet a sterner test than a classification resulting from economic or social regulation. A law like this would have to substantially relate to important government objectives. Increasingly, courts have nullified government sex classifications as societal concern with gender equality has grown. (See Shannon Faulkner's case against The Citadel, an all-male state school.)[31]

Suppose, however, that the city of New Orleans decided that no one of Middle Eastern heritage could drive a taxicab or be a street vendor. That kind of classification would be examined with strict scrutiny to see if there was any compelling justification for it. As noted, classifications such as this one are almost never upheld. The law would be upheld only if it were necessary to promote a compelling state interest. Very few laws that have a racial or ethnic classification meet that test.

However, claiming that people from several mostly Muslim countries posed a "national security threat," President Trump's executive order banning them from U.S. entry was upheld (5–4) by the Supreme Court in June, 2018.[32]

The strict scrutiny test will be applied to classifications involving racial and ethnic criteria as well as classifications that interfere with a fundamental right. In *Palmore v. Sidoti*, the state refused to award custody to the mother because her new spouse was racially different from the child.[33] This practice was declared unconstitutional because the state had made a racial classification; this was presumptively invalid, and the government could not show a compelling need to enforce such a classification through its law.

In *Obergefell v Hodges* (2015)[34] the Supreme Court applied the strict scrutiny test to same-sex marriages. Concluding that the liberty and equality of same-sex couples was unduly burdened by prohibitions against same-sex marriage, the Court held (by a 5–4 vote) that prohibitions against same-sex marriage violated the Equal Protection Clause;[35] there was no "compelling state interest" in denying to same-sex couples the privileges afforded to heterosexual couples. Justice Kennedy closed with this:

> No union is more profound than marriage, for it embodies the highest ideals of love, fidelity, devotion, sacrifice, and family. In forming a marital union, two people become something greater than once they were. As some of the petitioners in these cases demonstrate, marriage embodies a love that may endure even past death. It would misunderstand these men and women to say they disrespect the idea of marriage. Their plea is that they do respect it, respect it so deeply that they seek to find its fulfillment for themselves. Their hope is not to be condemned to live in loneliness, excluded from one of civilization's oldest institutions. They ask for equal dignity in the eyes of the law. The Constitution grants them that right.

Cases

The First Amendment, Corporate Free Speech, and Campaign Finance

Citizens United v. Federal Election Commission

U.S. Supreme Court case, 2010, holding that corporations' First Amendment free-speech rights allows them to make unlimited campaign contributions.

Citizens United v. Federal Election Commission

588 U.S. 310 (U.S. Supreme Court, 2010)

Kennedy, J.[36]

Federal law prohibits corporations and unions from using their general treasury funds to make independent expenditures for speech defined as an "electioneering communication" or for speech expressly advocating the election or defeat of a candidate. 2 U.S.C. §441b. Limits on electioneering communications were upheld in *McConnell v. Federal Election Comm'n*, [citation]. The holding of *McConnell* rested to a large extent on an earlier case, *Austin v. Michigan Chamber of Commerce* [Citation] (1990)]. *Austin* had held that political speech may be banned based on the speaker's corporate identity.

In this case we are asked to reconsider *Austin* and, in effect, *McConnell*. It has been noted that "*Austin* was a significant departure from ancient First Amendment principles," [Citation]. We agree with that conclusion and hold that stare decisis does not compel the continued acceptance of *Austin*. The Government may regulate corporate political speech through disclaimer and disclosure requirements, but it may not suppress that speech altogether. We turn to the case now before us.

Citizens United is a nonprofit corporation. It has an annual budget of about $12 million. Most of its funds are from donations by individuals; but, in addition, it accepts a small portion of its funds from for-profit corporations.

In January 2008, Citizens United released a film entitled *Hillary: The Movie*. We refer to the film as *Hillary*. It is a 90-minute documentary about then-Senator Hillary Clinton, who was a candidate in the Democratic Party's 2008 Presidential primary elections. *Hillary* mentions Senator Clinton by name and depicts interviews with political commentators and other persons, most of them quite critical of Senator Clinton. * * *

In December 2007, a cable company offered, for a payment of $1.2 million, to make *Hillary* available on a video-on-demand channel called "Elections '08." * * * Citizens United was prepared to pay for the video-on-demand; and to promote the film, it produced two 10-second ads and one 30-second ad for *Hillary*. Each ad includes a short (and, in our view, pejorative) statement about Senator Clinton, followed by the name of the movie and the movie's Website address. Citizens United desired to promote the video-on-demand offering by running advertisements on broadcast and cable television.

* * * It feared, however, that both the film and the ads would be covered by §441b's ban on corporate-funded independent expenditures, thus subjecting the corporation to civil and criminal penalties. In December 2007, Citizens United sought declaratory and injunctive relief against the FEC. It argued that (1) §441b is unconstitutional as applied to *Hillary*; and (2) [another section's] disclaimer and disclosure requirements are unconstitutional as applied to *Hillary* and to the three ads for the movie.

The District Court denied Citizens United's motion for a preliminary injunction, and then granted the FEC's motion for summary judgment.

The court held that §441b was facially constitutional under *McConnell*, and that §441b was constitutional as applied to *Hillary* because it was "susceptible of no other interpretation than to inform the electorate that Senator Clinton is unfit for office, that the United States would be a dangerous place in a President Hillary Clinton world, and that viewers should vote against her." [Citation]. The court also rejected Citizens United's challenge to disclaimer and disclosure requirements. It noted that "the Supreme Court has written approvingly of disclosure provisions triggered by political speech even though the speech itself was constitutionally protected under the First Amendment." * * *

The First Amendment provides that "Congress shall make no law . . . abridging the freedom of speech." Laws enacted to control or suppress speech may operate at different points in the speech process. * * * The law before us is an outright ban, backed by criminal sanctions. Section 441b makes it a felony for all corporations—including nonprofit advocacy corporations—either to expressly advocate the election or defeat of candidates or to broadcast electioneering communications within 30 days of a primary election and 60 days of a general election. Thus, the following acts would all be felonies under §441b: The Sierra Club runs an ad, within the crucial phase of 60 days before the general election, that exhorts the public to disapprove of a Congressman who favors logging in national forests; the National Rifle Association publishes a book urging the public to vote for the challenger because the incumbent U.S. Senator supports a handgun ban; and the American Civil Liberties Union creates a website telling the public to vote for a Presidential candidate in light of that candidate's defense of free speech. These prohibitions are classic examples of censorship.

Section 441b is a ban on corporate speech notwithstanding the fact that a PAC created by a corporation can still speak. PACs are burdensome alternatives; they are expensive to administer and subject to extensive regulations. For example, every PAC must appoint a treasurer, forward donations to the treasurer promptly, keep detailed records of the identities of the persons making donations, preserve receipts for three years, and file an organization statement and report changes to this information within 10 days.

And that is just the beginning. PACs must file detailed monthly reports with the FEC, which are due at different times depending on the type of election that is about to occur. . . .

PACs have to comply with these regulations just to speak. This might explain why fewer than 2,000 of the millions of corporations in this country have PACs. PACs, furthermore, must exist before they can speak. Given the onerous restrictions, a corporation may not be able to establish a PAC in time to make its views known regarding candidates and issues in a current campaign.

Section 441b's prohibition on corporate independent expenditures is thus a ban on speech. As a "restriction on the amount of money a person or group can spend on political communication during a campaign," that statute "necessarily reduces the quantity of expression by restricting the number of issues discussed, the depth of their exploration, and the size of the audience reached." [Citation.]

Speech is an essential mechanism of democracy, for it is the means to hold officials accountable to the people. See [Citation]: ("In a republic where the people are sovereign, the ability of the citizenry to make informed choices among candidates for office is essential.") The right of citizens to inquire, to hear, to speak, and to use information to reach consensus is a precondition to enlightened self-government and a necessary means to protect it. The First Amendment "has its fullest and most urgent application' to speech uttered during a campaign for political office."

For these reasons, political speech must prevail against laws that would suppress it, whether by design or inadvertence. Laws that burden political speech are "subject to strict scrutiny," which requires the Government to prove that the restriction "furthers a compelling interest and is narrowly tailored to achieve that interest." * * *

The Court has recognized that First Amendment protection extends to corporations. This protection has been extended by explicit holdings to the context of political speech. Under the rationale of these precedents, political speech does not lose First Amendment protection "simply because its source is a corporation."[Citation]. The Court has thus rejected the argument that political speech of corporations or other associations should be treated differently under the First Amendment simply because such associations are not "natural persons." * * *

The purpose and effect of this law is to prevent corporations, including small and nonprofit corporations, from presenting both facts and opinions to the public. * * *

When Government seeks to use its full power, including the criminal law, to command where a person may get his or her information or what distrusted source he or she may not hear, it uses censorship to control thought. This is unlawful. The First Amendment confirms the freedom to think for ourselves. * * *

Due consideration leads to this conclusion: *Austin* should be and now is overruled. We return to the principle established in *Buckley* and *Bellotti* that the Government may not suppress political speech on the basis of the speaker's corporate identity. No sufficient governmental interest justifies limits on the political speech of nonprofit or for-profit corporations. * * *

Some members of the public might consider *Hillary* to be insightful and instructive; some might find it to be neither high art nor a fair discussion on how to set the Nation's course; still others simply might suspend judgment on these points but decide to think more about issues and candidates. Those choices and assessments, however, are not for the Government to make. "The First Amendment underwrites the freedom to experiment and to create in the realm of thought and speech. Citizens must be free to use new forms, and new forums, for the expression of ideas. The civic discourse belongs to the people, and the Government may not prescribe the means used to conduct it." [Citation.]

The judgment of the District Court is reversed with respect to the constitutionality of 2 U.S.C. §441b's restrictions on corporate independent expenditures. The case is remanded for further proceedings consistent with this opinion.

It is so ordered. [This was a 5–4 decision.]

Case Questions

1. What does the case say about disclosure? Corporations have a right to free speech under the First Amendment and may exercise that right through unrestricted contributions of money to political parties and candidates. Can the government condition that right by requiring that the parties and candidates disclose to the public the amount and origin of the contribution? What would justify such a disclosure requirement?

2. Are a corporation's contributions to political parties and candidates tax deductible as a business expense? Should they be?

3. How is the donation of money equivalent to speech? Is it a strict construction of the Constitution to hold that it is?

4. Conservatives mostly cheered the Citizens' United case because it withdrew "meddling government" from restricting corporate free speech. If free speech is a good thing, why did President Trump in 2017 refer to the press as "the enemy of the people"?[37] President Trump repeatedly invokes the phrase "fake news" about any media reporting that is critical of him. Does such thinking comport with the values of the First Amendment?

Free Speech: Selling Violent Video Games to Children

Brown v. Entertainment Merchants Association

564 U.S. 786 (U.S. Supreme Court, 2011).

Brown v. Entertainment Merchants Association

U.S, Supreme Court, 2011, setting forth limits on state governments' censorship of violent children's video games.

Scalia, J.

We consider whether a California law imposing restrictions on violent video games comports with the First Amendment.

California Assembly Bill 1179 (2005), prohibits the sale or rental of "violent video games" to minors, and requires their packaging to be labeled "18." The Act covers games "in which the range of options available to a player includes killing, maiming, dismembering, or sexually assaulting an image of a human being, if those acts are depicted" in a manner that "a reasonable person, considering the game as a whole, would find appeals to a deviant or morbid interest of minors," that is "patently offensive to prevailing standards in the community as to what is suitable for minors," and that "causes the game, as a whole, to lack serious literary, artistic, political, or scientific value for minors." Violation of the Act is punishable by a civil fine of up to $1,000.

Respondents, representing the video-game and software industries, brought a pre-enforcement challenge to the Act in the United States District Court for the Northern District of California. That court concluded that the Act violated the First Amendment and permanently enjoined its enforcement. The Court of Appeals affirmed, and we granted *certiorari* [discretionary review].

California correctly acknowledges that video games qualify for First Amendment protection. The Free Speech Clause exists principally to protect discourse on public matters, but we have long recognized that it is difficult to distinguish politics from entertainment, and dangerous to try. "Everyone is familiar with instances of propaganda through fiction. What is one man's amusement, teaches another's doctrine." [Citation] (1948)]. Like the protected books, plays, and movies that preceded them, video games communicate ideas—and even social messages—through many familiar literary devices (such as characters, dialogue, plot, and music) and through features distinctive to the medium (such as the player's interaction with the virtual world). That suffices to confer First

Amendment protection. Under our Constitution, "esthetic and moral judgments about art and literature . . . are for the individual to make, not for the Government to decree, even with the mandate or approval of a majority" [Citation]." And whatever the challenges of applying the Constitution to ever-advancing technology, "the basic principles of freedom of speech and the press, like the First Amendment's command, do not vary" when a new and different medium for communication appears. [Citation.]

The most basic of those principles is this: "[A]s a general matter, government has no power to restrict expression because of its message, its ideas, its subject matter, or its content." [Citation.] There are of course exceptions. [Citations to cases involving obscenity, incitement, fighting words, defamation, etc.] which represent "well-defined and narrowly limited classes of speech, the prevention and punishment of which have never been thought to raise any Constitutional problem" [Citation]. * * *

The [federal] Government argued in *U.S. v Stevens* [Citation, 2010] that lack of a historical warrant [precedent for banning videos of cruel treatment of animals] did not matter; that it could create new categories of unprotected speech by applying a "simple balancing test" that weighs the value of a particular category of speech against its social costs and then punishes that category of speech if it fails the test. We emphatically rejected that "startling and dangerous" proposition. "Maybe there are some categories of speech that have been historically unprotected, but have not yet been specifically identified or discussed as such in our case law." [Citation.] But without persuasive evidence that a novel restriction on content is part of a long . . . tradition of proscription, a legislature may not revise the "judgment of the American people," embodied in the First Amendment, "that the benefits of its restrictions on the Government outweigh the costs." [Citation.] That holding controls this case. * * *

California does not argue that it is empowered to prohibit selling offensively violent works *to adults*—and it is wise not to, since that is but a hair's breadth from the argument rejected in *Stevens*. Instead, it wishes to create a wholly new category of content-based regulation that is permissible only for speech directed at children.

That is unprecedented and mistaken. "Minors are entitled to a significant measure of First Amendment protection, and only in relatively narrow and well-defined circumstances may government bar public dissemination of protected materials to them." [Citation.] No doubt a State possesses legitimate power to protect children from harm, [Citations] but that does not include a free-floating power to restrict the ideas to which children may be exposed. "Speech that is neither obscene as to youths nor subject to some other legitimate proscription cannot be suppressed solely to protect the young from ideas or images that a legislative body thinks unsuitable for them." [Citation.]

California's argument would fare better if there were a longstanding tradition in this country of specially restricting children's access to depictions of violence, but there is none. Certainly the *books* we give children to read—or read to them when they are younger—contain no shortage of gore. Grimm's Fairy Tales, for example, are grim indeed. As her just deserts for trying to poison Snow White, the wicked queen is made to dance in red hot slippers "till she fell dead on the floor, a sad example of envy and jealousy." *The Complete Brothers Grimm Fairy Tales*, 198 (2006 ed.). Cinderella's evil stepsisters have their eyes pecked out by doves. And Hansel and Gretel (children!) kill their captor by baking her in an oven.

High-school reading lists are full of similar fare. Homer's Odysseus blinds Polyphemus the Cyclops by grinding out his eye with a heated stake. *The Odyssey of Homer*, Book IX, p. 125 (S. Butcher & A. Lang translations, 1909) ("Even so did we seize the fiery-pointed brand and whirled it round in his eye, and the blood flowed about the heated bar. And the breath of the flame singed his eyelids and brows all about, as the ball of the eye burnt away, and the roots thereof crackled in the flame"). In the Inferno, Dante and Virgil watch corrupt politicians struggle to stay submerged beneath a lake of boiling pitch, lest they be skewered by devils above the surface. Canto XXI, pp. 187–189 [etc., with other examples from "classic literature"]. * * *

Because the Act imposes a restriction on the content of protected speech, it is invalid unless California can demonstrate that it passes strict scrutiny—that is, unless it is justified by a compelling government interest and is narrowly drawn to serve that interest. The State must specifically identify an "actual problem" in need of solving, [Citation], and the curtailment of free speech must be actually necessary to the solution. * * * That is a demanding standard. "It is rare that a regulation restricting speech because of its content will ever be permissible." [Citation.]

California cannot meet that standard. At the outset, it acknowledges that it cannot show a direct causal link between violent video games and harm to minors. Rather, relying upon our decision in *Turner Broadcasting System, Inc. v. FCC,* [Citation, 1994], the State claims that it need not produce such proof because the legislature can make a predictive judgment that such a link exists, based on competing psychological studies. But reliance on *Turner Broadcasting* is misplaced. That decision applied *intermediate scrutiny* to a content-neutral regulation. California's burden is much higher, and because it bears the risk of uncertainty, ambiguous proof will not suffice.

The State's evidence is not compelling. California relies primarily on the research of Dr. Craig Anderson and a few other research psychologists whose studies purport to show a connection between exposure to violent video games and harmful effects on children. These studies have been rejected by every court to consider them, and with good reason: They do not prove that violent video games *cause* minors to *act* aggressively (which would at least be a beginning). Instead, "Nearly all of the research is based on correlation, not evidence of causation, and most of the studies suffer from significant, admitted flaws in methodology." [Citation.] They show at best some correlation between exposure to violent entertainment and minuscule real-world effects, such as children's feeling more aggressive or making louder noises in the few minutes after playing a violent game than after playing a nonviolent game.

Even taking for granted Dr. Anderson's conclusions that violent video games produce some effect on children's feelings of aggression, those effects are both small and indistinguishable from effects produced by other media. In his testimony in a similar lawsuit, Dr. Anderson admitted that the "effect sizes" of children's exposure to violent video games are "about the same" as that produced by their exposure to violence on television. And he admits that the *same* effects have been found when children watch cartoons starring Bugs Bunny or the Road Runner, or when they play video games like Sonic the Hedgehog that are rated "E" (appropriate for all ages), or even when they "view a picture of a gun."

Of course, California has (wisely) declined to restrict Saturday morning cartoons, the sale of games rated for young children, or the distribution of pictures of guns. The consequence is that its regulation is wildly under-inclusive when judged against its asserted justification, which in our view is alone enough to defeat it. Under-inclusiveness raises serious doubts about whether the government is in fact pursuing the interest it invokes, rather than disfavoring a particular speaker or viewpoint. [Citations.] Here, California has singled out the purveyors of video games for disfavored treatment—at least when compared to booksellers, cartoonists, and movie producers—and has given no persuasive reason why.

The Act is also seriously under-inclusive in another respect—and a respect that renders irrelevant the contentions of the concurrence and the dissents that video games are qualitatively different from other portrayals of violence. The California Legislature is perfectly willing to leave this dangerous, mind-altering material in the hands of children so long as one parent (or even an aunt or uncle) says it's OK. And there are not even any requirements as to how this parental or avuncular relationship is to be verified; apparently the child's or putative parent's, aunt's, or uncle's say-so suffices. That is not how one addresses a serious social problem.

California claims that the Act is justified in aid of parental authority—by requiring that the purchase of violent video games can be made only by adults, the Act ensures that parents can decide what games are appropriate. At the outset, we note our doubts that punishing third parties for conveying protected speech to children *just in case* their parents disapprove of that speech is a proper governmental means of aiding parental authority. Accepting that position would largely vitiate the rule that "only in relatively narrow and well-defined circumstances may government bar public dissemination of protected materials to [minors]." [Citation.]

But leaving that aside, California cannot show that the Act's restrictions meet a substantial need of parents who wish to restrict their children's access to violent video games but cannot do so. The video-game industry has in place a voluntary rating system designed to inform consumers about the content of games. * * * In 2009, the Federal Trade Commission (FTC) found that, as a result of this system, "the video game industry outpaces the movie and music industries" in "(1) restricting target-marketing of mature-rated products to children; (2) clearly and prominently disclosing rating information; and (3) restricting children's access to mature-rated products at retail." [Citation.] This system does much to ensure that minors cannot purchase seriously violent games on their own, and that parents who care about the matter can readily evaluate the games their children bring home. Filling the remaining modest gap in concerned-parents' control can hardly be a compelling state interest.

And finally, the Act's purported aid to parental authority is vastly over-inclusive. Not all of the children who are forbidden to purchase violent video games on their own have parents who *care* whether they purchase violent video games. While some of the legislation's effect may indeed be in support of what some parents of the restricted children actually want, its entire effect is only in support of what the State thinks parents *ought* to want. This is not the narrow tailoring to "assisting parents" that restriction of First Amendment rights requires. * * *

California's legislation straddles the fence between (1) addressing a serious social problem and (2) helping concerned parents control their children. Both ends are legitimate, but when they affect First Amendment rights they must be pursued by means that are neither seriously under-inclusive nor seriously over-inclusive. [Citation, 1993]. As a means of protecting children from portrayals of violence, the legislation is seriously under-inclusive, not only because it excludes portrayals other than video games, but also because it permits a parental or avuncular veto. And as a means of assisting concerned parents it is seriously over-inclusive because it abridges the First Amendment rights of young people whose parents (and aunts and uncles) think violent video games are a harmless pastime. And the overbreadth in achieving one goal is not cured by the underbreadth in achieving the other. Legislation such as this, which is neither fish nor fowl, cannot survive strict scrutiny.

We affirm the judgment below.

Justice Thomas, dissenting.

The Court's decision today does not comport with the original public understanding of the First Amendment. The majority strikes down, as facially unconstitutional, a state law that prohibits the direct sale or rental of certain video games to minors because the law "abridges the freedom of speech." U.S. Const., Amendment 1. But I do not think the First Amendment stretches that far. The practices and beliefs of the founding generation establish that "the freedom of speech," as originally understood, does not include a right to speak to minors (or a right of minors to access speech) without going through the minors' parents or guardians. I would hold that the law at issue is not facially unconstitutional under the First Amendment and reverse and remand for further proceedings.

When interpreting a constitutional provision, "the goal is to discern the most likely public understanding of [that] provision at the time it was adopted." [Citation, 2010.] Because the Constitution is a written instrument, "its meaning does not alter." [Citation] "That which it meant when adopted, it means now." [Citation.]

As originally understood, the First Amendment protection against laws "abridging the freedom of speech" did not extend to *all* speech. "There are certain well-defined and narrowly limited classes of speech, the prevention and punishment of which have never been thought to raise any Constitutional problem." [Citations.] Laws regulating such speech do not "abridge the freedom of speech" because such speech is understood to fall outside "the freedom of speech." [Citations.]

In my view, the "practices and beliefs held by the Founders" reveal another category of excluded speech—speech to minor children bypassing their parents. [Citation.] The historical evidence shows that the founding generation believed parents had absolute authority over their minor children and expected parents to use that authority to direct the proper development of their children. It would be absurd to suggest that such a society understood "the freedom of speech" to include a right to speak to minors (or a corresponding right of minors to access speech) without going through the minors' parents. [Citation.] The founding generation would not have considered it an abridgment of "the freedom of speech" to support parental authority by restricting speech that bypasses minors' parents.

[Justice Breyer wrote a separate dissent. He stated that the majority's opinion conflicted with prior decisions in *Ginsberg* and *Miller*. He asked what sense it made to forbid selling an image of a nude woman but allow violent video games: "But what sense does it make to forbid selling to a 13-year-old boy a magazine with an image of a nude woman, while protecting a sale to that 13 year-old of an interactive video game in which he actively, but virtually, binds and gags the woman, then tortures and kills her?" Breyer saw the case as less about censorship and the First Amendment and more about education, and that "California's law imposes no more than a modest restriction on expression." As to the industry's voluntary program of labeling video games, he noted that self-regulation of the industry still allowed for 20% of minors to purchase mature video games, and as high as 50% in the case of one nationwide chain, based on the 2011 FTC study.]

Case Questions

1. What about the distinction the Court makes between depictions of sexual conduct and depictions of violence? Is the majority actually saying that the First Amendment's exception for "obscenity" (*Miller v. California*, holding that some depictions and descriptions are beyond First Amendment protection) does *not* apply to depictions as detailed here—maiming and killing in a game?

2. What would a "strict constructionist" say? Does the express language of the First Amendment resolve the case in any straightforward way?

3. What sense does it make to say that what the Constitution "meant when adopted, it means now"? The Constitution does not authorize an Air Force, but we have one; the Constitution refers to the president only as a male—"he"—does that mean a woman cannot be president? And if the answer is no, the Constitution does not mean no Air Force and no women presidents, then how *does* one determine when it means today what it meant when it was adopted, and when it does not?

Key Takeaway

The Bill of Rights has applied to federal actions from the start. Through the Fourteenth Amendment, its provisions largely apply to state actions, too. Both the Bill of Rights and the Fourteenth Amendment apply to business in various ways, but the rights conferred are rights against governmental action and not the actions of private enterprise or private persons.

Exercises

1. John Hanks works at ProLogis. The company decides to institute a drug-testing policy. John is a good and longtime employee but enjoys smoking marijuana on the weekends. The drug testing will involve urine samples and, semiannually, a hair sample. It is nearly certain that the drug-testing protocol that ProLogis proposes will find that Hanks is a marijuana user. The company has made it clear that it will have zero tolerance for any kind of nonprescribed con-

trolled substances. John and several fellow employees wish to go to court to challenge the proposed testing as "an unreasonable search and seizure." Can he possibly succeed?

2. Larry Reed, majority leader in the Senate, is attacked in his reelection campaign by a series of ads sponsored by a corporation (Global Defense, Inc.) that does not like his voting record. The corporation is upset that Reed would not write a special provision that would favor Global Defense in a defense appropriations bill. The ads run constantly on television and radio in the weeks immediately preceding election day and contain numerous falsehoods. For example, in order to keep the government running financially, Reed found it necessary to vote for a bill that included a last-minute rider that defunded a small government program for the handicapped, sponsored by someone in the opposing party that wanted to privatize all programs for the handicapped. The ad is largely paid for by Global Defense and depicts a handicapped child being helped by the existing program and large letters saying "Does Larry Reed Just Not Care?" The ad proclaims that it is sponsored by Citizens Who Care for a Better Tomorrow. Is this protected speech? Why or why not? Can Reed sue for defamation? Why or why not?

3. The "compelling state interest" test is that the Constitutional mandate that a government should not abridge (limit) a fundamental right (free speech, freedom of religious practice) unless there is a compelling reason. What was the compelling state interest in prohibiting same-sex marriage?

3.6 Summary and Exercises

Summary

The U.S. Constitution sets the framework for all other laws of the United States, at both the federal and the state level. It creates a shared balance of power between states and the federal government (federalism) and shared power among the branches of government (separation of powers), establishes individual rights against governmental action (Bill of Rights), and provides for federal oversight of matters affecting interstate commerce and commerce with foreign nations. Knowing the contours of the U.S. legal system is not possible without understanding the role of the U.S. Constitution.

The Constitution is difficult to amend. Thus, when the Supreme Court uses its power of judicial review to determine that a law is unconstitutional, it actually shapes what the Constitution means. New meanings that emerge must do so by the process of amendment or by the passage of time and new appointments to the court. Because justices serve for life, the court changes its philosophical outlook slowly.

The Bill of Rights is an especially important piece of the Constitutional framework. It provides legal causes of action for infringements of individual rights by state or federal government. Through the due process clause of the Fifth Amendment and the Fourteenth Amendment, both procedural and (to some extent) substantive due process rights are given to individuals.

Exercises

1. For many years, the Supreme Court believed that "commercial speech" was entitled to less protection than other forms of speech. One defining element of commercial speech is that its dominant theme is to propose a commercial transaction. This kind of speech is protected by the First Amendment, but the government is permitted to regulate it more closely than other forms of speech. However, the government must make reasonable distinctions, must

narrowly tailor the rules restricting commercial speech, and must show that government has a legitimate goal that the law furthers.

Edward Salib owned a Winchell's Donut House in Mesa, Arizona. To attract customers, he displayed large signs in store windows. The city ordered him to remove the signs because they violated the city's sign code, which prohibited covering more than 30 percent of a store's windows with signs. Salib sued, claiming that the sign code violated his First Amendment rights. What was the result, and why?

2. Jennifer is a freshman at her local public high school. Her sister, Jackie, attends a nearby private high school. Neither school allows them to join its respective wrestling team; only boys can wrestle at either school. Do either of them have a winning case based on the equal protection clause of the Fourteenth Amendment?

3. The employees of the U.S. Treasury Department that work the border crossing between the United States and Mexico learned that they will be subject to routine drug testing. The customs bureau, which is a division of the treasury department, announces this policy along with its reasoning—since customs agents must routinely search for drugs coming into the United States, it makes sense that border guards must themselves be completely drug-free. Many border guards do not use drugs, have no intention of using drugs, and object to the invasion of their privacy. What is the constitutional basis for their objection?

4. Happy Time Chevrolet employs Jim Bydalek as a salesman. Bydalek takes part in a Gay Pride March in Los Angeles, is interviewed by a local news camera crew, and reports that he is gay and proud of it. His employer is not, and he is fired. Does he have any constitutional causes of action against his employer?

5. You begin work at the Happy-Go-Lucky Corporation on Halloween. On your second day at work, you wear a political button on your coat, supporting your choice for U.S. senator in the upcoming election. Your boss, who is of a different political persuasion, looks at the button and says, "Take that stupid button off or you're fired." Has your boss violated your constitutional rights?

6. David Lucas paid $975,000 for two residential parcels on the Isle of Palms near Charleston, South Carolina. His intention was to build houses on them. Two years later, the South Carolina legislature passed a statute that prohibited building on beachfront properties. The purpose was to leave the dunes system in place to mitigate the effects of hurricanes and strong storms. The South Carolina Coastal Commission created the rules and regulations with substantial input from the community and from experts and with protection of the dune system primarily in mind. People had been building on the shoreline for years, with harmful results to localities and the state treasury. When Lucas applied for permits to build two houses near the shoreline, his permits were rejected. He sued, arguing that the South Carolina legislation had effectively "taken" his property. At trial, South Carolina conceded that because of the legislation, Lucas's property was effectively worth zero. Has there been a taking under the Fifth Amendment (as incorporated through the Fourteenth Amendment), and if so, what should the state owe Lucas? Suppose that Lucas could have made an additional $1 million by building a house on each of his parcels. Is he entitled to recover his original purchase price or his potential profits?

Self-Test Questions

1. Harvey filed a suit against the state of Colorado, claiming that a Colorado state law violates the commerce clause. The court will agree if the statute:

    a. places an undue burden on interstate commerce

    b. promotes the public health, safety, morals, or general welfare of Colorado

    c. regulates economic activities within the state's borders

    d. a and b

    e. b and c

2. The state legislature in Maine enacts a law that directly conflicts with a federal law. Mapco Industries, located in Portland, Maine, cannot comply with both the state and the federal law.

    a. Because of federalism, the state law will have priority, as long as Maine is using its police powers.

    b. Because there's a conflict, both laws are invalid; the state and the federal government will have to work out a compromise of some sort.

    c. The federal law preempts the state law.

    d. Both laws govern concurrently.

3. Hannah, who lives in Ada, is the owner of Superior Enterprises, Inc. She believes that certain actions in the state of Ohio infringe on her federal constitutional rights, especially those found in the Bill of Rights. Most of these rights apply to the states under:

    a. the supremacy clause

    b. the protection clause

    c. the due process clause of the Fourteenth Amendment

    d. the Tenth Amendment

4. Minnesota enacts a statute that bans all advertising that is in "bad taste," "vulgar," or "indecent." In Michigan, Aaron Calloway and his brother, Clarence "Cab" Calloway, create unique beer that they decide to call Old Fart Ale. In their marketing, the brothers have a label in which an older man in a dirty T-shirt is sitting in an easy chair, looking disheveled and having a three-day growth of stubble on his chin. It appears that the man is in the process of belching. He is also holding a can of Old Fart Ale. The Minnesota liquor commission orders all Minnesota restaurants, bars, and grocery stores to remove Old Fart Ale from their shelves. The state statute and the commission's order are likely to be held by a court to be:

    a. a violation of the Tenth Amendment

    b. a violation of the First Amendment

    c. a violation of the Calloways' right to equal protection of the laws

    d. a violation of the commerce clause, since only the federal laws can prevent an article of commerce from entering into Minnesota's market

5. Raunch Unlimited, a Virginia partnership, sells smut whenever and wherever it can. Some of its material is "obscene" (meeting the Supreme Court's definition under *Miller v. California*) and includes child pornography. North Carolina has a statute that criminalizes obscenity. What are possible results if a store in Raleigh, North Carolina, carries Raunch merchandise?

    a. The partners could be arrested in North Carolina and may well be convicted.

    b. The materials in Raleigh may be the basis for a criminal conviction.

    c. The materials are protected under the First Amendment's right of free speech.

    d. The materials are protected under state law.

    e. a and b

Self-Test Answers

1. a
2. c
3. c
4. b
5. e

Endnotes

1. U.S. Constitution, Article VI. There is a bit more to the sentence; it goes on like this: "but no religious test shall ever be required as a qualification to any office or public trust under the United States."

2. And you might consider why President Trump's critics are frankly alarmed at his apparent interpretations of the role of the president, the judiciary, and the press in American society.

3. In *Scott v. Sanford* (the Dred Scott decision), the court held that Scott should remain a slave; that as a slave he was not a citizen of the United States and thus not eligible to bring suit in a federal court, and that as a slave he was personal property and thus had never been free.

4. *Roe v. Wade*, 410 U.S. 113 (1973).

5. The U.S. Senate.gov page provides an intriguing history on the cloture rule.

6. Eight states and D.C. have legalized marijuana for recreational use; it is illegal under federal law. Now what? U.S. attorney general Jeff Sessions is an outspoken opponent of legalized marijuana.

7. *Kimel v. Florida Board of Regents*, 528 U.S. 62 (2000).

8. William O. Douglas (1898–1980) was 40 years old when Franklin Roosevelt nominated him to serve on the Supreme Court. Douglas retired in 1975; he was the longest-serving Supreme Court justice in U.S. history. He was an ardent environmentalist.

9. Up until the mid-1970s "Indian Law" was a quiet legal backwater, not considered very important. In 1974 a federal judge in Washington state ruled that the state was abusing Native Americans' treaty rights, from treaties made with the U.S. in 1855, by denying them access to fishing grounds and prohibiting them from using certain types of fishing gear. The decison was affirmed by the 9th Circuit Court of Appeals, and the U.S. Supreme Court declined to hear it. The consequence has been, as the non-Indian capitalists see it, that the Indians are interfering with Growth and Progress by denying non-Indians the "right" to exploit natural resources, including fish, water, minerals, and access to land for laying pipe. The states cannot regulate "Indian law," and they cannot regulate foreign commerce—those areas are exclusively federal.

10. As FDR has a "court packing plan" that would add more Justices to the Supreme Court (there was nothing in the Constitution that mandated only 9 Justices), the switch of Justice Owen Roberts has been called "the switch in time that saved nine."

11. *Katzenbach v. McClung*, 379 U.S. 294 (1964).

12. 514 U.S. 549 (1995)

13. In 1994, while enrolled at Virginia Polytechnic Institute (Virginia Tech), Christy Brzonkala alleged that Antonio Morrison and James Crawford, both students and varsity football players at Virginia Tech, had raped her. In 1995, Brzonkala filed a complaint against Morrison and Crawford under Virginia Tech's sexual assault policy. After a hearing, Morrison was found guilty of sexual assault and sentenced to immediate suspension for two semesters. Crawford was not punished. A second hearing again found Morrison guilty. After an appeal through the university's administrative system, Morrison's punishment was set aside, as it was found to be "excessive." Brzonkala dropped out of the university. She then sued Morrison, Crawford, and Virginia Tech in federal district court, alleging that Morrison's and Crawford's attack violated 42 U.S.C. Section 13981 (part of the VAWA), which provides a federal civil remedy for the victims of gender-motivated violence. Morrison and Crawford moved to dismiss Brzonkala's suit on the ground that Section 13981's civil remedy was unconstitutional. In dismissing the complaint, the district court found that Congress lacked authority to enact Section 13981 under either the commerce clause or the Fourteenth Amendment, which Congress had explicitly identified as the sources of federal authority for the VAWA. Ultimately, the court of appeals affirmed, as did the Supreme Court.

14. The goal of the legal challenge to the Agricultural Adjustment Act was to gut the entire federal crop-support program by declaring it unconstitutional, and by extension to undermine the whole New Deal.

15. Kassell v. Consolidated Freightways, 450 U.S. 662 (1981).

16. *Oregon Waste Systems v. Department of Environmental Quality*, 511 U.S. 93 (1994).

17. *Fort Gratiot Sanitary Landfill v. Michigan Dep't of Natural Resources*, 504 U.S. 353 (1992).

18. Hunt v. Washington State Apple Advertising Commission, 432 U.S. 333 (1977).

19. The cigarette warning legislation of the 1960s (where the federal government required warning labels on cigarette packages) effectively preempted state negligence claims based on failure to warn. When the family of a lifetime smoker who had died sued in New Jersey court, one cause of action was the company's failure to warn of the dangers of its product. The Supreme Court reversed the jury's award: the federal legislation preempted any successful claim against the tobacco companies based on any state law imposing liability for failure to warn. *Cippolone v. Liggett Group*, 505 U.S. 504 (1993)

20. 545 U.S. 1 (2005)

21. See Bradley Steinman, The Medical Use of Marijuana v. The Use of Marijuana for Medical Purposes http://www.americanbar.org/publications/tyl/topics/health-law/medical-use-marijuana-versus-use-marijuana-medical-purposes.html

22. The U.S. Bill of Rights is patterned after the English Bill of Rights of 1689.

23. *Jackson v. Metropolitan Edison Co.*, 419 U.S. 345 (1974).

24. *N.Y. Times v. Sullivan*, 376 U.S. 254. The case was brought against the Times by the chief of police of the city of Montgomery, Alabama who complained that the Times' coverage of Alabama police brutality against civil rights activists defamed him. What he wanted was to silence Northern critics of pro-segregationist state government officials. But he lost (9–0): the Supreme Court held that, to promote robust public discussion of government officials and others who are "public figures," the bar for defamation suits should be raised. Public figures must prove the offensive statements were made with "actual malice."

25. *Buckley v. Valeo*, 424 U.S. 1 (1976).

26. We cannot leave the First Amendment without observing that in addition to its free speech provisions, it includes other fundamentally important protections: freedom of religion, and the right of the people to peaceably assemble and petition the government for a redress of grievances.

27. Also in the "closely regulated" category are pawn shops, liquor stores, gun stores and coal mines, among others.

28. *Kelo v. City of New London*, 545 U.S. 469 (2005).

29. *BMW of North America, Inc. v. Gore*, 517 U.S. 559 (1996).

30. *Plessy v. Ferguson*, 163 U.S. 537 (1896).

31. *United States v. Virginia*, 518 U.S. 515 (1996).

32. *Donald Trump v Hawaii, et al.* 585 U.S. ____ (2018).

33. *Palmore v. Sidoti*, 466 U.S. 429 (1984).

34. 576 U.S. ___ (2015).

35. The opinion also addressed issues of due process under the 14th Amendment.

36. Justice Kennedy also wrote *Obergefell v Hodges*. He retired in 2018, replaced by Brett Kavanaugh.

37. https://www.nytimes.com/2017/02/17/business/trump-calls-the-news-media-the-enemy-of-the-people.html

CHAPTER 4
Introduction to Law Making

Chapter Learning Objectives

After reading this chapter, you should be able to:

1. Understand how law is made by the "traditional" three branches of government: the legislature, executive, and judiciary branches.
2. Understand how law is made by two other entities: administrative agencies and the people directly (in many states) via initiative or referendum.

This chapter first takes up law-making by the traditional three branches: legislature, executive and judiciary. Second, it takes up administrative agencies—the so-called "fourth branch of government" as well as initiatives and referendums that purport to give people the power to make law directly.

4.1 Law-Making by the Three Traditional Branches

Learning Objectives

1. Understand that government makes law by the legislature, through the legislative process (however, the law—a statute or ordinance—is subject to interpretation by the courts.)
2. Understand that government makes law by the executive by veto, presentation of budget, and by executive order.
3. Understand that government makes law by the judiciary by judicial review, judicial interpretation of legislation, and by developing ("discovering") the common law.

Law by the Legislature

Introduction

In the early days of English law—where the U.S. legal system originated—there was no legislature. There was an executive (the king or queen—"the Crown") and the Crown's ministers. The ministers carried out the Crown's directives, and there were courts with judges appointed by the Crown. The Crown also had members of the nobility (both ecclesiastical and lay) as advisors. In the 12th century the nobility began to chafe at some of the Crown's demands for money and men (prominent was the Crown's need to prosecute wars in France), and the nobility let the king know that if he wanted more such money and men he would have to do some things they wanted. Thus began Parliament (from the French, "a place to meet and talk"). When the American colonies declared independence from Britain in 1776 they retained a kind of parliament (Congress), but with differences. The Americans created a new governing system (the first system under the 1776 Articles of Confederation was replaced in June of 1788 by the Constitution). Under the Constitution, federal legislative power is assigned primarily to Congress, and at the state and local levels to the state legislatures and the city and county councils or commissions. The federal legislature and most state legislatures have two houses, an upper house (the Senate), and a lower house, (the House of Representatives); only Nebraska has a one-chamber—unicameral—legislature.

The Legislative Process

The legislative process, similar at both federal and state levels of government in the U.S., is not designed to make it easy to adopt legislation; rather, it is designed to make the process deliberative. Legislation is always the result of a perceived need to address some problem, as, for example, the problem of air pollution. A preliminary draft of a plan in response—usually called a "bill"—is introduced (or "read") and the matter is delegated to one or more committees whose elected members and their staffs have some experience with the issue. The committee invites interested people to attend and testify, works to understand the problem, and considers how the proposed response would address it. The committee may drop the bill entirely (the bill "never emerges from committee"), or it may amend the bill, and ultimately forwards its recommendations to the full body, which debates the bill's provisions and may make further amendments.

statute

A written law adopted by a federal or state legislative body.

ordinance

A written law adopted by a county or city legislative body.

In jurisdictions with bicameral legislatures (Congress and most state legislatures), the resulting bill is reconciled with the version from the other house, and the matter is presented to the executive (president, governor, mayor, county executive) for signature and approval. It is then a **statute** (at the federal or state level) or an **ordinance** (at the county and city level—most counties and cities are not bicameral); government employees—department heads and subordinates—("bureaucrats" has the connotation of a lot of red tape) implement the policies. The executive may veto the legislation; the veto can be overridden by the legislature by a two-thirds vote.

FIGURE 4.1 The Making of Legislation

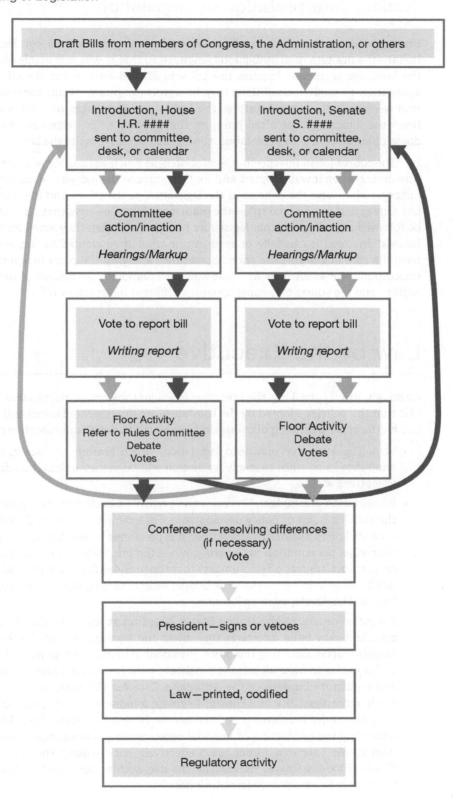

Judicial Interpretation of Legislation

Provisions in a statute or an ordinance may be ambiguous or unclear. Sometimes this is intentional—the drafters used ambiguous language so that it was acceptable to all parties. Sometime, the language is unclear because the bill was drafted hastily and sloppily. If it's an old law, its application to modern conditions may be uncertain. In any event, somebody has to say what it means—somebody has to interpret the legislation. That takes us right away to a *judicial* function—the judiciary must often interpret the meaning of contested legislation. If the legislature doesn't like the courts' interpretation, the legislature can re-write the law.

plain meaning rule

In interpreting the meaning of legislation, the judiciary should use the ordinarily understood meaning of the words and language of the statute.

The courts' job in interpreting legislation is, as much as possible, to determine what the legislature meant when it was adopted, and for this purpose the judges may be briefed on the legislative history—what were the debates in the legislature at the time? And there are several rules courts use. One generally accepted rule—the **plain meaning rule**—says that a statute's plain meaning will be followed regardless of what legislators had in mind when they voted for it. If some of the legislators didn't read it carefully or read into it what they wanted to see, application of the plain meaning rule might surprise them. Sometimes applying the plain meaning rule gives rise to an unacceptable (or absurd) result—that was the situation in the *Church of the Holy Trinity v. United States*—and the courts may come up with a different interpretation. [1]

Law by the Executive

Although, strictly speaking, the executive (president, governor, mayor, county executive) only sees to it that the policies adopted by the legislature are implemented (executed), in practice the executive has far more political (policy-making) power than that. Some executive powers are:

- Veto. The executive may veto legislation, which entirely undoes it, or the executive may announce in advance that any legislation will be vetoed unless it conforms to certain of the executive's wishes.

- Presentation of a budget. The executive presents a budget to the legislature which is (at least) the starting point of policy development. For example, President Donald Trump campaigned for a wall on the southern U.S. border; it is presumed he will include funding for such a wall in his budget presentation to Congress. When the president and Congress are of different political parties, Congress often trumpets that the president's budget is "dead on arrival"—Congress won't follow it. But even then, the budget reflects some governmental priorities affecting what laws will be developed or enforced.

- Executive orders. In the United States, based on at least two Constitutional provisions, the president may issue directives that affect the management of the federal government. For example, upon assuming the office, President Trump issued an executive order directing federal agencies to "take all actions consistent with law to minimize the unwarranted economic and regulatory burdens of the Affordable Care Act ['Obamacare'], and prepare to afford the states more flexibility and control to create a more free and open health care market." Any executive order is subject to judicial review. In 1952 the United Steel Workers went on strike, imperiling the production of materiel necessary to prosecute the Korean War. President Truman issued Executive Order 10340 effectively nationalizing the steel mills. In *Youngstown Sheet & Tube C. v Sawyer*[2] (known as "the steel seizure case") the Supreme Court declared President Truman's actions unconstitutional.

- Nominations to the federal courts. The president of the United States nominates people to serve with lifetime tenure on the federal courts. These are really political appointees, and their influence on law and politics will usually far outlast the president's time in office.

- Appointment or nomination of agency heads. The president (governor, county executive) has significant authority to shape the nature of the legal and regulatory environment by choosing department heads who share his or her political philosophy.

Law by the Judiciary

The judiciary makes law in three ways: judicial review, judicial interpretation of legislation, and development of the common law.

Judicial Review

In the United States, any decision by any government entity is subject to review by the judiciary to test the decision's legality. The courts, then, can review acts of the legislature, executive, lower courts, administrative agencies, or of the people themselves acting through the initiative or referendum processes (direct democracy).

Judicial Review of Acts of the Legislature

The legislature—federal, state, or local—is given its authority by the federal and state constitutions and, at the local level, by city or county charters. When the legislature's acts are challenged as without authority, somebody has to determine whether the act was within its powers—whether the legislature's act was constitutional; such a determination is a judicial function. The United States Constitution does not expressly give the Supreme Court the power to declare acts of Congress unconstitutional; but the Court assumed that power for itself in the landmark case **Marbury v. Madison.**[3]

> **Marbury v. Madison**
>
> U.S. Supreme Court case, 1803, establishing the power of judicial review: that the Court could declare acts of Congress unconstitutional.

Thomas Jefferson, of the liberal party (Democratic Republicans), won the bitterly contested presidential election of 1800 against the conservative party (Whigs, ancestor of today's Republican Party), whose president was the outgoing John Adams. In accordance with the Judiciary Act of 1789 which had established the lower federal court system, President Adams during the last days of his administration signed a commission (granting authority to somebody to act) appointing William Marbury as a judge in the District of Columbia. Several weeks after President Jefferson was inaugurated, Mr. Marbury approached James Madison, secretary of state, whose job in those days included delivering commissions to presidential appointees. Mr. Madison refused to give Mr. Marbury the commission. Marbury sued, asking the Supreme Court to issue a writ of mandamus (an order directing a public official to do his or her job). Congress had given the Supreme Court power to issue such writs in the previously-noted Judiciary Act. The real issue in the case was whether Congress could give the Court a power that the Constitution did not give it—could Congress effectively amend the Constitution by Congressional law-making? Chief Justice John Marshall said no, that Congress's act was unconstitutional. Justice Marshall wrote:

The question, whether an act, repugnant to the constitution, can become the law of the land, is a question deeply interesting to the United States; but, happily, not of an intricacy proportioned to its interest. The powers of the legislature are defined and limited; and that those limits may not be mistaken or forgotten, the constitution is written. To what purpose are powers limited, and to what purpose is that limitation committed to writing; if these limits may, at any time, be passed by those intended to be restrained? . . . It is a proposition too plain to be contested, that the constitution controls any legislative act repugnant to it; or, that the legislature may not alter the constitution by an ordinary act. . . . It is emphatically the province and duty of the judicial department to say what the law is . . . the constitution is superior to any ordinary act of the legislature; the constitution, and not such ordinary act, must govern the case to which they both apply.

In *Marbury* the Supreme Court rejected Congress' attempt to give it a bit of authority (to issue writs of mandamus), but assumed for itself the larger power to declare acts of Congress unconstitutional. The power was sparingly used for a hundred years, but in the early 20th century the Court struck down scores of state and federal laws, most of them passed to address abuses of concentrated economic power that had grown with rapid post-Civil War industrialization. States passed various laws about child labor, working hours, and minimum wages. In defense of "substantive due process," (discussed in Chapter 3) the Court struck down such laws. As Lawrence Friedman wrote in his history of American law, "Whatever the economic impact, clearly the Supreme Court had developed a dangerous appetite for power. From 1906 it was like a man-eating tiger; everyone in its shadow had to cope with its awesome and lethal tastes."[4] The tiger was stopped in 1935 when the Court did an about-face and began using the Interstate Commerce Clause to uphold federal regulation of abusive market practices.

Judicial Review of Acts of the Executive

Courts are also called upon from time to time to review acts of the executive (president, governor, mayor, county executive or commission), and the same standard applies as reviewing acts of the legislature—though each branch gives great deference to others, the Constitution sets out executive powers, and it is up to the courts, not the executive, to say what the Constitution means. That is, the courts determine the president's powers, not the president. We observed that the Supreme Court declared President Truman's attempts to nationalize the steel mills unconstitutional—without authority under the law. And in the famous *U.S. v. Nixon*, the question, whether the president, claiming executive privilege, could withhold evidence and remain entirely immune from judicial review, was decided against the president. Quoting directly from *Marbury*, the unanimous Court reiterated that determining the reach of presidential authority was "emphatically the province and duty of the judicial department," not of the executive department.

Judicial Review of Acts of Lower Courts

It is not very common for courts to overturn acts of the legislature or of the executive on review. But it is very common for courts of appeal to review what the lower courts did to determine that the lower court acted according to the correct rule of law. Such a determination does not get an appeals court into the murky waters of separation of powers. A court, on review, might take issue with various lower-court findings. Perhaps the lower court applied incorrect rules on what evidence could be admitted; or the lower court applied an incorrect rule of substantive law, or—sometimes—the appeals court recognizes that the lower court applied the right law as it stood, but the law should be changed, and existing precedent overruled.

Judicial Review of Acts of Administrative Agencies

Administrative agencies (like the I.R.S., the Social Security Administration, the Food and Drug Administration, the Department of Corrections) have procedural and substantive rules to follow. The decisions of an administrative agency are subject to judicial review for the same purpose that any decision is so subject—did the lower-level decision-maker use the correct rule of law?

We take up administrative agencies below, but here's an example. Administrative agencies cannot act beyond the authority granted to them by the legislature that created the agency. That's a rule of law. During the Vietnam War, by law, male university students could not be drafted to serve in the military as long as they were enrolled full time in college—they got a student deferment. Peter Wolff and Richard Shortt were so enrolled, but they protested against the war at the office of a local Selective Service board in Ann Arbor, Michigan. The board then reclassified them as I-A (draftable) asserting they had become "delinquents" by acting "knowingly to hinder or interfere" with the work of the local draft board (a federal offense). On appeal, the Federal Court of Appeals for New York (the Second Circuit) held:

> *As these two students have never been indicted or tried or convicted of [hindering and interfering] in a District Court, the two Local Boards [defendants] exceeded their jurisdiction by reclassifying the two students I-A.*
>
> *There is nothing to prevent the prosecution of registrants or others for conduct by them in violation of either federal or state criminal laws, subject to such defenses as may be alleged and established. What we hold in this case is that it is not the function of local boards in the Selective Service System to punish these registrants by reclassifying them I-A because they protested as they did over the Government's involvement in Vietnam.*[5]

Judicial Review of Acts of Direct Democracy

In twenty-six states the people themselves can make law by initiative and/or referendum (sometimes called a "veto referendum"). That is, if enough voters sign a petition so demanding, an issue will be put on the ballot for a public vote, or—in the case of the referendum—a law adopted by the legislature will be approved or nullified by the voters. These laws (taken up in more detail below) are subject to judicial review just as are acts of the legislature.

Judicial Interpretation of Legislation

Aside from judicial review, a second mechanism by which the judiciary makes law is by the interpretation of legislation. A statute or ordinance does not necessarily mean what the legislature thought it meant when it was passed; its meaning can be interpreted by litigants, and, ultimately, it is up to the courts to decide which interpretation to apply to the facts of cases that litigants bring. Otherwise, U.S. courts have no power to examine legislation that is not part of ongoing litigation. We discussed this above in the section on law by legislation; again, the matter is illustrated in the *Church of the Holy Trinity* case.

Judicial Development (or "Discovery") of the Common Law

Development of the Common Law

common law

Rules of law are determined by high-court judges, recorded in cases, and serve as precedent whereby that rule will be applied to similar fact situations in the future.

The third mechanism by which the judiciary makes law is by "discovering" (developing or making up) the **common law**.

In general, if an issue is presented by litigants to a court (a judge), the court *must* decide it. The court cannot say, "Well, well, that is a difficult problem. We won't take it up." And even if there is no statute adopted by the legislature, the court must decide anyway (otherwise people will take the matter into their own hands, not infrequently resulting in violence). In the early development of the common law, this happened frequently, for there *was* no legislature until Parliament was created, and even then, English legislatures let judges decide issues (defining arson, rape, burglary, or degrees of homicide, for example) without writing legislation. In making common law, then, judges created rules for society, but these "made up" rules had to be reasonable, meaning that they had to be acceptable to the community—they were based on custom and tradition.

stare decisis

Latin, "precedent governs," the rule of law articulated in one case will be used to decide future cases based on the same facts; it is the basis of the common law.

When the Normans settled into the kingdom they conquered in 1066 (England) they soon understood a need to end local law peculiarities—the Anglo-Saxon folk courts, urban borough courts, merchant courts, royal courts, college and manorial and ecclesiastical (religious) courts all operated differently. In 1154 Henry II began the institutionalization of the law by creating a system of law common throughout the kingdom. Judges appointed by the Crown from the central court—learned, respectable men—were sent (or appointed from among local lawyers) to resolve disputes throughout the kingdom by applying what they understood to be general rules of local custom. Anglo-Saxon law was not too different from Norman law anyway. When they returned to London they discussed their decisions among themselves; they recorded the decisions, filed them, and devised an indexing system for them. Predictability is a very important thing in the law, so over time the concept of **stare decisis** developed: in deciding a case, judges are bound—required—to follow the rules determined (or discovered) in previous cases involving the same basic facts.[6] In this way, judicial decisions became common to the entire realm of England.

There are many areas of law governed entirely or almost entirely by common-law rules. Contract, tort, agency, much property law, much domestic relations law—these are common-law areas. In the U.S., state legislatures have never tried to entirely supplant common law on these matters. Where it does legislate, in doing "tort reform" for example, a new statute will modify only those parts of the common law that are directly addressed in the statute; the rest of the common law of torts remains valid.

Problems with Common Law

Plessy v. Ferguson

U.S. Supreme Court case, 1896, interpreting the 14th Amendment's Equal Protection clause and establishing the "separate but equal" doctrine (overruled in 1954).

Stare decisis has the great benefit of providing some predictability, and it stands as the basis for a court's authority in announcing a result—a judge says, in effect, "Here's my decision, and it's based on applying a rule of law to the facts here. I did not make up this rule; it was made long ago, but it is still valid." But relying on the old rules presents problems, too—social conditions and technology change, and we come to understand things differently than in the past as customs and morals change. So, sometimes courts will overrule precedent—they change the law. This happens at both the state and federal level. On the federal levels, *Brown v. Board of Education* (1954), is one of the Supreme Court's most important decisions and probably the classic historical example of overruling a precedent (the overturned case was **Plessy v. Ferguson**, 1896) that had found *separate* public facilities for African-Americans to be acceptable if they were equal to the facilities provided for white people—"equal" enough for purposes of the Equal Protection clause of the 14th Amendment. Time, experience, and moral sensibilities proved the cultural assumptions of the *Plessy* court to be mistaken.

Aside from the problem that common law can become *outdated*, it has two other short comings.

One is the problem of lack of uniformity. In the United States, much of the responsibility in making laws that affects people's daily lives falls upon the states, but each state has the right to make its own laws, with a resulting lack of uniformity. For example, in the early automobile age there were no traffic laws as we know them. The common law was that drivers should stay to the right[7] and drive carefully—that was pretty much it. When accidents happened, courts in one state decided whether the driver had been careful, and came up with a rule about—say—who has the right of way at intersections. Courts in other states developed a slightly different rule. State-by-state differences in automobile intersection rules can have significant and deadly consequences, especially where driver's licenses are reciprocally recognized as valid in every state. It became obvious that there should be uniform traffic rules throughout the United States. In 1924 at a national traffic conference attended by representatives from every state, a group of attendees, headed by then-Secretary of Commerce Herbert Hoover, drafted, and in 1926 presented to the states, "A Suggested Model for a Uniform Vehicle Code."[8] The Code, as variously amended over the years, has been adopted in whole or in part by all U.S. jurisdictions. But the lack of uniformity in our federal system will continue. Rules regarding "driverless vehicles" are likely to be governed by state law; different states will no doubt develop different rules and standards for driverless vehicles, until such time as the federal government, through Congress, sees the need for uniformity.

The second shortcoming with the common law is the "case or controversy" test. The Constitution provides that federal judicial power extends to various "cases [and] controversies,"[9] which the federal courts have interpreted to mean that a plaintiff must *suffer some actual damage* that affords the plaintiff **standing to sue**. Federal courts will not issue advisory opinions—you have to suffer damages first, and then sue the defendant for a remedy. Generally speaking, the same rule is true in state courts (although some states do allow, by constitutional provision, their Supreme Courts to issue such opinions to the governor or legislature; those opinions are not binding). If your neighbor wants to set up a pig farm in a residential neighborhood, you cannot go to court and say, "Your Honor, this pig-farm operation will smell really bad. Stop it from happening—issue an injunction." The judge would say, "After you've suffered from the smell and have a real dispute, come back and we'll see."

Legally, then, a limitation of the common law is that it rarely provides preventive remedies (a **prophylactic**, a common term in law and medicine, is something that prevents the undesired result from happening in the first place). What's needed is a state statute or local land-use ordinance prohibiting pig farms in residential neighborhoods *in advance*. But even remedial legislation that operates prospectively—preventing future harms—will typically only come after harms and complaints have accumulated enough to attract the legislators' attention. Still, once the standards for well-regulated pig farms are in place, it would be possible to get injunctive relief if the operator's plans were contrary to the regulations. The "case or controversy" that didn't exist prior to the statute would give jurisdiction to courts to apply the new standards.

standing to sue

The Constitutional requirement that the plaintiff present an actual case or controversy before the plaintiff can have judicial relief. The plaintiff must be aggrieved, and arguably within the zone of interests protected by a statute.

prophylactic

That which prevents the undesired result from happening in the first place.

Cases

Judicial Review of Acts of the Executive

United States v. Nixon

418 U.S. 683 (1974)

United States v. Nixon

U.S. Supreme Court case, 1974, determining the reach of executive privilege.

Burger, C. J.

* * * Although he was not designated as such in the indictment, the grand jury named the President, among others, as an unindicted co-conspirator. On April 18, 1974, upon motion of the Special Prosecutor, a subpoena was issued to the President by the District Court [requiring] the production of certain tapes, memoranda, papers, transcripts, or other writings relating to certain precisely identified meetings between the President and others. * * * The President's counsel filed a motion to quash the subpoena. This motion was accompanied by a formal claim of privilege. * * * The District Court denied the motion to quash and further ordered "the President or any subordinate officer, official, or employee with custody or control of the documents or objects subpoenaed," to deliver to the District Court, on or before May 31, 1974, the originals of all subpoenaed items. * * *

The District Court held that the judiciary, not the President, was the final arbiter of a claim of executive privilege. * * * [The president appealed.]

[W]e turn to the claim that the subpoena should be quashed because it demands "confidential conversations between a President and his close advisors that it would be inconsistent with the public interest to produce." * * *

In the performance of assigned constitutional duties, each branch of the Government must initially interpret the Constitution, and the interpretation of its powers by any branch is due great respect from the others. The President's counsel, as we have noted, reads the Constitution as providing an absolute privilege of confidentiality for all Presidential communications. Many decisions of this Court, however, have unequivocally reaffirmed the holding of *Marbury v. Madison*, (1803), that "[i]t is emphatically the province and duty of the judicial department to say what the law is." * * *

Our system of government "requires that federal courts on occasion interpret the Constitution in a manner at variance with the construction given the document by another branch." * * * [Citation.]

[Citation]: "Deciding whether a matter has in any measure been committed by the Constitution to another branch of government, or whether the action of that branch exceeds whatever authority has been committed, is itself a delicate exercise in constitutional interpretation, and is a responsibility of this Court as ultimate interpreter of the Constitution."

Notwithstanding the deference each branch must accord the others, the "judicial Power of the United States" vested in the federal courts by Art. III, § 1, of the Constitution can no more be shared with the Executive Branch than the Chief Executive, for example, can share with the Judiciary the veto power, or the Congress share with the Judiciary the power to override a Presidential veto. Any other conclusion would be contrary to the basic concept of separation of powers and the checks and balances that flow from the scheme of a tripartite government.

We therefore reaffirm that it is the province and duty of this Court "to say what the law is" with respect to the claim of privilege presented in this case. *Marbury v. Madison.* [The President's counsel argued (1) there is a need for protection of communications between high Government officials and those who advise and assist them in the performance of their manifold duties, and (2) the President has absolute privilege to decide what will be revealed to the judicial branch.]

[As to (1):] The importance of this confidentiality is too plain to require further discussion. Human experience teaches that those who expect public dissemination of their remarks may well temper candor with a concern for appearances and for their own interests to the detriment of the decision-making process. Whatever the nature of the privilege of confidentiality of Presidential communications in the exercise of Art. II powers, the privilege can be said to derive from the supremacy of each branch within its own assigned area of constitutional duties. Certain powers and privileges flow from the nature of enumerated powers; the protection of the confidentiality of Presidential communications has similar constitutional underpinnings.

The second ground asserted by the President's counsel in support of the claim of absolute privilege rests on the doctrine of separation of powers. Here it is argued that the independence of the Executive Branch within its own sphere [Citations] insulates a President from a judicial subpoena in an ongoing criminal prosecution, and thereby protects confidential Presidential communications.

However, neither the doctrine of separation of powers nor the need for confidentiality of high-level communications, without more, can sustain an absolute, unqualified Presidential privilege of immunity from judicial process under all circumstances. The President's need for complete candor and objectivity from advisers calls for great deference from the courts. However, when the privilege depends solely on the broad, undifferentiated claim of public interest in the confidentiality of such conversations, a confrontation with other values arises. Absent a claim of need to protect military, diplomatic, or sensitive national security secrets, we find it difficult to accept the argument that even the very important interest in confidentiality of Presidential communications is significantly diminished by production of such material for *in camera* inspection with all the protection that a district court will be obliged to provide.

The impediment that an absolute, unqualified privilege would place in the way of the primary constitutional duty of the Judicial Branch to do justice in criminal prosecutions would plainly conflict with the function of the courts under Art. III. In designing the structure of our Government and dividing and allocating the sovereign power among three co-equal branches, the Framers of the Constitution sought to provide a comprehensive system, but the separate powers were not intended to operate with absolute independence. * * *

The interest in preserving confidentiality is weighty indeed, and entitled to great respect. However, the allowance of the privilege to withhold evidence that is demonstrably relevant in a criminal trial would cut deeply into the guarantee of due process of law and gravely impair the basic function of the court. A President's acknowledged need for confidentiality in the communications of his office is general in nature, whereas the constitutional need for production of relevant evidence in a criminal proceeding is specific and central to the fair adjudication of a particular criminal case in the administration of justice. Without access to specific facts, a criminal prosecution may be totally frustrated. The President's broad interest in confidentiality of communications will not be vitiated by disclosure of a limited number of conversations preliminarily shown to have some bearing on the pending criminal cases. * * *

The generalized assertion of privilege must yield to the demonstrated, specific need for evidence in a pending criminal trial.

Affirmed.

Case Questions

1. The lower court issued an order (subpoena) directing the president to do what?
2. The president refused to obey the subpoena: what two arguments did he make?
3. What did the Supreme Court say about the president's arguments and why?
4. What was the president afraid would be discovered if the subpoenaed material were produced?
5. What happened to President Nixon after the evidence was surrendered to the courts? Watch this video to learn more.

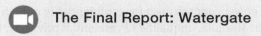

The Final Report: Watergate

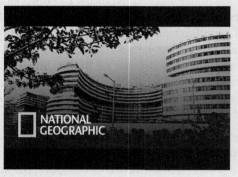

View the video online at: //www.youtube.com/embed/vC9PE2CiSGA?rel=0

Judicial Interpretation of Legislation

Church of the Holy Trinity v. United States

U.S. Supreme Court case, 1892, interpreting the meaning of the Congressional act which prohibited employers from hiring contract laborers from foreign countries.

Church of the Holy Trinity v. United States

143 U.S. 457 (1892)

[In the 1870s there was much resentment against Chinese laborers who were imported into the United States under contract to work on—among other things—the railroads. The imported labor depressed wage rates, and while the tens of thousands of healthy young Chinese men (hard-working laborers, waiters, laundry workers) did not use government schools and hospitals, they congregated in enclaves like San Francisco, and, absent the civilizing influence of women, some of them joined gangs. Public opinion came to demonize the Chinese. In 1885 Congress passed the Alien Contract Labor Law Act which provided:

> *It shall be unlawful for any person, company, partnership, or corporation, in any manner whatsoever, to prepay the transportation, or in any way assist or encourage the importation or migration of any alien or aliens, any foreigner or foreigners, into the United States . . . under contract . . . to perform labor or service of any kind in the United States.*

In 1887, Dr. E. W. Warren, an English pastor, was hired by the Holy Trinity Church in New York City to act as its rector (a cleric in charge of an Episcopal parish) and pastor. The government sued to recover the $1,000 penalty prescribed by the Act (about $28,000 in 2018 dollars). The church argued that the statute was not intended to prohibit the importation of this kind of learned, educated contract employee; the government argued the plain meaning of the statute made the contract illegal, and that although there were listed exceptions (for professional actors, singers, lecturers, artists, and so on) pastors were *not* included. The lower courts ruled for the government; the church appealed. The law at issue was repealed in 1924.]

Brewer, J.

* * * While there is great force to [the government's] reasoning, we cannot think Congress intended to denounce with penalties a transaction like that in the present case. It is a familiar rule that a thing may be within the letter of the statute and yet not within the statute because not within its spirit nor within the intention of its makers. This has been often asserted, and the reports are full of cases illustrating its application. This is not the substitution of the will of the judge for that of the legislator, for frequently words of general meaning are used in a statute, words broad enough to include an act in question, and yet a consideration of the whole legislation, or of the circumstances surrounding its enactment, or of the absurd results which follow from giving such broad meaning to the words, makes it unreasonable to believe that the legislator intended to include the particular act. [Citation.] * * * In [Citation] the Court says:

All laws should receive a sensible construction. General terms should be so limited in their application as not to lead to injustice, oppression, or an absurd consequence. It will always therefore be presumed that the legislature intended exceptions to its language which would avoid results of this character. The reason of the law in such cases should prevail over its letter. The common sense of man approves the judgment [where a law provided] "that whoever drew blood in the streets should be punished with the utmost severity" did not extend to the surgeon who opened the vein of a person that fell down in the street in a fit. The same common sense accepts the ruling * * * where the law provides that a prisoner who breaks prison shall be guilty of felony, does not extend to a prisoner who breaks out when the prison is on fire, "for he is not to be hanged because he would not stay to be burnt." * * *

The intent of Congress with respect to the act was gathered partially at least, from its title. Now the title of this act is

"An act to prohibit the importation and migration of foreigners and aliens under contract or agreement to perform labor in the United States, its territories, and the District of Columbia."

Obviously the thought expressed in this reaches only to the work of the manual laborer, as distinguished from that of the professional man. No one reading such a title would suppose that Congress had in its mind any purpose of staying the coming into this country of ministers of the gospel, or, indeed, of any class whose toil is that of the brain. The common understanding of the terms "labor" and "laborers" does not include preaching and preachers, and it is to be assumed that words and phrases are used in their ordinary meaning. So whatever of light is thrown upon the statute by the language of the title indicates an exclusion from its penal provisions of all contracts for the employment of ministers, rectors, and pastors.

Again, another guide to the meaning of a statute is found in the evil which it is designed to remedy, and for this the court properly looks at contemporaneous events, the situation as it existed, and as it was pressed upon the attention of the legislative body. * * * The situation which called for this statute was briefly but fully stated [in another case]:

It had become the practice for large capitalists in this country to contract with their agents abroad for the shipment of great numbers of an ignorant and servile class of foreign laborers, under contracts by which the employer agreed, upon the one hand, to prepay their passage, while, upon the other hand, the laborers agreed to work after their arrival for a certain time at a low rate of wages. The effect of this was to break down the labor market and to reduce other laborers engaged in like occupations to the level of the assisted immigrant. The evil finally became so flagrant that an appeal was made to Congress for relief by the passage of the act in question, the design of which was to raise the standard of foreign immigrants and to discountenance the migration of those who had not sufficient means in their own hands, or those of their friends, to pay their passage.

* * * It was this cheap, unskilled labor which was making the trouble, and the influx of which Congress sought to prevent. It was never suggested that we had in this country a surplus of brain toilers, and least of all that the market for the services of Christian ministers was depressed by foreign competition. * * *

We find, therefore, that the title of the act, the evil which was intended to be remedied, the circumstances surrounding the appeal to Congress, the reports of the committee of each house, all concur in affirming that the intent of Congress was simply to stay the influx of this cheap unskilled labor. * * * It is the duty of the courts under [these] circumstances to say that, however broad the language of the statute may be, the act, although within the letter, is not within the intention of the legislature, and therefore cannot be within the statute.

The judgment will be reversed, and the case remanded for further proceedings in accordance with this opinion.

Case Questions

1. The statute clearly prohibited exactly what Holy Trinity Church did: it hired a foreigner under contract to perform services in the U.S. How did the Court determine Holy Trinity was not liable for violation of the statute?
2. What tools did the Court use in interpreting the statute?
3. Why did Congress pass this legislation? How does it relate to the current debate about immigration into the United States?

The Common Law: Overturning Precedent

Brown v. Board of Education

U.S. Supreme Court case, 1954, holding that the 14th Amendment's Equal Protection clause forbids racial segregation in public schools (overruling Plessey v. Ferguson).

Brown v. Board of Education

347 U.S. 483 (1954)

Warren, C. J.

[Several cases were consolidated; they all had a common legal question.] In each of the cases, minors of the Negro race, through their legal representatives, seek the aid of the courts in obtaining admission to the public schools of their community on a non-segregated basis. In each instance, they had been denied admission to schools attended by white children under laws requiring or permitting segregation according to race. This segregation was alleged to deprive the plaintiffs of the equal protection of the laws under the Fourteenth Amendment. In [the cases] a district court denied relief to the plaintiffs on the so-called "separate but equal" doctrine announced by this Court in *Plessy v. Ferguson*, [Citation, 1896]. Under that doctrine, equality of treatment is accorded when the races are provided substantially equal facilities, even though these facilities be separate.

The plaintiffs contend that segregated public schools are not "equal" and cannot be made "equal," and that hence they are deprived of the equal protection of the laws.

In the first cases in this Court construing the Fourteenth Amendment, decided shortly after its adoption, the Court interpreted it as proscribing all state-imposed discriminations against the Negro race. The doctrine of "separate but equal" did not make its appearance in this Court until 1896 in the case of *Plessy v. Ferguson*, involving not education but transportation. American courts have since labored with the doctrine for over half a century. In this Court, there have been six cases involving the "separate but equal" doctrine in the field of public education. * * *

In the instant cases, that question is directly presented. Here, unlike *Sweatt v. Painter* [citation], there are findings below that the Negro and white schools involved have been equalized, or are being equalized, with respect to buildings, curricula, qualifications and salaries of teachers, and other "tangible" factors. Our decision, therefore, cannot turn on merely a comparison of these tangible factors in the Negro and white schools involved in each of the cases. We must look instead to the effect of segregation itself on public education.

Today, education is perhaps the most important function of state and local governments. Compulsory school attendance laws and the great expenditures for education both demonstrate our recognition of the importance of education to our democratic society. * * * In these days, it is doubtful that any child may reasonably be expected to succeed in life if he is denied the opportunity of an education. Such an opportunity, where the state has undertaken to provide it, is a right which must be made available to all on equal terms.

We come then to the question presented: does segregation of children in public schools solely on the basis of race, even though the physical facilities and other "tangible" factors may be equal, deprive the children of the minority group of equal educational opportunities? We believe that it does.

In *Sweatt v. Painter, supra*, in finding that a segregated law school for Negroes could not provide them equal educational opportunities, this Court relied in large part on "those qualities which are incapable of objective measurement but which make for greatness in a law school." In *McLaurin v. Oklahoma State Regents*, [Citation] the Court, in requiring that a Negro admitted to a white graduate school be treated like all other students, again resorted to intangible considerations: ". . . his ability to study, to engage in discussions and exchange views with other students, and, in general, to learn his profession."

Such considerations apply with added force to children in grade and high schools. To separate them from others of similar age and qualifications solely because of their race generates a feeling of inferiority as to their status in the community that may affect their hearts and minds in a way unlikely ever to be undone. The effect of this separation on their educational opportunities was well stated by a finding in the Kansas case by a court which nevertheless felt compelled to rule against the Negro plaintiffs:

> *Segregation of white and colored children in public schools has a detrimental effect upon the colored children. The impact is greater when it has the sanction of the law, for the policy of separating the races is usually interpreted as denoting the inferiority of the negro group. A sense of inferiority affects the motivation of a child to learn. Segregation with the sanction of law, therefore, has a tendency to [retard] the educational and mental development of negro children and to deprive them of some of the benefits they would receive in a racial[ly] integrated school system.*

Whatever may have been the extent of psychological knowledge at the time of *Plessy v. Ferguson*, this finding is amply supported by modern authority. Any language in *Plessy v. Ferguson* contrary to this finding is rejected.

We conclude that, in the field of public education, the doctrine of "separate but equal" has no place. Separate educational facilities are inherently unequal. Therefore, we hold that the plaintiffs and others similarly situated for whom the actions have been brought are, by reason of the segregation complained of, deprived of the equal protection of the laws guaranteed by the Fourteenth Amendment. * * * It is so ordered.

Case Questions

1. In 1896 the Court decided that it was no violation of the 14th Amendment's Equal Protection Clause for the government to require legal separation of the races so long as the government services or facilities provided for the races were equal. Why did the Court decide that in 1896?
2. What is "equal protection of the laws"?
3. In this case the Court reversed a decision it had made fifty years before. Why did it? What had changed?
4. What happened when the Supreme Court ordered desegregation of schools? Check out this video: https://www.youtube.com/watch?v=xERXusiEszs .

Key Takeaway

There are three traditional law-making entities. The primary law-making entity in our system is the legislature which, following the legislative process, adopts statutes (at the federal and state level) or ordinances (at the local level). The executive affects what laws are made by presentation of a budget, veto, nominations to courts (at the federal level), nominations and appointments to agencies, and executive orders. The judiciary makes law by judicial review of acts of all branches of government, by judicial interpretation of legislation, and—in the absence of legislation—by developing the common law.

Exercises

1. If you and 100 other people were—as the old story goes—cast upon a deserted (unpopulated) island and compelled to live your lives there, which of the three traditional law-making entities would you need to establish for your governance?
2. Why is the legislature considered the most powerful law-making entity in our system?
3. The executive's veto cancels out a statute adopted by the legislature. How could such "cancelling out" be considered a way to *make* law?
4. When the president or a governor issues an executive order, what does it affect? Would the president act without authority if she or he directed the Justice Department, say, to de-prioritize the deportation of undocumented aliens who were brought to the U.S. as children?
5. The common law is based on precedent: a judge deciding today's case looks to the already-existing rules that were applied in similar situations in the past. Why is that a reasonably useful approach to law-making in the absence of legislation?
6. The Constitution does not provide that the Supreme Court should be able to declare acts of Congress or the president unconstitutional. Why is it acceptable that the Court should have that power? And what remedy is there if the Court declares a Congressional statute (or policy) unconstitutional if it has very broad public support and is perceived to be vitally important for the national welfare?
7. Why are federal judges appointed and granted lifetime tenure?

4.2 Law by Administrative Agencies and Direct Democracy

We have reviewed the three traditional law-making entities: legislature, executive, and judicial. There are two more. The fourth is law by administrative agencies—sometimes called "the fourth branch of government," and the fifth is law made by the people themselves, in some states, by initiative or referendum.

Learning Objectives

1. Understand that administrative agencies are created and delegated power (typically in accordance with the enabling statute) by the legislative or executive branch to carry out functions assigned to that branch.
2. Recognize that administrative agencies may often have three powers: quasi-legislative, quasi-executive, and quasi-judicial.
3. Know what legislative, executive, and judicial constraints exist on agency power and authority.
4. Understand that those who seek judicial review of administrative actions must have standing to sue, and that the judiciary grants significant deference to agency decisions.
5. Know what "corporate capture" of administrative agencies means.
6. Understand that in many states the people themselves can make law by the initiative or referendum process, but this process is also subject to "corporate capture."

Law by Administrative Agencies

Introduction: Why Have Administrative Agencies?

An "agent" is one who acts on behalf of another; an "administration" is a group of people working together to achieve some goal or pursue some objective (in this context, on behalf of the public). So, an **administrative agency** is a government entity—other than the constitutionally-mandated legislative, executive, or judicial branches—that carries out tasks assigned to one of those branches of government. There are also significant nongovernmental organizations (NGOs) that are usually non-profit, independent of governments, but often funded by them, that do work in the educational, humanitarian, human rights, environmental areas to affect social change. These are agents of its donors and benefactors, but are not public in the way that administrative agencies are.

The U.S. Constitution mentions only three branches of government: legislative, executive, and judicial (Articles I, II, and III). There is no mention of agencies in the Constitution, though federal administrative agencies are sometimes referred to as "the fourth branch of government." The Supreme Court has recognized the legitimacy of federal administrative agencies to make rules that have the same binding effect as statutes by Congress. State governments have agencies, too (*e.g.*, the Department of Health and Social Services, the Gambling Commission, the Liquor and Cannabis Control Board), and so do local cities and counties (for example, the Building and Codes Department, or the Health Department).

administrative agency

A government entity —other than the constitutionally-mandated legislative, executive, or judicial branches—that carries out tasks assigned to one of those branches of government.

Agencies are a practical necessity: (1) Congress or the president (or the state, or county legislature) does not have the expertise, time, or continuity to develop specialized knowledge in various areas (e.g., communications, the environment, aviation). (2) Because of this, it makes sense for the legislature to set forth broad statutory guidance to an agency and delegate authority to the agency to propose rules that further the statutory purposes. (3) As long as the legislature makes this delegating guidance sufficiently clear, it is not delegating improperly. If legislative guidelines are too vague or undefined, it is (in essence) giving away its constitutional power to some other group, and this it cannot do.[10]

Among other functions, regulatory administrative agencies exist to curb the potential excesses of capitalism. The "free market" in reality is commerce that is *legally constrained* by what is economically and socially desirable. In a completely free market, a thirteen-year-old could purchase machine guns, cigarettes, heroin, alcohol, pornography, and much more. Abortion services would be completely unregulated. Such sales are limited by laws that aim to serve public policy objectives in the social arena—ensuring equal opportunity in employment, protecting employees from unhealthy or unsafe work environments, preserving environmental quality and resources, and protecting consumers from unsafe products and false advertising. Sometimes these objectives are met by giving individuals statutory rights that can be used in bringing a complaint (e.g., Title VII of the Civil Rights Act of 1964, for employment discrimination), and sometimes they are met by creating agencies with the right to investigate, monitor, and enforce statutory law and the regulations created to enforce such law (e.g., the Environmental Protection Agency, for bringing a lawsuit against a polluting company or setting enforceable standards for greenhouse gas emissions).[11]

Because agencies are empowered by legislatures to do what legislatures have delegated to them, their final rules have the same force and effect as statutory law; these final rules are most often referred to as "regulations." Again, final federal agency regulations are published in the Code of Federal Regulations, and cannot be undone by executive order if the agency is created by Congress. At all times, however, Congress has the power to un-delegate or to legislatively change an agency rule, and the president (or governor, or mayor) can press the agency to be vigorous in its enforcement, or not. (President Obama issued an executive order deferring prosecution of illegal aliens who were brought to the U.S. when they were infants; that worked. As of this writing we will see what becomes of these "Dreamers.")

How Agencies Are Created

enabling statute

The legislation by which an administrative agency is created and given power.

Agencies are created because problems—like air pollution or fairly allocating limited radio frequencies for broadcasting (the Environmental Protection Agency and the Federal Communications Commission, respectively—are recognized which requires a response by group of people with expertise in the area. Most agencies are created by the legislature via an **enabling statute**, the law that creates the agency and gives it its powers. For example, the Federal Trade Commission was created in 1914 by Congress concerned about monopolization, price fixing, and other anti-competitive devices and authorized to "prevent persons, partnerships, or corporations . . . from using unfair methods of competition in or affecting commerce and unfair or deceptive acts or practices in or affecting commerce."[12]

Types of Agencies

We may count (1) legislative agencies, (2) independent executive and executive agencies, (3) and judicial agencies among the types. Each branch of government has agencies to further its work.

Legislative Agencies

Legislative agencies carry out functions assigned to *Congress* (or the state legislature, or city council, etc.). But Congress doesn't really have very many functions beyond the critically important one of budgeting and determining policy—it's up to others to carry out the policy. Here is a partial list of legislative agencies:

> Architect of the Capitol
>
> Congressional Budget Office
>
> Congressional Research Service
>
> Copyright Office
>
> Government Accountability Office
>
> Government Publishing Office
>
> Joint Congressional Committee on Inaugural Ceremonies
>
> Library of Congress
>
> U.S. Botanic Garden
>
> U.S. Capitol Police
>
> U.S. Capitol Visitor Center

Independent Executive Agencies

These are agencies charged with the responsibility to carry out functions constitutionally assigned to the executive (president). We may call out two types of executive agencies.

Executive Branch Agencies

Independent executive agencies carry out a task assigned to the president. Congress said a hundred years ago that we need to curb anti-competitive behavior and made such behavior illegal; theoretically it is the president's job to execute the law, but Congress created an agency to carry out that function. These agencies almost always have a commission or board consisting of five to seven members who make policy. The president appoints the commissioners or board subject to Senate confirmation, and members serve staggered terms, often for longer than a usual four-year presidential term. They cannot be removed by the president except for "good cause" (why they are called "independent"). This means that most presidents will not get to appoint all the commissioners of a given independent agency. Most independent agencies have a statutory requirement of bipartisan membership. Examples include the Federal Communications Commission (1934), Securities and Exchange Commission (1934), National Labor Relations Board (1935), and Environmental Protection Agency (1970).

   Executive branch agencies are also created by Congress, and they also carry out functions theoretically assigned to the executive. Directors and members of these agencies—unlike independent executive agencies—serve at the pleasure of the president; they are political appointees, although Congress typically must approve the president's nominations to head these agencies.[13] The rules that independent agencies promulgate may not be reviewed by the president or his staff—only Congress may directly overrule them—whereas the White House or officials in the various cabinet departments may oversee the work of the executive-branch agencies contained within them (unless specifically denied the power by Congress). Executive branch agencies include these:

> Department of Agriculture (USDA)
>
> Department of Commerce (DOC)
>
> Department of Defense (DoD)

Department of Education (ED)

Department of Energy (DOE)

Dept. of Health & Human Services (HHS)

Dept. of Housing and Urban Development (HUD)

Department of the Interior (DOI)

Department of Justice (DOJ)

Department of Labor (DOL)

Department of State (DOS)

Department of Transportation (DOT)

Department of the Treasury

Department of Veterans Affairs (VA)

Judicial Agencies

judicial agencies

More often actually committees of the federal or state bar associations, carrying out functions assigned to the judicial branch.

Judicial agencies are sometimes, but not always, created by statute; some judicial "agencies" are really committees of the state or federal bar associations. Here are the agencies within the federal judicial branch that are authorized by statute (the members of these agencies are independent of the executive or Congress; they are often appointed by the chief justice):

Supreme Court Police

U.S. Probation and Pretrial Services System

Marshal of the U.S. Supreme Court

Administrative Office of the United States Courts

Federal Judicial Center

Judicial Conference of the United States

Judicial Panel on Multidistrict Litigation

United States Sentencing Commission

In general, the federal or state Supreme Courts are responsible for court administration in their jurisdictions. The judges themselves do not have the time or expertise to address the details of running the judicial branch, so committees of the bar association do that work—lawyers volunteer their services and adopt policies and rules that have the force of law. Here is a list of some of the Washington State Bar Association committees:[14]

Board of Bar Examiners

Budget & Audit Committee

Bylaws Work Group

Character and Fitness Board

Civil Litigation Rules Drafting Task Force

Client Protection Fund Board

Committee on Professional Ethics

Continuing Legal Education Committee

Council on Public Defense

Court Rules and Procedures Committee

Disciplinary Board

Diversity Committee

Editorial Advisory Committee

Cost of Civil Litigation Task Force

Powers of Administrative Agencies

Administrative agencies have three powers: quasi-legislative, quasi-executive, and quasi-judicial.

Quasi-legislative power means the agency acts as if it were a legislature. It promulgates regulations, which are like laws, *except* they are not adopted by the legislature, but rather—again—by the agency acting as if it were a legislature. Just as there is a process by which the legislature itself makes law, so there is a process by which agencies make (or "**promulgate**"—to make known or public the terms of a proposed regulation). At the federal level the 1946 Administrative Procedure Act (APA) is the statute that governs how administrative agencies propose and establish regulations. Many states have similar acts to govern administrative procedures.

Here's how it works. Suppose a problem within the agency's jurisdiction needs to be addressed. For example, when the voters in Washington State legalized recreational marijuana by initiative in 2012, the process of setting up the rules on retailing marijuana was consigned to a revised agency, the Washington State Liquor Board. When the legislature added "cannabis" to the agency's name, the agency became the Washington State Liquor and Cannabis Board. The agency's board members toured the state, reached out through various media, and said to the state's residents, "We need to come up with regulations that conform to the authorizing statute. What ideas do you have for how to administer the sale of legalized marijuana?" The agency got a lot of feedback that it incorporated into preliminary regulations; these were published, and further feedback sought. More comments came in, and the agency re-wrote the regulations. It again published the proposed regulations, and got further feedback. Final regulations were adopted in 2013, subject to further amendments in the future. Final agency regulations are published at the federal level in the Code of Federal Regulations ("CFR"); at the state level, publication of final regulations are governed by the state administrative codes.[15]

This is how the agency effectively makes law—if you don't sell marijuana according to the regulations, you will be prohibited from selling any; if you don't build your house according to the local building regulations promulgated by the Building and Codes Department, you cannot occupy the house; that's the law. But strictly speaking it is regulation, not "law," because the mandates are from an agency, not the legislature. Agencies also dictate to some businesses how much they can charge. If the water in your city is not provided by the city itself by collective action to create public goods (that's the theory of socialism), it is either your own well water or is provided by a company whose rates are regulated by an agency. The same is true for electricity, natural gas, garbage pickup, and other such services that are more efficient with some degree of monopolization. (For example, it would be inefficient to have competing electric companies with two or three separate electrical lines running all over town.).

Quasi-executive power. The quasi-legislative division of the agency makes the rules, and the quasi-executive division enforces them, as the executive branch of government enforces legislation adopted by the legislature. So, for example, the Food and Drug Administration has agents who check to see that meat-processing plants adhere to proper sanitary protocols (failing to do so can result in outbreaks of serious disease, like e-coli poisoning). If protocols are not followed the agency may issue a citation, impose a fine, suspend operations at the plant, and require correction.

quasi-legislative power

The agency acts as if it were a legislature and promulgates regulations having the force of law.

promulgate

To issue forth or proclaim as an official statutory or administrative law or regulation following the appropriate procedure.

quasi-executive

The section or branch of the administrative agency that carries out the agency's regulations, as the executive carries out the legislatures mandates.

Quasi-judicial power functions are found in some agencies, as well. This third power is exercised by the agency's **administrative law judge**, (usually known as "**hearing examiners**" at the city and county level), who does not have lifetime tenure like a federal judge, but is rather an employee of the agency. Adversely affected parties (usually called "the respondent" in administrative law) may contest the citation issued by the agency. Internal appeals within the agency are possible, and once the agency makes a final order, that order is appealable to the federal courts. The process works in a similar way in state administrative law.

Constraints on Agency Action

Administrative agencies are powerful government entities. In our daily lives we are much more likely to deal with the effects of administrative regulation than we are with legislation itself. (Who says that the cold-water faucet should be on the right and the hot-water faucet on the left? An administrative agency.) There are, however, constraints on agency action; these constraints are—not surprisingly—legislative, executive, and judicial constraints.

Legislative Constraints

There are several legislative constraints; five may be called out here:

- The power to abolish the agency. Because most agencies are created by the legislature, the legislature has the power to abolish them. For example, in 1887 the first U.S. administrative agency (besides the Post Office) was created. The Interstate Commerce Commission was intended to regulate railroads (and later trucking, bus lines, and telephone companies), to ensure fair rates, eliminate discrimination, and otherwise regulate, theoretically for the public good. In 1995, after Congress had transferred most of the ICC's power to other agencies (U.S. Surface Transportation Board, the Motor Carrier Safety Administration) the ICC was abolished.

- The power to dictate to the agency what regulations it promulgates. An "agent" is one who acts for a principal, but the principal doesn't surrender the right to step in and take over directly.[16] The legislature can forgo agency involvement and act by itself directly, and can legislatively overturn any agency rule it does not like.

- The power of the purse. If the legislature likes an agency, it gets more money (e.g., Immigration and Custom Enforcement ("ICE") received $2.8 billion in 2012; in 2018 President Trump wanted more detention facilities, more immigration officers, and more enforcement, so in its 2018 budget the administration requested a funding increase of $900 million over FY 2017 for ICE.[17] If the legislature doesn't like the agency, it gets less money and does less (fewer employees, fewer resources, etc.).

- The power to approve administrative agency leadership. The executive nominates agency heads and the legislature (the Senate at the federal level) usually approves the nomination. Sometimes the legislature signals that it won't approve the nomination, and the candidate is withdrawn from consideration; sometimes the legislature simply refuses to approve the nomination.

- The power of constituent watch-dog work. If your grandmother doesn't get her Social Security check, or the city lets the street by your house deteriorate, you might contact your member of Congress or your city councilmember. Elected officials can often help ensure appropriate agency response to citizens' needs.

Executive Constraints

The executive—president, governor, mayor—exercises some constraint over agencies. She or he nominates agency leadership, proposes budget allocations, and can exercise the threat and power of a veto to get the legislature to approve enabling statute language. The leadership of executive-branch agencies, as noted above, serve at the pleasure of the executive—people get fired. However, a president that removes highly-visible leaders of executive branch agencies—such as the Federal Bureau of Investigation or the Department of Justice—may pay a political price for firing someone without defensible reasons.

Judicial Constraints

Discussing judicial review, above, we noted that courts have the power to declare acts of administrative agencies invalid. But before the respondent can have a court hearing, the respondent must have **standing to sue**. Standing is required for any litigant in any judicial proceeding, but it becomes particularly important in administrative law because administrative agencies affect people's daily lives more often than legislation does. The standing issue helps explain why people who are alarmed about environmental destruction (or the number of people killed on highways, or by guns in the hands of crazies, or the repeated scandals on Wall Street) are very often helpless to do anything about it—the doors of the administrative hearing room are closed except to those who have directly suffered. Then it is often too late—because the damage is done.

There are three requirements for standing: (1) the respondent must have exhausted administrative remedies, (2) must be aggrieved in fact, and (3) must be "arguably within the zone of interest protected by the statute" (the enabling statute).

First, before a person can complain to the courts, she or he, or it (in the case of corporate entities) must usually have **exhausted administrative remedies**. If relief is available at the local, regional, or national administrative agency level, the litigant must (usually) pursue those avenues of redress before complaining to the courts. That is to allow the agency to correct its own errors, if any, and to create a record for judicial review. However, if it is clear the agency will not reconsider the citation so that exhaustion of remedies would be futile, a court may allow a petitioner's case to proceed in court.

Second, to have standing the complainant must be "**aggrieved in fact**," complaining of injury, actual or threatened, because of what the agency has done. The injury may be economic or non-economic. For example, in environmental cases a person has suffered injury in fact if she shows that she has "an aesthetic or recreational interest in a particular place or animal, and that interest is impaired by a defendant's conduct."[18] The injury must be "concrete and particularized," and "actual or imminent, not conjectural or hypothetical."

Third, to have standing the complainant must be "arguably within the zone of interest protected by a statute"—in the words of the Supreme Court—there must be "an invasion of a legally protected interest," that is, you can't complain, say, about all the litter in orbit around Earth—space ship junk[19]—because, among other things, you have no *right* to be protected from it by any statute. You are not "arguably within the zone of interest protected by a statute."

The standard of review. Assuming the complainant has standing and a court will hear the argument, start with this—courts give significant deference to administrative agencies' decisions.[20] It's not easy to prove the agency made a mistake. The agency, after all, is the one with the expertise. A decision rendered by an agency may be challenged where it is:

- outside the scope of the agency's authority.
- unconstitutional or a violation of the APA (Administrative Procedure Act).
- not supported by substantial evidence.

standing to sue

The Constitutional requirement that the plaintiff present an actual case or controversy before the plaintiff can have judicial relief. The plaintiff must be aggrieved, and arguably within the zone of interests protected by a statute.

exhausted administrative remedies

The general requirement that before a person can appeal from an administrative agency to the courts, the person must first have gone through the entire appeals procedure within the agency itself.

aggrieved in fact

Actually suffered some cognizable harm; a requirement for standing.

- unwarranted by the facts.
- arbitrary, capricious, an abuse of discretion, or otherwise unlawful.

Note that if you called the IRS for tax advice and got incorrect advice, you would lose. Mistakes made by the government are generally held against the complainant, not the government (there are exceptions). But this makes sense—if the rule were otherwise, people would seek out the least knowledgeable relevant agency employee and claim reliance on that person's advice.

In sum, most administrative agencies are set up to protect the public against the inherent abuses of capitalism. However, over time they almost inevitably come to instead represent the interests of the industry they are supposed to be overseeing. John Kenneth Galbraith (1908–2006), a Canadian-born economist and diplomat (ambassador to India during the Kennedy Administration) wrote:

> *Regulatory agencies, like the people who comprise them, have a marked life cycle. In youth they are vigorous, aggressive, evangelist, and even intolerant. Later they mellow, and in old age—after a matter of ten or fifteen years—they become, with some exceptions, either an arm of the industry they are regulating or senile.*[21]

revolving door

Administrative heads are drawn from the industry they are called upon to regulate, and then when they quit government work, they are employed by the industry they previously regulated.

The agencies are prey to persistent, well-funded lobbyists and to the "**revolving door**": men and women are hired to work as regulators of the very industries they formerly worked in as private-sector employees, and former government employees get jobs for the firms they formerly regulated.[22] Who better to know how things work and where the bodies are buried? Critics of the current regulatory system suggest that between corporate or regulatory capture and the revolving door, we now have a kind of "corporate crony capitalism."[23]

Law by Direct Democracy

initiative

A mechanism by which voters themselves can directly originate and approve legislation, if a sufficient number of them sign a petition.

referendum

The legislature, or a group of petitioners following a signature drive, invite the electorate to vote on a particular proposal; a type of direct democracy.

The fifth mechanism of law-making is direct democracy—the people themselves make law. You may be familiar with how the **initiative** works—you are headed into the supermarket and a woman with a clipboard stops you. "Would you like to sign this petition to legalize marijuana in our state?" You say, "Well, I don't know much about that really." "That's okay," says the signature gatherer, "if we get people to sign, it'll go on the ballot and there'll be like a political campaign. Arguments will be made back and forth." So you sign, a lot of people do, the signatures are validated, and there is a campaign, and marijuana is legalized, or not, depending on the vote. A **referendum** happens when the legislature refers to the voters a single political question for a direct decision by ballot. The people cannot invalidate a law that is already operative, but they can by vote annul a law that has not yet gone into effect. In this sense, referendum is similar to a governor's veto power.

This all seems robustly democratic, but as the history of the Constitution's adoption and its construction make clear, at the federal level, the Framers were wary of popular democracy—perhaps with good reason. As the Constitution was originally conceived, only the House of Representatives was democratically elected (by some white males). The Senate was indirectly elected by state legislatures until 1913 (the 17th Amendment brought in direct election of senators); the president is indirectly elected by the Electoral College (in 2000 and 2016 the U.S. presidential candidate who garnered more popular votes than the other side *lost* the election). The federal judiciary and the federal bureaucracy is entirely appointed. Maybe it is a bit misleading to tout the U.S. political system as comprehensively democratic when it is significantly not, and indeed the Framers wanted no such a thing. They were propertied men (women could not vote in federal elections until 1920[24]) and they wanted to maintain and secure their privileged status. But, by the late

19th century social conditions of post-Civil War capitalism in the United States caused unrest and pressure for reform.

The Progressive Era in U.S. politics (roughly 1890 to 1920) was a response to some of the economic problems presented by the transformation of society, particularly the problem of robber-baron capitalism and corrupt state legislatures. The progressives agitated for direct democracy, which, they thought, would "re-establish democratic forms, which have been lost through the complexity of our life, the great increase in population, the misuse of federal and state patronage, and the illegal combination of the boss with the privileged interests."[25] Twenty-five states now allow the initiative process.[26]

But democratic norms have not carried the day for many recent Progressive-style initiatives. In 1995 David Lagasse observed that corporations had successfully torpedoed environmental initiative measures in Massachusetts, Oregon, California, and Ohio that had overwhelming early support. For example, corporate manufacturers of non-recyclable materials, including Exxon, Mobil Oil, Dow Chemical, and DuPont, contributed more than $5 million to defeat a Massachusetts recycling initiative in 1992.[27] Twenty years later, armed with paid signature-gathers, giant corporations weighed in on Washington state with much more money. In 2009 the American Beverage Association and candy companies poured nearly $11 million into a successful campaign to convince Washington voters that candy and soda pop are "groceries" and should not be taxed.[28] And in 2011 when Costco decided it could make money on liquor sales, it spent $22 million in Washington state to abolish state-run liquor stores and get what it wanted (liquor sold retail) via an initiative,[29] which, it turned out, was not really what the people thought they were getting when they voted for it.[30] Direct democracy "has increasingly become the province of special interests, big business and unions. 'The old purpose of the (initiative) process is being subverted,' said Blaine Gavin, professor of political science at Gonzaga University. 'Interest groups recognize there's another way to make law, and big powerful interests know how to conduct good advertising campaigns.'"[31] Authentic citizen-activists can generate real popular support for public policy changes. This is called "grass roots" activism—it grows from the soil, so to say. To disguise their affiliations with their corporate industry backers, "astro-turf" organizations *seem* to be citizen driven, but they are really corporate driven—fake grass-roots, hence the play on "AstroTurf," a synthetic carpeting that looks somewhat like natural grass.

Case

Judicial Review of Acts of Administrative Agencies: The Requirement of Standing

Lujan v. Defenders of Wildlife 504 U.S. 555 (1992)	**Lujan v. Defenders of Wildlife** U.S. Supreme Court opinion, 1992, defining who has standing to sue an administrative agency.

Scalia, J.

[The Endangered Species Act (ESA) of 1973 prohibited federal funding for projects that would be likely to harm species; a joint ruling in 1979 by the Interior Department and the Commerce Department (both federal administrative agencies) limited the geographic scope of the Act to affected species in the United States and the high seas. Defenders of Wildlife and other environmental organizations ("respondents") sued in district court, complaining that the departments' ruling—an interpretation of the ESA—was in error. They claimed some U.S. projects in Africa would harm local species in violation of the ESA. Following a lower-court ruling that the respondents had standing and could sue the departments, the Department of Interior (Lujan, director) appealed to the U.S. Supreme Court.

The U.S. Constitution extends federal judicial power to "cases and controversies," which are disputes appropriately resolved through the judicial process. If there is no case or controversy, a would-be litigant has no standing and cannot sue.]

* * * Over the years, our cases have established that the irreducible constitutional minimum of standing [requires that] the plaintiff must have suffered an "injury in fact"—an invasion of a legally protected interest which is concrete and particularized [Citations] "actual or imminent, not 'conjectural' or 'hypothetical,'" [Citation]. * * * By particularized, we mean that the injury must affect the plaintiff in a personal and individual way.

Of course, the desire to use or observe an animal species, even for purely esthetic purposes, is undeniably a cognizable interest for purpose of standing. "But the 'injury in fact' test requires more than an injury to a cognizable interest. It requires that the party seeking review be himself among the injured." To survive the Secretary's summary judgment motion, respondents had to submit affidavits or other evidence showing, through specific facts, not only that listed species were in fact being threatened by funded activities abroad, but also that one or more of respondents' members would thereby be "directly" affected apart from their "special interest' in the subject."

With respect to this aspect of the case, the Court of Appeals focused on the affidavits of two Defenders' members. Joyce Kelly and Amy Skilbred. Ms. Kelly stated that she traveled to Egypt in 1986 and "observed the traditional habitat of the endangered Nile crocodile there and intend[s] to do so again, and hope[s] to observe the crocodile directly," and that she "will suffer harm in fact as the result of [the] American ... role ... in overseeing the rehabilitation of the Aswan High Dam on the Nile ... and [in] develop[ing] ... Egypt's ... Master Water Plan." Ms. Skilbred averred that she traveled to Sri Lanka in 1981 and "observed the[e] habitat" of "endangered species such as the Asian elephant and the leopard" at what is now the site of the Mahaweli project funded by the Agency for International Development (AID), although she "was unable to see any of the endangered species"; "this development project," she continued, "will seriously reduce endangered, threatened, and endemic species habitat including areas that I visited ... [, which] may severely shorten the future of these species"; that threat, she concluded, harmed her because she "intend[s] to return to Sri Lanka in the future and hope[s] to be more fortunate in spotting at least the endangered elephant and leopard." When Ms. Skilbred was asked at a subsequent deposition if and when she had any plans to return to Sri Lanka, she reiterated that "I intend to go back to Sri Lanka," but confessed that she had no current plans: "I don't know [when]. There is a civil war going on right now. I don't know. Not next year, I will say. In the future."

We shall assume for the sake of argument that these affidavits contain facts showing that certain agency-funded projects threaten listed species—though that is questionable. They plainly contain no facts, however, showing how damage to the species will produce "imminent" injury to Mses. Kelly and Skilbred. That the women "had visited" the areas of the projects before the projects commenced proves nothing. * * * And the affiants'[32] profession of an "inten[t]" to return to the places they had visited before—where they will presumably, this time, be deprived of the opportunity to observe animals of the endangered species—is simply not enough. Such "some day" intentions—without any description of concrete plans, or indeed even any specification of when the some day will be—do not support a finding of the "actual or imminent" injury that our cases require.

Besides relying upon the Kelly and Skilbred affidavits, respondents propose a series of novel standing theories. The first, inelegantly styled "ecosystem nexus," proposes that any person who uses any part of a "contiguous ecosystem" adversely affected by a funded activity has standing even if the activity is located a great distance away. This approach, as the Court of Appeals correctly observed, is inconsistent with our opinion in National Wildlife Federation, which held that a plaintiff claiming injury from environmental damage must use the area affected by the challenged activity and not an area roughly "in the vicinity" of it. [Citations.] It makes no difference that the general-purpose section of the ESA states that the Act was intended in part "to provide a means whereby the ecosystems upon which endangered species and threatened species depend may be conserved," To say that the Act protects ecosystems is not to say that the Act creates (if it were possible) rights of action in persons who have not been injured in fact, that is, persons who use portions of an ecosystem not perceptibly affected by the unlawful action in question.

Respondents' other theories are called, alas, the "animal nexus" approach, whereby anyone who has an interest in studying or seeing the endangered animals anywhere on the globe has standing; and the "vocational nexus" approach, under which anyone with a professional interest in such animals can sue. Under these theories, anyone who goes to see Asian elephants in the Bronx Zoo, and anyone who is a keeper of Asian elephants in the Bronx Zoo, has standing to sue because the Director of the Agency for International Development (AID) did not consult with the Secretary regarding the AID-funded project in Sri Lanka. This is beyond all reason. Standing is not "an ingenious academic exercise in the conceivable," [Citation] (1973), but as we have said requires, at the summary judgment stage, a factual showing of perceptible harm. It is clear that the person who observes or works with a particular animal threatened by a federal decision is facing perceptible harm, since the very subject of his interest will no longer exist. It is even plausible—though it goes to the outermost limit of plausibility—to think that a person who observes or works with animals of a particular species in the very area of the world where that species is threatened by a federal decision is facing such harm, since some animals that might have been the subject of his interest will no longer exist, see *Japan Whaling Assn.* v. *American Cetacean Society* [Citation, (1986)]. It goes beyond the limit, however, and into pure speculation and fantasy, to say that anyone who observes or works with an endangered species, anywhere in the world, is appreciably harmed by a single project affecting some portion of that species with which he has no more specific connection.

"It is an established principle," we said, "that to entitle a private individual to invoke the judicial power to determine the validity of executive or legislative action he must show that he has sustained or is immediately in danger of sustaining a direct injury as the result of that action and it is not sufficient that he has merely a general interest common to all members of the public." [Citation.] * * *

We hold that respondents lack standing to bring this action and that the Court of Appeals erred in denying the summary judgment motion filed by the United States. The opinion of the Court of Appeals is hereby reversed, and the cause is remanded for proceedings consistent with this opinion. It is so ordered.

[Two justices dissented at length; three concurred in the result but disagreed that the respondents lacked standing.]

Case Questions

1. Given the vigorous and learned dissents (not reproduced here), how reasonable is it for Justice Scalia to dismiss respondents' arguments as "novel," and "beyond the limit . . . and into pure speculation and fantasy"? After all, several justices *accepted* those arguments. Why did Justice Scalia use the word "alas" here: "Respondents' other theories are called, alas, the 'animal nexus' approach"?

2. In concluding his dissent, Justice Blackmun wrote, "I cannot join the Court on what amounts to a slash-and-burn expedition through the law of environmental standing. In my view, '[t]he very essence of civil liberty certainly consists in the right of every individual to claim the protection of the laws, whenever he receives an injury.' Marbury v. Madison, [citation], (1803)." Why does Justice Blackmun describe the majority opinion as "a slash-and-burn expedition through the law of environmental standing"? What is "slash-and-burn"?

3. What does the majority opinion do to the ability of Americans to complain about the effect of U.S. overseas projects that seriously damage the environment?

Key Takeaway

To the three "traditional" 18th century law-making entities established in the Constitution (legislature, executive, judicial), two additional entities have been added since the early 20th century. Administrative agencies make law when—usually acting based on authority granted by the legislature's enabling statute—they exercise quasi-legislative, quasi-executive, and (sometimes) quasi-judicial power. These agencies are subject to legislative, executive, and judicial constraints. A person who challenges agency action must have standing to sue, and should be aware that the courts grant significant deference to agency decisions. Not infrequently agencies eventually come to act, not in the interest of the public, but in the interest of the industries they are supposed to regulate—they are subject to "corporate capture."

The second non-traditional source of law-making is direct democracy. In half the states the people themselves can make law by the initiative or referendum process. Direct democracy, like administrative agencies, often becomes a tool of big business.

Exercises

1. Where does Congress (or the state legislature) get the authority to create and empower administrative agencies? Congress could not give *all* its power "to regulate commerce among the several states" to an administrative agency, and then close the book on that issue for, say, decades. It can't delegate its entire authority away. Why not?

2. The first administrative agency was the Post Office, created in 1792. Why did Congress feel that the Post Office was very important? The next administrative agency wasn't created until 1887 (the Interstate Commerce Commission); why was it 100 years until that happened, and why was the object of regulation the railroads?

3. What is "corporate capture" and why does it happen?

4. What is "the revolving door"? What problems does the concept create in government—or is it a problem at all?

5. What spurred the states to adopt the initiative process so that citizens could make the law directly themselves?

6. What relatively recent problems have arisen with direct democracy that makes some people think it has been corrupted, and by whom?

4.3 Summary and Exercises

Summary

Law is made by five entities. The "traditional" three are the legislature, the executive, and the courts. Courts make law by judicial review of other government entities' decisions, by judicial interpretation of legislation (a statute means what the courts say it does), and by developing the common law (where there is no legislation).

The "fourth branch" of government is the administrative agencies; the legislature, executive, and judicial branches have, effectively, administrative agencies to help them do their work. Administrative rules and regulations constitute the largest body of laws that directly affect business. These regulations, issued according to the relevant Administrative Procedure Act by dozens of federal and state agencies, regulate virtually every aspect of modern business life, including the natural environment, corporate finance, transportation, telecommunications, energy, labor relations, and trade practices. Agencies generally derive their power to promulgate regulations from statutes passed by Congress or state legislatures (enabling statutes). Agencies can license companies to carry on certain activities or prohibit them from doing so, lay down codes of conduct, set rates that companies may charge for their services, and supervise various aspects of business.

Agencies have quasi-legislative, quasi-executive and (in many cases) quasi-judicial power. The traditional three branches of government exercise constraint on agency action. To obtain judicial review of such action a petitioner needs standing to sue, and once review is granted the courts give significant deference to the agency's decision.

Exercises

1. What is the common law? Where do the courts get the authority to interpret it and to change it?

2. After World War II ended in 1945, there was an international tribunal at Nuremberg that prosecuted various officials in Germany's Third Reich who had committed "crimes against humanity." Many of them claimed that they were simply "following orders" of Adolf Hitler and his chief lieutenants. What law, if any, have they violated? Watch this video: https://www.ushmm.org/wlc/en/media_fi.php?ModuleId=0&MediaId=5710 .

3. What does *stare decisis* mean, and why is it basic to the common-law legal tradition?

4. The Equal Employment Opportunity Commission seeks data about the racial composition of Terrific Textiles' labor force. Terrific refuses on the grounds that inadvertent disclosure of the numbers might cause certain "elements" to picket its factories. The EEOC takes Terrific to court to get the data. What is the result?

5. In order to police the profession, the state legislature has just passed a law permitting the State Plumbers' Association the power to hold hearings to determine whether a particular plumber has violated the plumbing code of ethics, written by the association. Sam, a plumber, objects to the convening of a hearing when he is accused by Roger, a fellow plumber, of acting unethically by soliciting business from Roger's customers. Sam goes to court, seeking to enjoin the association's disciplinary committee from holding the hearing. What is the result? How would you argue Sam's case? The association's case?

6. Assume that a president of the United States was elected overwhelmingly by pledging to "do away with bureaucrats who interfere in your lives." Discuss which of the following courses he or she may lawfully follow: (a) Fire all incumbent commissioners of federal agencies in order to install new appointees. (b) Demand that all pending regulations being considered by federal agencies be submitted to the White House for review and redrafting, if necessary. (c) Interview potential nominees for agency positions to determine whether their regulatory philosophy is consistent with his or hers.

7. Dewey owned a mine in Wisconsin. He refused to allow Department of Labor agents into the mine to conduct warrantless searches to determine whether previously found safety violations had been corrected. The Federal Mine Safety and Health Act of 1977 authorizes four warrantless inspections per year. Is the provision for warrantless inspections by this agency constitutional?[33]

8. Where does the U.S. Supreme Court get the power to declare acts of Congress unconstitutional?

9. Why are administrative agencies practical necessities for a modern government?

10. If the United States were a parliamentary democracy like Britain, who would be the president?

11. Why was direct democracy adopted by many states (mostly in the early 20th century)? What has happened to direct democracy in the early 21st century?

12. As you may recall from Chapter 3 on the Bill of Rights, in 2010 the U.S. Supreme Court (by a 5–4 decision) determined that corporations' First Amendment rights allows them to make donations to political campaigns, pretty much without limit. What has been the consequence of this decision on U.S. elections? What relationship does this decision have to a discussion (as in Chapter 2) of business ethics and social responsibility?

Self-Test Questions

1. *Marbury v. Madison* (1803), one of the most important cases ever decided by the Supreme Court, established what precedent?

    a. Acts of Congress may be declared unconstitutional by the Court.

    b. Act of the executive may be declared unconstitutional.

    c. High courts may review what lower courts have done to determine if it was legally correct.

    d. Congress may establish administrative agencies to carry out tasks assigned to the executive.

    e. There is no constitutional provision for direct democracy at the federal level.

2. Jane Judge, a California trial court judge, heard a contract dispute case. She established a logical relationship between the case at hand (the "instant case") and a case decided by the state's Supreme Court five years before (the *Smith* case). She compared the facts of the instant case to the *Smith* case, and to the extent the facts were similar, applied the same rule to reach her decision. This is:

    a. deductive reasoning

    b. stare decisis

    c. linear objectivizing

    d. a case of first impression.

3. Moore is a state court judge in Colorado. He also heard a contract-dispute case. But there was no Colorado Supreme Court or court of appeals decision that set forth a rule that could be applied. However, the *Smith* case from California was "very close" on the facts and set forth a rule of law that could be applied in the case before him. What process must Moore follow in considering whether to use *Smith* as precedent? Judge Moore:

    a. is free to decide the case any way he wants, but he may not look at decisions and reasons in similar cases from other states.

    b. must wait for the Colorado legislature and the governor to pass a law that addresses the issues raised in the California case.

    c. must follow the California case if that is the best precedent.

    d. may follow the California case if he believes that it offers the best reasoning for a similar case.

4. Most federal administrative agencies are created by:

    a. an executive order by the president

    b. a Supreme Court decision

    c. the passage of enabling legislation by Congress, signed by the president

    d. subcommittees of Congress.

5. The Federal Trade Commission, like most administrative agencies of the federal government, is part of the:

    a. executive branch of government

    b. legislative branch of government

    c. judicial branch of government

    d. administrative branch of government

6. In the Clean Water Act, Congress sets broad guidelines, but it is the Environmental Protection Agency that proposes rules to regulate industrial discharges. Where do proposed rules finally appear?

    a. Congressional Record

    b. Federal Reporter

    c. Code of Federal Regulations

    d. United States Code

7. The legal basis for all administrative law, including regulations of the Federal Trade Commission, is found in the:

   a. Administrative Procedure Act

   b. U.S. Constitution

   c. commerce clause

   d. they do not appear in any of the above.

8. The Federal Trade Commission, like other administrative agencies, has the power to:

   a. issue regulations that have the force of law

   b. undertake investigations of firms that may have violated FTC regulations

   c. prosecute firms that have violated FTC regulations

   d. all of these

   e. none of these

Self-Test Answers

1. a
2. b
3. d
4. c
5. a
6. c
7. b
8. d

Endnotes

1. For more on statutory interpretation, see this discussion by the Colorado Office of Legislative Legal Services: https://leg.colorado.gov/agencies/office-legislative-legal-services/commonly-applied-rules-statutory-construction.

2. 343 U.S. 579 (1952)

3. 5 U.S. 137 (1803).

4. Lawrence M. Friedman, A History of American Law, (1973), 301-02.

5. Wolff v. Selective Service Local Board No. 16, 372 F. 2d 817 - Court of Appeals, 2nd Circuit 1967

6. See, Frederick G. Kempin, Jr., Historical Introduction to Anglo-American Law, Chapter V, "Custom and Cases," (1973).

7. For an explanation of why 35% of the world population drives on the left, and 65% drives on the right, see https://www.worldstandards.eu/cars/driving-on-the-left/.

8. You can read the 1926 Report by the National Conference on Street and Highway Safety here: https://catalog.hathitrust.org/Record/001348876

9. United States Constitution, Article III, Section 2.

10. See also the discussion of this issue as it applies to environmental law in Chapter 11.

11. The United States Government Manual lists all the federal administrative agencies; access it here: https://www.gpo.gov/fdsys/browse/collection.action?collectionCode=GOVMAN

12. 15 U.S. Code § 45 - Unfair methods of competition unlawful; prevention by Commission

13. Through the beginning of the twenty-first century, however, no overarching principles dictate precisely when, and under what conditions, presidents can remove executive officials. Presidents enjoy broad discretion to fire cabinet secretaries and political appointees within the executive office. The president's freedom to dismiss directors of administrative agencies, however, is usually subject to terms set by Congress. The legislation creating some agencies, such as the President's Commission on Civil Rights and the Environmental Protection Agency, does not place any restrictions on the president's removal powers. For other agencies, however, the enacting legislation establishes certain guidelines. For example, the president can remove members of the Nuclear Regulatory Commission for "inefficiency, neglect of duty, or malfeasance in office," but can remove members of the Consumer Product Safety Commission "for neglect of duty or malfeasance in office but for no other cause." When all is said and done, the president's power to remove executive officials may depend less upon formal principles than it does upon the practice of everyday politics. Congressional leaders, interest groups, and public opinion exert considerable influence over whether, and when, presidents opt to remove executive officials from office, and when they choose to withstand their continued service.

14. https://www.wsba.org/connect-serve/committees-boards-other-groups

15. You can find the Washington state marijuana regulations at http://apps.leg.wa.gov/wac/default.aspx?cite=314 .

16. For the history of how the Federal Communications Commission was told to stop attempting to regulate children's television cartoon shows, see https://www.awn.com/animationworld/dr-toon-when-reagan-met-optimus-prime.

17. https://www.dhs.gov/sites/default/files/publications/DHS   FY18   BIB Final.pdf .

18. National Wildlife Federation v. Norton, 386 F. Supp. 2d 553 (D. Vt. 2005)

19. See https://www.theguardian.com/science/2010/aug/22/pollution-litter-space-edde-darpa

20. United States v. Mead Corporation, 533 U.S. 218 (2001).

21. John Kenneth Galbraith, The Great Crash: 1929 (1997)

22. See, e.g., Timothy J. Burger, The Lobbying Game: Why the Revolving Door Won't Close, Time Magazine, Feb. 16, 2006.

23. Luigi Zinagles: A Capitalism for the People: Recapturing the Lost Genius of American Prosperity (2012)

24. U.S. Const. amend. XIX .

25. Frederic C. Howe, The City: The Hope of Democracy, 171–71 (1967)(1905).

26. See Nat'l Conf. St. Legislatures, http://www.ncsl.org/legislatures-elections/elections/chart-of-the-initiative-states.aspx . Accessed 11-13-15.

27. David Lagasse, Undue Influence: Corporate Political Speech, Power and the Initiative Process, 61 Brook. L. Rev. 1347, 1348 (1995).

28. Joey Peters, Soda Tax Fizzles in Wake of Industry Lobbying, Wash. Post, July 13, 2010. http://www.washingtonpost.com/wp-dyn/content/article/2010/07/13/AR2010071303494.html .

29. Melissa Allison, Costco's $22M for Liquor Initiative Sets Record, *Seattle Times*, October 19, 2011. http://seattletimes.com/html/localnews/2016553052_costco20m.html .

30. The result has been higher liquor prices. See e.g., David Groves, Liquor Privatization's False Promises Already Exposed, *The Stand*, June 5, 2013, http://www.thestand.org/2012/06/liquor-privatizations-false-promises-exposed/; See also Alexis Krell, State Liquor Workers Leaving for other Jobs, *Tacoma News Tribune*, April 16, 2012, http://www.thenewstribune.com/2012/04/   15/2109190/state-liquor-workers-leaving-for.html/ (describing the loss of good-paying state jobs for 700 former state liquor-industry employees); see also John Gillie, Cracking Down on Liquor Theft, *Tacoma News Tribune*, December 16, 2012 (describing the increased theft of liquor from stores), http://www.thenewstribune.com/2012/12/16/2394271/cracking-down-on-liquor-theft.html#storylink=mire-lated).

31. Jim Camden, Spin Control: Money Pours into Initiative Campaigns, Spokesman Review, September 5, 2010, http://www.spokesman.com/blogs/spincontrol/2010/sep/05/money-pours-initiative-campaigns/

32. An "affiant" is one who makes an affidavit, a written statement, which the writer swears under oath is true.

33. Donovan v. Dewey, 452 U.S. 594 (1981).

CHAPTER 5
Introduction to Courts and the Legal Process

Chapter Learning Objectives

After reading this chapter, you should be able to:

1. Describe the two different court systems in the United States, and explain why some cases can be filed in either court system.
2. Explain the importance of subject-matter jurisdiction and personal jurisdiction and know the difference between the two.
3. Understand the various stages of a civil action: from pleadings, to discovery, to trial, and to appeals.
4. Describe two alternatives to litigation: mediation and arbitration.

In the United States, law and government are interdependent. The Constitution establishes the basic framework of government and imposes certain limitations on the powers of government. In turn, the various branches of government are intimately involved in making, enforcing, and interpreting the law. Today, much of the law comes from Congress and the state legislatures. But it is in the courts that legislation is interpreted and prior case law is interpreted and applied.

5.1 State and Federal Court Systems in the United States

Learning Objective

1. Understand the different but complementary roles of state and federal court systems.

Although it is sometimes said that there are two separate U.S. court systems, the reality is more complex. There are, in fact, fifty-two court systems—those of the fifty states, the local court system in the District of Columbia, and the federal court system. At the same time, these are not entirely separate; they all have several points of contact.

State courts cannot disobey federal law, as we saw in examining the Constitution's Supremacy Clause. Moreover, states are required to provide to all persons due process of the law (14th Amendment), and the U.S. Supreme Court decides what due process is. That said, the Framers of the Constitution did not completely strip state courts of their historical omnipotence; state courts are to some extent independent of the federal regime, that's part of the idea of federalism—state courts can act as a check on the federal judicial system, and vice-versa.

State Court Systems

original jurisdiction

The jurisdiction that a judge has to hear witnesses and receive evidence in a trial proceeding.

appellate jurisdiction

The jurisdiction of an appellate court to review whether the parties received a fair trial in accordance with applicable law. Appellate jurisdiction does not include hearing witnesses or receiving new evidence.

limited jurisdiction courts

Courts, either federal or state, whose jurisdiction or authority to hear and decide cases is limited to certain kinds of cases.

The vast majority of civil lawsuits in the United States are filed in state courts. Two aspects of civil lawsuits are common to all state courts: trials and appeals. A court exercising a trial function has **original jurisdiction**—that is, its job is to determine the facts of the case and apply the law to them. A court that hears appeals from the trial court is said to have **appellate jurisdiction**—it must accept the facts as determined by the trial court and limit its review to the lower court's theory of the applicable law. Understanding these last two sentences will help you get a good grip on the important difference between facts and law, and how trial and appellate courts work together.

State Limited Jurisdiction Courts

In most large urban states and many smaller states, there are four and sometimes five levels of courts. The lowest level is that of the **limited jurisdiction courts**. These are usually county or municipal courts with original jurisdiction to hear minor criminal cases (petty assaults, traffic offenses, and breach of peace, among others) and small claims civil cases involving monetary amounts up to a fixed ceiling (up to $25,000 in Tennessee, with limits of $5,000 to $10,000 being most common; and a low of $3,000 in Alabama and Ohio). The advantage of the small claims court is that its procedures are informal, it is often located in a neighborhood outside the business district, it is usually open after business hours, and it is speedy. Lawyers are not necessary to present the case and in some states are not allowed to appear in court (unless, of course, they are litigants—a party to the lawsuit).

Many states have specialized courts that hear only a certain type of case, such as landlord-tenant disputes, divorce cases, or probate of wills. Decisions by judges in specialized courts are usually final, although any party dissatisfied with the outcome may be able to get a new trial in a court of general jurisdiction. Because there has been one trial already, this is known as a trial de novo. It is not an appeal, since the case essentially starts over.

State General Jurisdiction (Trial) Courts

courts of general jurisdiction

A trial court that can hear (almost) any kind of case.

All other civil and criminal cases are heard in the general trial courts, or **courts of general jurisdiction**. These go by a variety of names: superior, circuit, district, or common pleas court (New York confusingly calls its general trial court the Supreme Court). These are the courts in which people seek redress for incidents such as automobile accidents and injuries, or breaches of contract. These state courts also prosecute those accused of murder, rape, robbery, and other serious crimes.

The purpose of a trial is to determine the facts, if the facts are disputed. The factfinder in these general jurisdiction courts is a jury (unless a jury trial is waived, then a judge alone hears the case and finds the facts).

Although courts of general jurisdiction can hear all types of cases, in most states more than half involve family matters (divorce, child custody disputes, and the like). A third were commercial cases, and slightly over 10 percent were devoted to car accident cases and other torts (as discussed in Chapter 7).

State Appellate Courts

The losing party in a general jurisdiction court can almost always appeal to either one or two higher courts. These intermediate appellate courts—usually called **courts of appeal**—have been established in forty states. They do not retry the evidence (they do not find facts), but rather determine whether the trial was conducted in a procedurally correct manner and whether the appropriate law was applied. For example, the appellant (the losing party who appeals) might complain that the judge wrongly instructed the jury on the meaning of the law, or improperly allowed testimony of a particular witness, or misconstrued the law in question. The **appellee** (who won in the lower court) will ask that the **appellant** be denied any relief—usually this means that the appellee wants the lower-court judgment affirmed. The appellate court has several choices: it can affirm, modify, reverse, or reverse and remand the lower court (return the case to the lower court for retrial).

State Supreme Courts

The last type of appeal within the state courts system is to the highest court, the state Supreme Court, which is composed of a single panel of between five and nine judges and is usually located in the state capital. The intermediate appellate courts are usually composed of panels of three judges and are situated in various locations around the state. In a few states, the highest court goes by a different name—in New York, it is known as the court of appeals. In certain cases, appellants to the highest court in a state have the right to have their appeals heard, but more often the state's Supreme Court selects the cases it wishes to hear. For most litigants, the ruling of the state Supreme Court is final. In a relatively small class of cases—those in which federal constitutional claims are made—appeal to the U.S. Supreme Court to issue a writ of *certiorari* (the order issued by a higher court that grants review of the decision of a lower court). In the United States, the Supreme Court's writ of *certiorari* is highly sought by those who would have the court review a state Supreme Court judgment or that of a federal circuit court of appeals. Most of the limited number of cases heard by the Supreme Court are through the granting of a petitioner's appeal to have the writ issued; at least four Justices must support granting the writ for the case to be appealed to the Supreme Court.

The Federal Court System

Federal Courts of Limited ("Specialized") Jurisdiction

Similar to the state system, the federal court system also has—starting at the lowest level—courts of limited jurisdiction[1] (more commonly referred to as "specialized jurisdiction"). These include the quasi-judicial "courts" embedded in administrative agencies (Chapter 4 Section 2), tax courts of various sorts, bankruptcy courts, courts of appeals for Armed Forces Review, Claims Courts (to hear claims brought against the U.S. government), and the Court of International Trade—among others. Judges on these courts are distinguished from members of the federal judiciary (those judges have lifetime tenure). Judges, hearing examiners, administrative law judges, and the attorney can develop special expertise in dealing with arcane administrative regulations.

court of appeals

An intermediary court, between the general trial court and the jurisdiction's supreme or highest court.

appellee

One against whom an appeal is taken.

appellant

One who, dissatisfied with the judgment rendered in a lower court or an Administrative Agency, asks a superior court to review the decision.

Federal General Trial (District) Courts

federal district court

Trial court in the federal judicial system.

The federal judicial system is uniform throughout the United States and consists of three levels (not including the specialized courts noted above). At the first level are the **federal district courts**, which are the trial courts in the federal system. Every state has one or more federal districts; the less populous states have one, and the more populous states (California, Texas, and New York) have four. The federal court with the heaviest commercial docket is the U.S. District Court for the Southern District of New York (Manhattan). There are forty-four district judges and fifteen magistrates in this district. The district judges throughout the United States commonly preside over all federal trials, both criminal and civil.

Federal Courts of Appeal

circuit courts of appeal

The intermediary federal courts of appeals; there are thirteen federal circuit courts (often just "federal courts of appeals").

Cases from the district courts can then be appealed to the **circuit courts of appeal**, of which there are thirteen (Figure 5.1). Each circuit oversees the work of the district courts in several states. For example, the U.S. Court of Appeals for the Second Circuit hears appeals from district courts in New York, Connecticut, and Vermont. The U.S. Court of Appeals for the Ninth Circuit hears appeals from district courts in California, Oregon, Nevada, Montana, Washington, Idaho, Arizona, Alaska, Hawaii, and Guam, and Northern Mariana Islands. The U.S. Court of Appeals for the District of Columbia Circuit hears appeals from the district court in Washington, DC, as well as from numerous federal administrative agencies. The U.S. Court of Appeals for the Federal Circuit, also located in Washington, DC, hears appeals in patent and customs cases. Appeals are usually heard by three-judge panels, but sometimes there will be a rehearing at the court of appeals level, in which case all judges sit to hear the case "en banc."

United States Supreme Court

U.S. Supreme Court

The highest—most authoritative—court in the U.S.

Overseeing all federal courts is the **U.S. Supreme Court**, in Washington, DC. It consists of nine justices—the chief justice and eight associate justices. This number is not constitutionally required; Congress can establish any number. It has been set at nine since after the Civil War. The Supreme Court has selective control over most of its docket. By law, the cases it hears represent only a tiny fraction of the cases that are submitted. In 2008, the Supreme Court had numerous petitions (over 7,000, not including thousands of petitions from prisoners) but heard arguments in only 87 cases. The Supreme Court does not sit in panels. All the justices hear and consider each case together, unless a justice has a conflict of interest and must withdraw from hearing the case.

FIGURE 5.1 The Federal Judicial Circuits

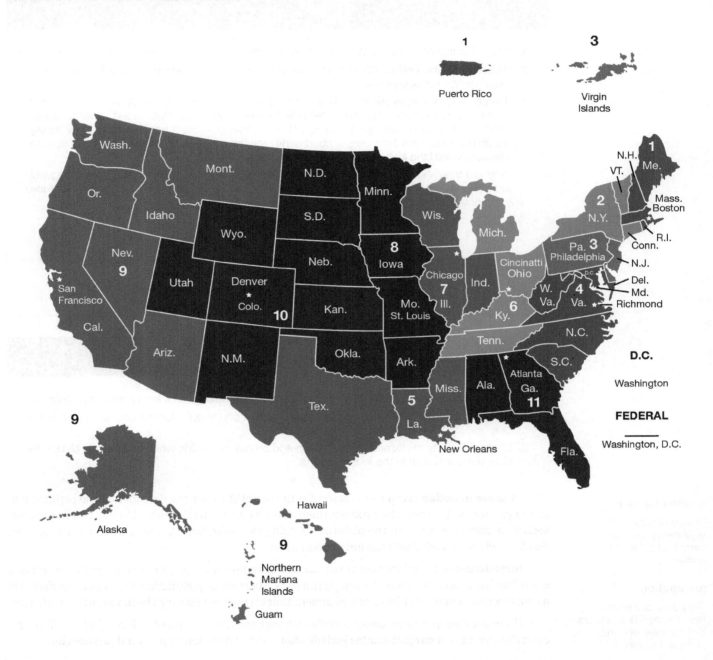

Federal judges—including Supreme Court justices—are nominated by the president and must be confirmed by the Senate. Unlike state judges, who are usually elected and preside for a fixed term of years, federal judges sit for life unless they voluntarily retire or are impeached.

Key Takeaway

The general structure of the state and federal court systems are similar; starting at the lower-level courts, the array is this—courts of limited jurisdiction (or specialized courts), courts of general trial jurisdiction, appeals courts, and supreme courts.

The two court systems—state and federal—are independent, yet also interdependent—for example, the U.S. Supreme Court dictates to states what state legislatures and courts can do consistently with the U.S. Constitution.

Exercises

1. Why all of this complexity? Why isn't there just one court system in the United States?
2. Where does the United States Supreme Court get the authority to dictate to state courts what constitutes due process?
3. James, a New Jersey resident, is sued by Jonah, an Iowa resident. After a trial in which James appears and vigorously defends himself, the Iowa state court awards Jonah $136,750 dollars in damages for his tort claim. In trying to collect from James in New Jersey, Jonah must have the New Jersey court certify the Iowa judgment. Why, under the U.S. Constitution, would the New Jersey court readily do so?
4. Why are there "specialized courts" like divorce court, bankruptcy, tax, and in-house quasi-judicial bodies like the Social Security Administration Appeals Board? Why not just hire more state or federal trial-court judges and let them hear these cases?

5.2 The Issue of Jurisdiction

Learning Objectives

1. Explain the concept of subject-matter jurisdiction and distinguish it from personal jurisdiction.
2. Know which kinds of cases must be heard in state courts only, federal courts only, or either one.
3. Explain diversity of citizenship jurisdiction and be able to decide whether a case is eligible for diversity jurisdiction in the federal courts.

cause of action

The set of facts or the legal theory giving one party the right to sue another.

jurisdiction

The power of a court to hear and decide a case (so that the loser feels the process was fair).

subject-matter jurisdiction

Legal authority to hear and decide a case or controversy.

personal jurisdiction

The ability of a court to exercise judicial power over the person of the defendant.

Once a **cause of action** accrues—a reason for the plaintiff to sue the defendant—the plaintiff will (if the parties can't resolve the problem themselves) want to sue.[2] As noted below and in the next section, a lawsuit starts with the plaintiff notifying the defendant that he, she, or it, is being sued. But first, *where* to sue? That's the jurisdiction issue.

Jurisdiction is a combination of two Latin words: *juris* (law) and *diction* (to speak). Whether a court has the power "to speak the law" is the basic question of jurisdiction. Or, to put it differently, a court cannot render or enforce any judgment unless the court hearing the matter has jurisdiction.

There are two questions about jurisdiction that must be answered before a judge will hear a case: the question of **subject-matter jurisdiction** and the question of **personal jurisdiction**.

Subject-Matter Jurisdiction

We will consider the question of subject-matter jurisdiction first, because that's what judges do. A court must have subject-matter jurisdiction to hear and decide a case, and thus we first address state court subject matter jurisdiction and then federal court subject matter jurisdiction.

State Court Subject-Matter Jurisdiction

In general—with some exceptions—the state courts can hear any kind of case that can be brought up; they are said to have "plenary" (all-encompassing) jurisdiction." That's because state courts have their origins in colonial-era courts when they *had* to hear any kind of case, as there were no other courts available. Because states sanction marriages and divorce, state courts would deal with domestic (family) issues. States deal with birth and death records, so it stands to reason that litigants in paternity suits, probate disputes, and the like would go to state courts. You wouldn't go to the federal building or courthouse to get a marriage license, ask for a divorce, or probate a will—these matters have traditionally been dealt with by the states (and the thirteen original colonies before them).

Matters that have historically been settled in state courts under state law include not only domestic and probate matters but also cases related to torts (like automobile accidents), corporations, partnerships, agency, contracts, property, torts, and commercial dealings generally. You cannot get married or divorced in federal court, because federal courts have no jurisdiction over matters that are historically (and are still exclusively) within the domain of state law. Likewise, with one important exception discussed below, you cannot take a typical auto-accident case to federal court.

The Framers of the Constitution of course intended the state courts to exercise jurisdiction unless it would be inappropriate for them to do so; the Framers wanted to separate power between the state and federal judiciaries. They wanted **federalism** or joint federal-state power.

federalism

The idea that the United States legal and political system would be one of governance shared between the states and the federal government.

Federal Court Subject-Matter Jurisdiction

Federal Courts Are of Limited Jurisdiction

The Constitution, Article III, is clear that federal courts are courts of limited power or jurisdiction. The only kinds of cases federal courts are authorized to deal with have strong federal connections. Here are areas of federal-court jurisdiction:

- **Federal questions**. That is, the case involves federal law, Constitutional questions, military law, admiralty law, cases concerning ambassadors, foreign ministers; also cases where one state sues another state or the federal government, or a person sues the federal government, or the question is about federal taxes, immigration, and so on. Federal courts are empowered to act where the issues raised by the parties have a clear federal connection.

- **Diversity of citizenship**. State court judges are (mostly) elected, and usually want to get re-elected. Therefore, they have a natural tendency to rule in favor of their own citizens or resident as against an "outsider" (because the outsider can't vote anyway). To address this problem of the home-court advantage, the Constitution provides that where the plaintiff(s) and defendant(s) come from different states, the matter may be heard in federal court, even though there is no federal question at all. If a resident of California and a resident of Ohio get into an auto accident, a federal judge in, say, Ohio, could hear the case. Congress has added a wrinkle though: in cases where monetary damages are the paramount issue, the plaintiff's claim must be for at least $75,000.[3] This typically removes the case from a specific county to a more regional pool of jurors and a federal judge not affected by local politics. In 1938 the Supreme Court clarified one vexing point: when a matter is in federal court for diversity, the judge will apply the substantive law of the state where he or she is sitting (procedural law remains federal).

federal questions

For the subject-matter jurisdiction of federal courts, federal questions are matters where litigants appropriately use federal law in their pleadings

diversity of citizenship

A category of civil procedure subject-matter jurisdiction where a federal district court has the power to hear a case when the amount in controversy exceeds $75,000 and the parties are "diverse" in citizenship or state of incorporation (corporations are legal persons).

Exclusive Jurisdiction in Federal Courts

exclusive jurisdiction

Where one court, or one court system, is the sole forum for determination of a particular type of case.

We noted that state courts are of plenary jurisdiction—they can hear any kind of case. Well, not quite. Federal courts have **exclusive jurisdiction** over certain cases. The reason for this comes directly from the Constitution, Article III of which provides the following:

> *The judicial Power shall extend to all Cases, in Law and Equity, arising under this Constitution, the Laws of the United States, and Treaties made, or which shall be made, under their Authority; to all Cases affecting Ambassadors, other public Ministers and Consuls; to all Cases of admiralty and maritime Jurisdiction; to Controversies to which the United States shall be a Party; to Controversies between two or more States; between a State and Citizens of another State; between Citizens of different States; between Citizens of the same State claiming Lands under Grants of different States, and between a State, or the Citizens thereof, and foreign States, Citizens or Subjects.*

Based on the Constitution, we can assemble a list of cases that can *only* be heard in federal courts:

1. *Suits between states.* Cases in which two or more states are a party.
2. *Cases involving ambassadors and other high-ranking public figures.* Cases that are brought by or against foreign ambassadors and other high-ranking public officials.
3. *Federal crimes.* Crimes defined by, or mentioned in, the U.S. Constitution or those defined or punished by federal statute. Such crimes include treason against the United States, piracy, counterfeiting, crimes against the law of nations, and crimes relating to the federal government's authority to regulate interstate commerce. However, most crimes are state matters.
4. *Bankruptcy.* The statutory procedure, usually triggered by insolvency, by which a person is relieved of most debts and undergoes a judicially supervised reorganization or liquidation for the benefit of the person's creditors.
5. *Intellectual-property*: patent, copyright, or trademark.
6. *Admiralty.* The system of laws that has grown out of the practice of admiralty courts—courts that exercise jurisdiction over all maritime contracts, torts, injuries, and offenses.
7. *Antitrust.* Federal laws designed to protect trade and commerce from restraining monopolies, price fixing, and price discrimination.
8. *Securities and banking regulation.* The body of law protecting the public by regulating the registration, offering, and trading of securities and the regulation of banking practices.
9. *Other cases specified by federal statute.* Any other cases specified by a federal statute where Congress declares that federal courts will have exclusive jurisdiction.

Concurrent Jurisdiction

concurrent jurisdiction

Where both state and federal courts could properly take subject-matter jurisdiction over a plaintiff's case.

Concurrent jurisdiction arises where more than one court system could have jurisdiction over a case. When a plaintiff takes a case to state court, it will be because state courts typically hear that kind of case (i.e., there is subject-matter jurisdiction). If the plaintiff's main cause of action comes from a certain state's constitution, statutes, or court decisions, of course the state courts have subject-matter jurisdiction. But state courts can also have subject-matter jurisdiction over certain cases that have only a federal-based cause of action; remember that state courts have plenary jurisdiction unless Article III points to exclusive federal jurisdiction). The Supreme Court has made clear that state courts have **concurrent jurisdiction** of any federal cause of action unless Congress has given exclusive jurisdiction to federal courts.

In short, a case with a federal question can often be heard in *either* state or federal court, and a case that has parties with a diversity of citizenship can be heard in state courts or in federal courts where the tests of complete diversity and amount in controversy are met.

Whether a case will be heard in a state court or moved to a federal court will depend on the parties. If a plaintiff files a case in state trial court where concurrent jurisdiction applies, a defendant may (or may not) ask that the case be removed to federal district court.

Personal Jurisdiction

Personal Jurisdiction in General

The first step in determining whether a court has the authority to hear and decide a case is whether it has subject-matter jurisdiction. If it doesn't, the case is not heard; if it does, the next question is whether the court has personal jurisdiction.

Personal jurisdiction is, fundamentally, a matter of fairness—of due process. The fundamental elements of due process are that the defendant receive *notice* that she is being sued, and that she have *an opportunity to be heard* by a disinterested person, whether that be a judge or a magistrate or some other public official.

Notice that the defendant is being sued, the mechanism by which personal jurisdiction is obtained, is by **service of process**. Most commonly the defendant is personally handed (served) the "**process**" by a disinterested person (often a professional process server). The "process" consists of two items, a **summons** (it says, in effect, "You are being sued! Pay attention and respond on time or you may lose by default!"), and the complaint (which spells out what the plaintiff says the defendant did that caused the plaintiff loss or damages).

Sometimes the defendant is difficult to find, or may deliberately be avoiding the process server—usually a sheriff for state courts and the U.S. Marshall for federal courts. The rules spell out a variety of ways by which individuals and corporations can be served. These include using the U.S. Postal Service's certified mail, or serving someone already designated to receive service of process. A corporation or partnership, for example, is often required by state law to designate a "registered agent" for purposes of getting public notices or receiving a summons and complaint.

Personal Jurisdiction Over Non-Resident Defendants

Suppose you lived in Seattle; your car and a car driven by somebody from Denver collided in Seattle. Suppose, too, that there were serious personal injuries as well as property damage. What would you think if a couple of weeks later you got notice you were being sued in Denver? You'd think, "That's not fair! I've never even *been* to Denver!" The jurisdiction of a state court over a person in the state is clear, but if the plaintiff claims that an out-of-state defendant injured him in some way, must the plaintiff sue where the accident occurred and the defendant resides (Washington State)? It depends, but most often, the answer is yes.

If the Colorado plaintiff believes you are at fault for the Seattle accident, the suit will ordinarily be heard in a Washington state court. But many defendants who do not reside in the state where the lawsuit is filed—and who never go to that state—would rather not be put to the inconvenience of contesting a lawsuit in a distant forum. Fairness—and the due process clause of the Fourteenth Amendment—dictates that nonresidents should not be required to defend lawsuits far from their home base, especially where there is little or no contact or connection between the nonresident and the state where a lawsuit is brought.

personal jurisdiction

The ability of a court with subject-matter jurisdiction to exercise power over a particular defendant or item of property.

service of process

The mechanism of delivering to a defendant the summons and complaint informing him, her, or it that a lawsuit has been started and that failure to respond can result in a loss by default.

process

The summons and complaint that is served on a defendant.

summons

The paper informing a defendant that he or she is being sued and asserts the power of the court to hear and determine the case.

International Shoe v. Washington State

Landmark 1945 U.S. Supreme Court case testing whether states' long-arm statutes comport with the 14th Amendment's due process requirements.

minimum contacts

A nonresident defendant's connections with the forum state (the state where the lawsuit is brought) that are sufficient for jurisdiction over that defendant to be fair.

In 1945 the U.S. Supreme Court weighed in on what constitutes due process for hauling a non-resident defendant into an out-of-state court. In the landmark case **International Shoe v. Washington State**[4] the Supreme Court had these facts: the defendant was an out-of-state corporation that had salesmen living and working (taking orders for shoes) in Washington. The state sued International Shoe in Washington State for failure to pay taxes; the defendant denied Washington's jurisdiction, asserting that the state would have to bring the case where the defendant corporation resided (Missouri). The Supreme Court ruled for Washington. It said that the state's long-arm statute was fair, complying with due process standards. (Each state has a long-arm statute, setting forth what the state believes is fair for taking personal jurisdiction over non-resident defendants. The Court said a non-resident defendant can fairly be sued in a jurisdiction if the defendant has at least "**minimum contacts**" with the forum jurisdiction.

For example, it would be fair for General Motors to be sued in Idaho if an Idaho plaintiff claimed her GM car was defective, because GM does business in Idaho, it advertises there, and expects its cars to be sold and "consumed" there. But, if GM did no business at all in the state, and only had, say, a bank account, that would not constitute "minimum contacts." Similarly, you do not have to go to Japan if you had cause to sue Toyota; that firm has minimum contacts in all U.S. jurisdictions. Driving on the roads within a state is sufficient minimum contacts for exercise of the state's jurisdiction (as to road-related lawsuits, at least). If you, as a Seattle resident, were to bring suit in Washington State against the Colorado driver for an accident in Seattle, the state court would have personal jurisdiction over the non-resident driver.

Venue

venue

The proper geographic place to bring a lawsuit against a defendant.

Before we leave the topic of jurisdiction, there is one final wrinkle to note: the topic of venue.

Suppose that Washington state has subject-matter and personal jurisdiction over the Colorado driver who is negligently driving in Seattle. The state is fairly large geographically, and it matters to the defendant *where* in Washington he may have to appear in court. Every county in Washington or any other state has a district trial court, but if the accident takes place in Seattle and you later move to Spokane, should the trial against the Colorado driver be in Spokane? The plaintiff is not free to pick any county or any city, and the court in Spokane would likely not be the proper venue. **Venue** is the answer to where in the state of Washington the trial should be. State statutes will generally make clear to which court the plaintiff must go (e.g., the county in which the plaintiff resides, the county in which the contract was made or the tort committed, or the county in which the defendant resides or maintains an office). This again is a matter of due process—fairness to the defendant.[5]

Likewise, where there is federal subject-matter and personal jurisdiction, there is still a question of the proper venue for the trial. Where in the very large geographic area of the U.S. will the case be heard—in which courthouse?

Choice of Law and Choice of Forum Clauses

The whole problem of jurisdiction and venue can be pretty easily obviated by contract. Parties to a lawsuit can choose what state (or country) they want the case heard in; they choose what law will apply. In a series of cases, the Supreme Court has made clear that U.S. courts will honor contractual choices of parties in a lawsuit. Suppose the parties to a contract wind up in court arguing over the application of the contract's terms. If the parties are from two different states, the judge may have difficulty determining which law to apply.[6] But if the contract says that a particular state's law will be applied if there is a dispute, then ordinarily the judge will apply that state's law as a rule of decision in the case. (The same rule applies in international contracts.)

Ordinarily, a **choice-of-law clause** will be accompanied by a **choice-of-forum clause**. In a choice-of-forum clause, the parties in the contract specify which court they will go to in the event of a dispute arising under the terms of contract. For example, Harold (a resident of Virginia) rents a car from Alamo at the Denver International Airport. He does not look at the fine print on the contract. He also waives all collision and other insurance that Alamo offers at the time of his rental. While driving back from the Telluride Bluegrass Festival, he has an accident in Idaho Springs, Colorado, and his rented Nissan Altima is badly damaged. On returning to Virginia, he would like to settle up with Alamo, but his insurance company and Alamo cannot come to terms. He realizes, however, that he has agreed to hear the dispute with Alamo in a specific court in San Antonio, Texas. In the absence of fraud or bad faith, any court in the United States is likely to uphold the choice-of-forum clause and require Harold (or his insurance company) to litigate in San Antonio, Texas.

> **choice-of-law clause**
>
> A term in a contract that specifies what law will be used to interpret it.
>
> **choice-of-forum clause**
>
> A term in a contract specifying what court will hear a dispute.

Case

State Jurisdiction Over Non-Resident Defendants

> *Burger King Corp. v. Rudzewicz*
>
> 471 U.S. 462 (U.S. Supreme Court, 1985)

> **Burger King Corp. v. Rudzewicz**
>
> U.S. Supreme Court (1985) case examining the extent to which the Due Process Clause allows a state to exercise jurisdiction over non-resident defendants.

[John Rudzewicz was a resident of Michigan; he and Brian MacShara started a Burger King franchise in the Drayton Plains, Michigan, area in 1979. The franchise application (the contract) had been approved at Burger King's offices in Miami, and MacShara attended the Miami Burger King University to learn how to run the business. The partners bought $165,000 of restaurant equipment from Davmore Industries, a Burger King corporate division located in Miami (about $640,000 in 2019 dollars).

The franchise agreement required the defendants to remit franchise fees and royalties to Burger King's Florida headquarters. The Michigan economy soured and the defendants could not pay their franchise fees. Burger King sued in the Florida Federal District Court in Miami in a diversity of citizenship case, claiming breach of contract and infringement of Burger King's trade and service marks after the defendants received notice to terminate the franchise. They continued to use Burger King's trademarks and confidential business information after receiving notice of termination, and Florida-based Burger King sued in Florida Federal District Court in a diversity of citizenship action to establish termination of the franchise. Rudzewicz challenged the court's personal jurisdiction. The District Court (applying Florida law) ruled for Burger King, holding that Florida had jurisdiction based on the state's long-arm statute that extended state jurisdiction to anyone breaching a contract in the state. The defendants appealed; the 11th Circuit reversed, holding that Florida's exercise of jurisdiction was a violation of the 14th Amendment's due process clause.]

Brennan, J.

The Due Process Clause protects an individual's liberty interest in not being subject to the binding judgments of a forum with which he has established no meaningful "contacts, ties, or relations." [Citation: *International Shoe Co. v. Washington*.] By requiring that individuals have "fair warning that a particular activity may subject them to the jurisdiction of a foreign sovereign," [Citation]. The Due Process Clause "gives a degree of predictability to the legal system that allows potential defendants to structure their primary conduct with some minimum assurance as to where that conduct will and will not render them liable to suit," [Citation, (1980)].

Where a forum seeks to assert specific jurisdiction over an out-of-state defendant who has not consented to suit there, this "fair warning" requirement is satisfied if the defendant has "purposefully directed" his activities at residents of the forum, and the litigation results from alleged injuries that "arise out of or relate to" those activities, Thus "the forum State does not exceed its powers under the Due Process Clause if it asserts personal jurisdiction over a corporation that delivers its products into the stream of commerce with the expectation that they will be purchased by consumers in the forum State" and those products subsequently injure forum consumers [Citation]. Similarly, a publisher who distributes magazines in a distant State may fairly be held accountable in that forum for damages resulting there from an allegedly defamatory story. [Citation.] * * *

The constitutional touchstone remains whether the defendant purposefully established "minimum contacts" in the forum State. * * * In defining when it is that a potential defendant should "reasonably anticipate" out-of-state litigation, the Court frequently has drawn from the reasoning of *Hanson v. Denckla*, 357 U.S. 235, 253 (1958):

> The unilateral activity of those who claim some relationship with a nonresident defendant cannot satisfy the requirement of contact with the forum State. The application of that rule will vary with the quality and nature of the defendant's activity, but it is essential in each case that there be some act by which the defendant purposefully avails itself of the privilege of conducting activities within the forum State, thus invoking the benefits and protections of its laws.

This "purposeful availment" requirement ensures that a defendant will not be hauled into a jurisdiction solely as a result of "random," "fortuitous," or "attenuated" contacts, or of the "unilateral activity of another party or a third person," [Citations]. Jurisdiction is proper, however, where the contacts proximately result from actions by the defendant himself that create a "substantial connection" with the forum State. [Citations.] Thus where the defendant "deliberately" has engaged in significant activities within a State, or has created "continuing obligations" between himself and residents of the forum, he manifestly has availed himself of the privilege of conducting business there, and because his activities are shielded by "the benefits and protections" of the forum's laws it is presumptively not unreasonable to require him to submit to the burdens of litigation in that forum as well. * * *

In this case, no physical ties to Florida can be attributed to Rudzewicz other than MacShara's brief training course in Miami. Rudzewicz did not maintain offices in Florida and, for all that appears from the record, has never even visited there. Yet this franchise dispute grew directly out of "a contract which had a substantial connection with that State." Eschewing the option of operating an independent local enterprise, Rudzewicz deliberately "reach[ed] out beyond" Michigan and negotiated with a Florida corporation for the purchase of a long-term franchise and the manifold benefits that would derive from affiliation with a nationwide organization. Upon approval, he entered into a carefully structured 20-year relationship that envisioned continuing and wide-reaching contacts with Burger King in Florida. In light of Rudzewicz' voluntary acceptance of the long-term and exacting regulation of his business from Burger King's Miami headquarters, the "quality and nature" of his relationship to the company in Florida can in no sense be viewed as "random," "fortuitous," or "attenuated." Rudzewicz' refusal to make the contractually required payments in Miami, and his continued use of Burger King's trademarks and confidential business information after his termination, caused foreseeable injuries to the corporation in Florida. For these reasons it was, at the very least, presumptively reasonable for Rudzewicz to be called to account there for such injuries.

Because Rudzewicz established a substantial and continuing relationship with Burger King's Miami headquarters, received fair notice from the contract documents and the course of dealing that he might be subject to suit in Florida, and has failed to demonstrate how jurisdiction in that forum would otherwise be fundamentally unfair, we conclude that the District Court's exercise of jurisdiction pursuant to [the Florida long-arm statute] did not offend due process. The judgment of the Court of Appeals is accordingly reversed, and the case is remanded for further proceedings consistent with this opinion.

Case Questions

1. Why did Burger King sue in Florida rather than in Michigan?
2. If Florida has a long-arm statute that tells Florida courts that it may exercise personal jurisdiction over someone like Rudzewicz, why is the court talking about the due process clause?
3. Why is this case in federal court rather than in a Florida state court?
4. How does this case help explain what is "minimum contacts" as articulated in *International Shoe*?
5. If this case had been filed in state court in Florida, would Rudzewicz be required to come to Florida? Explain.
6. Why would Burger King sue to stop the defendants from using the company trade and service marks after their franchise was terminated?

Key Takeaway

There are two court systems in the United States. It is important to know which system—the state court system or the federal court system—has the power to hear and decide a particular case.

A court must have (1) jurisdiction over the subject matter of the case, and it must have (2) personal jurisdiction over the person of the defendant. As to subject matter, state courts have plenary (broad) jurisdiction (with some constitutional restrictions); federal courts are of limited jurisdiction—they have the power to hear federal-related cases. And sometimes either state or federal courts have jurisdiction concurrently.

For in-state defendants, personal jurisdiction is no problem. For out-of-state defendants, the Constitution compels an inquiry to make sure that no court extends its reach unfairly. A person is subject to a state's jurisdiction (via its long-arm statute) if she, he, or it has some minimum contact with the state. What is "minimum contacts" is up to the U.S. Supreme Court to decide, because it is an issue of Constitutional due process.

Once jurisdiction is established, it is necessary to determine where within the jurisdiction—what specific city—the case should be brought. Rules governing venue dictate this.

Contracting parties can put into their agreements choice-of-law and choice-of-forum terms and these will be recognized as binding by courts.

Exercises

1. The Constitution specifies that federal courts have exclusive jurisdiction over admiralty claims. Mr. and Mrs. Shute have a claim against Carnival Cruise Lines for the negligence of the cruise line. Mrs. Shute sustained injuries as a result of the company's negligence. Mr. and Mrs. Shute live in the state of Washington. Can they bring their claim in state court? Must they bring their claim in federal court?
2. Congress passed Title VII of the Civil Rights Act of 1964. In Title VII, employers are required not to discriminate against employees on the basis of race, color, sex, religion, or national

origin. In passing Title VII, Congress did not require plaintiffs to file only in federal courts. That is, Congress made no statement in Title VII that federal courts had "exclusive jurisdiction" over Title VII claims. Mrs. Harris wishes to sue Forklift Systems, Inc. of Nashville, Tennessee, for sexual harassment under Title VII. She has gone through the Equal Employment Opportunity Commission process and has a right-to-sue letter, which is required before a Title VII action can be brought to court. Can she file a complaint that will be heard by a state court?

3. Mrs. Harris fails to go to the Equal Employment Opportunity Commission to get her right-to-sue letter against Forklift Systems, Inc. She therefore does not have a viable Title VII cause of action against Forklift. She does, however, have her rights under Tennessee's equal employment statute and various court decisions from Tennessee courts regarding sexual harassment. Forklift is incorporated in Tennessee and has its principal place of business in Nashville. Mrs. Harris is also a citizen of Tennessee. Explain why, if she brings her employment discrimination and sexual harassment lawsuit in a federal court, her lawsuit will be dismissed for lack of subject-matter jurisdiction.

4. The Robinsons bought a new Audi from Seaway Volkswagen, a car dealer in New York. While traveling through Oklahoma en route to Arizona, the Audi was rear-ended and the gas tank exploded, causing the Robinsons serious injury. They sued in Oklahoma. Now, suppose Mr. and Mrs. Robinson find in the original paperwork with Seaway Volkswagen that there is a contractual agreement with a provision that says "all disputes arising between buyer and Seaway Volkswagen will be litigated, if at all, in the county courts of Westchester County, New York." Will the Oklahoma court take personal jurisdiction over Seaway Volkswagen, or will it require the Robinsons to litigate their claim in New York?

5.3 Trial Procedure

Learning Objectives

1. Explain the function of these two pleadings: complaint and answer.
2. Understand how a lawsuit can be dismissed prior to trial.
3. Recognize the purpose and types of discovery before a trial.
4. Know something of the pre-trial, trial, and post-trial stages of litigation.

The purpose of a trial is to determine the facts of the case (we discussed in Chapter 4 who determines what the law is). If there is no factual dispute and no significant question as to what the law is, a motion for summary judgment is appropriate. If that fails, and following a pre-trial conference, the trial begins.

Initial Pleadings and Motions to Dismiss

After the cause of action accrues, and if the matter can't be settled, a lawsuit commences[7] with the filing of pleadings, defendants often have grounds for asking the court to dismiss the matter before witnesses are called.

Pleadings

The first papers filed in a lawsuit are called the pleadings.[8] These include the plaintiff's **complaint** and then (usually after thirty days or more) the **answer** from the defendant. The answer may be coupled with a counterclaim against the plaintiff. (In effect, the defendant becomes a plaintiff for the claims she has against the original plaintiff.) The plaintiff may reply to any counterclaim by the defendant. By comparing the answer to the complaint, it is possible to determine what issues of fact are in dispute (if the defendant's answer admits an allegation made in the complaint, obviously the plaintiff doesn't have to prove that allegation).

State and federal rules of civil procedure require that the complaint must state the nature of the plaintiff's claim, the jurisdiction of the court, and the nature of the relief that is being asked for (usually an award of money, but sometimes an injunction, or a declaration of legal rights). In an answer, the defendant will often deny all the allegations of the complaint or will admit to certain of its allegations and deny others.

Motions to Dismiss Before Trial

After the initial exchange of pleadings, a trial may begin. Or it may not. Or it may begin and be cut short. One party may request that the judge dismiss the case, or decide it outright without the jury weighing in at all. These are the ways:

1. Dismissal on Default Judgment. A case can be decided on the pleadings alone. If the defendant fails to answer the complaint, the court can enter a **default judgment**, awarding the plaintiff what he seeks.
2. Dismissal for **failure to state a claim upon which relief can be granted**. The defendant can move to dismiss the complaint on the grounds that the plaintiff failed to "state a claim on which relief can be granted," or on the basis that there is no subject-matter jurisdiction for the court chosen by the plaintiff, or on the basis that there is no personal jurisdiction over the defendant. The defendant is saying, in effect, that even if all the plaintiff's allegations are true, they do not amount to a legal claim that can be heard by the court. For example, a claim that the defendant induced a woman to stop dating the plaintiff (a so-called "alienation of affections cause of action" that was viable in many Eastern common law states) is no longer actionable in U.S. state courts, and any court will dismiss the complaint without any further proceedings. (This type of dismissal is still called a "demurrer" in some states.)
3. Motion for **summary judgment**. Sometimes a judgment may be granted upon a party's motion when the pleadings and evidence show that there is no issue of material fact and that the party is entitled to judgment in its favor as a matter of law.

Discovery

If the matter is not dismissed and there is a factual dispute, the case will usually involve some degree of **discovery**, where each party tries to get as much information out of the other party as the rules allow. Until the 1940s, when discovery became part of civil procedure rules, a lawsuit was frequently a game in which each party hid as much information as possible and tried to surprise the other party in court.

Beginning with a change in the Federal Rules of Civil Procedure adopted by the Supreme Court in 1938 and subsequently followed by many of the states, the parties are entitled to learn the facts of the case before trial. The basic idea is to help the parties determine what the evidence might be,

---

complaint

The plaintiff's document that details what the defendant did to harm the plaintiff—the plaintiff's "beef" against the defendant.

answer

The defendant's response to the plaintiff's complaint, admitting or denying the plaintiff's allegations.

default judgment

Judgment entered against a party who has failed to defend against a claim brought by another party.

failure to state a claim upon which relief can be granted

Dismissal of a lawsuit because the complaint failed to properly allege one or more of the required elements of an action.

summary judgment

A judgment granted upon a party's motion when the evidence shows there is no issue of material fact and that the party is entitled to judgment in its favor as a matter of law.

discovery

The process in U.S. litigation by which parties to a lawsuit can find out (discover) in advance of any trial what facts and evidence the other side will present at trial.

who the potential witnesses are, and what specific issues are relevant. Discovery can proceed by several methods.

- Interrogatories. A party may serve an interrogatory on the adversary. This is a written request for answers to specific questions. (For example: "In the four hours before your car and the plaintiffs car collided in the intersection, had you consumed any alcohol or cannabis?")
- Deposition. A deposition is a live question-and-answer session at which the witness answers, under oath, questions put to him by one of the parties' lawyers. His answers are recorded verbatim and may be used at trial.
- Inspection of books and documents. Each party is also entitled to inspect books, documents, records, and other physical items in the possession of the other. This is a broad right, as it is not limited only to evidence that would be relevant and admissible at trial. Discovery of physical evidence means that a plaintiff may inspect a company's accounts, customer lists, assets, profit-and-loss statements, balance sheets, engineering and quality-control reports, sales reports, and virtually any other document.

The lawyers, not the court, run the discovery process. For example, one party simply makes a written demand, stating the time at which the deposition will take place or the type of documents it wishes to inspect and make copies of. A party unreasonably resisting discovery methods (whether depositions, written interrogatories, or requests for documents) can be challenged, however, and judges are often brought into the process to push reluctant parties to make more disclosures or to protect a party from irrelevant or unreasonable discovery requests. For example, the party receiving the discovery request can apply to the court for a protective order if it can show that the demand is for privileged material (e.g., a party's lawyers' records are not open for inspection) or that the demand was made to harass the opponent.

In complex cases between companies, the discovery of documents can run into tens of millions of pages and can take years. Depositions can consume days or even weeks of a business executive's time. The whole process can be very expensive, and demands for discovery can be used to harass the other side.

The Pretrial and Trial Phases

Litigation has several components, including pre-trial and trial phases.

Pretrial Phase

Motion for summary judgment. After discovery, one party may believe that there is no triable issue of law or fact for the court to consider and may file a motion with the court for summary judgment—discussed just above. Unless there clearly is no triable issue of law or fact, the judge will generally deny a summary judgment motion, because that ends the case at the trial level; it is a "final order" in the case that tells the plaintiff "no" and leaves no room to bring another lawsuit against the defendant for that particular set of facts.[9] If the plaintiff successfully appeals a summary judgment motion, the case will come back to the trial court.

Settlement conference. Prior to the trial, the judge may also convene the parties in an effort to investigate the possibilities of settlement. Usually, the judge will probe the strengths and weaknesses of each party's case with the attorneys, and sometimes make probing inquiries to the attorney for a party whose case appears weak. The attorney may realize that the opposing party's offer of settlement is a better risk than going to trial, and could recommend that to her client. Ultimately, though, the client decides whether to take the risk of trial, or settle.

Trial Phase

Jury Selection

At **trial**, the first order of business is to select a jury. (In a civil case of any consequence, either party can request one, based on the Sixth Amendment to the U.S. Constitution; in criminal cases a defendant is entitled to a jury, but may waive the right.) The judge, and sometimes the lawyers, are permitted to question the jurors to be sure that they are unbiased. This questioning is known as the **voir dire** (pronounced vwahr-DEER). This is an important process, and a great deal of thought goes into selecting the jury, especially in high-profile cases. A jury panel can be as few as six persons, or as many as twelve, with alternates selected and sitting in court in case one of the jurors is unable to continue. In a long trial, having alternates is essential; even in shorter trials, most courts will have at least two alternate jurors.

In both criminal and civil trials, each side has opportunities to challenge potential jurors for cause. Challenges to jurors are of two types. **Challenges for cause** arise where there is good reason to think a juror is biased, or has pre-judged the matter. The judge, at her discretion, can either accept the for-cause reason or reject it.

The second challenge to a juror is a **peremptory challenge**; it results in the exclusion of a potential juror without the need for any reason or explanation (but it cannot be used to exclude a juror on account of race, religion, sex, or ethnicity). A trial attorney may develop a sixth sense about a potential juror and, consulting the client, decide to use a peremptory challenge to avoid having that juror on the panel. The number of peremptory challenges is limited.

Opening Statement, Evidence, Examination and Cross-Examination

After the jury is sworn and seated, the plaintiff's lawyer makes an opening statement, laying out the nature of the plaintiff's claim, the facts of the case as the plaintiff sees them, and the evidence that the lawyer will present. The defendant's lawyer may also make an opening statement or may reserve his right to do so at the end of the plaintiff's case.

The plaintiff's lawyer then calls witnesses and presents the physical evidence that is relevant to her proof. The direct testimony at trial is usually far from a smooth narration. The rules of evidence (that govern the kinds of testimony and documents that may be introduced at trial) and the question-and-answer format tend to make the presentation of evidence choppy and difficult to follow.

Anyone who has watched an actual televised trial or a television melodrama featuring a trial scene will appreciate the nature of the trial itself: witnesses are asked questions about a number of issues that may or may not be related, the opposing lawyer will frequently object to the question or the form in which it is asked, and the jury may be sent from the room while the lawyers argue at the bench before the judge.

After direct testimony of each witness is over, the opposing lawyer may conduct **cross-examination.** This is a crucial constitutional right; in criminal cases it is preserved in the Constitution's Sixth Amendment (the right to confront one's accusers in open court). The formal rules of direct testimony are then relaxed, and the cross-examiner may probe the witness more informally, asking questions that may not seem immediately relevant. This is when the opposing attorney may become harsh, casting doubt on a witness's credibility, trying to trip her up and show that the answers she gave are false or not to be trusted. This use of cross-examination, along with the requirement that the witness must respond to questions that are at all relevant to the questions raised by the case, distinguishes common-law courts from those of authoritarian regimes around the world.

trial

That part of litigation in which the parties present their case to the factfinder (judge or jury) and the various procedures related to that.

voir dire

The questioning of potential jurors before trial by lawyers or the judge to assure their apparent suitability to serve fairly.

challenge for cause

A trial-lawyer's request that a juror be dismissed from the jury pool because he or she cannot be impartial regarding the matter at hand.

peremptory challenge

A request that a juror be dismissed from the jury pool without giving any reason.

cross-examination

The questioning of one party's witness by the other's attorney, usually to cast doubt on the witness's credibility.

Following cross-examination, the plaintiff's lawyer may then question the witness again: this is called redirect examination and is used to demonstrate that the witness's original answers were accurate and to show that any implications otherwise, suggested by the cross-examiner, were unwarranted. The cross-examiner may then engage the witness in re-cross-examination, and so on. The process usually stops after cross-examination or redirect.

During the trial, the judge's chief responsibility is to see that the trial is fair to both sides. One big part of that responsibility is to rule on the admissibility of evidence. A judge may rule that a particular question is out of order—that is, not relevant or appropriate—or that a given document is irrelevant. Where the attorney is convinced that a particular witness, a particular question, or a particular document (or part thereof) is critical to her case, she may preserve an objection to the court's ruling by saying "exception," in which case the court stenographer will note the exception; on appeal, the attorney may cite any number of exceptions as adding up to the lack of a fair trial for her client and may request a court of appeals to order a retrial.[10]

At the end of the plaintiff's case, the defendant presents his case, following the same procedure just outlined. The plaintiff is then entitled to present rebuttal witnesses, if necessary, to deny or argue with the evidence the defendant has introduced. The defendant in turn may present "surre-buttal" witnesses.

Post-Examination Motions, Closing Arguments, Jury Instructions, and Verdict

directed verdict

A verdict decided by the judge without advice from the jury.

At the close of the plaintiff's case, or—more often—when all testimony has been presented, either party may ask the judge for a **directed verdict**. A judge will direct a verdict if there is no real issue of fact for reasonable jurors to consider and if the law as applied to the facts in evidence clearly favors the party who requests the directed verdict. For example, the plaintiff alleges that the defendant owes him money and introduces a signed promissory note. The defendant cannot show that the note is invalid. The defendant must lose the case unless he can show that the debt has been paid or otherwise discharged. Directed verdicts are not usually granted, since it is the jury's job to determine the facts in dispute.

If the judge refuses to grant a directed verdict, each lawyer will then present a closing argument to the jury (or, if there is no jury, to the judge alone). The closing argument is used to tie up the loose ends, as the attorney tries to bring together various seemingly unrelated facts into a story that will make clear and convincing sense.

jury instructions

The judge's explanation to the jury of the law they should apply after they find the facts of the case.

After closing arguments, the judge will give **jury instructions** to explain the law as it relates to the issues they are considering and to tell the jurors what facts they must determine if they are to give a verdict for one party or the other. Each lawyer will have prepared a set of written instructions that she hopes the judge will give to the jury. These will be tailored to advance her client's case. Many a verdict has been overturned on appeal because a trial judge has wrongly instructed the jury. The judge will carefully determine which instructions to give and often will use a set of pattern instructions provided by the state bar association or the supreme court of the state. These pattern jury instructions are usually safe because they are patterned after language that appellate courts have used previously, and appellate courts are less likely to find reversible error in the instructions.

After all instructions are given, the jury will retire to a private room and discuss the case and the answers requested by the judge for as long as it takes to reach a **verdict**. Criminal cases require a unanimous verdict; civil cases usually require that ten out of twelve agree. If the jury cannot reach a decision, this is called a **hung jury**, and the case will have to be retried. When a jury does reach a verdict, it delivers it in court with both parties and their lawyers present. The jury is then discharged, and control over the case returns to the judge. (If there is no jury, the judge will usually announce in a written opinion his findings of fact and how the law applies to those facts. Juries just announce their verdicts and do not state their reasons for reaching them.)

Post-Trial Motions

After the verdict, the losing party can still try to get a better result. The lawyers for the losing side may ask the court for a **judgment notwithstanding the verdict** ("j.n.o.v."), saying, in effect, "Your honor, no disrespect to the jury, but its verdict is clearly and palpably unreasonable. We ask the court to change it." Judges are reluctant to second-guess juries (that would kind of destroy the jury system), but sometimes juries are moved by passion or prejudice; sometimes they come up with off-the-wall verdicts that would not withstand an appeal. *Ferlito v. Johnson & Johnson* (below) illustrates the judgment n.o.v. process in a case where the judge allowed the case to go to a jury that was apparently overly sympathetic to the plaintiffs.

Case

Judgment Notwithstanding the Verdict (Judgment N.O.V.)

Ferlito v. Johnson & Johnson Products, Inc.

771 F. Supp. 196 (U.S. District Ct., Eastern District of Michigan, 1991)

Gadola, J.

Plaintiffs Susan and Frank Ferlito, husband and wife, attended a Halloween party in 1984 dressed as Mary (Mrs. Ferlito) and her little lamb (Mr. Ferlito). Mrs. Ferlito had constructed a lamb costume for her husband by gluing cotton batting manufactured by defendant Johnson & Johnson Products ("JJP") to a suit of long underwear. She had also used defendant's product to fashion a headpiece, complete with ears. The costume covered Mr. Ferlito from his head to his ankles, except for his face and hands, which were blackened with Halloween paint. At the party Mr. Ferlito attempted to light his cigarette by using a butane lighter. The flame passed close to his left arm, and the cotton batting on his left sleeve ignited. Plaintiffs sued defendant for injuries they suffered from burns which covered approximately one-third of Mr. Ferlito's body.

Following a jury verdict entered for plaintiffs November 2, 1989, the Honorable Ralph M. Freeman entered a judgment for plaintiff Frank Ferlito in the amount of $555,000 [about $1.2 million in 2018 dollars] and for plaintiff Susan Ferlito in the amount of $70,000 [about $139,000 in 2018 dollars]. Judgment was entered November 7, 1989. Subsequently, on November 16, 1989, defendant JJP filed a timely motion for judgment notwithstanding the verdict pursuant to Fed.R.Civ.P. 50(b) or, in the alternative, for a new trial. Plaintiffs filed their response to defendant's motion December 18, 1989; and defendant filed a reply January 4, 1990. Before reaching a decision on this motion, Judge Freeman died. The case was reassigned to this court April 12, 1990.

---

verdict

The decision announced by the spokesperson for a jury following trial.

hung jury

A jury that fails to arrive at the necessary consensus to find guilt (in a criminal case) or liability (in a civil case).

judgment notwithstanding the verdict

A motion arguing that no reasonable jury could reach the verdict that the jury in this case did, and requesting that the verdict be reversed or changed in favor of the other side. From the Latin, "*non obstante veredicto.*"

Ferlito v. Johnson & Johnson Products, Inc.

Federal District Court case, 1991, examining when a court may disregard a jury verdict and issue a judgment notwithstanding the verdict (and taking up some issues of product liability).

Motion for judgment notwithstanding the verdict ["j.n.o.v."].

Defendant JJP filed two motions for a directed verdict, the first on October 27, 1989, at the close of plaintiffs' proofs, and the second on October 30, 1989, at the close of defendant's proofs. Judge Freeman denied both motions without prejudice. Judgment for plaintiffs was entered November 7, 1989; and defendant's instant motion, filed November 16, 1989, was filed in a timely manner.

The standard for determining whether to grant a j.n.o.v. is identical to the standard for evaluating a motion for directed verdict [Citation]:

> *In determining whether the evidence is sufficient, the trial court may neither weigh the evidence, pass on the credibility of witnesses nor substitute its judgment for that of the jury. Rather, the evidence must be viewed in the light most favorable to the party against whom the motion is made, drawing from that evidence all reasonable inferences in his favor. If after reviewing the evidence . . . the trial court is of the opinion that reasonable minds could not come to the result reached by the jury, then the motion for j.n.o.v. should be granted.*

To establish a *prima facie case* that a manufacturer's breach of its duty to warn was a proximate cause of an injury sustained, a plaintiff must present evidence that the product would have been used differently had the proffered ["proffered" means to put before a person something for acceptance] warnings been given.[11] In the absence of evidence that a warning would have prevented the harm complained of by altering the plaintiff's conduct, the failure to warn cannot be deemed a proximate cause of the plaintiff's injury as a matter of law. [In accordance with procedure in a diversity of citizenship case such as this one, the court cites Michigan case law as the basis for its legal interpretation.] * * *

A manufacturer has a duty "to warn the purchasers or users of its product about dangers associated with intended use." Conversely, a manufacturer has no duty to warn of a danger arising from an unforeseeable misuse of its product. [Citation] Thus, whether a manufacturer has a duty to warn depends on whether the use of the product and the injury sustained by it are foreseeable. [Citations.] Whether a plaintiff's use of a product is foreseeable is a legal question to be resolved by the court. [Citation.] Whether the resulting injury is foreseeable is a question of fact for the jury.[12] [Citations.]

In the instant action no reasonable jury could find that JJP's failure to warn of the flammability of cotton batting was a proximate cause of plaintiffs' injuries because plaintiffs failed to offer any evidence to establish that a flammability warning on JJP's cotton batting would have dissuaded them from using the product in the manner that they did.

Plaintiffs repeatedly stated in their response brief that plaintiff Susan Ferlito testified that "she would never again use cotton batting to make a costume." * * * However, a review of the trial transcript reveals that plaintiff Susan Ferlito never testified that she would never again use cotton batting to make a costume. More importantly, the transcript contains no statement by plaintiff Susan Ferlito that a flammability warning on defendant JJP's product would have dissuaded her from using the cotton batting to construct the costume in the first place. At oral argument counsel for plaintiffs conceded that there was no testimony during the trial that either plaintiff Susan Ferlito or her husband, plaintiff Frank J. Ferlito, would have acted any different if there had been a flammability warning on the product's package. The absence of such testimony is fatal to plaintiffs' case; for without it, plaintiffs have failed to prove proximate cause, one of the essential elements of their negligence claim.

In addition, both plaintiffs testified that they knew that cotton batting burns when it is exposed to flame. Susan Ferlito testified that she knew at the time she purchased the cotton batting that it would burn if exposed to an open flame. Frank Ferlito testified that he knew at the time he appeared at the Halloween party that cotton batting would burn if exposed to an open flame. His additional testimony that he would not have intentionally put a flame to the cotton batting shows that he recognized the risk of injury of which he claims JJP should have warned. Because both plaintiffs were already aware of the danger, a warning by JJP would have been superfluous. Therefore, a reasonable jury could not have found that JJP's failure to provide a warning was a proximate cause of plaintiffs' injuries.

The evidence in this case clearly demonstrated that neither the use to which plaintiffs put JJP's product nor the injuries arising from that use were foreseeable. Susan Ferlito testified that the idea for the costume was hers alone. As described on the product's package, its intended uses are for cleansing, applying medications, and infant care. Plaintiffs' showing that the product may be used on occasion in classrooms for decorative purposes failed to demonstrate the foreseeability of an adult male encapsulating himself from head to toe in cotton batting and then lighting up a cigarette.ORDER

It is ordered that defendant JJP's motion for judgment notwithstanding the verdict is GRANTED.

And that the judgment entered November 2, 1989, is set aside.

The clerk will enter a judgment in favor of the defendant JJP.

Case Questions

1. The opinion focuses on proximate cause. As we will see in Chapter 7, a negligence case cannot be won unless the plaintiff shows that the defendant has breached a duty and that the defendant's breach has actually and proximately caused the damage complained of. What, exactly, is the alleged breach of duty by the defendant here?
2. What was the defect in the plaintiffs' case that caused the verdict to be tossed?
3. Explain why Judge Gadola reasoned that JJP had no duty to warn in this case. After this case, would it then have a duty to warn, knowing that someone might use its product in this way?
4. When would it be appropriate for a judge to disregard the jury's verdict and render a judgment notwithstanding the verdict?

Key Takeaway

The purpose of a trial is to determine the facts. Many cases never get to trial. They are disposed of by motions to dismiss or are settled after extensive discovery makes clear to the parties the strengths and weaknesses of the parties to the dispute.

Trial procedures involve jury selection, opening statements, evidence gathered from examination and cross examination of witnesses, and presentation of other items of evidence (photos, documentation, etc.).

After evidence is presented, motions may be made for directed verdicts; after a jury verdict, motions may be made for judgment notwithstanding the verdict.

Exercises

1. Under contributory negligence, the negligence of any plaintiff that causes or contributes to the injuries a plaintiff complains of will be grounds for dismissal. Suppose that in discovery, Mr. Ferlito in *Ferlito v. Johnson & Johnson,* admits that he brought the cigarette lighter dangerously close to his costume, saying, "Yes, you could definitely say I was being careless; I had a few drinks under my belt." Also, suppose in discovery that Mrs. Ferlito admits that she

never reads product instructions from manufacturers. If the case is brought in a state where contributory negligence is the law, will Johnson & Johnson succeed in a summary judgment motion? (See Chapter 7 Section 3 on contributory negligence.) Explain.

2. Do you think it was ethical for the Ferlitos to even bring this action, or for their attorneys to file the lawsuit? Why, or why not? Why didn't the judge approve Johnson & Johnson's motion for a directed verdict?

3. Legal systems based on the English model—as in the U.S.—conduct trials by the "adversarial system": attorneys examine and cross examine. In many countries the judge alone asks questions (the "inquisitional system"). What are the advantages and disadvantages of each? Is one fairer than the other?

5.4 Judgment, Appeal, and Execution

Learning Objectives

1. Understand the post-trial process—how appellate courts process appeals.
2. Explain how a court's judgment is translated into relief for the winning party.

Judgment or Order

judgment

The decision rendered by a court (usually after a trial).

At the end of a trial, the judge will enter a **judgment** or an order that reports on what facts were found (often with the help of a jury), and conclusions of law are drawn (for example, the *fact* was the defendant was negligent, and the *conclusion of law* is he is liable to the plaintiff). The judge will also make a judgment as to what relief or remedy should be given. Often, it is an award of money damages to one of the parties. The losing party may ask for a new trial at this point or within a short period of time following. Once the trial judge denies any such request, the judgment—in the form of the court's order—is final.

Appeal

If the loser's motion for a new trial or a judgment n.o.v. is denied, the losing party may appeal but must ordinarily post a bond sufficient to ensure that there are funds to pay the amount awarded to the winning party.[13] In an appeal, the appellant aims to show that there was some prejudicial error committed by the trial judge. There will be errors, of course, but the errors must be significant (i.e., not harmless). The basic idea is for an appellate court to ensure that a reasonably fair trial was provided to both sides. Enforcement of the court's judgment—an award of money, an injunction—is usually stayed (postponed) until the appellate court has ruled. As noted earlier, the party making the appeal is called the appellant, and the party defending the judgment is the appellee (or in some courts, the petitioner and the respondent).

During the trial, the losing party may have objected to certain procedural decisions by the judge. In compiling a record on appeal, the appellant needs to show the appellate court some examples of mistakes made by the judge—for example, having erroneously admitted evidence, having failed to admit proper evidence that should have been admitted, or having wrongly instructed the jury. The appellate court must determine if those mistakes were serious enough to amount to prejudicial error.

Appellate and trial procedures are different—the appellate court does not hear witnesses or accept evidence. It reviews the *record* of the case—the transcript of the witnesses' testimony and the documents received into evidence at trial—to try to find a legal error on a specific request of one or both of the parties. The parties' lawyers prepare briefs (written statements containing the facts in the case), the procedural steps taken, and the argument or discussion of the meaning of the law and how it applies to the facts. After reading the briefs on appeal, the appellate court may dispose of the appeal without argument, issuing a written opinion that may be very short or very long. Often, though, the appellate court will hear oral argument. (This can be months, or even more than a year after the briefs are filed.) Each lawyer is given a short period of time, usually no more than thirty minutes, to present his client's case. The lawyer rarely gets a chance for an extended statement because he is usually interrupted by questions from the judges. Through this exchange between judges and lawyers, specific legal positions can be tested and their limits explored.

Depending on what it decides, the appellate court will *affirm* the lower court's judgment, *modify* it, *reverse* it, or *remand* it to the lower court for retrial or other action directed by the higher court. The appellate court itself does not take specific action in the case; it sits only to rule on contested issues of law. The lower court must issue the final judgment in the case.

Like trial judges, appellate judges must follow previous decisions, or precedent. But not every previous case is a precedent for every court. Courts in one state are not bound by decisions of courts in other states, and are not bound by decisions of federal district or circuit courts, except on points of federal law that come from federal courts within the state (or from the federal circuit court of appeals supervising federal district courts in that state). Still, a supreme court in one state with a type of case it has not previously dealt with may find *persuasive* reasoning in decisions of other state supreme courts or in the federal courts generally. In any case, relevant parts of decisions by the U.S. Supreme Court would be binding on all courts, state or federal. As noted in Chapter 4, the Supreme Court itself will, on occasion, reverse a long-standing precedent, as it did in *Brown v. Board of Education*, and is often urged to do with *Roe v. Wade*.

Execution

In civil cases, when a party has no more possible appeals, it usually pays up voluntarily, and the decision is said to be "executed." If not voluntarily, then the losing party's assets can be seized ("attached") or its wages or other income garnished to satisfy the judgment. If the final judgment is an injunction, failure to follow its dictates can lead to a contempt citation, with a fine or jail time imposed. "**Execution**" is the process of performing a judgment or sentence of a court (it also refers to signing a legal document to give it effect, as in "this deed was executed on July 1").

In criminal cases, when appeals are exhausted the defendant must pay fines, go to jail or prison (or to his death), and sometimes make restitution.

execution

The process of performing a judgment or sentence of a court, or of signing a legal document to give it effect.

Key Takeaway

The process of conducting a civil trial has many aspects, starting with pleadings and continuing with motions, discovery, more motions, pretrial conferences, and finally the trial itself. At all stages, the rules of civil procedure attempt to give both sides plenty of notice, opportunity to be heard, discovery of relevant information, cross-examination, and the preservation of procedural objections for purposes of appeal. All of these rules and procedures are intended to provide each side with a fair trial.

Exercises

1. Regarding the exploding Audi automobile, Mrs. Robinson has a key witness on auto safety that the judge believes is not qualified as an expert. The judge examines the witness while the jury is in the jury room and disqualifies him from testifying. The jury does not get to hear this witness. Her attorney objects. She loses her case. What argument would you expect Mrs. Robinson's attorney to make in an appeal?

2. Why don't appellate courts need a witness box for witnesses to give testimony under oath?

3. A trial judge in Nevada is wondering whether to enforce a surrogate motherhood contract. Penelope Barr, of Reno, Nevada, has contracted with Reuben and Tina Goldberg to bear the in vitro fertilized egg of Mrs. Goldberg. After carrying the child for nine months, Penelope gives birth, but she is reluctant to give up the child, even though she was paid $20,000 at the start of the contract and will earn an additional $20,000 on handing over the baby to the Goldbergs. (Barr was an especially good candidate for surrogate motherhood: she had borne two perfect children, and at age 28, drinks no wine, does not smoke or use drugs of any kind, practices yoga, and maintains a largely vegetarian diet with just enough meat to meet the needs of the fetus within.)

   The Goldbergs have asked the judge for an order compelling Penelope to give up the baby, who was five days old when the lawsuit was filed. The baby is now a month old as the judge looks in vain for guidance from any Nevada statute, federal statute, or any prior case in Nevada that addressed the issue of surrogate motherhood. He does find several well-reasoned cases, one from New Jersey, one from Michigan, and one from Oregon. Are any of these "precedent" that he must follow? May he adopt the reasoning of any of these courts, if he should find that reasoning persuasive?

4. When would a court on appeal *remand* a case as opposed to simply reversing the lower court's judgment?

5.5 When Can Someone Bring a Lawsuit?

Learning Objectives

1. Explain the requirements for standing to bring a lawsuit in U.S. courts.
2. Describe the process by which a group or class of plaintiffs can be certified to file a class action case.

Almost anyone can bring a lawsuit, assuming they have the filing fee and the help of an attorney. But the court may not hear it, for a number of reasons. There may be no case or controversy, there may be no law to support the plaintiff's claim, it may be in the wrong court, too much time might have elapsed (a statute of limitations problem), or the plaintiff may not have standing.

Case or Controversy: Standing to Sue

Article III of the U.S. Constitution provides limits to federal judicial power. For some cases, the Supreme Court has decided that it has no power to adjudicate because there is no "case or controversy." For example, perhaps the case has settled or the "real parties in interest" are not before the court. In such a case, a court might dismiss the case on the grounds that the plaintiff does not have "standing" to sue.

For example, suppose you see a sixteen-wheel moving van drive across your neighbor's flower bed, destroying her beloved roses. You have enjoyed seeing her roses every summer for years. She is forlorn and tells you that she is not going to raise roses there anymore. She also tells you that she has decided not to sue, because she has made the decision to never deal with lawyers if at all possible. Incensed, you decide to sue on her behalf. But you will not have standing to sue because your person or property was not directly injured by the moving van. Standing means that only the person whose interests are directly affected has the legal right to sue (this issue is also discussed in Chapter 4 Section 2, in the context of administrative law).

The **standing doctrine** is easy to understand in straightforward cases such as this but is often a fairly complicated matter. For example, can fifteen or more state attorneys general bring a lawsuit for a declaratory judgment that the healthcare legislation passed in 2010 is unconstitutional? What particular injury have they (or the states) suffered? Are they the best set of plaintiffs to raise this issue? Time—and the Supreme Court—will tell. (The "standing issue" is also discussed in Chapter 4 as it relates to administrative law, and in Chapter 11 as it relates to environmental law—it is a fundamental legal doctrine.)

standing doctrine

The requirement that no one can maintain a lawsuit unless they can demonstrate a particular injury to their own interests caused by the defendant's actions.

Class Actions

Most lawsuits concern a dispute between two people or between a person and a company or other organization. But it can happen that someone injures more than one person at the same time. A driver who runs a red light may hit another car carrying one person or many people. If several people are injured in the same accident, they each have the right to sue the driver for the damage that he caused them. Could they sue as a group? Usually not, because the damages would probably not be the same for each person, and different facts would have to be proved at the trial. Plus, the driver of the car that was struck might have been partially to blame, so the defendant's liability toward him might be different from his liability toward the passengers.

If, however, the potential plaintiffs were all injured in the same way, whether at the same time (an airplane accident caused by the airline's negligence, for example) or even at different times, a single lawsuit might be a far more efficient way of determining liability and deciding financial responsibility than many individual lawsuits.

How could such a suit be brought? All the injured parties could hire the same lawyer, and she could present a common case. With a group numbering more than a handful of people, it could become exceedingly complicated, yet many individuals suing alone in many different jurisdictions for the same civil wrongs can frustrate the orderly and fair resolution of the common dispute. In revising the Federal Rules of Civil Procedure in 1966, Congress tried to create a rule for "**class actions**" that would serve the interests not only of a large "class" of plaintiffs, but also be manageable by the courts and fair to defendants.

class action

A lawsuit that allows a large number of people with a common interest in a matter to sue or be sued as a group.

Thus, the class action was provided for in the Federal Rules of Civil Procedure (Rule 23) and in the separate codes of civil procedure in the states. These rules can differ and are often complex, but in general anyone can file a class action in an appropriate case, subject to approval of the court. Once the class is "certified," or judged to be a legally adequate group with common injuries, the lawyers for the named plaintiffs become, in effect, lawyers for the entire class.

Usually a person who doesn't want to be in the class can decide to leave. If she does, she will not be included in an eventual judgment or settlement. But a potential plaintiff who is included in the class cannot, after a final judgment is awarded, seek to relitigate the issue if she is dissatisfied with the outcome, even though she did not participate at all in the legal proceeding.

Corporate defendants do not like being sued in class actions. If they can prevent those who contract with them from bringing class actions, they can often prevent a lawsuit being filed against them altogether. The reason is that a single plaintiff rarely has the money to bring a complex civil case against a corporate defendant—thousands of plaintiffs need to join together. In *American Express v. Italian Colors*, however, the Supreme Court held that no-class-action-lawsuit clauses in contracts are enforceable (See Section 7).

Key Takeaway

Anyone can file a lawsuit, with or without the help of an attorney, but only those lawsuits where a plaintiff has standing will be heard by the courts. Standing has become a complicated question and is used by the courts to ensure that civil cases heard are being pursued by those with tangible and particular injuries. Class actions are a way of aggregating claims that are substantially similar and arise out of the same facts and circumstances.

Exercise

1. Fuchs Funeral Home is carrying the body of Charles Emmenthaler to its resting place at Forest Lawn Cemetery. Charles's wife, Chloe, and their two children, Chucky and Clarice, are following the hearse when the coffin falls on the street, opens, and the body of Charles Emmenthaler falls out. The wife and children are shocked and aggrieved and later sue in civil court for damages. Assume that this is a viable cause of action based on "negligent infliction of emotional distress" in the state of California and that Charles's brother, sister-in-law, and multiple cousins also were in the funeral procession and saw what happened. The brother of Charles, Kingston Emmenthaler, also sees his brother's body on the street, but his wife, their three children, and some of Charles's other cousins do not.

   Charles was actually emotionally closest to Kingston's oldest son, Nestor, who was studying abroad at the time of the funeral and could not make it back in time. He is as emotionally distraught at his uncle's passing as anyone else in the family and is especially grieved over the description of the incident and the grainy video shot by one of the cousins on his cell phone. Who has standing to sue Fuchs Funeral Home, and who does not?

5.6 Relations with Lawyers

Learning Objectives

1. Understand the various ways that lawyers charge for services.
2. Describe the contingent fee system in the United States.
3. Know the difference between the American rule and the British rule with regard to who pays attorneys' fees.

Legal Fees

Lawyers charge for their services in one of three different ways: flat rate, hourly rate, and contingent fee. A flat rate is usually used when the work is relatively routine and the lawyer knows in advance approximately how long it will take her to do the job. Drawing, a will or doing a real estate closing are examples of legal work that is often paid a flat rate. The rate itself may be based on a percentage of the worth of the matter—say, 1 percent of a home's selling price.

Lawyers generally charge by the hour for courtroom time and for ongoing representation in commercial matters. Virtually every sizable law firm bills its clients by hourly rates, which in large cities can range from $300 for an associate's time to $600 and more for a senior partner's time.

A **contingent fee** is one that is paid only if the lawyer wins—that is, it is contingent, or depends upon, the success of the case. This type of fee arrangement is used most often in personal injury cases (e.g., automobile accidents, product liability, and professional malpractice). Although used quite often, the contingent fee is controversial. Trial lawyers justify it by pointing to the high cost of preparing for such lawsuits. A typical automobile accident case can cost at least ten thousand dollars to prepare, and a complicated product-liability case can cost tens of thousands of dollars. Few people have that kind of money or would be willing to spend it on the chance that they might win a lawsuit. Corporate and professional defendants complain that the contingent fee gives lawyers a license to go big game hunting, or to file suits against those with deep pockets in the hopes of forcing them to settle.

contingent fee

A fee paid to a lawyer only if the lawyer wins the client's case.

Trial lawyers respond that the contingent fee arrangement forces them to screen cases and weed out cases that are weak, because it is not worth their time to spend the hundreds of hours necessary on such cases if their chances of winning are slim or nonexistent.

Costs

In England and in many other countries, the losing party must pay the legal expenses of the winning party, including attorneys' fees. That is not the general rule in the U.S. In the U.S., each party must pay most of its own costs, including (and especially) the fees of lawyers. Certain relatively minor costs, such as filing fees for various documents required in court, are chargeable to the losing side, if the judge so decides. This type of fee structure is known as the American rule (in contrast to the British rule).

There are three exceptions to the American rule. By statute, Congress and the state legislatures have provided that the winning party in particular classes of cases may recover its full legal costs from the loser—for example, the federal antitrust laws so provide and so does the federal Equal Access to Justice Act. The second exception applies to litigants who either initiate lawsuits in bad faith, with no expectation of winning, or who defend them in bad faith, in order to cause the plaintiff great expense. Under these circumstances, a court has the discretion to award attorneys' fees to the winner. But this rule is not infinitely flexible, and courts do not have complete freedom to award attorneys' fees in any amount, but only "reasonable" attorney's fees. The third situation—and it is very common—arises where the contract between the parties provides that the loser must pay the winner's attorney's fees.

Key Takeaway

Litigation is expensive. Getting a lawyer can be costly, unless you get a lawyer on a contingent fee. Not all legal systems allow contingent fees basis. In many legal systems, the loser pays attorneys' fees for both parties.

Exercises

1. Mrs. Robinson's attorney estimates that they will recover a million dollars from the defendant in her suit against it for gas-tank design defects. She has Mrs. Robinson sign a contract that gives her firm one-third of any recovery after the firm's expenses are deducted. The judge does, in fact, award a million dollars, and the defendant pays. The firm's expenses are $100,000. How much does Mrs. Robinson get?

2. Harry Potter brings a lawsuit against Draco Malfoy in Chestershire, England, for slander, a form of defamation. Potter alleges that Malfoy insists on calling him a mudblood. Ron Weasley testifies, as does Neville Chamberlain. But Harry loses, because the court has no conception of wizardry and cannot make sense of the case at all. In dismissing the case, however, who (under English law) will bear the costs of the attorneys who have brought the case for Potter and defended the matter for Malfoy?

3. What is the effect on a party's willingness to sue—on access to justice—under the British rule as opposed to the American rule, as relates to the obligation to pay lawyers' fees?

5.7 Alternative Means of Resolving Disputes

Learning Objectives

1. Understand how arbitration and mediation are frequently-used alternatives to litigation.
2. Describe the differences between arbitration and mediation.
3. Explain why arbitration is final and binding.

Problems with Litigation

Disputes do not have to be settled in court. No law requires parties who have a legal dispute to seek judicial resolution if they can resolve their disagreement privately or through some other public forum. In fact, the threat of a lawsuit can frequently motivate parties toward private negotiation. Filing a lawsuit may convince one party that the other party is serious. Or the parties may decide that they will come to terms privately rather than wait the three or four years it can frequently take for a case to move up on the court calendar. There are significant problems with litigation, among them these:

- It is expensive. To hire lawyers and for the litigants to drop their daily lives to deal with lawyers and courts. It is emotionally expensive for the litigants, too—being sued is awful.

- It is time consuming. Because criminal cases have priority, it may take two or three years for a civil case to get docketed for trial. Plus, as noted above in the discussion on discovery (Section 3), the entire process takes a lot of the parties' time—time away from work, time answering discovery demands, time fretting about the whole thing.
- It is public. Often, people don't want the details of their legal disputes laid out in the newspapers.
- Somebody loses. If you sue somebody and win, the loser probably won't like you very much, and if you lose, you won't like the winner. When parties have to deal with each other in the future, an alternative to litigation might be a better solution.

Alternatives to Litigation

Arbitration

Beginning around 1980, a movement toward alternative dispute resolution began to gain force throughout the United States. Bar associations, other private groups, and the courts themselves wanted to find quicker and cheaper ways for litigants and potential litigants to settle certain types of quarrels than through the courts. As a result, neighborhood justice centers or dispute resolution centers have sprung up in communities, where people can come for help in settling disputes that should not consume the time and money of the parties or courts in lengthy proceedings.

These alternative forums use a variety of methods, including arbitration, mediation, and conciliation, to bring about agreement or at least closure of the dispute. These methods are not all alike, and their differences are worth noting.

Arbitration is a type of adjudication. The parties use a private decision maker, the arbitrator, and the rules of procedure are considerably more relaxed than those that apply in the courtroom. Arbitrators might be retired judges, lawyers, or anyone with the kind of specialized knowledge and training that would be useful in making a final, binding decision on the dispute. In a contractual relationship, the parties can decide even before a dispute arises to use arbitration when the time comes. Or parties can decide after a dispute arises to use arbitration instead of litigation. In a pre-dispute arbitration agreement (often part of a larger contract), the parties can spell out the rules of procedure to be used and the method for choosing the arbitrator. For example, they may name the specific person or delegate the responsibility of choosing to some neutral person, or they may each designate a person and the two designees may jointly pick a third arbitrator.

> **arbitration**
>
> A process agreed to by disputing parties, involving an arbitrator or arbitral panel (usually three), in which a final and binding award is made, enforceable through the courts if necessary.

Many arbitrations take place under the auspices of the American Arbitration Association, a private organization headquartered in New York, with regional offices in many other cities. The association uses published sets of rules for various types of arbitration (e.g., labor arbitration or commercial arbitration); parties who provide for arbitration through the association in contracts are agreeing to be bound by the association's rules. Similarly, the National Association of Securities Dealers provides arbitration services for disputes between clients and brokerage firms. International commercial arbitration often takes place through the auspices of the International Chamber of Commerce. A multilateral agreement known as the Convention on the Recognition and Enforcement of Arbitral Awards provides that agreements to arbitrate—and arbitral awards—will be enforced across national boundaries.

Arbitration has two advantages over litigation. First, it is usually much quicker, because the arbitrator does not have a backlog of cases and because the procedures are simpler. Second, in complex cases, the quality of the decision may be higher, because the parties can select an arbitrator with specialized knowledge.

Under both federal and state law, arbitration is favored, and a decision rendered by an arbitrator is binding by law and may be enforced by the courts. The arbitrator's decision is final and binding, with very few exceptions (such as fraud or manifest disregard of the law by the arbitrator or panel of arbitrators), and there is no appeal. Saying that arbitration is favored means that if you have agreed to arbitration, you can't go to court if the other party wants you to arbitrate. Under the Federal Arbitration Act, the other party can go to court and get a stay against your litigation and also get an order compelling you to go to arbitration.

Employers and business firms that deal with the public have been using arbitration clauses more and more in the past twenty years, and one continuing controversy is that arbitration clauses may exclude any class actions. In class actions, small losses writ large over thousands or millions of customers would ordinarily mean that bringing an individual lawsuit would be cost prohibitive, even if the amount claimed were $1,000 to $5,000. For example, Wells Fargo opened up to 3.5 million fake bank and credit card accounts from 2002 to 2015 without customers' consent. People tried to sue Wells Fargo starting in 2013, but the bank was able to get lawsuits dismissed in favor of arbitration, and also blocked both class action litigation and arbitration. Prior to President Trump's election, the Consumer Financial Protection Bureau (CFPB) was considering regulation that would prohibit financial firms from blocking class action arbitrations. But under the new CFPB agency chief, that initiative no longer has support.

In 2018, the Supreme Court ruled in the *Italian Colors* case that potential plaintiffs wishing to arbitrate as a class could not do so if their employer's arbitration agreements forbid joining others in a class action. The National Labor Relations Board had argued that individual lawsuits for violations of the Fair Labor Standards Act's requirements on wages and working hours could not practically be brought except through a class action, either in litigation or arbitration. Employer violations of the FLSA as to each individual employee would not be of interest to any attorney because the costs of representing an individual in arbitration would greatly exceed any recovery in an arbitral award. That argument and others failed in a 5–4 decision that emphasized the court's view that the only grounds for setting aside an agreement to arbitrate (and all of its specific terms) are the same grounds that would invalidate any contract—fraud, duress or unconscionability. That employer's arbitration agreements are always non-negotiable, take-it-or-leave-it "offers," does not amount to "duress," however.

The *Italian Colors* case also provides some indication that the Supreme Court is "pro-business" rather than "pro-market" in its leanings. In a free market where "voluntary consent" is valued as a core principle, we can ask whether the Supreme Court majority believes it is upholding that principle, and in the *Italian Colors* case whether Congressional anti-trust law is being supported by the Court's upholding arbitration agreements unless they are obtained by fraud, duress, or unconscionability.

Mediation

mediation

A process where disputing parties agree to bring their differences to an experienced mediator, knowledgeable about the type of dispute involved, and in which the mediator's recommendations may be accepted or rejected by either or both parties.

Unlike adjudication, **mediation** gives the neutral party no power to impose a decision. The mediator is a go-between who attempts to help the parties negotiate a solution. The mediator will communicate the parties' positions to each other, will facilitate the finding of common ground, and will suggest outcomes. But the parties have complete control: they may ignore the recommendations of the mediator entirely, settle in their own way, find another mediator, agree to binding arbitration, go to court, or forget the whole thing!

Other Alternatives

Besides arbitration and mediation there are various other ways parties to a dispute can get resolution (not including fighting it out in the streets). These include the following:

- Mock trial. The parties present their case to an advisory (kind of a "pretend") jury, whose "verdict" is not binding, but may affect negotiations.

- Mini-trial. Mostly used for corporate disputes, this involves limited discovery and the presentation of evidence to a panel of managers from each company, plus a neutral third party. The managers try to solve the dispute after the presentation without the lawyers, and they may consult with the third party.

- Cyber settlements. Parties can agree to use the 'Net as a mechanism of presenting their cases. Here's a bit from one such website, Cybersettle: "Contending parties submit confidential offers and demands on-line from most computers, smart phones or tablets. Cybersettle instantly compares the parties' submissions to determine if they are in range of a mutually-acceptable settlement. If not, it prompts the parties to submit their next offer. If yes, the parties arrange payment. Neither party sees the other party's offer or demands (double-blind) unless and until a settlement is reached." http://www.cybersettle.com/

- Change the law. Say you were the parent (or brother or sister) of a child killed in a school shooting. Well, you can go after the shooter, all right (he's probably dead), but you won't get any relief—he's got no money. And you can't go after the gun companies that make the guns, however obvious it is that widespread sale of semi-automatic weapons is likely to cause harm, because of the federal Protection of Lawful Commerce in Arms Act, signed into law by President Bush in 2005. It says that gun manufacturers cannot be sued when people commit crimes with their products. Maybe you could get the law changed. But probably you couldn't. Recourse to the legislature for relief is pretty much available only to large industry groups and wealthy people, who can hire lobbyists. Whether their interest is the same as the public interest is worth considering.

Case

Validity of Arbitration Clause and No-Class-Action Clauses

American Express v. Italian Colors

570 U.S. 133 S. Ct. 2304 (U.S. Supreme Court, 2013)

American Express v. Italian Colors

U.S. Supreme Court case from 2013, upholding the validity of contractual clauses that prevented class action arbitration.

[Italian Colors Restaurant (the respondents here, but plaintiff at the trial court level) accepted American Express cards. Their contract with American Express contained a clause that requires all disputes between the parties to be resolved by arbitration. The contract also provided that "[t]here shall be no right or authority for any Claims to be arbitrated on a class action basis." As plaintiffs, Italian Colors brought a class action lawsuit against American Express for violations of the federal antitrust laws, alleging that American Express had used its monopoly power in the market for charge cards to force merchants to accept credit cards at rates approximately 30% higher than the fees for competing credit cards.

As defendants, American Express (Petitioners before the Supreme Court) moved the trial court to compel individual arbitration under the Federal Arbitration Act ("FAA"; the FAA became law in 1925). This motion, if accepted by the trial court, would effectively bar Italian Colors from bringing any kind of lawsuit, whether individually or as a lead plaintiff in a class action because—as no one disputed—it would cost more for Italian Colors, all alone or as lead, to bring an antitrust action against American Express than it would get if it won.

The District Court granted the motion to compel arbitration and dismissed the lawsuit. But the Court of Appeals reversed and remanded for further proceedings. It held that because respondents had established that "they would incur prohibitive costs if compelled to arbitrate under the class action waiver," the waiver was unenforceable and the arbitration could not proceed. [14]

The Supreme Court granted certiorari, and—following further rather complex procedures, took up the case. Notice that the issue could also have been phrased, "Can a credit card firm exercise its monopoly power to charge excessive fees and effectively prevent retailers and merchants from suing collectively under U.S. antitrust laws or, if the credit card company insists on arbitration rather than litigation, can it by contract preclude retailers and merchants from using class arbitration?"]

Scalia, J.

Congress enacted the FAA in response to widespread judicial hostility to arbitration. As relevant here, the Act provides:

"A written provision in any maritime transaction or contract evidencing a transaction involving commerce to settle by arbitration a controversy thereafter arising out of such contract or transaction . . . shall be valid, irrevocable, and enforceable, save upon such grounds as exist at law or in equity for the revocation of any contract." 9 U.S.C. §2.

This text reflects the overarching principle that arbitration is a matter of contract. And consistent with that text, courts must "rigorously enforce" arbitration agreements according to their terms, including terms that "specify *with whom* [the parties] choose to arbitrate their disputes," and "the rules under which that arbitration will be conducted," [Citation (1989)]. That holds true for claims that allege a violation of a federal statute, unless the FAA's mandate has been "overridden by a contrary congressional command.'" [Citation (2012)].

No contrary congressional command requires us to reject the waiver of class arbitration here. Respondents argue that requiring them to litigate their claims individually—as they contracted to do—would contravene the policies of the antitrust laws. But the antitrust laws do not guarantee an affordable procedural path to the vindication of every claim. Congress has taken some measures to facilitate the litigation of antitrust claims—for example, it enacted a multiplied-damages remedy [15 U.S.C. §15 (treble damages)]. In enacting such measures, Congress has told us that it is willing to go, in certain respects, beyond the normal limits of law in advancing its goals of deterring and remedying unlawful trade practice. But to say that Congress must have intended whatever departures from those normal limits advance antitrust goals is simply irrational. "[N]o legislation pursues its purposes at all costs." [Citation (1987)].

The antitrust laws do not "evinc[e] an intention to preclude a waiver" of class-action procedure. [Citation.] The Sherman and Clayton Acts make no mention of class actions. In fact, they were enacted decades before the advent of Federal Rule of Civil Procedure 23, which was "designed to allow an exception to the usual rule that litigation is conducted by and on behalf of the individual named parties only." [Citation (1979)]. The parties here agreed to arbitrate pursuant to that "usual rule," and it would be remarkable for a court to erase that expectation. * * *

Our finding of no "contrary congressional command" does not end the case. Respondents invoke a judge-made exception to the FAA which, they say, serves to harmonize competing federal policies by allowing courts to invalidate agreements that prevent the "effective vindication" of a federal statutory right. Enforcing the waiver of class arbitration bars effective vindication, respondents contend, because they have no economic incentive to pursue their antitrust claims individually in arbitration.

But the fact that it is not worth the expense involved in *proving* a statutory remedy does not constitute the elimination of the *right to pursue* that remedy. The class-action waiver merely limits arbitration to the two contracting parties. It no more eliminates those parties' right to pursue their statutory remedy than did federal law before its adoption of the class action for legal relief in 1938,* * * Or, to put it differently, the individual suit that was considered adequate to assure "effective vindication" of a federal right before adoption of class-action procedures did not suddenly become "ineffective vindication" upon their adoption.

In *Gilmer v. Interstate Johnson Lane*, 500 U.S. 20 (1991), we had no qualms in enforcing a class waiver in an arbitration agreement even though the federal statute at issue, the Age Discrimination in Employment Act, expressly permitted collective actions. We said that statutory permission did "'not mean that individual attempts at conciliation were intended to be barred.'" *[Citations], where* we held that requiring arbitration in a foreign country was compatible with the federal Carriage of Goods by Sea Act. That legislation prohibited any agreement "relieving" or "lessening" the liability of a carrier for damaged goods, [Citations]—which is close to codification of an "effective vindication" exception. The Court rejected the argument that the "inconvenience and costs of proceeding" abroad "lessened" the defendants' liability, stating that "it would be unwieldy and unsupported by the terms or policy of the statute to require courts to proceed case by case to tally the costs and burdens to particular plaintiffs in light of their means, the size of their claims, and the relative burden on the carrier." [Citation]. Such a "tallying of the costs and burdens" is precisely what the dissent would impose upon federal courts here.

The regime established by the Court of Appeals' decision would require—before a plaintiff can be held to contractually agreed bilateral arbitration—that a federal court determine (and the parties litigate) the legal requirements for success on the merits claim-by-claim and theory-by-theory, the evidence necessary to meet those requirements, the cost of developing that evidence, and the damages that would be recovered in the event of success. Such a preliminary litigating hurdle would undoubtedly destroy the prospect of speedy resolution that arbitration in general and bilateral arbitration in particular was meant to secure. The FAA does not sanction such a judicially created superstructure.

The judgement of the Court of Appeals is reversed.

It is so ordered.

Justice Sotomayor took no part in the consideration or decision of this case.

Justice Kagan, with whom Justice Ginsburg and Justice Breyer join, dissenting. [What follows here is an excerpt from the dissenting judges]:

Here is the nutshell version of this case, unfortunately obscured in the Court's decision. The owner of a small restaurant (Italian Colors) thinks that American Express (Amex) has used its monopoly power to force merchants to accept a form contract violating the antitrust laws. The restauranteur wants to challenge the allegedly unlawful provision (imposing a tying arrangement), but the same contract's arbitration clause prevents him from doing so. That term imposes a variety of procedural bars that would make pursuit of the antitrust claim a fool's errand. So, if the arbitration clause is enforceable, Amex has insulated itself from antitrust liability—even if it has in fact violated the law. The monopolist gets to use its monopoly power to insist on a contract, effectively depriving its victims of all legal recourse.

And here is the nutshell version of today's opinion, admirably flaunted rather than camouflaged: Too darn bad.

That answer is a betrayal of our precedents, and of federal statutes like the antitrust laws. Our decisions have developed a mechanism—called the effective-vindication rule—to prevent arbitration clauses from choking off a plaintiff's ability to enforce congressionally created rights. * * * As applied here, the rule would ensure that Amex's arbitration clause does not foreclose Italian Colors from vindicating its right to redress antitrust harm.

The majority barely tries to explain why it reaches a contrary result. It notes that we have not decided this exact case before—neglecting that the principle we have established fits this case hand in glove. And it concocts a special exemption for class-arbitration waivers—ignoring that this case concerns much more than that. Throughout, the majority disregards our decisions' central tenet: An arbitration clause may not thwart federal law, irrespective of exactly how it does so. Because the Court today prevents the effective vindication of federal statutory rights, I respectfully dissent. * * * I would follow our precedents and decline to compel arbitration. * * *

Case Questions

1. How can Supreme Court justices, or any judge, know what Congress meant or "intended" in 1925?

2. From the case, it's clear that the Justices have made many interpretations of the FAA in recent decades, and that they very much tend to favor the arbitration process. Why do you think they do?

3. These many interpretations add meaning and context to the FAA so that the public (and business, in particular) understands what kinds of contractual agreements to arbitrate will be upheld by the courts. Could Congress invalidate these interpretations if they chose to do so?

4. Here's a hoary Latin phrase for you: *Ubi Jus Ibi Remedium*. It means, For every wrong, the law provides a remedy. This was a principle of Roman law, known to the common law, and part of "equity" jurisprudence (that is, where the law courts in England did not provide a remedy, the equity courts did). Law and equity rules and principles are now merged in U.S. law. Which opinion, majority or dissent, takes this principle more seriously?

5. Would you say this opinion favors or disfavors small businesses, "the little guy"?

6. If Italian Colors (the restaurant plaintiff here) didn't like Amex's no-litigation and no-class-action policies, why did it contract with Amex at all?

Key Takeaway

Litigation is not the only way to resolve disputes. Informal negotiation between the disputants usually comes first, but both mediation and arbitration are available. Arbitration, though, is final and binding. Once you agree to arbitrate, you will have a final, binding arbitral award that is enforceable through the courts, and courts will almost never allow you to litigate after you have agreed to arbitrate.

Other types of non-litigation dispute resolution include mock trials, mini-trials and—for big companies and rich people—getting the law itself changed.

Exercises

1. Suppose that when Mrs. Robinson buys her Audi (the one with the exploding gas tank) from Seaway, there is a paragraph in the bill of sale, which both the dealer and Mrs. Robinson sign, that says, "In the event of any complaint by customer/buyer against Seaway regarding the vehicle purchased herein, such complaint shall not be litigated, but may only be arbitrated under the rules of the American Arbitration Association and in accordance with New York law." Mrs. Robinson did not see the provision, doesn't like it, and wants to bring a lawsuit in Oklahoma against Seaway. What do you think is the result?

2. Hendrik Koster (Netherlands) contracts with Automark, Inc. (a U.S. company based in Illinois) to supply Automark with a large quantity of valve cap gauges. He does, and Automark fails to pay. Koster thinks he is owed $66,000. There is no agreement to arbitrate or mediate. Can Koster make Automark mediate or arbitrate? (See Chapter 6 as well.)

3. Suppose that there is an agreement between Koster and Automark to arbitrate. It says, "The parties agree to arbitrate any dispute arising under this agreement in accordance with the laws of the Netherlands and under the auspices of the International Chamber of Commerce's arbitration facility." The International Chamber of Commerce has arbitration rules and will appoint an arbitrator or arbitral panel in the event the parties cannot agree on an arbitrator. The arbitration takes place in Geneva. Koster gets an arbitral award for $66,000 plus interest. Automark does not participate in any way. Will a court in Illinois enforce the arbitral award?

5.8 Summary and Exercises

Summary

The United States has two different court systems—state and federal. This can create issues about which system has "jurisdiction" (the power to hear and decide a case). Federal courts generally hear cases whose causes of action are based in federal law or the U.S. Constitution, but also can have jurisdiction over state-law causes of action where the parties are from different states (diversity jurisdiction). Civil cases begin with a complaint by a plaintiff or group of plaintiffs, served on a defendant with a summons, and defendants will either answer the complaint or move to dismiss if there are grounds to dismiss, such as the court's lack of jurisdiction, or the running of a statute of limitations, or an existing agreement between plaintiff and defendant to arbitrate.

If the civil action survives such motions, the discovery phase of the litigation takes place, and the parties may settle at any time prior to (or even during) trial, although during and after discovery, defendants will often ask for summary judgment if there are no triable issues of fact or law. At trial, the rules of evidence and procedure are many, and the judge's role in a "bench" trial or a jury trial is to insure that the proceedings are fair to both sides. A judgment (or order) will issue from the presiding judge at the end of the trial, incorporating the verdict of the jury, if there is one. Parties will typically appeal a trial court judgment where there is "prejudicial error" in the way the judge has handled the proceeding. Often, an appellate court will find "harmless error" and the trial court's judgment will be affirmed.

Where disputes go to arbitration, the findings of the arbitrator (or panel) are typically "final and binding" on the parties, even if the arbitrator has made significant errors in finding facts or applying the relevant law. Arbitrators need not be lawyers or have experience as a judge, but often are.

Exercises

1. Colorado and Nebraska have a dispute over water rights from the North Platte River. Nebraska, after trying to negotiate with the Colorado Governor's office, decides to bring a lawsuit to enforce its water rights. Can they bring a lawsuit in Nebraska? Colorado? To which court? Who has "original jurisdiction" in this case?

2. Explain why a state-based product liability action (the New York family Robinsons on their way to Arizona) could be heard in a federal court. Could it also be heard in Oklahoma state court? Would a state court in Oklahoma have personal jurisdiction over a New York City area Volkswagen dealer? Why, or why not?

3. Somewhere in the waters near Staten Island, New York, two merchant vessels collide, and one of them is "at fault." The vessel that is not at fault is owned by a Chinese state-owned enterprise that was about to dock in Port Newark, New Jersey. The vessel that is at fault flies a Panamanian "flag of convenience," but is actually owned by a New York corporation. Can the Chinese company bring a lawsuit in the U.S.? Should it file in state or federal court? Does it matter that on the dotted line on the map, the vessels were straddling the New Jersey portion of the harbor as well as the New York portion, and that it's hard to tell which part of the harbor the boats were in when they collided? Does it matter at all that the Chinese vessel was heading to a dock in New Jersey rather than New York?

4. Using *Robinson* again (the exploding gas tank on their Audi), suppose the Robinsons fail to get a judgment from a New York state court that Worldwide Volkswagen (a New York corporation) sold them a "lemon." The judge (or jury) decides there was no "product liability." Can they try again in federal court in New York's southern district? What is most likely to happen procedurally if they file there, and why?

5. In their case against the defendants, will the Robinsons have to prove their case beyond a reasonable doubt? Why, or why not?

6. Suppose that when the Robinsons bought their car, the sales contract specified that the parties must arbitrate any and all disputes before an arbitrator in Westchester County, N.Y. under the rules of the American Arbitration Association. Their lawyer advises them that they should sue in New York, instead. On the car dealer's motion to dismiss after getting the complaint and summons, what is the trial court likely to do? Explain.

Self-Test Questions

1. A brings a lawsuit against B in a court of general jurisdiction in your state. A loses, but finds another attorney who thinks the same cause of action will succeed if you just try again. But in the same court, the case will be dismissed because of:

   a. lack of jurisdiction

   b. no full faith and credit

   c. due process

   d. res judicata

   e. a motion to direct the verdict

2. Most often, when the Supreme Court decides to take a case on appeal, it will issue:

   a. a writ of subpoena

   b. a writ of certiorari

   c. a writ of res judicata

   d. a writ of jurisdiction

   e. a writ of habeas corpus

3. In *Burger King v. Rudzewicz*, the issue before the Supreme Court was mainly:

   a. subject-matter jurisdiction

   b. personal jurisdiction

   c. admiralty jurisdiction

   d. original jurisdiction

   e. a "venue" question

4. In most state courts, when a party loses at the trial level and appeals, they are officially known as:

   a. appellants

   b. appellees

   c. petitioners

   d. respondents

   e. losers

5. Suppose you win a judgment in your state against a non-resident corporation whose principal place of business is not in your state, nor were they incorporated in your state. The corporation argued the case in your state, but lost. Still, they refuse to pay the judgment until you file the judgment in either the state of their incorporation or where they have their principal place of business. The company wants to re-litigate the dispute, but the trial court there will enforce the judgment from your state:

   a. if there was no issue as to jurisdiction, either subject-matter or personal

   b. because the full faith and credit clause in the Constitution requires states to honor the judgments and orders of "sister states" in our federal system.

   c. because corporations are not "persons" under the law

   d. a and b

   e. a, b, and c

Self-Test Answers

1. d
2. b
3. b
4. a
5. d

Endnotes

1. As noted in the section on jurisdiction, all federal courts are of limited jurisdiction, but there are specialized federal courts which are assigned specific judicial or judicial-like functions.
2. There are some alternatives to suing—they're taken up in Section 5.7.
3. 28 U.S. Code § 1332
4. 326 U.S. 310 (1945)
5. We might note in passing that for criminal cases, the Constitution requires that the prosecution be brought at the place where the crime is alleged to have been committed. The Constitution dictates the venue so that criminal defendants are not unduly prejudiced by being tried at some place distant from where they (usually) have any support system, witnesses, etc. In either civil or criminal cases, either side can ask for a "change of venue" if it seems a fair trial can't be had at the usually-applicable venue.
6. This involves the rather complex matter of "conflict of laws," which is beyond the scope of this text to take up.
7. There are various alternatives to lawsuits—to suing somebody. They are taken up in the section below, "Alternative Means of Resolving Disputes."
8. The term "pleadings" derives from the early days of English law when judges had more discretion in dispensing justice: parties would, in effect, "plead"—ask—for relief from the court.
9. The doctrine of res judicata ("the thing is adjudicated") holds that a cause of action may not be relitigated once it has been judged on the merits; it is the civil equivalent of the 5th Amendment's prohibition against double jeopardy.
10. For the most part, courts of appeal will not reverse and remand for a new trial unless the trial court judge's errors are "prejudicial," or "an abuse of discretion." In short, neither party is entitled to a perfect trial, but only to a fair trial, one in which the trial judge has made only "harmless errors" and not prejudicial ones.
11. By "prima facie case," the court means a case in which the plaintiff has presented all the basic elements of the cause of action alleged in the complaint. If one or more elements of proof are missing, then the plaintiff has fallen short of establishing a prima facie case, and the case should be dismissed (usually on the basis of a directed verdict).
12. Note the division of labor here: questions of law are for the judge, while questions of "fact" are for the jury. Here, "foreseeability" is a fact question, while the judge retains authority over questions of law. The division between questions of fact and questions of law is not an easy one, however.
13. In criminal cases, if the plaintiff (the government) loses, it cannot appeal because of the 5th Amendment's prohibition against double jeopardy (a person can only be tried once for the same offense).
14. *In re American Express Merchants' Litigation*, 554 F. 3d 300, 315–316 (CA2 2009).

CHAPTER 6
Introduction to International Law

Chapter Learning Objectives

After reading this chapter, you should understand:

1. The sources of international law.
2. Important doctrines in nation-state (domestic, internal) judicial decision making that affect international relations, including jurisdiction, *forum non conveniens*, sovereign immunity, and the Act of State doctrine.
3. Aspects of import and export controls.
4. Several different methods of business organization for international business.

Nation-states can adopt laws and enforce them within their borders, but no nation-state can control the laws of another. International law is the mechanism by which nation-states order their foreign legal relationships. In this chapter we take up how international law is made and enforced, consider some limits on the scope of international law, and examine different methods of organizing to do international business.

6.1 Sources of International Law

Learning Objectives

1. Understand the executive branches, and how presidents, prime ministers, and "supreme leaders" effectively make and enforce laws.
2. Understand the judiciary branch.
3. Understand how nation-state governmental agencies, international governmental agencies, and nongovernmental agencies ("NGOs") affect international law.
4. Understand how voters themselves, in some countries, make or affect international law.

Here we briefly examine the sources of international law. When we examined law-making in the United States (Chapter 4) we observed that the law is made by five entities: the legislature, the executive, the judiciary, administrative agencies, and in some states, by the people themselves through direct democracy. The same five entities, or closely analogous ones, make international law, too.

International Law by Legislation—Treaties

Nation-states adopt **treaties**[1] or conventions in response to perceived international problems, just as nations themselves adopt domestic legislation as a response to a perceived problem. In most nation-states the national legislature, or part of it, must approve treaties negotiated by the executive's foreign affairs department.

In the United States, the Executive Branch normally negotiates treaties and agreements with other nation-states, and the Senate must approve treaties by a two-thirds vote (politically, a difficult number to achieve). Once ratified, a treaty has the same force of law within the United States as any statute that Congress might pass. There are hundreds of treaties and conventions to which the United States is a party—https://www.state.gov/documents/organization/282222.pdf.

The most basic kind of treaty is an agreement between, or among, nation-states on matters of trade and friendly relations. Treaties of friendship, commerce, and navigation (FCN treaties) are common; they provide mutual respect for each nation-state's citizens in (1) rights of entry, (2) practice of professions, (3) right of navigation, (4) acquisition of property, (5) matters of expropriation or nationalization, (6) access to courts, and (7) protection of patent rights. Bilateral investment treaties (BITs) are similar but are more focused on commerce and investment. There are also treaties dealing with outer space, earthly environmental issues and pollution, joint maintenance of waterways, mutual defense, bomb-testing, and extradition, to mention just a few. We will look in greater detail at peace and land-claims treaties, treaties affecting exports and imports, and treaties addressing international property rights.

Peace and Land-Claims Treaties

No war lasts forever and usually the formal end of a war between, or among, nation-states is marked by a treaty. In rare cases, there may be an "armistice"—a cease fire with no surrender, and no treaty—as with the Korean War. Nation-states have for centuries made weapons-limitation treaties, like the Strategic Arms Limitation Treaty (SALT) between the U.S. and Russia in 1991 and 2011, and have made treaties to resolve territorial disputes. One example is the treaty between Russia and the U.S., which ceded Alaska to the U.S. in 1867).[2]

The most important peace treaty of modern times is the UN Charter Treaty of 1945. As of 2018, 193 parties (nation-states) have signed on to the treaty creating the United Nations (the treaty is the Charter of the UN—its Constitution), including the United States, Uzbekistan, Ukraine, Uganda, United Arab Emirates, United Kingdom of Great Britain and Northern Ireland, and Uruguay (just to name a few of the nations starting with the letter *U*).[3]

The United States also has land-claims and peace treaties with American Indian tribes, or Indian nations, dating mostly from the mid-19th century; these treaties have the effect of law, and are today significantly affecting various development projects, particularly in the western states.

Free-Trade Treaties

Nation-states naturally wish to protect their domestic industries. Historically, protectionism has come in the form of import taxes, or tariffs, also called duties. The tariff is simply a tax imposed on goods when they enter a country. Tariffs change often and vary from one nation-state to another.

But after World War II, the international community attempted to promote economic prosperity and prevent another terrible depression (the Great Depression of the 1930s was arguably made worse by trade protectionism, and became one of the precipitating causes of WWII). Implementation of free trade began with the General Agreement on Tariffs and Trade (GATT) in 1947 and is now effected through the World Trade Organization (WTO). The GATT and the WTO have sought, through successive rounds of trade talks, to decrease the number and extent of tariffs that hinder the free flow of commerce from one nation-state to another. The theory of comparative advantage espoused by David Ricardo (1772–1823) a British political economist, is the basis for the gradual but steady reduction of tariffs, from early rounds of talks under the GATT to the Uruguay Round, which established the WTO in 1994.

And tariff reduction has been significant—in 1948, the worldwide average tariff on industrial goods was around 40 percent; now it's more like 4 percent. WTO proponents claim that globalization has increased general well-being, especially by reducing prices, while opponents claim that free trade has brought outsourcing, industrial decline, and the hollowing-out of the U.S. manufacturing base. The same criticisms have been directed at the regional North American Free Trade Agreement (NAFTA) among Mexico, the U.S., and Canada (1994).

There are a number of regional trade agreements other than NAFTA. The European Union (EU), formerly the Common Market, provides for the free movement of member nations' citizens throughout the EU and sets union-wide standards for tariffs, subsidies, transportation, human rights, and many other issues. Another regional trade agreement is Mercosur—an organization formed by Brazil, Argentina, Uruguay, and Paraguay to improve trade and commerce among those South American nations. Almost all trade barriers between the four nations have been eliminated, and the organization has also established a broad social agenda focusing on education, culture, the environment, and consumer protection. International agreements regarding recognition of patents, trademarks, and copyright can also be included in the list of "free trade treaties."

Of course, no treaty works unless the signatories agree to be bound by it. No nation-state can be forced by another to do anything, except by war. The force and authority of a government in any given territory is fundamental to sovereignty. Historically, that was understood to mean a nation's right to issue its own currency, make and enforce laws within its borders without interference from other nations (the "right of self-determination" that is noted in the Charter of the United Nations), and to defend its territory with military force, if necessary.

International Law by the Executive

Usually a nation-state's office of foreign affairs (in the U.S. it is the State Department) negotiates foreign policy and diplomatic relations with direction from the president, who may also authorize agents to negotiate (or re-negotiate) treaties. The State Department also had authority over treaties for U.S. trade relations with other nation-states but in the Trade Expansion Act of 1962, Congress called for the president to appoint a Special Representative for Trade Negotiations to conduct U.S. trade negotiations. The Act specified that the Special Trade Representative would serve as chair of a new interagency organization that would make recommendations to the president on the U.S. trade agreement program. Congress' intent in 1962 was to achieve a better balance between competing domestic and international interests in creating and maintaining the federal government's positions on trade.

The executive can also withdraw a nation-state from a treaty (sometimes with the approval of the national legislature, sometimes without.). Regarding free-trade treaties, President Trump has imposed or has threatened to impose new and very large tariffs (taxes) on goods imported from our biggest trading partners, including China, Mexico, and Canada (among others). These tariffs are unprecedented in their scope.[4]

International Law by the Judiciary

As we saw in Chapter 4, the American judiciary has several law-making functions. International tribunals similarly make law, and nation-state judges sometimes decide matters of international law as well.

International Tribunals

Where a nation-state feels that a treaty to which it is a party is not being recognized by a treaty partner, it may bring an action in an international court. The Statute of the International Court of Justice (part of the United Nations charter) can enforce treaty provisions. The ICJ has fifteen judges elected for nine-year terms by UN members. The ICJ only has jurisdiction in cases where both nation-states willingly submit to its jurisdiction and other than what the Security Council might do, the ICJ has no enforcement mechanism, so a nation-state can disregard its decision. Other international courts include the European Court of Justice and the International Criminal Court, which the United States refuses to recognize.

International Custom ("Common Law")

In common-law countries (like the U.S., England, and former British Colonies in the Commonwealth), courts may apply rules of custom and tradition as a source of law where there is no legislation. That is true in international law also. Custom is practice followed by two or more nations in the course of dealing with each other. These practices can be found in diplomatic correspondence, policy statements, or official government statements. To become custom, a consistent and recurring practice must prevail over a significant period of time, nations must recognize that the practice or custom is binding, and must follow it because of legal obligation and not mere courtesy. As an example, courts in many nations have believed that sovereign immunity (one nation-state is immune from legal claims absent its agreement to accept the claim) was an established principle of international law. However, a more restrictive doctrine began to take hold after World War II, one that denied sovereign immunity for a sovereign's commercial or private acts. What had been customary had ceased to be so. Eventually, the U.S. and other trading nations adopted a restrictive theory of sovereign immunity, where commercial acts of governments could not be dismissed for lack of subject-matter jurisdiction over "the sovereign."

Scholarly Teachings as Part of International Law

Another type of international "common law," besides custom, is based on scholarly teachings (scholarly teachings from time to time become part of American common law, too). The Statute of the International Court of Justice recognizes that international tribunals may refer to the teachings of preeminent scholars on international law. The ICJ, for example, often referred to the scholarly writings of Sir Hersh Lauterpacht[5] in its early decisions. Generally, international tribunals are not bound by stare decisis (i.e., they may decide each case on its merits without reference to their prior decisions), but some, such as the ICJ, do refer to their own past decisions for guidance. Notice that in the *Bremen* case, below, the U.S. Supreme Court refers to "noted scholars" in making its opinion.

Nation-State Judges Sometimes Decide Issues of International Law

Corporations or individuals with disputes that cross national boundaries must usually resort to national (domestic) court systems or arbitration; there is no international civil court. A disputant may turn to a nation-state's judiciary where questions arise about the fairness of procedures used in foreign courts to acquire the judgment. Perhaps the defendant was not notified or did not have ample time in which to prepare a defense, or perhaps some measure of damages was assessed that seemed distinctly unfair. If a foreign state makes a judgment against a U.S. company, the judgment will not be recognized and enforced in the United States unless the U.S. court believes that the foreign judgment provided the U.S. company with due process.

But skepticism about a foreign judgment works the other way, as well. For example, if a U.S. court were to assess punitive damages against a Belgian company, and the successful plaintiff were to ask for enforcement of the U.S. judgment in Belgium, the Belgian court would reject that portion of the award based on punitive damages. Compensatory damages would be allowed, but as Belgian law does not recognize punitive damages, it might not recognize that portion of the U.S. court's award.

International Arbitration

When we examined "Courts and the Legal Process" in Chapter 5, we observed that disputants may agree to forgo litigation and resolve their problem by arbitration. That's true in international disputes, as well. In international arbitration, parties can select, either before or after a dispute arises, an arbitrator or arbitral panel that will hear the dispute. As in all arbitration, the parties agree that the arbitrator's decision will be final and binding. Arbitration is generally faster, can be less expensive, and is always private, being a proceeding not open to media scrutiny.

Typically, an arbitration clause in the contract will specify the arbitrator or the means of selecting the arbitrator. For that purpose, there are many organizations that conduct international arbitrations, including the American Arbitration Association, the International Chamber of Commerce, the International Centre for Settlement of Investment Disputes, and the United Nations Commission on International Trade Law. Arbitrators need not be judges or lawyers; they are usually businesspeople, lawyers, or judges who are experienced in global commercial transactions. In essence, an arbitration clause is a kind of forum-selection clause and usually includes a choice of law for the arbitrator or arbitral panel to follow. For example, a contract for Sudanese groundnuts between buyer and seller might specify that "all disputes arising shall be arbitrated according to the rules of the International Chamber of Commerce, and heard in London, England, with the application of U.S. admiralty law."

Any arbitral award from the London arbitrator will be more easily recognized and enforced; almost every country that is engaged in international commerce has ratified the United Nations Convention on the Recognition and Enforcement of Foreign Arbitral Awards, sometimes known as the New York Convention. The United States adopted this convention in 1970 and has amended the Federal Arbitration Act accordingly. Anyone who has an arbitral award subject to the convention can satisfy the award by attaching property of the loser, as long as the property is located in a country that has signed the convention.

International Law by Administrative Agencies

When we examined U.S. law-making processes (again, in Chapter 4) we counted administrative agencies as a "fourth branch" of law-making entities. Such agencies make and enforce regulations based on policy adopted by their governments, and there are also nongovernmental administrative agencies.

Nation-State International Administrative Agencies

Many nation-states have administrative agencies to help develop or to implement international policies, political, military, and business. In the U.S., for example here are some agencies or committees that do that:

- Advisory Committee for Study of Eastern Europe and the Independent States of the Former Soviet Union (https://2001-2009.state.gov/r/pa/prs/ps/2003/18811.htm)
- Advisory Committee on International Economic Policy (https://www.state.gov/e/eb/adcom/aciep/)
- Advisory Committee on International Postal and Delivery Services (https://2001-2009.state.gov/p/io/ipp/110066.htm)
- Cuba Internet Task Force (https://www.state.gov/p/wha/ci/cu/citf/index.htm)
- Defense Trade Advisory Group (https://www.pmddtc.state.gov/)

Other U. S. "administrative agencies" that affect international law and relations include the following.[6]

- Records of the National Security Council (RG 273) (https://www.archives.gov/research/foreign-policy/related-records/rg-273.html)
- Records of the Office of the United States Trade Representative (RG 364) (https://www.archives.gov/research/foreign-policy/related-records/rg-364.html)
- Records of the Central Intelligence Agency (RG 263) (https://www.archives.gov/research/foreign-policy/related-records/rg-263.html)
- Records of the Office of the Secretary of Defense (RG 330)(https://www.archives.gov/research/foreign-policy/related-records/rg-330.html)
- Records of the Foreign Agricultural Service (RG 166) (https://www.archives.gov/research/foreign-policy/related-records/rg-166.html)

There are similar "agencies" or committees in other nation-states that are repositories of custom and tradition and to which nation-state governments look for guidance in international relations.

International NGOs

International nongovernmental organizations are another type of "administrative agency." Here is a definition of NGOs by the Executive Committee of Non-Governmental Organizations Associated with the United Nations Department of Public Information:

A non-governmental organization (NGO) is any non-profit, voluntary citizens' group which is organized on a local, national or international level. Task-oriented and driven by people with a common interest, NGOs perform a variety of service and humanitarian functions, bring citizen concerns to Governments, advocate and monitor policies and encourage political participation through provision of information. Some are organized around specific issues, such as human rights, environment or health. They provide analysis and expertise, serve as early warning mechanisms and help monitor and implement international agreements. Their relationship with offices and agencies of the United Nations system differs depending on their goals, their venue and the mandate of a particular institution.[7]

NGOs address international issues involving such things as world hunger, blindness, health (Doctors without Borders may be familiar to you, or the International Rescue Committee), water, children's issues, education, and human rights (Amnesty International is an example). There are many others. You can explore this area of international NGOs at the website of the World Association of Non-Governmental Organizations ("WANGO") here: https://www.wango.org/about.aspx. NGOs draft their own regulations to implement their missions. Here you can read "Principles and Rules for Red Cross and Red Crescent Disaster Relief": http://www.ifrc.org/docs/idrl/I280EN.pdf.

International Law by Direct Democracy

In the U.S., 26 states allow the people themselves to make law by initiative or referendum (see Chapter 4 Section 2). Some nation-states also allow citizens to vote on matters affecting international law. For example, in 2016 a majority of British citizens who voted in a referendum, supported Britain's withdrawal from the European Union—a major foreign policy change.[8] In 2014 voters in the Crimea region of Ukraine voted to secede from their country and join Russia, though many international observers condemned the referendum as illegitimate.[9] In 2017 voters in the Spanish state of Catalonia voted to leave Spain;[10] the Spanish government declared the referendum illegal. In 1861 Southern U.S. states voted to secede from the U.S. The government in Washington, when Abraham Lincoln was president, declared the secession unconstitutional, and civil war followed.

Case

Due Process for Asserting Jurisdiction over a Foreign Defendant

Koster v. Automark

640 F.2d 77 (U.S. Court of Appeals, 7th Circuit, 1981)[11]

Koster v. Automark

U.S. Court of Appeals, 7th Cir, 1981, examining what constitutes due process for asserting personal jurisdiction over a foreign defendant.

Wood, J.

This diversity case involves the appeal of defendant Automark Industries, Inc. ("Automark"), a corporation doing business in Illinois, from the district court's determination on motion for summary judgment in favor of plaintiff Hendrik Koster, a citizen of the Netherlands. The district court's decision granted enforcement of a default judgment obtained in district court in Amsterdam by Koster against Automark in a case brought on a claimed breach of contract. Finding that Automark did not have sufficient contact with the Netherlands to vest that country's courts with personal jurisdiction over Automark so as to permit enforcement of the default judgment in United States courts, we reverse.

Whether a court may, under American law, assert jurisdiction over a foreign defendant-company depends upon whether the company "purposefully avails itself of the privilege of conducting activities within the forum State." [Citation, 1977]. This means that the company must pass a threshold of minimum contacts with the forum state so that it is fair to subject it to the jurisdiction of that state's courts. *International Shoe v. Washington*, [U.S. Supreme Court, 1945].

The parties agree that the document alleged to be Automark's contract to purchase up to 600,000 units of Koster's valve cap gauges[12] was executed in Milan, Italy. The Milan meeting between Koster and Automark followed preliminary inquiry and discussion between the two parties during a period of five months. The discussion was carried on via mail between Koster's Amsterdam office and Automark's Illinois address. * * *

In November 1970, Automark's vice-president, J. L. Bohmrich, wrote that he would like to meet with Koster in Amsterdam or at the Swiss factory during a European trip Bohmrich planned to take later in the month. Koster replied that he would instead be willing to meet in Milan, and would telephone Bohmrich's Illinois office to make arrangements. As noted, the Milan meeting resulted in execution of the document involved in this case.

The business contacts described above are insufficient to reach the minimum level needed to satisfy due process requirements prerequisite to enforcement of the Dutch default judgment. A recent opinion of this court, *Lakeside Bridge & Steel Co. v. Mountain State Construction Co.*, [Citation, 7th Cir. (1979)], thoroughly analyzed the due process requirements of minimum contacts in concluding that a federal court sitting in a diversity case arising in Wisconsin did not have personal jurisdiction of a West Virginia defendant. Whether it be Wisconsin or the Netherlands, the standard of minimum contacts is the same. [Citations.] The facts in the *Lakeside* case were similar to those involved here, and if anything, presented a more compelling case for recognizing personal jurisdiction.

In *Lakeside*, the defendant construction company had ordered structural assemblies from plaintiff Lakeside, a Wisconsin company. Several letters and telephone calls had been exchanged between the two businesses, and a contract concluded by mail. The assemblies were delivered, and Lakeside sued when the defendant withheld part of the purchase price. The court assumed that the defendant believed that Lakeside would perform the contract in Wisconsin, the forum state. Focusing on the nature and quality of the contacts between the two companies, the court nevertheless concluded that Wisconsin could not assert jurisdiction over the West Virginia company because the defendant's Wisconsin contacts did not show that it "purposefully avail[ed] itself of the privilege of conducting activities within the forum state."

The document at issue in the case before us was executed in Italy and involved the purchase of goods manufactured in Switzerland. While the document contains language that might be construed as an agreement to pay, which payment Koster claims was to take place in the Netherlands, such a promise even if so interpreted is not sufficient contact to confer personal jurisdiction. * * * In comparison to the facts in the *Lakeside* case, Automark's only contacts with the Netherlands were eight letters, and possibly a telegram and a transatlantic telephone call all preliminary to the meeting in Italy. In *Lakeside*, the court notes that such contacts cannot be held to satisfy jurisdictional requirements, otherwise "use of the interstate telephone and mail service to communicate with [an out-of-state] plaintiff, if constituting contacts supporting jurisdiction, would give jurisdiction to any state into which communications were directed." Such a result would make virtually every business subject to suit in any state with which it happened to communicate in some manner. That clearly would not satisfy the demands of due process. *Lakeside* emphasizes that "the best interests of the international and state systems" of commerce should be considered when making determinations about minimum contacts in individual cases.

This consideration weighs in favor of Automark, since it "is based on the proposition that `a state should not improperly impinge upon the interests of other states by trying in its courts a case with which it has no adequate relationship.'" [Citation]. The Netherlands lacks an adequate relationship to defendant's presence and conduct to justify trial of the case in that country. The interests of international business are better served by protecting potential international purchasers from being unreasonably called to defend suits commenced in foreign courts which lack jurisdiction according to our recognized standards of due process.

Moreover, the *Lakeside* opinion stresses that where the nature of a defendant's business contact in the forum state does not involve activities dangerous to persons and property, the propriety of vesting personal jurisdiction in that state must be considered in light of its relationship with the defendant other than that at issue in the lawsuit. [Citation.] The purchase and shipment of valve gauges is not a dangerous activity. And here, there are no allegations that Automark had any relationship with the Netherlands beyond the letters, telegram, and telephone call involved in its business contact with Koster.

On these facts, Automark did not have the minimum contacts necessary to show that it purposefully utilized the privilege to conduct business activities in the Netherlands sufficient to confer on that country's courts personal jurisdiction over Automark. The district court concluded that cases decided under the Illinois long-arm statute supported his finding that Automark satisfied the requirement of minimum contacts to support the Dutch court's jurisdiction. We disagree.

Absent personal jurisdiction over Automark in the Dutch case that resulted in a default judgment, the courts of this country lack jurisdiction to enforce the foreign default judgment.

The decision of the district court accordingly is reversed and the case is remanded with directions to dismiss the complaint.

Case Questions

1. What does the court mean when it talks about a court "sitting in diversity"? (Hint: See Chapter 5 Section 2)
2. The U.S. Constitution says "No person shall be denied due process of law." What is the "due process" question or issue regarding the long-arm statute?
3. What is necessary for one jurisdiction to exercise judicial authority over a person from another jurisdiction?
4. What contact did the defendant here have with Holland? Suppose the same sequence of events happened today, only instead of phone calls, Automark and Koster had used emails? Would that confer jurisdiction on Koster?
5. Assume this is a debt that Automark simply doesn't want to pay; what else could Koster do to collect? What kind of agreement signed in Milan would have protected him?

Key Takeaway

International law is made by five entities: the legislature (approves treaties), the executive, the judiciary (including international tribunals, international custom, and the teachings of scholars), administrative agencies (both nation-state and nongovernmental) and—sometimes—by direct democracy.

Exercises

1. Argentina sells bonds (it borrows money from lenders and promises to repay the loans) on the open market, and buyers all around the world buy them. Five years later, Argentina declares that it will default on paying interest or principal on these bonds. Assume that Argentina has assets in the United States. Is it likely that a bondholder in the United States can bring an action in U.S. courts that will not be dismissed for lack of subject-matter jurisdiction?

2. During the Falkland Island war (1982) between Argentina and Great Britain, neutral tanker traffic was at risk of being involved in hostilities. Despite diplomatic cables from the United States assuring Argentina of the vessels' neutrality, an oil tanker leased by Amerada Hess, traveling from Puerto Rico to Valdez, Alaska, was repeatedly bombed by the Argentine air force. The ship had to be scuttled, along with its contents. Will a claim by Amerada Hess be recognized in U.S. courts?

6.2 Important Doctrines in Nation-State Judicial Decisions Affecting International Law

Learning Objectives

1. Define and describe the three traditional bases for a nation's jurisdiction over those individuals and entities from other nation-states.
2. Explain *forum non conveniens* and be able to apply that in a case involving citizens from two different nation-states.
3. Understand how forum-selection clauses operate in international contracts.
4. Describe and explain the origins of both sovereign immunity and the Act of State doctrine, and be able to distinguish between the two.

A fundamental element of any legal system anywhere is that a court cannot exercise authority over a person—natural or corporate—unless the court has jurisdiction. In Chapter 5 we discussed issues of jurisdiction in domestic U.S. law. In international law jurisdiction is no less important, but it is complicated because nation-states are sovereign entities with the right to make their own law, and to recognize (or not) the laws and authority of other nation-states.

Bases for National Jurisdiction under International Law

We touched on the sources of international law above; as we saw, in appropriate cases, courts apply international law to resolve disputes. Also relevant in international law is the question of when one nation-state may apply its *own* law when international disputes arise.

A nation-state has jurisdiction to make and enforce laws:

- within its own borders,
- with respect to its citizens ("nationals") wherever they might be, and
- with respect to actions taking place outside the territory but having an objective or direct impact within the territory.

The Restatement (Third) of Foreign Relations Law, labels these three jurisdictional bases as (1) the territorial principle, (2) the nationality principle, and (3) the objective territoriality principle.

The Territorial Principle

A nation-state has the power to make and enforce laws with regard to events taking place within its political/geographic territory. Anything that happens within a nation's borders is subject to its laws. A German company that makes direct investment in a plant in Spartanburg, South Carolina, is subject to South Carolina law and U.S. law as well.

The Nationality Principle

Nationality jurisdiction (the second jurisdictional basis) often raises problems. Under customary international law, nation-states may exercise jurisdiction over their citizens (nationals) even when the citizens' actions take place beyond their borders; the citizens of a nation-state are subject to its laws while within the nation and abroad. The United States has passed several laws that specifically govern the conduct of U.S. nationals abroad. United States companies operating abroad may not, for example, bribe public officials of foreign countries in order to get contracts (Foreign Corrupt Practices Act of 1976). Title VII of the Civil Rights Act also applies extraterritorially. Where a U.S. citizen is employed abroad by a U.S. company it is a violation of U.S. law for the employer to discriminate against employees on account of race, religion, color, sex, national origin, and so on.

Where the U.S. laws conflict with local or host country laws, extraterritorial application of U.S. law is problematic. In *Kern v. Dynalectron*,[13] Wade Kern, a Baptist pilot (U.S. citizen) sought employment with a company that provided emergency services to Muslims on pilgrimage to Mecca. The job required helicopter pilots to occasionally land in Mecca. However, Saudi law required that all who set foot in Mecca be Muslim; violators were to be beheaded. Kern wanted the job and tried to convert to Islam, but couldn't give up his Baptist roots. Dynalectron (a U.S. company) refused to hire hi, and he sued Dynalectron for discrimination under Title VII, claiming that he was denied the job because of his religion. Dynalectron did not deny that it had discriminated on account of his religion but argued that because of the Saudi law, it had no choice. Kern lost on the Title VII claim; the court ruled that being Muslim was a bona fide occupational qualification for an employee that might set foot in Mecca. The court understood that although Title VII of the Civil Rights Act of 1964 gave him a cause of action, the same law carved out an exception that a foreign state's laws might create a bona fide occupational qualification (a "BFOQ").

The Objective Territoriality Principle

The principle of objective territoriality is that nation-states may exercise jurisdiction over non-citizens when the actions of those non-citizens have a direct and foreseeable impact on the nation-state claiming jurisdiction. Nation-states act appropriately when they make and enforce law against actors whose conduct has such direct effects. A lawsuit in the United States against Osama bin Laden and his relatives in the Middle East was based on objective territoriality—bin Laden, based in Afghanistan, claimed credit for attacks in the United States on September 11, 2001.

The U.S. Sherman Antitrust Act has extraterritorial reach—if two Italian olive oil manufacturers conspire in Italy to fix the price of olive oil sold in the U.S., the manufacturers could be sued in the U.S. The 1977 Foreign Corrupt Practices Act has some extra-territorial application, as well; since 1998, the FCPA's anti-bribery provisions have applied to foreign persons and entities that, either directly or through an agent, engage in any act in furtherance of a corrupt payment (or an offer, promise, or authorization to pay) while in the territory of the United States.

Doctrines Limiting Nation-States' Jurisdiction

Once jurisdiction is established in U.S. courts in cases involving parties from two different nations, there are some important limiting doctrines that business leaders should be aware of. The doctrines can result in a court with jurisdiction refusing to hear the case. They are as follows:

- *forum non conveniens* (here, note that businesspeople can avoid the problem of conflicting forums by inserting forum selection clauses into their agreements);
- the act of state doctrine; and
- the sovereign immunity doctrine.

Forum Non Conveniens

Forum non conveniens (Latin: "forum not agreeing," abbreviated "FNC") is a common-law doctrine by which a court that *could* exercise jurisdiction in a case declines to do so because there is a more appropriate forum available to the parties. The doctrine works in both domestic law (a court in California may decide the better forum is Ohio), and for international litigants. The American application of the doctrine regarding international disputes first appeared in 1801 when a federal district court in Philadelphia refused to exercise jurisdiction over a Danish sea captain who was sued for back wages by a Danish crew member.[14] In 1947 the U.S. Supreme Court set out some of the factors relevant to *forum non conveniens* applications:

> An interest to be considered, and the one likely to be most pressed, is the private interest of the litigant. Important considerations are the relative ease of access to sources of proof; availability of compulsory process for attendance of unwilling, and the cost of obtaining attendance of willing witnesses; possibility of view of premises, if view would be appropriate to the action; and all other practical problems that make trial of a case easy, expeditious and inexpensive. There may also be questions as to the enforceability of a judgment if one is obtained.[15]

The International Forum-Choice Problem

As just noted, the *forum non conveniens* doctrine applies in U.S. domestic cases where two different federal court systems have both subject-matter jurisdiction and personal jurisdiction over the parties. And the doctrine may be applied when the court systems of two nation-states have jurisdiction to hear a case: a court may refuse to hear a case if there is an alternative forum in another country that is available and adequate, and if public and private interest factors point to the other nation's legal system as the proper venue.

For example, when Union Carbide's plant in Bhopal, India, exploded and killed or injured thousands of workers and local citizens, the injured Indian plaintiffs could sue Union Carbide in India, since Indian negligence law had territorial effect in Bhopal and Union Carbide was doing business in India. The plaintiffs could also sue Union Carbide in the United States, since Union Carbide was organized and incorporated in the United States. Which nation's courts should take a primary role? That, in essence, is the question that the *forum non conveniens* doctrine tries to answer.

The question can be complex, and a simple solution in a contracts case is the presence of a forum-selection clause by which the parties specify in advance where a lawsuit is to be heard. In a negligence case such as with Union Carbide's operations in India, however, there is no contract to enforce, and no forum selection provision to resolve the choice of forum issue.

Forum Selection Clauses

Bremen v. Zapata (below) is known for its holding that in cases where sophisticated parties engage in arms-length bargaining and select a forum in which to settle their disputes, the courts will not second-guess that selection unless there is fraud or unless one party has overwhelming bargaining power over the other. In *Bremen*, Zapata was held to its choice; this tells you that international contracting requires careful attention to the forum-selection clause. Since *Bremen*, the use of arbitration clauses in international contracting has grown exponentially. The arbitration clause is just like a forum-selection clause; instead of the party's selecting a judicial forum, the arbitration clause points to resolution of the dispute by an arbitrator or an arbitral panel.

In short, parties to an international contract can select a forum (a national court system and even a specific court within that system), or an arbitral forum to resolve any disputes that might arise.

Where there is no forum-selection clause, as in most tort cases (because, of course, torts are never agreed to in advance!) corporate defendants often find it useful to invoke *forum non conveniens* to avoid a lawsuit in the United States, knowing that the lawsuit elsewhere cannot as easily result in a dollar-value judgment and might face procedural problems, and they can challenge any foreign judgment as lacking in due process. In theory, at least, a U.S. court's finding that the foreign forum is "adequate"—one of the four requirements for a judge to grant *forum non conveniens* in the U.S.—should mean that there is some semblance of due process. Consider *Gonzalez v. Chrysler Corporation*, below.

Act of State Doctrine

In the United States, the government may sometimes constitutionally seize private property, but must pay "just compensation" for property so taken. Frequently, however, foreign governments have seized the assets of U.S. corporations without compensation. If the seizure violates the standards of international law—as, for example, by failing to pay just compensation—the question arises whether the former owners may sue in U.S. courts. One problem with permitting the courts to hear such claims is that by time of suit, the property may have passed into the hands of bona fide purchasers from the foreign government. Such asset seizures are also called "expropriations."

The Supreme Court has enunciated the act-of-state doctrine as follows: "Every sovereign State is bound to respect the independence of every other sovereign State, and the courts of one country will not sit in judgment on ... the acts of the government of another done within its own territory."[16] This means that U.S. courts will "reject private claims based on the contention that the damaging act of another nation violates either U.S. or international law."[17]

The Act of State doctrine attracted considerable attention when, in 1959, the new communist government in Cuba, under Fidel Castro, expropriated without compensation, American businesses on the island. In *Banco Nacional de Cuba v. Sabbatino* (1964) the Court held that if the foreign state exercises its own jurisdiction to give effect to its public interests, however the government defines those interests, the expropriated property will be held to belong to that country or to bona fide purchasers. For the Act of State doctrine to be invoked, the act of the foreign government must have been completely executed within the country—for example, by having enacted legislation expropriating the property. The Supreme Court said that the Act of State doctrine applies in this case, meaning that the U.S. businesses could not recover in U.S. courts from Cuba's official public acts, even though the United States had severed diplomatic relations with Cuba and even though Cuba would not reciprocally apply the Act of State doctrine in its own courts.[18]

Sovereign Immunity

sovereign immunity

The legal doctrine that the sovereign or state cannot commit a legal wrong and, absent its consent, is immune from civil criminal liability; the government cannot be sued.

For many years, sovereigns (governments) enjoyed complete immunity for their own acts. A king who established courts for citizens to resolve their disputes would generally not retain judges who allowed subjects to sue the king (the sovereign) and collect money from the treasury of the realm. If a subject sued a foreign sovereign, any judgment would have to be collectible in the foreign realm, and no king thought it advisable politically to allow his subjects to get a judgment on a foreign sovereign's treasury. Even if a sovereign's citizens were allowed to get such judgments, a judgment in one nation-state against the sovereign of another state would usually have to be collected in the other state, and the foreign sovereign could quickly put an end to that. In effect, claims against sovereigns at home or abroad just didn't get very far. Judges, seeing a case against a sovereign, would generally dismiss it on the basis of "**sovereign immunity**." This became customary international law.

In the twentieth century, the rise of communism led to state-owned companies that began trading across national borders. But, when a state-owned company failed to deliver the quantity or quality of goods agreed upon, could the disappointed buyer sue? Many tried, but sovereign immunity was often invoked as a reason why the court should dismiss the lawsuit, and motions to dismiss were freely granted. Gradually, however, a few courts began distinguishing between governmental acts and commercial acts—where a state-owned company was acting like a private, commercial entity, the court would not grant immunity. This became known as the "restrictive" version of sovereign immunity, in contrast to "absolute" sovereign immunity. In U.S. courts, decisions as to sovereign immunity after World War II were often political in nature, with the U.S. State Department giving advisory letters on a case-by-case basis, recommending that the court either grant immunity to the foreign state or not. Congress moved to clarify matters in 1976 by passing the Foreign Sovereign Immunities Act, which legislatively recognized the restrictive theory.

Sovereign Immunity vs. Act of State Doctrine

Sovereign immunity and the Act of State doctrine rest on different legal principles and have different legal consequences. The doctrine of sovereign immunity bars a suit altogether—once a foreign-government defendant shows that sovereign immunity applies to the claims the plaintiff has raised, the court has no jurisdiction even to consider them and must dismiss the case. By contrast, the Act of State Doctrine rests on notions of the separation of powers in the U.S. Constitution—the judiciary does not wish to intrude on foreign policy, regarding that as the primary responsibility of the President and Congress. Declaring foreign sovereign acts as "illegal" would be politically sensitive, so judges must decide cases without deciding whether a foreign act of state is legal or not. The doctrine, unlike sovereign immunity, does not require dismissal in a case properly before a court; indeed, the doctrine may be invoked by plaintiffs as well as defendants. Instead, it precludes anyone from arguing against the legal validity of an act of a foreign government.

Here is a simple example: suppose a widow living in the United States is sued by her late husband's family to prevent her from inheriting his estate. They claim she was never married to the deceased. She shows that while citizens of another country, they were married by proclamation of that country's legislature. Although legislatures do not marry people in the United States, the Act of State Doctrine would bar a court from denying the legal validity of the marriage entered into in their home country.

Cases

Forum Non Conveniens

> ### Gonzalez v. Chrysler Corporation
> 301 F.3d 377 (5th Cir., 2002)

[Note: This opinion was appealed to the Supreme Court, but the Court did not take the case, so the decision stands as good precedent regarding FNC.]

Jolly, C. J.

In this *forum non conveniens* case, we first consider whether the cap imposed by Mexican law on the recovery of tort damages renders Mexico an inadequate forum for resolving a tort suit by a Mexican citizen against an American manufacturer and an American designer of an air bag. Holding that Mexico—despite its cap on damages—represents an adequate alternative forum, we next consider whether the district court committed reversible error when it concluded that the private and public interest factors so strongly pointed to Mexico that Mexico, instead of Texas, was the appropriate forum in which to try this case. Finding no reversible error, we affirm the district court's judgment dismissing this case on the ground of *forum non conveniens*.

In 1995, while in Houston, the plaintiff, Jorge Gonzalez ("Gonzalez") saw several magazine and television advertisements for the Chrysler LHS. The advertisements sparked his interest, so Gonzalez decided to visit several Houston car dealerships. Convinced by these visits that the Chrysler LHS was a high quality and safe car, Gonzalez purchased a Chrysler LHS upon returning to Mexico.

On May 21, 1996, the wife of the plaintiff was involved in a collision with another moving vehicle while driving the Chrysler LHS in Atizapan de Zaragoza, Mexico. The accident triggered the passenger-side air bag, and the force of the air bag's deployment instantaneously killed Gonzalez's three-year-old son, Pablo.

Gonzalez brought suit in Texas district court against (1) Chrysler, as the manufacturer of the automobile; (2) TRW, Inc. and TRW Vehicle Safety Systems, Inc., as the designers of the front sensor for the air bag; and (3) Morton International, Inc., as designer of the air bag module. Gonzalez asserted claims based on products liability, negligence, gross negligence, and breach of warranty. As noted, Gonzalez chose to file his suit in Texas, which has a tenuous connection to the underlying dispute. Neither the car nor the air bag module was designed or manufactured in Texas. The accident took place in Mexico, involved Mexican citizens, and only Mexican citizens witnessed the accident. Moreover, Gonzalez purchased the Chrysler LHS in Mexico (although he shopped for the car in Houston, Texas). Because of these factors, the district court granted the defendants' identical motions for dismissal on the ground of *forum non conveniens*. Gonzalez now appeals.

The primary question we address today involves the threshold inquiry in the *forum non conveniens* analysis: Whether the limitation imposed by Mexican law on the award of damages renders Mexico an inadequate alternative forum for resolving a tort suit brought by a Mexican citizen against a United States manufacturer. * * *

Gonzalez contends that a Mexican forum would provide a clearly unsatisfactory remedy because (1) Mexican tort law does not provide for a strict liability theory of recovery for the manufacture or design of an unreasonably dangerous product and (2) Mexican law caps the maximum award for the loss of a child's life at approximately $2,500 (730 days' worth of wages at the Mexican minimum wage rate). Thus, according to Gonzalez, Mexico provides an inadequate alternative forum for this dispute.

Gonzalez's first contention may be quickly dismissed based on the explicit principle stated in *Piper Aircraft* [U.S. Supreme Court, 1981]. There the Supreme Court held that Scotland's failure to recognize strict liability in an airplane crash case did not render Scotland an inadequate alternative forum. There is no basis to distinguish the absence of a strict products liability cause of action under Mexican law from that of Scotland. *Piper Aircraft* therefore controls. Accordingly, we hold that the failure of Mexican law to allow for strict liability on the facts of this case does not render Mexico an inadequate forum.

Gonzalez's second contention—that the damage cap renders the remedy available in a Mexican forum "clearly unsatisfactory"—is slightly more problematic. Underlying this contention are two distinct arguments: First, Gonzalez argues that if he brings suit in Mexico, the cap on damages will entitle him to a *de minimis* recovery only—a clearly unsatisfactory award for the loss of a child. Second, Gonzalez argues that because of the damage cap, the cost of litigating this case in Mexico will exceed the potential recovery. As a consequence, the lawsuit will never be brought in Mexico. Stated differently, the lawsuit is not economically viable in Mexico. It follows, therefore, that Mexico offers no forum (much less an adequate forum) through which Gonzalez can (or will) seek redress. We address each argument in turn.

In addressing Gonzalez's first argument, we start from basic principles of comity [courtesy between nations, as in respect shown by one country for the laws, judicial decisions, and institutions of another]. Mexico, as a sovereign nation, has made a deliberate choice in providing a specific remedy for this tort cause of action. In making this policy choice, the Mexican government has resolved a trade-off among the competing objectives and costs of tort law, involving interests of victims, of consumers, of manufacturers, and of various other economic and cultural values. In resolving this trade-off, the Mexican people, through their duly-elected lawmakers, have decided to limit tort damages with respect to a child's death. It would be inappropriate—even patronizing—for us to denounce this legitimate policy choice by holding that Mexico provides an inadequate forum for Mexican tort victims. In another *forum non conveniens* case, the District Court for the Southern District of New York made this same point—observing (perhaps in a hyperbolic choice of words) that "to retain the litigation in this forum, as plaintiffs request, would be yet another example of imperialism, another situation in which an established sovereign inflicted its rules, its standards and values on a developing nation." In re *Union Carbide Corp. Gas Plant Disaster* at Bhopal, India in December, 1984, [Citation, S.D.N.Y., 1986]. In short, we see no warrant for us, a United States court, to replace the policy preference of the Mexican government with our own view of what is a good policy for the citizens of Mexico.

Based on the considerations mentioned above, we hold that the district court did not err when it found that the cap on damages did not render the remedy available in the Mexican forum clearly unsatisfactory.

We now turn our attention to Gonzalez's "economic viability" argument—that is, because there is no economic incentive to file suit in the alternative forum, there is effectively no alternative forum.

The practical and economic realities lying at the base of this dispute are clear. At oral argument, the parties agreed that this case would never be filed in Mexico. In short, a dismissal on the ground of *forum non conveniens* will determine the outcome of this litigation in Chrysler's favor. We nevertheless are unwilling to hold as a legal principle that Mexico offers an inadequate forum simply because it does not make economic sense for Gonzalez to file this lawsuit in Mexico. Our reluctance arises out of two practical considerations.

[Discussion of the first consideration is omitted.]

Second, if we allow the economic viability of a lawsuit to decide the adequacy of an alternative forum, we are further forced to engage in a rudderless exercise of line drawing with respect to a cap on damages: At what point does a cap on damages transform a forum from adequate to inadequate? Is it, as here, $2,500? Is it $50,000? Or is it $100,000? Any recovery cap may, in a given case, make the lawsuit economically unviable. We therefore hold that the adequacy inquiry under *Piper Aircraft* does not include an evaluation of whether it makes economic sense for Gonzalez to file this lawsuit in Mexico.

The district court found that almost all of the private and public interest factors pointed away from Texas and toward Mexico as the appropriate forum. It is clear to us that this finding does not represent an abuse of discretion. After all, the tort victim was a Mexican citizen, the driver of the Chrysler LHS (Gonzalez's wife) is a Mexican citizen, and the plaintiff is a Mexican citizen. The accident took place in Mexico. Gonzalez purchased the car in Mexico. Neither the car nor the air bag was designed or manufactured in Texas. In short, there are no public or private interest factors that would suggest that Texas is the appropriate forum for the trial of this case.

For the foregoing reasons, the district court's dismissal of this case on the ground of *forum non conveniens* is AFFIRMED.

Case Questions

1. How can an alternative forum be "adequate" if no rational lawyer would take Gonzalez's case to file in a Mexican state court?
2. To what extent does it strike you as "imperialism" for a U.S. court to make a judgment that a Mexican court is not "adequate"?
3. Why did the plaintiff want to file suit in the United States instead of Mexico?

Forum-Selection Clauses

In re the Bremen
407 U.S. 1 (1972)

In re the Bremen

U.S. Supreme Court case, 1972, enforcing an international forum-selection clause in a contract between a U.S. firm and a German firm.

[The parties entered into an agreement for a drilling rig owned by Zapata, a U.S. corporation based in Houston, to be towed from Louisiana to Italy by Unterweser, a German corporation; Unterwser's ocean-going tugboat—a huge ship—was named the Bremen. Zapata was to drill oil wells in the Adriatic Sea. The parties' contract included a choice of forum clause:

"Any dispute arising must be treated before the London Court of Justice."

A storm seriously damaged the rig and forced the Bremen to make land in Tampa, Florida. Notwithstanding the choice of forum clause, Zapata sued Unterweser in the U.S. district court in Tampa for $3.5 million in damages (about $25 million in 2019 dollars). The Florida federal district court (trial court) refused to recognize the choice of forum clause (that the matter should be heard in Britain), relying on a previous court of appeals case, *Carbon Black Export, Inc.*, which had held "agreements in advance of controversy whose object is to oust the jurisdiction of the courts are contrary to public policy and will not be enforced." Unterweser appealed, and a divided federal court of appeals affirmed, agreeing that the U.S. courts had jurisdiction and that the choice of forum clause was not enforceable.]

Burger, C. J. [Chief judge]

We granted certiorari to review a judgment of the United States Court of Appeals for the Fifth Circuit declining to enforce a forum-selection clause governing disputes arising under an international towage contract between petitioners and respondent. The circuits have differed in their approach to such clauses. For the reasons stated hereafter, we vacate the judgment of the Court of Appeals. * * *

We hold, with the six dissenting members of the Court of Appeals, that far too little weight and effect were given to the forum clause in resolving this controversy. For at least two decades we have witnessed an expansion of overseas commercial activities by business enterprises based in the United States. The barrier of distance that once tended to confine a business concern to a modest territory no longer does so. Here we see an American company with special expertise contracting with a foreign company to tow a complex machine thousands of miles across seas and oceans. The expansion of American business and industry will hardly be encouraged if, notwithstanding solemn contracts, we insist on a parochial concept that all disputes must be resolved under our laws and in our courts. * * * In an era of expanding world trade and commerce, the absolute aspects of the doctrine of the *Carbon Black* case have little place and would be a heavy hand indeed on the future development of international commercial dealings by Americans. We cannot have trade and commerce in world markets and international waters exclusively on our terms, governed by our laws, and resolved in our courts.

Forum-selection clauses have historically not been favored by American courts. Many courts, federal and state, have declined to enforce such clauses on the ground that they were "contrary to public policy," or that their effect was to "oust the jurisdiction" of the court. Although this view apparently still has considerable acceptance, other courts are tending to adopt a more hospitable attitude toward forum-selection clauses. This view is that such clauses are prima facie valid and should be enforced unless enforcement is shown by the resisting party to be "unreasonable" under the circumstances.

We believe this is the correct doctrine to be followed by federal district courts sitting in admiralty. It is merely the other side of the proposition recognized by this Court in [Citation, 1964], holding "It is settled that parties to a contract may agree in advance to submit to the jurisdiction of a given court, to permit notice to be served by the opposing party, or even to waive notice altogether."

This approach is substantially that followed in other common-law countries, including England. It is the view advanced by noted scholars and that adopted by the Restatement of the Conflict of Laws. It accords with ancient concepts of freedom of contract and reflects an appreciation of the expanding horizons of American contractors who seek business in all parts of the world. Not surprisingly, foreign businessmen prefer, as do we, to have disputes resolved in their own courts, but if that choice is not available, then in a neutral forum with expertise in the subject matter. Plainly, the courts of England meet the standards of neutrality and long experience in admiralty litigation. The choice of that forum was made in an arm's-length negotiation by experienced and sophisticated businessmen, and absent some compelling and countervailing reason it should be honored by the parties and enforced by the courts. * * *

The judgment of the Court of Appeals is vacated and the case is remanded for further proceedings consistent with this opinion. [One justice dissented.]

Case Questions

1. Why do parties insert choice of forum clauses in their contracts?
2. If the contract called for a forum in a country whose judiciary is lacking in "due process" as we in the U.S. think of it, would the Court have approved of the clause?
3. Why did the Court hold that approving the choice of forum clause here was a good policy as relates to American international trade contracts?

Act of State Doctrine

W. S. Kirkpatrick & Co., Inc. v. Environmental Tectonics Co.[19]

493 U.S. 400 (1990)

W. S. Kirkpatrick & Co., Inc. v. Environmental Tectonics Co.

U.S. Supreme Court, 1990, analyzing the application of the Act of State doctrine to the act of a public official taking a bribe from an American firm operating in Nigeria.

Scalia, J.

In 1981, Harry Carpenter, then Chairman of the Board and Chief Executive Officer of defendant W. S. Kirkpatrick & Co., Inc. (Kirkpatrick) learned that the Republic of Nigeria was interested in contracting for the construction and equipment of an aeromedical center at Kaduna Air Force Base in Nigeria. He made arrangements with Benson Akindele, a Nigerian citizen, whereby Akindele would endeavor to secure the contract for Kirkpatrick. It was agreed that in the event the contract was awarded to Kirkpatrick, Kirkpatrick would pay Akindele an amount equal to 20% of the contract price, which would in turn be given as a bribe to officials of the Nigerian government. In accordance with this plan, the contract was awarded to defendant Kirkpatrick; Kirkpatrick paid the promised "commission" and those funds were disbursed as bribes. All parties agree that Nigerian law prohibits both the payment and the receipt of bribes in connection with the award of a government contract.

Plaintiff Environmental Tectonics Corporation, International, an unsuccessful bidder for the Kaduna contract, learned of the 20% "commission" and brought the matter to the attention of the Nigerian Air Force and the United States Embassy in Lagos. Following an investigation the United States Attorney for the District of New Jersey brought charges against both Kirkpatrick and Carpenter for violations of the Foreign Corrupt Practices Act of 1977 and both pleaded guilty.

Plaintiff then brought this civil action in the United States District Court in New Jersey against Carpenter, Akindele, petitioners, and others, seeking damages under the Racketeer Influenced and Corrupt Organizations Act, the Robinson-Patman Act, and the New Jersey Anti-Racketeering Act.[20] The defendants moved to dismiss the complaint on the ground that the action was barred by the act of state doctrine.

The District Court concluded that the act of state doctrine applies "if the inquiry presented for judicial determination includes the motivation of a sovereign act which would result in embarrassment to the sovereign or constitute interference in the conduct of foreign policy of the United States." Applying that principle to the facts at hand, the court held that respondents suit had to be dismissed because in order to prevail respondents would have to show that "the defendants intended to wrongfully influence the decision to award the Nigerian contract by payment of a bribe, that the government of Nigeria, its officials or other representatives knew of the bribe, that the bribe was actually received or anticipated and that but for the bribe, Plaintiff would have been awarded the Nigerian contract."

The Court of Appeals for the Third Circuit reversed. [That is, the 3rd Circuit reversed the trial (district court), holding that the act-of-state doctrine did not apply and the U.S. court should hear the case]. * * *

In every case in which we have held the act of state doctrine applicable, the relief sought or the defense interposed would have required a court in the United States to declare invalid the official acts of a foreign sovereign performed within its own territory. * * * In *Sabbatino*, upholding the defendant's claim to the funds would have required a holding that Cuba's expropriation of goods located in Havana was null and void. In the present case, by contrast, neither the claim nor any asserted defense requires a determination that Nigeria's contract with Kirkpatrick International was, or, was not effective.

Petitioners point out, however, that the facts necessary to establish respondent's claim will also establish that the contract was unlawful. Specifically, they note that in order to prevail respondent must prove that defendant Kirkpatrick made, and Nigerian officials received, payments that violate Nigerian law, which would, they assert, support a finding that the contract is invalid under Nigerian law. Assuming that to be true, it still does not suffice. The act of state doctrine is not some vague doctrine of abstention but a "principle *of decision* binding on federal and state courts alike." As we said in [Citation], "the act within its own boundaries of one sovereign State . . . becomes a rule of decision for the courts of this country." Act of state issues only arise when a court *must* decide—that is, when the outcome of the case turns upon—the effect of official action by a foreign sovereign. When that question is not in the case, neither is the act of state doctrine. This is the situation here. Regardless of what the court's factual findings may suggest as to the legality of the Nigerian contract, its legality is simply not a question to be decided in the present suit, and there is thus no occasion to apply the rule of decision that the act of state doctrine requires. * * *

The short of the matter is this: Courts in the United States have the power, and ordinarily the obligation, to decide cases and controversies properly presented to them. The act of state doctrine does not establish an exception for cases and controversies that may embarrass foreign governments, but merely requires that, in the process of deciding, the acts of foreign sovereigns taken within their own jurisdictions shall be deemed valid. The doctrine has no application to the present case because the validity of no foreign sovereign act is at issue.

The judgment of the Court for the Third Circuit is affirmed.

Case Questions

1. Why is this case not about sovereign immunity? (Hint: was taking the bribe an "official action" of the Nigerian government?)
2. On what basis does the U.S. court take jurisdiction over an event or series of events that takes place in Nigeria?
3. If the court goes on to the merits of the case and determines that an unlawful bribe took place in Nigeria, is it likely that diplomatic relations between the United States and Nigeria will be adversely affected?
4. Why would a U.S. firm engage in bribery in the first place?

Key Takeaway

Each nation-state has several bases of jurisdiction to make and enforce laws, including the territorial principle, nationality jurisdiction, and objective territoriality.

However, nation-states will not always choose to exercise their jurisdiction: the doctrines of *forum non conveniens*, sovereign immunity, and act of state limit the amount and nature of judicial activity in one nation that would affect nonresident parties and foreign sovereigns. Parties to an international contract may specify what country will hear any dispute, and this obviates the FNC problem.

Exercises

1. Argentina sells bonds on the open market, and buyers all around the world buy them. Five years later, Argentina declares that it will default on paying interest or principal on these bonds. Assume that Argentina has assets in the United States. Is it likely that a bondholder in the United States can bring an action in U.S. courts that will not be dismissed for lack of subject-matter jurisdiction?

2. During the Falkland Islands war between Argentina and Great Britain, neutral tanker traffic was at risk of being involved in hostilities. Despite diplomatic cables from the United States assuring Argentina of the vessels' neutrality, an oil tanker leased by Amerada Hess, traveling from Puerto Rico to Valdez, Alaska, was repeatedly bombed by the Argentine Air Force. The ship had to be scuttled, along with its contents. Will a claim by Amerada Hess be recognized in U.S. courts?

6.3 Regulating Trade

Learning Objectives

1. Understand why nation-states have sometimes limited imports but not exports.
2. Explain why nation-states have given up some of their sovereignty by lowering tariffs in agreement with other nation-states.

Before globalization, nation-states traded with one another, but they did so with a significant degree of protectiveness. For example, one nation might have imposed very high tariffs (taxes on imports from other countries) while not taxing exports in order to protect its own industries or to encourage a favorable "balance of trade." The balance of trade is an important statistic for many countries; for many years, the U.S. balance of trade has been negative because it imports far more than it exports (even though the United States, with its very large farms, is the world's largest exporter of agricultural products). This section will explore import and export controls in the context of global agreement to reduce import controls in the name of free trade.

Export Controls

Notwithstanding the post-WWII free-trade movement, the United States maintains restrictions on some products sold to other nations and to individuals and firms within those nations. For example, the Export Administration Act of 1985 has controlled certain exports that would endanger national security, drain scarce materials from the U.S. economy, or harm foreign policy goals. The U.S. Secretary of Commerce has a list of controlled commodities that meet these criteria.

The United States imposes export controls to protect national security interests and promote foreign policy objectives. The U.S. also participates in various multilateral export control regimes to prevent the proliferation of weapons of mass destruction and prevent destabilizing accumulations of conventional weapons and related material. The Bureau of Industry and Security (BIS)—part of the Department of Commerce—administers American laws, regulations, and policies governing the export, reexport, and transfer (in-country) of commodities, software, and technology (collectively "items") falling under the jurisdiction of the Export Administration Regulations (EAR).

More specifically, the Arms Export Control Act permits the president to create a list of controlled goods related to military weaponry, and no person or firm subject to U.S. law can export any listed item without a license. When the United States has imposed sanctions, the International Emergency Economic Powers Act (IEEPA) has often been the legislative basis; and the act gives the president considerable power to impose limitations on trade. For example, in 1979, President Carter, using IEEPA, was able to impose sanctions on Iran after the diplomatic hostage crisis. The United States still imposes travel restrictions and other sanctions on Cuba, North Korea, and many other countries.

Free Trade and Import Controls

The International Free-Trade Movement

Nation-states naturally wish to protect their domestic industries. Historically, protectionism has come in the form of import taxes or tariffs, also called duties, and by non-tariff barriers. The tariff is simply a tax imposed on goods when they enter a country. Tariffs change often and vary from one nation-state to another.

Efforts to implement free trade began after WWII with the General Agreement on Tariffs and Trade (GATT) and are now enforced through the World Trade Organization (WTO). The GATT and the WTO have sought, through successive rounds of trade talks, to eliminate non-tariff barriers and also to decrease the number and extent of tariffs that would hinder the free flow of commerce from one nation-state to another. The theory of comparative advantage espoused by David Ricardo is the basis for the gradual but steady decline of tariffs, from early rounds of talks under the GATT to the Uruguay Round, which established the WTO.

The GATT was a huge multilateral treaty negotiated after World War II and signed in 1947. Nation-states agreed to give up some of their sovereignty (the right to restrict international trade) if other nation-states did the same. After various "rounds" of re-negotiation, the Uruguay Round ended in 1994 with the United States and 125 other nation-states signing the treaty that established the WTO. In 1948, the worldwide average tariff on industrial goods was around 40 percent. That number is now more like 4 percent, as globalization has taken root. Free-trade proponents claim that globalization has increased general well-being, while opponents claim that free trade has brought outsourcing, industrial decline, and the hollowing-out of the U.S. manufacturing base. The same kinds of criticisms have been directed at the North American Free Trade Agreement (NAFTA).

The Uruguay Round was to be succeeded by the Doha Round, but that round has not concluded because developing countries have not been satisfied with the proposed reductions in agricultural tariffs imposed by the more developed economies. Developing countries have been resistant to further agreements unless and until the United States and the European Union lower their agricultural tariffs.

There are a number of regional trade agreements other than NAFTA. The European Union (EU), formerly the Common Market, provides for the free movement of member nations' citizens throughout the EU, and sets union-wide standards for tariffs, subsidies, transportation, human rights, and many other issues. Another regional trade agreement is Mercosur—an organization formed by Brazil, Argentina, Uruguay, and Paraguay to improve trade and commerce among those South American nations. Almost all trade barriers between the four nations have been eliminated, and the organization has also established a broad social agenda focusing on education, culture, the environment, and consumer protection.

Import Controls

We discussed the trend toward limiting tariffs to encourage free trade, above, but tariffs yet abound. They are imposed because of concerns about the national economy, the preservation of animal or plant life, and consumer health and well-being.

Other controls ("non-tariff barriers") include prohibitions against importation, or limits on importation. For example, a nation-state that wishes to preserve its textile industry may forbid or limit textile importation. In 2001, the U.S. prohibited all European imports of livestock to prevent the spread of hoof and mouth disease in the U.S., which had sickened large numbers of animals in Europe. The U.S. has prohibited the importation of elephant ivory from Africa (to discourage poaching of threatened species).[21] Specific and sometimes intentionally laborious paperwork, inspection, and other obscure rules may be unfairly imposed on some goods (such as food, livestock, footwear, audio/visual equipment), and some labeling and special packaging requirements may impede the free flow of goods.

Controls can be imposed unilaterally by any nation-state, and can be imposed differentially, depending on the country of origin. Beef from Korea may be given more lenient tariffs or other non-tariff barriers than beef from Argentina. Much of this is political, driven by the executive branch, often with little consultation or oversight from Congress. In 2018, President Trump imposed differential tariffs on steel and aluminum, with higher tariffs on those goods for certain targeted countries. But such actions can be challenged if there are treaties or conventions that obligate the U.S. not to do so. By being part of the WTO, the U.S. is subject to having the WTO dispute resolution process invoked by affected WTO member states.

Key Takeaway

Historically, import controls were more common than export controls; nation-states would typically impose tariffs (taxes) on goods imported from other nation-states. Since WWII, most nation-states have voluntarily given up some of their sovereignty in order to gain the advantages of bilateral and multilateral trade and investment treaties. The most prominent example of a multilateral trade treaty is the GATT, now administered by the WTO. There are also regional free-trade agreements, such as NAFTA and Mercosur, that provide additional relaxation of tariffs beyond those agreed to under the WTO.

Some nation-states, the United States included, nevertheless maintain certain export controls for national security, humanitarian, and military purposes.

Exercises

1. Look at various sources and describe, in one hundred or fewer words, why the Doha Round of WTO negotiations has not been concluded.

2. President Trump has imposed, or threatened to impose, tariffs on the importation into the United States of goods from many countries, including China and our ally and immediate neighbor, Canada. Why has he done that? What imported goods have been hit with tariffs? (Hint: https://www.businessinsider.com/trump-china-tariff-product-list-trade-war-2018-4/)

3. What U.S. industries have been targeted by Canada in retaliation, and why those? (Hint: https://www.fin.gc.ca/activty/consult/cacsap-cmpcaa-eng.asp).

6.4 Organizing for International Business

Learning Objectives

1. Understand the most common methods of business organization for international business.
2. Recognize that many firms do significant amounts of international business outside of their home nation-state.

Common Methods of Doing Business Abroad

Any firm in the U.S. can do business abroad. Businesspeople may do that to market to foreign customers, avoid tariffs, reduce transportation costs, and meet local-content requirements. Here are the seven most common ways firms do that.

1. Simple import-export relationships. A customer in New York might order apples from a Washington state firm; the New Yorker could also order apples from Chile or Japan and have them shipped to New York.
2. Product-use licensing. A U.S. firm can license a foreign company to produce its product in a foreign country and earn income from those sales. The U.S. firm does not have to establish a foreign manufacturing facility.
3. Sales representatives. A sales rep in, say, South Korea, solicits orders for ball bearings made in the U.S. and sends the order to the U.S. for approval and shipping. The agent is not an employee of the U.S. firm; he or she is paid a commission on the ball bearings sold in South Korea.
4. Agents. A sales agent is an employee of the U.S. firm, working abroad.
5. Branch offices. A U.S. company may set up a foreign branch office, an extension of the home office, and not independent.
6. Joint ventures. A joint venture is a partnership between a U.S. and foreign firm to do business in the foreign country or in a third country.
7. Subsidiaries or foreign affiliates. A U.S. company may set up a foreign-based firm according to the laws of the foreign country, but under the control of a U.S. parent. Or, a U.S. firm may establish a presence abroad, but retain less than 50% interest in it.

The Importance of Cross-Border Ownership

Many large U.S. companies invest heavily in foreign markets. General Motors has invested billions in China, and indeed, makes one of the best-selling cars sold in China (Buick). Ford, and its joint-venture partner Changan Ford Mazda, set up a Ford Focus plant in Chongqing in 2012, investing almost $500 million.[22]

And of course foreign companies sell goods and services in the U.S., too, employing millions of workers. Airbus, the arch-rival of Boeing, employs hundreds of employees in Mobile, Alabama; BMW has set up a huge auto-making plant[23] in South Carolina, as has the Mexican cement-making giant Cemex. In 2008 *Forbes* estimated that 4% (five million) U.S. workers were employed in the U.S. by overseas companies.[24] The reference just cited has a very long list of foreign firms doing business in the U.S., including BP (British Petroleum), Toyota, Honda, Nestlé, Sony, Unilever, and Bayer. Burger King is owned by a Brazilian firm, and Heinz's top management is Brazilian. Miller Beer is owned by the South African Brewing Company (but, happily, local craft beers are flourishing in America). "Made in the USA" is a popular label for many foreign firms, and the United States is seen as an "oasis of stability—political, economic and infrastructural—in an uncertain world."[25]

We might add, though, that the United States' reputation for legal stability, democratic elections, and peaceful transfers of power between political parties is currently subject to remarkable stress. For the past dozen years at least there has been a lack of compromise in Congress[26] and increasing partisan politicization of the third branch of government, the judiciary.[27]

Key Takeaway

There are several mechanisms by which business owners in one nation-state can do business in another to sell goods and services, from simple import-export relationships to setting up entire production facilities. Foreign business is a big part of the U.S. economy. U.S. firms do business abroad, and foreign firms have significant presence in the U.S.

Exercises

1. Why do firms headquartered in one nation-state do business abroad?
2. A private textile and clothing manufacturing firm in Bangladesh decided to upgrade its sophisticated computer technology systems, but it lacked the capital for research and development to get it. Also, the firm figured that the Bangladeshi government could not effectively handle such a development project. What business forms might it consider, and what are the benefits and pitfalls of the options?
3. Why does the "increasing partisan politicization of the third branch of government"—the U.S. judiciary—in any way threaten foreigners who might want to do business in the United States?

6.5 Summary and Exercises

Summary

International law is the mechanism by which nation-states secure their own interests in the international arena. This body of law is made by mechanisms analogous to how law is made domestically. It is made by the legislature, the executive, the judiciary, administrative agencies, and sometime by direct democracy. There is an International Court of Justice, but it only hears cases between nation-states. There is no international court for the resolution of civil disputes, and no regional courts for that purpose, either.

The lack of unified law and prevalence of global commerce means that local and national court systems must find ways to enforce judgments from one national court system in another, to deal with claims against sovereigns, and to factor in diplomatic considerations; domestic judicial systems must deal with disputes that involve (directly or indirectly) the political and diplomatic prerogatives of sovereigns. Three doctrines that have been devised are sovereign immunity, Act of State, and *forum non conveniens*. The recognition of forum-selection clauses in national contracting has also aided the use of arbitration clauses, making international commercial dispute resolution more efficient. Because of existing treaties, arbitration awards are more easily enforceable than judgments from national court systems.

In regulating global trade, the traditional practice of imposing taxes (tariffs) on imports from other countries (and not taxing exports to other countries) has been substantially modified by the emergence of the General Agreement on Tariffs and Trade (GATT) rules as now enforced by the World Trade Organization (WTO). The United States has recently revived some tariffs, and it also regulates exports, for national security and other foreign policy considerations.

Exercises

1. Assume that the United States enters into a multilateral treaty with several third-world countries under which then-existing private claims to molybdenum and certain other minerals in the United States are assigned to an international agency for exploitation. When the owner of a U.S. mine continues to dig for ore covered by the treaty, the Justice Department sues to enjoin further mining. What is the result? Why?

2. A foreign government enters into a contract with a U.S. company to provide computer equipment and services for the intelligence arm of its military forces. After the equipment has been supplied, the foreign government refuses to pay. The U.S. company files suit in federal court in the United States, seeking to attach a U.S. bank account owned by the foreign government. The foreign government claims that the U.S. court has no jurisdiction and that even if it does, the government is immune from suit. What is the result?

3. Would the result in Exercise 2 be any different if the U.S. company had maintained its own equipment on a lease basis abroad and the foreign government had then expropriated the equipment and refused to pay the U.S. company its just value?

4. Canada and Russia have competing claims over fishing and mining rights in parts of the Arctic Ocean. Assuming they cannot settle their competing claims through diplomatic negotiation, where might they have their dispute settled?

Self-Test Questions

1. International law derives from:
   a. the U.S. Constitution
   b. the common law
   c. treaties
   d. customary international law
   e. c and d

2. Foreign nations are generally immune from suit in U.S. courts for governmental acts because of:
   a. the international sovereign immunity treaty
   b. a United Nations law forbidding suits against foreign sovereigns
   c. the Foreign Sovereign Immunities Act
   d. precedent created by the U.S. Supreme Court

3. A foreign government's expropriation of private assets belonging to a nonresident is:

   a. a violation of international law

   b. a violation of the U.S. Constitution

   c. permitted by the domestic law of most nation-states

   d. in violation of the Act of State doctrine

4. Arbitration of business disputes is:

   a. frowned upon by courts for replacing public dispute resolution with private dispute resolution

   b. permissible when a country's laws permit it

   c. permissible if the parties agree to it

   d. a and b

   e. b and c

Self-Test Answers

1. e
2. c
3. c
4. e

Endnotes

1. Treaties typically are between two or more nation-states but may also be multilateral if others join, as when the first European nations signed the Treaty of Rome (1960), and others signed on later. A convention, unlike a treaty process, usually begins with the convening multiple nation-states with a common interest in resolving an international problem. Like a treaty, a convention must be acted upon by the nation's legislature, unless it is "self-executing." See https://www.law.cornell.edu/wex/self_executing_treaty

2. Among famous treaties to which the U.S. is a party are these: Second Treaty of Paris, 1783 (ended American Revolution); Louisiana Purchase Treaty, 1803 (acquiring real estate from France); Treaty of Ghent, 1814 (ended War of 1812); Treaty of 1818 (resolved boundary issues between U.S. and Great Britain); Oregon Treaty, 1846 (ended competing U.S. and British claims to Oregon Territory); Treaty of Guadalupe Hidalgo, 1848 (ended Mexican-American War); Treaty of Tientsin; 1858 (peace, amity and commerce with China); Alaska Purchase Treaty, 1867 (U.S. bought Alaska from Russia); Treaty of Berlin, 1921 (U.S. peace with Germany after WWI); Paris Peace Accords, 1973 (with N. Vietnam, ending Vietnam War); International Convention Against Torture, 1988; and so on.

3. Here is the Preamble to the Charter ("constitution") of the United Nations, adopted by treaty in San Francisco in 1945: We the Peoples of the United Nations, Determined—to save succeeding generations from the scourge of war, which twice in our lifetime has brought untold sorrow to mankind, and—to reaffirm faith in fundamental human rights, in the dignity and worth of the human person, in the equal rights of men and women and of nations large and small, and—to establish conditions under which justice and respect for the obligations arising from treaties and other sources of international law can be maintained, and—to promote social progress and better standards of life in larger freedom, And for these Ends—to practice tolerance and live together in peace with one another as good neighbors, and—to unite our strength to maintain international peace and security, and—to ensure by the acceptance of principles and the institution of methods, that armed force shall not be used, save in the common interest, and—to employ international machinery for the promotion of the economic and social advancement of all peoples, Have Resolved to Combine Our Efforts to Accomplish these Aims. Accordingly, our respective Governments, through representatives assembled in the city of San Francisco, who have exhibited their full powers found to be in good and due form, have agreed to the present Charter of the United Nations and do hereby establish an international organization to be known as the United Nations.

4. The U.S. president can do this unilaterally—without Congressional approval—in three circumstances. (1) "During time of war" under the Trading with the Enemy Act of 1917; the U.S. doesn't have to be at war with any specific nation, just being "at war" someplace is good enough. Because the Korean War never ended with surrender and a treaty, in 1971 President Nixon imposed a 10% general import tax, citing the Korean War which ended in 1952. (2) The president can impose tariffs under the International Emergency Economic Powers Act of 1977. The definition of a "national emergency" is vague; perhaps losing manufacturing jobs to China and Mexico is sufficient, but federal courts have never rejected a president's reasoning here. (3) Also, the Trade Act of 1974 gives the president the authority to impose tariffs if there is "an adverse impact on national security from imports." Lost jobs might qualify, or the concern that certain American industries critical to national security (steel, say) are in decline because of cheaper imports. China and Canada will, of course, retaliate with tariffs against U.S. products. That becomes a trade war, with unforeseen consequences.

5. Hersch Lauterpacht (1897–1960) was a Polish-British lawyer and judge at the International Court of Justice.

6. https://www.archives.gov/research/foreign-policy/other-agencies.html

7. http://www.ngo.org/index3.htm

8. For a "Brexit" (Britain's exit from the EU) primer see https://www.bbc.com/news/uk-politics-32810887.

9. http://time.com/26537/crimea-ukraine-russia-referendum-results/.

10. https://www.cnbc.com/2017/10/01/catalan-independence-referendum-government-says-90-percent-voted-to-leave-spain.html.

11. The 7th Circuit's jurisdiction includes parts of Illinois, Indiana, and Wisconsin; it is based in Chicago.

12. A valve-cap gauge measures tire pressure at the tire stem valve (where the tire is inflated).

13. 77 F. Supp.1196 (N.D. Tex 1983)

14. Willendson v. Forsoket [29 Fed Cas 1283 (DC Pa 1801)] (No 17,682)

15. *Gulf Oil Corp. v. Gilbert*, 330 U.S. 501 (1947)

16. *Underhill v. Hernandez*, 168 U.S. 250, 252 (1897).

17. *Mannington Mills, Inc. v. Congoleum Corp.*, 595 F.2d 1287 (3d Cir. 1979).

18. 376 U.S. 398 (1964)

19. This case also appears in Chapter 2, Introduction to Business Ethics.

20. A racket is an organized criminal act; the criminal act is a form of business or a way to earn illegal or extorted money regularly or briefly but repeatedly. Federal and state law make racketeering illegal.

21. https://www.npr.org/sections/thetwo-way/2016/06/02/480494835/new-u-s-ban-on-ivory-sales-to-protect-elephants

22. Gady Epstein and Robyn Meredith, "U.S. Companies that Invest Big in China," *Forbes*, July 5, 2010. https://www.forbes.com/2010/07/05/us-investments-china-markets-emerging-markets-fdi.html#650da7a64822 .

23. Paul Davidson, "Foreign Manufacturers Bringing Jobs to U.S.," USA Today, May 15, 2013.

24. Deborah Orr, "The Largest Foreign Investments in the U.S.," Forbes, April 10, 2008. https://www.forbes.com/2008/04/10/foreign-investment-stocks-2000global08-biz-cx_do_0410investments.html#333f03e2b1f4

25. Paul Davidson, "Foreign Manufacturers Bringing Jobs to U.S.," *USA Today*, May 15, 2013.

26. Thomas Mann and Norman Ornstein, The Broken Branch: How Congress is failing American and how to get it back on track (2006).

27. James D. Zirin, Supremely Partisan: How Raw Politics Tips the Scales in the U.S. Supreme Court (2016)

CHAPTER 7
Tort Law

Chapter Learning Objectives

After reading this chapter, you should be able to:

1. Know why most legal systems have tort law.
2. Identify the three kinds of torts.
3. Explain how tort law relates to criminal law and contract law.
4. Understand negligent torts and defenses to claims of negligence.
5. Understand strict liability torts and the reasons for them in the U.S. legal system.

In U.S. civil litigation, contract and tort claims are by far the most numerous. The law tries to compensate for harms done to individuals and firms by awarding damages to plaintiffs who can demonstrate that the defendant was the cause of the plaintiff's losses. Damages are of two types: a person can cause harm to another by breaking a promise (contract law), or a person can cause harm to another in ways other than breaking a promise (tort law). Torts can be intentional torts, negligent torts, or strict liability torts. Employers must be aware that in many circumstances, their employees may create liability in tort.

In some countries at some times there is no functioning judicial system. Then, people seek redress for torts by seeking revenge, and civil society deteriorates.

This chapter explains the different kind of torts, as well as available defenses to tort claims.

7.1 Purpose of Tort Laws

Learning Objectives

1. Explain why a sound market system requires tort law.
2. Define a tort and give two examples.
3. Explain the moral basis of tort liability.
4. Understand the purposes of damage awards in tort.

Definition of Tort and Purpose of Tort Law

Definition of Tort

tort

A civil wrong other than a breach of contract.

The term **tort** is the French equivalent of the English word *wrong*. The word *tort* is also derived from the Latin word *tortum*, which means twisted, crooked, or wrong, in contrast to the word *rectum*, which means straight (*rectitude* uses that Latin root). Thus, conduct that is not straight (that is "twisted" or "crooked") is a tort. The term was introduced into the English law by the Norman jurists from France in 1066. (Roman law and, subsequently, European law—"civil" or "continental" law—also recognized "torts" as actionable in public courts.) The person or firm who causes a tort is often referred to by courts as the "tortfeasor."

A tort, in short, is a civil wrong other than a breach of contract.

Long ago, *tort* was used in everyday speech; today it is left to the legal system. A judge will instruct a jury that a tort is usually defined as a wrong for which the law will provide a remedy, most often in the form of monetary damages. The law does not remedy all "wrongs." There are wrongs in the moral sphere that are not remedied in the legal sphere. For example, the law will not provide a remedy for saying something false and cruel to someone *directly*, while it may provide a remedy for "defaming" someone (saying something false about them, orally or in writing, that becomes known to *others*).

Although the word is no longer in general use, tort suits are the stuff of everyday headlines. More and more people injured by exposure to a variety of risks now seek "redress" (that is, some sort of remedy through the courts). Headlines boast of multi-million dollar jury awards against doctors who bungled operations, against newspapers and other media that have libeled people or invaded their privacy, and against oil companies that devastate entire ecosystems. All are examples of tort lawsuits.

The law of torts developed almost entirely in the common-law courts; that is, plaintiffs would rely on the common law rather than statutes passed by legislatures. Over many years, the courts have fashioned a series of rules that govern the conduct of individuals in their non-contractual dealings with each other. Beyond consented-to contract obligations, tort law holds individuals accountable for the consequences of their actions. Those who suffer losses at the hands of others can often be compensated if the wrong fits within a legally established form of tort.

Many acts (like homicide) are both criminal and tortious. But torts and crimes are different—a crime is an act against society as a whole. In a criminal case, society punishes the murderer; it does not usually compensate the family of the homicide victim. In contrast, tort law views the death as a private wrong for which damages are owed. In a civil case, the tort victim or her family, not the state, brings the action. The judgment against a defendant in a civil tort suit is usually expressed in monetary terms, not in terms of prison times or fines, and is the way that the legal system tries to make up for the victim's loss.

Purpose of Tort Law

The purpose of tort law is to compensate individuals and firms that have been harmed; as with contract law, the purpose is to make the plaintiff whole—to put her in the position, as much as possible, as she would have been had there been no tort. If a nation-state had no tort law, or ineffective tort law, people would tend to seek personal vengeance against those who have hurt them; violence would ensue.

Dimensions of Tort Liability

The chart below illustrates several dimensions of tort law. We can talk about (1) the tortfeasor's degree of fault, (2) the type of harm or injury caused, (3) the type of damages, and (4) defenses or excuses raised by the tortfeasor-defendant.

FIGURE 7.1 Dimensions of Tort Liability

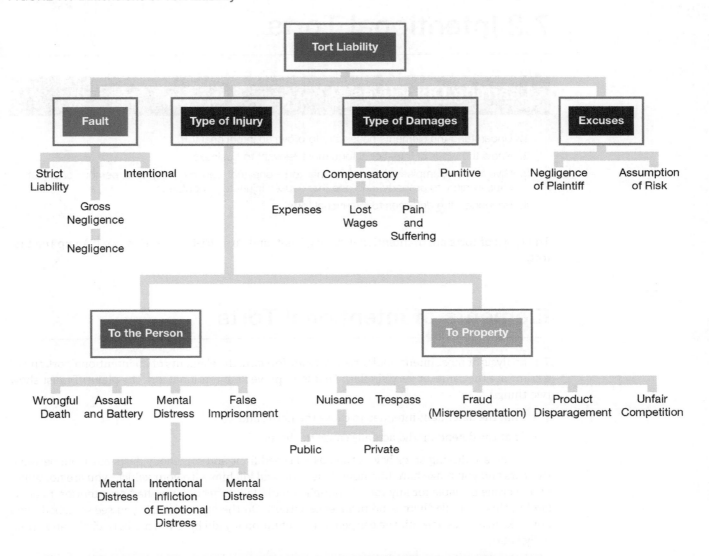

Key Takeaway

A tort is a civil wrong other than a breach of contract. Tort law is intended to compensate injured parties by putting them in the position they would have been in had there been no tort. Thereby, people are satisfied and do not resort to vengeance as a remedy. Torts may be analyzed along four dimensions: (1) the tortfeasor's degree of fault, (2) the type of harm or injury caused, (3) the type of damages, and (4) defenses or excuses that are raised by the tortfeasor-defendant.

Exercises

1. What would happen if there were no tort law?
2. When it is said that tort law is almost entirely common law, what does that mean?

7.2 Intentional Torts

Learning Objectives

1. Understand the elements necessary to prove an intentional tort.
2. Know the types of intentional torts most relevant to business.
3. Give three examples of an intentional tort—one that causes injury to a person, one that causes injury to property, and one that causes injury to a reputation.
4. Recognize the defenses to intentional torts.

The types of torts are (1) intentional, (2) negligent, and (3) strict-liability. Here we take up the first tort.

Elements of Intentional Torts

The analysis of most intentional torts is straightforward; the elements of an intentional tort and of a crime are the same (or very similar). That is, to prove an intentional tort, the plaintiff must show two things:

- That the defendant intended to cause the harm, and
- That the defendant did actually cause the harm.

If you are driving at, or below, the posted speed limit and somebody darts out from between two cars and you brake hard but, nonetheless, hit and kill him with your vehicle, you are not guilty of any crime or liable for any tort. Although you did kill somebody, you had no intention to do so (and in this example there is no negligence, either). On the other hand, if you see somebody you don't like in a crosswalk, hit the gas pedal, and intentionally kill him, you are both civilly and criminally liable.

Note again the rather obvious point: an intentional tort like this is also a crime, but the state will bring criminal charges, while the family of the deceased will likely bring the civil action in tort.

Certain intentional torts are worth noting for their relevance to business. Here we take up (1) assault and battery, (2) false imprisonment, (3) intentional infliction of emotional distress, (4) intentional interference with contractual relationships, (5) malicious prosecution, (6) conversion and fraud, (7) defamation, and (8) invasion of privacy. A few other types are noted in passing.

Types of Intentional Torts

Assault

One of the most obvious intentional torts is assault and battery. Both criminal law and tort law serve to restrain individuals from using physical force on others. **Assault** is (1) the threat of immediate harm or offense of contact, or (2) any act that would arouse reasonable apprehension of imminent harm. **Battery** is unauthorized and harmful or offensive physical contact with another person that causes injury. It is also possible to have an assault without battery (a frightening attempt to hit somebody; the attempt fails), or battery without assault (man hit from behind with skateboard—never saw it coming). Sexual assault (much in the news of late) is a subset of the common-law tort of assault; it is also illegal under employment discrimination statutory law.

False Imprisonment

The tort of false imprisonment originally implied a locking up, as in a prison, but today it can occur if a person is restrained in a room or a car or even if his or her movements are restricted while walking down the street. People generally have a right to be free to go as they please, and anyone who without cause deprives another of personal freedom has committed a tort. Damages are allowed for time lost, discomfort and resulting ill health, mental suffering, humiliation, loss of reputation or business, and expenses such as attorneys' fees incurred as a result of the restraint (such as a false arrest). But as the case below, *Lester v. Albers Super Markets, Inc.*, makes clear, the defendant must be shown to have restrained the plaintiff in order for damages to be allowed.

Intentional Infliction of Emotional Distress

Until recently, the common-law rule was that there could be no recovery for acts, even though intentionally undertaken, that caused purely mental or emotional distress. For a case to go to the jury, the courts required that the mental distress result from some physical injury. In recent years, many courts have overthrown the older rule and now recognize the so-called new tort. In an employment context, however, it is rare to find a case where a plaintiff is able to recover. The most difficult hurdle is proving that the conduct was "extreme" or "outrageous."

In an early California case, bill collectors came to the debtor's home repeatedly and threatened the debtor's pregnant wife. Among other things, they claimed that the wife would have to deliver her child in prison. The wife miscarried and had emotional and physical complications. The court found that the behavior of the collection company's two agents was sufficiently outrageous to prove the tort of intentional infliction of emotional distress.

In *Roach v. Stern* (a New York case), the famous cable television talk show host Howard Stern had tastelessly discussed the remains of Deborah Roach, a topless dancer and cable access television host.[1] The remains had been brought to Stern's show by a close friend of Roach, Chaunce Hayden, and a number of crude comments by Stern and Hayden about the remains were videotaped and broadcast on a national cable television station. Roach's sister and brother sued Howard Stern and Infinity broadcasting and survived the defendant's motion to dismiss so that a jury could consider their claim.

A plaintiff's burden in these cases is to show that the mental distress is severe. Many states require that this distress must result in physical symptoms such as nausea, headaches, ulcers, or, as in the case of the pregnant wife, a miscarriage. Other states have not required physical symptoms, finding that shame, embarrassment, fear, and anger constitute severe mental distress. Freedom of

assault

The threat of immediate harm or offense of contact; any act that would arouse reasonable apprehension of imminent harm.

battery

Unauthorized and harmful or offensive physical contact with another person that causes injury.

speech, as protected in the First Amendment, can create interesting conflicts between tort law and Constitutional law. *Hustler* magazine printed a false advertisement showing Reverend Jerry Falwell, and describing him as having lost his virginity to his mother in an outhouse while he was drunk. Suing for intentional infliction of emotional distress, he won at the trial court, but the Supreme Court overturned, holding that parodies of public figures were protected under the First Amendment.[2] The "public figure" standard also applies to defamation lawsuits. See *New York Times v. Sullivan*, in Chapter 3).

Trespass and Nuisance

Trespass[3] happens when a person goes onto another's land or causes some tangible thing to 'invade' the land, contrary to the owner's wishes. This part of tort law shows how strongly the law values the rights of property owners. The right to enjoy your property without interference from others is also found in common law of nuisance. There are limits to property owners' rights, however. In *Katko v. Briney*, for example, the plaintiff was injured by a spring gun while trespassing on the defendant's property.[4] The defendant had set up No Trespassing signs after ten years of trespassing and housebreaking events, with the loss of some household items. Windows had been broken, and there was "messing up of the property in general." The defendants had boarded up the windows and doors of a small outbuilding on his property in order to stop the intrusions. At some point, he set up a shotgun trap in the north bedroom of the outbuilding. The defendant had cleaned and oiled his 20-gauge shotgun and taken it to the old house where it was secured to an iron bed with the barrel pointed at the bedroom door. "It was rigged with wire from the doorknob to the gun's trigger so would fire when the door was opened." The angle of the shotgun was adjusted to hit an intruder in the legs. The spring could not be seen from the outside, and no warning of its presence was posted.

The plaintiff, Katko, had been hunting in the area for several years and considered the property abandoned. He knew it had long been uninhabited. He and a friend had been to the house and found several old bottles and fruit jars that they took and added to their collection of antiques. When they made a second trip to the property, they entered by removing a board from a porch window. When the plaintiff opened the north bedroom door, the shotgun went off and struck him in the right leg above the ankle bone. Much of his leg was blown away. While Katko knew he had no right to break and enter the house with intent to steal bottles and fruit jars, the court held that a property owner could not protect an unoccupied boarded-up building by using a spring gun capable of inflicting death or serious injury.

In *Katko*, there is an intentional tort. But what if someone who is trespassing is injured by the negligence of the landowner? States have differing rules about trespass and negligence. In some states, a trespasser is only protected against the gross negligence of the landowner. In other states, trespassers may be owed the duty of due care on the part of the landowner. The burglar who falls into a drained swimming pool, for example, may have a case against the homeowner unless the courts or legislature of that state have made it clear that trespassers can only sue for gross negligence. Suppose a young child wanders off his own property and falls into a gravel pit on a nearby property and suffers death or serious injury; if the owner of the gravel pit (in the exercise of due care) should have filled in the pit or had some barrier erected around it, then there was negligence. But if the state law holds that the duty to trespassers is only to avoid gross negligence, the child's family would lose, unless the state law makes an exception for very young trespassers. In general, guests, licensees, and invitees are owed a duty of due care; a trespasser may not be owed such a duty, but states have different rules on this.

Intentional Interference with Contractual Relations

Tortious interference with a contract can be established by proving four elements:

1. There was a contract between the plaintiff and a third party.
2. The defendant knew of the contract.
3. The defendant improperly induced the third party to breach the contract or made performance of the contract impossible.
4. There was injury to the plaintiff.

In a famous case of contract interference, Texaco was sued by Pennzoil for interfering with an agreement that Pennzoil had with Getty Oil. After complicated negotiations between Pennzoil and Getty, a takeover share price was struck, a memorandum of understanding was signed, and a press release announced the agreement in principle between Pennzoil and Getty. Texaco's lawyers, however, believed that Getty Oil was "still in play," and before the lawyers for Pennzoil and Getty could complete the paperwork for their agreement, Texaco announced it was offering Getty shareholders an additional $12.50 per share over what Pennzoil had offered.

Texaco later increased its offer to $228 per share, and the Getty board of directors soon began dealing with Texaco instead of Pennzoil. Pennzoil decided to sue Texaco in Texas state court for tortious interference with a contract. After a long trial, the jury returned an enormous verdict against Texaco: $7.53 billion in actual damages and $3 billion in punitive damages. The verdict was so large that it would have bankrupted Texaco. Appeals from the verdict centered on an obscure rule of the Securities and Exchange Commission (SEC), Rule 10(b)-13, and Texaco's argument was based on that rule and the fact that the contract had not been completed. If there was no contract, Texaco could not have legally interfered with one. After the SEC filed a brief that supported Texaco's interpretation of the law, Texaco agreed to pay $3 billion to Pennzoil to dismiss its claim of tortious interference with a contract.

Malicious Prosecution

Malicious prosecution is the tort of causing someone to be prosecuted for a criminal act, knowing that there was no probable cause to believe that the plaintiff committed the crime. The plaintiff must show that the defendant acted with malice or with some purpose other than bringing the guilty to justice. A mere complaint to the authorities is insufficient to establish the tort, but any official proceeding will support the claim—for example, a warrant for the plaintiff's arrest. The criminal proceeding must terminate in the plaintiff's favor in order for his suit to be sustained.

A related cause of action is for **abuse of process.** A majority of U.S. courts permit a suit for wrongful civil proceedings. Civil litigation is usually costly and burdensome, and someone who forces another to defend himself against baseless accusations should not be permitted to impose the costs of defending against such accusations. But, because civil litigation is a socially favored way to vindicate legal rights, a plaintiff in an abuse of process case must meet a heavy burden. The mere dismissal of the original lawsuit against the plaintiff is not sufficient proof that the suit was unwarranted. The plaintiff in a suit for wrongful civil proceedings must show that the defendant (who was the plaintiff in the original suit) filed the action for an improper purpose and had no reasonable belief that his cause was legally or factually well grounded.

abuse of process

An intentional tort arising when a person deliberately misuses a court process that is not justified by the underlying civil or criminal legal action.

Conversion and Fraud

Conversion is the taking or using of someone else's property without their consent. Personal property is discussed in detail in Chapter 9. But in brief, personal property is any tangible or intangible thing that is not a physical structure, such as a house or building ("real property"), and is not attached to real property. Priya's cellphone, Justin's backpack, or even your roommate's six pack that was left in the shared refrigerator—all of these are personal property that can be "converted." Conversion is the tort counterpart to the crime of theft. But recall that with any tort, proving a criminal

conversion

Taking or using someone else's personal property without their consent.

intent to permanently deprive the owner of the use and possession of her personal property is not required. The person converting may intend only to "borrow" the item before losing or damaging it.

In practice, the one whose property is stolen or borrowed is unlikely to bring an action for conversion unless the item is one of considerable value. The costs of hiring an attorney would likely exceed the value of many items of personal property. But note that personal property can be intangible as well: software codes, designs, customer lists, trade secrets, and intellectual property (copyrights, trademarks, and patents) can all be taken and used by others, depriving the owner of exclusive use. (See Chapter 9).

Fraud is a tortious injury to another by deliberate deception. Fraud is actionable in civil courts for a variety of misrepresentations, without the need to demonstrate criminal "mens rea" or criminal intent. The types of fraud are as varied as human nature. Phony checks, online misrepresentations, phone solicitations for free cruises to the Bahamas, organizations that pretend to be charities but aren't, Ponzi schemes (such as chain letters), and many more. Securities fraud—a particularly important aspect of how law deals with fraud—will be covered in Chapter 14.

Defamation

Defamation is injury to a person's good name or reputation. In general, if the harm is done through the spoken word—one person to another, by telephone, by radio, or on television—it is called slander. If the defamatory statement is published in written form, it is called libel. Defamation is not protected by the First Amendment.

The Restatement (Second) of Torts defines a defamatory communication as one that "so tends to harm the reputation of another as to lower him in the estimation of the community or to deter third persons from associating or dealing with him."[5]

A statement is not defamatory unless it is false. Truth is an absolute defense to a charge of libel or slander. Moreover, the statement must be "published"—that is, communicated to a third person. You cannot be libeled by one who sends you a letter full of false accusations and scurrilous statements about you unless a third person opens it first (your roommate, perhaps). Any living person is capable of being defamed, but the dead are not. Corporations, partnerships, and even non-profit oganizations can also be defamed, if the statements tend to injure their ability to do business or to garner contributions.

The statement must have reference to a particular person, but he or she need not be identified by name. A statement that "the company president is a crook" is defamatory, as is a statement that "the major network weathermen are imposters." The company president and the network weathermen could show that the words were aimed at them. But statements about large groups will not support an action for defamation (e.g., "all doctors are butchers" is not defamatory of any particular doctor).

The law of defamation is largely built on strict liability. That a person did not intend to defame is ordinarily no excuse; a typographical error that converts a true statement into a false one in a newspaper, magazine, or corporate brochure can be sufficient to make out a case of libel. Even the exercise of due care is usually no excuse if the statement is in fact communicated. Repeating a libel is itself a libel; a libel cannot be justified by showing that you were quoting someone else.

fraud

The intentional perversion of truth in order to induce another to part with something of value or to surrender a legal right.

defamation

Injury to a person's reputation by intentional or reckless dissemination of falsehoods, either orally (slander) or in writing (libel).

Publishing false information about another business's product constitutes the tort of **slander of quality**, or **trade libel**. In some states, this is known as the tort of **product disparagement**. It may be difficult to establish damages, however. A plaintiff must prove that actual damages proximately resulted from the slander of quality and must show the extent of the economic harm as well. Sometimes the person claimed liable for defamation can raise defenses of privilege.

Absolute Privilege

Statements made during the course of judicial proceedings are absolutely privileged, meaning that they cannot serve as the basis for a defamation suit. Accurate accounts of judicial or other proceedings are absolutely privileged; a newspaper, for example, may pass on the slanderous comments of a judge in court. "Judicial" is broadly construed to include most proceedings of administrative bodies of the government. The Constitution exempts members of Congress from suits for libel or slander for any statements made in connection with legislative business. The courts have constructed a similar privilege for many executive branch officials.

Qualified Privilege

Absolute privileges pertain to those in the public sector. A narrower privilege exists for private citizens. In general, a statement that would otherwise be actionable is held to be justified if made in a reasonable manner and for a reasonable purpose. Thus, you may warn a friend to beware of dealing with a third person, and if you had reason to believe that what you said was true, you are privileged to issue the warning, even though false. Likewise, an employee may warn an employer about the conduct or character of a fellow or prospective employee, and a parent may complain to a school board about the competence or conduct of a child's teacher. Although many employers fear to give accurate accounts of their experiences with ex-employees to other employers, they do have a qualified privilege if the statements are made in good faith and the publication is limited to those who have a legitimate interest in the communications.

The "public figure" exception as a kind of qualified privilege is by now well established. In 1964, the Supreme Court handed down its historic decision in *New York Times v. Sullivan*, holding that under the First Amendment a libel judgment brought by a public official against a newspaper cannot stand unless the plaintiff has shown "actual malice," which in turn was defined as "knowledge that [the statement] was false or with a reckless disregard of whether it was false or not."[6] In subsequent cases, the court extended the constitutional doctrine further, applying it not merely to government officials but to **public figures**, people who voluntarily place themselves in the public eye or who involuntarily find themselves the objects of public scrutiny. This would include politicians, entertainers, professional athletes, and others who are in the public eye. Whether a private person is, or is not, a public figure is a difficult question that has so far eluded rigorous definition and has been answered only from case to case. A CEO of a private corporation ordinarily will be considered a private figure unless he puts himself in the public eye—for example, by starring in the company's television commercials. Former Secretary of Labor Robert Reich labels himself a "public figure" on his blog, and Kim Kardashian is a public figure because of her desire to put herself in the public eye.

Invasion of Privacy

The right of privacy—the right "to be let alone"—did not receive judicial recognition until the twentieth century, and its legal formulation is still evolving. In fact there is no single right of privacy. Courts and commentators have discerned at least four different types of interests: (1) the right to control the appropriation of your name and picture for commercial purposes, (2) the right to be free of intrusion on your "personal space" or seclusion, (3) freedom from public disclosure of embarrassing and intimate facts of your personal life, and (4) the right not to be presented in a "false light." If

---

slander of quality

The tort of defaming another's business product; also called "product disparagement" or "trade libel."

trade libel

The tort of defaming another's business product; also called "product disparagement."

product disparagement

The tort of defaming another's business product.

public figures

Based on the First Amendment of the U.S. Constitution, a public figure cannot recover in a defamation case unless the plaintiff's defamation was done with actual malice.

you consent to have your image or information used by Google or Facebook, you may find that you have waived your right of privacy. Of course, whether the waiver was obtained ethically, with your full consent of what you were giving up, is a question that is now receiving greater attention.

Appropriation of Name or Likeness

The earliest privacy interest recognized by the courts was appropriation of name or likeness—someone else placing your photograph on a billboard or cereal box as a model or using your name as endorsing a product or in the product name. A New York statute makes it a misdemeanor to use the name, portrait, or picture of any person for advertising purposes or for the purposes of trade (business) without first obtaining written consent. The law also permits the aggrieved person to sue and to recover damages for unauthorized profits and also to have the court enjoin (judicially block) any further unauthorized use of the plaintiff's name, likeness, or image. This is particularly useful to celebrities.

Personal Space

One form of intrusion upon a person's solitude—trespass—has long been actionable under common law. Physical invasion of a home or other property is not a new tort. But in recent years, the notion of intrusion has been broadened considerably. Now, taking photos of someone else with your cell phone in a locker room could constitute invasion of the right to privacy. Reading someone else's mail or e-mail could also constitute an invasion of the right to privacy. Photographing someone on a city street is not tortious, but subsequent use of the photograph could be. Whether the invasion is in a public or private space, the amount of damages will depend on how the image or information is disclosed to others.

Public Disclosure of Embarrassing Facts

Circulation of false statements that do injury to a person are actionable under the laws of defamation. What about true statements that might be every bit as damaging—for example, disclosure of someone's income tax return, revealing how much he earned? The general rule is that if the facts are truly private and of no "legitimate" concern to the public, then their disclosure is a violation of the right to privacy. But a person who is in the public eye cannot claim the same protection.

Media companies now pay close attention to this aspect of privacy law. In a case against Gawker Media, Terry Gene Bollea (known generally by his professional wrestling name, "Hulk Hogan") sued for invasion of privacy and infliction of emotional distress when Gawker published 2 minutes of a 30-minute video showing consensual sexual acts by Hulk Hogan with the wife of radio personality "Bubba the Love Sponge." In March of 2016, a state jury awarded Bollea $115 million in damages, including $60 million for emotional distress and $25 million in punitive damages. While Gawker appealed the judgment and the amounts, it also filed for bankruptcy within three months.

False Light

A final type of privacy invasion is that which paints a false picture in a publication. Though false, it might not be libelous, since the publication need contain nothing injurious to reputation. Indeed, the publication might even glorify the plaintiff, making him seem more heroic than he actually is. Subject to the First Amendment requirement that the plaintiff must show intent or extreme recklessness, statements that put a person in a false light, like a fictionalized biography, are actionable.

Other Types of Intentional Torts

In addition to those called out above, we might note others, as follows:

- Unfair competition. This includes various common-law restraints of trade, some of which are encompassed in antitrust law or addressed by the Federal Trade Commission, the Food and Drug Administration, and the like.
- False advertising.
- Palming off (also "product imitation"). Leading the public to believe your product is made by someone else, as if you were to bottle soda pop in a container that looks a lot like a Coca-Cola bottle.
- Trade name infringement. This is a common-law tort, and also encompassed in federal trademark law.
- Trade secret infringement.

Defenses to Intentional Torts

A person can raise one or more defenses to a claim that he, she, or it caused damages by committing and intentional tort.

- Consent. If you voluntarily engage in a kick-boxing contest, you of course consent to have your opponent kick you. In years past it was said that a wife always gave consent to have intimate relations with her husband. That is, a wife could not claim her husband raped her. That certainly is no longer true. However that a woman consented to have sex is a common defense raised by men accused of assault (the tort) or rape (the crime). If you get on a crowded subway you impliedly consent to be jostled by your fellow passengers, but such jostling might not be acceptable on a nearly deserted sidewalk at 10:30 pm.
- Self-defense and defense of others and of property. A person has a right to use appropriate force to defend herself or others or her property. Whether the force was "appropriate" is a fact question. We have traditionally thought the first line of "defense" is to run away, and we have traditionally thought that lethal force cannot be used to defend mere property.
- Privilege. A shopkeeper has a limited privilege to detain suspected shoplifters (see the *Albers* case below); a police officer has privilege to use reasonable force to subdue a suspected criminal.

Case

Intentional Torts: False Imprisonment

Lester v. Albers Super Markets, Inc.

94 Ohio App. 313, 114 N.E.2d 529 (Ohio, 1952)

Lester v. Albers Super Markets, Inc.

Ohio Supreme Court case, 1952, analyzing defenses to the tort of false imprisonment.

[The plaintiff, carrying a bag of rolls purchased at another store, entered the defendant's grocery store to buy some canned fruit. Seeing her bus outside, she stepped out of line and put the can on the counter. The store manager intercepted her and repeatedly demanded that she submit the bag to be searched. Finally she acquiesced; he looked inside and said she could go. She testified that several people witnessed the scene, which lasted about fifteen minutes, and that she was humiliated. The jury awarded her $800 (about $7,600 in 2019 dollars). She also testified that no one laid a hand on her or made a move to restrain her from leaving by any one of numerous exits.]

Matthews, J.

As we view the record, it raises the fundamental question of what is imprisonment. Before any need for a determination of illegality arises there must be proof of imprisonment. In [Citation], it is said: "Submission to the mere verbal direction of another, unaccompanied by force or by threats of any character, cannot constitute a false imprisonment, and there is no false imprisonment where an employer interviewing an employee declines to terminate the interview if no force or threat of force is used and false imprisonment may not be predicated on a person's unfounded belief that he was restrained."

Many cases are cited in support of the text. * * *

In *Fenn v. Kroger Grocery & Baking Co.*, [Citation], the court said:

> *A case was not made out for false arrest. The plaintiff said she was intercepted as she started to leave the store; that Mr. Krause stood where she could not pass him in going out. She does not say that he made any attempt to intercept her. She says he escorted her back to the desk, that he asked her to let him see the change. . . . She does not say that she went unwillingly. . . . Evidence is wholly lacking to show that she was detained by force or threats. It was probably a disagreeable experience, a humiliating one to her, but she came out victorious and was allowed to go when she desired with the assurance of Mr. Krause that it was all right. The demurrer to the evidence on both counts was properly sustained.*

The result of the cases is epitomized in [a legal encyclopedia], as follows:

> *A customer or patron who apparently has not paid for what he has received may be detained for a reasonable time to investigate the circumstances, but upon payment of the demand, he has the unqualified right to leave the premises without restraint, so far as the proprietor is concerned, and it is false imprisonment for a private individual to detain one for an unreasonable time, or under unreasonable circumstances, for the purpose of investigating a dispute over the payment of a bill alleged to be owed by the person detained for cash services.*

For these reasons, the judgment is reversed and final judgment entered for the defendant-appellant.

Case Questions

1. The court begins by saying what false imprisonment is not. What is the legal definition of false imprisonment?

2. What kinds of detention are permissible for a store to use in accosting those that may have been shoplifting?

3. Jody broke up with Jeremy and refused to talk to him. Jeremy saw Jody get into her car near the business school and parked right behind her so she could not move. He then stood next to the driver's window for fifteen minutes, begging Jody to talk to him. She kept saying, "No, let me leave!" Has Jeremy committed the tort of false imprisonment?

Key Takeaway

There are several kinds of intentional torts. Some of them involve harm to the physical person or to his or her property, reputation or feelings, or economic interests. In each case of intentional tort, the plaintiff must show that the defendant intended harm, but the intent to harm does not need to be directed at a particular person and need not be malicious, as long as the resulting harm is a direct consequence of the defendant's actions.

There are defenses to intentional torts: consent, self-defense, defense of others, and of property and privilege are among them.

Exercises

1. Name two kinds of intentional torts that could result in damage to a business firm's bottom line.

2. Name two kinds of intentional torts that are based on protection of a person's property.

3. Intentional torts are more likely to result in a verdict, not only for compensatory damages, but also for punitive damages (to punish the defendant). Why?

4. What kinds of intentional tort might spell the end of a famous sports, television, radio, or business personality? Why should the public care about what private persons do to their individual "victims"?

7.3 Negligence

Learning Objectives

1. Understand how the duty of due care relates to negligence.
2. Distinguish between actual and proximate cause.
3. Explain the primary defenses to a claim of negligence.

The second type of tort, and by far the most common, is negligence.

Elements of Negligence

negligence

A breach of the duty of due care. If such a breach causes damages to a plaintiff, all the elements of a negligence tort have been established.

Physical harm need not be intentionally caused. A pedestrian knocked over by an automobile does not hurt less because the driver intended no wrong but was merely careless. The law imposes a duty of care on all of us in our everyday lives. Accidents caused by **negligence** are actionable.

The tort of negligence has three elements:

1. The defendant had a duty of care;
2. Which duty the defendant unreasonably breached;
3. The breach was the proximate cause of the plaintiff's damages.

Even if a plaintiff can prove each of these aspects, the defendant may be able to show that she has a defense and is not liable. We examine each of these factors below.

Defendant Has a Duty of Care

The law does not impose on us a duty to care for every person. If the rule were otherwise, we would all, in this interdependent world, be our brothers' keepers, constantly unsure whether any action we took might subject us to liability for its effect on someone else. The law copes with this difficulty by limiting the number of people toward whom we owe a duty to be careful. The general rule is this: We owe a duty to be careful toward other people if it is reasonably foreseeable that whatever we are planning to do might cause harm to others.

negligence per se

An act of the defendant that violates a statute (regulation) or ordinance can be used to establish a breach of the duty of due care.

Sometimes the duty of care is spelled out by statute or regulation—if Juan drives over the center line, he is by definition negligent—the traffic laws say so; this is **negligence per se** or "negligence as such," without need for the plaintiff to show a breach of a legal duty. Cleo, whose car Juan crashed into, will not have to prove that Juan had a duty of care and that he breached it if she puts forth credible evidence that he was "over the line" at the time of impact. (Juan could rebut with his own expert witness, but lacking an effective rebuttal on his part, the first two elements of a negligence tort would be established by **negligence per se**.

But any action that would be likely to cause harm could be negligent. For example, a gun-store owner ought not to sell a gun to an obviously intoxicated customer, and may be liable for the death of the customer's victim if the store owner does sell the gun. Why? It is reasonably foreseeable that an intoxicated person who gets a gun could kill somebody.[7]

In general, the law imposes no obligation to act in a situation to which we are strangers. We may pass the drowning child without risking a lawsuit. But if we do act, then the law requires us to act carefully. The law of negligence requires us to behave with due regard for the foreseeable consequences of our actions in order to avoid unreasonable risks of injury.

Which Duty the Defendant Unreasonably Breached

The second element necessary to prove the defendant is liable for negligence is that—assuming the defendant had a duty of care—the defendant unreasonably breached the duty.

Not every unintentional act that causes injury is negligent. If you hit a pedestrian who has darted out into the street between two parked cars, you have not acted negligently. Yes, you do have a duty to pedestrians on the street, but here you did nothing unreasonable that caused the harm.

Given the infinite variety of human circumstances and conduct, no general statement of what is "reasonable care" is possible. Nevertheless, the law has tried to encapsulate it in the form of the famous standard of "the reasonable person." This fictitious person "of ordinary prudence" is the model that juries are instructed to use in assessing whether those defendants have acted negligently. Analysis of this mythical personage has baffled several generations of commentators. How much knowledge must she have of events in the community, of technology, of cause and effect? With what physical attributes, courage, or wisdom is this nonexistent person supposedly endowed? If the defendant is a person with specialized knowledge, like a doctor or an automobile designer, must the jury also treat the "reasonable man" as having this knowledge in the case before it, even though the average person in the community will not? (Answer: in most cases, yes.)

Despite its many difficulties, the concept of the reasonable person is one on which most negligence cases ultimately turn. If a defendant has acted "unreasonably under the circumstances" and his conduct posed an unreasonable risk of injury, then he is liable for injury caused by his conduct. A.P. Herbert (Alan Patrick Herbert, 1890–1971, was an English humorist and novelist) described the reasonable man (we would now say the reasonable person) like this:

> *He is one who invariably looks where he is going, and is careful to examine the immediate foreground before he executes a leap or bound; who neither star-gazes nor is lost in meditation when approaching trap-doors or the margin of a dock; . . . who never mounts a moving omnibus, and does not alight from any car while the train is in motion; who investigates exhaustively the bona fides of every mendicant [beggar] before distributing alms, and will inform himself of the history and habits of a dog before administering a caress; who believes no gossip, nor repeats it, without firm basis for believing it to be true; who never drives his ball till those in front of him have definitely vacated the putting-green which is his own objective; who never from one year's end to another makes an excessive demand upon his wife, his neighbours, his servants, his ox, or his ass; who in the way of business looks only for that narrow margin of profit which twelve men such as himself would reckon to be 'fair', contemplates his fellow-merchants, their agents, and their goods, with that degree of suspicion and distrust which the law deems admirable; who never swears, gambles, or loses his temper; who uses nothing except in moderation, and even while he flogs his child is meditating only on the golden mean.[8]*

Juries are not likely to take this description literally, and no judge has ever instructed a jury with Herbert's description. A typical "pattern instruction" on negligence and due care is provided by New Mexico courts as follows, and juries would take this into the jury room as they consider a negligence case before it:

> *Negligence: The term 'negligence' may relate either to an act or a failure to act. An act, to be 'negligence,' must be one which a reasonably prudent person would foresee as involving an unreasonable risk of injury to [himself] [herself] or to another and which such a person, in the exercise of ordinary care, would not do. A failure to act, to be 'negligence,' must be a failure to do an act which one is under a duty to do and which a reasonably prudent person, in the exercise of ordinary care, would do in order to prevent injury to [himself] [herself] or to another.*
>
> *Ordinary care: Ordinary care is that care which a reasonably prudent person would use in the conduct of that person's own affairs. What constitutes 'ordinary care' varies with the nature of what is being done. As the risk of danger that should reasonably be foreseen increases, the amount of care required also increases. In deciding whether ordinary care has been used, the conduct in question must be considered in the light of all the surrounding circumstances.*

The Breach was the Proximate Cause of Plaintiff's Damages

The third requirement is that the plaintiff must show the defendant's breach was the proximate cause of plaintiff's damages.

actual cause (causation in fact)

The actual cause of negligence is sometimes called the "but for" event that is a breach of duty on the part of the defendant.

proximate cause

Sometimes known as legal cause, proximate cause must be shown as well as actual cause, so that an act of the defendant will not result in liability if the consequences of the negligent act are too remote or unforeseeable.

"For want of a nail, the kingdom was lost," as the old saying has it. Virtually any cause of an injury can be traced to some preceding cause. The problem for the law is to know when to draw the line between causes that are immediate and causes too remote for liability to be reasonably assigned to them. In tort theory, there are two kinds of causes that a plaintiff must prove: actual cause and proximate cause. **Actual cause (causation in fact)** can be found if the connection between the defendant's act and the plaintiff's injuries passes the "but for" test—if an injury would not have occurred "but for" the defendant's conduct, then the defendant is the cause of the injury. Still, this is not enough causation to create liability. The injuries to the plaintiff must also be foreseeable, or not "too remote," for the defendant's act to create liability. This is **proximate cause**—a cause that is not too remote or unforeseeable. (We use the word "approximate" often, meaning "not exact"; "*proximate*" means "exact, or exact enough to impose liability").

Suppose that someone you negligently injured was not anyone you could have expected or imagined would be harmed by your action. If you had failed to properly secure a large barge on the docks in Pittsburgh and it broke free of its moorings with no pilot aboard, you might imagine that there would be possible collisions on the Ohio River as other vessels were also out there, not realizing the barge had no pilot. But if drawbridges around the city all went up to account for the commotion of the river, you would not imagine that a pregnant woman on her way to the hospital would consequently be delayed and give birth in a traffic jam with no professional help. "But for" your negligence, she would almost surely have given birth at the hospital; if she or the baby suffers damages as a result, would there also be "proximate cause"? It's a question of fact to be determined by the jury, but it does seem "remote" or "unforeseeable" that your negligence proximately caused the damages.

The landmark proximate cause case is *Palsgraf v. Long Island Railroad*, below, which was decided by the highly regarded Judge Benjamin Cardozo. Although Judge Cardozo persuaded four of his seven brethren to side with his position, the closeness of the case demonstrates the difficulty that unforeseeable consequences and unforeseeable plaintiffs present.

As to damages—obviously there would be no lawsuit if the plaintiff suffered no damages—the plaintiff must allege and prove that she was injured. The fear that she might be injured in the future is not usually a sufficient basis for a suit. [9]

Problems of Proof

The plaintiff in a tort suit, as in any other lawsuit, has the burden of proving each of the essential elements of the cause of action in the complaint.

The plaintiff's evidence must show that the defendant did the acts complained of as negligent, demonstrate the circumstances that make the actions negligent, and prove the fact and extent of injury. Factual issues are for the jury to resolve. Since it is frequently difficult to make out the requisite proof, the law allows certain presumptions and rules of evidence that ease the plaintiff's task, on the ground that without them, justice could not be done. One important rule goes by the Latin phrase **res ipsa loquitur**, meaning "the thing speaks for itself." The best evidence is always the most direct evidence—an eyewitness account of the acts in question. But eyewitnesses are often unavailable, and in any event they frequently cannot testify directly to the reasonableness of someone's conduct, which inevitably can only be inferred from the circumstances.

In many cases, then, **circumstantial evidence** (evidence that is indirect) will be the only evidence or will constitute the bulk of the evidence. Circumstantial evidence can often be quite telling—though no one saw anyone leave the building, muddy footprints tracing a path along the sidewalk are fairly conclusive. Res ipsa loquitur is a rule of circumstantial evidence that permits the jury to draw an inference of negligence. A common statement of the rule is the following: "There must be reasonable evidence of negligence but where the thing is shown to be under the management of the defendant or his servants, and the accident is such as in the ordinary course of things does not happen if those who have the management use proper care, it affords reasonable evidence, in the absence of explanation by the defendants, that the accident arose from want of care."[10]

If a barrel of flour rolls out of a factory window and hits someone, or a soda bottle explodes, or an airplane crashes, courts in every state permit juries to conclude, in the absence of contrary explanations by the defendants, that there was negligence. The plaintiff is not put to the impossible task of explaining precisely how the accident occurred. A defendant can always offer evidence that he acted reasonably—for example, that the flour barrel was securely fastened and that a bolt of lightning, for which he was not responsible, broke its bands, causing it to roll out the window. But testimony by the factory employees that they secured the barrel, in the absence of any further explanation, will not usually serve to rebut the inference. But, application of res ipsa loquitur does not automatically entitle the plaintiff to a judgment. The plaintiff would still have to show proximate cause, actual cause, and damages. Also, tort law provides the defendant with several defenses, some of which are discussed briefly in the next section.

Defenses

There are more defenses than are listed here, but contributory negligence or comparative negligence, assumption of risk, and act of God are among the principal defenses that will completely or partially excuse the negligence of the defendant.

Contributory and Comparative Negligence

At common law, it was ordinarily a complete defense to show that the plaintiff in a negligence suit was himself negligent. Even if the plaintiff was only a little bit negligent, with most of the fault being chargeable to the defendant, the court would dismiss the suit if the plaintiff's conduct contributed to his injury. In a few states today, this rule of **contributory negligence** is still in effect.

res ipsa loquitur

Literally, "the thing speaks for itself." In tort cases, res ipsa loquitur creates a presumption that the defendant was negligent because he or she was in exclusive control of the situation and that the plaintiff would not have suffered injury but for someone's negligence. Res ipsa loquitur shifts the burden to the defendant to prove that he or she was not negligent.

circumstantial evidence

Evidence that is not "direct" but that provides judges and juries with facts that tend to show legal liability.

contributory negligence

Actions of a plaintiff that contribute to his or her own injuries. In a few states, comparative negligence is a complete bar to the plaintiff's recovery.

comparative negligence

In most states, the negligence of the plaintiff is weighed against the negligence of the defendant, and where the defendant's negligence outweighs the plaintiff's, the plaintiff can recover against the defendant even though the plaintiff has partly caused some of his or her own injuries.

This rule operated to defeat many claims even where the defendant's negligence greatly outweighed the plaintiff's, and most states, either by statute or judicial decision, have changed to some version of **comparative negligence**. Under the rule of comparative negligence, damages are apportioned according to the defendant's degree of culpability. For example, if the plaintiff has sustained a $100,000 injury, and the defendant is 80% responsible and the plaintiff is 20 percent responsible in the jury's formal estimation, the defendant will be liable for $80,000 in damages. In a state where contributory negligence remains the operative doctrine, the plaintiff's negligence will cause her to lose the case and recover nothing.

The case of *Whitlock v. University of Denver*, below, illustrates one application of the comparative negligence doctrine.

Assumption of Risk

Risk of injury pervades the modern world, and plaintiffs should not win a lawsuit simply because they took a risk and lost. The law provides, therefore, that when a person knowingly takes a risk, he or she must suffer the consequences.

The assumption of risk doctrine comes up in three ways. The plaintiff may have formally agreed with the defendant before entering a risky situation that he will relieve the defendant of liability should injury occur. ("You can borrow my car if you agree not to sue me if the brakes fail, because they're worn and I haven't had a chance to replace them.") Or, the plaintiff may have entered into a relationship with the defendant knowing that the defendant is not in a position to protect him from known risks (the fan who is hit by a line drive in a baseball park). Or, the plaintiff may act in the face of a risky situation known in advance to have been created by the defendant's negligence (getting into an automobile when the driver is known to be drunk).

The difficulty in many such cases is to determine what the injured party knew or should have known. If the plaintiff had no actual knowledge of the risk, he cannot be held to have assumed it. On the other hand, if you file a negligence tort case, you might claim that you did not appreciate the danger, but the courts will apply an objective standard of community knowledge in some situations (a test more like "but you should have known"). But when the plaintiff has no real alternative, assumption of risk fails as a defense (e.g., the landlord who negligently fails to light the exit to the street cannot claim that all tenants assumed the risk of using it).

At the turn of the 20th century, courts applied assumption of risk in industrial cases to bar relief to workers injured on the job. They were said to assume the risk of dangerous conditions or equipment. This rule has been abolished by workers' compensation statutes in most states.

Act of God

Technically, the rule that no one is responsible for an "act of God," or *force majeure* as it is sometimes called, is not an excuse but a defense premised on a lack of causation. If a force of nature caused the harm, then the defendant was not negligent in the first place. A marina, obligated to look after boats moored at its dock, is not liable if a sudden and fierce storm against which no precaution was possible destroys someone's vessel. However, if it is foreseeable that harm will flow from a negligent condition triggered by a natural event, then there is liability. For example, a work crew failed to remove residue explosive gas from an oil barge. Lightning hit the barge, exploded the gas, and injured several workmen. The plaintiff recovered damages against the company because the negligence consisted in the failure to guard against any one of a number of chance occurrences that could ignite the gas.[11]

Vicarious Liability

Liability for negligent acts does not always end with the one who was negligent. Under certain circumstances, the liability is imputed to others. For example, an employer is responsible for the negligence of his employees if they were acting in the scope of employment. This rule of vicarious liability is often called *respondeat superior*, meaning that the higher authority must respond to claims brought against one of its agents. *Respondeat superior* is not limited to the employment relationship but extends to a number of other agency relationships as well.

Legislatures in many states have enacted laws that make people vicariously liable for acts of certain people with whom they have a relationship, though not necessarily one of agency. It is common, for example, for the owner of an automobile to be liable for the negligence of one to whom the owner lends the car. So-called dram shop statutes place liability on bar and tavern owners and others who serve too much alcohol to a patron who gets drunk and later causes injury to others. In these situations, although the injurious act of the drinker stemmed from negligence, the one whom the law holds vicariously liable (the bartender and his employer) is not himself necessarily negligent—but the law holds them *strictly liable*, and to this concept we now turn.

Cases

Negligence: Proximate Cause

Palsgraf v. Long Island R.R.

248 N.Y. 339, 162 N.E. 99 (N.Y., 1928)

> **Palsgraf v. Long Island R.R.**
>
> A famous 1928 case from the high court of New York analyzing the issue of "proximate cause."

Cardozo, C. J.

Plaintiff was standing on a platform of defendant's railroad after buying a ticket to go to Rockaway Beach [a park on the Atlantic Ocean maintained by the City of New York Parks Department]. A train stopped at the station, bound for another place. Two men ran forward to catch it. One of the men reached the platform of the car without mishap, though the train was already moving. The other man, carrying a package, jumped aboard the car, but seemed unsteady as if about to fall. A guard on the car, who had held the door open, reached forward to help him in, and another guard on the platform pushed him from behind. In this act, the package was dislodged, and fell upon the rails. It was a package of small size, about fifteen inches long, and was covered by a newspaper. In fact it contained fireworks, but there was nothing in its appearance to give notice of its contents. The fireworks when they fell exploded. The shock of· the explosion threw down some scales [here, a tall coin-operated device for weighing things] at the other end of the platform many feet away. The scales struck the plaintiff, causing injuries for which she sues. [Some witnesses said the jostling of the startled or paniced passengers on the platform caused the scales to topple on to Mrs. Palsgraf.]

The conduct of the defendant's guard, if a wrong in its relation to the holder of the package, was not a wrong in its relation to the plaintiff, standing far away. Relatively to her it was not negligence at all. Nothing in the situation gave notice that the falling package had in it the potency of peril to persons thus removed. Negligence is not actionable unless it involves the invasion of a legally protected interest, the violation of a right. "Proof of negligence in the air, so to speak, will not do." * * *

A guard stumbles over a package on the floor. It seems to be a bundle of newspapers. It turns out to be a can of dynamite. To the eye of ordinary vigilance, the bundle is abandoned waste, which may be kicked or trod on with impunity. Is a passenger at the other end of the platform protected by the law against the unsuspected hazard concealed beneath the waste? If not, is the result to be any different, so far as the distant passenger is concerned, when the guard stumbles over a valise which a truckman or a porter has left upon the walk? * * * The orbit of the danger as disclosed to the eye of reasonable vigilance would be the orbit of the duty. One who jostles one's neighbor in a crowd does not invade the rights of others standing at the outer fringe when the unintended contact casts a bomb upon the ground. The wrongdoer as to them is the man who carries the bomb, not the one who explodes it without suspicion of the danger. Life will have to be made over, and human nature transformed, before prevision so extravagant can be accepted as the norm of conduct, the customary standard to which behavior must conform.

The argument for the plaintiff is built upon the shifting meanings of such words as "wrong" and "wrongful" and shares their instability. For what the plaintiff must show is a "wrong" to herself; i.e., a violation of her own right, and not merely a "wrong" to someone else, nor conduct "wrongful" because unsocial, but not a "wrong" to anyone. We are told that one who drives at reckless speed through a crowded city street is guilty of a negligent act and therefore of a wrongful one, irrespective of the consequences.

Negligent the act is, and wrongful in the sense that it is unsocial, but wrongful and unsocial in relation to other travelers, only because the eye of vigilance perceives the risk of damage. If the same act were to be committed on a speedway or a race course, it would lose its wrongful quality. The risk reasonably to be perceived defines the duty to be obeyed, and risk imports relation; it is risk to another or to others within the range of apprehension. This does not mean, of course, that one who launches a destructive force is always relieved of liability, if the force, though known to be destructive, pursues an unexpected path. * * * Some acts, such as shooting are so imminently dangerous to anyone who may come within reach of the missile however unexpectedly, as to impose a duty of prevision not far from that of an insurer. * * * Negligence, like risk, is thus a term of relation.

Negligence in the abstract, apart from things related, is surely not a tort, if indeed it is understandable at all. * * * One who seeks redress at law does not make out a cause of action by showing without more that there has been damage to his person. If the harm was not willful, he must show that the act as to him had possibilities of danger so many and apparent as to entitle him to be protected against the doing of it though the harm was unintended. * * *

The judgment of the Appellate Division and that of the Trial Term should be reversed, and the complaint dismissed, with costs in all courts.

Case Questions

1. Is there actual cause in this case? How can you tell?
2. Why should Mrs. Palsgraf (or her insurance company) be made to pay for injuries that were caused by the negligence of the Long Island Railroad?
3. How is this accident *not* foreseeable?
4. This case is recognized as probably the most analyzed and commented-upon civil case in American law. The man carrying the package was never identified—he got on the train and left the facts and commentary to history.

Negligence: Duty of Due Care

> **Whitlock v. University of Denver**
> 744 P.2d 54 (Supreme Court of Colorado, 1987)

Whitlock v. University of Denver

1987 Supreme Court of Colorado case analyzing the liability in negligence of a university for damages to a student who was injured while playing on a trampoline.

On June 19, 1978, at approximately 10:00 p.m., plaintiff Oscar Whitlock suffered a paralyzing injury while attempting to complete a one-and-three-quarters front flip on a trampoline. The injury rendered him a quadriplegic. The trampoline was owned by the Beta Theta Pi fraternity (the Beta house) and was situated on the front yard of the fraternity premises, located on the University campus. At the time of his injury, Whitlock was twenty years old, attended the University of Denver, and was a member of the Beta house, where he held the office of acting house manager. The property on which the Beta house was located was leased to the local chapter house association of the Beta Theta Pi fraternity by the defendant University of Denver.

Whitlock had extensive experience jumping on trampolines. He began using trampolines in junior high school and continued to do so during his brief tenure as a cadet at the United States Military Academy at West Point, where he learned to execute the one-and-three-quarters front flip. Whitlock testified that he utilized the trampoline at West Point every other day for a period of two months. He began jumping on the trampoline owned by the Beta house in September of 1977. Whitlock recounted that in the fall and spring prior to the date of his injury, he jumped on the trampoline almost daily. He testified further that prior to the date of his injury, he had successfully executed the one-and-three-quarters front flip between seventy-five and one hundred times.

During the evening of June 18 and early morning of June 19, 1978, Whitlock attended a party at the Beta house, where he drank beer, vodka, and scotch until 2:00 a.m. Whitlock then retired and did not awaken until 2:00 p.m. on June 19. He testified that he jumped on the trampoline between 2:00 p.m. and 4:00 p.m., and again at 7:00 p.m. At 10:00 p.m., the time of the injury, there again was a party in progress at the Beta house, and Whitlock was using the trampoline with only the illumination from the windows of the fraternity house, the outside light above the front door of the house, and two street lights in the area. As Whitlock attempted to perform the one-and-three-quarters front flip, he landed on the back of his head, causing his neck to break.

Whitlock brought suit against the manufacturer and seller of the trampoline, the University, the Beta Theta Pi fraternity and its local chapter, and certain individuals in their capacities as representatives of the Beta Theta Pi organizations. Whitlock reached settlements with all of the named defendants except the University, so only the negligence action against the University proceeded to trial. The jury returned a verdict in favor of Whitlock, assessing his total damages at $7,300,000 [about $25.5 million in 2019 dollars]. The jury attributed twenty-eight percent of causal negligence to the conduct of Whitlock and seventy-two percent of causal negligence to the conduct of the University. The trial court accordingly reduced the amount of the award against the University to $5,336,000 [about $17 million in 2019 dollars].

The University moved for judgment notwithstanding the verdict, or, in the alternative, a new trial. The trial court granted the motion for judgment notwithstanding the verdict, holding that as a matter of law, no reasonable jury could have found that the University was more negligent than Whitlock, and that the jury's monetary award was the result of sympathy, passion, or prejudice.

The court of appeals reversed * * * by a divided vote [Citation]. The court of appeals held that the University owed Whitlock a duty of due care to remove the trampoline from the fraternity premises or to supervise its use. * * * The case was remanded to the trial court with orders to reinstate the verdict and damages as determined by the jury. The University then petitioned for certiorari review, and we granted that petition.

The present case involves the alleged negligent failure to act, rather than negligent action. The plaintiff does not complain of any affirmative action taken by the University, but asserts instead that the University owed to Whitlock the duty to assure that the fraternity's trampoline was used only under supervised conditions comparable to those in a gymnasium class, or in the alternative to cause the trampoline to be removed from the front lawn of the Beta house. * * * If such a duty is to be recognized, it must be grounded on a special relationship between the University and Whitlock. According to the evidence, there are only two possible sources of a special relationship out of which such a duty could arise in this case: the status of Whitlock as a student at the University, and the lease between the University and the fraternity of which Whitlock was a member. We first consider the adequacy of the student-university relationship as a possible basis for imposing a duty on the University to control or prohibit the use of the trampoline, and then examine the provisions of the lease for that same purpose.

The Student-University Relationship

The student-university relationship has been scrutinized in several jurisdictions, and it is generally agreed that a university is not an insurer of its students' safety. [Citations] The relationship between a university and its students has experienced important change over the years. At one time, college administrators and faculties stood in loco parentis [in the place of parents] to their students, which created a special relationship "that imposed a duty on the college to exercise control over student conduct and, reciprocally, gave the students certain rights of protection by the college." [Citation.] However, in modern times there has evolved a gradual reapportionment of responsibilities from the universities to the students, and a corresponding departure from the in loco parentis relationship. [Citation.] Today, colleges and universities are regarded as educational institutions rather than custodial ones. [Citation.] (contrasting colleges and universities with elementary and high schools). * * *

By imposing a duty on the University in this case, the University would be encouraged to exercise more control over private student recreational choices, thereby effectively taking away much of the responsibility recently recognized in students for making their own decisions with respect to private entertainment and personal safety. Such an allocation of responsibility would "produce a repressive and inhospitable environment, largely inconsistent with the objectives of a modern college education." [Citation.]

The evidence demonstrates that only in limited instances has the University attempted to impose regulations or restraints on the private recreational pursuits of its students, and the students have not looked to the University to assure the safety of their recreational choices. Nothing in the University's student handbook, which contains certain regulations concerning student conduct, reflects an effort by the University to control the risk-taking decisions of its students in their private recreation. Indeed, fraternity and sorority self-governance with minimal supervision appears to have been fostered by the University. * * *

Aside from advising the Beta house on one occasion to put the trampoline up when not in use, there is no evidence that the University officials attempted to assert control over trampoline use by the fraternity members. We conclude from this record that the University's very limited actions concerning safety of student recreation did not give Whitlock or the other members of campus fraternities or sororities any reason to depend upon the University for evaluation of the safety of trampoline use. Therefore, we conclude that the student-university relationship is not a special relationship of the type giving rise to a duty of the University to take reasonable measures to protect the members of fraternities and sororities from risks of engaging in extra-curricular trampoline jumping.

The plaintiff asserts, however, that we should recognize a duty of the University to take affirmative action to protect fraternity members because of the foreseeability of the injury, the extent of the risks involved in trampoline use, the seriousness of potential injuries, and the University's superior knowledge concerning these matters. The argument in essence is that a duty should spring from the University's natural interest in the welfare and safety of its students, its superior knowledge of the nature and degree of risk involved in trampoline use, and its knowledge of the use of trampolines on the University campus. The evidence amply supports a conclusion that trampoline use involves risks of serious injuries and that the potential for an injury such as that experienced by Whitlock was foreseeable. It shows further that prior injuries resulting from trampoline accidents had been reported to campus security and to the student clinic, and that University administrators were aware of the number and severity of trampoline injuries nationwide.

The record, however, also establishes through Whitlock's own testimony that he was aware of the risk of an accident and injury of the very nature that he experienced. * * *

We conclude that the relationship between the University and Whitlock was not one of dependence with respect to the activities at issue here, and provides no basis for the recognition of a duty of the University to take measures for protection of Whitlock against the injury that he suffered.

Does the Lease between the University and the Fraternity Create a Special Relationship between the Parties?

We next examine the lease between the University and the fraternity to determine whether a special relationship between the University and Whitlock can be predicated on that document. The lease was executed in 1929, extends for a ninety-nine year term, and gives the fraternity the option to extend the term for another ninety-nine years. The premises are to be occupied and used by the fraternity "as a fraternity house, clubhouse, dormitory and boarding house, and generally for religious, educational, social and fraternal purposes." Such occupation is to be "*under control of the tenant.*" (emphasis added) The annual rental at all times relevant to this case appears from the record to be one dollar. The University has the obligation to maintain the grounds and make necessary repairs to the building, and the fraternity is to bear the cost of such maintenance and repair. * * *

We conclude that the lease, and the University's actions pursuant to its rights under the lease, provide no basis of dependence by the fraternity members upon which a special relationship can be found to exist between the University and the fraternity members that would give rise to a duty upon the University to take affirmative action to assure that recreational equipment such as a trampoline is not used under unsafe conditions.

Considering all of the factors presented, we are persuaded that under the facts of this case the University of Denver had no duty to Whitlock to eliminate the private use of trampolines on its campus or to supervise that use. There exists no special relationship between the parties that justifies placing a duty upon the University to protect Whitlock from the well-known dangers of using a trampoline. Here, a conclusion that a special relationship existed between Whitlock and the University sufficient to warrant the imposition of liability for nonfeasance would directly contravene the competing social policy of fostering an educational environment of student autonomy and independence.

We reverse the judgment of the court of appeals and return this case to that court with directions to remand it to the trial court for dismissal of Whitlock's complaint against the University.

Case Questions

1. How are comparative negligence numbers calculated by the trial court? How can the jury say that the university is 72 percent negligent and that Whitlock is 28 percent negligent?
2. Why is this not an assumption of risk case?
3. Is there any evidence that Whitlock was contributorily negligent? If not, why would the court engage in comparative negligence calculations?

4. Why does the court examine whether there is a "special relationship" created by the student-university relationship? Why does it examine whether there is a "special relationship" created by the relationship of landlord and tenant?
5. What public-policy reason is there to deny any "special relationship" between the university and its students?

Key Takeaway

The most common tort claim is based on the negligence of the defendant. In each negligence claim, the plaintiff must establish by a preponderance of the evidence that (1) the defendant had a duty of due care, (2) the defendant breached that duty, (3) that the breach of duty both actually and approximately has caused harm to the plaintiff, and (4) that the harm is measurable in money damages.

It is also possible for the negligence of one person to be imputed to another, as in the case of respondeat superior, or in the case of someone who loans his automobile to another driver who is negligent and causes injury. There are many excuses (defenses) to claims of negligence, including assumption of risk and comparative negligence. In those few jurisdictions where contributory negligence has not been modified to comparative negligence, plaintiffs whose negligence contributes to their own injuries will be barred from any recovery.

Exercises

1. Explain the difference between comparative negligence and contributory negligence.
2. How is actual cause different from probable cause?
3. What is an example of assumption of risk?
4. How does res ipsa loquitur help a plaintiff establish a case of negligence?

7.4 Strict Liability

Learning Objectives

1. Understand how strict liability torts differ from negligent torts.
2. Understand the historical origins of strict liability under common law.
3. Be able to apply strict liability concepts to liability for defective products.
4. Distinguish strict liability from absolute liability, and understand the major defenses to a lawsuit in products-liability cases.

After intentional torts and negligent torts, the third kind of tort is strict-liability tort.

Historical Basis of Strict Liability: Animals and Ultrahazardous Activities

Up to this point, we have considered principles of liability that in some sense depend upon the "fault" of the tortfeasor. This fault does not always imply serious moral blame, especially with negligence lawsuits, but some moral blame is part and parcel of intentional torts. There is, however, no ascription of moral blame where "strict liability" torts are involved. The earliest examples of **strict liability** at common law involved animals; an owner of any animal that escaped from its pastures and caused damage to neighboring property may be liable, even if the reason for their escape was beyond the power of the owner to stop (e.g., a fire started by lightning that burns open a barn door). Another well-established common law principle is that those who engage in ultra-hazardous (sometimes termed "abnormally dangerous") activities are liable for damage that they cause, even though they have taken every possible precaution to avoid harm to others.

> **strict liability**
>
> The imposition of tort liability upon a defendant even though the defendant was without fault in the incident.

In such cases, the courts invoke the principle of strict liability, or, as it is sometimes called, liability without fault. The reason for the rule is explained in *Klein v. Pyrodyne Corporation*, below, but basically it is this: somebody has to pay when one person's fault-free actions nevertheless cause another harm, and it ought to be the one who can buy liability insurance to compensate the "victims."

Strict Liability for Products

Strict liability moved well beyond animals and ultrahazardous activities in the 20th Century. In the United States the doctrine of strict liability was created (or "discovered") in a California Supreme Court decision—the seminal *Greenman v. Yuba Power Products, Inc.* (1962).

In *Greenman*, the plaintiff had used a home power saw and bench, the Shopsmith, designed and manufactured by the defendant. He was experienced in using power tools and was injured while using the approved lathe attachment to the Shopsmith to fashion a wooden chalice. The case was decided on the premise that Greenman had done nothing wrong in using the machine but that the machine had a defect that was "latent" (not easily discoverable by the consumer). Rather than decide the case based on warranties, or requiring that Greenman prove how the defendant had been negligent, Justice Traynor found for the plaintiff based on the overall social utility of strict liability in cases of defective products. According to his decision, the purpose of such liability is to ensure that the "cost of injuries resulting from defective products is borne by the manufacturers . . . rather than by the injured persons who are powerless to protect themselves."

Today, the majority of U.S. states recognize strict liability for defective products, although some states limit strict liability actions to damages for personal injuries rather than property damage. Injured plaintiffs have to prove the product caused the harm but do not have to prove exactly how the manufacturer was careless. Purchasers of the product, as well as injured guests, bystanders, and others with no direct relationship with the product, may sue for damages caused by the product.

The Restatement of the Law of Torts, Second, Section 402(a), was originally issued in 1964. It is a widely accepted statement of the liabilities of sellers of goods for defective products. The Restatement specifies six requirements, all of which must be met for a plaintiff to recover using strict liability for a product that the plaintiff claims is defective:

1. The product must be in a defective condition when the defendant sells it.
2. The defendant must normally be engaged in the business of selling or otherwise distributing the product.

3. The product must be unreasonably dangerous to the user or consumer because of its defective condition.

4. The plaintiff must incur physical harm to self or to property by using or consuming the product.

5. The defective condition must be the proximate cause of the injury or damage.

6. The goods must not have been substantially changed from the time the product was sold to the time the injury was sustained.

Section 402(a) also explicitly makes clear that a defendant can be held liable even though the defendant has exercised "all possible care." Thus, it becomes clear that in a strict liability case in the U.S., the plaintiff does not need to show "fault" (or negligence).

Defenses to Strict Liability

You might think there are no defenses to strict liability, after all, the liability is strict. But for defendants, who can include the entire range of businesspeople, corporations, and regular folks, there are a number of defenses that are available:

- Assumption of the risk (we already looked at this one);
- Product misuse (like trimming a hedge with a rotatory lawnmower)[12];
- Comparative negligence (we examined that above);
- Knowledgeable user doctrine: If the parents of obese teenagers bring a lawsuit against McDonald's, claiming that its fast-food products are defective and that McDonald's should have warned customers of the adverse health effects of eating its products, a defense based on the knowledgeable user is available. In one case, the court found that the high levels of cholesterol, fat, salt, and sugar in McDonald's food are well known to users. The court stated, "If consumers know (or reasonably should know) the potential ill health effects of eating at McDonald's, they cannot blame McDonald's if they, nonetheless, choose to satiate their appetite with a surfeit of supersized McDonald's.[13]

Case

Strict Liability

Klein v. Pyrodyne Corporation

Washington State Supreme Court case analyzing the application of strict liability in tort for damages caused during a public fireworks show.

Klein v. Pyrodyne Corporation

810 P.2d 917 (Supreme Court of Washington, 1991)

Guy, J.

The plaintiffs in this case are persons injured when an aerial shell at a public fireworks exhibition went astray and exploded near them. The defendant is the pyrotechnic company hired to set up and discharge the fireworks. The issue before this court is whether pyrotechnicians are strictly liable for damages caused by fireworks displays. We hold that they are.

Defendant Pyrodyne Corporation (Pyrodyne) is a general contractor for aerial fireworks at public fireworks displays. Pyrodyne contracted to procure fireworks, to provide pyrotechnic operators, and to display the fireworks at the Western Washington State Fairgrounds in Puyallup, Washington, on July 4, 1987. All operators of the fireworks display were Pyrodyne employees acting within the scope of their employment duties.

As required by Washington statute, Pyrodyne purchased a $1 million insurance policy prior to the fireworks show. The policy provided $1 million coverage for each occurrence of bodily injury or property damage liability. Plaintiffs allege that Pyrodyne failed to carry out a number of the other statutory and regulatory requirements in preparing for and setting off the fireworks. * * *

During the fireworks display, one of the 5-inch mortars was knocked into a horizontal position. From this position an aerial shell inside was ignited and discharged. The shell flew 500 feet in a trajectory parallel to the earth and exploded near the crowd of onlookers. Plaintiffs Danny and Marion Klein were injured by the explosion. Mr. Klein's clothing was set on fire, and he suffered facial burns and serious injury to his eyes. * * *

[The trial court held] that Pyrodyne was strictly liable without fault and ordered summary judgment in favor of the Kleins on the issue of liability. * * * Pyrodyne is appealing solely as to the trial court's holding that strict liability is the appropriate standard of liability for pyrotechnicians. A strict liability claim against pyrotechnicians for damages caused by fireworks displays presents a case of first impression in Washington.

Section 520 of the Restatement lists six factors that are to be considered in determining whether an activity is "abnormally dangerous." The factors are as follows:

  a. existence of a high degree of risk of some harm to the person, land or chattels of others;
  b. likelihood that the harm that results from it will be great;
  c. inability to eliminate the risk by the exercise of reasonable care;
  d. extent to which the activity is not a matter of common usage;
  e. inappropriateness of the activity to the place where it is carried on; and
  f. extent to which its value to the community is outweighed by its dangerous attributes.

We find that the factors stated in clauses (a), (b), and (c) are all present in the case of fireworks displays. Anytime a person ignites aerial shells or rockets with the intention of sending them aloft to explode in the presence of large crowds of people, a high risk of serious personal injury or property damage is created. That risk arises because of the possibility that a shell or rocket will malfunction or be misdirected. Furthermore, no matter how much care pyrotechnicians exercise, they cannot entirely eliminate the high risk inherent in setting off powerful explosives such as fireworks near crowds.

The dangerousness of fireworks displays is evidenced by the elaborate scheme of administrative regulations with which pyrotechnicians must comply. Pyrotechnicians must be licensed to conduct public displays of special fireworks. [Citing regulations under Washington law.] To obtain such a license, the pyrotechnician must take and pass a written examination administered by the director of fire protection, and must submit evidence of qualifications and experience, including "participation in the firing of at least six public displays as an assistant, at least one of which shall have been in the current or preceding year." [Citation.] * * * Regulations also govern such matters as the way in which the fireworks at public displays are constructed, stored, installed, and fired. The necessity for such regulations demonstrates the dangerousness of fireworks displays.

Pyrodyne argues that if the regulations are complied with, then the high degree of risk otherwise inherent in the displays can be eliminated. Although we recognize that the high risk can be reduced, we do not agree that it can be eliminated. Setting off powerful fireworks near large crowds remains a highly risky activity even when the safety precautions mandated by statutes and regulations are followed. The Legislature appears to agree, for it has declared that in order to obtain a license to conduct a public fireworks display, a pyrotechnician must first obtain a surety bond or a certificate of insurance, the amount of which must be at least $1 million for each event [Citation]. * * *

[The defendant argued plaintiffs' damages were caused by the negligence of the Chinese fireworks manufacturer, and that therefore strict liability should not apply.] We note that the Restatement (Second) of Torts takes a position contrary to that advocated by Pyrodyne. Section 522 of the Restatement provides that: "One carrying on an abnormally dangerous activity is subject to strict liability for the resulting harm although it is caused by the unexpectable (a) innocent, negligent or reckless conduct of a third person . . . ." * * *

In sum, we find that setting off public fireworks displays satisfies four of the six conditions under the Restatement test; that is, it is an activity that is not "of common usage" and that presents an ineliminably high risk of serious bodily injury or property damage. We therefore hold that conducting public fireworks displays is an abnormally dangerous activity justifying the imposition of strict liability. * * *

This conclusion is consistent with the results reached in cases involving damages caused by detonating dynamite. This court has recognized that parties detonating dynamite are strictly liable for the damages caused by such blasting. [Citations.]

Policy considerations also support imposing strict liability on pyrotechnicians for damages caused by their public fireworks displays, although such considerations are not alone sufficient to justify that conclusion. Most basic is the question as to who should bear the loss when an innocent person suffers injury through the nonculpable but abnormally dangerous activities of another. In the case of public fireworks displays, fairness weighs in favor of requiring the pyrotechnicians who present the displays to bear the loss rather than the unfortunate spectators who suffer the injuries. * * *

We hold that Pyrodyne Corporation is strictly liable for all damages suffered as a result of the July 1987 fireworks display. Detonating fireworks displays constitutes an abnormally dangerous activity warranting strict liability. Public policy also supports this conclusion. Judgment below affirmed.

Case Questions

1. Why would certain activities be deemed ultrahazardous or abnormally dangerous so that strict liability is imposed?
2. If the activities are known to be abnormally dangerous, did Klein assume the risk?
3. Assume that the fireworks were negligently manufactured in China, as the defendant asserted. Why is the general rule (the Restatement) that such is immaterial to the imposition of strict liablilty?
4. There are sound public policy reasons for imposing strict liability on an "innocent" defendant. What are they? What is the role that insurance plays here?

Key Takeaway

Common-law courts have long held that certain activities are inherently dangerous and that those who cause damage to others by engaging in those activities will be held strictly liable. More recently, courts in the United States have applied strict liability to defective products. Strict liability, however, is not absolute liability, as there are defenses available to defendants in lawsuits based on strict liability, such as comparative negligence and product abuse.

7.5 Tort Remedies, Limitations on Remedies, and Tort Reform

Learning Objectives

1. Understand the purpose of remedies in tort.
2. Recognize the distinction between legal remedies and equitable remedies, and what the remedies are.
3. Know that there are several limitations on tort recovery.
4. Understand why "tort reform" is argued for, and by what entities.

Once it is established that the defendant is liable in tort (intentional, negligent, or strict liability) the plaintiff is, as we noted in the discussion of the purpose of tort law, entitled to remedies to put her in the situation she would have been in had the tortfeasor not committed the tort. Notice again, if there were no tort law people would tend to take revenge, and violence would ensue.

Here we look at the two major categories of remedies: damages (in law) and equitable remedies (in equity), we note briefly some limits on recovery, and touch briefly on tort reform.

Remedies in Tort

Legal Remedies

Legal *remedies* in tort or contract refer to **damages**, money paid by (typically) the defendant to the plaintiff, because the plaintiff has suffered some loss as a result of the defendant's actions. (Damages are to be distinguished from *costs* which refer to expenses incurred as a result of bringing the lawsuit. A plaintiff may be entitled to both.)

There are three main types of damages.

> **damages**
>
> Monetary compensation that is awarded by a court in a civil action to an individual who has been injured through the wrongful conduct of another party.

special damages

In tort law, damages for which the plaintiff has a receipt—specific expenses.

Special damages. Special damages are damages for which there is a receipt; these are also referred to as "damages for economic loss." If you crash into my car I am entitled to damages to repair it; I am entitled to damages to pay my hospital bills, and any other expenses I can prove. Special damages would include:

- Replacement or repair of damaged or destroyed property;
- Loss of income;
- Medical expenses, past and future.

general damages

In tort, damages where plaintiff cannot demonstrate monetary, out of pocket expense caused by the tort.

General damages. General damages are damages for which there is no receipt, but for which, nevertheless, compensation is recognized as owing. It is up to the artful lawyer to explain to the jury what and how much compensation should be awarded for general damages. Here are examples of general damages:

- Pain and suffering;
- Physical impairment;
- Physical disfigurement;
- Mental anguish;
- Loss of companionship (of one's family members in wrongful death cases, and today may include loss of one's pet dog or cat).

punitive damages

Monetary compensation awarded to an injured party that goes beyond that which is necessary to compensate the individual for losses and that is intended to punish the wrongdoer.

Punitive damages are a third type of damages intended to deter others from similar wrongdoing; they are sometimes called "exemplary damages"—as in the word "example." Contrary to the normal purpose of civil-law remedies, punitive damages are indeed intended to punish the defendant. They are almost never awarded except in cases of intentional torts as a deterrent to the tortfeasor and an example the world: don't do that.

Equitable Remedies

injunction

An equitable remedy in the form of a court order that compels a party to do or refrain from specific acts.

A plaintiff who claims she has suffered harm as the result of a tort might not always want money. If your neighbor's cows are tramping your garden, you might get money damages for your squashed pumpkins, but that won't stop the cows from getting into your yard again. Equitable remedies are non-monetary. The most common equitable remedy in tort is an **injunction**. (You will remember that we discussed equity in Chapter 1—recall the case where Campbell's Soup Company sued the carrot farmers.)

An injunction is an order signed by a judge directing a person to stop doing what he ought not do because what he's doing is a tort. For example, if somebody was trespassing on your land you might not like the invasion of privacy or loss of quietude. What you want is not that the trespasser pay you, but that he stop trespassing; same with the cow example. Notice that an injunction does not require a person to do anything, but rather *not* to do something.

If a person is enjoined ("to enjoin" is the verb) and disobeys the injunction, she can be held in contempt of court ("contempt" is to disrespect). She may be fined or even spend some time in jail for it.

Limitations on Remedies

Of course a plaintiff will get no remedy at all if he fails to prove the necessary elements of tort. For example, plaintiff was injured when struck in a crosswalk; he claimed that because of his injury he could not care for his cattle. Because he could not care for his cattle, he had to sell them at a loss. The court determined the loss on the cattle was not proximately caused by the defendant's action, and there was no recovery for that.[14]

But beyond failure to prove the case at all, we may call out several limitations on tort remedies.

Certainty of damages. If you can't prove whether your tort loss was $600 or $60,000, you might well get nothing at all. The plaintiff doesn't have to prove the damages to the penny, but rather with reasonable certainty. Courts have said things like this in regard to certainty of damages:

> *Damages need not be measured with exactness and precision. When defendant is liable for some damages, the amount may be fixed when circumstances permit intelligent estimate.*[15]
>
> *Proof of damages to absolute certainty as to amount of damages is not essential when existence of loss is established and facts are such as permit intelligent estimate of damages.*[16]
>
> *One should not be allowed to escape liability simply because precise amount of damages is uncertain; however, there must be sufficient facts and circumstances to permit intelligent and probable estimate of damages.*[17]

Mitigation of damages. Suppose your neighbor fails to attend to his garden-pruning burn pile; sparks land on your roof and burn part of it. But instead of getting it fixed promptly, you put a blue plastic tarp over it. Two weeks later your house is damaged when the tarp blows off the roof and rain water gets inside. You will not recover the damage to your furniture, drapes, rugs, and so on because you failed to make a reasonable effort to mitigate your damages. ("To mitigate" means to make less bad.) Similarly, if after the defendant causes you injury you fail to get medical attention, you will not recover for the costs of treating the subsequent infection (or amputation).

Defenses. We have already observed that a defendant in a tort case can raise various defenses that can limit or defeat the plaintiff's recovery: self defense, consent, privilege, comparative negligence, assumption of the risk, and so on.

Tort Reform

Many businesses see tort lawsuits as a nuisance at best and ruinous at worst, and would like to see them disappear altogether; they advocate for **tort reform**.

Over thirty years ago, in 1988, The Conference Board[18] published a study: a survey of more than 500 chief executive officers from large and small companies regarding the effects of tort-claim liability on their firms concluded that U.S. companies are less competitive in international business because of these effects and that products-liability laws must be reformed.

The reform effort has been under way ever since, with varying degrees of alarms and finger-pointing as to who is to blame for the "tort crisis," if there even is one. Business and professional groups beat the drums for tort reform as a means to guarantee "fairness" in the courts as well as spur U.S. economic competitiveness in a global marketplace, while plaintiffs' attorneys and consumer advocates claim that businesses simply want to externalize costs by denying recovery to victims of greed and carelessness.

Here are some of the reforms:

- Statutes of repose. These are like statutes of limitation that preclude plaintiffs from filing tort-claim suits after a period of time. For example, in 1994 President Clinton signed the General Aviation Revitalization Act into law, imposing an eighteen-year statute of repose on product liability claims brought against general aviation aircraft manufacturers such as Cessna and

---

certainty of damages

The requirement that the plaintiff in a civil case, generally, must articulate with some evidence—not just speculation—what her damages are as a result of the defendant's breach of duty.

mitigation of damages

The duty owed by one who has suffered a loss to try to make it as small as possible; failure to mitigate damages precludes recovery for such damages as would otherwise have been avoided.

tort reform

The effort undertaken by or at the behest of "perennial defendants," and moderately successful, to limit the availability or reach of tort law so that the cost of doing business (buying insurance) is reduced.

Piper. The law allowed these manufacturers to once again launch new light aircraft production in the United States.

- A cap on punitive damages. President George W. Bush supported a nationwide punitive damage cap of $250,000 for medical malpractice claims, but Congress did not pass any such law.
- Eliminating, by legislation, "defective design" as a basis for recovery. In particular, federal pre-emption may be invoked to preclude state courts from entering judgments against firms whose products have been approved by a federal agency. For example, the FDA approves medical devices and--the pre-emption argument goes--if the FDA rules that a device is safe, that ruling cannot be challenged in state court.
- Allowing "state-of-the-art defenses" (if something was "state of the art" at the time it was produced then no strict liability can apply).
- Federal reform. Piecemeal reform of tort law, especially product-liability torts, in each state has contributed to the basic lack of uniformity from state to state, giving it a crazy-quilt effect. In the nineteenth century, this might have made little difference, but today most manufacturers sell in the national market and are subjected to the varying requirements of the law in every state. For years there has been talk in and out of Congress of enacting a federal products-liability law that would include reforms adopted in many states, as discussed earlier. So far, these efforts have been without much success.

Each side vilifies the other in very unseemly language—pro-business advocates call consumer-oriented states "judicial hell-holes" and complain of "well-orchestrated campaigns by tort-lawyer lobbyists and allies to undo years of tort reform at the state level,"[19] while pro-plaintiff interests claim that there is "scant evidence" of any tort abuse at all.[20] It would be more amusing if it were not so shrill and partisan. Perhaps the most one can say with any certainty is that peoples' perceptions of reality are highly colored by their self-interests. In any event, there have been reforms (or, as the detractors say, "deforms").

Key Takeaway

Remedies in tort are legal and equitable. In law, tort remedies are damages—money paid by one side to the other; the damages can be special (for which there is a receipt) or general (no receipt, but compensation is recognized as allowed). The main equitable remedy is an injunction, by which a court orders the defendant to stop doing what is a tort.

A plaintiff's tort remedies may be limited if she cannot with reasonable certainty articulate the amount of the loss suffered, or if she has failed to mitigate damages, or if she is determined to have been contributorily negligent herself.

The perennial defendants, especially big corporations, don't like being sued in tort and have well-funded campaigns to constrain such cases with "tort reform." Plaintiffs' lawyers claim the perennial defendants are just trying to avoid responsibility for their own carelessness. And so the argument goes.

Exercises

1. Plaintiff was injured when the blade on his rotary lawnmower broke and a piece of it hit his ankle. The manufacturer showed that it had an entirely up-to-date factory and that the apparent defect in the lawnmower blade was not discoverable by the inspection it received, which was the same sort of inspection all lawnmower manufacturers give such blades before they are installed on the machine. On these facts, what theory of tort liability should plaintiff pursue? Who will win and why?
2. Deborah Defendant's dog dug under its back-yard fence, ran into Paul Plaintiff's yard, and attacked and killed Plaintiff's cat, a companion of Plaintiff for fifteen years. Defendant asserted that she maintained a reasonable fence, and that she never anticipated that her dog

would dig under it and escape. Moreover, she said, the plaintiff could go to the humane society and adopt another cat for only $50, so in any event that's all she would owe. Is defendant right? Explain. Would it matter if Defendant had significant homeowner's insurance?

3. Plaintiff approached defendant's newly-acquired horse from the back to pet it; as she passed its flank, the horse shied, kicking plaintiff and breaking her leg. Who wins if plaintiff sues defendant for her injuries?

4. Jason took a shortcut to the bus stop every day, trampling on plaintiff's vegetable garden quite noticeably. To what remedy or remedies is plaintiff entitled?

5. What is the argument raised by "perennial defendants" (like automobile companies) in favor of tort reform, and what argument to the contrary is raised by the plaintiffs' bar (attorneys representing plaintiffs)?

7.6 Summary and Exercises

Summary

The principles of tort law pervade modern society because they spell out the duties of care that we owe each other in our private lives. Tort law has had a significant impact on business because modern technology poses significant dangers and the modern market is so efficient at distributing goods to a wide class of consumers.

Unlike criminal law, tort law does not require the tortfeasor to have a specific intent to commit the act for which he or she will be held liable to pay damages. Negligence—that is, carelessness—is a major factor in tort liability. In some instances, especially in cases involving injuries caused by products, a no-fault standard called strict liability is applied.

What constitutes a legal injury depends very much on the circumstances. A person can assume a risk or consent to the particular action, thus relieving the person doing the injury from tort liability. To be liable, the tortfeasor must be the proximate cause of the injury, not a remote cause. On the other hand, certain people are held to answer for the torts of another—for example, an employer is usually liable for the torts of his employees, and a bartender might be liable for injuries caused by someone to whom he sold too many drinks. Two types of statutes—workers' compensation and no-fault automobile insurance—have eliminated tort liability for certain kinds of accidents and replaced it with an immediate insurance payment plan.

Among the torts of particular importance to the business community are wrongful death and personal injury caused by products or acts of employees, misrepresentation, defamation, and interference with contractual relations.

Exercises

1. What is the difference in objectives between tort law and criminal law?

2. A woman fell ill in a store. An employee put the woman in an infirmary but provided no medical care for six hours, and she died. The woman's family sued the store for wrongful death. What arguments could the store make that it was not liable? What arguments could the family make? Which seem the stronger arguments? Why?

3. The signals on a railroad crossing were defective. Although the railroad company was notified of the problem a month earlier, the railroad inspector failed to come by and repair them. Seeing the all-clear signal, a car drove up and stalled on the tracks as a train rounded the bend. For the past two weeks the car had been stalling, and the driver kept putting off taking the car to the shop for a tune-up. As the train rounded the bend, the engineer was distracted

by the conductor and didn't see the car until it was too late to stop. Who is negligent? Who must bear the liability for the damage to the car and its driver, and to the train?

4. Suppose the owners of an abandoned building on their farmland were ticked off because people are going into the building, and doing who knows what in there! The owners rigged a spring gun so that when an intruder opened a door, his legs were blown off. The owners would be liable to the trespasser: "Spring guns and other man-killing devices are not justifiably against a mere trespasser"[21] Now suppose that instead of setting such a device, the defendants had simply let the floor immediately inside the front door rot until it was so weak that anybody who came in and took two steps straight ahead would fall through the floor and to the cellar. Will the defendant be liable in this case? What if they invited a realtor to appraise the place and did not warn her of the floor? Does it matter whether the injured person is a trespasser or an invitee?

5. Plaintiff's husband died in an accident, leaving her with several children and no money except a valid insurance policy by which she was entitled to $5,000. Insurance Company refused to pay, delaying and refusing payment and meanwhile "inviting" Plaintiff to accept less than $5,000, hinting that it had a defense. Plaintiff was reduced to accepting housing and charity from relatives. She sued the insurance company for bad-faith refusal to settle the claim and for the intentional infliction of emotional distress. The lower court dismissed the case. Should the court of appeals allow the matter to proceed to trial?

6. The plaintiff, shopping for produce in a supermarket and pushing a shopping cart, noticed some water and some leaves of lettuce on the floor; moving around a display rack, she slipped and fell. She looked at the floor where she had slipped and saw a squashed cherry pit on the floor, and the pit was on her shoe, but she did not know how long the cherry had been on the floor. After the plaintiff presented her case on this fact situation, essentially without more, the trial judge dismissed the case without sending it to the jury. The court of appeals and the state supreme court affirmed. Why did the plaintiff lose this tort case? What crucial piece of evidence was missing?[22]

7. When a big corporation like Boeing or Disney gets "hit" with a multimillion dollar tort judgment, who really pays? The corporation's insurance company? The shareholders?

8. How do insurance companies play a role in "policing" their insureds' activities and premises to promote the safe maintenance of the premises and safe carrying-on of those activities?

9. The defendant rock radio station had a large teenage listening audience in the greater Los Angeles area. It ran a contest that rewarded the first contestant to physically locate a traveling disk jokey who drove, at legal speeds, a conspicuous car, broadcasting from the vehicle as he moved about L.A.'s freeways, streets, and byways. Two teenagers, in separate cars and independently, followed the DJ, reaching speeds of over 80 mph to catch up with him. As the cars closed in on the DJ's vehicle, one of them forced the decedent's car off the road. It rolled over onto the median and the driver was killed. The decedent's widow and children sued the radio station. What argument would the plaintiffs make; what defense would the station raise?[23]

Self-Test Questions

1. Catarina falsely accused Jeff of stealing from their employer. The statement is defamatory only if:

   a. a third party hears it

   b. Nick suffers severe emotional distress as a result

   c. the statement is the actual and proximate cause of his distress

   d. the statement is widely circulated in the local media and on Twitter

2. Garrett filed a suit against Colossal Media Corporation for defamation. Colossal has said that Garrett is a "sleazy, corrupt public official" (and provided some evidence to back the claim). To win his case, Garrett will have to show that Colossal acted with:

   a. malice

   b. ill will

    c. malice aforethought

    d. actual malice

3. Big Burger begins a rumor, using social media, that the meat in Burger World is partly composed of ground-up worms. The rumor is not true, as Big Burger well knows. Its intent is to get some customers to shift loyalty from Burger World to Big Burger. Burger World's best cause of action would be:

    a. trespass on the case

    b. nuisance

    c. product disparagement

    d. intentional infliction of emotional distress

4. Wilfred Phelps, age 65, is driving his Nissan Altima down Main Street when he suffers the first seizure of his life. He loses control of his vehicle and runs into three people on the sidewalk. Which statement is true?

    a. He is liable for an intentional tort.

    b. He is liable for a negligent tort.

    c. He is not liable for a negligent tort.

    d. He is liable under strict liability, because driving a car is abnormally dangerous.

5. Jonathan carelessly bumped into Amanda, knocking her to the ground. He will be held liable for a negligence tort:

    a. only if Amanda is injured

    b. only if Amanda is not injured

    c. whether or not Amanda is injured

Self-Test Answers

1. a
2. d
3. c
4. c
5. a

Endnotes

1. *Roach v. Stern*, 675 N.Y.S.2d 133 (1998).
2. *Hustler Magazine, Inc. v. Falwell*, 485 U.S. 46, 108 S.Ct. 876 (1988).
3. Trespass is here discussed as a tort; in Chapter 9 it is discussed as an element of Property Law, and in Chapter 12 as an element of Environmental Law.
4. *Katko v. Briney*, 183 N.W.2d 657 (Iowa 1971).
5. Restatement (Second) of Torts, Section 559 (1965).
6. *Times v. Sullivan*, 376 US 254 (1964).
7. *Bernethy v. Walt Failor's, Inc.*, 653 P2d 280 (Wash. 1982).
8. A.P. Herbert, *Misleading Cases in the Common Law* (1930), 12, 16.
9. This rule has proved troublesome in medical malpractice and industrial disease cases. A doctor's negligent act or a company's negligent exposure of a worker to some form of contamination might not become manifest in the body for years. In the meantime, the tort statute of limitations might have run out, barring the victim from suing at all. An increasing number of courts have eased the plaintiff's predicament by ruling that the statute of limitations does not begin to run until the victim discovers that she has been injured or contracted a disease.
10. *Scott v. London & St. Katherine Docks Co.*, 3 H. & C. 596, 159 Eng.Rep. 665 (Q.B. 1865).
11. *Johnson v. Kosmos Portland Cement Co.*, 64 F.2d 193 (6th Cir. 1933).
12. Consider the urban (or Internet) legend of Merv Grazinski, who supposedly put his Winnebago on autopilot to go back and make coffee in the kitchen, and then recovered millions after his Winnebago turned over and he suffered serious injuries. There are multiple defenses to this alleged action; these would include the defenses of contributory negligence, comparative negligence, and product misuse. There was never any such case, and certainly no such recovery; it is not known who started this legend, or why, although "tort reform" was on the agenda of many individuals and firms that felt "frivolous lawsuits" were hurting business and commerce generally. It was, as we now say, "fake news."
13. *Pellman v. McDonald's Corp.*, 237 F.2d 512 (S.D.N.Y. 2003).
14. *Phillips v. Stewart*, 148 S.E.2d 784 (VA, 1966).
15. *M & B Constr. Co. v. Mitchell*,195 S.E.2d 873 (VA, 1973).
16. *Silvey v. Johnston*, 70 S.E.2d 280 (VA, 1952).
17. *Jefferson Std. Ins. Co. v. Hedrick*, 27 S.E.2d 198 (VA, 1943).
18. https://www.conference-board.org/about/index.cfm?id=1980
19. American Tort Reform Association, http://www.atra.org.
20. Ross Eisenbrey, "The Frivolous Case for Tort Law Change," Economic Policy Institute, May 16, 2005. https://www.epi.org/publication/bp157/
21. *Katko v. Briney*, 282 NW 2d 657 (1971).
22. *Moultrey v. A&P*, 442 A.2d 593 (PA, 1981).
23. *Weirum v. RKO General*, 539 P.2d 36 (CA, 1975).

CHAPTER 8
Contract Law

Chapter Learning Objectives

After reading this chapter, you should understand:

1. What role contracts play in society today.
2. What a contract is.
3. The sources of contract law.
4. Some basic contract taxonomy.
5. The required elements of a contract: mutual assent, consideration, legality, and capacity.
6. The circumstances when a contract needs to be in writing to be enforceable.
7. The remedies for breach of contract, and limitations on remedies.

The two fundamental concepts considered the twin cornerstones of business relationships are contract and tort. Although both involve the concept of duty, creation of the duty differs in a manner that is important to business. The parties create *contract* duties through a bargaining process—they *agree* to deal with each other. The key element in the process is control; individuals are in control of a situation because they have the freedom to decide whether to enter into a contractual relationship. *Tort* duties, in contrast, are obligations the law imposes when harm is caused in a relationship to which the parties did not agree.

That is, we have two fundamental duties to our fellow humans and their property: the duty to avoid causing harm by breaking our promises (that's contract law), and the duty to avoid causing harm by means other than breaking our promises (that's tort law).

8.1 Introduction to Contract Law

Learning Objectives

1. Understand the role of contract in society—it moves society from status to contract.
2. Know the definition of a contract.
3. Recognize the sources of contract law: the common law, the Uniform Commercial Code (UCC), and the Convention on the International Sale of Goods (CISG)—a treaty.
4. Understand some fundamental contract taxonomy and terminology.

The Role of Contract in Modern Society

This chapter takes up the law of contracts for real estate and services, and touches on the law of contracts for the sale of goods.

Contract is probably the most familiar legal concept in our society because it is central to a deeply-held conviction about the essence of our political, economic, and social life. Commonly speaking, the term is used interchangeably with agreement, bargain, undertaking, or deal; but whatever the word, it embodies our notion of freedom to make choices about how we live. Contract is central because it is the means by which people in a free society order their affairs. You are reading this book because you made a contract to buy it.

So commonplace is the concept of contract—and our freedom to make contracts with each other—that it is difficult to imagine a time when contracts were rare, an age when people's everyday associations with one another were not freely determined. Yet in historical terms, it was not so long ago that contracts were rare, entered into by very few, if at all. In "primitive" societies and in medieval Europe, from which our institutions sprang, the relationships among people were largely fixed; traditions spelled out duties that each person owed to family, tribe, or manor. That's feudalism—you are *born* into a status which is, pretty much, unchangeable, and you don't have much use for contracts. Sir Henry Maine (1822–1888), a nineteenth century English historian, sketched the development of society in his classic book *Ancient Law*. *As* he put it:

> [F]rom a condition of society in which all the relations of Persons are summed up in the relations of Family, we seem to have steadily moved towards a phase of social order in which all these relations arise from the free agreement of Individuals. Thus the status of the Slave has disappeared—it has been superseded by the contractual relation of the servant [employee] to his master [employer]. The status of the female under tutelage [guardianship] has also ceased to exist. . . . So too the status of the son under power [adult son subordinate to a parent] has no true place in the law of modern European societies. We may say that the movement of the progressive societies has hitherto been a movement from Status to Contract.[1]

Maine's optimism about the inevitable march of progress seems somewhat overblown (he was writing in "the Age of Optimism," before World War I), but the idea that change necessarily involves freeing individuals from their *assigned* status stations—freeing them from stations assigned by skin color, family name, sex, religion, sexuality, nationality—and thereby allowing individuals to determine as best as they can their own course through voluntary choices—that is, through contract—seems right. This movement "from status to contract" was not accidental. It developed with the emerging industrial order; from the fifteenth to the nineteenth centuries, as England, especially, evolved into a booming mercantile economy with all that that implies—flourishing trade, growing cities, an expanding monetary system, commercialization of agriculture, mushrooming manufacturing—contract law was created of necessity.

Contract law did not develop, however, according to a conscious, far-seeing plan. It was a response to changing conditions, and the judges who created it frequently resisted, preferring the quieter, imagined pastoral life of their forefathers. Not until the nineteenth century, in both the United States and England, did a full-fledged law of contracts arise, together with modem capitalism.

Contract Defined

The legal definition of "**contract**" is formalistic ("formalistic" means strictly adhering to, or observing of, prescribed or traditional forms). The Restatement[2] says: "A contract is a promise or a set of promises for the breach of which the law gives a remedy, or the performance of which the law in some way recognizes as a duty." Similarly, the Uniform Commercial Code says: "'Contract' means the total legal obligation which results from the parties' agreement as affected by this Act and any other applicable rules of law."

A short-hand definition is: "A contract is a legally enforceable promise." This implies that not every promise or agreement creates a binding contract; if every promise did, the simple definition set out in the preceding sentence would read, "A contract is a promise." But, again, a contract is not simply a promise: it is a legally enforceable promise.

contract
A legally enforceable promise.

Sources of Contract Law

The most important sources of contract law are two: state case law and state statutes (though there are also various federal statutes governing how contracts are made by, and with, the federal government). And we need to mention a third source, too: the Convention on the International Sale of Goods.

Common Law: Judge-Made Law (Case Law)

Common law (or case law, the terms are synonymous) governs contracts for the sale of real estate and services. "Services" refer to acts or deeds (like plumbing, drafting documents, driving a car) as opposed to the sale of property. Judges have made up (or "discovered") the rules of contract over time; the decisions of the highest court in the jurisdiction on what is correct law to apply in a case binds subsequent judges in similar cases: they are expected to follow precedent (though not slavishly).

The Restatement of Contracts. Because it would not be convenient for practitioners to comb through scores (or indeed, thousands) of contract cases to extract the rules of law related to the many possible fact situations, legal scholars, lawyers, and judges have done that for us all. The Restatement of Contracts is a summary of the law abstracted from the case books; it is not a statement of the law (that's in the cases), rather, it is a handy, organized re-statement of the law.[3]

You will see references to the Restatement from time to time, and you can take a look at it here: https://www.nylitigationfirm.com/files/restat.pdf.

common law

Rules of law are determined by high-court judges, recorded in cases, and serve as precedent whereby that rule will be applied to similar fact situations in the future.

Statutory Law: The Uniform Commercial Code

Uniform Commercial Code

A uniform law of commerce developed by the National Conference of Commissioners on Uniform State Laws (NCCUSL) and the American Law Institute (ALI). It was first published in 1953 and has been adopted by most American jurisdictions.

Article 2

That section of the Uniform Commercial Code dealing with contracts for the sale of goods.

Because of the historical development of the English legal system, contracts for the sale of goods came to be governed by a different body of legal rules. In its modern American manifestation, that body of rules is an important statute: the **Uniform Commercial Code** (UCC), especially **Article 2**, which deals with contracts for the sale of goods.

A bit of history is in order. Before the UCC was written, commercial law varied, sometimes greatly, from state to state. This first proved to be a nuisance and then a serious impediment to business, as the American economy became nationwide during the twentieth century. Although there had been some uniform laws concerned with commercial deals—including the Uniform Sales Act, first published in 1906—few were widely adopted and none nationally. As a result, the law governing sales of goods, negotiable instruments, warehouse receipts, securities, and other matters crucial to doing business in an industrial market economy was a crazy quilt of untidy provisions that did not mesh well from state to state.

The UCC is one of many uniform model laws developed by the American Law Institute and the National Conference of Commissioners on Uniform State Laws; it has been adopted in one form or another by the legislatures in all fifty states, the District of Columbia, and the American territories. It is a "national" law not enacted by Congress—it is not federal law but uniform state law. Initial drafting of the UCC began in 1942 and was ten years in the making. It is now a basic law of relevance to every business and business lawyer in the United States (although it is not entirely uniform because different states have adopted it at various stages of its evolution—an evolution that continues).

FIGURE 8.1 The UCC and Common Law

Type of Contract	Source of Law	
	Common Law	UCC
Real Estate	✔	
Services	✔	
Sale of Goods		✔

Common law and Article 2 rules are basically similar, though the Code (Article 2) is in various ways simpler and less formalistic than the common law. Also, common law applies to anybody who makes a contract, while some parts of Article 2 apply only to merchants—people who have special knowledge or skill or who deal in the goods involved in the transaction.

The Convention on the International Sale of Goods

The third source of contract law is the Convention on Contracts for the International Sale of Goods (**CISG**); it was approved in 1980 at a diplomatic conference in Vienna. (A convention is a preliminary agreement that serves as the basis for a formal treaty.) The CISG has been adopted by more than forty countries, including the United States, and is significant for three reasons:

1. Contracting parties can choose to have it govern their contracts. It is an international law governing the sale of goods—in effect, an international Uniform Commercial Code. People can include in any contract a **choice-of-law clause**—you could make a contract in New York and have it governed by the law of California, China, or the CISG. The court deciding the case will apply the law the parties chose.

2. A major goal of the drafters was to produce a uniform law acceptable to countries with different legal, social, and economic systems. It is very interesting to see what kind of contract law people come up with when—unlike the common law and the UCC—it is not drafted by a bunch of white men sitting in a room. Although provisions in the CISG are generally consistent with the UCC, there are significant differences. For instance, under the CISG, consideration (discussed below) is not required to form a contract, and there is no requirement that certain contracts ever be evidenced by a writing (that requirement in U.S. law is rather unfortunately called "the statute of frauds"—it doesn't have to do with fraud as we usually think of it, but again, is a requirement that, in some cases, a contract be evidenced by a writing to be enforceable).

3. The CISG represents the first attempt by the U.S. Senate (the Senate has to ratify treaties) to reform the private law of business through its treaty powers, for the CISG preempts the UCC. Again, the CISG is not mandatory—parties to an international contract for the sale of goods may choose to have their agreement governed by different law, perhaps the UCC, or perhaps, say, Japanese contract law. But if they chose the CISG, they are bound by it.

The CISG does not apply to contracts for the sale of (1) ships or aircraft, (2) electricity, or (3) goods bought for personal, family, or household use, nor does it apply (4) where the party furnishing the goods does so only incidentally to the labor or services part of the contract.

> **CISG**
>
> The Convention on the International Sale of Goods; if parties so designate, the Convention's rules on sales contracts will govern their contract.
>
> **choice-of-law clause**
>
> A term in a contract specifying what law will be applied in case of dispute.

Basic Contract Taxonomy

In order to talk about, say, automobile design, you would need to know what these words mean: A-pillar, B-pillar, sail panel, rear deck, rocker panel, green house, belt line, and so on. To talk about contracts you need to know the vocabulary. Because contracts can be formed, expressed, and enforced in a variety of ways, a taxonomy[4] of contracts has developed to identify what's being discussed. In general, contracts are classified along four dimensions: explicitness, mutuality, enforceability, and degree of completion.

- *Explicitness* is concerned with the degree to which the agreement was objectively made.
- *Mutuality* takes into account whether promises are exchanged by two parties or only made by one.
- *Enforceability* is the degree to which a given contract is binding.
- *Degree of Completion* considers whether the contract is yet to be performed or the obligations have been fully discharged by one or both parties.

We will examine each of these concepts in turn.

Explicitness

Express Contract

express contract

A contract in words, orally or in writing.

An **express contract** is one in which the terms are spelled out directly, in words; the parties to an express contract, whether written or oral, are conscious that they are making an enforceable agreement. For example, an agreement to "purchase Raul's car for $1,500 and to take title next Monday" is an express contract whether the agreement is oral or written.

Implied Contract

implied contract

A contract not expressed but inferred from the parties' actions.

An **implied contract** is one that is inferred from the actions of the parties. Although no discussion of terms took place, an implied contract exists if it is clear (to outsiders) from the conduct of both parties that they intended there to be one. A delicatessen patron who asks for a "turkey sandwich to go" has made a contract and is obligated to pay when the sandwich is made. By ordering the food, the patron is implicitly agreeing to the price, whether posted or not.

Contract Implied in Law: Quasi-Contract

quasi-contract

A contract imposed on a party when there was none, to avoid unjust enrichment.

Both express and implied contracts embody an actual agreement of the parties. A **quasi-contract**, by contrast, is an obligation said to be "imposed by law" in order to avoid unjust enrichment of one person at the expense of another. A quasi-contract is not a contract at all; it is a fiction that the courts created to prevent injustice. Suppose, for example, that a carpenter mistakenly believes you have hired him to repair your porch; in fact, it is your neighbor who has hired him. One Saturday morning he arrives at your doorstep and begins to work. Rather than stop him, you let him proceed, pleased at the prospect of having your porch fixed for free (since you have never talked to the carpenter, you figure you need not pay his bill). Although it is true there is no contract, the law imposes a contract for the value of the work. You should have stopped him if you didn't want to pay.

Mutuality

bilateral contract

A contract where each party makes a promise to the other.

The garden-variety contract is one in which the parties make *mutual* promises. Each is both promisor and promisee; that is, each pledges to do something (called the "detriment") and each is the recipient of such a pledge (the "benefit"). This type of contract is called a **bilateral contract**. But mutual promises are not necessary to constitute a contract.

unilateral contract

A contract that is accepted by the performance of the requested action, not by a promise.

Unilateral contracts, in which only one party makes a promise, are equally valid but depend upon performance of the promise to be binding. If Charles says to Fran, "I will pay you fifteen dollars if you wash my car," Charles is contractually bound to pay once Fran washes the car. *Fran* never made a promise, but by actually performing, she makes Charles liable to pay. A common example of a unilateral contract is the offer "$50 for the return of my lost dog Kapok." Fran's acceptance of the offer is not to promise Charles that she will look for the dog; her acceptance would be finding Kapok, and if she finds him, she is entitled to the $50.

Enforceability

Not every agreement between two people is a binding contract. An agreement that is lacking one of the legal elements of a contract is said to be **void**—that is, not a contract at all. An agreement that is illegal—for example, a promise to commit a crime in return for a money payment—is void. Neither party to a void "contract" may enforce it.

By contrast, a **voidable contract** is one that is unenforceable by one party but enforceable by the other. For example, a minor (any person under eighteen, in most states) may "avoid" a contract with an adult; the adult may not enforce the contract against the minor, if the minor refuses to carry out the bargain. But the adult has no choice if the minor wishes the contract to be performed. (A contract may be voidable by both parties if both are minors.) Ordinarily, the parties to a voidable contract are entitled to be restored to their original condition. Suppose you agree to buy your seventeen-year-old neighbor's car. He delivers it to you in exchange for your agreement to pay him next week. He has the legal right to terminate the deal and recover the car, in which case you will of course have no obligation to pay him. If you have already paid him, he still may legally demand a return to the *status quo ante* (previous state of affairs). You must return the car to him; he must return the cash to you.

A voidable contract remains a valid contract until it is voided. Thus, a contract with a minor remains in force unless the minor decides she does not wish to be bound by it. When the minor reaches her majority, she may "ratify" the contract—that is, agree to be bound by it—in which case the contract will no longer be voidable and will thereafter be fully enforceable.

An **unenforceable contract** is one that some rule of law bars a court from enforcing. For example, Tom owes Pete money, but Pete has waited too long to collect it and the statute of limitations has run out. The contract for repayment is unenforceable and Pete is out of luck, unless Tom makes a new promise to pay or actually pays part of the debt. (However, if Pete is holding collateral as security for the debt, he is entitled to keep it; not all rights are extinguished because a contract is unenforceable.)

void contract

An agreement that never was a contract.

voidable contract

A contract that can be annulled.

unenforceable contract

A contract for which the non-breaching party has no remedy for its breach.

Degree of Completion

In medieval England, contract—defined as a set of promises—was not an intuitive concept. The courts gave relief to one who wanted to collect a debt, for in such a case the creditor presumably had already given the debtor something of value, and the failure of the debtor to pay up was seen as manifestly unjust. But the issue was less clear when neither promise had yet been fulfilled. Suppose John agrees to repair Humpty's wall for $500. On the appointed day, John has done no repairs. Contract law holds that a valid contract exists even though no wall was repaired and no money exchanged: Humpty will have somebody else repair the wall and charge John for the difference in price between what he and John agreed to and what Humpty had to pay somebody else.

executory contract

A contract that has yet to be completed.

partially executed contract

A contract in which one party has performed, or partly performed, and the other has not.

executed contract

A contract that has been completed.

An agreement consisting of a set of promises is called an **executory contract** before either promise is carried out. Most executory contracts are enforceable. If one promise or set of terms has been fulfilled—if, for example, Humpty had paid John, but John hadn't done any repairs—the contract is called **partially executed**. A contract that has been carried out fully by both parties is called an **executed contract**.

Suffixes

There is one other vocabulary issue we should touch on. It is the use of suffixes in the English language to designate one person's relationship to another. A promis*or* is one who makes a promise; a promis*ee* is one to whom a promise is made. An offer*or* is one who makes an offer; an offer*ee* is one to whom and offer is made. An oblig*or* is one who makes an obligation; an oblig*ee* is one to whom and obligation is made. An assign*or* is one who makes an assignment; an assign*ee* is one to whom an assignment is made. And so on. You get the point. But, you have to be careful to pick up on the suffix (whether in print or orally) or you will get all confused about who's who.

Case

Explicitness: Implied Contract

Roger's Backhoe Service, Inc. v. Nichols

Iowa Supreme Court case, 2004, analyzing the common-law doctrine of implied contract.

Roger's Backhoe Service, Inc. v. Nichols	
681 N.W.2d 647 (Iowa, 2004)	

Carter, J.

Defendant, Jeffrey S. Nichols, is a funeral director in Muscatine. * * * In early 1998 Nichols decided to build a crematorium on the tract of land on which his funeral home was located. In working with the Small Business Administration, he was required to provide drawings and specifications and obtain estimates for the project. Nichols hired an architect who prepared plans and submitted them to the City of Muscatine for approval. These plans provided that the surface water from the parking lot would drain onto the adjacent street and alley and ultimately enter city storm sewers. These plans were approved by the city.

Nichols contracted with Roger's Backhoe Service, Inc. for the demolition of the foundation of a building that had been razed to provide room for the crematorium and removal of the concrete driveway and sidewalk adjacent to that foundation. Roger's completed that work and was paid in full.

After the new building construction began, city officials came to the job site and informed Roger's that the proposed drainage of surface water onto the street and alley was unsatisfactory. The city required that an effort be made to drain the surface water into a subterranean creek, which served as part of the city's storm sewer system. City officials indicated that this subterranean sewer system was about fourteen feet below the surface of the ground. * * * Roger's conveyed the city's mandate to Nichols when Mr. Nichols visited the job site that same day.

It was Nichols' testimony at trial that, upon receiving this information, he advised * * * Roger's that he was refusing permission to engage in the exploratory excavation that the city required.

Nevertheless, it appears without dispute that for the next three days Roger's did engage in digging down to the subterranean sewer system, which was located approximately twenty feet below the surface. When the underground creek was located, city officials examined the brick walls in which it was encased and determined that it was not feasible to penetrate those walls in order to connect the surface water drainage with the underground creek. As a result of that conclusion, the city reversed its position and once again gave permission to drain the surface water onto the adjacent street and alley.

[T]he invoices at issue in this litigation relate to charges that Roger's submitted to Nichols for the three days of excavation necessary to locate the underground sewer system and the cost for labor and materials necessary to refill the excavation with compactable materials and attain compaction by means of a tamping process. * * * The district court found that the charges submitted on the * * * invoices were fair and reasonable and that they had been performed for Nichols' benefit and with his tacit approval. * * *

[Nichols appealed.]

The court of appeals * * * concluded that a necessary element in establishing an implied contract is that the services performed be beneficial to the alleged obligor. It concluded that Roger's had failed to show that its services benefited Nichols.

In describing the elements of an action on an implied contract, the court of appeals stated in [Citation], that the party seeking recovery must show: (1) the services were carried out under such circumstances as to give the recipient reason to understand: (a) they were performed for him and not some other person, and (b) they were not rendered gratuitously, but with the expectation of compensation from the recipient; and (2) the services were beneficial to the recipient.

The services were carried out under such circumstances as to give the recipient reason to understand:

   a. they were performed for him and not some other person;

   b. they were not rendered gratuitously, but with the expectation of compensation from the recipient; and

   c. the services were beneficial to the recipient.

In applying the italicized language to the present controversy, it was the conclusion of the court of appeals that Roger's services conferred no benefit on Nichols. We disagree. There was substantial evidence in the record to support a finding that, unless and until an effort was made to locate the subterranean sewer system, the city refused to allow the project to proceed. Consequently, it was necessary to the successful completion of the project that the effort be made.

The fact that examination of the brick wall surrounding the underground creek indicated that it was unfeasible to use that source of drainage does not alter the fact that the project was stalemated until drainage into the underground creek was fully explored and rejected. The district court properly concluded that Roger's services conferred a benefit on Nichols. * * *

Decision of court of appeals vacated; district court judgment affirmed.

Case Questions

1. What are the elements necessary to have an implied contract? Who says those are the elements—what is the authority for that?
2. Did you find Mr. Nichols' assertion that he refused Roger's permission to dig the huge hole very credible? If it *were* true—if we throw that fact into the case—that would change the result; why would it?
3. What argument did Nichols make at the court of appeals that caused the court to reverse the trial court and rule for Mr. Nichols?
4. How would the facts have to be changed to make an express contract?

Key Takeaway

Contract is the mechanism by which people in modern society make choices for themselves, as opposed to being born or placed into a status as is common in feudal societies. A contract is a legally enforceable promise. The law of contract is the common law (for contracts involving real estate and services), statutory law (the Uniform Commercial Code for contracts involving the sale or leasing of goods), and treaty law (the Convention on the International Sale of Goods). Contracts may be described based on the degree of their explicitness, mutuality, enforceability, and degree of completion. The manipulation of suffixes in English designates the role a person plays in a relationship.

Exercises

1. What did Sir Henry Maine mean when he wrote of society's movement "from status to contract?
2. We might hope this is not true, but hypothetically: When a man and woman in the United States marry, it might be expected that the wife assume a certain pre-ordained status without negotiation with the husband. That is, she might be expected to do most of the child-rearing, shopping, cleaning, cooking, and laundry; the husband is expected to earn money, watch ballgames on TV and drink beer. Is there a contract here setting out the expectations? What if the wife doesn't like to cook? What does that do to the expected status relationship?
3. Are all promises "contracts"?
4. What is the source of law for contracts involving real estate? For contracts involving the sale of goods?
5. In contract taxonomy, what are the degrees of explicitness, mutuality, enforceability, and of completion?
6. Is "change" always accompanied by "progress"?

8.2 Contract Formation

Learning Objectives

1. Understand the elements of common-law contracts, including agreements, acceptance, and consideration.
2. Learn when a contract must be in writing—or evidenced by some writing—to be enforceable.

For a contract to exist, five elements must be present:

1. The parties reached an *agreement* (offer and acceptance);
2. There was *real acceptance*—it was the product of free will, knowledge, and capacity on both sides;
3. *Consideration* was present (some "price" was paid for what was received in return);
4. The agreement was *legal*;
5. The agreement was in the *proper form* (something in writing, if required).

    Here we examine these elements—what is necessary to prove for a contract to exist.

The Agreement: Offer and Acceptance

The core of a legal contract is the agreement between the parties: there must be, as is said, "a meeting of the minds."

Definition of *Offer* and *Acceptance*

Although agreements may take any form, including unspoken conduct between the parties, they are usually structured in terms of an **offer** and and **acceptance**. Certainly, people can reach an agreement without forming a contract. For example, people may agree that the weather is pleasant or that it would be preferable to go out for Chinese food rather than seeing a foreign film; in neither case has a contract been formed. One of the major functions of the law of contracts is to sort out those agreements that are legally binding (those that are contracts) from those that are not.

An offer is a manifestation of willingness to enter into a bargain such that it would be reasonable for another individual to conclude that assent to the offer would complete the bargain. Offers must be communicated to the offeree and must be reasonably definite; that is, they must spell out terms to which the offeree can assent.

An *acceptance* (a "manifestation of the willingness to be bound by the terms of the offer") is required to form a contract. The offeree must manifest his assent to the terms of the offer in a manner invited or required by the offer. Complications arise when an offer is accepted indirectly through correspondence. Although offers and revocations of offers are not effective until received, an acceptance is deemed accepted when sent if the offeree accepts in the manner specified by the offeror.

offer

The proposal upon which a contract is based.

acceptance

A manifestation of willingness to be bound by the terms of an offer.

When Is the Acceptance Effective?

If the offeror specifies no particular mode, then acceptance is effective when transmitted, as long as the offeree uses a reasonable method of acceptance. It is implied that the offeree can use the same means used by the offeror or a means of communication customary to the industry. For example, the use of the postal service was so customary that acceptances are considered effective when mailed, regardless of the method used to transmit the offer. Indeed, the so-called "**mailbox rule**" (the acceptance is effective upon dispatch) has an ancient lineage, tracing back nearly two hundred years to the English courts.[5] It is still the rule that an acceptance is in effect when it is dispatched, not when it is received (unless otherwise stipulated in the agreement).

mailbox rule

At common law, that, absent stipulations contrary, an acceptance is effective when it is dispatched (not when it is received).

Was There a Serious Intent to Make an Offer and Acceptance?

In interpreting whether there really was an offer and acceptance, courts generally apply an **objective standard**. The *Restatement (Second) of Contracts* defines agreement as a *"manifestation of mutual assent by two or more persons to one another."* The UCC defines agreement as "the bargain of the parties in fact as found in their language or by implication from other circumstances including course of dealing or usage of trade or course of performance." (Section 1-201(3).) The critical question is what the parties said or did, not what they thought they said or did.

The distinction between objective and subjective standards crops up occasionally when one person claims he spoke in jest in making an offer or an acceptance. (See *Barnes v. Treece*, below.)

objective standard

Judging something as an outsider would understand it; not subjective.

Real Acceptance: Free Will, Knowledge, and Capacity

A contract is a voluntary agreement between parties. An "agreement" is no good unless everybody is acting of free will, with knowledge, and has the capacity to make the agreement.

Free Will: Duress

When a person is forced to do something against his or her will, that person is said to have been the victim of duress—compulsion. Relative to contract, there are two types of duress: physical duress and duress by improper threat.

Physical Duress

If a person is forced into entering a contract on threat of physical bodily harm, he or she is the victim of physical duress (the threat of physical harm that wrongfully induces a party to contract). It is defined by the Restatement (Second) of Contracts in Section 174: "If conduct that appears to be a manifestation of assent by a party who does not intend to engage in that conduct is physically compelled by duress, the conduct is not effective as a manifestation of assent." A contract induced by physical violence is void, but since the contract defense here, physical duress, is usually also a crime (extortion), not many private litigants seek judicial assistance to resolve such matters.

Duress by Threat

The second kind of duress is duress by threat, and it is more common than physical duress. Here the perpetrator coerces the victim, who feels there is no reasonable alternative but to assent to the contract. The threat must be improper, and the "victim" must feel—subjectively—that he or she had no alternative but to submit. "If you do not agree to sell me that antique carpet for $600 I will tell the police you are trafficking in stolen property" (when there is no evidence of such trafficking.) Any such agreement is void.

Free Will: Undue Influence

undue influence

The improper use of power or trust in persuading a person to make a contract, so as to deprive the person of free will, and that substitutes another's objective.

Undue influence is unfair persuasion of a party who is under the domination of the person exercising the persuasion or who, by virtue of the relation between them, is justified in assuming that that person will not act in a manner inconsistent with his welfare.

Undue influence is characterized by "unfair" persuasion (improper pressure) that may fall short of constituting actual duress. The facts in the cases typically involve abuse of trust by the "perpetrator," high-pressure persuasion tactics, which tactics exploit the "victim's" mental, moral, or emotional vulnerability to such an extent that it approaches the boundaries of coercion, and the isolation of the victim from outside counsel.[6]

Knowledge: Misrepresentation

It is not fair if one party is misled into an agreement because the other side has not been truthful about the facts and circumstances involved. A contract entered into based on misrepresentation is voidable by the "victim" (the word "victim" is really more appropriate in criminal cases). Generally speaking, these are the elements of misrepresentation:

- The defendant made a material misstatement of fact
  - Note: a "misstatement of fact" is not sales puff or opinion (unless the opinion-stater is an expert); it is something the truth of which is now ascertainable.
  - Note: technically the misstatement does not have to be "material" if it is intentionally made.
- The misstatement was made
  - intentionally—for fraudulent misrepresentation;
  - negligently—for negligent misrepresentation; or
  - innocently—for innocent misrepresentation.
- The plaintiff justifiably relied on the misstatement.

Failure to disclose a fact that a reasonable person would think important to disclose may constitute a "misstatement of fact."[7]

The remedy for misrepresentation is, generally speaking, rescission.

Knowledge: Mistake

Mistakes may be unilateral (one side makes a mistake), or mutual (both sides make a mistake).

Unilateral mistake. The general rule is that a person who makes a mistake—buys the wrong style door, orders a window that doesn't fit, pays too much for a car—is out of luck (assuming no fraud or overreaching by the other side). People are usually bound by the contracts they make, oral or written. However, if the non-mistaken party knew, or should have known, of the mistake, relief may be granted. A lumber yard mistakenly bids one-half what it should have for Contractor's job; Contractor cannot accept that bid and demands its enforcement.

Mutual mistake. Where both parties are mistaken, relief usually will be granted. Efrem bought a violin from Seller for $80,000, both of them believing it was a Stradivarius (built by a member of a famous Italian family in the 1700s). Unknown to either party, it was not genuine; Efrem can rescind.

Junk store Dealer sells Buyer what they both agree is "a nice painting but not remarkable" for $35. It turns out to be a masterpiece by the Spaniard El Greco (1541–1614). Buyer discovers its true value; local newspaper runs story "City Man Buys Greco Masterpiece for $35!" Dealer reads the story. Can she claim mutual mistake and rescind? No. If Buyer could discover the truth (apparently by having an expert examine the painting), Dealer could also have discovered the truth. If there is a mutual mistake, but one party bears the risk of it (here Dealer), that party loses.[8]

Capacity

A contract is a meeting of minds. If someone lacks mental **capacity** to understand what he is assenting to—or that he is assenting to anything—it is unreasonable to hold him to the consequences of his act. Issues of incapacity arise relating to (1) contracts entered into by youngsters (<18 years, legally "infants"), and (2) contracts entered into by insane or intoxicated persons.

capacity

The mental state of mind sufficient to understand that a contract is made and its consequences.

Infancy

The general rule is that a person younger than eighteen (legally an "infant," though of course this does not mean a baby or toddler) can avoid his or her contracts[9] up to and within a reasonable time after reaching majority. The rationale is pretty obvious: young people—not yet mature adults—often exercise poor judgment, and sometimes get taken advantage of. It is not unreasonable that people dealing with a minor do so at their own risk.

A minor's contract is voidable, not void. A child wishing to avoid the contract need do nothing positive to disaffirm; the defense of minority to a lawsuit is sufficient. Although the adult cannot enforce the contract, the child can (which is why it is said to be voidable, not void).

When the minor becomes an adult, she has two choices: she may ratify the contract or **disaffirm** it. She may ratify expressly; no further consideration is necessary. She may also do so by impliedly—for instance, by continuing to make payments or retaining goods for an unreasonable period of time. If the young person has not disaffirmed the contract while still a minor, she may do so within a reasonable time after reaching majority.[10]

In most cases of disaffirmation, the only obligation is (usually) to return the goods (if he still has them) or repay the consideration, unless it has been dissipated. However, in two situations, a minor might incur greater liability: contracts for necessities (food, clothing, shelter, etc.) may be enforced against the minor,[11] and the minor will (usually) be liable for contracts he made if he misrepresented his age when making the contract.

Insanity or Intoxication

Contracts made by an *insane* or *intoxicated* person are also said to have been made by a person lacking capacity. In general, such contracts are voidable by the person when capacity is regained (or by the person's legal representative if capacity is not regained). The person must be so incapacitated as to be "unable to understand the nature of the business at hand." Voluntary intoxication (a person getting drunk) is an unfavored defense.

Consideration

Consideration, is the quid pro quo (something given or received for something else) between the contracting parties in the absence of which the law will not (usually) enforce the promise or promises made. Consider the following three agreements:

1. Betty offers to give a book to Lou. Lou accepts.
2. Betty offers Lou the book in exchange for Lou's promise to pay $15. Lou accepts.
3. Betty offers to give Lou the book if Lou promises to pick it up at Betty's house. Lou accepts.

The question is which, if any, is a binding contract? In American law, only situation 2 is a binding contract, because only that contract contains a set of mutual promises in which each party pledges to give up something to the benefit of the other.

The question of what constitutes a binding contract has been answered differently throughout history and in other cultures. For example, under Roman law, any contract that was reduced to writing was binding, whether or not there was consideration in our sense. Moreover, in later Roman times, certain promises of gifts were made binding, whether written or oral; these would not be binding in the United States. At one time in the U.S. contracts "under seal" did not need consideration, but seals are out of fashion.

---

disaffirm

To legally disavow or avoid a contract.

---

consideration

The surrender of any legal right in return for the promise of some benefit; the "price" paid for what is received.

The existence of consideration is determined by examining whether the person against whom a promise is to be enforced (the **promisor**) received something in return from the person to whom he made the promise (the **promisee**). That may seem a simple enough question, but as with much in the law, the complicating situations are never very far away. The "something" that is promised or delivered cannot just be anything—a feeling of pride, warmth, amusement, or friendship. It must be something known as a **legal detriment**—an act, a forbearance, or a promise of such from the promisee. The detriment need not be an actual detriment; it may, in fact, be a benefit to the promisee, or at least not a loss. At the same time, the "detriment" to the promisee need not confer a tangible benefit on the promisor; the promisee can agree to forego something without that something being given to the promisor. Whether consideration is legally sufficient has nothing to do with whether it is morally or economically adequate to make the bargain a fair one ("courts do not inquire into the adequacy of consideration"[12]). Moreover, legal consideration need not even be certain; it can be a promise contingent on an event that may never happen. Consideration is a *legal* concept, and it centers on the giving up of a *legal* right or benefit: each side gives up a legal right, and each side gets a benefit.

Consideration has two elements. The first, as just outlined, is whether the promisee has incurred a legal detriment. (Some courts—although a minority—take the view that a bargained-for legal benefit to the promisor is sufficient consideration.) The second is whether the legal detriment was *bargained for*: did the promisor specifically intend the act, forbearance, or promise in return for his promise? Applying this two-pronged test to the three examples given at the outset about Betty and Lou, we can easily see why only in the example is there legally sufficient consideration. In the first, Lou incurred no legal detriment; he made no pledge to act or to forbear from acting, nor did he in fact act or forbear from acting. In the third example, what might appear to be such a promise is not really so. Betty made a promise on a condition that Lou come to her house; the intent clearly is to make a gift. Betty was not seeking to induce Lou to come to her house by promising the book.

Exceptions. There are several exceptions to the requirement of consideration; let us call out one. In cases of promissory estoppel, the courts (in equity) will enforce promises without consideration. Simply stated, **promissory estoppel** (or more completely, promissory estoppel with detrimental reliance) means that the courts will stop the promisor from claiming that there was no consideration because the promisee relied on the promise and incurred some loss (detriment). The doctrine of promissory estoppel is invoked in the interests of justice when three conditions are met:

1. The promise is one the promisor should reasonably expect to induce the promisee to take, or forbear from taking, action of a definite and substantial nature;
2. The action or forbearance is taken;
3. Injustice can only be avoided by enforcing the promise.

Timko served on the board of trustees of a school. He recommended that the school purchase a building for a substantial sum of money, and to induce the trustees to vote for the purchase, he promised to help with the purchase and to pay at the end of five years the purchase price less the down payment. At the end of four years, Timko died. The school sued his estate, which defended on the ground that there was no consideration for the promise. Timko was promised or given nothing in return, and the purchase of the building was of no direct benefit to him (which would have made the promise enforceable as a unilateral contract). The court ruled that under the three-pronged promissory estoppel test, Timko's estate was liable.[13]

Final thoughts on consideration: the requirement of consideration is not known in all contract systems (it is not part of Scottish law, for example). It is formalistic and can be complex, but (or perhaps *therefore*) no one who understands it has much incentive to change this venerable common law requirement. Lawyers and judges (and other well-educated people, like attentive students) understand it. State legislatures, who could change contract law by statute (they adopted the UCC after all), also have little incentive to change it (a lot of legislators are lawyers, too). And consideration actually does have a useful purpose: if you have to *give up* something in return for what you get in an agreement, you might give the matter some consideration—you might think about it some.

promisor

The one who makes a promise.

promisee

The one to whom a promise is made.

legal detriment

The giving up by a person of that which she had a right to retain.

promissory estoppel

To be prohibited from denying a promise when another has subsequently relied upon it.

Legality

Illegal contracts[14] are unenforceable, and the courts will, generally, offer no relief to either party. The courts must grapple with two types of illegalities: (1) statutory violations (e.g., the practice of law by a non-lawyer is forbidden by statute), and (2) violations of public policy not expressly declared unlawful by statute, but so declared by the courts (common-law illegality).

- Illegal by statute includes: practicing certain trades or professions without a license (a medical doctor has to pass the medical boards or won't get a license; an unlicensed "doctor" cannot collect a fee for service, even if she cures the patient); gambling statutes (regulating gambling); usury statutes (limiting legal interest rates that can be charged).
- Illegal by public policy includes: unreasonable non-compete agreements in employment contracts (employee agrees not to compete with her former employer when she quits) or in contracts for the sale of a business (seller of business agrees not to open a business to compete with the buyer); unreasonable exculpatory clauses (one party is excused in advance for his own tortious conduct); unconscionable contracts (contracts that are grossly unfair).

There are some exceptions, of course, to the rule that courts will grant parties to an illegal agreement no relief. If one party withdraws from the agreement before performance, relief may be granted: Able delivers $500 to Sally, the stakeholder (who holds the monies for delivery to the winner of an illegal game), but then thinks better of gambling, and gets out before the game starts; he gets his $500 back. And, if a party is protected by statute against suffering the consequence of having entered into an illegal agreement, relief may be granted: Ingrid Investor pays Baker $30,000 to buy unregistered securities (in violation of Blue Sky laws); Ingrid can rescind the sale and get her money back. Also, courts may grant relief if one party is excusably ignorant that the agreement is illegal; courts may, if reasonable, enforce legal parts of an agreement and not enforce illegal parts.

Is a contract legally enforceable when it effectively deprives one side of any legal redress for a long-recognized, serious, federal statutory offense? Yes, if the agreement is validly entered into: parties can put pretty much whatever they want into contracts. If you want to waive your right to some contractual right or relief, you can do that in the contract you make.[15] Be careful what you agree to.

Form and Meaning

Form

As a general rule, a contract need not be in writing to be enforceable. Oral agreements are okay—the problem with them is not legal, but factual: was there really an intention for the oral understanding to be a contract, and if so, what are its terms if there is a dispute. For centuries a large exception has grown up around the rule that oral contracts are good: **Statute of Frauds**, first enacted in England in 1677 under the formal name "An Act for the Prevention of Frauds and Perjuries" requires some agreements be evidenced by a writing to be enforced.

The purpose of the statute of frauds is to prevent the fraud that occurs when one party is forced to answer for performance (or breach) of an agreement that the party denies was enforceable. Where applicable, the statute provides that no agreement is enforceable unless some memo or writing regarding it is signed by the party called to perform. An oral contract to sell real estate is not enforceable. The contracts affected by the statute of frauds include these:

- agreements (contracts) affecting a transfer of interest in real estate;
- contracts that cannot be performed within one year of their making;

- contracts whereby a secondary obligor promises to perform a contractual duty to the obligee if the primary obligor fails to do so (suretyship contracts).
- contracts of marriage where part of the agreement is to transfer property--that part must be in writing.
- Under Article 2 of the UCC, agreements for the sale of goods in an amount equal to or greater than $500 must be evidenced by some writing.

Again, as may be evident from the title of the act and its language, the general purpose of the law is to provide evidence, in areas of some complexity and importance, that a contract was actually made. To a lesser degree, the law serves to caution those about to enter a contract and "to create a climate in which parties often regard their agreements as tentative until there is a signed writing."[16]

Because the statute can sometimes be used by people who want to wriggle out of oral agreements that they really did make (that's called "using the statute of frauds as a sword, not a shield"), there are exceptions to all the statute's applications. However, here is an easy rule: get it in writing.

Meaning

Two issues arise (1) if the written contract is ambiguous, how is its meaning determined, and (2) can one side or the other "amend" the signed agreement--assert that what's on the paper is not what they intended? ("we left something out").

Contractual interpretation. As to the first bit, if a contract is ambiguous or unclear it is the court's job to give meaning to the parties' intention when they made the contract. This is "contractual interpretation." It the same idea as we discussed in the chapter on Making the Law as to statutory interpretation.

Parol evidence rule. As to the second bit, the "parol evidence rule" provides (somewhat simplifying) that if the parties have a written agreement that is their full understanding, no evidence of oral ("parol") discussions that took place during the negotiation will be allowed to change it. The four corners of the document control.

Sales: Contracts for the Sale of Goods

We have observed that contracts for real estate and services are (with the statutory intrusion of the statute of frauds aside) governed by the common law—judge-made law. We noted that contracts for the sale of *goods* are governed by state statute: all of the states[17] and the District of Columbia have adopted the Uniform Commercial Code, Article 2 of which deals with contracts for the sale of goods. Article 2 applies to any contract for the sale of goods in the United States (unless the parties agree to have the contract interpreted by some other law—we touched on the Convention for the International Sale of Goods above).

It is beyond the scope of this text to discuss in detail Article 2. There are certainly some differences between the common law and Article 2. Here are two: (1) Under Article 2 an acceptance may vary from the offer, if the difference is not material or objected to (no "mirror image rule"); (2) consideration is required to make a sales contract, but—unlike at common law—no consideration is required to modify a sales contract. Article 2 does have a writing requirement (a statute of frauds), but there are robust exceptions.

Cases

Objective Intention

Barnes v. Treece

549 P.2d 1152 (Wash., 1976)

Callow, J.

Vend-A-Win is a Washington corporation engaged primarily in the business of distributing punchboards [gambling devices found in bars and taverns]. Warren Treece served as vicepresident, was a member of the board of directors, and owned 50 percent of the stock of Vend-A-Win. On July 24, 1973, Treece spoke before the Washington State Gambling Commission in support of punchboard legitimacy and Vend-A-Win's particular application for a temporary license to distribute punchboards. During the testimony, as stated by the trial judge, Treece made a statement to the following effect:

"I'll put a hundred thousand dollars to anyone to find a crooked board. If they find it, I'll pay it!" [$100,000: about $570,000 in 2019 dollars.]

The statement brought laughter from the audience.

The next morning the plaintiff Barnes was watching a television news report of the proceedings before the gambling commission and heard Treece's statement that $100,000 would be paid to anyone who could produce a crooked punchboard. Barnes also read a newspaper report of the hearings that quoted Treece's statement.

A number of years earlier, while employed as a bartender, Barnes had purchased two fraudulent punchboards. After learning of Treece's statement, Barnes searched for and located his two punchboards. Barnes telephoned Treece, announced that he had two crooked punchboards, and asked Treece if his earlier statement had been made seriously. Treece assured Barnes that the statement had been made seriously, advised Barnes that the statement was firm, and further informed Barnes that the $100,000 was safely being held in escrow. Treece also specifically directed Barnes to bring the punchboard to the Seattle office of Vend-A-Win for inspection.

On July 28, 1973, Barnes traveled to Seattle, met Treece and Vend-A-Win's secretary-treasurer in Vend-A-Win's offices, produced one punchboard, and received a receipt for presentation of the board written on Vend-A-Win stationery, signed by Treece, and witnessed by Vend-A-Win's secretary-treasurer. Barnes was informed that the punchboard would be taken to Chicago for inspection.

Both Treece and Vend-A-Win refused to pay Barnes $100,000. Barnes then initiated this breach of contract action against both defendants. The trial court found that the two punchboards were rigged and dishonest, that Treece's statements before the gambling commission and reiterated to Barnes personally on the telephone constituted a valid offer for a unilateral contract, and that Barnes' production of two dishonest punchboards constituted an acceptance of the offer. The trial court also found that Vend-A-Win had not manifested any apparent authority in Treece to make the offer, had not impliedly ratified the contract, and therefore was not liable on the contract.

The first issue is whether the statement of Treece was the manifestation of an offer which could be accepted to bind the offeror to performance of the promise. Treece contends that no contract was formed. He maintains that his statement was made in jest and lacks the necessary manifestation of a serious contractual intent.

When expressions are intended as a joke and are understood or would be understood by a reasonable person as being so intended, they cannot be construed as an offer and accepted to form a contract. However, if the jest is not apparent and a reasonable hearer would believe that an offer was being made, then the speaker risks the formation of a contract which was not intended. It is the objective manifestations of the offeror that count and not secret, expressed intentions. [Citations.] If a party's words or acts, judged by a reasonable standard, manifest an intention to agree in regard to the matter in question, that agreement is established, and it is immaterial what may be the real but unexpressed state of the party's mind on the subject. [Citations.]

The trial court found that there was an objective manifestation of mutual assent to form a contract. This was a matter to be evaluated by the trier of fact. The record includes substantial evidence of the required mutual assent to support the finding of the trial court. Although the original statement of Treece drew laughter from the audience, the subsequent statements, conduct, and the circumstances show an intent to lead any hearer to believe the statements were made seriously. In present day society it is known that gambling generates a great deal of income and that large sums are spent on its advertising and promotion. In that prevailing atmosphere, it was a credible statement that $100,000 would be paid to promote punchboards. The statements of the defendant and the surrounding circumstances reflect an objective manifestation of a contractual intent by Treece and support the finding of the trial court.

The trial court properly categorized Treece's promise of $100,000 as a valid offer for a unilateral contract. The offer made promised that a contract would result upon performance of the act requested. Performance of the act with the intent to accept the offer constituted acceptance. The trial judge entered a specific finding that Barnes performed the requested act of acceptance when he produced a rigged and fraudulent punchboard. We concur with the trial court's holding that a binding unilateral contract was formed between Barnes and Treece and uphold the conclusions of the trial court in that regard.

The last question presented is whether Vend-A-Win is also liable on the contract, either because of the claim that the contract was made within an apparent authority given Treece, or because of an implied ratification of the contract by Vend-A-Win.

In order for a corporation to be bound by the apparent authority of its officers, it must have acted or conducted itself in a manner that manifested to third persons that the agent had authority. [Citation.] To constitute a manifestation of an agent's apparent authority by the principal, the circumstances must be such that a prudent person would have believed that the agent possessed the authority to do the particular act in question. [Citation.] The manifestation must be sufficient to mislead a reasonable person, to deter further inquiry, and to cause reliance on the manifestation of apparent authority. [Citations.]

The corporation did not manifest to Barnes that Treece had authority to offer $100,000 for the production of an illegal punchboard. Barnes, as a reasonable, prudent individual, did contact Treece to ascertain whether the offer was serious, but he never inquired of Vend-A-Win concerning whether Treece had any authority to bind the corporation. Whether an agent has apparent authority to make a contract depends upon the circumstances and is to be decided by the trier of fact. [Citations.]

[Treece also asserted that the corporation had ratified his unauthorized contract offer by its subsequent silence in not disaffirming it. The court held that the trial court's finding of no ratification by the corporation was supported by substantial evidence.]

Judgment affirmed.

Case Questions

1. Why did Treece make the statement that he'd pay $100,000 to anybody who produced a crooked board?

2. Suppose the defendant really did think the whole thing was a kind of joke. Would that make any difference?

3. Treece argued his "offer" was not seriously intended, and was so ridiculous that it could not be taken seriously by third parties. Why did the court disagree?

4. As a matter of public policy, why does the law use an objective standard to determine the seriousness of intention, instead of a subjective standard?

5. Treece also argued he was merely an agent of the corporate principal (this anticipates an issue involving Agency Law, see Chapter 10), and therefore he was not personally liable. Why did that argument fail?

6. Mr. Treece is ordered to pay—in 2019 dollars—$570,000! Whoa! What lesson do we take from this case about making jokey contract offers?

Consideration: Preexisting Obligation

Denney v. Reppert

Kentucky Supreme Court opinion, 1968, analyzing the application of the "pre-existing obligation" concept as to consideration in contract law.

Denney v. Reppert

432 S.W.2d 647 (Ky., 1968)

Myre, Special Commissioner[18]

The sole question presented in this case is which of several claimants is entitled to an award for information leading to the apprehension and conviction of certain bank robbers.

On June 12th or 13th, 1963, three armed men entered the First State Bank, Eubank, Kentucky, and with a display of arms and threats robbed the bank of over $30,000 [about $208,000 in 2010 dollars]. Later in the day they were apprehended by State Policemen Garret Godby, Johnny Simms, and Tilford Reppert, placed under arrest, and the entire loot was recovered. Later all of the prisoners were convicted and Garret Godby, Johnny Simms, and Tilford Reppert appeared as witnesses at the trial.

The First State Bank of Eubank was a member of the Kentucky Bankers Association which provided and advertised a reward of $500.00 for the arrest and conviction of each bank robber. Hence the outstanding reward for the three bank robbers was $1,500.00 [about $12,000 in 2019 dollars]. Many became claimants for the reward and the Kentucky State Bankers Association being unable to determine the merits of the claims for the reward asked the circuit court to determine the merits of the various claims and to adjudge who was entitled to receive the reward or share in it. All of the claimants were made defendants in the action.

At the time of the robbery the claimants Murrell Denney, Joyce Buis, Rebecca McCollum, and Jewell Snyder were employees of the First State Bank of Eubank and came out of the grueling situation with great credit and glory. Each one of them deserves approbation and an accolade. They were vigilant in disclosing to the public and the peace officers the details of the crime, and in describing the culprits, and giving all the information that they possessed that would be useful in capturing the robbers. Undoubtedly, they performed a great service. It is in the evidence that the claimant Murrell Denney was conspicuous and energetic in his efforts to make known the robbery, to acquaint the officers as to the personal appearance of the criminals, and to give other pertinent facts.

The first question for determination is whether the employees of the robbed bank are eligible to receive or share in the reward. The great weight of authority answers in the negative. [Citation] states the rule thusly:

'To the general rule that, when a reward is offered to the general public for the performance of some specified act, such reward may be claimed by any person who performs such act, is the exception of agents, employees and public officials who are acting within the scope of their employment or official duties."

At the time of the robbery the claimants Murrell Denney, Joyce Buis, Rebecca McCollum, and Jewell Snyder were employees of the First State Bank of Eubank. They were under duty to protect and conserve the resources and moneys of the bank, and safeguard every interest of the institution furnishing them employment. Each of these employees exhibited great courage, and cool bravery, in a time of stress and danger. The community and the county have recompensed them in commendation, admiration and high praise, and the world looks on them as heroes. But in making known the robbery and assisting in acquainting the public and the officers with details of the crime and with identification of the robbers, they performed a duty to the bank and the public, for which they cannot claim a reward.

The claims of Corbin Reynolds, Julia Reynolds, Alvie Reynolds and Gene Reynolds also must fail. According to their statements, they gave valuable information to the arresting officers. However, they did not follow the procedure as set forth in the offer of reward in that they never filed a claim with the Kentucky Bankers Association. It is well established that a claimant of a reward must comply with the terms and conditions of the offer of reward. [Citation]

State Policemen Garret Godby, Johnny Simms, and Tilford Reppert made the arrest of the bank robbers and captured the stolen money. All participated in the prosecution. At the time of the arrest, it was the duty of the state policemen to apprehend the criminals. Under the law they cannot claim or share in the reward and they are interposing no claim to it.

This leaves the defendant, Tilford Reppert, the sole eligible claimant. The record shows that at the time of the arrest he was a deputy sheriff in Rockcastle County, but the arrest and recovery of the stolen money took place in Pulaski County. He was out of his jurisdiction, and was thus under no legal duty to make the arrest, and is thus eligible to claim and receive the reward. In [Citation] it was said:

"It is * * * well established that a public officer with the authority of the law to make an arrest may accept an offer of reward or compensation for acts or services performed outside of his bailiwick or not within the scope of his official duties." [Citation.]

It is manifest from the record that Tilford Reppert is the only claimant qualified and eligible to receive the reward. Therefore, it is the judgment of the circuit court that he is entitled to receive payment of the $1,500.00 reward now deposited with the Clerk of this Court.

The judgment is affirmed.

Case Questions

1. Why did the Bankers Association put the resolution of this matter into the court's hands?
2. Several claimants came forward for the reward; only one person got it. What was the difference between the person who got the reward and those who did not?
3. Contract consideration aside, why would it be a bad idea if police officers were able to claim rewards for catching crooks?

Key Takeaway

Five elements are necessary to form a contract: offer, acceptance, real acceptance (with free will, knowledge, and capacity), consideration, and legality.

Proper form: sometimes a writing is required under the statute of frauds or there is no contract at all. If the meaning of a contract is disputed, a court will interpret the contract so as to give effect to the parties' intention when they made is, using various tools of interpretation. Under the parol evidence rule, in general, parties to a complete and unambiguous written contract are not allowed to introduce evidence that when they were making the agreement, they decided upon terms which were not in the writing (if you intended those terms to be in the writing, you should have put it in there).

Exercises

1. What are the required elements of a contract?
2. Why are infants—persons <18 years old—allowed to avoid their contracts? When can they *not* avoid them?
3. When was the Statute of Frauds first enacted, by whom, and why?
4. Basically, what does the Statute of Frauds require?
5. Why might it be said that *because* of its complexity, the people who understand consideration have little incentive to change it?
6. A, an unlicensed architect (she had not passed the architect board exams as required to obtain the license) designed a house for B. The design was entirely acceptable according to relevant building standards, and B liked it. B refused to pay A. A sued B; what result obtains?
7. A received and offer from B. A wrote a letter rejecting the offer and dropped it in the mail. The next morning A had second thoughts. He telephoned B: "B, tomorrow you will get a letter from me rejecting your offer. Disregard the letter—I accept." Is there a contract?
8. A found B's lost dog and returned it to B, who was very grateful. B said, "I am grateful. I have to go to my office for an appointment. Come by here tomorrow and I'll give you a $20 reward." But when A appeared at B's place for the $20, B said, "Oh, I'm sorry, I changed my mind. But thank you," and gently but firmly closed the door. Is A legally entitled to the $20?
9. Julio bought an outboard motor for his recreational fishing boat. It was too big—too many horsepower—to idle slowly for trolling. Can he return it and get his money back?
10. Sherwood agreed to buy a cow from Walker, both of them understanding that the cow was sterile, and worth only the price of a beef cow. But when Sherwood went to Walker's farm to take the cow home, she was pregnant, and worth much more as a milk and breed cow. Can Walker rescind on the basis of mutual mistake?
11. The Mitchells, owners of an antique store, bid on at auction and purchased for $50 a safe from the estate of deceased person whose family was disposing of the items. The auctioneer mentioned that the safe had a locked compartment inside and that he had no access to it. The Mitchells took the safe to a locksmith; when the inside compartment was opened, it was found to contain (in 2019 dollars) $124,000. Both the Mitchells and the estate claimed the money. Who gets it?[19]

8.3 Excuses for Non-Performance

Learning Objectives

1. Understand that a person may indeed have a contract, but can still have an excuse for failure to perform, and so not be liable for breach.
2. Recognize these excuses for non-performance, and understand why they have developed in contract law.

A contracting party who fails to perform might have a valid excuse for non-performance and not be liable for breach. Here we take up several of those "excuses" for non-performance.

Discharge by Breach

Material breach by one side discharges the non-breaching party and gives that party a cause of action against the breaching party. If Justin agrees to re-roof Peggy's house for $15,000, and doesn't do it, or does just a little bit, Justin has materially breached the contract. Peggy doesn't owe him anything at all, and she'll sue him for the difference between what Justin agreed to do it for and how much Peggy had to pay for a substitute (in the event the substitute cost her less, Justin doesn't benefit).

Where a promisor has somewhat performed, enough to confer some benefit on the promisee, the promisor may still be entitled to compensation for such benefit as was conferred, under the doctrine of **substantial performance.**

Discharge by Conditions

Frequently, the obligation of a party to perform a contract is conditioned, or depends upon, something else. Conditions are terms in a contract that affect the obligation to perform it; they may be express or implied. Here are some examples of conditions:

* **condition precedent**. A term in a contract that says a party's obligation to perform does not ripen until the happening of some other event: "I will buy your house if I get financing." That "I get financing" is a condition precedent to my obligation to you to buy your house.
* **condition subsequent**. A term that ends a party's ongoing contract upon the happening of some event: "I will manage your hotel for five years, so long as the railroad serves the downtown station." If the railroad stops using the station, my contract to manage your hotel is over.
* **condition of satisfaction**. "You must be satisfied or your money back." Such satisfaction can be objective or—within reason—subjective; it may be to the satisfaction of a third party (like an architect).
* **condition of timeliness**. Usually, failure to perform on time is not a material breach (it is substantial performance), but if exact timeliness is critical, the contract might say, "time is of the essence"; any failure to perform on time is a material breach").[20]

Discharge by Agreement of the Parties

Parties are free to put pretty much whatever they want in their contracts, and they are free to agree to end the contract if they want. Here are several ways.

material breach

Complete, or very nearly complete, failure of a promisor's consideration flowing to the promisee; the promisee is discharged from contract obligations and can sue the promisor for breach.

substantial performance

Performance of a contract by an obligor that is not complete performance, but is enough so that it would be unjust for the obligee to give the obligor zero compensation. The obligee can recover whatever damages she suffered by failure of complete performance.

condition precedent

A term in a contract that a party's obligation to perform does not arise until the happening of some other event.

condition subsequent

A term in a contract that, upon the happening of some specified event, legal rights or duties are ended.

condition of satisfaction

A term in a contract requiring that the obligee be satisfied with the obligor's performance, or the obligation is not discharged.

condition of timeliness

A term in a contract requiring performance on time or the contract is breached.

mutual rescission

Parties to a contract agree to release each other from its obligations.

waiver

The surrender of a legal right.

novation

Replacing a party in a contract with another, or replacing one contractual obligation with another; it requies the consent of all parties involved.

accord and satisfaction

An agreement by parties to a contract to settle the matter by compromise; if the agreement is satisfied, the matter is closed.

- **Mutual rescission**. Each side agrees to release the other from contract obligation.
- **Waiver**. A party voluntarily gives up a right she has under a contract, but doesn't give up the entire right to performance by the other side; it is permission to deviate from the contract.
- **Novation**. The substitution of a new obligation for an old one, usually by the substitution of a new debtor or of a new creditor.
- **Accord and Satisfaction**. The parties to a disputed agreement agree to suspend demands for performance pending the satisfactory performance of a compromise (that's the "accord") and if the compromise is carried out, the deal is satisfied. If the compromise is not satisfied, the accord is of no effect.

Discharge by Difficulty of Performance

Sometimes it becomes so difficult to perform the contract that parties are excused. Here are some such circumstances.

- Death or incapacity of a personal services promisor. Artist contracts to sculpt Mrs. Ace's dog, Patches, in marble. Artist dies. The estate of Artist is discharged. (Though note if Mrs. Ace had contracted with Artist's business in *general*—as a partnership or a corporation—the business would still be liable to perform; Artist would be merely an agent for the business).
- Destruction of thing essential for performance of the contract. Landowner contracts with Contractor for the latter to use his machine to harvest Landowner's trees; the machine is destroyed in a fire; Contractor is discharged. (Though note this would only be so if it were specifically understood that Contractor was to use his own machine; otherwise Contractor would be required to find another machine).
- Performance prohibited by government regulation or order. After the contract is made, the government prohibits such contracts (e.g., for shipment of goods to Iran).
- Impossibility. Traditionally this meant, "It cannot be done," not, "I cannot do it." But modernly the difficulty of performance need not be so absolute: if it is commercially unreasonable to require performance, it may be excused (called "commercial impracticablity"). For example, Obligor's gravel pit, from which he was to sell gravel to Obligee, unexpectedly floods. It *is* possible to extract gravel from under water, but it is a whole different job (it would involve an entire different value of consideration than the parties had agreed to). Obligor could be discharged.
- Frustration of purpose. When an unforeseen event undermines a party's principal reason for entering into a contract, and both parties knew of this purpose, the obligations may be discharged.[21]

Case

Substantial Performance and Conditions Precedent

TA Operating Corp. v. Solar Applications Engineering, Inc.

191 S.W.3d 173 (Tex. Ct. App., 2005)

> **TA Operating Corp. v. Solar Applications Engineering, Inc.**
>
> Texas Court of Appeals case, 2005, analyzing whether a contractual condition precedent trumps the doctrine of substantial performance.

TA Operating Corporation, a truck stop travel center company, contracted with Solar Applications Engineering, Inc. to construct a prototype multi-use truck stop in San Antonio for a fixed price of $3,543,233 [about $5 million in 2019 dollars].* * * [When the project was near] completion, TA sent Solar a "punch list" of items that needed to be finished to complete the building. Solar disputed several items on the list and delivered a response to TA listing the items Solar would correct. * * * Solar began work on the punch list items and filed a lien [a property that carries a lien can be forced into sale by the creditor in order to collect what is owed] against the project on October 2, 2000 in the amount of $472,392.77. TA understood the lien affidavit to be a request for final payment.

On October 18, 2000, TA sent notice to Solar that Solar was in default for not completing the punch list items, and for failing to keep the project free of liens. TA stated in the letter that Solar was not entitled to final payment until it completed the remainder of the punch list items and provided documentation that liens filed against the project had been paid. Solar acknowledged at least two items on the punch list had not been completed, and submitted a final application for payment in the amount of $472,148.77. * * * TA refused to make final payment, however, contending that Solar had not complied with section 14.07 of the contract, which expressly made submission of a lien-release affidavit[22] a condition precedent to final payment: * * *

> *The final Application for Payment shall be accompanied by: … complete and legally effective releases or waivers … of all lien rights arising out of or liens filed in connection with the work.*

Although Solar did not comply with this condition precedent to final payment, Solar sued TA for breach of contract under the theory of substantial performance. * * * TA [asserts that] the doctrine of substantial performance does not excuse Solar's failure to comply with an express condition precedent to final payment.

The first issue we must resolve is whether the doctrine of substantial performance excuses the breach of an express condition precedent to final payment that is unrelated to completion of the building. TA acknowledges that Solar substantially performed its work on the project, but contends its duty to pay was not triggered until Solar pleaded or proved it provided TA with documentation of complete and legally effective releases or waivers of all liens filed against the project. * * * TA contends that when the parties have expressly conditioned final payment on submission of [a liens-release] affidavit, the owner's duty to pay is not triggered until the contractor pleads or proves it complied with the condition precedent.

While the common law did at one time require strict compliance with the terms of a contract, this rule has been modified for building or construction contracts by the doctrine of substantial performance. "Substantial performance" was defined by the Texas [court] in [Citation]:

> *To constitute substantial compliance the contractor must have in good faith intended to comply with the contract, and shall have substantially done so in the sense that the defects are not pervasive, do not constitute a deviation from the general plan contemplated for the work, and are not so essential that the object of the parties in making the contract and its purpose cannot without difficulty, be accomplished by remedying them. Such performance permits only such omissions or deviation from the contract as are inadvertent and unintentional, are not due to bad faith, do not impair the structure as a whole, and are remediable without doing material damage to other parts of the building in tearing down and reconstructing.*

Solar argues that by agreeing substantial performance occurred, TA acknowledged that Solar was in "full compliance" with the contract and any express conditions to final payment did not have to be met. [Citation]: "A finding that a contract has been substantially completed is the legal equivalent of full compliance, less any offsets for remediable defects." Solar argues that TA may not expressly provide for substantial performance in its contract and also insist on strict compliance with the conditions precedent to final payment. We disagree. While the substantial performance doctrine permits contractors to sue under the contract, it does not ordinarily excuse the non-occurrence of an express condition precedent, [Citation]:

> *The general acceptance of the doctrine of substantial performance does not mean that the parties may not expressly contract for literal performance of the contract terms. . . . Stated otherwise, if the terms of an agreement make full or strict performance an express condition precedent to recovery, then substantial performance will not be sufficient to enable recovery under the contract.*

TA, seeking protection from double liability and title problems, expressly conditioned final payment on Solar's submission of a [liens-release] affidavit. Solar did not dispute that it was contractually obligated to submit the affidavit as a condition precedent to final payment, and it was undisputed at trial that $246,627.82 in liens had been filed against the project. Though the doctrine of substantial performance permitted Solar to sue under the contract, Solar did not plead or prove that it complied with the express condition precedent to final payment. Had Solar done so, it would have been proper to award Solar the contract balance minus the cost of remediable defects. While we recognize the harsh results occasioned from Solar's failure to perform this express condition precedent, we recognize that parties are free to contract as they choose and may protect themselves from liability by requesting literal performance of their conditions for final payment. * * *

[T]he trial court erred in awarding Solar the contract balance [as] damages, and we render judgment that Solar take nothing on its breach of contract claim.

Case Questions

1. Why did Solar believe it was entitled to the contract balance here?
2. Why did the court determine that Solar should not have been awarded the contract damages it claimed, even though it substantially complied with the terms of the contract?
3. Why would a party in Solar's situation want to obtain a lien at all?

4. The common law used to say, "If you don't fulfill the terms of the contract completely, you breach it and are liable for damages." How has the common law changed in demanding strict performance of contract terms? Why has it changed?

5. What facts must a claimant show to be entitled to relief under the doctrine of substantial performance?

Key Takeaway

Even where the elements of a contract are satisfied, one side might have excuses for nonperformance and still not be liable for breach. These include: breach by the other side, the happening or non-happening of one or more conditions, agreements by the parties to waive contract performance, or discharge by difficulty of performance (impossibility, etc.).

Exercises

1. Theresa hired Contractor to construct a large office building. Theresa's duty to pay Contractor was conditioned on receipt of a statement from her architect that the building complied with the terms of the contract. Contractor completed the building but used the wrong color fixtures in the bathrooms. The architect refused to approve the work, but under state law, Contractor was considered to have substantially performed the contract. Is he entitled to payment, less damages for the improper fixtures? Explai.

2. In early 1987, Larry McLanahan submitted a claim to Farmers Insurance for theft of his 1985 Lamborghini while it was on consignment for sale in the Los Angeles area. The car had sustained extensive damage, which McLanahan had his mechanic document. The insurance policy contained this language: "Allow us to inspect and appraise the damaged vehicle before its repair or disposal." But after considerable delay by Farmers, McLanahan sold the car to a cash buyer without notifying Farmers. He then sued Farmers for its refusal to pay for damages to his car. Upon what legal theory did Farmers get a summary judgment in its favor?

3. Plaintiff sold a tavern to Defendants. Several months later, Defendants began to experience severe problems with the septic tank system. They informed Plaintiff of the problem and demanded the return of their purchase money. Plaintiff refused. Defendants took no formal action against Plaintiff at that time, and they continued to operate the tavern and make their monthly payments under the contract. Some months later, Defendants met with state officials from the Departments of Environmental Quality, Health, and Liquor Control Commission. The officials warned Defendants that because of the health hazards posed by the septic tank problems, Defendants' licenses might not be renewed. As a result, Defendants decided to close the tavern and attempt to reopen when the septic tank was repaired. Defendants advertised a going-out-of-business sale. The purpose of the sale was to deplete the tavern's inventory before closing. Plaintiff learned about the sale and discovered that Defendants had removed certain personal property from the tavern. He sued the Defendants, claiming, among other things, that they had anticipatorily breached their contract with him, though he was receiving payments on time. Did the Defendants' actions amount to an anticipatory breach?[23]

4. Julius, a manufacturer of neckties, contracted to supply neckties to a wholesaler. When Julius's factory burned, he failed to supply any, and the wholesaler sued. Is Julius excused from performance by impossibility?

5. The Plaintiff (a development corporation) contracted to buy Defendant's property for $1.8 million. A term in the contract read: "The sale…shall be closed at the office of Community Title Company on May 16th at 10:00 am….Time is of the essence in this contract." Defendant appeared at the office at 10:00 a.m. on the day designated, but the Plaintiff's agent was not there. Defendant waited for twenty minutes, then left. Plaintiff's agent arrived at 10:30 a.m. and announced that he would not have funds for payment until 1:30 p.m., but Defen-

dant refused to return; she had already made other arrangements to finance her purchase of other real estate. Plaintiff sued Defendant for specific performance. Who wins, and why?

6. A contract between the Koles and Parker-Yale provided for completion of the Koles's condominium unit within 180 days. It also authorized the Koles to make written changes in the plans and specifications. Construction was not completed within the 180-day period, and the Koles, prior to completion, sent a letter to Parker-Yale rescinding the contract. Were the Koles within their rights to rescind the contract?

7. Defendant contracted to buy Plaintiff's commercial property for $1,265,000. Under the terms of the agreement, Defendant paid $126,000 as an earnest-money deposit, which would be retained by Plaintiff as liquidated damages if Defendant failed to close by the deadline. Defendant's husband died four days before the closing deadline, and she was not able to close by the deadline. She was relying on her husband's business to assist her in obtaining the necessary financing to complete the purchase, and after his death, she was not able to obtain it. Plaintiff sued for the $126,000; Defendant argued that the purpose of the contract was frustrated due to the untimely death of her husband. Is this a good argument?

8. Buyer contracted to buy Seller's house for $290,000; the contract included a representation by Buyer "that he has sufficient cash available to complete this purchase." Buyer was a physician who practiced with his uncle. He had received assurances from his uncle of a loan of $200,000 in order to finance the purchase. Shortly after the contract was executed, the uncle was examined by a cardiologist, who found his coronary arteries to be dangerously clogged. As a result, the uncle immediately had triple bypass surgery. After the operation, he told Buyer that his economic future was now uncertain and that therefore it was impossible for him to finance the house purchase. Meanwhile, Seller, who did not know of Buyer's problem, committed herself to buy a house in another state and accepted employment there as well. Buyer was unable to close; Seller sued. Buyer raised as a defense impossibility or impracticability of performance. Is the defense good?

9. Pursuant to a contract for the repair and renovation of a swimming pool owned by Defendant (City of Fort Lauderdale), Plaintiff commenced the work, which included resurfacing the inside of the pool, and had progressed almost to completion. Overnight, vandals damaged the work Plaintiff had done inside the pool, requiring that part of the work be redone. Plaintiff proceeded to redo the work and billed Defendant, who paid the contract price but refused to pay for the additional work required to repair the damage. Did the damage constitute destruction of subject matter discharging Plaintiff from his obligation to complete the job without getting paid extra?

10. Apache Plaza (the landlord) leased space to Midwest Savings to construct a bank building in Apache's shopping mall, based on a prototype approved by Apache. Midwest constructed the building and used it for twelve years until it was destroyed by a tornado. Midwest submitted plans for a new building to Apache, but Apache rejected the plans because the new building was larger and had less glass than the old building or the prototype. Midwest built it anyway. Its architect claimed that certain changes in the structure of the new building were required by new regulations and building codes, but he admitted that a building of the stipulated size could have been constructed in compliance with the applicable codes. Apache claimed $210,000 in damages over the term of the lease because the new building consumed more square feet of mall space and required more parking. Midwest claimed it had substantially complied with the lease requirements. Is this a good defense?[24]

8.4 Remedies

Learning Objectives

1. Know the types of legal remedies: damages of various kinds.

2. Understand the types of equitable remedies: injunction, specific performance, and restitution.
3. Recognize that there can be limits to remedies.
4. Recognize the interplay between contract and tort as a cause of action.

At *common law*, monetary awards (called "damages") of various types are the remedies for contract breach. In *equity*, specific performance, injunction, and restitution are the three principal remedies for breach of contract.

In the development of English law, only money damages were recognized as compensation for breach of contract. If the plaintiff wanted something other than money, resort had to be to equity (more about which below).

Legal Remedies: Damages

If the non-breaching party can articulate its monetary losses adequately, that party has the right to **damages** (money paid by one side to another) when the other party has breached the contract unless, of course, the contract itself or other circumstances suspend or discharge the obligation.

damages
Money paid by one party to another to discharge a liability.

Compensatory Damages

Compensatory damages are those awarded to the non-breaching party (the plaintiff) for the immediate loss suffered. If Rufus contracts to re-roof Owner's house, and does a poor job, Owner will hire Substitute to do it right, and charge Rufus the difference in price between what Owner had agreed to pay Rufus and how much Owner ended up paying to get the job done.

compensatory damages
A sum of money awarded in a civil action by a court to indemnify a person for the particular loss, detriment, or injury suffered as a result of a breach of contract.

Consequential Damages

Consequential damages are those damages that flow as a foreseeable consequence of the breach. For example, if you hire a roofer to fix a leak in your roof, and he does a bad job, so that the interior of your house suffers water damage, the roofer is liable not only for the poor roofing job, but also for the ruined drapes, damaged flooring and walls, and so on. These damages are a foreseeable consequence of the breach. As noted below, consequential damages must be foreseeable.

consequential damages
Damages that flow as a foreseeable but indirect result of the breach of contract.

Incidental Damages

Suppose City College hires Prof. Blake on a two-year contract, after an extensive search. After one year the professor quits to take a job elsewhere, in breach of her contract. If City College has to pay $5,000 more to find a replacement for one year, Blake is liable for that amount—that's compensatory damages. But what if it costs City College $1,200 to search for, bring to campus and interview a replacement? City College can claim that, too, as **incidental damages**, which include additional costs incurred by the non-breaching party after the breach in a reasonable attempt to avoid further loss, even if the attempt is unsuccessful.

incidental damages
Money paid to the non-breaching party in an attempt to avoid further loss on account of the breach.

Liquidated Damages

liquidated damages

A term in a contract that specifies in advance what the damages will be in case of a specific breach. E.g.: "For every day the house is not completed, contractor will owe homeowner $500."

We have seen that parties to a contract can put pretty much whatever they want in the agreement (as long as it's not illegal). They can agree in advance what the damages will be in the event of a breach—that's **liquidated damages** (to "liquidate" means to reduce something of uncertain value to a dollar amount). At common law, liquidated damages are allowed if the actual amount of the damages is difficult to ascertain (or else they don't need to be figured up in advance, just do it after the loss), and if the amount set is not a penalty (again, the purpose of contract remedies is not usually to punish anyone). Liquidated damages are allowable in contracts for the sale of goods, too.

Punitive Damages

punitive damages

Money awarded to the non-breaching party in excess of any loss suffered to punish the breaching party.

Punitive damages are those awarded for the purpose of punishing a defendant in a civil action, in which criminal sanctions may be unavailable. They are not part of the compensation for the loss suffered; they are proper in cases in which the defendant has acted willfully and maliciously and are thought to deter others from acting similarly.

Since the purpose of contract law is compensation, not punishment, punitive damages have not traditionally been awarded (except for cases of fraudulent misrepresentation).

Nominal Damages

nominal damages

A token amount of money paid when the breach has caused no loss.

If the breach caused no loss, or the plaintiff cannot prove it with reasonable certainty, the plaintiff is nevertheless entitled to a minor sum, perhaps one dollar, called **nominal damages**. When, for example, a buyer could purchase the same commodity at the same price as that contracted for, without spending any extra time or money, there can be no real damages in the event of breach.

Equitable Remedies

equity

As a legal system, a body of law addressing concerns that fall outside the jurisdiction of common law. Most generally, equity means "fairness."

As suggested above (and discussed in more detail in Chapter 1—remember the case about Campbell's Soup Company and the carrot farmers?), in the development of the English court system, judges were constrained by tradition and law to give redress (relief) only for certain kinds of cases. Aggrieved plaintiffs found that otherwise valid complaints were sometimes dismissed on technicalities; they turned to the king (as the fundamental source of fairness and justice in the kingdom) for help. The king assigned the cases the law courts would not hear to a royal court (the Chancery) with the power to settle disputes according to the chancellor's sense of what was fair—what was equitable—as opposed to what was legal. That was a broad grant of discretion; moreover, chancellors of equity relied not on precedent to guide decision making, but on equitable maxims (a maxim is a handy little saying, like "look before you leap"—an equitable maxim is "one who seeks equity must have behaved equitably"). **Equity** uses no jury, and courts of law and of equity competed for business in England in separate courthouses, but by the late 1600s equity and law were effectively folded into one court system.

Equity is alive and well in the United States today. The primary distinction of interest here between what a judge "sitting in equity" can do compared to one "sitting in law" is that equity affords non-monetary relief. If what the plaintiff wants is not money, the plaintiff seeks equitable relief.

The major types of equitable relief are (1) specific performance, (2) injunctions, and (3) restitution.

Specific Performance

Specific performance is a judicial order to the promisor that he deliver something that he promised he would. It is the remedy for breach of contract for the sale of a unique (or very rare) item. Emily signs a contract to sell Charlotte an antique French painting. Emily then repudiates the contract while still executory. A court may properly grant Charlotte an order of specific performance against Emily: Emily may be required to deliver the item as she promised.

specific performance

An order directing a person to deliver the exact property (real or personal) that she contracted to sell to the buyer.

Specific performance is necessarily the remedy for breach of contract to sell real estate: all real estate is unique. But notice, while specific performance is an attractive remedy, it is limited in availability: it is only good for breach of contract to sell a unique item (if the item is not unique, the disappointed buyer can always find another one and charge the breaching seller with the difference in price between what they had agreed and what the buyer had to pay for it on the market). It will not be used to force somebody to *perform* as required in a contract.

Injunction

An **injunction** is an order signed by a judge directing a person to stop doing that which is a breach of contract; it does not order a person to do anything (though sometimes it seems like it)—it orders a person to stop.

injunction

An order signed by a judge directing a person to stop doing that which he or she should not legally do.

Primo Carnera (1906–67) was an Italian professional boxer and the world heavyweight champion in 1933–34. In 1931 he contracted with Madison Square Garden Corporation to box in a contest to be set up by the Garden; he was contractually prohibited from boxing anybody else (except sparring) for the duration of his contract—he had agreed to a negative covenant (promised not to do something), and when, in violation of that promise, he contracted to box in a match outside the Garden's purview, the court agreed that an injunction should issue to enforce the contract: "A negative covenant in a contract for personal services is enforceable by injunction where the damages for breach are incapable of ascertainment."[25]

Courts might issue an injunction where a labor union is on strike in violation of its contract with the employer, or where one ex-spouse is contacting the other in violation of the divorce agreement.

Restitution

As the word implies, **restitution** is a restoring to one party of what he gave to the other—the purpose of restitution is to put the party suffering loss back to where he was before the contract was made. Therefore, only to the extent that the injured party conferred a benefit on the other party may the injured party be awarded restitution. Restitution works in these kinds of cases:

restitution

To restore to one party what was delivered to the other.

- Party suffers losses by breach. Able agrees to sell Baker a parcel of real estate for $300,000 and she makes a $30,000 down payment; Able wrongfully refuses to sell; as an alternative to damages or specific performance, Baker may recover the money in restitution.

- Party in default. Able agrees to build a fence for Baker and Baker agrees to, and does indeed, deliver to Able a 1958 Edsel convertible in payment. Able breaches—doesn't build the fence. Baker gets the car back in restitution (and can pursue Able for damages).

- Voidable contracts. A party who has avoided a contract (infancy, undue influence, duress, mistake) is entitled to restitution insofar as some benefit has been conferred on the other side. Able fraudulently convinces Baker that she has great potential as a dancer and induces her to sign up for $250,000 in dance lessons. Baker realizes she has been duped; she is entitled to the return of such amount of the lessons' values as she did not use.

Limitations on Remedies

Contract remedies are intended, insofar as possible, to put the non-breaching party into the position that he, she, or it would have been in had there been no breach. However, there are circumstances in which the non-breaching party will be denied a remedy, or can get only a partial remedy. Limitations on remedies include the following:

- Liquidated damages. We observed above that parties to a contract can agree in advance what the damages will be in case of breach. They can limit damages, within reason.
- Certainty of damages. If the non-breaching party cannot prove with some degree of certainty what the loss was from the breach, she will get nothing (or maybe nominal damages). Professor Freund signed a contract to have a book he wrote published; the publisher breached the contract by not publishing, but Freund was awarded nothing because "he provided no stable foundation for a reasonable estimate of the royalties he would have earned had the defendant not breached its promise to publish. His claim for royalties fails for uncertainty.[26]
- Mitigation of damages. A non-breaching party has a duty to attempt to mitigate (to make less serious) damages suffered. If tenants skip out of a 12-month lease after two months, the landlord cannot sit back and let the damages accrue against them; she has to make a reasonable effort to mitigate by trying to re-rent the premises. If she doesn't make a reasonable effort, she will not be able to collect the unpaid rent.
- Foreseeability. A person enters a contract with certain expectations about what the liability will be in case he breaches, and he will not be liable for damages which—based on an objective test—were not foreseeable. Tire Company repairs Tavis' tire, but not well; it goes flat on the LA freeway. Exerting himself in the hot weather to change the tire, Tavis dies of a heart attack. Tire company breached, all right, but it is not liable for Tavis' death because that was not forseeable when they contracted to repair the tire. (See *EBWS v. Britly Corp.*, below.)

Tort versus Contract Remedies; Knowing Breaches

Tort vs. Contract

Frequently, a contract breach may also amount to tortious conduct. A physician warrants her treatment as perfectly safe but performs the operation negligently, scarring the patient for life. The patient could sue for malpractice (tort) or for breach of warranty (contract). The choice involves at least four considerations:

1. *Statute of limitations.* Most statutes of limitations prescribe longer periods for contract than for tort actions.
2. *Allowable damages.* Punitive damages are more often permitted in tort actions, and certain kinds of injuries are compensable in tort but not in contract suits—for example, pain and suffering.
3. *Expert testimony.* In most cases, the use of experts would be the same in either tort or contract suits, but in certain contract cases, the expert witness could be dispensed with, as, for example, in a contract case charging that the physician abandoned the patient.
4. *Insurance coverage.* Most policies do not cover intentional torts, so a contract theory that avoids the element of willfulness would provide the plaintiff with a surer chance of recovering money damages.

Knowing Breaches

A person always has the power to breach a contract, but not the right: you will, usually, suffer the consequences if you breach a contract. But sometimes people knowingly breach—they do it intentionally. If the cost of adhering to a contract outweighs the benefit of adhering to it (including the benefit of maintaining a good reputation), it may make economic sense to breach. If, for example, the price of natural gas drops very significantly, a coal-fired electric utility may find it cheaper to dump the long-term coal contract, pay the coal company its lost profits, and make the switch to natural gas.

Case

Consequential Damages

EBWS, LLC v. Britly Corp.

928 A.2d 497 (Vt., 2007)

EBWS, LLC v. Britly Corp.

Vermont Supreme Court, 2007, analyzing the elements of consequential damages in contract.

Reiber, C. J.

The Ransom family owns Rock Bottom Farm in Strafford, Vermont, where Earl Ransom owns a dairy herd and operates an organic dairy farm. In 2000, the Ransoms decided to build a creamery on-site to process their milk and formed EBWS, LLC to operate the dairy-processing plant and to market the plant's products. In July 2000, Earl Ransom, on behalf of EBWS, met with Britly's president to discuss building the creamery. In January 2001, EBWS and Britly entered into a contract requiring Britly to construct a creamery building for EBWS in exchange for $160,318. * * * The creamery was substantially completed by April 15, 2001, and EBWS moved in soon afterward. On June 5, 2001, EBWS notified Britly of alleged defects in construction. [EBWS continued to use the creamery pending the necessity to vacate it for three weeks when repairs were commenced].

On September 12, 2001, EBWS filed suit against Britly for damages resulting from defective design and construction. * * *

Following a three-day trial, the jury found Britly had breached the contract and its express warranty, and awarded EBWS: (1) $38,020 in direct damages, and (2) $35,711 in consequential damages.

The jury's award to EBWS included compensation for both direct and consequential damages that EBWS claimed it would incur while the facility closed for repairs. Direct damages [i.e., compensatory damages] are for "losses that naturally and usually flow from the breach itself," and it is not necessary that the parties actually considered these damages. [Citation]. In comparison, special or consequential damages "must pass the tests of causation, certainty and foreseeability, and, in addition, be reasonably supposed to have been in the contemplation of both parties at the time they made the contract."

The trial court ruled that EBWS could not recover for lost profits because it was not a going concern at the time the contract was entered into, and profits were too speculative. The court concluded, however, that EBWS could submit evidence of other business losses, including future payment for unused milk and staff wages. * * *

At trial, Huyffer, the CEO of EBWS, testified that during a repairs closure the creamery would be required to purchase milk from adjacent Rock Bottom Farm, even though it could not process this milk. She admitted that such a requirement was self-imposed as there was no written output contract between EBWS and the farm to buy milk. In addition, Huyffer testified that EBWS would pay its employees during the closure even though EBWS has no written contract to pay its employees when they are not working. The trial court allowed these elements of damages to be submitted to the jury, and the jury awarded EBWS consequential damages for unused milk and staff wages.

On appeal, Britly contends that because there is no contractual or legal obligation for EBWS to purchase milk or pay its employees, these are not foreseeable damages. EBWS counters that it is common knowledge that cows continue to produce milk, even if the processing plant is not working, and thus it is foreseeable that this loss would occur. We conclude that these damages are not the foreseeable result of Britly's breach of the construction contract and reverse the award.

[W]e conclude that it is not reasonable to expect Britly to foresee that its failure to perform under the contract would result in this type of damages. While we are sympathetic to EBWS's contention that the cows continue to produce milk, even when the plant is closed down, this fact alone is not enough to demonstrate that buying and dumping milk is a foreseeable result of Britly's breach of the construction contract. Here, the milk was produced by a separate and distinct entity, Rock Bottom Farm, which sold the milk to EBWS.

Similarly, EBWS maintained no employment agreements with its employees obligating it to pay wages during periods of closure for repairs, dips in market demand, or for any other reason. Any losses EBWS might suffer in the future because it chooses to pay its employees during a plant closure for repairs would be a voluntary expense and not in Britly's contemplation at the time it entered the construction contract. It is not reasonable to expect Britly to foresee losses incurred as a result of agreements that are informal in nature and carry no legal obligation on EBWS to perform. "[P]arties are not presumed to know the condition of each other's affairs nor to take into account contracts with a third party that is not communicated." [Citation] * * * Under these circumstances, this business decision is beyond the scope of what Britly could have reasonably foreseen as damages for its breach of contract. * * *

Award for consequential damages is reversed.

Case Questions

1. Why, according to EBWS's CEO, would EBWS be required to purchase milk from adjacent Rock Bottom Farm, even though it could not process this milk?
2. Surely it is well known in Vermont dairy country that dairy farmers can't simply stop milking cows when no processing plant is available to take the milk—the cows will not just stop producing. Why was EBWS then not entitled to those damages which it will certainly suffer when the creamery is down for repairs?
3. Britly (the contractor) must have known EBWS had employees that would be idled when the creamery shut down for repairs. Why was it not liable for their lost wages?
4. What could EBWS have done at the time of contracting to protect itself against the damages it would incur in the event the creamery suffered downtime due to faulty construction?

Key Takeaway

The purpose of remedies in contract is, usually, to put the non-breaching party in the position he or she would have been in had there been no breach. The remedies are: compensatory damages (money paid to compensate the non-breaching party for the losses caused by the breach), which also include sub-categories of incidental and nominal damages; punitive damages (to punish the breaching party) are sometimes allowed where the breach is egregious and intentional.

Where loses suffered by one party may be attributed to either breach of contract or tort, the plaintiff usually needs to make a choice about which cause of action to take. And sometimes defendants knowingly and intentionally breach contracts because that makes economic sense.

Exercises

1. What are compensatory damages?
2. When is specific performance an appropriate remedy? Will it be used to require a person to perform a service (such as properly repair a leaky roof)?
3. When is restitution used?
4. How could a breach of contract also be a tort, and when is one cause of action chosen over the other?
5. What is the purpose of punitive damages?

8.5 Summary and Exercises

Summary

In this chapter we have seen that two fundamental sources of contract law are the common law as developed in the state courts and as summarized in the *Restatement (Second) of Contracts,* and the Uniform Commercial Code for the sale of goods. (We observed there is international contracts law for the sale of goods, too: the CISG.)

Sales law is a special type of contract law, governed by Article 2 of the UCC. Article 2 governs the sale of goods only, defined as things movable at the time of identification to the contract for sale.

Types of contracts can be distinguished along these axes: (1) express and implied, including quasi-contracts implied by law; (2) bilateral and unilateral; (3) enforceable and unenforceable; and (4) completed (executed) and uncompleted (executory). To understand contract law, it is necessary to master these distinctions and their nuances.

For parties to have a contract, the following elements are required:

- There was an agreement (offer and acceptance);
- The agreement was real (there was no lack of free will, knowledge, or capacity);
- There was consideration;
- The agreement was legal.

For the agreement to be enforceable, in some situations there must be something in writing signed by the party to be bound (to be held to the agreement) in accordance with the statute of frauds.

If the parties did have a contract, nevertheless, one side might have a defense (excuse) and not be held liable for breach. Excuses include the happening or non-happening of conditions, agreement by the parties to limit liability, and impossibility of performance (and its relatives), among others.

Remedies available against someone who breaches a contract include damages, specific performance, and restitution. Frequently, the party who is not in breach must choose between tort and contract remedies. Sometimes, where economically beneficial, a party knowingly and intentionally breaches (that party's reputation may suffer, though).

Exercises

1. On November 26, Joe wrote to Kate offering to purchase a farm that she owned. Upon receiving the letter on November 28, Kate immediately sent Joe a letter of acceptance. However, shortly after mailing the letter, Kate had second thoughts and called Joe to advise him that she was rejecting his offer. The call was made before Joe received the letter of acceptance. Has a contract been formed? Why?

2. On a busy day just before April 15, Albert Accountant received a call from a local car dealer. The dealer said, "Hi, Mr. Accountant. Now, while you have income from doing clients' taxes, I have an excellent offer for you. You can buy a new Buick Century automobile, completely loaded, for $36,000. Al, I know you're busy. If I don't hear from you by the end of the day, I'll assume you want the car." Albert, distracted, did not respond immediately, and the dealer hung up. Then followed an exhausting day of working with anxiety-ridden tax clients, and Albert forgot about the conversation. Two days later a statement arrived from the dealer with instructions on how Albert should pick up the car at the dealership. Is there a contract? Explain.

3. Bert purchased Ernie's car. Before selling the car, Ernie had stated to Bert, "This car runs well and is reliable. Last week I drove the car all the way from Seattle to San Francisco to visit my mother and back again to Seattle." In fact, Ernie was not telling the truth—he had driven the car to San Francisco to visit his paramour, not his mother. Upon discovery of the truth, may Bert void the contract? Why?

4. Langstraat was seventeen when he purchased a motorcycle. When applying for insurance, he signed a "Notice of Rejection," declining to purchase uninsured motorist coverage. He was involved in an accident with an uninsured motorist and sought to disaffirm his rejection of the uninsured motorist coverage on the basis of infancy. May he do so?

5. Richard promised to have Darlene's deck awning constructed by July 10. On June 20, Darlene called him and asked if he could get the job done by July 3, in time for Independence Day. Richard said he could, but he failed to do so, and Darlene had to rent two canopies at some expense. Darlene claims that because Richard breached his promise, he is liable for the cost of awning rental. Is she correct—was his promise binding? Why?

6. After taking a business law class at State U, Elke entered into a contract to sell her business law book to a classmate, Matthew, for $45. As part of the same contract, she agreed to prepare a will for Matthew's mother for an additional $110. Elke prepared the will and sent the book to Matthew, but he refused to pay her. Is she entitled to any payment? Explain.

7. Sara Hohe, a fifteen-year-old junior at Mission Bay High School in San Diego, was injured during a campus hypnotism show sponsored by the PTSA as a fund-raiser for the senior class. Hypnotism shows had been held annually since 1980, and Sara had seen the previous year's show. She was selected at random from a group of many volunteers. Her participation in the "Magic of the Mind Show" was conditioned on signing two release forms. Hohe's father signed a form entitled "Mission Bay High School PTSA Presents Dr. Karl Santo." Hohe and her father both signed a form titled "Karl Santo Hypnotist," releasing Santo and the school district from all liability. During the course of the show, while apparently hypnotized, Hohe slid from her chair and also fell to the floor about six times and was injured. She, through her father, then sued the school district. The Hohes claimed the release was contrary to public policy; the trial court dismissed the suit on summary judgment. Was the release contrary to public policy? Decide.

8. Schiff, a self-styled "tax rebel," appeared on a late-night TV show and asserted that people don't have to pay income taxes. He said, "If anybody calls this show—I have the [tax] code—and cites any section of this code that says an individual is required to file a tax return, I'll pay them $100,000." Newman, a tax lawyer, heard an excerpt of the late-night show on morning television. He researched the issue at his office, contacted the television studio that day, and then demanded the money from Schiff. When Schiff refused, Newman sued him. Who wins and why? *Newman v Schiff*, 778 F.2d 460 (8th Cir., 1985).

9. Owner of an auto repair shop hires Contractor to remodel his shop but does not mention that two days after the scheduled completion date, Owner is to receive five small U.S. Army personnel carrier trucks for service, with a three-week deadline to finish the job and turn the trucks over to the army. The contract between Owner and the army has a liquidated-damages clause calling for $300 a day for every day trucks are not operable after the deadline.

Contractor is five days late in finishing the remodel. Can Owner claim the $1,500 as damages against Contractor as a consequence of the latter's tardy completion of the contract? Explain.

10. Calvin, a promising young basketball and baseball player, signed a multiyear contract with a professional basketball team after graduating from college. After playing basketball for one year, he decided he would rather play baseball and breached his contract with the basketball team. What remedy could the team seek?

11. It's 85 degrees in July and 5:00 p.m., quitting time. The battery in Mary's car is out of juice again. Mary says, "Arrgh! I will sell this stupid car for $50!" Jason, walking to his car nearby, whips out his checkbook and says, "It's a deal. Leave your car here. I'll give you a ride home and pick up your car after you give me the title." Do the parties have a contract?

Self-Test Questions

1. An implied contract:

   a. must be in writing

   b. is one in which the terms are spelled out

   c. is one inferred from the actions of the parties

   d. is imposed by law to avoid an unjust result

   e. may be avoided by one party.

2. The Convention on Contracts for the International Sale of Goods is:

   a. an annual meeting of international commercial purchasing agents.

   b. contract law used in overseas U.S. federal territories

   c. a customary format or template for drafting contracts

   d. a kind of treaty setting out international contract law, to which the United States is a party

   e. the organization that develops uniform international law.

3. Consideration:

   a. can consist of a written acknowledgment of some benefit received, even if in fact the benefit is not delivered

   b. cannot be nominal in amount

   c. is a bargained-for act, forbearance, or promise from the promisee

   d. is all of the above

4. An example of valid consideration is a promise:

   a. by a seventeen-year-old to refrain from drinking alcohol

   b. to refrain from going to court

   c. to cook dinner if the promisor can get around to it

   d. to repay a friend for the four years of free legal advice he had provided.

5. A contract to pay a lobbyist to influence a public official is generally illegal.

   a. true

   b. false

Self-Test Answers

1. c

2. d

3. c

4. b
5. false

Endnotes

1. Sir Henry Maine, *Ancient Law* (1869), 180–82.
2. The Restatement of Contracts is an abstracted, organized, presentation of the common law of contracts taken from the many cases expressing contract law. It is not the law; it is a restatement of it by legal scholars.
3. The Restatement is "one of the most widely recognized and most frequently cited legal treatises that is part of jurisprudence in the United States. . . . The Restatement of Contracts is not legally binding, but it carries a great deal of weight and is highly persuasive because it represents the thoughts of prominent legal professors, practicing attorneys, and judges. The Restatement of Contracts is a reflective consensus reached by the American legal system and professionals, both of what the law is and, in rare cases, what the law should be.https://contract-law.laws.com/contract-law/restatement-of-contracts
4. taxonomy is an orderly arrangement of names of things; "tax" here means an orderly arrangement, and "nomy" is "word" or "name" (like a taxidermist is one who makes an orderly arrangement of an animals epidermis—surface of the skin).
5. *Adams v. Lindsell*, 1 Barnewall & Alderson 681 (K.B. 1818).
6. Restatement, Second, of Contracts sec. 177.
7. In *Reed v. King*, 193 Cal. Rptr. 130 (Calif. Ct. App. 1983), the court held the defendants' failure to disclose to the plaintiff that the house she bought from them had been the site of a grisly mass murder of a woman and four children ten years before was misrepresentation by concealment (the defendant had argued the decade-old event was "immaterial").
8. Here is the Restatement's take: Sec. 152. When Mistake of Both Parties Makes a Contract Voidable Where a mistake of both parties at the time a contract was made as to a basic assumption on which the contract was made has a material effect on the agreed exchange of performances, the contract is voidable by the adversely affected party unless he bears the risk of the mistake under the rule stated in R2C § 154. Sec. 154. When a Party Bears the Risk of a Mistake A party bears the risk of a mistake when the risk is allocated to him by agreement of the parties, or he is aware, at the time the contract is made, that he has only limited knowledge with respect to the facts to which the mistake relates but treats his limited knowledge as sufficient, or the risk is allocated to him by the court on the ground that it is reasonable in the circumstances to do so.
9. Although the age of majority was lowered in most states during the 1970s to correspond to the Twenty-sixth Amendment (ratified in 1971, guaranteeing the right to vote at eighteen), some states still put the age of majority at twenty-one. Legal rights for those under twenty-one remain ambiguous, however. Although eighteen-year-olds may assent to binding contracts, not all creditors and landlords believe it, and they may require parents to cosign. For those under twenty-one, there are also legal impediments to holding certain kinds of jobs, signing certain kinds of contracts, marrying, leaving home, and drinking alcohol. There is as yet no uniform set of rules.
10. How long is "reasonable" is a fact question. In one case of the authors' recollection a court held that the plaintiff, at age 23, could disaffirm a contract she made when she was 13.
11. The theory is that the rule allowing minors to disaffirm their contracts is to protect them against their lack of good judgment, but if the contract is for a necessity, the minor *needs* the contracted-for thing, and if the adult refused to contract with the minor because of his age, the minor would not be "protected" at all—he would suffer harm.

12. In one well-known case a young man promised his uncle the would not smoke, drink, swear, or play pool for some years in return for the uncle's promise to give him a significant amount of money at the end of that time. The court held the young man had given good consideration to enforce the promise: he had a right to smoke, drink, swear and play pool, and he gave that right up.
13. *Estate of Timko v. Oral Roberts Evangelistic Assn.*, 215 N.W.2d 750 (Mich. App. 1974).
14. Actually there is no such thing as an "illegal contract." If the agreement is illegal, it's not a contract at all.
15. Italian Colors Restaurant contracted with American Express to accept the latter's credit cards. (This case is set out in Chapter 5.8, as you may recall.) The contract provided that all disputes between them be arbitrated (not litigated) and that no claims can "be arbitrated on a class action basis." Italian Colors brought a class action against Amex alleging Amex was abusing its market power to maintain a monopoly, in violation of the federal Sherman Act of 1890. The majority opinion held that the plaintiff made the bargain and was stuck. The dissent said Amex had effectively deprived its "victims" (the dissent's word) "of all legal recourse. And here is the nutshell version of today's opinion, admirably flaunted rather than camouflaged: 'Too darn bad.'"
16. Restatement (Second) of Contracts Chapter 5, statutory note.
17. Louisiana has not adopted *all* of the UCC because its legal system is based on the Napoleonic Code and not English common law. The law in all states that have adopted the Uniform Commercial Code are not, actually, entirely uniform: some states have adopted amendments that others have not.
18. A "special commissioner" is a lawyer appointed by judges to hear a case, usually because the lawyer has expertise regarding the subject matter of the case.
19. 631 P.2d 366 (WA, 1981).
20. Where installment payments are being made, like rent or payment on a promissory note, the "time is of the essence" clause is usually accompanied by an "acceleration clause" which says that failure to make one payment on time terminates the entire contract: the tenant is evicted or the whole amount of the outstanding debt immediately becomes payable.
21. The classic illustration of frustration of purpose is the litigation that gave birth (or caused the discovery of) the rule: the cornonation cases. In 1902 when King Edward VII was to be crowned following the death of his mother Queen Victoria, the parade route was announced for the royal show. Scores of people rented rooms in buildings lining the route in downtown London, at exorbitant prices, to see the grand parade. But the king fell ill and the procession had to be postponed. Many expectant viewers failed to pay for the spaces they'd rented. The court declared the would-be viewers were not liable because the purpose of the contract had been frustrated.
22. A *lien* (from the French "string") is a claim of interest that a creditor has in another's property, lasting ususally until a debt or duty that it secures is satisfied. An *affidavit* is a sworn-to statement (usually notarized).
23. *Crum v. Grant*, 692 P.2d 147 (Or. App., 1984).
24. *Apache Plaza, Ltd. v. Midwest Sav. Ass'n*, 456 N.W.2d 729 (Minn. App. 1990).
25. *Madison Square Garden Corp. v. Carnera*, 52 F.2d 47 (2d Cir. Ct. App., 1931).
26. *Freund v. Washington Square Press*, 314 NE 2d 419 (NY, 1974)

CHAPTER 9
Property Law

Chapter Learning Objectives

After studying this chapter you should:

1. Understand what "property" is, and a little of its legal history.
2. Recognize that property can be variously categorized, as real, personal, tangible, intangible, and intellectual, among other possible categories.
3. Know something about real property law and how one's interest in it can be acquired, owned, mortgaged, and disposed of.
4. Understand some basic concepts in personal property such as acquisition, disposition, and bailments.
5. Recognize what a fixture is.
6. Be somewhat familiar with the law of estates and trusts (what happens to peoples' property when they die).
7. Recognize intellectual property, how it is created, and how it is protected under common-law and statutory regimes.

One of the most important aspects of free-market capitalism (although as we note here and there, no society has ever had a truly free market) is the right to own private property and enjoy its uses. Property is wealth and security; property is a matter of urgent interest to us all and, not surprisingly, a lot of law has grown up around it over centuries. Here, we take up the law of real property (land), and various kinds of personal property (not land), and we examine the rights and duties associated with property.

9.1 Introduction to Property Law

Learning Objectives

1. Understand why property law was very important when the English legal system (from which the United States' legal system devolved) was in its infancy.
2. Know the definition of "property": it is a legal concept, not a thing.
3. Know the classifications of property.

This chapter is a quick study on property law. We say "quick study" because property law is very old and very complex, so we offer here only the most prominent features of property law. Without laws regarding property, business as we know it in the U.S. would not be possible. Lack of adequate property laws has also been shown to hinder business development in many countries,[1] and without property law, theft or misappropriation of property could only be redressed by counter-theft, revenge, and violence.

History of Property Law

Property law is old because in an agricultural and feudal society—as was England in the 12th century, following the Norman Conquest—how a person held real property (real estate) was *the* big deal.[2] The king (or queen) was the source of power and prestige because the Crown—in theory, and early on much in practice—owned, or had the legal right to dispose of, all the land. The Crown parceled out rights to the land's use and possession to the nobility, and—the Crown promised—"we will also provide military security to protect you from disloyal warlords, if you pledge in return loyalty, periodic monetary contributions, and men to serve in our military." The people to whom these rights were "parceled out" were the dukes and counts and bishops (the Church participated), and they in turn divided up their parcels, granting other lower-ranked members of the nobility use of the land (estates), again, in return for loyalty to the dukes.[3]

What rights a person has in property are defined politically—in a purely Communist country, for example, only the state can own property. In the People's Republic of China, citizens' rights to compensation for land taken by the government have been entirely up to the government.[4] Back in the 13th century the English nobility got tired of the Crown's heavy-handed demands: money to maintain the royal household and to prosecute increasing unpopular wars in France; King John raised taxes, including inheritances taxes, levied new ones, and threatened to interfere with what the nobility thought was their right to dispose of their estates as they saw fit. The powerful nobility at last rebelled and, after a serious threat of civil war, a peace deal was brokered by the Archbishop of Canterbury, and King John signed the Magna Carta on June 15, 1215. The "great charter" curbed the Crown's powers, guaranteed property rights, and is considered a major part of the foundation of English law, government, and politics.

Personal property is everything a person can own that is not real property or affixed to real property. The concept of personal property developed before that of real property, so the concept of owning a thing is universal and pre-historic. Cavemen made flint scrapers to de-hair animal skins, and doubtless became upset if somebody stole their favorite tool without permission. The concept of owning real estate, on the other hand, is different; can a person own part of the Earth itself? In our system, yes; but many indigenous cultures have no concept of land ownership. Personal property can be tangible or intangible: while the caveman's flint scraper or your iPad are material (tangible), intellectual property—such as a song, a novel, or a computer program—is intangible, and its existence, which cannot be pinned to one location, must be documented properly. Moreover, the one who created the intellectual property may or may not be its legal owner, as we shall see. That suggests that personal property is "assignable" or "transferable," which is also true of real property.

Definition of Property

Restatement of the Law of Property defines property as the "legal relationship between persons with respect to a thing."

Property is not the thing itself; it is a *legal relationship*, the power of one person to use things in ways that affect others, to exclude others from the property, and to acquire and transfer them. We can own personal objects like iPods and DVDs, and even more complex objects like homes and minerals under the ground. Property also embraces objects whose worth is representative or symbolic. Ownership of stock in a corporation is valued not for the piece of paper called a stock certificate, but for dividends, the power to vote for directors, and the right to sell the stock on the open market. Wholly intangible things or objects like copyrights, patents, and bank accounts are capable of being owned as property. The list of things that can be property is not fixed—our concept of property continues to evolve. Collateralized debt obligations (CDOs) and structured investment vehicles

(SIVs), prime players in the subprime mortgage crisis, were not on anyone's list of possible properties even twenty years ago.

Classifications of Property

Property can be classified in various ways, as follows:

- **Tangible property** is what physically exists—buildings, a hair dryer, an automobile, or a meadow.
- **Intangible property** is something without physical reality that entitles the owner to certain benefits; stocks, bonds, and intellectual property are common examples.
- **Public property** is that which is owned by any branch of government.
- **Private property** is that which is owned by a person or persons (including corporations), not the government.
- **Real property** is land and the things affixed to it—it is immoveable. This includes items of personal property that become affixed to the real estate. (For example, a bathroom cabinet purchased at Home Depot and screwed into the bathroom wall may become part of the real property when it is affixed.)
- **Personal property** (at common law, called "chattels") is moveable stuff, like desks, chairs, clothing, groceries, books, and appliances.

The distinction between the latter two classifications—real and personal property—is significant in several ways.

For example, the sale of personal property, but not real property, is governed by Article 2 of the Uniform Commercial Code (UCC). Real estate transactions, by contrast, are governed by the general law of contracts. Suppose goods are exchanged for realty. Section 2-304 of the UCC says that the transfer of the goods and the seller's obligations with reference to them are subject to Article 2, but not the transfer of the interests in real property.

The form of transfer depends on whether the property is real or personal. Real property is normally transferred by a deed, which must meet formal requirements imposed by state law. By contrast, transfer of personal property (other than motor vehicles) can often occur without just a handshake and a mutually satisfactory exchange of value.

Another difference relates to the transfer of property on death. A person's heirs depend on the law of the state for distribution of his property if he dies "intestate"—that is, without a will that takes legal effect. Who the heirs are and what their share of the property will be may depend on whether the property is real or personal. For example, in some states a widow whose husband has died intestate will be entitled to a different percentage of real property than personal property.

Tax laws also differ in their approach to real and personal property. In particular, the rules of valuation, depreciation, and enforcement depend on the nature of the property. Real property depreciates more slowly than personal property, and real property owners generally have a longer time than personal property owners to make good unpaid taxes before the state seizes the property.

tangible property

Personal property (not real estate) that can be touched; e.g., tables, automobiles, books.

intangible property

Personal property that cannot actually be touched; e.g., patents, copyrights, good will.

public property

Property belonging to the government.

private property

Property not belonging to the government but rather owned by a private person (human being or corporation).

real property

Real estate; land.

personal property

All property that is not real estate (e.g., books, cows, tables, patents, stocks, copyrights).

Case

What Is Property?

> ### *In Re Marriage of Washburn*
> 677 P.2d 152 (Wash., 1968)

Dimmick, J.

[Two cases with similar facts were consolidated for decision.]

The cases at bar are representative of a situation which is so familiar as to be almost a cliché. A husband and wife make the mutual decision that one of them will support the other while he or she obtains a professional degree. The educational years will be lean ones for the family not only because of heavy educational expenses, but also because the student spouse will be able to earn little or nothing. Moreover, the supporting spouse may be called upon to postpone his or her own education or forgo promotions and other valuable career opportunities in order to find a job near the student spouse's school. These sacrifices are made in the mutual expectation that the family will enjoy a higher standard of living once the degree is obtained. But dissolution of the marriage intervenes. Because the family spent most of its financial resources on the degree, there may be few or no assets to be distributed. The student spouse has the degree and the increased earning potential that it represents, while the supporting spouse has only a dissolution decree.

Other courts have responded to this all too common situation in a variety of ways.

A few appellate courts adopt the view that the professional degree (or the enhanced earning potential which it represents) is property which must be valued and distributed upon dissolution of the marriage. These courts differ in their valuation of the degree or earning potential. *See* [Citations.]

Another line of cases holds that, although a professional degree is not property, the supporting spouse is entitled to restitution of the money he or she spent toward the attainment of the degree, in order to prevent unjust enrichment of the student spouse. The formula used to determine the amount of restitution varies from court to court. *See* [Citations.]

Still other courts find the solution in an award of maintenance to the supporting spouse. One court grants "reimbursement alimony" equal to the amount spent by the supporting spouse toward the education. [Citation]. Others recognize the contribution of the supporting spouse as a basis for awarding maintenance, but do not prescribe a formula for determining the amount. [Citations.]

Another approach is to consider the supporting spouse's contribution to the attainment of the professional degree when dividing marital assets between the parties. [Citations.]

Finally, some courts simply deny any recovery to the supporting spouse. [Citations.] Generally, these courts deny recovery because they cannot find a legal label for the requested award which seems to fit. Designation of the degree as "property" which may be valued and equitably divided is rejected because the degree, which cannot be sold, assigned or inherited, lacks the traditional attributes of property. [Citation.] Unjust enrichment, which would place a value on the supporting spouse's contribution, is rejected as inappropriate in the context of marriage, which is "more than an economic undertaking." [Citation.] Maintenance is rejected because the supporting spouse is capable of self-support. [Citation.] The ability to consider the supporting spouse's contribution in dividing marital assets is acknowledged, but proves useless because there are no assets. [Citation.]

In view of the fact that fault is an impermissible consideration in a dissolution proceeding in this state, we are disinclined to compensate the supporting spouse under the theory of unjust enrichment, as was done in [Citations]. Unjust enrichment is a contract implied at law requiring a person to make restitution to the extent he has been unjustly enriched. Not only must the person be enriched, but the enrichment must be unjust. [Citation] To require trial courts to determine whether the student spouse had been *unjustly* enriched by the efforts of the supporting spouse would invite the introduction of evidence as to who was at fault in the termination of the marriage before the fruits of the degree could be realized. Nor are we inclined to address at this time the somewhat metaphysical question of whether a professional degree is "property." However, we need not join the ranks of those courts which deny recovery. The liberal provisions of our dissolution of marriage act, codified in RCW 26.09, provide a flexible way for courts to fairly compensate supporting spouses in the state of Washington. * * *

When a person supports a spouse through professional school in the mutual expectation of future financial benefit to the community, but the marriage ends before that benefit can be realized, that circumstance is a "relevant factor" which must be considered in making a fair and equitable division of property and liabilities pursuant to [Washington law], or a just award of maintenance pursuant to [Washington law]. A professional degree confers high earning potential upon the holder. The student spouse should not walk away with this valuable advantage without compensating the person who helped him or her obtain it. * * *

The trial court may consider the supporting spouse's contribution and exercise its broad discretion to grant maintenance, thereby in effect allowing the supporting spouse to share, temporarily, in the lifestyle which he or she helped the student spouse to attain.

Case Questions

1. What difference does it make whether the degree and its future earning potential is "a factor to be considered" or "property subject to distribution"?
2. What if the parties had established, and were thought by their friends and family, to have a "committed" non-marital relationship, and that relationship broke up as here—what would the court do then?

Key Takeaway

Property law is old and complex because in a feudal, agricultural society (as England was after the Norman Conquest in 1066) property ownership was the source of status and wealth. Who had it, how it could be disposed of, and the rights associated with it, was a political issue. Property is not a thing; rather, it is a legal relationship between a person and a thing, by which the owner can exclude others from its use or possession. There are various classifications of property: public property, private property; tangible property, intangible property; and, most importantly, real property and personal property. These distinctions have legal consequences.

Exercises

1. Kristen buys a parcel of land on Marion Street, a new and publicly-maintained roadway. Her town's ordinances say that each property owner on a public street must also provide a sidewalk within ten feet of the curb. A year after buying the parcel, Kristen commissions a house to be built on the land, and the contractor begins by building a sidewalk in accordance with the town's ordinance. Is the sidewalk public property or private property? If it snows, and if Kristen fails to remove the snow, and it melts and ices over, and a pedestrian slips and falls, who is responsible for the pedestrian's injuries?
2. When can private property become public property? Does public property ever become private property?

9.2 The Law of Real Property

Learning Objectives

1. Understand how the ownership interest in real property may be acquired, financed, disposed of, and lost.
2. Know what forms property ownership may take—what "estates in land" a person may hold.
3. Understand what rights are connected with the possession and ownership of real estate.
4. Understand how non-owners may acquire the use of part of someone's property by right of an easement.

Acquiring and Disposing of Interests in Real Property

A hallmark of the idea of property is that it is a transferable interest, voluntarily or involuntarily.

Voluntary Transfers of Title

•

Voluntary Title Transfer in General

title

The right of ownership in property.

deed

A written instrument by which the ownership and title of land is conveyed.

"**Title**" to real estate means a person has legitimately acquired it from a predecessor, either from a previous private owner or—where most land titles originated in the United States—from the government.[5]

The **deed** is the formalized written document showing land ownership (title), a copy of which is filed with the local government land records office (usually the county auditor).

How Title is Voluntarily Transferred

- Sale
- Gift
- Testamentary Transfer: Upon the owner's death, through inheritance by a **will** (**testamentary transfer**—a "testament" is a will); if no will was left, title passes to logical heirs (children, grandchildren, cousins) by **intestacy** ("**intestate transfer**") according to the state's laws on intestacy.

Financing

Most people do not have enough money to buy land with cash; they buy it on time. There are three primary mechanisms.

- A real estate **mortgage** is one means by which a creditor gets security guaranteeing (more or less) that the debtor will pay up. The borrower/buyer/debtor/mortgagor signs a **promissory note** (usually just called a "note") which is a promise to repay the creditor the amounts borrowed, takes the borrowed money, buys the property, and gets title. To secure the loan, the creditor/**mortgagee** (bank) accepts from the debtor a mortgage by which the debtor says, "If I don't pay—if I default—you can sue me, get a judgment against me, and my interest in the property will be judicially foreclosed. Then you can sell it."[6] Here is an example of a mortgage (observe the reference to the promissory note):

will

A document signed and witnessed by which a person describes how his/her property should be disposed of upon death.

testamentary transfer

Transfer of property by will.

intestacy

The state of dying without a will; to "die intestate" is to leave no will.

intestate transfer

Transfer of the property of a deceased person according to the law when there is no will.

mortgage

A security interest in real property held by a creditor; if the debtor (mortgagor) defaults on the loan, the creditor (mortgagee) can take the property to satisfy the debt.

promissory note

Often simply a "note," a legal financial and debt instrument by which the debtor (maker) promises to pay the creditor money to satisfy an obligation.

mortgagee

One who holds a mortgage on real estate; if the mortgage debt is not paid, the mortgagee can foreclose (sell the property to satisfy the debt).

FIGURE 9.1 Sample Mortgage

Mortgage

This mortgage is made the _____ day of _____, 20 _____, between the mortgagor, [name of mortgagor], at [insert residence], and [name of mortgagee], mortgagee, at [insert residence].

To secure the payment of an indebtedness of $[numbers] _____ [written out] _____ dollars, to be paid on starting on the _____ day of _____, 20 _____ with interest to be computed from _____ at the rate of _____ % per year, and to be paid monthly, according to the promissory note of today's date, the mortgagor hereby mortgages to the mortgagee.

[address and legal description of the property].

And the mortgagor promises the mortgagee as follows:

1. That the mortgagor will pay the debt as provided.
2. That the mortgagor will keep the buildings on the premises insured against loss by fire for the benefit of the mortgagee; that s/he will assign and deliver the policies to the mortgagee; and that s/he will reimburse the mortgagee for any premiums paid for insurance made by the mortgagee on the mortgagor's default in insuring the buildings.
3. That no building on the premises shall be removed or demolished without the consent of the mortgagee.
4. That the whole principal sum and interest shall become due at the option of the mortgagee:
   - After default in the payment of any installment of principal or of interest for _____ days;
   - Or after default in the payment of any tax, water rate or assessment for _____ days, after notice and demand;
   - Or after default after notice and demand either in assigning and delivering the policies insuring the buildings against loss by fire to the mortgage;
   - Or in reimbursing the mortgagee for premiums paid on such insurance, as provided here;
5. That the mortgagor will pay all taxes, assessments or water rates, and if s/he defaults, the mortgagee may pay instead.
6. That the mortgagor within _____ days upon request in person or _____ days upon request by mail will furnish a written statement, properly acknowledged, of the amount due on this mortgage and whether any offsets or defenses exist against the mortgage debt.
7. That any notice and demand or request shall be in writing and may be served in person or by mail.
8. That the mortgagor warrants the title to the premises.

As evidence of this agreement between the parties, this mortgage is signed below by them.

_____ Mortgagor.

_____ Mortgagee.

- A deed of trust. Like a mortgage, a **deed of trust** secures a debt by placing a lien on the debtor's property, but with a deed of trust no lawsuit is needed if the debtor defaults and the creditor wants to take possession. Instead, the trustee—a disinterested third party who nominally holds title (often a title insurance company)—sells the property without judicial intervention for the benefit of the beneficiary/creditor. Foreclosing on a deed of trust is faster and less expensive than foreclosing on a mortgage.

- A real estate sales contract (also called a "**land contract**," or an "installment sales contract") is a sale where—unlike a mortgage or deed of trust—the seller retains title until the buyer completely performs; the buyer typically makes monthly installment payments. These kinds of contracts have been criticized as unfair, and are historically predatory. In these contracts for deed, the buyer makes payments directly to the seller over a period of time—often 30 years—and the seller promises to convey legal title to the home only when the full purchase price has been paid. If the buyer defaults at any time, the seller can cancel the contract through a process known as forfeiture, keep all payments, and evict the buyer. Where a mortgage arrangement would build equity for the mortgagor, the contract for deed builds none, and there are no rights to redeem at a foreclosure because the person making payments never had legal title. [7]

Involuntary Transfers of Title

Title to real estate is ordinarily "alienated"—disposed of—by voluntary sale, gift, or inheritance. Title can also be alienated *involuntarily* in four ways.

- Mortgage foreclosure, deed of trust foreclosure, sales contract cancellation, material or labor liens, judicial sale. If the buyer/owner fails to make payments or otherwise perform, he or she can lose the property to satisfy creditors' demands. If a "materialman" (an older legal term; perhaps today we would say "materialperson"?) supplies building materials for your remodel, or the contractor spends four weeks on the job, and you don't pay, the material- or service-provider usually has a lien under most states' laws, and may enforce that lien by executing on the property. While not a foreclosure as such, it has a similar effect; unless the owner pays off the lien, a sale would proceed to satisfy the amount of the lien.

- **Accession** is the addition of value to one's real (or personal) property. For example, by adding an addition to the house, or by a change in the meander of a river where the owner's rights "extend to the middle of the river" (or by a person spending time or money improving personal property, as where an artist changes marble from a rock into a statue).

- **Eminent domain** is the power of the government to take private property for public use with just compensation. Suppose Omar's property is taken by the government to expand the city airport; Omar will get paid for his land in a civil "condemnation proceeding," but he will lose title and right of possession..

- **Tax lien foreclosure**. If the land owner doesn't pay property taxes, the government will eventually seize the land and sell it at a tax foreclosure auction to get the money owed.

- **Adverse possession**. If a person goes on to and makes use of another's real estate, openly, and notoriously and hostile to the owner's interest, after a number of years (21 is common) the ownership and title transfer to the interloper. The number of years is less—as little as seven—if the interloper has some sort of quitclaim deed or other "color of title" on the public record. The point is to encourage owners to be vigilant about their ownership interest, and though the concept seems like something out of the Old West, it happens quite often. Gosling uses land he thinks is his, fences it off and uses it as if it were his for ten years. Then, he discovers the land is—or was—the neighbors. Not anymore: depending on the number of years specified by the state's statutes on real property, it may be Gosling's by adverse possession.

deed of trust

Title to real property is transferred to a trustee who (nominally) holds it as security for a debt; if the debt is not paid by the borrower, the trustee sells the property for the benefit of the lender.

land contract

The seller of real estate agrees to accept periodic (monthly) purchase payments from the buyer; at the end of the agree-to time if the buyer has paid, the seller delivers the deed.

accession

The addition of value to property, real or personal, whether by labor or naturally, as where an addition to a house is made, or an adjoining river changes course and ownership to the middle of the river creates additional contiguous land.

eminent domain

The right of the government to take private property for public use with just compensation.

tax lien foreclosure

The sale of a property by the government resulting from the property owner's failure to pay tax liabilities.

adverse possession

The involuntary transfer of title to land from its owner to one who has occupied the land according to the law; "squatters' rights."

Estates in Land

estate in land

Ownership interest in real estate.

In real property law, an **estate in land** is an interest in real property, ranging from absolute dominion and control to bare possession. Ordinarily when we think of property, we think of only one kind: absolute ownership. The owner of a car has the right to drive it, rebuild it, repaint it, sell it, or scrap it. The thought that an owner might lose her property when something happens doesn't fit with our concepts of personal property; but real property is different. You would probably think it very odd if you were sold a used car subject to the condition that you not paint it a different color—and that if you did, you would automatically be stripped of ownership; but land can be sold that way. Estates in land—ownership—can be sliced and diced in lots of ways.

Possessory Interests

present estate

A present ownership interest in real estate.

future estate

A property interest in which the privilege of possession is in the future.

fee simple

Complete ownership of real estate in the broadest property interest in the law.

non-freehold estate

Something less than complete ownership of real estate, e.g., a tenancy.

fee simple determinable

Complete ownership of real estate which, however, the ownership interest may be terminated by the happening of a future event ("To Sally, as long as she remains married to John.")

life estate

The ownership of land for the duration of a person's life.

easement

The right granted to one person to go onto or make some use of another's realty.

A person may have the *present* use of land (a **present estate**), or a *future* use (a **future estate**). The use may be complete, partial, or contingent.

- **Fee simple.**[8] This is full ownership of land, the highest interest; the owner can sell it, give it away, devise it (leave it to somebody in a will), or allow others to use the land now or in the future.
- **Non-freehold estate**. A person has some right to use land, but no ownership. This includes a leasehold, what a tenant gets for paying rent.
- **Fee simple determinable** (or defeasible). A person is granted rights in land, but the right may terminate upon the happening of some future event. Example: To the Southern Pacific Railroad so long as the property is used for rail lines." One hundred years later the railroad abandons the line; the property right reverts to the original owner's successors in interest (the people who own the underlying land today).
- **Life estate**. The ownership of land for the duration of a person's life; upon death the ownership may revert to the original owner, or pass to a third person. Example: Owner grants rights "To Deborah for her life and then to the Humane Society." The Humane Society has a future estate.
- **Easement**. A non-possessory right to use and/or enter onto the realty of another without possessing it.

Concurrent (Simultaneous) Possessory Interests

You do not have to form a corporation, limited partnership, or other type of business to acquire property with others; many other forms are available for personal or investment purposes.

- **Joint tenancy**. An estate in land owned by two or more persons. When one dies, the interest passes to the others.

- **Tenancy by the entireties**. About half the states permit husbands and wives to hold property as tenants by the entirety. This form of ownership is similar to joint tenancy, but is restricted to married persons. Neither party can dispose of the interest without the other's consent.

- **Tenancy in common**. A tenant in common holds an individual, undivided ownership interest in the property. Each party has the right to alienate (transfer) her ownership interest by deed, will, or otherwise.

- **Community property**. In ten states—Alaska, Arizona, California, Idaho, Louisiana, Nevada, New Mexico, Texas, Washington, and Wisconsin—property acquired during a marriage is said to be community property. With certain exceptions, each spouse has an undivided equal interest in property acquired while the spouses are married to each other.

- **Condominiums**. A form of joint ownership or control of real estate. Modernly, it refers to a form of housing involving two elements of ownership: first, the living space itself, and second, the common space in the building (roof, land under the structure, hallways, swimming pool, etc.). The common space is held by all purchasers as tenants in common.

- **Cooperatives**. The tenant of a cooperative does not own a particular unit. Instead, she owns a share of the entire building. Since the building is usually owned by a corporation (a cooperative corporation, hence the name), this means that the tenant owns stock in the corporation. A tenant occupies a unit under a lease from the corporation.

- **Time share**. A time-share is an arrangement by which several people can own the same property while being entitled to occupy the premises exclusively at different times on a recurring basis. In the typical vacation property, each owner has the exclusive right to use the apartment unit or cottage for a specified period each year—for example, the Smiths may have possession from December 15 through December 22, and the Jacksons from December 23 through December 30, and so on.

Key Takeaway

Property may be acquired or alienated (disposed of) voluntarily by transfer of title; usually a buyer will finance the purchase by a mortgage, deed of trust, or installment real estate contract. Property may also be acquired (or title to it alienated) involuntarily, by foreclosure of a real property security interest (mortgage foreclosure, deed of trust sale); by tax lien; the government's exercise of eminent domain (though it must pay); and by adverse possession.

Estates in land refers to the quality of one's rights as to real estate. A person may acquire the complete interest in land (fee simple), or less than the complete interest (life estate, leasehold, easement, etc.). And more than one person can have interest in the same real estate at the same time: joint tenancy, tenancy in common, community property, among others.

Exercises

1. Able's dog flushed a rabbit out of the underbrush; whereupon Baker, hunting rabbit, shot and killed it. Whose property is the rabbit now?

2. In the example above, what if Able's dog chased the (poor) rabbit until the rabbit was prostrate (on the ground) with exhaustion, and then Baker took (a euphemism for "killed") the rabbit; whose property is it now?

3. What is the difference between a mortgage and a deed of trust?

4. How is title to real property involuntarily alienated from its owner?

5. What is "adverse possession"? Why does the doctrine remain viable in the 21st century?

6. What kind of a property interest does a tenant have?

---

joint tenancy

Co-ownership of real estate; when one joint tenant dies, the interest passes to the others.

tenancy by the entireties

Co-ownership of land by a married couple (in states that do not have community property).

tenancy in common

Co-ownership of land; when one tenant dies, the interest passes to that person's heirs, not the other tenants in common.

community property

Co-ownership of land by a married couple.

condominiums

A multiple-unit complex wherein individual units are separately owned and all owners share in joint ownership of common areas.

cooperatives

A business owned and run by its members jointly; they share in the profits and benefits (or losses).

time share

Co-ownership of real estate, with each owner allotted a specific time to use the property; sometimes called "vacation ownership."

7. Able made a will giving Baker the right to use Blackacre for as long as Baker lives, and upon Baker's death, title shifts to Carr. What is the name of the interest that Baker got?
8. Why was community property introduced in the American western states?
9. What is the difference between joint tenancy and tenancy in common (and why would anybody care)?

9.3 Rights and Duties Incident to Possession and Ownership of Real Estate

Learning Objectives

1. Understand that property owners have certain rights in the airspace above their land, in the minerals beneath their land, and in water that adjoins their land.
2. Recognize that landowners have rights and duties as relates to their ownership.

Rights to Airspace, the Depths, and Water

At common law it was traditionally thought (or imagined) that a property owner owned a "wedge" of property from the center of the earth to the sky, that's not really the rule today.

Rights to Airspace

The traditional rule was stated by Lord Coke: "Whoever owns the soil owns up to the sky." Ownership of the sky can cause problems and it is subject to various limitations.

Is it a trespass when an airplane—or an earth satellite—flies over your backyard? The courts must balance the public interest in air travel and satellite transmission against landowners' rights. In *U.S. v. Causby*,[9] the Court determined that flights over private land may constitute a diminution in the property value if they are so low and so frequent as to be a direct and immediate interference with the enjoyment and use of land, but nobody has the right to shoot down an airplane. The low-flying of drones over residential property is also creating interesting legal issues.[10]

Rights to the Depths

Lord Coke's dictum applies to the depths as well as the sky. The owner of the surface has the right to the oil, gas, and minerals below it, although this right can be severed and sold separately. Perplexing questions may arise in the case of oil and gas, which can flow under the surface. Some states say that oil and gas can be owned by the owner of the surface land; others say that they are not owned until actually extracted—although the property owner may sell the exclusive right to extract them from his land.

Rights to Water

Water is of course essential for all life on Earth, and has long been recognized as a right. The Eastern states generally follow the English common-law **riparian system**[11] under which water is like sunlight or air; it is not "owned" by anybody, but the right to take it comes along with the land it falls upon, or then travels along the surface, and all landowners have a right to make reasonable use of it. If there's not enough water for everyone, water rights are allocated in proportion to frontage on the water source.

Western states have adopted a different system, the **prior appropriation doctrine**. This rule looks not to equality of interests but to priority in time—first in time is first in right. The first person to use the water for a beneficial purpose has a right superior to latecomers. This rule applies even if the first user takes all the water for his own needs and even if other users are riparian owners. This rule developed in water-scarce states in which development depended on incentives to use, rather than hoard, water.[12]

FIGURE 9.2 Water Rights

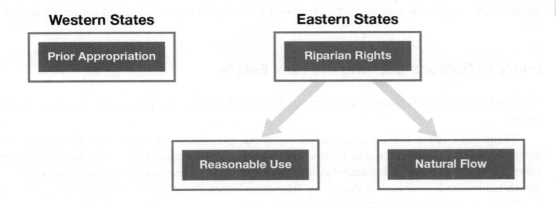

As the population relentlessly (and unsustainably) increases in the most apparently desirable places (like Seattle, San Francisco, and Boston) and demands on the finite supply of water multiply, legislation and lawsuits boil up with ever-increasing frequency, and increasing government regulation is necessary and inevitable.

Regulation of Land Use by Tort and by Private Agreement

Land use regulation falls into three broad categories: (1) restriction on the use of land through tort law (see Chapter 7); (2) private regulation by agreement (restrictive covenants, such as a neighborhood for residents "55 and older"); and (3) public ownership or regulation through the powers of eminent domain and zoning (eminent domain is taken up in Chapter 3).

riparian system water rights

A type of interest attaching to real estate ownership pertaining to the rights to use adjacent bodies of water; riparian rights are awarded to landowners whose property is located along flowing bodies of water such as rivers or streams.

prior appropriation doctrine

The first person to use water for a beneficial use has a right superior to latecomers.

Regulation of Land Use by Tort Law

Tort law is used to regulate land use in two ways: (1) The owner may become liable for certain activities carried out on the real estate that affect others beyond the real estate. (2) The owner may be liable to persons who, upon entering the real estate, are injured.

Landowner's Activities that Affect Others Beyond the Real Estate

The two most common torts in this area are nuisance and trespass.

nuisance

At common law, a thing or activity that substantially interferes with the use and enjoyment of an owner's property.

A common-law **nuisance** is an interference with the use and enjoyment of one's land. Examples of nuisances are excessive noise (especially late at night), polluting activities, and emissions of noxious odors. But the activity must produce substantial harm, not fleeting, minor injury, and it must produce those effects on the reasonable person, not on someone who is peculiarly allergic to the complained-of activity. A person who suffered migraine headaches at the sight of croquet or badminton being played on a neighbor's lawn would not likely win a nuisance lawsuit. While the meaning of nuisance is difficult to define with any precision, this common-law cause of action is a primary means for landowners to obtain damages for invasive environmental harms.[13]

trespass

The wrongful physical invasion of or entry upon land possessed by another.

A **trespass** is the wrongful physical invasion of, or entry upon, land possessed by another. Loud noise blaring out of speakers in the house next door might be a nuisance but could not be a trespass, because noise is not a physical invasion. But spraying pesticides on your gladiolas could constitute a trespass on your neighbor's property if some of the pesticide drifts across the boundary.

Injury to Persons Entering the Real Estate

Traditionally, liability for injury has depended on the status of the person who enters the real estate.

Trespassers. If the person is an intruder without permission—a trespasser—the landowner owes him no duty of care unless he knows of the intruder's presence, in which case the owner must exercise reasonable care in his activities and warn of hidden dangers on his land of which he is aware. Laura Landowner knows that Terry Trespasser habitually takes a shortcut along a corner of Laura's property; she must warn him if, say, she sprays dangerous insecticides on the path.

attractive nuisance

Something not naturally occurring on a landowner's property that is likely to attract children, to their injury; the landowner is liable for not protecting them.

Children. A landowner has a duty to protect children from being injured by structures or non-natural conditions that are likely to attract them (they have poor judgment). Old refrigerators, open gravel pits, or mechanisms that a curious child would find inviting are all examples of **attractive nuisance**. A child will clamber into an old rotted-out buggy on Farmer Brown's property, fall through the floor, and Mr. Brown will be liable—he should have seen it coming. Its ornamentation value is not comparable to the child's probably injury.

licensee

A non-trespasser who comes onto the land without invitation, or for purposes not connected with any business on the premises; e.g., a person soliciting door-to-door.

Licensees. A **licensee** is a non-trespasser who comes onto the land without invitation, or for purposes not connected with any business on the premises. That is, (1) social guests (people you invite to your home for a party); (2) a salesman, not invited by the owner, who wishes to sell something to the owner or occupier of the property; and (3) persons visiting a building for a purpose not connected with the business on the land (e.g., students who visit a factory to see how it works). The landowner owes the same duty of care to licensees that he owes to known trespassers.

Invitees. A final category of persons entering land is that of **invitee**. This is one who has been invited onto the land, usually, though not necessarily, for a business purpose of potential economic benefit to the owner or occupier of the premises. You'd think a social guest would be an invitee, but they are traditionally considered licensees. Invitees include customers of stores, users of athletic and other clubs, customers of repair shops, strollers through public parks, restaurant and theater patrons, hotel guests, and the like. The owner has an ordinary duty of care to avoid harming the invitee.

A Modern Trend. All this said, in recent years, some courts have moved away from the rigidities and sometimes perplexing differences between trespassers, licensees, and invitees. By court decision, several states have now abolished such distinctions and hold the proprietor, owner, or occupier liable for failing to maintain the premises in a reasonably safe condition.

Regulation of Land Use by Private Agreement

Tort law effectively can regulate, to some extent, what landowners do with their land by imposing liability for negligent use of land or for negligence in treating persons who enter the land. Private agreements—contracts—may also regulate land use.

An **easement** is an interest in land created by agreement between land owners. An easement permits one person to make use of another's estate. An easement must be distinguished from a mere license, which is permission, revocable at the will of the owner, to make use of the owner's land. An easement is an estate; a license is personal to the grantee and is not assignable.

The two main types of easements are affirmative and negative. An **affirmative easement** gives a landowner the right to use the land of another (e.g., crossing it or using water from it), while a **negative easement**, by contrast, prohibits the landowner from using his land in ways that would affect the holder of the easement. For example, the builder of a solar home would want to obtain negative easements from neighbors barring them from building structures on their land that would block sunlight from falling on the solar home. With the growth of solar energy, some states have begun to provide stronger protection by enacting laws that regulate one's ability to interfere with the enjoyment of sunlight. These laws range from a relatively weak statute in Colorado, which sets forth rules for obtaining easements, to the much stronger statute in California, which says in effect that the owner of a solar device has a vested right to continue to receive the sunlight.

Easements may be created by express agreement, either in deeds or in wills. The owner of the land benefited by the easement (the "dominant tenement"), may buy the easement from the owner of the the land "burdened" by the easement (the "servient tenement") or may reserve the easement for herself when selling part of her land.

An easement can also be implied from prior use. Suppose a seller of land has two lots, with a driveway connecting both lots to the street. The only way to gain access to the street from the back lot is to use the driveway, and the seller has always done so. If the seller now sells the back lot, the buyer can establish an easement in the driveway through the front lot if the prior use was (1) apparent at the time of sale, (2) continuous, and (3) reasonably necessary for the enjoyment of the back lot. The rule of implied easements through prior use operates only when the ownership of the dominant and servient tenements was originally in the same person.

The servient owner may use the easement—remember, it is on or under or above his land—as long as his use does not interfere with the rights of the easement owner. Suppose you have an easement to walk along a path on your neighbor's property to a lake. When you bought the easement the owner did not use the lake; now she wants to swim in it herself. You have no valid complaint: her swimming in the lake does not interfere with your right to swim. But if she proposed to clear the woods and build a mill on the land, obliterating the path and polluting the lake, you could get an injunction to stop her from interfering with your easement.

invitee

One who goes onto another's property, premises, or business establishment upon invitation, though the invitation need not be expressly made to an individual. An invitation will be implied when the premises is open and the public is expected to enter to inspect, purchase, or otherwise do business on the premises.

easement

The right given by a landowner permitting another person to make some use of the landowner's property.

affirmative easement

A grant by a landowner to another, allowing the other some right to use the land.

negative easement

A prohibition restraining a landowner from making some use of her real estate.

covenant

A term in a contract for land (usually in the deed) granting the landowner certain rights or curtailing certain rights of the landowner.

A **covenant** is a contract (in the old days solemnized by affixing a seal to the document, making it "formal"); it is a promise made in a deed or implied by law that creates an obligation burdening or favoring a landowner and applying to anybody who acquires ownership. For example, Able sells Baker real estate, Baker promising not to sell liquor on the premises, or Baker promising not to erect any buildings over two stories. If the covenant is intended to bind only the immediate party (Baker) it is "a covenant of a purely personal nature"; if the covenant is intended to bind all future owners of the land, it is said to be "a covenant running with the land."

Regulation of Land Use by the Government: Government Ownership, Eminent Domain, and Zoning

Government ownership. The U.S. federal government obtained ("took"? "acquired"? "stole"?) land from native peoples ("American Indians") in the 19th and early 20th centuries. The government as owner of that land can do what it wants with it, subject to the pressures of politics. National parks are federal land on which the landowner (the government) restricts what can go on there.

Eminent domain. The government—federal, state, local—can take private property for public use, as long as it pays the landowner just compensation. Issues of eminent domain are discussed in Chapter 3 and Chapter 12 Section 1.

Zoning. The government may restrict what uses a landowner may make of his, her, or its land through zoning (discussed in Chapter 12 Section 2).

Key Takeaway

Ownership interest in real property (an estate in land) takes various forms, and can be acquired by deed, inheritance, gift, easement, or adverse possession. Financing may be by cash, mortgage, deed of trust, or land contract. Loss of the estate may occur when the owner deeds (by sale or gift), devises (wills) the land, or if the government takes the land by eminent domain, or on tax foreclosure, or if the owner loses her interest (or part thereof) by adverse possession or upon foreclosure of a material or contractors' lien.

Property owners have certain rights in the airspace above their land, in subsurface minerals (like oil and gas). Property owners who have bodies of water adjacent to their land will also have rights to withdraw or impound water for their own use.

Property owners' rights to do what they want with their land can be restricted by tort law, contract law, and by government action.

Exercises

1. Jessa owns a house and lot on 9th Avenue. She sells the house to the Hartley family, who wish to have a conveyance from her that says, "to Harriet Hartley for life, remainder to her son, Alexander Sandridge." Alexander is married to Chloe, and they have three children, Carmen, Sarah, and Michael. Who has a future interest, and who has a present interest? What is the correct legal term for Harriet's estate? Do Alexander, Carmen, Sarah, or Michael have any part of the estate at the time Jessa conveys to Harriet using the stated language?

2. After Harriet dies, Alexander wants to sell the property. Alexander and Chloe's children are all eighteen years of age or older. Can he convey the property by his signature alone? Who else needs to sign?

3. Miguel and Maria Ramirez own property in Hendersonville, North Carolina as tenants by the entirety. Miguel is a named defendant in a lawsuit that alleges defamation, and an award is made for $245,000 against Miguel. The property he owns with Maria is worth $320,000 and is owned free of any mortgage interest. To what extent can the successful plaintiff recover damages by forcing a sale of the property?

4. Miguel and Maria Ramirez own property in Hendersonville, N.C. as tenants by the entirety; they divorce. At the time of the divorce, there are no new deeds signed or recorded. Are they now tenants in common or joint tenants?

5. David and Roger, a married couple in a community-property state, each come into the marriage with significant separately-owned property. Upon their marriage, do each of them now own the other's formerly separate property?

6. Steve Hannaford farms in western Nebraska. The farm has passed to succeeding generations of Hannafords, who use water from the North Platte River for irrigation purposes. The headlands of the North Platte are in Colorado, but use of the water from the North Platte by Nebraskans preceded use of the water by settlers in Colorado. What theory of water rights governs Nebraska and Colorado residents? Can the state of Colorado divert and use water in such a way that less of it reaches western Nebraska and the Hannaford farm? Why or why not?

7. Ricky Cava decides to put solar panels on the south face of his roof. Ricky lives on a block of one- and two-bedroom bungalows in South Miami, Florida. In 2018, someone purchased the house next door and within two years decided to add a second and third story. This proposed addition would significantly decrease the utility of Ricky's solar array. Does Ricky have any rights that would limit what his new neighbors can do on their own land?

9.4 The Law of Personal Property

Learning Objectives

1. Understand how rights in personal property are acquired and or lost.
2. Know what a fixture is, how some kinds of personal property can become real property, and how to determine who has rights in fixtures that are a part of real property.
3. Know what is meant by a "bailment" and some basics of bailment law.

The previous section took up the law of real property—land. This section takes up the law of personal property—things like books, barbecues, beach balls, and cement mixers.

Definition of Personal Property

Personal property is, again, all that is not real property.

Most legal issues about personal property center on its acquisition.

personal property

All property that is not real estate (e.g., books, cows, tables, patents, stocks, copyrights).

How Personal Property Is Acquired

Acquisition by purchase is the most common way we acquire personal property, but there are at least four other ways to legally acquire it:

accession

The addition of value to property, real or personal, whether by labor or naturally, as where an addition to a house is made, or an adjoining river changes course and ownership to the middle of the river creates additional contiguous land.

- Possession. It is often said that "possession is nine-tenths of the law." There is some truth to this, but it's not the whole truth. The more important question is, what is meant by "possession"? Its meaning is not intuitively obvious, as a moment's reflection will reveal. For example, you might suppose than you possess something when it is physically within your control, but what do you say when a hurricane deposits a boat onto your land? Or what if you give your class ring to a friend to examine; does the friend have possession? No, the friend has custody. Possession or physical control must usually be understood as the power to exclude others from using the personal property.

- Finding lost, misplaced, or abandoned property. "Finders keepers, losers weepers" is, at best, only partially true, and more often false. The owner of lost property is entitled to the return of the property (you don't get to keep the lost wallet you found on the street). If the owner fails to claim the property within the time allowed by statute or has abandoned it, then the property goes to the owner of the real estate on which it was found, or to the finder.[14] Obviously, a person can dispose of ownership of personal property by hopelessly losing it or throwing it away.

- Gift. This is of course a voluntary transfer of property without consideration; a person can give a gift (alienate the property) or receive a gift.

- **Accession**. An accession is something that is added to what one already possesses. The owner of the thing owns the additional thing that comes to be attached to it. For example, the owner of a cow owns her calves when she gives birth. But when one person adds value to another person's property, either through labor alone or by adding new materials (when goods are added to goods) the owner of the principal property or goods becomes the owner of the enhanced product. For example, a garage uses its paint to repaint its customer's automobile. The car owner, not the painter, is the owner of the finished product.[15]

Note that this is not an exhaustive list.

Fixtures

Definition

fixture

An object that was once personal property but that has become so affixed to land or structures that it is considered legally a part of the real property because the real estate is not useful without it (e.g., a door, window, or furnace).

A **fixture** is an object that was once personal property but that has become so affixed to land or structures that it is considered legally a part of the real property. For example, a stove bolted to the floor of a kitchen and connected to the gas lines is usually considered a fixture, either in a contract for sale, or for testamentary transfer (by will). For tax purposes, fixtures are treated as real property.

No clear line can be drawn between what is, and what is, not a fixture. In general, the courts look to three tests to determine whether an object has become a fixture. A fixture must be:

- *annexed* or affixed to the real property;

- *adapted to the use* of the real property, like home furnaces, power equipment in a mill, or computer systems in a bank; and

- *intended* that the object be a permanent part of the real estate.

FIGURE 9.3 Personal Property versus Real Property

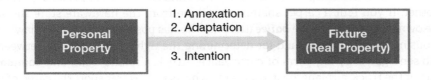

Disputes About Fixtures

Because fixtures have a hybrid nature (they are first personal property, then become real property, and may again be personal property), they generate a large number of disputes. We call out two here:

- Transfer of real estate. When a house or factory sells, the problem frequently crops up as to whether certain items in the place have been sold also, or may be removed by the seller. Is a refrigerator, which simply plugs into the wall, a fixture or an item of personal property? If a dispute arises, the courts will apply the three tests—annexation, adaptation, and intention. Of course, the simplest way of avoiding the dispute is to make clear reference to questionable items in the contract for sale, indicating whether they remain with the real property or not.

- Tenant's fixtures. Tenants frequently install fixtures in the buildings they rent or the property they occupy. A company may install tens of thousands of dollars' worth of equipment; a tenant in an apartment may bolt a bookshelf into the wall or install window shades. Who owns the fixtures when the tenant's lease expires? The older rule was that any fixture, determined by the usual tests, must remain with the landlord. Today, however, certain types of fixtures—known as tenant's fixtures—stay with the tenant: (1) trade fixtures—articles placed on the premises to enable the tenant to carry on his or her trade or business in the rented premises; (2) agricultural fixtures—devices installed to carry on farming activities (e.g., milling plants and silos); (3) domestic fixtures—items that make a tenant's personal life more comfortable (carpeting, screens, doors, washing machines, bookshelves, and the like). But the tenant will be liable for any damage caused in installing or removing such fixtures.

Bailments

We have touched on how personal property may be acquired and lost (ownership changes), and how it may become part of the real estate. Here we touch on bailments, which involves what happens to personal property when someone other than its owner has it or uses it (with the owner's permission).

Definition

A **bailment**[16] arises where one person has rightful use and possession of personal property belonging to another. If you rent a carpet shampoo machine from the hardware store the store is the **bailor** (the owner), and you are the **bailee** (the one who has possession). Bailment law is important for warehousing (a big business), and for determining the rights and liabilities between **shippers** (those who send goods by any form of conveyance—truck, airplane, boat) and **common carriers** (the owners of the truck, airplane, boat, train, etc.), who as bailees transport the cargo of people and firms paying for the transport.

Liabilities

Bailee's liability. To simplify somewhat, bailment disputes usually arise in application of this rule:

> *The bailee must return the bailed goods to the bailor according to their contract, or, in the case of common carriers, to deliver the goods as directed. Failure to do so gives rise to a presumption that the bailee was negligent, but the presumption may be rebutted if the bailee can show the loss was not caused by its negligence.*

For example, you take your down comforter to the dry cleaners, but when you go to pick it up it cannot be found; it is presumed the dry cleaner people were negligent (after all, they had custody of it, not you). But they might be able to show they were not—that it was stolen notwithstanding their reasonable security protocols. However, common carriers (those who transport goods for others) have strict liability—they are not only presumed negligent if the goods aren't delivered properly, they have no defense (well, limited defenses[17]).

Less often this rule comes into play: the bailor must give the bailee notice of dangers associated with the bailed goods. Suppose the bailor contracts to store goods in a warehouse but does not tell the warehouser that the goods are likely to off-gas potentially flammable fumes. The fumes accumulate in an unventilated space and cause an explosion. The bailor is liable for damages to the bailee's place; the bailee would have stored the goods with ventilation if it had known of the danger.

The potential liability of bailees is large in theory, but not so much in practice: almost always bailees, including common carriers, limit their liability in the contract with the bailor to a small amount (maybe $50). However, the bailor could declare to the bailee that the property is worth more, and pay to raise that limit if the bailee agrees.

Case

Found Property

Bishop v. Ellsworth

234 N.E. 2d 49 (Ill., 1968)

Stouder, J.

Dwayne Bishop, plaintiff, filed a complaint alleging that on July 21, 1965, defendants, Mark and Jeff Ellsworth and David Gibson, three small boys, entered his salvage yard premises at 427 Mulberry Street in Canton, without his permission, and while there happened upon a bottle partially embedded in the loose earth on top of a landfill, wherein they discovered the sum of $12,590 in U.S. currency [just about $100,000 in 2019 dollars]. It is further alleged that the boys delivered the money to the municipal chief of police who deposited it with defendant, Canton State Bank. The complaint also alleges defendants caused preliminary notices to be given as required by [the relevant Illinois statute], but that such statute or compliance therewith does not affect the rights of the plaintiff. [The trial court dismissed the plaintiff's complaint.]

It is defendant's contention that the provisions of [the Illinois Revised Statutes] * * * govern this case. The relevant portions of this statute are as follows:

> *Lost goods:*
>
> *The finder shall return lost goods to their owner; if the owner is unknown, the finder shall deposit the goods with the court. If the value of the goods is more than $15, the county clerk shall publish a notice for three weeks in a public newspaper in the state, and post a notice on the courthouse door and in three other public places for three weeks. If nobody claims the goods after one year, the finder becomes the owner.*

We think it apparent that the statute to which defendants make reference provides a means of vesting title to lost property in the finder where the prescribed search for the owner proves fruitless. * * * [The statute is] designed to provide a procedure whereby the discoverer of "lost" property may be vested with the ownership of the property even as against the true owner thereof, a right which theretofore did not exist at common law.

In the absence of any language in the statute from which the contrary can be inferred it must be assumed that the term "lost" was used in its generally accepted legal sense and no extension of the term was intended. Thus, the right to possession of discovered property still depends upon the relative rights of the discoverer and the owner of the *locus in quo* [scene of the event] and the distinctions which exist between property which is abandoned, mislaid, lost or is treasure trove.

* * * There is a presumption that the owner or occupant of land or premises has custody of property found on it or actually imbedded in the land. * * * If the premises on which the property is discovered are private it is deemed that the property discovered thereon is and always has been in the constructive possession of the owner of the premises and in a legal sense the property can be neither mislaid nor lost. [Citation.] The question of whether the property is mislaid or lost in a legal sense depends upon the intent of the true owner. The ownership or possession of the premises is an important factor in determining such intent. If the property be determined to be mislaid, the owner of the premises is entitled to the possession thereof against the discoverer. It would also appear that if the discoverer is a trespasser such trespasser can have no claim to possession of such property even if it might otherwise be considered lost.

* * * The facts as alleged are that the Plaintiff was the owner and in possession of real estate, that the money was discovered in a private area of said premises in a bottle partially imbedded in the soil and that such property was removed from the premises by the finders without any right or authority and in effect as trespassers. We believe the averment [claim] of facts in the complaint * * * is sufficient to state a cause of action. [The trial court's dismissal of the Plaintiff's complaint is reversed and the case is remanded.]

Case Questions

1. What is the actual result in this case? Do the young boys get any of the money that they found? Why or why not?

2. Who is Dwayne Bishop, and why is he a plaintiff here? Was it Bishop that put nearly $100,000 (in 2018 dollars) in U.S. currency in a bottle in the landfill at the salvage yard? If not, then who did?

3. If Bishop is not the original owner of the currency, what are the rights of the original owner in this case? Did the original owner "lose" the currency? Did the original owner "misplace" the currency? What difference does it make whether the original owner "lost" or "misplaced" the currency? Can the original owner, after viewing the legal advertisement, have a claim superior to Dwayne Bishop's claim?

Key Takeaway

Personal property is everything that is not real estate—land. It is acquired by purchase, devise, gift, accession, or—in some cases—it is acquired by finding it. Personal property can be converted to real property when it is affixed to real property; it is then a fixture, depending on the relevant circumstances of annexation, adaptation, and intention. Disputes over fixtures often arise in the transfer of real property and in landlord-tenant relations. The owner of goods—a bailor—may consign them to the custody and use of a bailee; the bailee has a duty to return the bailed goods as contracted, and is liable for failure to do so, unless it can show the loss was not the bailee's fault. A bailor may be liable for failure to warn the bailee of dangers associated with the bailed goods.

Exercises

1. Jim and Donna Wittmer contracted to sell their house in Charlevoix, Michigan, to Clem and Clara Hovenkamp. Clara thought that the decorative chandelier in the entryway was lovely and gave the house an immediate appeal. The chandelier was a gift from Donna's mother, "to enhance the entryway" and provide "a touch of beauty" for Jim and Donna's house. Clem and Clara assume that the chandelier will stay, and nothing specific is mentioned about the chandelier in the contract for sale. Clem and Clara are shocked when they move in and find the chandelier is gone. If the dispute cannot be mediated, on what basis would a court decide that the chandelier is a fixture, or not?

2. Blaine Goodfellow rented a house from Associated Properties in Abilene, Texas. He was there for two years, and during that time he installed a ceiling fan, custom-built a bookcase for an alcove on the main floor, and replaced the screening on the front and back doors, saving the old screening in the furnace room. When his lease expired, he leaves, and the bookcase remains behind. Blaine did, however, take the new screening after replacing it with the old screening, and he removed the ceiling fan and put back the light. He caused no damage to Associated Properties' house in doing any of this. Discuss who is the rightful owner of the screening, the bookcase, and the ceiling fan after the lease expires.

3. Paula Plaintiff took a valuable oriental rug to Rug Cleaners. When she went to pick it up, it could not be found. Which side bears the burden of proof in arguing about this case of negligence (or breach of contract)?

9.5 The Law of Estates and Trusts

Learning Objectives

1. Describe how property, both real and personal, can be devised and bequeathed to named heirs in a will.
2. Understand what happens to property when the decedent leaves no valid will.
3. Explain the requirements for "testamentary capacity"—the requisite mental state for someone to make a will that can be admitted to probate.
4. Describe the steps in the probate and administration of a will.
5. Understand some basic points about trusts, how they differ from a will, and how they are created and function.

Transfer of Property by Will

A **will** declares a person's wishes about the disposition of her assets when she dies. The will names the persons who are to receive specific items of real and personal property. A will has no effect as long as the person making the will lives. Wills have served their present function for virtually all of recorded history. The earliest known will is from 1800 BC (see Figure 9.4)[18]:

will

A document signed and witnessed by which a person describes how his/ her property should be disposed of upon death.

FIGURE 9.4 Sample Will

[Will of Uah] "I, Uah, devise to my wife Sheftu, the woman of Gesab called Teta, daughter of Sat Sepdu, all properties given to me by my brother Ankh-ren. She shall give it to whomsoever she may see fit of her issue born to me.

"I devise to her the Eastern slaves, 4 persons, that my brother Ankh-ren gave me. She shall give them to whomsoever she may see fit of her children.

"As to my tomb, let me be buried in it with my wife alone.

"Moreover, as to the house built for me by my brother Ankh-ren, my wife shall dwell therein and shall not be evicted by any person."

"The deputy Sebu shall act as guardian of my son. Done in the presence of these witnesses:

"Kemen, Decorator of Columns,

"Apu, Doorkeeper of the Temple,

"Senb, son of Senb, Doorkeeper of the Temple."

Usually, wills are written in standard form, but some special types of wills are enforceable in many states (e.g., oral wills declared in front of witnesses are only valid where the testator is dying as she declares the will; holographic wills, entirely in the testator's handwriting, not witnessed; soldiers' and sailors' wills, enforceable no matter how informal while the testator is in active service;) Wills can be changed expressly, or by operation of law.

Will Requirements

A valid will has four requirements. (1) The testator must have capacity—18 years old and of sound mind. (2) The will must be in writing.[19] (3) It must be signed. (4) There must be witnesses to the testator's signature.

Transfer of Property by Intestacy (Without a Will)

intestacy

The state of dying without a will; to "die intestate" is to leave no will.

Intestacy means dying without a will, and happens all too frequently. Even those who know the consequences for their heirs often put off making a will until it is too late—Abraham Lincoln, for one, who as an experienced lawyer knew very well the hazards to heirs of dying intestate. On his death, Lincoln's property was divided, with one-third going to his widow, one-third to a grown son, and one-third to a twelve-year-old son.

If you die without a will, the state dictates what happens to your property. Commonly, property of the deceased goes to the people she would probably want to get it: spouse, descendants, parents, grandparents, descendants of parents, children or grandchildren of grandparents, or great-grandchildren of grandparent—but the rules vary from state to state. If there are no such potential recipients, the property escheats The reversion of property—especially real property—to the state if the deceased left no will and no heirs. to the state.

Estate Administration

probate

The legal process of proving the validity of a will to the satisfaction of a court.

Probate is the process by which a deceased's estate is managed under the supervision of a court and probate laws vary considerably from state to state. In most states, the court supervising this process is a specialized probate court. Probate follows a general pattern in which the assets of an estate are located, collected, and disbursed according to the will or, if there is no will, according to the law of intestate succession. The National Conference of Commissioners on Uniform State Laws issued a Uniform Probate Code (UPC) in 1969; however, by 2018 it had been adopted in its entirety in only sixteen states,[20] while other states have adopted parts of the UPC.

executor

The person appointed in a will to wind up the affairs of the deceased and see that the terms of the will are followed.

If named in the will, the person who carries out the deceased's will is an **executor**. If the decedent dies intestate, the court will appoint an **administrator**, usually a close member of the family. The UPC uses the term **personal representative** for the executor or administrator.

administrator

A person who winds up the affairs of the deceased and oversees the distribution of the assets if there is no will, or executor.

The personal representative assembles the estate's assets, decides how and when to dispose of the assets (should a business be sold, liquidated, or kept going? Should securities be sold, and if so, when?), pays outstanding debts based on claims submitted by creditors, and pays appropriate federal and state taxes owed by the estate. (The inheritance tax—called the "death tax" by its opponents—seems to be fading away in the U.S. as part of an anti-tax enthusiasm prevalent since about 1980; its proponents worry about a revival of an aristocracy that the American colonies threw off in 1776 by the transfer of enormous wealth from one generation to the next). Then the assets can be distributed according to the will.

personal representative

An executor or administrator of an estate.

Trusts

The basic idea of a trust is that one person, the grantor (or settlor), designates assets she or he owns or controls (the assets of the trust are called the *res* to be administered by another, the trustee—a fiduciary—for the benefit of a third party, the beneficiary.

There are various kinds of trusts. Parents might set up a trust for their children upon reaching 35 years of age; a spendthrift trust constrains the trustee to limit the beneficiaries' access to the trust assets so they are not wasted; the blind trust is used by high government officials who are required by the Ethics in Government Act of 1978 to put their assets in trusts over which they have no control, or abstain from making decisions that affect any companies in which they have a financial stake. A charitable trust is one where the assets are devoted to some public purpose.

Trusts may be created expressly. Express trusts may be testamentary (effective upon the trustor's death) or *inter vivos* (living) trusts, which are effective during the testator's life. A trust may be revocable or irrevocable.

Trusts may also be created by implication. An implied trust arises without any agreement when it is fair and equitable that a person could be said to hold property for the benefit of another. Suppose you give $1 to an agent to purchase a lottery ticket for you, but the agent buys the ticket in his own name instead and wins $1,000,000, payable into an account in amounts of $50,000 per year for twenty years. Since the agent had violated his fiduciary obligation and unjustly enriched himself, the court would impose an implied or constructive trust on the account (the fact situation is *construed* to create a trust), and the agent would find himself holding the funds as trustee for you as beneficiary.

Key Takeaway

Any person with the requisite capacity may make a will and bequeath property to named heirs. Throughout the United States, there are some common requirements to be met for a will to qualify for probate. The law of each state sets forth certain formalities, such as the number of witnesses, to which written wills must adhere. In general, anyone over eighteen and of sound mind may make a will. It must be signed by the testator, and two or three others must witness the signature. A will may always be modified or revoked during the testator's lifetime, either expressly through certain actions, such as a subsequent marriage and the birth of children, not contemplated by the will. Wills are managed through the probate process, which varies from state to state, although many states have now adopted the Uniform Probate Code. An executor (or executrix) is the person named in the will to administer the estate and render a final accounting. Estate and inheritance taxes may be owed if the estate is large enough.

Intestacy statutes will govern where there is no will, and an administrator will be appointed by the probate court. Intestacy statutes will dictate which relatives will get what portion of the decedent's estate, portions that are likely to differ from what the decedent would have done had he or she left a valid will. Where there are no heirs, the decedent's property escheats to the state.

A trust is a relationship in which one person holds legal title to certain property and another person has the use and benefit of it. The settlor or grantor creates the trust, giving specific property (the res) to the trustee for the benefit of the beneficiary. Express trusts come in many forms: living or testamentary, revocable or irrevocable, fixed or discretionary. Trusts may also be imposed by law; constructive trusts are designed to redress frauds, prevent unjust enrichment, or see to it that the intent of the parties is carried out

Exercises

1. Governor-elect Mason has significant business interests throughout the state. What kind of a trust would she use to minimize any appearance of conflict of interest?
2. Roswald has income from a patent. He assigns the right to receive the income to Alice Able, but by mistake the licensee pays Roswald the royalty. Alice says to him, "You are a constructive trustee holding my money." What does that mean, and is Alice correct?
3. Roswald is worried that his daughter Rosalina will spend her eventual inheritance from him wastefully. What can he do to minimize that possibility?

9.6 Intellectual Property

Learning Objectives

1. Understand what a patent is, and what copyright means, how patents and copyrights are obtained, and how they differ from trademarks.
2. Understand the difference between patents and trade secrets, and why a company might choose to rely on trade secrets rather than obtain a patent.
3. Know why some "marks" may not be eligible for trademark protection, and how to obtain trademark protection for those that are.

Few businesses of any size could operate without being able to protect their rights to a particular type of intangible personal property—intellectual property. The major forms of intellectual property are:

- patents,
- copyrights,
- trademarks,
- trade secrets.

Unlike tangible personal property (machines, inventory) or real property (land, office buildings), intellectual property has no physicality. It is the product of the human intellect that is embodied in the goods and services a company offers and by which the company is known. An intellectual property right is the right to exclude others from gaining economic benefit from your own intellectual creation. The government protects intellectual property by granting the owners of patents, copyrights, and trademarks the right to the exclusive use of their property for limited periods of time, and infringers are subject to damages and injunctions.

Patents

Source of Authority and Duration

Patent (and copyright) law is federal, enacted by Congress under the power given by Article I of the Constitution "to promote the Progress of Science and useful Arts, by securing for limited Times to

Authors and Inventors the exclusive Right to their respective Writings and Discoveries." Under current law, a patent gives an inventor exclusive rights to make, use, or sell an invention for twenty years. (If the patent is a design patent—protecting the appearance rather than the function of an item—the period is fourteen years.) In return for this limited-time monopoly, the inventor must fully disclose, in papers filed in the U.S. Patent and Trademark Office (PTO), a complete description of the invention.

What Can Be Patented

Not just anything can be patented—laws of nature, scientific principles, mathematical algorithms and formulas are not patentable. A patent is not available just for an idea, but for its tangible, practical application. Patent law provides that to be patentable the invention must be:

> *any new and useful process, machine, manufacture, or composition of matter, or any new and useful improvement thereof . . . [A]ny new, original and ornamental design for an article of manufacture . . . [any asexual reproduction of a] distinct new variety of plant, including cultivated sprouts, mutants, hybrids[.]*

Patents can cover such innovations as gene sequence patenting and other biological patenting, provided that the patent applicant has in some way modified what was a "naturally occurring" gene or gene sequence. In the 2013 case of *Association for Molecular Pathology v. Myriad Genetics*, the U.S. Supreme Court ruled unanimously that "a naturally" occurring DNA segment is a product of nature and not patent eligible merely because it has been isolated."[21] Yet, an Australian high court had come to the opposite conclusion just months earlier.[22] Remarkably, animals can be patented—the first such patent was for a mouse whose genes were modified so it was very sensitive to cancer-causing agents; it is a valuable research tool.

If the invention satisfies the requirements noted, it must also be: (1) useful, (2) novel, and (3) unobvious; as one judge memorably put it, the thing must reflect "a flash of thought," not something (like a porcelain doorknob) that would be thought of by "any mechanic acquainted with the business."[23]

Obtaining a Patent

Obtaining a patent is an expensive and time-consuming process, and the inventor will need the services of a patent attorney, a highly specialized lawyer. In today's global market, obtaining a U.S. patent is important but is not usually sufficient protection. The inventor will often need to secure patent protection in other countries as well. The World Trade Organization's Agreement on Trade-Related Aspects of Intellectual Property Rights (TRIPS) established standards for protecting intellectual property rights (patents, trademarks, and copyrights) and provides that each member nation must have laws that protect intellectual property rights with effective access to judicial systems for pursuing civil and criminal penalties for violations of such rights. A patent issued by the PTO means that preliminary tests have been met, and usually, this indicates a valid, protectable patent, though it is not uncommon for patents to be disputed by other parties in litigation and sometimes declared invalid.

Rights of the Patentee

patentee

One who is awarded a patent by the U.S. Patent Office.

The patent holder, **patentee**, (the federal government is the "patentor") is entitled to make and market the invention and to exclude others from doing so. And, because the patent is a species of property, it may be transferred. The inventor may assign part or all of his interest in the patent, or keep the property interest and license others to manufacture or use the invention, in return for payments known as royalties, or as security for a loan.

Infringement Suits

infringement

Unauthorized use of patented material.

The patentee may claim its patent has been infringed on ("somebody's stealing my intellectual property!"); the "infringer" may deny the validity of the claimed patent. Following litigation, the court may grant the winner reimbursement for attorneys' fees and costs. If the **infringement** is adjudged to be intentional, the court can triple the amount of damages. Courts have the discretion to determine whether justice requires a permanent injunction, but they may conclude that the public interest and equitable principles may be better satisfied with compensatory damages only.

Copyright

Source and Duration

copyright law

Federal law giving authors and other creators of original works in a fixed medium a limited-time monopoly on profits from the works.

Copyright law is federal; like patent law, its source lies in the Constitution. Copyright protects the expression of ideas in some tangible form; it does not protect the ideas themselves. For example, the basic idea in the films *Freaky Friday*, *Dream a Little Dream*, and *Like Father Like Son* is that there is a comedic "body swap" of some sort (sister and sister, or parent and child) but the expressions of this basic idea are different, and so there is no copyright infringement.

A copyright in any work begins when the work is fixed in tangible form—for example, when a book is written down or a picture is painted—and generally lasts for the life of the author plus 70 years after his or her death. If there is co-authorship, the 70 years begins after the death of the second author.

public domain

Works that would be copyrightable if current, but which are so old as to be beyond the reach of copyright law (e.g., Shakespeare's plays are public domain).

For copyrights owned by corporations, copyright expires 95 years from the date of publication or 120 years from the date of creation, whichever is first. For works created before 1978, such as many of Walt Disney's movies and cartoons, the Sonny Bono Copyright Term Extension Act of 1998 retroactively provided additional protection of up to 95 years from publication date. Thus, works created in 1923 by Disney entered the **public domain** (free for anybody to use) in 2019. It seems likely that Disney will convince Congress to extend Disney's monopoly over Mickey Mouse for even longer.

In 1989, the United States signed the Berne Convention,[24] an international copyright treaty (conforming American law eliminated the need to place the symbol © or the word *Copyright* or the abbreviation *Copr.* on the work itself) which affords international copyright protection.

What Can Be Copyrighted

To be subject to copyright, three requirements apply:

1. The work must be "fixed" in some "tangible medium of expression." The Copyright Act protects literary works (books, newspapers, and magazines), music, drama, choreography, films, art,

sculpture, and sound recordings. Because expression is protected, not the material or physical object, a book may be copyrighted whether it is on paper, microfilm, tape, or computer file. Computer programs are copyrightable,[25] and so are two- or three-dimensional layouts or topographies of integrated circuits (called "mask works").[26]

2. The work also must be creative, at least to a minimal degree. Words and phrases, such as names, titles, and slogans, are not copyrightable; nor are symbols or designs familiar to the public. But an author who contributes her own creativity—like taking a photograph of nature—may copyright the resulting work, even if the basic elements of the composition were not of her making.

3. Finally, the work must be "original,"–it must have originated with the author. The law does not require that it be novel or unique. This requirement was summarized by Judge Learned Hand: "If by some magic a man who had never known it were to compose anew Keats's "Ode on a Grecian Urn," he would be an author, and, if he copyrighted it, others might not copy that poem, though they might of course copy Keats's."[27]

The Copyright Act *excludes* copyright protection for any "idea, procedure, process, system, method of operation, concept, principle, or discovery, regardless of the form in which it is described, explained, illustrated, or embodied." The *way* an idea is expressed (like this text's expression of business law) are copyrightable; *ideas* themselves (the laws affecting business) are not copyrightable.

How a Copyright Is Obtained

An idea that is fixed in some medium, adequately creative, and original, is *automatically* copyrighted when it is so fixed, but—notwithstanding the Berne Convention—use of the notice, "Copyright," or "Copr.," or ©, is still advisable to prevent an infringer from claiming innocent infringement (that the infringer did not know and should not have known that the conduct constituted infringement—it is a heavy burden of proof for the defendant[28]). *Registration* with the PTO, however, provides these benefits: it establishes a record of the holder's ownership, enables the owner to sue in federal court, allows the owner to claim statutory damages and attorneys' fees, and gives the owner protection against importation into the U.S. of infringing copies. Registration requires: (1) an application with the PTO, (2) a non-refundable filing fee (from $35–150), and (3) a non-returnable copy or copies deposited with the Copyright Office.[29]

Rights of the Copyright Holder

A copyright gives its holder the right to prevent others from copying the work. The holder has the exclusive right to reproduce the work in any medium (paper, film, sound recording), to perform it (e.g., in the case of a play), to display it (a painting or film), and to prepare derivative works based on the copyrighted work. Thus, a playwright could not adapt to the stage a novelist's book without the latter's permission.

A major exception to the copyright monopoly is the **fair use doctrine**.

Section 107 of the Copyright Act provides as follows:

Fair use of a copyrighted work, including such use by reproduction in copies or phonorecords or by any other means specified by section 106 of the copyright, for purposes such as criticism, comment, news reporting, teaching (including multiple copies for classroom use), scholarship, or research, is not an infringement of copyright. In determining whether the use made of a work in any particular case is a fair use, the factors to be considered shall include–

1. the purpose and character of the use, including whether such use is of a commercial nature or is for nonprofit educational purposes;

2. the nature of the copyrighted work;

fair use doctrine

Minimal use of copyrighted material for critical comment, review, or brief quotations that are exempt from copyright law.

3. the amount and substantiality of the portion used in relation to the copyrighted work as a whole; and

4. the effect of the use upon the potential market for, or value of, the copyrighted work.

These are broad guidelines; any copying could potentially be an infringement, and fair use becomes a question of fact on a case-by-case basis. In determining fair use, however, courts have often considered the fourth factor (effect of the use upon the potential market for the copyrighted work) to be the most important.

Clear examples of fair use would be when book reviewers or writers quote passages from copyrighted books. Without fair use, most writing would be useless because it could not readily be discussed. But fair use grew more troublesome with the advent of plain-paper copiers and is now even more troublesome with electronic versions of copyrighted materials that are easily copied and distributed. The 1976 act took note of the new copier technology, listing "teaching (including multiple copies for classroom use)" as fair use. The Copyright Office issues guidelines specifying just how far the copying may go—for example, multiple copies of certain works may be made for classroom use, but copies may not be used to substitute for copyrighted anthologies.

Infringement and Damages

Verbatim use of a copyrighted work is easily provable. The more difficult question arises when the copyrighted work is altered in some way. As in patent law, the test is whether there is substantial similarity between the original and the alleged infringement version. Courts may enjoin further infringement from the defendant, order destruction of the infringing material, and require the defendant/infringer to pay damages, profits earned, and attorney's fees.

The plaintiff can recover "actual damages" suffered, plus the plaintiff can recover the *defendant's* profits from the infringement. If the copyright is registered, without showing specific damages, the plaintiff can recover "statutory damages" (up to $100,000 for willful infringement). Also the plaintiff may get attorneys' fees, and there may be injunctive relief and seizure of infringing material as well.[30] Criminal penalties are also sometimes levied against the infringer (although the government brings criminal cases, not the private plaintiff).

Trademarks

Definition

A **trademark** is defined in the federal Lanham Act of 1946 as "any word, name, symbol, or device or any combination thereof adopted and used by a manufacturer or merchant to identify his goods and distinguish them from goods manufactured or sold by others."[31]

Examples of well-known trademarks are Coca-Cola, Xerox, and Apple. A **service mark** is used in the sale or advertising of services to identify the services of one person and distinguish them from the services of others. Examples of service marks are McDonald's, BP, and Hilton. A **certification mark** shows that work or labor on the goods or services was performed by members of a union or other organization. Examples are the Good Housekeeping Seal of Approval and UL (Underwriters Laboratories, Inc.) approval mark. The owner of the certification is not the owner of the underlying product.

Trademarks and other kinds of marks may consist of words and phrases, pictures, symbols, shapes, numerals, letters, slogans, and sounds. Trademarks are a part of our everyday world: the sounds of a radio or television network announcing itself (NBC, NPR), the shape of a whiskey bottle (Haig & Haig's Pinch Bottle), a series of initials (GE, KPMG, IBM), or an animal's warning growl (MGM's lion).

> **service mark**
>
> A trademark that represents a service instead of a product.
>
> **certification mark**
>
> A mark (e.g., "UL"—Underwriters Laboratories certification mark on products) indicating that the product to which it is affixed complies with appropriate industry-recognized standards.

Limitations on Marks

To qualify for protection, a trademark must be used to identify and distinguish. The courts employ a four-part test: (1) Is the mark so arbitrary and fanciful that it merits the widest protection? (2) Is it "suggestive" enough to warrant protection without proof of secondary meaning? (3) Is it merely "descriptive," unprotected unless secondary meaning—where the notoriety of the mark with the public provides protection even though the words are generic—is proven? (4) Is the mark "generic" and thus unprotectable?

Certain words and phrases may not qualify at all for trademark protection. These include generic terms like "straw broom" (for a broom made of straw) and ordinary words like "fast food." In one case, a federal appeals court held that the word "Lite" is generic and cannot be protected by a beer manufacturer to describe a low-calorie brew.[32] Donald Trump's effort to trademark "You're fired!" (from the television show, *The Apprentice*) was also dismissed as being generic. "Shredded Wheat" cannot be trademarked, but "Rice Krispies" can because "Krispies" is not really a word—it is fanciful.

Securing Trademark Protection

Trademarks have been protected at common law for five hundred years, and state statutory law may provide additional benefits for marks used only in *one* state. But federal registration provides these benefits: (1) it shows trademark ownership; (2) provides notice of ownership for the PTO's online trademark search system[33]; (3) provides nationwide protection; (4) provides protection against importation into the U.S. of trademark-violating imports; and (5) allows access to federal court jurisdiction and enhanced damage awards. Registration can be obtained in advance by registering with the PTO an intention to use the mark within six months; once obtained the trademark will be protected for ten years and if after that time the mark is still being used, the registration can be renewed. Those who feel that their own marks would be hurt by registration of a proposed mark may file an opposition proceeding with the PTO.

Loss of Rights

Trademark owners may lose their rights if they abandon the mark, if a patent or copyright expires on which the mark is based, or if the mark becomes generic. A mark is abandoned if a company goes out of business and ceases selling the product.

The most widespread difficulty that a trademark holder faces is the prospect of too much success: if a trademark comes to stand generically for the product itself, it may lose exclusivity in the mark. Famous examples are aspirin (but Aspirin remains a trademark in Canada), escalator, and cellophane. The threat is a continual one. If enough people describe web searches as "Googling," Alphabet may lose its trademark protection over the "Google" trademark. In short, trademark holders must be vigilant.

Trade Secrets

Definition

A **trade secret** is a means to a monopoly that a company hopes to maintain by preventing public disclosure. Why not always take out a patent—couldn't Coca-Cola take out a patent on its secret formula? There are several reasons owners don't go the patent route. The trade secret might be one that is not patentable, such as a customer list or an improvement that does not meet the tests of novelty or non-obviousness. A patent can be designed around; but if the trade secret is kept, its owner will be the exclusive user of it. Patents are expensive to obtain, and the process is extremely time consuming. Patent protection expires in twenty years, after which anyone is free to use the invention, but a trade secret can be maintained for as long as the secret is kept.

However, a trade secret is valuable only so long as it is kept secret. Once it is publicly revealed, by whatever means, anyone is free to use it. Here is the difference between a patent and a trade secret: a patent gives its owner the right to enjoin anyone who infringes it from making use of it, whereas a trade secret is not public—as patents must be—and gives its "owner" the right to sue only the person who improperly took it or revealed it.

According to the Restatement of Torts, Section 757, Comment b, a trade secret may consist of:

> any formula, pattern, device or compilation of information which is used in one's business, and which gives him an opportunity to obtain an advantage over competitors who do not know or use it. It may be a formula for a chemical compound, a process of manufacturing, treating or preserving materials, a pattern for a machine or other device, or a list of customers....A trade secret is a process or device for continuous use in the operation of a business. Generally it relates to the production of goods, as, for example, a machine or formula for the production of an article.

Other types of trade secrets are customer information, pricing data, marketing methods, sources of supply, and secret technical know-how.

Elements of Trade Secrets

To be entitled to protection, a trade secret must be: (1) original, and (2) secret.

1. Original. The trade secret must have a certain degree of originality, although not as much as would be necessary to secure a patent. For example, a principle or technique that is common knowledge does not become a protectable trade secret merely because a particular company taught it to one of its employees who now wants to leave to work for a competitor.

2. Secret. Some types of information are obviously secret, like the chemical formula that is jealously guarded through an elaborate security system within the company. But a method is not secret simply because someone develops and uses it, if no steps are taken to guard it. A company that hopes to keep its processes and designs secret should affirmatively attempt to do

so—for example, by requiring employees to sign a nondisclosure agreement covering the corporate trade secrets with which they work. (However, a company need not go to every extreme to guard a trade secret.)

Trade-secrets espionage is a big business, and in order to protect industrial secrets, U.S. corporations spend billions on security arrangements. The line between competitive intelligence gathering and espionage can sometimes be difficult to draw. The problem is by no means confined to the United States; companies and nations all over the world have become concerned about theft of trade secrets to gain competitive advantage, and all governments are widely believed to be involved in espionage and cyberattacks.

The **Economic Espionage Act** (EEA) of 1996 makes the theft or misappropriation of commercial trade secrets a federal crime. Penalties for violation are fines of up to U.S.$500,000 per offense and imprisonment of up to fifteen years for individuals, and fines of up to U.S.$10 million for organizations. The EEA is meant to apply to companies worldwide, although getting jurisdiction over foreign firms or sovereigns who "hack" into company servers can be difficult.

> **Economic Espionage Act**
>
> Theft or misappropriation of a trade secret is a federal crime.

Right of Employees to Use Trade Secrets

A perennial source of lawsuits in the trade secrets arena is the employee who is hired away by a competitor, allegedly taking trade secrets along with her. Companies frequently seek to prevent piracy by requiring employees to sign confidentiality agreements. An agreement—express or implied—not to disclose particular trade secrets learned or developed on the job is generally enforceable—one of the duties of an agent is confidentiality. However, courts also hold that as a matter of public policy, every person has the right to earn a living. The courts do not prohibit people from using the general knowledge and skills they developed on the job elsewhere. Only specific trade secrets are protected. To get around this difficulty, some companies require their employees to sign agreements not to compete. But unless the agreements are limited in scope and duration, to protect a company against only specific misuse of trade secrets, they are unenforceable.

Case

Enforcing Trademark Protection

> ### *Dallas Cowboys Cheerleaders, Inc. v. Pussycat Cinema, Ltd.*
>
> 467 F. Supp. 366 (SDNY, 1979)

> **Dallas Cowboys Cheerleaders, Inc. v. Pussycat Cinema, Ltd.**
>
> New York Federal District Court case, 1979, analyzing trade mark misappropriation.

[Plaintiff obtained an injunction against defendant Pussycat Cinema, Ltd., prohibiting the showing of the movie here; enforcement for contempt resulted in the arrest of people responsible for its showing. Plaintiff Dallas Cowboys Cheerleaders then moved for an injunction against defendant Zaffarano, the owner of Pussycat Cinema, prohibiting his showing of the defendant's pornographic movie. This case is the trial court judge's brief.]

Griesa, J.

The Dallas Cowboys Cheerleaders came into being in 1972. They have appeared at professional football games since that time. At these games they perform choreographed cheerleading and dance routines. Through these games they have become known to millions of persons attending the games and watching them on television. They have become a highly popular entertainment group. * * *

Plaintiff also licenses the use of the Dallas Cowboys Cheerleaders name and the distinctive uniform used by the cheerleaders for use in connection with certain products such as posters, playing cards, calendars, and T shirts. Plaintiff derives substantial revenues from this licensing.

Plaintiff has exercised substantial effort and care to promote the popularity of the Dallas Cowboys Cheerleaders and to give them a particular public image. The members of the 36-member group are carefully chosen. Thousands have applied for the small number of positions available. Not only must the cheerleaders have physical beauty, but they must also have dancing ability and they must represent various occupations which can be thought to constitute something of the cross-section of the American woman.

The Dallas Cowboys Cheerleaders must meet standards regarding moral character. For instance, no one is accepted who has been photographed for magazines such as Playboy or Hustler.

The Dallas Cowboys Cheerleaders are also known by the somewhat shorter names of Dallas Cheerleaders and Dallas Cowgirls. The uniform in which they appear and perform consists of a blue bolero blouse, white vest decorated with three blue five-pointed stars on each side of the front of the vest and white fringe at the bottom of the vest, tight white shorts with a belt decorated with blue stars, and white boots.

The evidence shows that the names Dallas Cowboys Cheerleaders, Dallas Cheerleaders, and Dallas Cowgirls have become identified in the public mind with plaintiff's cheerleader group. The evidence further shows that the Dallas Cowboys Cheerleaders uniform has come to be identified as the distinctive uniform of plaintiff's group, and is associated with the Dallas Cowboys Cheerleaders as distinguished from other entertainment groups. This identification and association have been acquired through use of the uniform in Dallas Cowboys Cheerleaders performances and appearances, both live and on television, over a period of years, and through the use of the uniform in the licensed products already described.

It appears that the "world premiere" of Debbie Does Dallas occurred at the Pussycat Cinema at 49th and Broadway, New York City, in October 1978. Plaintiff hoped that the film would promptly pass out of existence and that no court action would be required. However, the film kept showing in New York City, and plaintiff learned of the arrangements for distribution elsewhere. Therefore this action was commenced. * * *

The film Debbie Does Dallas lasts for 90 minutes. It has no other purpose than to display sex acts in minute detail. * * * The main character of the film is Debbie, played by one Bambi Woods. * * * Debbie has been selected to become a cheerleader in Dallas. Although there is no explicit reference to Dallas Cowboys Cheerleaders as being the group she is to join, this idea is clearly intended to be conveyed to the viewer. Debbie needs to finance her trip to Dallas, and for some unexplained reason her six friends wish to accompany her to Dallas, and also need money for their expenses. They decide to offer sexual services to various local businessmen. * * *

While the film was playing at the original theater, Pussycat Cinema, there was a large marquee, each side of which contained a picture of Debbie in the uniform closely resembling the Dallas Cowboys Cheerleaders uniform. Also, the marquee contained the title of the film and the slogan "STARRING EX DALLAS COWGIRL CHEERLEADER BAMBI WOODS." Below the marquee, on each side of the theater entrance, was a large poster showing Debbie in the same uniform appearing on the marquee, with even more emphasis upon the features of the Dallas Cowboys Cheerleaders uniform. On these posters there was a quotation from Sir Magazine, starting with the phrase "Cheers for X-Dallas Cowgirl Bambi Woods!" * * * Bambi Woods is not now, and never has been, a Dallas Cowboys Cheerleader.

Section 43(a) of the Lanham Act, 15 U.S.C. § 1125(a) provides:

Anyone who sends goods or services into commerce, knowingly using false representations regarding their origin, or anyone who knowingly transports such goods, is civilly liable to any person who is likely damaged thereby.

New York General Business Law § 368-d, known as the Antidilution Law, provides:

Likelihood of injury to business reputation or of dilution of the distinctive quality of a mark or trade name shall be a ground for injunctive relief in cases of infringement of a mark registered or not registered or in cases of unfair competition, notwithstanding the absence of competition between the parties or the absence of confusion as to the source of goods or services.

Plaintiff contends that the showing and advertising of Debbie Does Dallas involves the misappropriation of plaintiff's service marks and trademarks, and further creates a misleading and confusing association of Debbie Does Dallas with plaintiff's cheerleader group, in violation of Section 43(a) of the Lanham Act. Plaintiff further contends that the showing and advertising of Debbie Does Dallas dilutes the quality of plaintiff's trade name and service marks and trademarks in violation of New York General Business Law § 368-d.

* * * The defense contends that the film is a parody or satire on female cheerleaders, and that, even though there is some reference to Dallas and some use of a uniform similar to that of the Dallas Cowgirls Cheerleaders in the film, no one could rationally believe that the film originated with plaintiff or is associated with plaintiff. The defense contends that the film violates neither of the statutes referred to, and is protected by the First Amendment. The defense argues that, even if certain elements of the advertising and promotion should be enjoined, the injunction should not reach the film itself.

We come to the question of whether plaintiff has a valid common law trademark and service mark in the uniform of the Dallas Cowboys Cheerleaders. The specific elements of the uniform their color, design, and ornamentation are distinctive and arbitrary, and thus susceptible of becoming a valid trademark and service mark. [Citations.] The evidence shows that the uniform has acquired a secondary meaning associated with the Dallas Cowboys Cheerleaders. [Citations.]

Defendant Zaffarano argues that color may not be trademarked. While a person cannot acquire a trademark by color alone, color taken in connection with other characteristics can be an element of a trademark. [Citations.]

I hold that the Dallas Cowboys Cheerleaders uniform is a valid trademark and service mark belonging to plaintiff. * * *

Section 43(a) of the Lanham Act makes illegal the use of "a false designation of origin" with respect to goods or services, "or any false description or representation, including words or other symbols tending falsely to describe or represent" the goods or services.

In considering the question of whether there is a tendency to deceive or a likelihood of confusion within the purview of the statute, it must be realized that the buying public includes the unthinking and the credulous. The public cannot be expected to analyze or carefully weigh what is presented to them in promotion and advertisements. The question is what is the likely ultimate *impression*, upon customers and potential customers of the relevant services and products which will be created by what is said and what is reasonably implied. * * *

In the copyright area, one means of accommodation between the conflicting interests [free speech v. copyright protection] is the "fair use" doctrine, which permits certain use of copyrighted material to be made for purposes such as news reporting, criticism, scholarship and parody and satire. [Citations.] * * *

Defendant Zaffarano argues that the doctrine of "fair use" is applicable in a trademark case and that the movie Debbie Does Dallas is a parody or satire not subject to legal restriction. * * *

I find that the movie is in no sense a parody or satire.

A parody is a work in which the language or style or another work is closely imitated or mimicked for comic effect or ridicule. A satire is a work which holds up the vices or shortcomings of an individual or institution to ridicule or derision, usually with an intent to stimulate change; the use of wit, irony or sarcasm for the purpose of exposing and discrediting vice or folly.

In the present case, there is no content, by way of story line or otherwise, which could conceivably place the movie Debbie Does Dallas within any definition of parody or satire. The purpose of the movie has nothing to do with humor; it has nothing to do with a commentary, either by ridicule or otherwise, upon the Dallas Cowboys Cheerleaders. * * *

The next question is whether there is a sufficient showing of likelihood of deception or confusion to bring the case within Section 43(a) of the Lanham Act. * * *

In the present case, I find that the movie Debbie Does Dallas and its advertising create a likelihood of confusing members of the public as to the sponsorship of the movie by the Dallas Cowboys Cheerleaders and the participation of a member of the group in the film. Consequently I hold that Debbie Does Dallas and its advertising violate Section 43(a) of the Lanham Act.

I also find that the showing and advertising of Debbie Does Dallas threaten irreparable harm to plaintiff. It is apparent that defendant Zaffarano, if not enjoined, will not only resume the showing of the film in New York, but will arrange for its distribution and exhibition throughout the country. It follows from the findings I have already made that these activities threaten widespread confusion in the public mind as to the association of plaintiff and its cheerleaders with pornographic films. The harm to plaintiff's reputation and standing is obvious.

I also hold that plaintiff has made out a valid case under the New York Anti-dilution Law. Defendant Zaffarano, and the others associated with him in the production, distribution and promotion of Debbie Does Dallas, have willfully misappropriated plaintiff's trade names and trademarks and service marks. If such activities are allowed to continue, there will inevitably be a dilution, or whittling down, of the reputation and good will associated with plaintiff's names and marks.

Certainly a preliminary injunction is warranted.

Case Questions

1. Do you agree that no one would rationally believe that the film originated with the Dallas Cowboys or the Dallas Cowgirls? If no one would rationally believe this, how could there be any damage suffered by, or any remedy, for the plaintiffs?
2. In creating judgment for the plaintiffs, is the Court actually infringing the right of free expression by the defendants? It's a "free country," right? The First Amendment says that Congress shall make no law infringing the right of free speech or the press. How can you reconcile the federal and state statutes here with the First Amendment?
3. Plaintiff's case for "dilution" under New York State law requires them to prove "likelihood of injury to business reputation or of dilution of the distinctive quality of a mark or trade name." Even if society as a whole might be better off without films like "Debbie Does Dallas," do you think that the narrative and evidence here show by a preponderance of the evidence that there is "injury" to the Dallas Cowboys business reputation? Dilution of the distinctive quality of the mark and/or trade name? Explain.
4. What is a "preliminary injunction"?

Key Takeaway

Products of the human mind are at the root of all business, but they are legally protectable only to a certain degree. Inventions that are truly novel may qualify for a twenty-year patent; the inventor may then prohibit anyone from using the art (machine, process, manufacture, and the like) or license it on her own terms. A business may sue a person who improperly gives away its legitimate trade secrets, but it may not prevent others from using the unpatented trade secret once publicly disclosed. Writers or painters, sculptors, composers, and other creative artists may generally protect the expression of their ideas for the duration of their lives plus seventy years, as long as the ideas are fixed in some tangible medium. That means that they may prevent others from copying their words (or painting, etc.), but they may not prevent anyone from talking about or using their ideas. Finally, one who markets a product or service may protect its trademark or service or other mark that is distinctive or has taken on a secondary meaning, but may lose it if the mark becomes the generic term for the goods or services.

Exercises

1. Samuel Morse filed claims in the U.S. Patent Office for his invention of the telegraph and also for the "use of the motive power of the electric or galvanic current…however developed, for marking or printing intelligible characters, signs or letters at any distances." For which claim, if any, was he entitled to a patent? Why?

2. In 1957, an inventor dreamed up and constructed a certain new kind of computer. He kept his invention a secret. Two years later, another inventor who conceived the same machine filed a patent application. The first inventor, learning of the patent application, filed for his own patent in 1963. Who is entitled to the patent, assuming that the invention was truly novel and "non-obvious"? Why?

3. A large company discovered that a small company was infringing one of its patents. It wrote the small company and asked it to stop. The small company denied that it was infringing. Because of personnel changes in the large company, the correspondence file was lost and only rediscovered eight years later. The large company sued. What would be the result? Why?

4. Clifford Witter was a dance instructor at the Arthur Murray Dance Studios in Cleveland. As a condition of employment, he signed a contract not to work for a competitor. Subsequently, he was hired by the Fred Astaire Dancing Studios, where he taught the method that he had learned at Arthur Murray. Arthur Murray sued to enforce the noncompete contract. What would be the result? What additional information, if any, would you need to know to decide the case?

5. Greenberg worked for Buckingham Wax as its chief chemist, developing chemical formulas for products by testing other companies' formulas and modifying them. Brite Products bought Buckingham's goods and resold them under its own name. Greenberg went to work for Brite, where he helped Brite make chemicals substantially similar to the ones it had been buying from Buckingham. Greenberg had never made any written or oral commitment to Buckingham restricting his use of the chemical formulas he developed. May Buckingham stop Greenberg from working for Brite? May it stop him from working on formulas learned while working at Buckingham? Why?

9.7 Summary and Exercises

Summary

The roots of real property law—the law governing real estate—go back to feudal England. Personal property law—the law governing things is not real estate or attached to real estate—also has ancient roots. But property is not a thing, rather, it is a power or relationship that a person has over something: to exclude others from them, to buy and sell and transfer ownership.

Property is classified as tangible (physically existing), intangible (like patents, stocks), public, private, real, and personal. The distinctions have legal implications.

Real property is usually acquired by purchase, but a person (including corporate person) can acquire it by gift, inheritance, and by adverse possession ("squatters' rights"). Financing to acquire real property is typically by mortgage, deed of trust, or installment land contract. Title to real property can be involuntarily lost by mortgage, tax, or lien foreclosure, by the government's exercise of eminent domain, or by adverse possession.

The interest a person has in real estate is an estate in land; the interest can be variously divided: present or future estate; fee simple or non-freehold (leasehold); or determinable, or for a person's life (life estate); or easement. Or, indeed, combinations of these. And there are concurrent estates in land: joint tenancy, community property, condominiums, among others.

The owner of land traditionally has rights to airspace above, to depths below, and to water. Water rights vary from state to state.

Personal property is all that's not real property. It may be acquired or lost by purchase; possession (sometimes); finding lost, misplaced, or abandoned property (sometimes); gift, or accession (an adding-on to something already owned).

Fixtures are items of personal property that have become attached to it so that it is part of the real estate (like windows, furnaces). An item is a fixture if it is annexed to, adapted for, and was intended to be part of the real estate. Disputes about fixtures arise when real estate is sold: does the air conditioner go as personal property, or stay as a fixture? And can a tenant who installs a fixture remove it when the tenancy ends?

A bailment arises where the owner of personal property (the "bailor") delivers the property into the custody or possession of another (the bailee). The bailee is presumed negligent if the bailed goods are not returned in reasonable condition, but the bailee may rebut the presumption by showing that the loss was not caused by the bailee's negligence. The bailor may be liable to the bailee for failure to warn of dangers associated with the bailed goods.

When a person dies his or her property is disposed of by will, or if no will, by the state laws governing intestacy. The executor or administrator assembles the estate, pays expenses and taxes, and distributes it to the beneficiaries. A trust is created when the owner of property ("trustor") consigns it to the hands of a trustee who administers it for the benefit of the beneficiary in accordance with the trustor's plan. Trust may be created expressly or by implication; they may be testamentary (effective upon the trustor's death) or inter vivos (between the living).

Patents are a kind of intangible intellectual property; patent law is exclusively federal. A person who successfully secures a patent for a new patentable thing (it's not easy) is given a temporary government monopoly to make money from it, and may sue infringers. Copyright is also federal intellectual property law. When a work is fixed in tangible form (book, recording) it is copyrighted and can't be copied (except for "fair use"), but broader benefits, including statutory damages for infringement, flow from registration of the copyrighted material.

Trademarks, service marks, and certification marks are protected at common law and by state statute, but registration under the federal Lanham Act (1946) provides nationwide protection, among other benefits. Trademarks may be lost if the mark becomes generic. Trade secrets are formulas, patterns, devices used in business that are original, secret, and that offer their owner a competitive advantage. They are protected under common law from unauthorized use; such a use is tort. Generally employees are not allowed to take trade secrets with them when they leave an employer.

Exercises

1. Owner hired Carpenter to remodel part of her old house. While demolishing a wall to enlarge the dining room, Carpenter found a metal box. He opened it; it contained gold and silver coins and 19th century U.S. currency. Carpenter gave the box to Owner, saying, "You won't be able to find the owner, so in a couple of months I claim the money. I found it." As between Carpenter and Owner, who gets the valuables and why?

2. Plaintiff, a licensed aircraft inspector employed by Ace Aviation, unscrewed several panels from the underside of an airplane as part of routine maintenance. The corporate plane was owned by Jensen, Inc. Two of the screws were so rusty they had to be broken off—the panels apparently had not been removed for several years. Inside the left wing Plaintiff discovered two packets about four inches high, carefully tied with twine, and wrapped in aluminum foil. Inside the packets was paper currency, tied in string and wrapped in hand-kerchiefs. The currency was predominately twenty-dollar bills with mint dates primarily in the 1950s; the bills smelled musty. Local police impounded the money. The court recognized that property can be: (1) *abandoned* (thrown away), and its finder is the owner; (2) *lost* (its owner involuntarily parts with it and does not know where it is), and the finder is the owner after statutory procedures are followed and the true owner makes no claim within 12 months; (3) *mislaid* (intentionally put someplace and the owner forgets where), and the owner of the premises upon which it is found is the owner; or (4) *treasure trove* (valuables concealed by the owner, with the element of antiquity about them), and the finder gets them. Who gets the money here, and why? *Benjamin v. Linder Aviation, Inc.*, 534 NW2d 400 (Iowa, 1995).

3. Plaintiff stored her grand piano with Senge Storage. Through no fault of either Senge or Plaintiff the warehouse caught fire and the piano was destroyed. Who suffers the loss, Senge or Plaintiff?

4. Plaintiff delivered her classic Mustang automobile to Garage for repairs; she parked it in Garage's lot which held about 80 cars and was fenced in on three sides, the street side excepting. It was not guarded at night, but—like all the car places on auto row—the police made periodic checks. During the night of April 4, thieves stole the hood, radiator cap, alternator and carburetor, a loss of some $2,800. The car remained on Garage's lot and the next day the rear lights, gas cap, and the steering wheel were stolen, a loss of about $850. Who suffers the loss for the first theft? The second theft? Explain.

5. Owner sold her real property (legally described) to her nephew Nephling. The land had on it a house containing beds, tables, chairs, and a built-in stereo case and built-in bookshelves in the study; a garage and shop containing extensive woodworking tools (planers, lathes, drill presses, built-in cabinets, and a toilet; a remodeled barn with a sink and numerous lawn and garden tools (rakes, shovels, axes); and a storage shed containing large amounts of valuable rough-sawn maple wood stacked to dry. Which of these items passed to Nephling and which did not?

6. Calvin Klein shipped $150,000 worth of blouses via Trylon Trucking Co. from New York City to Princeton, New Jersey. The contract provided "Trylon's liability is limited to $50 unless the shipper [Calvin Klein] declares greater value and pays an insurance surcharge." Trylon's driver stole the shipment and it was never recovered. Calvin Klein claimed the liability limitation was so low as to be unconscionable and sued Trylon for the lost goods. Who wins and why?

7. Dickens sold a farm to Able "for his life, and upon Able's death, to Baker." Some years later oil was discovered in the area, and Able contracted with an oil company to drill for it. Baker sued to enjoin (stop) the drilling. As between Able and Baker, who wins and why?

8. Wanda oversaw acquisitions for her company. Because water was important to company operations, Wanda bought a plant site on a river, and the company built a plant that used almost all the river water. Downstream owners brought suit to stop the company from using so much water. What is the result? Why?

9. After her last business law class, Ingrid casually threw her textbook into a trash can and muttered to herself, "I'm glad I don't have to read that stuff anymore." Tom immediately retrieved the book from the can. Days later, Ingrid realized that the book might come in handy, saw Tom with it, and demanded that he return the book. Tom refused. Who is entitled to the book? Why?

10. In the exercise above, suppose that Ingrid had accidentally left the book on a table in a restaurant. Tom found it, and chanting "Finders keepers, losers weepers," he refused to return the book. Is Ingrid entitled to the book? Why?

11. Above, if the owner of the book (Ingrid) were never found, who would be entitled to the book—the owner of the restaurant or Tom? Why?

12. Barbara has a substantial estate and no relatives. Is there any reason for her to consider a will or trust? Why? If she dies without a will, what will happen to her property?

Self-Test Questions

1. The person or institution holding a mortgage is called:
   a. the mortgagor
   b. the mortgagee
   c. the debtor
   d. none of the above

2. Mortgages are regulated by:
   a. the Truth in Lending Act
   b. the Equal Credit Opportunity Act
   c. the Real Estate Settlement Procedures Act
   d. all of the above

3. At the closing, a mortgagor signs:
   a. only a mortgage
   b. only a note
   c. either a note or the mortgage
   d. both a note and the mortgage

4. Mortgages are terminated by:
   a. repayment
   b. novation
   c. foreclosure
   d. any of the above

5. A lien ordered against a person's property to prevent its disposal during a lawsuit is called:
   a. a judgment lien
   b. an attachment lien
   c. a possessory lien
   d. none of the above

6. Which of the following cannot be protected under patent, copyright, or trademark law?
   a. a synthesized molecule
   b. a one-line book title
   c. a one-line advertising jingle
   d. a one-word company name

7. Which of the following does not expire by law?
   a. a closely guarded trade secret not released to the public
   b. a patent granted by the U.S. Patent and Trademark Office
   c. a copyright registered in the U.S. Copyright Office
   d. a federal trademark registered under the Lanham Act

8. A sculptor casts a marble statue of a three-winged bird. To protect against copying, the sculptor can obtain which of the following?

   a. a patent

   b. a trademark

   c. a copyright

   d. none of the above

9. A stock analyst discovers a new system for increasing the value of a stock portfolio. He may protect against use of his system by other people by securing:

   a. a patent

   b. a copyright

   c. a trademark

   d. none of the above

10. A company prints up its customer list for use by its sales staff. The cover page carries a notice that says "confidential." A rival salesman gets a copy of the list. The company can sue to recover the list because the list is:

    a. patented

    b. copyrighted

    c. a trade secret

    d. none of the above

11. A freehold estate is defined as an estate:

    a. with an uncertain duration

    b. due to expire at a definite time

    c. owned now but not yet available for use

    d. that is leased or rented

12. A fee simple defeasible is a type of:

    a. present estate

    b. future estate

    c. life estate

    d. leasehold estate

13. A reversion is:

    a. a present estate that prevents transfer of land out of the family

    b. a form of life estate

    c. a future estate that arises when the estate transferred has a duration less than that originally owned by the transferor

    d. identical to a remainder interest

14. An easement is an interest in land that may be created by:

    a. express agreement

    b. prior use

    c. necessity

    d. all of the above

15. The prior appropriation doctrine:

    a. tends to be applied by Eastern states

    b. holds that first in time is first in right

    c. gives those that live along a waterway special rights to use the water

    d. all of the above

16. Personal property is defined as property that is:

    a. not a chattel

    b. owned by an individual

    c. movable

    d. immovable

17. Personal property can be acquired by:

    a. accession

    b. finding

    c. gift

    d. all of the above

18. A gift causa mortis is:

    a. an irrevocable gift

    b. a gift made after death

    c. a gift made in contemplation of death

    d. none of the above

19. To make a gift effective,

    a. the donor must intend to make a gift

    b. the donor must either make out a deed or deliver the gift to the donee

    c. the donee must accept the gift

    d. all of the above are required

20. Tenant's fixtures:

    a. always remain as property of the landlord

    b. remain the property of the tenant in all cases

    c. remain the property of the tenant if they are removable without substantial damage to the landlord's property

    d. refer to any fixture installed by a tenant

Self-Test Answers

1. b
2. d
3. d
4. d
5. b
6. b
7. a
8. c
9. d
10. c
11. a
12. a
13. c
14. d
15. b
16. c
17. d
18. c
19. d
20. c

Endnotes

1. Hernando de Soto, The Mystery of Capital: Why Capitalism Triumphs in the West and Fails Everywhere Else (2000)

2. It is worth noting that property ownership is of course still a big deal: everything in our built environment—all the stuff in the world—is either grown on the land or mined from it (except maybe the odd trinket made from meteorites).

3. As of 1611, the British hierarchy was, from most august to least: King, Duke, Marquis, Earl (European "Count"). Viscount, Baron, Baronet. It is marvelously complicated. Check this out: http://dankoboldt.com/feudal-nobility-guide/.

4. Sarah Hsu, China is Finally Improving Property Rights Protections, *Forbes*, Nov. 30, 2016. https://www.forbes.com/sites/sarahsu/2016/11/30/china-improving-property-rights-protections/#7bb534096e5c

5. Where did the government get land title to give to private persons? Native Americans—Indians (that is actually the legal term, absurd as it is)—had no conception of land ownership as we know it. European settlers and their successors could not figure out how to acquire legal title to the land, so they simply took it by force, and prepared treaties for the Indians to sign by which the latter gave away the land, keeping for themselves "reservations"—land never taken by the conquerors, but left for the Indians to have.

6. Usually we think of a mortgage as a device to fund a real estate purchase: for a homeowner to buy her house, or for a commercial entity to buy real estate (e.g., an office building), or for a person to purchase farmland. But the value in real estate can be mortgaged for almost any purpose (a home equity loan): a person can take out a mortgage on land to fund a vacation. Indeed, during the period leading up to the recession in 2007–08, a lot of people borrowed money on their houses to buy things: boats, new cars, furniture, and so on. Unfortunately, it turned out that some of the real estate used as collateral was overvalued (cue bank scandals here): when the economy weakened and people lost income or their jobs, they couldn't make the mortgage payments. And, to make things worse, the value of the real estate sometimes sank too, so that the debtors owed more on the property than it was worth (that's called being "underwater"). They couldn't sell without taking a loss, and they couldn't make the payments. Some debtors just walked away, leaving the banks with a large number of houses, commercial buildings, and even shopping centers on their hands.

7. Between 1930 and the late 1960s, the exclusion of African Americans from the conventional mortgage market made it easy to sell land contracts with inflated prices and harsh terms to those in credit-starved communities of color and in impoverished rural areas. The "land contract" has made a comeback in post-2008 foreclosures; large companies, with backing from private equity, are buying up large numbers of foreclosed homes, many from Fannie Mae and Freddie Mac's bulk sales, and peddling them to credit-impaired people through land contracts.

8. "Fee simple" comes from the Latin "feudum," the core element of feudalism. It was the inheritable property or rights (in land, or in government offices, or to the right of exploiting as fishing, hunting, trade monopolies) granted by an overlord to a vassal who held it "in fealty" or "in fee" in return for feudal loyalty and services.

9. *U.S. v. Causby*, 328 U.S. 256 (1946).

10. Gary Wickert, Drone Wars: Airspace and Legal Rights in the Age of Drones. http://www.claimsjournal.com/news/national/2015/07/02/264216.htm.

11. "Riparian" relates to living or located on the bank of a natural watercourse. In England one might encounter a "riparian villa": a house on a river. In the U.S. it would be "a riverside house."

12. Alaska, Arizona, California, Colorado, Hawaii, Idaho, Kansas, Montana, Nebraska, Nevada, New Mexico, North Dakota, Oklahoma, Oregon, South Dakota, Utah, Washington, and Wyoming all use the prior appropriation doctrine.

13. See http://tort.laws.com/nuisance.

14. The personal property goes to the owner of real estate on which it was found if: (1) the finder was a trespasser, (2) the goods are found in a private place (though what exactly constitutes a private place is open to question: is the aisle of a grocery store a private place? the back of the food rack? the stockroom?), (3) the goods are buried, or (4) the goods are misplaced rather than lost. Otherwise it's finder's keepers.

15. But a problem arises when the converter has added to the value of that property. In general, the courts hold that when the conversion is willful, the owner is entitled to the full value of the goods as enhanced by the converter. Suppose that a carpenter enters a ten-acre forest that he knows belongs to his neighbor, cuts down one hundred trees, transports them to his shop, and cuts them up into standard lumber, thus increasing their market value. The owner is entitled to this full value, and the carpenter will get nothing for his trouble. Thus the willful converter loses the value of his labor or materials. If, on the other hand, the conversion was innocent, or at most negligent, the rule is somewhat more uncertain. Generally the courts will award the forest owner the value of the standing timber, giving the carpenter the excess attributable to his labor and transportation. A more favorable treatment of the owner is to give her the full value of the lumber as cut, remitting to the carpenter the value of his expenses.

16. The word "bailment" comes from the French for "to bear a burden" or "to carry a responsibility." If you bail out a boat, you carry the water in a pail; when the government bails out a bank, it assumes the bank's responsibility to its customers. If you bail a friend out of jail, you bear the burden of making sure he shows up for court next time. How come from the French? Goes back to the Norman Conquest of England in 1066. The Normans spoke (early) French.

17. There actually are defenses: (1) negligence of the shipper (your sister didn't package the crystal goblets she sent you properly, and they got broken en route; (2) inherent nature of the goods (fruits and vegetables spoil, living plants or animals may become diseased or die through no fault of the carrier); (3) act of the public enemy (foreigners drop bombs on the U.S.—not bad guys committing crimes; (4) act of God or nature (earthquake hits railroad tracks, train crashes, goods destroyed). And the carrier will almost always limit its liability by contract; the shipper can buy insurance to reduce the limitation of liability.

18. Source: John H. Wigmore, *A Panorama of the World's Legal Systems*, vol. 1, p. 22.

19. Typically, the written will has the following provisions: (1) a "publication clause," listing the testator's name and his or her intention to make a will; (2) a "revocation clause," revoking all previously made wills; (3) burial instructions; (4) debt payments, listing specific assets to be used; (5) bequests, which are gifts of personal property by will; (6) devises, which are gifts of real property by will; (7) a "residuary clause," disposing of all property not covered by a specific bequest or devise; (8) a "penalty clause," stating a penalty for anyone named in the will who contests the will; (9) the name of minor children's guardian; and (10) the name of the executor

20. Alaska, Arizona, Colorado, Florida, Hawaii, Idaho, Maine, Michigan, Minnesota, Montana, Nebraska, New Mexico, North Dakota, South Carolina, South Dakota, and Utah.

21. Adam Liptak, "Justices, 9–0, Bar Patenting Human Genes," *New York Times*, June 13, 2013.

22. Amy Corderoy, "Landmark patent ruling over breast cancer gene BRCA1," *Sydney Morning Herald*, Feb. 15, 2013.

23. *Brown v. Piper*, 91 U.S. 37 (1875).

24. Berne Convention: http://www.wipo.int/treaties/en/ip/berne/summary_berne.html

25. *Apple Computer, Inc. v. Franklin Computer Corp.*, 714 F.2d 1240 (3d Cir. 1983).

26. The 1998 Digital Millennium Copyright Act (DMCA) implements two 1996 treaties of the World Intellectual Property Organization. It criminalizes production and sale of devices or services intended to get around protective measures that control access to copyrighted works. In addition, the DMCA heightens the penalties for copyright infringement on the Internet. The DMCA amended Title 17 of the United States Code to extend the reach of copyright, while limiting the liability of the providers of online services for copyright infringement by their users.

27. *Sheldon v. Metro-Goldwyn Pictures Corp.*, 81 F.2d 49 (2d Cir. 1936).

28. *National Football League v. Primetime 24 Joint Venture*, 131 F.Supp.2d 458, 476 (S.D.N.Y. 2001)

29. The PTO has helpful information on its websites. Check out https://www.copyright.gov/docs/fees.html

30. 17 U.S.C. 504.

31. 15 U.S.C. 1127

32. *Miller Brewing Co. v. Falstaff Brewing Corp.*, 655 F.2d 5 (1st Cir. 1981).

33. Check it out: http://tmsearch.uspto.gov/bin/gate.exe?f=searchss&state=4809:2rjxx.1.1

CHAPTER 10
Agency Law

Chapter Learning Objectives

After reading this chapter, you should understand:

1. Why agency law is important.
2. How agency relationships are created.
3. Definitions of agency-related terminology.
4. The general rules for agency regarding torts, the rationale for the rules, and specific areas of concern including who is the employer, what is "the scope of employment," and liability for intentional torts and crimes.
5. The general rule for agency regarding contracts, the rationale for the rule, and specific areas of concern, including how the agent gets authority to act for the principal, and duties owed among the parties.
6. How agency relationships are terminated.

Agency law is the law of vicarious liability—how one legal entity (a person or a corporation) can be responsible for the torts or breaches of contract committed or made by another. Agency law is integral to understanding how business organizations (like partnerships or corporations) work, and it is the basis for imposing significant liability on persons who, superficially, did nothing "wrong" at all.

10.1 Introduction to Agency

Learning Objectives

1. Understand why agency law is important.
2. Understand how agency relationships are created.
3. Understand the basic agency rules, and the rationale for the rules.
4. Learn the appropriate terminology.

Why Agency Law Is Important and How Agencies are Created

An **agent** is a person who acts in the name of, and on behalf of, another, having been given and assumed some degree of authority to do so. Most organized human activity—and virtually all commercial activity—is carried on through agency. No corporation would be possible, even in theory,

agent

One who acts on behalf of another.

without such a concept. We might say "General Motors is building cars in China," for example, but we can't shake hands with General Motors. "The General," as people sometimes refer to the corporation, exists and works through agents. Likewise, partnerships and other business organizations rely extensively on agents to conduct their business. Indeed, it is no exaggeration to say that agency is the cornerstone of enterprise organization. In a partnership each partner is a general agent, while under corporation law the officers and all employees are agents of the corporation. Agency is from the common law, and the rules have grown up over seven hundred years and remain matters of everyday importance.

How Agency Relationships Are Created: Types of Agents

agency

A fiduciary relationship created expressly or impliedly by which one person (the agent) may legally act on behalf of another (the principal).

gratuitous agency

An agency wherein the agent is not compensated.

power of attorney

A written authorization by one person to act or represent on another's behalf.

implied agency

An agency created by an implied contract.

apparent agency

An agency created by an apparent contract.

An **agency** is a relationship between the principal (or employer) and the agent (or employee) whereby the principal becomes liable for the agent's actions. It can be created by any of the ways that a contract can be created: expressly, impliedly, apparently, or by ratification or operation of law; it can be created by agreement that does not amount to a contract. Contracts require consideration, but it is not unusual for one person to act as an agent for another without consideration. For example, Abe asks Byron to run some errands for him—to buy some lumber on his account at the local lumberyard. Even such a **gratuitous agency** creates legal results similar to the more common contractual agency.

An express agency is one created by contract orally or in writing. A **power of attorney**, whereby one person (the principal) authorizes another (the agent) to act in her stead, is a type of express, written agency contract; a power of attorney may be general or limited to a specific function. It is not necessary for the agent to be compensated for her actions to trigger the creations of an agency relationship.

An **implied agency** arises based on the parties' actions; actions that imply they have mutually agreed to the contractual agency relationship, based on custom and usage, or acquiescence. Suppose Robert goes to a coffee shop where the barista tells him if he orders a scone he gets a free latte. The barista has implied authority to make the offer because he works for the coffee shop and is acting on behalf of its manager, the principal. When an employee wears a badge, uniform, name tag, or has a business card with the name or logo of a company, it is implied that she is an employee with authority to do what is reasonably related to the business.

Apparent agency arises where a reasonable third party would understand that, under the circumstances, the person with whom he is dealing would be authorized to conduct business on behalf of the principal, when in fact the person so authorized is not an agent at all—there is no agency contract.

In *Weingart v. Directoire Restaurant* (NY, 1972), Buster Douglas was not a restaurant employee. Yet, with the clear knowledge of the Directoire Restaurant, he stationed himself in front of the restaurant, wore a doorman's uniform, and parked patrons' cars. He parked the plaintiff's 1967 Cadillac Coupe de Ville, but later, when the plaintiff called for it, it could not be found. The court held that "although Douglas was not an actual employee of the restaurant, defendant held him out as its authorized agent or 'employee' for the purpose of parking its customers' cars, by expressly consenting to his standing, in uniform, in front of its door to receive customers, to park their cars and issue receipts therefor—which services were rendered without charge to the restaurant's customers, except for any gratuity paid to Douglas. Clearly, under these circumstances, apparent authority has been shown and acted within the scope of this authority."

FIGURE 10.1 1967 Cadillac Coupe DeVille

Source: Sergey Kohl / Shutterstock.com

Or again, suppose Arthur is Paul's agent, employed through October 31. On November 1, Arthur buys materials at Lumber Yard—as he has been doing since early spring—and charges them to Paul's account. Lumber Yard, not knowing that Arthur's employment terminated the day before, bills Paul. Will Paul have to pay? Yes, because the termination of the agency was not communicated to Lumber Yard. It reasonably appeared to the seller that Arthur was an agent authorized to purchase the materials.

In some circumstances the law imposes an agency relationship upon the parties when they did not specifically agree to that; this is agency by operation of law. For example, in partnership law all of the partners are agents and principals of each other. Or, again, it may arise where for some reason the "agent" must act to preserve the principal's property or interests, as in an emergency.

Agency by ratification comes about when the principal subsequently approves of its agent's acts where the agent lacked actual authority to legally bind the principal.

Definitions

As always, definitions are key.

Agency. Agency is the fiduciary relationship that arises when one person (a "principal") manifests assent to another person (an "agent") that the agent shall act on the principal's behalf and subject to the principal's control, and the agent manifests assent or otherwise consents so to act.

Agent. An employee, one who is authorized to make contracts for the principal. Agents come in several types:

- A **general agent** has the authority to carry out a broad range of transactions in the name, and on behalf of the principal. The general agent may be the manager of a business or may have a more limited but nevertheless ongoing role—for example, as a purchasing agent or as a life insurance agent authorized to sign up customers for the home office. In either case, the general agent has authority to alter the principal's legal relationships with third parties. One who is designated a general agent has the authority to act in any way required by the principal's business. One common form of a personal general agent is where one holds another's power of attorney. This is a delegation of authority to another to act instead of the principal.

- A **special agent** is one who has authority to act only in a specifically designated instance or in a specifically designated set of transactions. For example, a residential real estate broker is usually a special agent hired to find a buyer for the principal's house.

- A **subagent** is an agent of the agent.

agency by ratification

An agency created when a person acts on behalf of another without agency authority, but the principal accepts and approves the act.

general agent

An agent authorized to represent a principal in matters of a general nature.

special agent

An agent with authority to do one thing, as buy a commercial building for the principal.

subagent

The agent of an agent.

FIGURE 10.2 General Power of Attorney

General Power of Attorney

I, _____, of (address) _____, hereby appoint
_____, of (address) _____, to be my agent and attorney
in fact. I grant my agent full authority and power to act on my behalf to do anything I
could do if I were personally present.

Signed _____; date _____.

In witness:

_____

_____

{Acknowledgement by notary}

employee

One who is hired by the employer to work, and whose work is subject to direct supervision and control by the employer.

Employee. The common-law term here was "servant," in the sense that the employer could tell the employee what, where, when, and how to do whatever the employee was hired to do. That is, a person is, or was, a "servant" when the hiring party controls, or has the right to control, the means and manner of the performance. Although "employer-employee" is more commonly used today, the hierarchy expressed in "master-servant" reflects the historical legal view in the U.S. that employees can be discharged from their service for no reason at all. "Employment at will" is the default relationship in U.S. law, only modified by judicial common law or by legislation that secures certain rights for employees, such as the Americans with Disabilities Act or the Civil Rights Act of 1964.[1]

independent contractor

One who is hired by contract to accomplish a task or do a job, but the one hiring has no direct control over how the job is done (as one would hire a plumber or lawyer).

Independent contractor. A hired person is an independent contractor when he "is not controlled by the other nor subject to the other's right to control with respect to his physical conduct in the performance of the undertaking" (quoting the Restatement of Agency)[2]. You hire a plumber to fix your leaky sink, but you don't tell him what tools to use or how to do the job. The plumber is an independent contractor.

The Basic Agency Rules

vicarious liability

Liability imposed upon one person (the principal) for torts committed by another (the agent or employee).

Agency law concerns **vicarious liability**—the liability of one person for what someone else did. Agency operates in two categories, tort and contract:

Tort. The **respondeat superior doctrine** (Latin for "let the superior—the boss—be responsible) says that the employer is liable for torts committed by the employee in the scope of employment (the employee is also liable). The doctrine is also sometimes known by its old common law term, "**master-servant doctrine**," the servant (now more aptly termed "employee") was doing the bidding of the master, and so the master as principal would be held liable. Today we would say that in the "employer-employee" relationship, the employer has vicarious liability for the employee's tort.

Contract. The **principal-agent doctrine** says that the principal who authorizes an agent to enter into contracts is liable for contracts made by the agent

Key Takeaway

Agency law is common law. An agent is one who acts on behalf of another; most business activity is carried on by agents. No corporation can do anything except through agents. Agencies are created by contract: (1) expressly, (2) impliedly, (3) apparently or by estoppel, or (4) by ratification. Agents may be general, special, or subagents. An employee (formerly called a "servant") is one who is controlled, or subject to control, by the employer (principal). An independent contractor is one hired to accomplish a result, but over whom the principal has no direct control and for whose torts the principal is not liable.

Exercises

1. Could express authority be established by silence on the part of the principal?
2. Why is the concept of implied authority very important in business situations?
3. What is the rationale for the doctrine of apparent authority—that is, why would the law impose a contract on a "principal" when, in fact, there was no principal-agent relationship with the "agent" at all?

10.2 Principal's Liability for Agent's (Employee's) Torts

Learning Objectives

1. Understand the basic agency law rules affecting liability for torts committed by the employee.
2. Be clear on the rationale for these rules.
3. Recognize some specific areas of concern: who is the employer? what is the scope of employment? and who is liable if the employee commits an intentional tort or crime?

Basic Agency Law Rules Affecting Liability for Torts Committed by the Employee

The general rule is this: the employer is liable for torts committed by the employee in the scope of employment; the employee is also liable.

Rationale for the Rule Imposing Vicarious Liability

There are several reasons why the employer should be liable for torts committed by the employee in the scope of employment.

But first, note that except under the most unusual circumstances, a person is always liable for his or her own torts; it would be bad public policy if that weren't true. Fundamental to "free market capitalism" is the concept that individuals will "earn" the consequences of their action, either positively or negatively. In agency law, the archaic "master-servant" language helps us to understand why no one would want to sue the "servant," who was typically without means to pay a judgment, either in tort or in contract. If "servants" could act on behalf of principals without consequence, trust in commerce would quickly break down.

Second, note that there is a difference between torts prompted by the principal himself and torts where the principal was innocent. If the principal directs the agent to commit a tort or knows that the agent's carrying out his instructions will likely bring harm to someone, the principal will be liable. This is an application of the general common-law principle that one cannot escape liability by delegating an unlawful act to another. The syndicate that hires a "hitman" is as guilty of murder as the man who pulls the trigger. Similarly, a principal who is negligent in his use of agents will be held liable for their negligence. This rule comes into play when the principal fails to supervise employees adequately, gives faulty directions, or hires incompetent or unsuitable people for a particular job.

But the principle of liability goes beyond negligence or intentionality to acts that the principal had no knowledge of; the principal may even have expressly prohibited the agent from engaging in such acts. Again, this goes to the principle of respondeat superior ("let the master answer"), which imposes vicarious liability on the principal (vicarious means "indirectly, as, by, or through a substitute"), as long as the acts are committed by the agent within the scope of the employment.

The moral rationale for the imposition of vicarious liability on the employer/principal is clear enough. First, the employer hires and trains employees and should be expected to choose competent workers, train them properly, and provide them with the tools and equipment to do the job. Second, the employer gets the benefit of the job well done, and should reasonably be expected to pay the cost when, as is inevitable, the employee commits a tort on the job. Third, the employer is the one with the money—the "deep pockets" that can satisfy a court's judgment of liability. The employer can, and almost certainly will, buy liability insurance to protect itself and the public from otherwise uncompensated losses, and the employer can add the cost of that insurance to the price of the goods or services being provided.

The "deep pocket" of the defendant-company is not always deep enough, however. For many small businesses, in fact, the principle of *respondeat superior* is one of life or death. One example was the closing in San Francisco of the much-beloved Larraburu Brothers Bakery—at the time, the world's second largest sourdough bread maker. The bakery was held liable for $2 million in damages after one of its delivery trucks injured a six-year-old boy. The bakery's insurance policy had a limit of $1.25 million, and the bakery could not absorb the excess. The Larraburu brothers had no choice but to cease operations. (See http://www.outsidelands.org/larraburu.php.)

Specific Areas of Concern

Several specific areas of concern arise related to *respondeat superior*: (1) who is the employer, (2) what is "the scope of employment," and (3) who is liable if the employee commits an intentional tort or a crime. They are taken up below.

Who Is the Employer?

This seems easy: the one who hires the employee is the employer, and the employer is liable. But two complications may be called out: (1) the "borrowed servant" (today we would say "borrowed employee") doctrine, and (2) the employee vs. independent contractor issue.

Borrowed employees. The **"borrowed servant" doctrine** holds that an employer may be liable for actions of a temporary employee. On a construction site, Contractor A realizes he needs two additional workers to move material. Contractor A says to Contractor B, "Do you have two people I could put to work for three hours this afternoon?" Contractor B: "Sure, that's fine. We're waiting on materials ourselves." Contractor A has borrowed two of Contractor B's employees; A is their temporary employer (called the "special employer") and the temporary employees are considered A's agents. The borrowed employees become A's agents for any torts committed, but A is also responsible under worker's compensation laws for any on-the-job injuries for those employees.

> **"borrowed servant" doctrine**
>
> If an employer borrows a worker from another employer, the borrowing employer can be held liable for the borrowed employee's actions, although there is not a permanent employer-employee relationship between them.

Independent Contractors. Ordinarily, an individual or a company is not vicariously liable for the tortious acts of independent contractors. The plumber who rushes to a client's house to repair a leak and causes a traffic accident does not subject the homeowner to liability (there are some exceptions to this rule.[2]) Also, most importantly, the employer hiring a true independent contractor is *not* liable for the contractor's torts, and is also not responsible for paying a contractor's Social Security taxes, unemployment taxes, workers' compensation, and the like. The independent contractor is carrying on his own enterprise. Many companies have created business plans that rely on independent contractors so as to avoid such expenses. Some will skirt ethical and legal lines to *mislabel* employees, to designate them "independent contractors" when in fact they are not. By misclassifying, an employer can save a lot of money; it will not have to pay the employer's share of Social Security and Medicare taxes, overtime pay, employee benefits, including vacation, holiday, disability and sick pay, unemployment compensation tax, and workers' compensation insurance.[3] Here's the federal government's Department of Labor on this issue:

> The misclassification of employees as independent contractors presents one of the most serious problems facing affected workers, employers and the entire economy. Misclassified employees often are denied access to critical benefits and protections they are entitled to by law, such as the minimum wage, overtime compensation, family and medical leave, unemployment insurance, and safe workplaces. Employee misclassification generates substantial losses to the federal government and state governments in the form of lower tax revenues, as well as to state unemployment insurance and workers' compensation funds.[4]

Whether a person is an employee or an independent contractor is not dependent upon what the people involved think about their relationship, or how they word their contract. It is a question of fact. The federal Department of Labor has helpful guidelines to make the determination: https://www.dol.gov/whd/regs/compliance/whdfs13.htm. Again, the primary issue is whether the person hired is subject to specific control by the one who does the hiring.

Was the Employee in the "Scope of Employment"?

A second area of concern is the "**scope of employment**." The employer is liable for torts committed by the employee in the scope of employment, but *not* liable for torts committed by the employee not in the scope of employment ("on a frolic of his own," as is said). Obviously, whether the employee was "in the scope" when the tort occurred is a very important fact, upon which may hinge a lot of money.

In *Edgewater Motels v Gatzke*,[5] the defendant Gatzke, a long-time Walgreen Drug Company employee and district supervisor, was staying at a motel in Duluth, Minnesota at his employer's expense while supervising the establishment of a drugstore restaurant. After a long day's work he sat at the small motel desk working up expense vouchers. He stubbed a cigarette out in the ashtray, dumped the ashes in the wastebasket, and retired. He escaped from the ensuing fire that caused over $1.1 million in damages to the motel (in 2019 dollars). The motel company sued Gatzke and Walgreen. Was Walgreen liable? It was if Gatzke was in the scope of employment. As to that issue, the court held: "The question of whether smoking can be within an employee's scope of employment is a close one, but after careful consideration of the issue we are persuaded by the reasoning of other courts which hold that smoking can be an act within an employee's scope of employment. It seems only logical to conclude that an employee does not abandon his employment as a matter of law while temporarily acting for his personal comfort when such activities involve only slight deviations from work that are reasonable under the circumstances, such as eating, drinking, or smoking."

Is a delivery driver outside the scope of employment if she stops at a fast-food restaurant for a quick lunch, going two blocks out of her way to the delivery destination, and gets into an accident leaving the order lane? No; almost certainly that's within the scope of her employment. Had she been on a "frolic," rather than a slight detour, the result would be different. Suppose, for example, that she is entitled to a lunch hour, packs a lunch, and goes to visit her ailing brother, making a three mile "detour" to get to his house, and has an accident after leaving his house. It's not a "frolic" in the ordinary sense—it might not be that much fun to visit her ailing brother—but she clearly goes beyond the slight detour of the fast-food stop. But test is always one of degree, and it is not always easy to decide when a detour has become so substantial that it becomes a "frolic."

The **Zone of Risk Test**. Court decisions in the last fifty years have moved toward a standard that looks to the foreseeability of the agent/employee's conduct. By this standard, an employer may be held liable for his employee's conduct as long as it was foreseeable that the agent might act as she did. This is the "zone of risk" test. The *employer* (the test is whether the *employer* is at risk, not the employee) will be within the zone of risk for vicarious liability if the employee is where she is supposed to be, doing—more or less—what she is supposed to be doing, and the incident arose from the employee's pursuit of the employer's interest (again, more or less). That is, the employer is within the zone of risk if the servant is in the place within which, if the employer were to send out a search party to find a missing employee, it would be reasonable to look.

Is the Principal Liable for an Agent's (Employee's) Intentional Torts or Crimes?

Generally, liability for intentional torts is imputed to the principal if the agent is acting to further the principal's business, and the "zone of risk" test applies.

As to criminal liability, a principal will generally not be held liable for an agent's unauthorized criminal acts if the crimes are among those requiring specific intent. For example, Larry Carlton drives a cab for Acme Cab Company in New York City. He gets into an altercation with another cab driver after they collide at an intersection. Because of his anger management issues, he decides to pull out his switchblade knife about 60 seconds after the yelling, pushing, and shoving, and kills the other cab driver. Will Acme Cab Company be liable for the tort of wrongful death of the other cab driver? Probably not.

There is a narrow exception to the broad policy of immunity. Courts have ruled that under certain regulatory statutes and regulations, an agent's criminality may be imputed to the principal, just as civil liability is imputed under Dramshop Acts (where a pub or tavern or restaurant may be liable for serving an obviously intoxicated person who later commits a tort). These include pure food and drug acts, speeding ordinances, building regulations, child labor rules, and minimum wage and maximum hour legislation. Misdemeanor criminal liability may be imposed upon corporations and individual employees for the sale or shipment of adulterated food in interstate commerce, even if the defendant had no actual knowledge that the food was adulterated at the time the sale or shipment was made.

FIGURE 10.3 Principal's Tort Liability

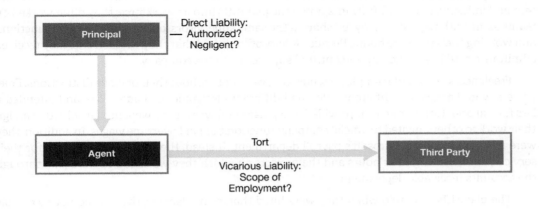

Cases

Employee versus Independent Contractor

Vizcaino v. Microsoft Corp. 97 F.3d 1187 (9th Cir., 1996)	**Vizcaino v. Microsoft Corp.** 9th Circuit case, 1996, analyzing who is an "independent contractor."

Reinhardt, J.

Large corporations have increasingly adopted the practice of hiring temporary employees or independent contractors as a means of avoiding payment of employee benefits, and thereby increasing their profits. This practice has understandably led to a number of problems, legal and otherwise. One of the legal issues that sometimes arises is exemplified by this lawsuit. The named plaintiffs, who were classified by Microsoft as independent contractors, seek to strip that label of its protective covering and to obtain for themselves certain benefits that the company provided to all of its regular or permanent employees. After certifying the named plaintiffs as representatives of a class of "common-law employees," the district court granted summary judgment to Microsoft on all counts. The plaintiffs * * * now appeal as to two of their claims: (a) the claim that they are entitled to savings benefits under Microsoft's Savings Plus Plan (SPP); and (b) that they are entitled to stock-option benefits under Microsoft's Employee Stock Purchase Plan (Stock Plan). In both cases, the claims are based on their contention that they are common-law employees.

Microsoft, one of the country's fastest growing and most successful corporations and the world's largest software company, produces and sells computer software internationally. It employs a core staff of permanent employees. It categorizes them as "regular employees" and offers them a wide variety of benefits, including paid vacations, sick leave, holidays, short-term disability, group health and life insurance, and pensions, as well as the two benefits involved in this appeal. Microsoft supplements its core staff of employees with a pool of individuals to whom it refuses to pay fringe benefits. It previously classified these individuals as "independent contractors" or "freelancers," but prior to the filing of the action began classifying them as "temporary agency employees." Freelancers were hired when Microsoft needed to expand its workforce to meet the demands of new product schedules. The company did not, of course, provide them with any of the employee benefits regular employees receive.

The plaintiffs performed services as software testers, production editors, proofreaders, formatters, and indexers. Microsoft fully integrated the plaintiffs into its workforce: they often worked on teams along with regular employees, sharing the same supervisors, performing identical functions, and working the same core hours. Because Microsoft required that they work on site, they received admittance card keys, office equipment, and supplies from the company.

Freelancers and regular employees, however, were not without their obvious distinctions. Freelancers wore badges of a different color, had different electronic-mail addresses, and attended a less formal orientation than that provided to regular employees. They were not permitted to assign their work to others, invited to official company functions, or paid overtime wages. In addition, they were not paid through Microsoft's payroll department. Instead, they submitted invoices for their services, documenting their hours and the projects on which they worked, and were paid through the accounts receivable department.

The plaintiffs were told when they were hired that, as freelancers, they would not be eligible for benefits. None has contended that Microsoft ever promised them any benefits individually. All eight named plaintiffs signed [employment agreements] when first hired by Microsoft or soon thereafter. [One] included a provision that states that the undersigned "agrees to be responsible for all federal and state taxes, withholding, social security, insurance and other benefits." The [other one] states that "as an Independent Contractor to Microsoft, you are self-employed and are responsible to pay all your own insurance and benefits." Eventually, the plaintiffs learned of the various benefits being provided to regular employees from speaking with them or reading various Microsoft publications concerning employee benefits.

In 1989 and 1990, the Internal Revenue Service (IRS)[,] * * * applying common-law principles defining the employer-employee relationship, concluded that Microsoft's freelancers were not independent contractors but employees for withholding and employment tax purposes, and that Microsoft would thereafter be required to pay withholding taxes and the employer's portion of Federal Insurance Contributions Act (FICA—Social Security]) tax. Microsoft agreed. * * *

After learning of the IRS rulings, the plaintiffs sought various employee benefits, including those now at issue: the Stock Plan and SPP benefits. The SPP [hereafter the Savings Plan] * * * is a cash or deferred salary arrangement under § 401k of the Internal Revenue Code that permits Microsoft's employees to save and invest up to fifteen percent of their income through tax-deferred payroll deductions. * * * Microsoft matches fifty percent of the employee's contribution in any year, with [a maximum matching contribution]. The Stock Plan [hereafter the Stock Plan] * * * permits employees to purchase company stock [with various rules].

Microsoft rejected the plaintiffs' claims for benefits, maintaining that they were independent contractors who were personally responsible for all their own benefits. * * *

The plaintiffs brought this action, challenging the denial of benefits.

Microsoft contends that the extrinsic evidence, including the [employment agreements], demonstrates its intent not to provide freelancers or independent contractors with employee benefits[.] * * * We have no doubt that the company did not intend to provide freelancers or independent contractors with employee benefits, and that if the plaintiffs had in fact been freelancers or independent contractors, they would not be eligible under the plan. The plaintiffs, however, were not freelancers or independent contractors. They were common-law employees. . .

We * * * hold that the plaintiffs are eligible to participate under the terms of the Savings Plan. [The court goes on to conclude that the plaintiffs, as common law employees, should also be covered under the Stock Plan. The court rejects Microsoft's arguments that the employment agreements signed by plaintiffs make them ineligible to participate in the Stock Plan.]

Microsoft next contends that the [employment agreements] signed by the plaintiffs render them ineligible to participate in the Stock Plan. First, the label used in the instruments signed by the plaintiffs does not control their employment status. Second, the employment instruments, if construed to exclude the plaintiffs from receiving Stock Plan benefits, would conflict with the plan's express incorporation of § 423. [That section extends Stock Plan participation to all common-law employees not covered by express exceptions.] Although Microsoft may have generally intended to exclude individuals who were in fact independent contractors, it could not, consistent with its express intention to extend participation in the Stock Plan to all common-law employees, have excluded the plaintiffs. Indeed, such an exclusion would defeat the purpose of including § 423 in the plan, because the exclusion of common-law employees not otherwise accepted would result in the loss of the plan's tax qualification.

Finally, Microsoft maintains that the plaintiffs are not entitled to Stock Plan benefits because the terms of the plan were never communicated to them and they were therefore unaware of its provisions when they performed their employment services. * * * In any event, to the extent that knowledge of an offer of benefits is a prerequisite, it is probably sufficient that Microsoft publicly promulgated the plan. * * *

There is a compelling reason, implicit in some of the preceding discussion, that requires us to reject the company's theory that the plaintiffs' entitlement to Stock Plan benefits is defeated by their previous lack of knowledge regarding their rights. * * * "[I]t is a principle of fundamental justice that if a promisor is himself the cause of the failure of performance, either of an obligation due him or of a condition upon which his own liability depends, he cannot take advantage of the failure." [Citation.] * * *

Applying these principles, we agree with the magistrate judge, who concluded that Microsoft, which created a benefit to which the plaintiffs were entitled, could not defend itself by arguing that the plaintiffs were unaware of the benefit, when its own false representations precluded them from gaining that knowledge. Because Microsoft misrepresented both the plaintiffs' actual employment status and their eligibility to participate in the Stock Plan, it is responsible for their failure to know that they were covered by the terms of the offer. It may not now take advantage of that failure to defeat the plaintiffs' rights to Stock Plan benefits. Thus, we reject Microsoft's final argument.

Conclusion

For the reasons stated, the district court's grant of summary judgment in favor of Microsoft and denial of summary judgment in favor of the plaintiffs is REVERSED and the case REMANDED for the determination of any questions of individual eligibility for benefits that may remain following issuance of this opinion and for calculation of the damages or benefits due the various class members.

Case Questions

1. In a 1993 *Wall Street Journal* article, James Bovard asserted that the IRS "is carrying out a sweeping campaign to slash the number of Americans permitted to be self-employed—and to punish the companies that contract with them . . . IRS officials indicate that more than half the nation's self-employed should no longer be able to work for themselves." Why did Microsoft want these employees to "be able to work for themselves"?

2. Why did the employees accept employment as independent contractors? If it was their free, voluntary choice, do you see it as unfair that the court is changing Microsoft's obligations? Was Microsoft being fair to the "freelancers" in the first place? Why, or why not?

3. It seems unlikely that the purpose of the IRS's campaign was really to keep people from working for themselves, despite Mr. Bovard's assumption. What was the purpose of the campaign?

4. On what basis did the IRS and the court determine that these "independent contractors" were in fact employees?

Employer's Liability for Employee's Intentional Torts: Scope of Employment

Lyon v. Carey

Cir. Ct. App. DC, 1976, analyzing "scope of employment" for employer's vicarious liability.

Lyon v. Carey

533 F.2d 649 (Cir. Ct. App. DC, 1976)

McMillan, J.

Corene Antoinette Lyon, plaintiff, recovered a $33,000.00 verdict [about $166,000 in 2019 dollars] in the United States District Court for the District of Columbia before Judge Barrington T. Parker and a jury, against the corporate defendants, George's Radio and Television Company, Inc., and Pep Line Trucking Company, Inc. The suit for damages arose out of an assault, including rape, committed with a knife and other weapons upon the plaintiff on May 9, 1972, by Michael Carey, a nineteen-year-old deliveryman for Pep Line Trucking Company, Inc. Three months after the trial, Judge Parker set aside the verdict and rendered judgment for both defendants notwithstanding the verdict. Plaintiff appealed. * * *

Although the assault was perhaps at the outer bounds of *respondeat superior*, the case was properly one for the jury. Whether the assault in this case was the outgrowth of a job-related controversy or simply a personal adventure of the deliveryman, was a question for the jury. This was the import of the trial judge's instructions. The verdict as to Pep Line should not have been disturbed.

Irene Lyon bought a mattress and springs for her bed from the defendant George's Radio and Television Company, Inc. The merchandise was to be delivered on May 9, 1972. Irene Lyon had to be at work and the plaintiff [Irene's sister] Corene Lyon, had agreed to wait in her sister's apartment to receive the delivery.

A C.O.D. balance of $13.24 was due on the merchandise, and Irene Lyon had left a check for $13.24 to cover that balance. Plaintiff had been requested by her sister to "wait until the mattress and the springs came and to check and make sure they were okay."

Plaintiff, fully clothed, answered the door. Her description of what happened is sufficiently brief and unqualified that it will bear repeating in full. She testified, without objection, as follows:

> *I went to the door, and I looked in the peephole, and I asked who was there. The young man told me he was a delivery man from George's. He showed me a receipt, and it said, "George's." He said he [needed cash on delivery—COD], so I let him in, and I told him to bring the mattress upstairs and he said, "No," that he wasn't going to lug them upstairs, and he wanted the COD first, and I told him I wanted to see the mattress and box springs to make sure they were okay, and he said no, he wasn't going to lug them upstairs [until he got the check].*
>
> *So this went back and forwards and so he was getting angry, and I told him to wait right here while I go get the COD. I went to the bedroom to get the check, and I picked it up, and I turned around and he was right there.*
>
> *And then I was giving him the check and then he told me that his boss told him not to accept a check, that he wanted cash money, and that if I didn't give him cash money, he was going to take it on my ass, and he told me that he was no delivery man, he was a rapist and then he threw me on the bed.*
>
> *[The Court] Talk louder, young lady, the jury can't hear you.*
>
> *[The witness] And then he threw me on the bed, and he had a knife to my throat.*
>
> *[Plaintiff's attorney] Then what happened?*
>
> *And then he raped me.*

Plaintiff's pre-trial deposition was a part of the record on appeal, and it shows that Carey raped plaintiff at knife point; that then he chased her all over the apartment with a knife and scissors and cut plaintiff in numerous places on her face and body, beat and otherwise attacked her. All of the physical injury other than the rape occurred after rather than before the rape had been accomplished. * * *

[Carey was convicted of rape and sent to prison. The court determined that George's was properly dismissed because Pep Line, Carey's employer, was an independent contractor over which George's had no control.]

The principal question, therefore, is whether the evidence discloses any other basis upon which a jury could reasonably find Pep Line, the employer of Carey, liable for the assault.

Michael Carey was in the employment of the defendant Pep Line as a deliveryman. He was authorized to make the delivery of the mattress and springs plaintiff's sister had bought. He gained access to the apartment only upon a showing of the delivery receipt for the merchandise. His employment contemplated that he visit and enter that particular apartment. Though the apartment was not owned by nor in the control of his employer, it was nevertheless a place he was expected by his employer to enter.

After Carey entered, under the credentials of his employment and the delivery receipt, a dispute arose naturally and immediately between him and the plaintiff about two items of great significance in connection with his job. These items were the request of the plaintiff, the customer's agent, to inspect the mattress and springs before payment (which would require their being brought upstairs before the payment was made), and Carey's insistence on getting cash rather than a check.

The dispute arose out of the very transaction which had brought Carey to the premises, and, according to the plaintiff's evidence, out of the employer's instructions to get cash only before delivery.

On the face of things, Pep Line Trucking Company, Inc. is liable, under two previous decisions of the Court of Appeals for the District of Columbia Circuit. [Citation (1953)] held a taxi owner liable for damages (including a broken leg) sustained by a customer who had been run over by the taxi in pursuit of a dispute between the driver and the customer about a fare. [Citation (1939)], held a restaurant owner liable to a restaurant patron who was beaten with a stick by a restaurant employee, after a disagreement over the service. The theory was that:

It is well established that an employer may be held responsible in tort for assaults committed by an employee while he is acting within the scope of his employment, even though he may act wantonly and contrary to his employer's instructions. [Citations] ".... having placed [the employee] in charge and committed the management of the business to his care, defendants may not escape liability either on the ground of his infirmity of temperament or because, under the influence of passion aroused by plaintiff's threat to report the circumstances, he went beyond the ordinary line of duty and inflicted the injury shown in this case. [Citations]"

Munick v. City of Durham ([Citation], Supreme Court of North Carolina, 1921), though not a binding precedent, is informative and does show that the theory of liability advanced by the plaintiff is by no means recent in origin. The plaintiff, Munick, a Russian born Jew, testified that he went to the Durham, North Carolina city water company office on April 17, 1919, and offered to pay his bill with "three paper dollars, one silver dollar, and fifty cents in pennies." The pennies were in a roll "like the bank fixes them." The clerk gave a receipt and the plaintiff prepared to leave the office. The office manager came into the room, saw the clerk counting the pennies, became enraged at the situation, shoved the pennies onto the floor and ordered Munick to pick them up. Bolton, the manager, "locked the front door and took me by the jacket and called me 'God damned Jew,' and said, 'I want only bills.' I did not say anything and he hit me in the face. I did not resist, and the door was locked and I could not get out." With the door locked, Bolton then repeatedly choked and beat the plaintiff, finally extracted a bill in place of the pennies, and ordered him off the premises with injuries including finger marks on his neck that could be seen for eight or ten days. Bolton was convicted of unlawful assault [but the case against the water company was dismissed].

The North Carolina Supreme Court reversed the trial court's dismissal and held that the case should have gone to the jury. The court * * * said [Citation]:

> 'It is now fully established that corporations may be held liable for negligent and malicious torts, and that responsibility will be imputed whenever such wrongs are committed by their employees and agents in the course of their employment and within its scope * * * in many of the cases, and in reliable textbooks * * * 'course of employment' is stated and considered as sufficiently inclusive; but, whether the one or the other descriptive term is used, they have the same significance in importing liability on the part of the principal when the agent is engaged in the work that its principal has employed or directed him to do and * * * in the effort to accomplish it. When such conduct comes within the description that constitutes an actionable wrong, the corporation principal, as in other cases of principal and agent, is liable not only for 'the act itself, but for the ways and means employed in the performance thereof.'

In 1 Thompson, Negligence, s 554[6], it is pointed out that, unless the above principle is maintained:

> It will always be more safe and profitable for a man to conduct his business vicariously than in his own person. He would escape liability for the consequences of many acts connected with his business, springing from the imperfections of human nature, because done by another, for which he would be responsible if done by himself. Meanwhile, the public, obliged to deal or come in contact with his agent, for injuries done by them must be left wholly without redress. * * * A doctrine so fruitful of mischief could not long stand unshaken in an enlightened jurisprudence.' This court has often held the master liable, even if the agent was willful, provided it was committed in the course of his employment. [Citation.]
>
> "The act of a servant done to effect some independent purpose of his own and not with reference to the service in which he is employed, or while he is acting as his own master for the time being, is not within the scope of his employment so as to render the master liable therefor. In these circumstances the servant alone is liable for the injury inflicted." [Citation.] The general idea is that the employee at the time of doing the wrongful act, in order to fix liability on the employer, must have been acting in behalf of the latter and not on his own account [Citation]."

The principal physical (as opposed to psychic) damage to the plaintiff is a number of disfiguring knife wounds on her head, face, arms, breasts and body. If the instrumentalities of assault had not included rape, the case would provoke no particular curiosity nor interest because it comes within all the classic requirements for recovery against the master. The verdict is not attacked as excessive, and could not be excessive in light of the physical injuries inflicted. * * *

It is, then, a question of fact for the trier of fact, rather than a question of law for the court, whether the assault stemmed from purely and solely personal sources or arose out of the conduct of the employer's business; and the trial judge so instructed the jury.

It follows that, under existing decisions of the District of Columbia Circuit, plaintiff has made out a case for the jury against Pep Line Trucking, Inc. unless the sexual character of one phase of the assault bars her from recovery for damages from all phases of the assault.

We face, then, this question: Should the entire case be taken from the jury because, instead of a rod of wood (as in [Citation]), in addition to weapons of steel (as in [one case, a knife]); and in addition to his hands (as in [the third case, regarding the dispute about the pennies]), Carey also employed a sexual weapon, a rod of flesh and blood in the pursuit of a job-related controversy?

The answer is, No. It is a jury's job to decide how much of plaintiff's story to believe, and how much if any of the damages were caused by actions, including sexual assault, which stemmed from job-related sources rather than from purely personal origins. * * *

The judgment is affirmed as to the defendant George's and reversed as to the defendant Pep Line Trucking Company, Inc.

Case Questions

1. What triggered the dispute here?
2. Is this a civil case or a criminal case?
3. The court observes, "On the face of things, Pep Line Trucking Company, Inc. is liable." But there are two issues that give the court cause for more explanation. (1) Why does the court discuss the point that the assault did not occur on the employer's premises? (2) Why does the court mention that the knife assault happened *after* the rape?
4. It is difficult to imagine that a sexual assault could be anything other than some "purely and solely personal" gratification, unrelated to the employer's business. How did the court address this?

5. What is the controlling rule of law as to the employer's liability for intentional torts here?

6. What does the court mean when it says, "the assault was perhaps at the outer bounds of respondeat superior"? Does Pep Line, or any other employer, have a duty to discover a potential employee's propensities for violent behavior? What if Carey had previously been convicted of rape? Or previously been charged with rape, only to be freed on a technicality?

7. Would the jury likely think about who had the "deep pocket" here? Who did have it?

8. How does a just legal system reliably compensate those who are injured through no fault of their own? If the damages from knife assault are minimal compared to the damages from the rape, should the courts allow her to recover damages only from the knife wounds? Does it make any sense that, somehow, he was in the scope of employment while administering knife wounds, but not in the scope of employment while raping Ms. Lyon?

Employer's Liability for Employee's Intentional Torts: Scope of Employment

Cockrell v. Pearl River Valley Water Supply Dist.

Mississippi Supreme Court case, 2004, analyzing "scope of employment" for vicarious liability.

Cockrell v. Pearl River Valley Water Supply Dist.

865 So.2d 357 (Miss., 2004)

Carlson, J.

The Pearl River Valley Water Supply District ("District") was granted summary judgment pursuant to the Mississippi Tort Claims Act (MTCA) dismissing with prejudice all claims asserted against it by Sandra Cockrell. Cockrell appeals. * * * Finding the motion for summary judgment was properly granted in favor of the District, this Court affirms the final judgment entered by the Circuit Court of Rankin County.

On June 28, 1998, Sandra Cockrell was arrested for suspicion of driving under the influence of alcohol by Officer Joey James who was employed as a security patrol officer with the Reservoir Patrol of the Pearl River Valley Water Supply District. Officer James then transported Cockrell to the Reservoir Patrol office and administered an intoxilyzer test. The results of the test are not before us; however, we do know that after the test was administered, Officer James apologized to Cockrell for arresting her, and he assured her that he would prepare her paperwork so that she would not have to spend much time in jail. As they were leaving the Reservoir Patrol office, Officer James began asking Cockrell personal questions such as where she lived, whether she was dating anyone and if she had a boyfriend.

Officer James then asked Cockrell for her cell phone number so that he could call and check on her. As they were approaching his patrol car for the trip to the Rankin County jail, Officer James informed Cockrell that she should be wearing handcuffs; however, he did not handcuff Cockrell, and he allowed her to ride in the front seat of the patrol car with him. In route to the jail, Cockrell became emotional and started crying. As she was fixing her makeup using the mirror on the sun visor, Officer James pulled his patrol car into a church parking lot and parked the car. He then pulled Cockrell towards him in an embrace and began stroking her back and hair telling her that things would be fine. Cockrell told Officer James to release her, but he continued to embrace her for approximately five minutes before continuing on to the jail.

On June 30, 1998, Cockrell returned to the Reservoir Patrol office to retrieve her driver's license. Officer James called Cockrell into his office and discussed her DUI charge with her. As she was leaving, Officer James grabbed her from behind, turned her around, pinned both of her arms behind her and pulled her to his chest. When Officer James bent down to kiss her, she ducked her head, thus causing Officer James to instead kiss her forehead. When Officer James finally released Cockrell, she ran out of the door and drove away. [Subsequently, Cockrell's attorney threatened civil suit against police department; James was fired in October 1998. At issue is whether James was in the scope of employment when he assaulted the plaintiff.]

* * * The trial court found that the police department could not be held liable under the MTCA for the conduct of Officer James which was both criminal and outside the course and scope of his employment. Cockrell appealed.

Summary judgment is granted in cases where there is "no genuine issue as to any material fact and that the moving party is entitled to a judgment as a matter of law." * * *

Cockrell contends there is a genuine issue of material of fact regarding whether Officer James was acting in the course and scope of his employment with the District during the incidents which occurred on the nights of June 28 and June 30, 1998. Cockrell argues Officer James's conduct, although inappropriate, did not rise to the level of criminal conduct. Cockrell contends Officer James's action of hugging Cockrell was similar to an officer consoling a victim of a crime. Cockrell does admit that Officer James's action of kissing her is more difficult to view as within the course and scope of his employment. * * *

The District argues that although Officer James acted within the course and scope of his duties when he arrested Cockrell, his later conduct, which was intended to satisfy his lustful desires, was outside the scope of his employment with it. * * *

"Mississippi law provides that an activity must be in furtherance of the employer's business to be within the scope and course of employment." [Citation] To be within the course and scope of employment, an activity must carry out the employer's purpose of the employment or be in furtherance of the employer's business. [Citations] Therefore, if an employee steps outside his employer's business for some reason which is not related to his employment, the relationship between the employee and the employer "is temporarily suspended and this is so 'no matter how short the time and the [employer] is not liable for [the employee's] acts during such time.'" "An employee's personal unsanctioned recreational endeavors are beyond the course and scope of his employment." [Citation]

[In one case cited,] Officer Kerry Collins, a Jackson Police officer, was on duty when he came upon the parked car of L.T., a minor, and her boyfriend, who were about to engage in sexual activity. [Citation] Officer Collins instructed L.T. to take her boyfriend home, and he would follow her to make sure she followed his orders. After L.T. dropped off her boyfriend, Officer Collins continued to follow her until he pulled L.T. over. Officer Collins then instructed L.T. to follow him to his apartment or else he would inform L.T.'s parents of her activities. L.T. followed Officer Collins to his apartment where they engaged in sexual activity. Upon returning home, L.T. told her parents everything that had happened. L.T. and her parents filed suit against Officer Collins, the City of Jackson and the Westwood Apartments, where Officer Collins lived rent free in return for his services as a security guard. * * * The district court granted summary judgment in favor of the City finding that Officer Collins acted outside the course and scope of his employment with the Jackson Police Department. [Citation.]

In [Citation] the plaintiff sued the Archdiocese of New Orleans for damages that allegedly resulted from his sexual molestation by a Catholic priest. The Fifth Circuit found that the priest was not acting within the course and scope of his employment. The Fifth Circuit held that "smoking marijuana and engaging in sexual acts with minor boys" in no way furthered the interests of his employer.

[Mississippi law holds] that sexual misconduct falls outside the course and scope of employment. There is no question that Officer James was within the course and scope of his employment when he first stopped Cockrell for suspicion of driving under the influence of alcohol. However, when Officer James diverted from his employment for personal reasons, he was no longer acting in the furtherance of his employer's interests. * * * Therefore, the District cannot be held liable * * * for the misconduct of Officer James which occurred outside the course and scope of his employment.

Affirmed.

Case Questions

1. How can this case and *Lyon v. Carey* be reconciled? Both involve an agent's unacceptable behavior—assault—but in *Lyon* the agent's actions were imputed to the principal, and in *Cockrell* the agent's actions were not imputed to the principal.
2. What is the controlling rule of law governing the principal's liability for the agent's actions?
3. The law governing the liability of principals for acts of their agents is well settled. Thus the cases turn on the facts. Who decides what are accepted as "facts" in a lawsuit?

Key Takeaway

The principal will be liable for the employee's torts in two circumstances: first, if the principal was directly responsible, as in hiring a person the principal knew or should have known was incompetent or dangerous; second, if the employee committed the tort in the scope of business for the principal. This is the master-servant doctrine or *respondeat superior*. It imposes vicarious liability on the employer: the master (employer) will be liable if the employee was in the zone of activity creating a risk for the employer ("zone of risk" test), that is—generally—if the employee was where he was supposed to be, when he was supposed to be there, and the incident arose out of the employee's interest (however perverted) in promoting the employer's business.

The independent contractor is not an employee; her activities are not specifically controlled by her client, and the contractor's client is not liable for payroll taxes or torts that the independent contractor may commit. For that reason, an employer will often claim workers are independent contractors when, in fact and law, they are employees. Because a lot of money is often at stake, such cases often depend on hard-fought factual arguments over the degree of control that the client/employer had over the independent contractor.

By statute, *employees* who, on behalf of their employers, sell alcohol or adulterated or short-weight foodstuffs, may be liable for—as an example—the employee who sells alcohol to minors will herself be liable. The employer of one who commits a crime is not usually liable unless the employer put the employee up to the crime or knew that a crime was being committed. But some prophylactic statutes impose liability on the employer for the employee's crime—even if the employee had no intention to commit it—as a means to force the employer to prevent such actions.

Exercises

1. What is the difference between an employer's direct and vicarious liability related to agency law?
2. What is the general rule for the master-servant doctrine?
3. What is the "zone of risk test"? Who is "at risk" under it?
4. What is the general rule for the principal-agent doctrine?
5. What distinguishes an employee from an independent contractor?
6. Why do employers not infrequently try to pass off employees as independent contractors?
7. Under what circumstances will the employer be liable for an employee's crimes?

10.3 Principal's Liability for Agent's Contracts

1. Understand that the principal's liability depends on whether the agent was authorized to make the contract.
2. Recognize how the agent's authority is acquired: expressly, impliedly, or apparently.
3. Know that the principal may also be liable—even if the agent had no authority—if the principal ratifies the agent's contract after the fact.

In the previous section we examined the vicarious liability of the employer for *torts* committed by the employee. Here, we take up the vicarious liability of the employer (or more properly in this context, principal) for contracts entered into by the employee (or agent).

Principal's Contract Liability Requires That the Agent Has Authority

Again, the general rule: the principal (employer) is liable for contracts entered into by authorized agents; the agent is not liable.

The key to determining whether a principal is liable for contracts made by his agent is authority—was the agent authorized to negotiate the agreement and close the deal? Obviously, it would not be sensible to hold a contractor liable to pay for a whole load of lumber merely because a stranger wandered into the lumberyard saying, "I'm an agent for ABC Contractors; charge this to their account." To be liable, the principal must have authorized the agent in some manner to act in his behalf, and that authorization must be communicated to the third party by the principal, or it must be apparent that, somehow, a reasonable vendor would conclude that the "stranger" was authorized to contract on behalf of the principal.

Types of Authority

Express Authority

The strongest form of authority is that which is expressly granted, often in written form. The principal consents to the agent's actions, and the third party may then rely on the document attesting to the agent's authority to deal on behalf of the principal. One common form of **express authority** is the standard signature card on file with banks allowing corporate agents to write checks on the company's credit. The principal bears the risk of any wrongful action of his agent, as demonstrated in *Allen A. Funt Productions, Inc. v. Chemical Bank*. Allen A. Funt submitted to his bank, through his production company, various certificates permitting his accountant to use the company's checking accounts. In fact, for several years the accountant embezzled money from the company by writing checks to himself and depositing them in his own account. The company sued its bank, charging it

express authority

Actual authority that an agent has, expressed to a third party in words, orally or in writing.

with negligence for failing to monitor the amount of money taken by the accountant. But the court dismissed the negligence complaint, citing a state statute based on the common-law agency principle that a third party is entitled to rely on the express authorization given to an agent; in this case, the accountant drew checks on the account within the monetary limits contained in the signature cards on file with the bank. Letters of introduction and work orders are other types of express authority.

Implied Authority

Not every detail of an agent's work can be spelled out. It is impossible to delineate step-by-step the duties of a general agent; at best, a principal can set forth only the general nature of the duties that the agent is to perform. If express authority were the only valid kind, there would be no efficient way to use an agent, both because the effort to describe the duties would be too great and because the third party would be reluctant to deal with him.

implied authority

Actual authority given by a principal to an agent that is expressed to the third party by circumstances that make it reasonable for the third party to assume such authority.

The law permits authority to be "implied" by the relationship of the parties, the nature and customs of the business, the circumstances surrounding the act in question, the wording of the agency contract, and the knowledge that the agent has of facts relevant to the assignment. The general rule is that the agent has implied authority to perform acts incidental to or reasonably necessary to carrying out the transaction. Thus, if a principal instructs her agent to "deposit a check in the bank today," the agent has **implied authority** to drive to the designated bank unless the principal specifically prohibits the agent from doing so.

The theory of implied authority is especially important to business in the realm of the business manager, who may be charged with running the entire business operation or only a small part of it. In either event, the business manager has a relatively large domain of implied authority. She can buy goods and services; hire, supervise, and fire employees; sell or junk inventory; take in receipts and pay debts; and in general, direct the ordinary operations of the business. The full extent of the manager's authority depends on the circumstances—what is customary in the particular industry, in the particular business, and among the individuals directly concerned.

On the other hand, a manager does not have implied authority to undertake unusual or extraordinary actions on behalf of his principal. In the absence of express permission, an agent may not sell part of the business, start a new business, change the nature of the business, incur debt (unless borrowing is integral to the business, as in banking, for example), or move the business premises. For example, the owner of a hotel appoints Andy as manager; Andy decides to rename the hotel and commissions an artist to prepare a new logo for the hotel's stationery. Andy has no implied authority to change the name or to commission the artist, though he does have implied authority to engage a printer to replenish the stationery supply—and possibly to make some design changes in the letterhead. Although, if unforeseen circumstances arise and it is not practical to communicate with the principal to find out what his wishes would be, the agent may do what is reasonably necessary in order to prevent substantial loss to the principal.

Apparent Authority

As long as an agent has authorization, either express or implied, she may bind the principal legally. Thus, the seller of a house may be ignorant of the buyer's true identity; the person he supposes to be the prospective purchaser might be the agent of an undisclosed principal. Nevertheless, if the agent is authorized to make the purchase, the seller's ignorance is not a ground for either seller or principal to void the deal.

But, if a person has no authority to act as an agent, or an agent has no authority to act in a particular way, is the principal free from all consequences? The answer depends on whether or not the agent has **apparent authority**—that is, on whether or not the third person reasonably believes from the principal's words, written or spoken, or from his conduct, that he has in fact consented to the agent's actions. Apparent authority is a manifestation of authority communicated to the third person; it runs from principal to third party, not to the agent.

Apparent authority is sometimes said to be based on the principle of **estoppel** commonly used to avoid injustice. Estoppel is the doctrine that a person will not now be allowed to deny a promise or assertion she previously made where there has been detrimental reliance on that promise or assertion.

Apparent authority can arise from prior business transactions. On July 10, Meggs sold his business to Spensley, the right to use the trade name Rose City Sheet Metal Works, and a list of suppliers he had used. Three days later, Spensley began ordering supplies from Central Supply Company, which was on Meggs's list, though it had been four years since Meggs had last dealt with Central Supply. On September 3, Central received a letter from Meggs notifying it of Meggs's sale of the business to Spensley. Later that month, Spensley failed to pay Central, which then sued Meggs. The court held that Rose City Sheet Metal Works had apparent authority to buy on Meggs's credit; Meggs was liable for supplies purchased between July 10 and September 3. In such cases, and in cases involving the firing of a general manager, actual notice should be given promptly to all customers and suppliers to avoid unwanted contractual obligations.

Ratification

Even if the agent possessed no actual authority and there was no apparent authority on which the third person could rely, the principal may still be liable if she ratifies or adopts the agent's acts before the third person withdraws from the contract. **Ratification** creates authority after the fact as though it had been legally established when the agent acted without authority. In most situations, ratification leaves the parties where they expected to be, correcting the agent's errors harmlessly and giving each party what was expected.

The following figure illustrates express, implied, and apparent authority.

FIGURE 10.4 Types of Authority

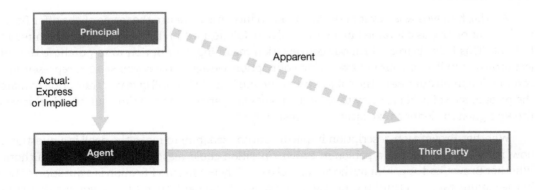

---

apparent authority

Authority in an agent conferred by some act or omission of the principal that reasonably causes a third party to believe the agent has authority when in fact there is no authority.

estoppel

To be prohibited now from denying a position or assertion made earlier, usually because someone has reasonably relied on that assertion.

ratification

The approval later of something done before.

Case

Implied Authority

> ### *Kanavos v. Hancock Bank & Trust Company*
>
> 439 N.E.2d 311 (Mass., 1982)

Kass, J.

At the close of the plaintiff's evidence in this contract litigation, the defendant moved for a directed verdict, which the trial judge allowed. The judge reasoned that the plaintiff had failed to introduce sufficient evidence tending to prove that the bank officer (who made the agreement with which the plaintiff sought to charge the bank) had any authority to make it. Upon review of the record we are of opinion that there was evidence that, if believed, warranted a finding that the bank officer had the requisite authority, or that the bank officer had apparent authority to make the agreement in controversy. We therefore reverse the judgment.

For approximately ten years prior to 1975, Harold Kanavos and his brother borrowed money on at least twenty occasions from the Hancock Bank & Trust Company (the Bank), and, during that period, the loan officer with whom Kanavos always dealt was James M. Brown. The aggregate loans made by the Bank to Kanavos at any given time went as high as $800,000.

Over that same decade, Brown's responsibilities at the Bank grew, and he had become executive vice-president. Brown was also the chief loan officer for the Bank, which had fourteen or fifteen branches in addition to its head office. Physically, Brown's office was at the head office, toward the rear of the main banking floor, opposite the office of the president—whose name was Kelley. Often Brown would tell Kanavos that he had to check an aspect of a loan transaction with Kelley, but Kelley always backed Brown up on those occasions. * * *

[The plaintiff, Harold Kanavos, entered into an agreement with the defendant Bank whereby stock owned by the Kanavos brothers was sold to the Bank and the plaintiff was given an option to repurchase the stock. Kanavos' suit against the Bank was based on a modification of the agreement offered by Brown.]

At trial, Kanavos was never permitted to introduce into evidence the terms of the offer Brown made. That offer was contained in a writing, dated July 16, 1976, on bank letterhead, which read as follows: "This letter is to confirm our conversation regarding your option to re-purchase the subject property. In lieu of your not exercising your option, we agree to pay you $40,000 representing a commission upon our sale of the subject property, and in addition, will give you the option to match the price of sale of said property to extend for a 60-day period from the time our offer is received." Brown signed the letter as executive vice-president. * * *

Whether Brown's job description impliedly authorized [him to make the deal] is a question of how, in the circumstances, a person in Brown's position could reasonably interpret his authority. Whether Brown had apparent authority to make the July 16, 1976, modification is a question of how, in the circumstances, a third person, e.g., a customer of the Bank such as Kanavos, would reasonably interpret Brown's authority in light of the manifestations of his principal, the Bank.

Titles of office generally do not establish apparent authority. Brown's status as executive vice-president was not, therefore, a badge of apparent authority to modify agreements to which the Bank was a party.

Trappings of office, e.g., office and furnishing, private secretary, while they may have some tendency to suggest executive responsibility, do not without other evidence provide a basis for finding apparent authority. Apparent authority is drawn from a variety of circumstances. Thus, in [Citation] (1940), it was held apparent authority could be found because an officer who was a director, vice-president and treasurer took an active part in directing the affairs of the bank in question and was seen by third parties talking with customers and negotiating with them. In [Citation] (1961), the executive director of a public housing authority was held to have apparent authority to vary specifications on the basis of the cumulative effect of what he had done and what the authority appeared to permit him to do.

In the instant case there was evidence of the following variety of circumstances: Brown's title of executive vice-president; the location of his office opposite the president; his frequent communications with the president; the long course of dealing and negotiations; the encouragement of Kanavos by the president to deal with Brown; the earlier amendment of the agreement by Brown on behalf of the Bank on material points, namely the price to be paid by the Bank for the shares and the repurchase price; the size of the Bank (fourteen or fifteen branches in addition to the main office); the secondary, rather than fundamental, nature of the change in the terms of the agreement now repudiated by the Bank, measured against the context of the overall transaction; and Brown's broad operating authority * * * all these added together would support a finding of apparent authority.

When a corporate officer, as here, is allowed to exercise general executive responsibilities, the "public expectation is that the corporation should be bound to engagements made on its behalf by those who presume to have, and convincingly appear to have, the power to agree." [Citation] This principle does not apply, of course, where in the business context, the requirement of specific authority is presumed, e.g., the sale of a major asset by a corporation or a transaction, which by its nature commits the corporation to an obligation outside the scope of its usual activity. The modification agreement signed by Brown and dated July 16, 1976, should have been admitted in evidence, and a verdict should not have been directed.

Judgment reversed.

Case Questions

1. Why are "titles of office" insufficient to establish apparent authority?
2. Why are "trappings of office" insufficient to establish apparent authority?
3. What is the relationship between apparent authority and estoppel? Who is estopped to do what, and why?
4. Did the appeals court decide Brown did have apparent authority here?

Key Takeaway

The principal is liable on an agent's contract only if the agent was authorized by the principal to make the contract. Such authority can be express, implied, or apparent. "Express" means that the authorization is made verbally (i.e., orally or in writing); "implied" means the agent has authority to perform acts incidental to or reasonably necessary to carrying out the transaction for which she has express authority. "Apparent authority" arises where the principal gives the third party reason to believe that the agent had authority. The reasonableness of the third party's belief is based on all the circumstances. Even if the agent has no authority, the principal may, after the fact, ratify the contract made by the agent.

Exercises

1. Could express authority be established by silence on the part of the principal?
2. Why is the concept of implied authority very important in business situations?
3. What is the rationale for the doctrine of apparent authority—that is, why would the law impose a contract on a "principal" when in fact there was no principal-agent relationship with the "agent" at all?

10.4 Duties Among the Parties

Learning Objectives

1. Learn the duties the employer/principal owes to agent/employees.
2. Understand the duties the agent owes to the principal.
3. Understand the duties owed by the agent to third parties

In any contract there is an implied duty that the parties will act in *good faith*—correctly and honestly (as much as possible). As the agency relationship is contractual, that good faith duty applies here. But the issue of duties among the parties in agency law has important finer points that involve, along with the good faith duty, a *fiduciary* duty. Here we take up three points: (1) the duty owed by the principal/employer to the agent/employee, (2) the duty owed by the agent to the principal, and (3) the duty owed by the agent to the third party.

Duties Owed by Principal/Employer to Agent/Employee

good-faith duty

The duty to act honestly; it is the normal duty we owe to our fellow humans.

In general, the principal owes the agent a duty in one category: the **good-faith duty**, to interact with the agent/employee honestly and properly. The duty plays out in tort and contract.

In tort, the principal owes the agent or employee, but not an independent contractor, a statutory duty to provide workers' compensation insurance, a matter taken up in Chapter 13. (As noted above, mislabeling of employees as "independent contractors" is not uncommon as employers wish to avoid liability through, and to, their employees based on agency rules.)

In contract, among other things, the principal has these duties:

- to refrain from unreasonably interfering with the agent's work (the principal is allowed, however, to compete with the agent unless the agreement specifically prohibits it).
- to inform the agent of risks of physical harm or pecuniary loss that inhere in the agent's performance of assigned tasks. For example, failure to warn an agent that travel in a particular neighborhood required by the job may be dangerous (a fact unknown to the agent but known to the principal) could under common law subject the principal to a suit for damages if the agent is injured while in the neighborhood performing her job.
- to provide accounts of monies due to the agent.

Duties Owed by Agent/Employee to Principal/Employer

The agent owes the principal duties in two categories: (1) a good-faith duty, and (2) a fiduciary duty.

(1) The good-faith duties owed by the agent to the principal include:

In tort:

- not to commit torts (obviously); the employee will be liable for his or her own torts. As we have seen, the employer is vicariously liable for the employee's torts in the scope of employment as affecting third parties, and usually the employer has liability insurance to protect itself here. If the employee commits a tort affecting another, workers' compensation laws usually apply. And if an employee's tort causes the employer to incur damages, the employee could be required to reimburse the employer. (No fiduciary duty issue arises in tort—only in contract.)

In contract:

- Duty of skill and care. The agent's legal duty is to perform his work with the care and skill that is "standard in the locality for the kind of work which he is employed to perform" and to exercise any special skills, if these are greater or more refined than those prevalent among those normally employed in the community.[7] In short, the agent may not lawfully do a sloppy job.
- Duty of good conduct. The agent is not at liberty to act with impropriety or notoriety, so as to bring disrepute on the business in which the principal is engaged. A lecturer at an alcohol rehabilitation clinic may be directed to refrain from frequenting bars. A bank cashier who becomes known as a gambler may be fired.
- Duty to keep and provide accounts. The agent must keep accurate financial records, take receipts, and otherwise act in conformity to standard business practices.
- Duty to act only as authorized. As long as the agent acts reasonably under the circumstances, he will not be liable for damages later if the principal ultimately repudiates what the agent has done.
- Duty to obey. The agent must obey reasonable directions concerning the manner of performance. A principal may prescribe uniforms for various classes of employees, for instance, and a manufacturing company may tell its sales force what sales pitch to use on customers. On the other hand, certain tasks entrusted to agents are not subject to the principal's control; for example, a lawyer may refuse to permit a client to dictate courtroom tactics.
- Duty to give information. Because the principal cannot be every place at once—that is why agents are hired, after all—much that is vital to the principal's business first comes to the attention of agents. If the agent has actual notice or reason to know of information that is relevant to matters entrusted to him, he has a duty to inform the principal. This duty is especially critical because information in the hands of an agent is, under most circumstances, imputed to the principal, whose legal liabilities to third persons may hinge on receiving information in timely fashion. Service of process, for example, requires a defendant to answer within a certain number of days; an agent's failure to communicate to the principal that a summons has been served may impair or bar the principal's right to defend a lawsuit. The imputation to the principal of knowledge possessed by the agent is strict: even where the agent is acting adversely to the principal's interests—for example, by trying to defraud his employer—a third party may still rely on notification to the agent, unless the third party knows the agent is acting adversely.
- Duty to give employer benefits of employee's work—the shop rights doctrine. An invention "developed and perfected in [a company's] plant with its time, materials, and appliances, and wholly at its expense" may be used by the company without payment of royalties. "Because the servant uses his master's time, facilities and materials to attain a concrete result, the employer is entitled to use that which embodies his own property and to duplicate it as often as he may find occasion to employ similar appliances in his business."[8]

fiduciary duty

The duty to act always in the interests of another, and not in one own's interest (as an attorney has a fiduciary duty to the client).

(2) The **fiduciary duty**. This duty—"fiduciary" derives from the Latin *fidere*, "to trust"—is imposed on people who have some control over another's welfare (money, business interests, personal welfare, etc.). It is the duty to act always in the beneficiary's welfare, and not in the fiduciary's (the agent's) own best interest; the agent must subordinate her interest to that of the principal. New York Judge Learned Hand (1872–1961—isn't that a great name!) famously described the fiduciary duty in 1928:

A trustee is held to something stricter than the morals of the market place. Not honesty alone, but the punctilio of an honor the most sensitive, is then the standard of behavior... the level of conduct for fiduciaries [has] been kept at a level higher than that trodden by the crowd.[9]

In this category are several duties owed by the agent to the principal. We call out two:

- Duty to avoid self-dealing. A fiduciary may not lawfully profit from a conflict between his personal interest in a transaction and his principal's interest in that same transaction. A broker hired as a purchasing agent, for instance, may not sell to his principal through a company in which he or his family has a financial interest. The penalty for breach of fiduciary duty is loss of compensation and profit and possible damages for breach of trust.

- Duty to preserve confidential information. To further his objectives, a principal will usually need to reveal a number of secrets to his agent—how much he is willing to sell or pay for property, marketing strategies, and the like. Such information could easily be turned to the disadvantage of the principal if the agent were to compete with the principal or were to sell the information to those who do. Or, as the Restatement puts it:

  An agent has a duty:

  (1) not to use property of the principal for the agent's own purposes or those of a third party; and

  (2) not to use or communicate confidential information of the principal for the agent's own purposes or those of a third party.[10]

Nor may the agent use confidential information after resigning his agency. Though he is free, in the absence of contract, to compete with his former principal, he may not use information learned in the course of his agency, such as trade secrets and customer lists.

The agent who breaches his or her fiduciary duty has breached the employment contract and will usually get fired, and she will have to account for any and all ill-gotten gains resulting from the disloyalty.

Duty Owed by Agent to Third Party

We may take up the duties owed by the agent to the third party in the familiar two categories of: (1) tort, and (2) contract, and also (3) where the agent lacks authority.

(1) Agent/employee's tort duties to third party.

Because a principal is held vicariously liable and must pay damages to an injured third person does not excuse the agent/employee who actually committed the tortious acts. A person is always liable for his or her own torts (unless the person is insane, involuntarily intoxicated, or acting under extreme duress).

The agent is personally liable for his wrongful acts; the principal may demand reimbursement for any damages the principal was forced to pay, as long as the principal did not authorize the wrongful conduct. However, any agent directed to commit a tort remains liable for his own conduct but is not obliged to repay the principal.

(2) Agent's contract duties to third party.

It makes sense that an agent should be liable for her own torts; it would be a bad social policy indeed if a person could escape tort liability based on her own fault merely because she acted in an agency capacity. It also makes sense that—as is the general rule—an agent is not liable on contracts she makes on the principal's behalf; the agent is not a party to a contract made by the agent on behalf of the principal. No public policy would be served by imposing liability, and in many cases it would not make sense. Suppose an agent contracts to buy $25 million of rolled aluminum for a principal, an airplane manufacturer. The agent personally could not reasonably perform such contract, and it is not intended by the parties that she should be liable.

But there are three exceptions to this rule: (1) if the agent is undisclosed or partially disclosed, (2) if the agent lacks authority or exceeds it, or (3) if the "agent" acts where there is actually no principal.

- Agent for undisclosed or partially disclosed principal. An agent need not, and frequently will not, inform the person with whom she is negotiating that she is acting on behalf of a principal. The secret principal is usually called an "undisclosed principal." Or the agent may tell the other person that he is acting as an agent but not disclose the principal's name, in which event the principal is "partially disclosed." If the third party wants to enforce the contract, both the principal and the agents are liable.

- Agent lacks authority or exceeds it. An agent who purports to make a contract on behalf of a principal, but who in fact has no authority to do so, is liable to the other party.[11] The theory is that the agent has warranted to the third party that he has the requisite authority. The principal is not liable in the absence of apparent authority or ratification. The implied warranty is that the agent has authority to make a deal, however, not that the principal will necessarily comply with the contract once the deal is made.

- "Agent" acting for non-existent principal. An "agent" also lacks authority and will be liable on contract if there is actually no principal. **Promoters** (people who work to start up a corporation) who so defectively form a corporation that it does not legally exist (as failing to submit documents of incorporation to the state) will be personally liable on contracts. There is no "principal" separate from the promoters, so they cannot be agents.

promoters

People who do the work necessary to establish a corporation or development project.

Case

Fiduciary Duty

Gilbert v. Otterson

Gilbert v. Otterson

550 A.2d 550 (PA, 1988)

Pennsylvania Supreme Court case, 1988, analyzing the extent of a former employee's fiduciary duty to his former employer.

[Donald Gilbert was employed by Harry Otterson, d/b/a Gettysburg Exterminating & Lawn Care Company. In August 1985, Gilbert quit and started a competing business, Fairfield Pest Control Corp. and he solicited some of the customers with whom he had become acquainted while in

Otterson's employ. Otterson claimed Gilbert had tortiously interfered with existing and prospective contractual relations by soliciting Otterson's customers and had stolen trade secrets.] * * *

WIEAND, J.

[Gilbert did solicit some of Otterson's customers.] There was no evidence, however, that he had caused any customer of Otterson to breach an existing contract. Therefore, the trial court properly refused to submit to the jury Otterson's claim for intentional interference with existing contractual relations.

In order for Otterson to prove a cause of action for interference with prospective contractual relations, it was essential for him to prove that Gilbert's conduct was improper. [Citation.] * * *

In this case, there was no evidence of a restrictive covenant which could have been enforced to prevent Gilbert from competing with Otterson upon termination of the employment relationship. Therefore, Gilbert could properly compete with Otterson after he was no longer employed by him. See Restatement (Second) of Agency [citation]. This right to compete included the right to divert business from Otterson. There was no evidence that Gilbert had exceeded the privilege of competing with his employer by tortiously interfering with the prospective contractual relations of his employer. The trial court did not err when it refused to submit to the jury Otterson's claim for intentional interference with his prospective contractual relations.

The trial court did submit to the jury the claim that Gilbert had been guilty of violating Otterson's confidence by stealing trade secrets consisting of his customer lists. The jury, however, returned a verdict which denied recovery. Otterson moved post-trial for the entry of judgment n.o.v. [notwithstanding the verdict], but his motion was denied. He argues on appeal that the denial of his motion was error. We disagree. * * * The jury in this case could find that Otterson failed to meet this dual burden as to customers who had been contacted by his former employee. It could find that the identity of Otterson's customers did not constitute a trade secret—they were not the product of any special work on the part of Otterson—and that Gilbert had not misappropriated such information in violation of a confidential relationship. See: [Citations].

Judgment Affirmed.

Case Questions

1. Why was Gilbert not found to have violated the fiduciary duty to his former employer?
2. Why was he not found to have misappropriated trade secrets? That would also have been a breach of the fiduciary duty.

Key Takeaway

The principal or employer owes the employee a duty to act in good faith—to treat the employee honestly and appropriately. In tort this encompasses providing workers' compensation (statutorily required); in contract it encompasses rendering and paying appropriate accounts as per their agreement, not interfering with the agent/employee's job, and warning the agent/employee of dangers associated with the job.

The agent or employee owes the principal duties in tort and contract. In tort, the agent has normal good-faith duties to act carefully, and may be required to reimburse the principal/employer for tort damages the agent/employee causes to third parties for which the employer had to pay under respondeat superior. In contract, the agent owes both good-faith and fiduciary duties. The good-faith duties are the normal sorts of things any employee owes her employer: to follow instructions, do the job well, render accounts, give the employer relevant information, among others. The fiduciary duties are to act always in the principal's best interest—e.g., to keep confidences, and to avoid self-dealing.

Exercises

1. Judge Learned Hand was quoted above regarding "The fiduciary duty is not the ordinary morals of the marketplace." How does the fiduciary duty differ from "the ordinary morals of the marketplace"? Why does the law impose a fiduciary duty on the agent?
2. What are the non-fiduciary duties owed by the agent to the principal?
3. What contract duties are owed by the principal to the agent?

10.5 Termination of Agency

Learning Objective

1. Understand how agency relationships are terminated.

The agency relationship is not permanent and will terminate by action of the parties or by operation of law.

By Action of the Parties

- Express Termination. The parties' agreement may stipulate when the agency ends. The most obvious of these circumstances is the expiration of a fixed period of time ("agency to terminate at the end of three months" or "on midnight, December 31")—an **express termination**. An agreement may also terminate on the accomplishment of a specified act ("on the sale of the house") or following a specific event ("at the conclusion of the last horse race").

- Mutual consent between the parties will end the agency. Moreover, the principal may revoke the agency or the agent may renounce it; such a revocation or renunciation of agency would be an express termination. Even a contract that states the agreement is irrevocable will not be binding, although it can be the basis for a damage suit against the one who breached the agreement by revoking or renouncing it. As with any contract, a person has the *power* to breach, even in absence of the *right* to do so.

- Implied Termination. There are a number of other circumstances that will spell the end of the relationship by implication. Unspecified events or changes in business conditions or the value of the subject matter of the agency might lead to a reasonable inference that the agency should be terminated or suspended. For example, suppose the principal desires the agent to buy bitcoin within a certain price range, but the silver market unexpectedly rises and silver doubles in price overnight. Other circumstances where there is **implied termination** include disloyalty of the agent (e.g., she accepts an agency relationship with another principal adverse to her first principal, or embezzles from the principal), bankruptcy of the agent or of the principal, or the outbreak of war in the place where the agent is working. (Here, it must be reasonable to infer that the principal, knowing that war had broken out, would not want the agent to continue to exercise agency authority. Finally, there could be a change in the law that would makes continued carrying out of the task illegal, or seriously interferes with the task.

express termination

A termination (as of employment or a lease) by words, orally or in writing.

implied termination

A termination (as of employment or a lease) because a reasonable interpretation of the facts indicates the legal relationship is over.

By Operation of Law

The most frequent termination by operation of law is the death of the principal or of the agent. The death of an agent also terminates the authority of subagents previously appointed, unless the principal has expressly consented to the continuing validity of their appointment. Similarly, if the agent or principal loses capacity to enter into an agency relationship, it is suspended or terminated. The agency terminates if its purpose becomes illegal.

Even though authority has terminated, whether by action of the parties or operation of law, the principal may still be subject to liability. Apparent authority in many instances will still exist; this is called **lingering authority**. A principal, on termination of authority, must notify all those who may still be in a position to deal with the agent. The only exceptions to this requirement are when termination is affected by death, loss of the principal's capacity, or an event that would make it impossible to carry out the object of the agency.

lingering authority

Apparent authority that arises when a former principal gives third parties cause to reasonably believe that a former agent still has authority when the agency is in fact terminated.

Key Takeaway

Agencies terminate expressly or impliedly or by operation of law. An agency terminates expressly by the terms of the agreement or mutual consent, or by the principal's revocation or the agent's renunciation. An agency terminates impliedly by any number of circumstances in which it is reasonable to assume one or both of the parties would not want the relationship to continue. An agency will terminate by operation of law when one or the other party dies or becomes incompetent, or if the object of the agency becomes illegal. However, an agent may have apparent lingering authority, so the principal, upon termination of the agency, should notify those who might deal with the agent that the relationship is severed.

Exercises

1. Under what circumstances will the agency terminate expressly?
2. Agent is hired by Principal to sell a new drug, Phobbot. Six months later, as it becomes apparent that Phobbot has nasty side effects (including death), the Food and Drug Administration orders the drug pulled from the shelves. Agent's agency is terminated; what terminology is appropriate to describe how?
3. Principal engages Agent to buy lumber, and in that capacity Agent deals with several large timber owners. Agent's contract ends on July 31; on August 1, Agent buys $150,000 worth of lumber from a seller with whom he had dealt previously on Principal's behalf. Who is liable and why?

10.6 Summary and Exercises

Summary

An agent is one who acts on behalf of another. The agency relationship is usually created by contract (express, implied, or apparent), but some agencies are created by operation of law.

The law recognizes several types of agents, including: (1) the general agent, one who possesses authority to carry out a broad range of transactions in the name of, and on behalf of, the principal; (2) the special agent, one with authority to act only in a specifically designated instance or set of transactions; (3) the subagent, one appointed by an agent with authority to do so; and (4) the servant ("employee" in modern English), one whose physical conduct is subject to control of the principal.

A servant or employee is distinguished from an independent contractor, whose work is not subject to the control of the principal. The difference is important for purposes of taxation, workers' compensation, and liability insurance.

The employer is liable for torts committed by an employee in the scope of employment; the employee is also liable. The principal is liable on contracts entered into by authorized agents.

An agent owes his principal the normal duty to act in good faith: the agent should perform the job at hand with skill and care, conduct her personal life so as not to bring disrepute on the business for which he acts as agent, keep and render accounts, and give appropriate information to the principal. But beyond the good-faith duty, the agent owes the highest duty of loyalty, that of a fiduciary. The agent must avoid self-dealing, and preserve confidential information. Although the principal is not the agent's fiduciary, the principal does have certain obligations toward the agent—for example, to refrain from interfering with the agent's work and to indemnify.

The agent has duties to the third party, too, of particular note in cases of non-disclosed or partially disclosed agencies, and where in fact there is no principal at all. In such cases the agent (or "agent") may be personally liable to the third party.

Exercises

1. A woman was involved in an automobile accident that resulted in the death of a passenger in her car. After she was charged with manslaughter, her attorney agreed to work with her insurance company's claims adjuster in handling the case. As a result of the agreement, the woman gave a statement about the accident to the claims adjuster. When the prosecuting attorney demanded to see the statement, the woman's attorney refused on the grounds that the claims adjuster was his—the attorney's—agent, and therefore the statement was covered by the attorney-client privilege. Is the attorney correct? Why?

2. A local hotel operated under a franchise agreement with a major hotel chain. Several customers charged the banquet director of the local hotel with misconduct and harassment. They sued the hotel chain (the franchisor) for acts committed by the local hotel (the franchisee), claiming that the franchisee was the agent of the franchisor. Is an agency created under these circumstances? Why?

3. A principal hired a mortgage banking firm to obtain a loan commitment of $10,000,000 from an insurance company for the construction of a shopping center. The firm was promised a fee of $50,000 for obtaining the commitment. The firm was successful in arranging for the loan, and the insurance company, without the principal's knowledge, agreed to pay the firm a finder's fee. The principal then refused to pay the firm the promised $50,000, and the firm brought suit to recover the fee. May the firm recover the fee? Why?

4. Based on his experience working for the CIA, a former CIA agent published a book about certain CIA activities in South Vietnam. The CIA did not approve of the publication of the book although, as a condition of his employment, the agent had agreed not to publish any information relating to the CIA without specific approval of the agency. The government brought suit against the agent, claiming that all the agent's profits from publishing the book should go to the government. Assuming that the government suffered only nominal damages because the agent published no classified information, will the government prevail? Why?

5. Upon graduation from college, Edison was hired by a major chemical company. During the time when he was employed by the company, Edison discovered a synthetic oil that could be manufactured at a very low cost. What rights, if any, does Edison's employer have to the discovery? Why?

6. A U.S. company hired MacDonald to serve as its resident agent in Bolivia. MacDonald entered into a contract to sell cars to Bolivia and personally guaranteed performance of the

contract as required by Bolivian law. The cars delivered to Bolivia were defective, and Bolivia recovered a judgment of $83,000 from MacDonald. If MacDonald sues in the U.S. for reimbursement of the $83,000, will the court agree that the U.S. company should reimburse MacDonald? Explain.

7. Principal engaged Agent to sell Principal's restored 1948 Packard convertible to Byers for $53,000. A few days later, Agent saw an advertisement showing that Collector was willing to pay $60,000 for a 1948 Packard convertible in "restored" condition. Agent sold the car to Byers, and subsequently Principal learned of Collector's interest. What rights, if any, has Principal against Agent?

8. What was wrong with common-law rules on employers' liability to employees injured on the job?

Self-Test Questions

1. One who has authority to act only in a specifically designated instance or in a specifically designated set of transactions is called:

   a. a subagent

   b. a general agent

   c. a special agent

   d. none of the above

2. An agency relationship may be created by:

   a. contract

   b. operation of law

   c. an oral agreement

   d. all of the above

3. An agent's duty to the principal includes:

   a. the duty to indemnify

   b. the duty to warn of special dangers

   c. the duty to avoid self dealing

   d. all of the above

4. A person whose work is not subject to the control of the principal, but who arranges to perform a job for him is called:

   a. a subagent

   b. a servant

   c. a special agent

   d. an independent contractor

5. The principal owes the agent:

   a. a duty of good faith

   b. a fiduciary duty

   c. two of these

   d. none of the above

6. Authority that legally may bind the principal includes:

   a. implied authority

   b. express authority

   c. apparent authority

   d. all of the above

7. As a general rule, a principal is not:

a. liable for tortious acts of an agent, even when the principal is negligent

b. liable for acts of a servant within the scope of employment

c. criminally liable for acts of the agent

d. liable for nondelegable duties performed by independent contractors

8. An agent may be held personally liable on contracts signed on behalf of a principal when:

a. the agent is serving an undisclosed or partially disclosed principal

b. the agent exceeds his authority

c. the agent entered into the contract in a personal capacity

d. all of the above are true

9. An agency relationship may be terminated by:

a. an implied agreement arising out of the circumstances

b. mutual consent of parties

c. death of the principal or agent

d. all of the above

10. The principal's liability for the agent's acts, which the principal did not specifically authorize, is:

a. contract liability

b. implied liability

c. respondeat superior

d. all of the above

Self-Test Answers

1. c
2. d
3. d
4. d
5. c
6. d
7. d
8. c
9. d
10. d

Endnotes

1. See Chapter 13 on Employment Law.
2. Restatement (Third) of Agency, sec. ____ (etc)
3. See, e.g., Department for Professional Employees, Misclassifications of Employees as Independent Contractors, http://dpeaflcio.org/programs-publications/issue-fact-sheets/misclassification-of-employees-as-independent-contractors/#_edn5.
4. https://www.dol.gov/whd/workers/Misclassification/.
5. 277 N.W.2d 11 (Minn., 1979)
6. This is a citation to a "hornbook," a primer; a book explaining the basics, fundamentals, or rudiments of any science or branch of knowledge (here, of the law of negligence).
7. Restatement (Third) of Agency, sec. 8.08 (2006). http://studylib.net/doc/8168533/restatement-of-the-law----agency-restatement--third--of-a...
8. *Grip Nut Co. v. Sharp*, 150 F.2d 192 (7th Cir. 1945).
9. *Meinhard v. Salmon*, 164 N.E. 545 (N.Y. 1928)
10. Restatement (Third) of Agency, Sec. 8.02 ff. (2006).
11. You may recall the *Barnes v. Treece* case in Chapter 8, where the defendant, vice president of a corporation that manufactured gambling machines, publicly asserted that he will pay $100,000 if anybody brought to his offices a rigged machine; the audience laughed. Barnes had such a machine and produced it. Not only did the court find that Treece's words constituted a legitimate offer, moreover, he was found personally liable: his employer, the corporation, gave him no authority to make such an offer.

CHAPTER 11
Business Organization Law

Chapter Learning Objectives

After reading this chapter, you should understand:

1. The laws governing sole proprietorships.
2. The laws governing partnerships.
3. The laws governing corporations.
4. The main types of and the laws governing hybrid business forms.

This chapter takes what we have examined in tort, contract, and agency law and applies these concepts to an examination of business organization law. It would be difficult to conceive of a complex society that did not operate its businesses through organizations. In this chapter we study sole proprietorships (which are not really "organizations"), partnerships, and corporations, and we touch on hybrid business forms, including limited partnerships, S-corporations, and limited liability companies.

11.1 Sole Proprietorships

Learning Objectives

1. Understand how a sole proprietorship is created, capitalized, and controlled.
2. Know how a sole proprietor is compensated.
3. Understand how a sole proprietorship creates liabilities on its owner for business debts.
4. Know how a sole proprietorship is treated for federal income tax purposes.
5. Understand how a sole proprietorship is terminated.

Here we consider some legal aspects of the first of the four business-organization types we examine. This is sole proprietorship law; the others are partnership, corporations, and hybrid business-organization forms.

Introduction to Sole Proprietorship

A sole proprietorship is an unincorporated business owned by one person. It is the simplest kind of business organization, though it is not an "organization" at all. Though the owner may have many employees, legally, the sole proprietorship is an **identity**—there is no legal distinction between the business and its owner. The "business" itself is not a legal entity; Jan Smith d/b/a ("doing business as") The Little Red School indicates that the school is a sole proprietorship owned by Jan Smith who

identity

A business form in which no legal distinction is made between the business and the owner of it.

is doing business as the Little Red School. Sole proprietorships make up, by far, the largest number of U.S. business organization types, but they are the smallest in terms of associated revenue.

FIGURE 11.1 Number of U.S. Business Organizations (1000s), 2013

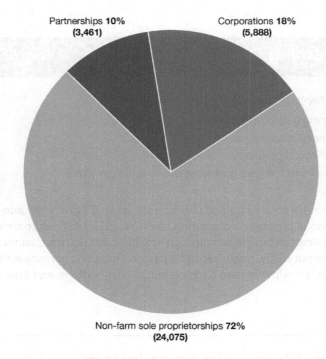

Partnerships **10%** (3,461)

Corporations **18%** (5,888)

Non-farm sole proprietorships **72%** (24,075)

Source for data: U.S. Census, Statistical Abstracts of the United States, Table 768 from 2013

FIGURE 11.2 Gross income U.S. Business Organizations ($billion), 2013

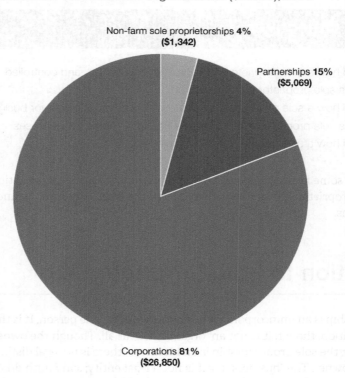

Non-farm sole proprietorships **4%** ($1,342)

Partnerships **15%** ($5,069)

Corporations **81%** ($26,850)

Source for data: U.S. Census, Statistical Abstracts of the United States, Table 768 from 2013

Creation and Capitalization

Creation

One benefit to the sole proprietorship is that it is easy to create: a person sets up and starts doing business. There are no formalities, and no state filing (however, the owner may be required to get a state, county or city business license).

Capitalization

Any business needs money to start up. A sole proprietor cannot issue stock, and must depend on her own start-up money, perhaps from family or friends who will pitch in. If a lot of capital is needed for the business to get started, the sole proprietorship is not the best business form to choose.

Control and Compensation

Control

The sole proprietorship is easy to control: there is only one owner, and that person is the boss. The boss can make decisions without conferring with partners or board members (there are none). Easy, however, is not always best. As is said, two heads (or three) are often better than one.

Compensation

The compensation of any business owner necessarily must come from the profits of the business. There is nobody to pay the owner wages or salary. In a sole proprietorship, the owner simply takes home as income whatever is left after paying expenses (or if expenses are greater than income, the owner will have to pay out of her own pocket).

Liabilities

The greatest disadvantage of the sole proprietorship is, again, related to its status as an identity, the liability issue—liability is personal and unlimited. The debts of the business are the owner's personal debts, and while the owner may buy liability insurance to protect against tort losses, contract losses may not be generally insurable. Bankruptcy is the sole proprietor's last refuge, and that might mean losing the house and other property taken to satisfy creditors' claims.

Taxation

Again, related to the "identity" point—there is no legal distinction between the owner and the business—the sole proprietorship as a business pays no federal income taxation. The owner pays income tax on whatever he or she takes from the business. The business is thus referred to as a "pass through" or a "mere conduit" (the "**conduit theory**," or the "**pass through theory**"); tax liabilities are owed not by "the business" but by the individual owner.

Termination

A sole proprietorship is easy to terminate: the owner just stops doing business; there are no partners or other interested parties involved directly. But two issues of note arise: (1) how easy is it to dispose of the business interest (called "ease of alienation"), and (2) what rights do creditors have to pursue payment if the business is terminated?

Ease of Alienation

An important feature of capitalism is the individual right to own property, real and personal, and to dispose of property by giving it away, willing it to heirs, or—most relevant here—selling it. Disposing of a business interest is referred to "**alienation of the interest**"—it is the capacity for property or a property right to be sold or otherwise transferred from one party to another. The sole proprietor owns the business, and when he calls it quits he may hope to sell it. The part owner of a corporation may own shares of stock; when the owner wants out, easy-peasy, just call a broker (dealer in stock) and sell the shares. But if you are the owner of a sole proprietorship it's not so easy: you have to find somebody who wants to run, hands-on, that business. How many people might want to own shares of stock in, say, Microsoft? Many millions. How many people want to own a manicure salon, or a veterinarian clinic? Not many at all. In brief, often it's not easy to alienate the ownership interest in a sole proprietorship.

Rights of Creditors

The second issue associated with termination of the business, after ease of alienation, is what rights do creditors have to pursue the former owner? Again, because there is no distinction between the person of the owner and the business (they are an identity), creditors have every right to pursue the former owner to satisfy outstanding debts. Even if the new owner has agreed to assume those debts, the former owner remains liable to creditors until the debts are paid (unless the former owner is discharged). Death of the sole proprietor dissolves and terminates the sole proprietorship, but the debts live on as part of the decedent/owner's estate.

Key Takeaway

A sole proprietorship is an unincorporated business owned and completely controlled by one person; it is *not* an entity separate from its owner—they are an identity. No formalities are needed to create the sole proprietorship, though capitalization of the business—with only one or a few interested parties to contribute—is difficult. Only the sole proprietor is taxed, and that person has unlimited liability for the business's debts. The interest in the business is freely transferable, except that the number of potential transferees is limited because whoever takes the business will have to run it hands-on. The death of the sole proprietor terminates the business, but debts are not extinguished.

Exercises

1. What does it mean to say the sole proprietorship is, legally, "an identity"?
2. What disadvantage does the sole proprietorship confront in capitalization?
3. Why is the sole proprietor personally liable without limit for the business's obligations?
4. When the sole proprietor quits, what happens to the business debts?
5. Why is it not so easy, in practice, for the sole proprietor to dispose of the business interest?

11.2 General Partnerships

Learning Objectives

1. Understand how partnership law has developed, and what the "entity" issue is all about.
2. Know how a partnership is created and capitalized.
3. Understand how a partnership is controlled and its owners compensated.
4. Recognize how a partnership creates liabilities for its owners for business debts.
5. See how a partnership is treated for federal income tax purposes.
6. Understand how a partnership terminates.

Introduction to Partnership Law

Definition of a Partnership

Partnership law defines a partnership as "the association of two or more persons to carry on as co-owners a business for profit."[1] In 2014, there were more than three million business firms in the United States as partnerships (see Table 10.1), and partnerships are traditionally a common form of organization among accountants, lawyers, doctors, and other professionals. When we use the word partnership, we are referring to the general business partnership. There are also limited partnerships and limited liability partnerships, which are discussed in subsequent sections. A **joint venture** is, essentially, a partnership for a specific project.[2]

> **joint venture**
>
> A partnership for a specific project (such as making a movie).

Because it is possible to become someone's partner without intending to, or even realizing that a partnership has been created, it is important to know about partnerships. If you have a partnership, however unintentionally, you may incur personal liability for what other partners did.

TABLE 11.1 Selected Data: Number of U.S. Partnerships, Limited Partnerships, and Limited Liability Companies

	1999	2002	2008	2014
Total number of active partnerships	1,936,919	2,242,169	3,146,006	3,611,255
Number of partners	15,353,154	13,328,108	19,300,250	27,714,478
Number of limited partnerships	354,295	376,963	411,698	414,338
Number of partners	8,944,693	6,918,515	7,054,319	12,250,817
Number of limited liability companies	589,403	946,130	1,898,178	2,432,303
Number of partners	2,256,062	3,737,899	7,524,172	10,202,627

Source: IRS, https://www.irs.gov/statistics/soi-tax-stats-historical-table-11

History of Partnership Law

Partnerships are ancient forms—one caveman says to another, "Together, let's hunt down this deer and split the meat;" that's a partnership. Partnership law developed in England over centuries as common law, and judges made up the rules as issues presented themselves. In the United States partnership law, like corporate law, is predominately the province of the 50 states. When the American Revolutionary War ended in 1783 the states began to develop partnership law, and not surprisingly, the states' common-law development was different from state to state. These differences caused uncertainty when commercial transactions crossed state borders, but they were largely reconciled by scholars and practitioners who drafted the Uniform Partnership Act (UPA), which was presented to the states for their adoption in 1914. All states have adopted the UPA (except Louisiana, which has a history of setting its own rules).[3] Federal tax and securities laws also affect partnerships (and corporations), but structures and rules for these business entities remain defined by state law.

The Entity Issue

aggregate theory

Under the 1914 Uniform Partnership Act, and from the common law, a partnership was not an entity, but a collection of individuals bound together by contract. (The revised act modifies this; some states still use the UPA.)

The drafters of the 1914 UPA debated over which of two partnership theories to adopt: should a partnership be a legal entity (separate from its owners), like a corporation, or should it be an aggregate (an aggregation of individuals) as it was at common law? UPA §6(1) in 1914 provided a neutral definition of partnership ("an association of two or more persons to carry on as co-owners a business for profit") and retained the common-law theory that a partnership is an aggregation of individuals—**the aggregate theory**.

But a revised act was adopted in 1997 that combined these theories. The aggregate approach was retained for some purposes, such as partners' "joint and several liability" (in modern English we would say joint and individual liability: all partners are liable, and each one is liable). Section 201(a) provides, "A partnership is an entity distinct from its partners." So, a partnership is an entity, but for some purposes, and not for others:

- Accounting purposes: the firm may keep business records as if it were a separate entity.
- Taxation: partnerships are *not* taxable entities, so they do not pay income taxes. The partners pay on their draws (income taken).

- Litigation: the UPA bows to the entity theory here—"A partnership may sue and be sued in the name of the partnership"[4]; and it bows to the aggregate side here—a plaintiff must still name the partnership and the partners individually to have access to both estates, the partnership's and the individuals' ("A judgment against a partnership is not by itself a judgment against a partner. A judgment against a partnership may not be satisfied from a partner's assets unless there is also a judgment against the partner.")[5] To this extent, the Revised UPA (RUPA) recognizes the entity.

- Owning real estate: RUPA provides that "property acquired by a partnership is property of the partnership and not of the partners individually."[6]

Thus, RUPA tends toward entity, and UPA stays aggregate. There are other differences, but for the purposes of this overview they will be noted only in passing.

Creation and Capitalization

Creation of the Partnership

A partnership is a contractual relationship among the owner-partners. As such it can be created in the same ways that any contract is created: expressly, impliedly, or apparently (this last one is also called "by estoppel").

Express Partnership. Usually partnerships are created expressly—that is, in words, orally or in writing. Such a partnership is called—reasonably enough—an **express partnership**. If parties have an express partnership with no partnership agreement, the relevant law—the Uniform Partnership Act (UPA) or the Revised Uniform Partnership Act (RUPA)—applies the governing rules.[7] That is, the agreement can be pretty much whatever the partners want; if their agreement does not address an issue, the relevant act is the default rule.

Implied Partnership. An **implied partnership** exists when, in fact, there are two or more persons carrying on a business as co-owners for profit, but they have not expressed the relationship.

Obviously, with an express agreement we know there is a partnership. But partnerships can come into existence informally—or accidentally. Courts use the definition of a partnership—not the parties' intentions—to determine if one exists.

express partnership

A partnership agreed to in words—orally or in writing.

implied partnership

A partnership that arises without any express agreement, but by the actions of the parties. Sharing decision making and profits are salient indicators of the existence of a partnership.

FIGURE 11.3 What Constitutes a Partnership?

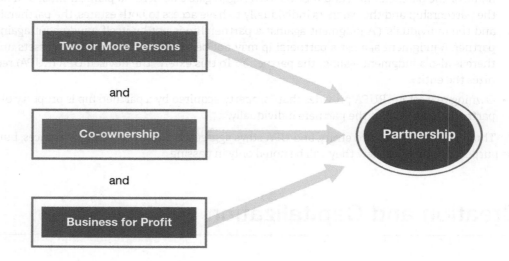

Association of persons. "'Person' means an individual, corporation, business trust, estate, trust, partnership, association, joint venture, government, governmental subdivision, agency, or instrumentality, or any other legal or commercial entity."[8] Thus a corporation can generally be a partner.

Co-ownership. Co-ownership comes in many guises, but to establish a partnership, the ownership must be of a business, not merely of property that might be used in the business.

Sharing of Profits. Partnership law provides that "a person who receives a share of the profits of a business is presumed to be a partner in the business," but this presumption can be rebutted by showing—among other possibilities—that the share of the profits paid out was to repay a debt, wages, or compensation to an independent contractor, or rent.

Partnership by Estoppel. Ordinarily, if two people are not legally partners, then third parties cannot so regard them. However, where there is a representation to a third party that there is in fact a partnership, and reliance by the third party on that representation, partnership law provides that the persons making the representation cannot deny it—they are estopped to do so: they have a **partnership by estoppel**

> **partnership by estoppel**
>
> A partnership that is imposed on the "partners" when third parties have reasonably relied on the appearance that there is a partnership; it is a "apparent partnership."

Capitalization of the Partnership

Partnerships get capital from the partners; they may organize their capital contributions by the agreement; they may agree that property owned by a partner before the formation of the partnership, but used by the firm, will or will not be partnership property. Raul may own a building, the use of which he contributes to the firm, but he retains its title and it is not partnership property. But, he could give the partnership title as part of his capital contribution.

New partners are expected to make a capital contribution which, often, is taken out of the funds they would otherwise be entitled to as income from the firm.

One drawback of the partnership form is that really large amounts of capital cannot usually be raised. Ten or even two hundred partners could not readily raise the hundreds of millions needed for a major capitalization (as, for example, to start a new automobile manufacturing company, like Tesla).

Control and Compensation

Most of the rules discussed in this section apply unless otherwise agreed, and they are really intended for the small firm. Again, the Uniform Partnership Act (UPA) and the Revised Uniform Partnership Act (RUPA) do not (with rare exceptions[9]) dictate what the relations among partners must be; the acts supply rules in the event that the partners have not done so for themselves.

Control of the Partnership

All partners are entitled to share equally in the management and conduct of the business, unless the partnership agreement provides otherwise.[10] The agreement could be structured to delegate more decision-making power to one class (senior partners) than to others (junior partners), or it may give more voting weight to certain individuals.

Because each partner has some control over the firm and the other partners' welfare, it is expected that the partners will behave as part of a team, working together. This imposes on the partners some duties and some rights. The "Official Comment" to UPA 301 observes: "a partner [is] a general managerial agent having both actual and apparent authority in scope with the firm's ordinary business."

Partnership Duties

Partners owe each other duties in two categories: the good-faith duty and the fiduciary duty. This is agency law—all partners are principals and agents of each other.

Good-Faith Duty

The **good-faith duty** is the duty to act as a prudent, honest person (here, the co-owner of the firm); it is the duty that we all owe to our fellow humans and their property. In this category four specific duties may be called out:

- Duty to serve. Generally, a partner is expected to work for the firm, and not just expect income from it.
- Duty of obedience. A partner is responsible to the partners for damages or losses arising from unauthorized activities that violate the terms of their agreement. Partners have a duty to make capital contributions as per their agreement.
- Duty to inform co-partners. A partner must inform co-partners of notices and matters coming to her attention that would be of interest to the partnership.
- Duty to allow inspection of books and records of the firm.

good-faith duty

The normal duty imposed by law that people should act honestly.

Fiduciary Duty

The **fiduciary duty** is the duty to always act in the best interest of another (here, the firm and co-partners) and not in one's own best interest. Here, we may call out two aspects of this duty (there are others).

- Duty of loyalty. Partners must put the firm's interests ahead of their own. Partners are fiduciaries as to each other and as to the partnership, and as such, they owe a fiduciary duty to each other and the partnership. Breach of the fiduciary duty gives rise to a claim for compensatory, consequential, and incidental damages; recoupment of compensation; and—although rarely—punitive damages. Loyalty to the firm includes not competing with it or acting as or on behalf of a party with an adverse interest to the firm; no partner may make secret profits

fiduciary duty

The duty to always act in the best interests of another, and not in one's own best interest.

while doing partnership business; all partners must maintain the confidentiality of partnership information.

- Duty to account to the partnership and hold as trustee for it any property, profit, or benefit derived by the partner in the conduct of, or the winding up of, the partnership business. This includes the value of any use by the partner of partnership property, including the appropriation of a partnership opportunity.[11]

Partnership Rights

Here we note the following salient rights that general partners have (additional detail lurks in some of the endnotes):

Right to distributions of profits. Profits and losses will be shared according to any formula the partners agree; if there is no agreement, they share equally.

Right to management. Absent agreement contra, all partners share equally in the management and conduct of the business.

Right to choose fellow partners. A business partnership is often analogized to a marriage. In both there is a relationship of trust and confidence between (or among) the parties; in both, the poor judgment, negligence, or dishonesty of one can create liabilities on the other(s). Thus, no one is compelled to accept a partner against his or her will: "A person may become a partner only with the consent of all of the partners." (But consent cannot be denied merely because of race, religion, national origin, or sex—employment discrimination is not allowed.[12])

Right to use property of the partnership.[13]

Right to assign partnership interest. A partner may assign some interest in the partnership—the interest entitling her to a share of the profits and distributions (personal property). She cannot assign management and other rights to outsiders.[14]

Right to information and inspection of books, including the right to an accounting.[15]

Partnership Compensation

As always, the only way owners of a business can get compensated is from the profits of the business. The general rule is that, absent an agreement contra, all of the partners share equally in the profits (or losses) of the firm.

In express partnerships the partners usually do *not* share equally—usually there is a formula upon which partner compensation is calculated. For example, a partner's draw (the amount a partner takes as income) may be based on billable hours, or numbers of new clients obtained in the last year, or compensation may increase based on years of service. In any event, the reason people want to "make partner" is because they share in the profit, even if they didn't directly participate in earning it. Able, Baker, Carr, and Donkers are partners in a law firm; they share profits equally. Able settles a case and the firm gets $1 million. Baker, Carr, and Donkers each get $250,000 (as does Able who did the deal).

Taxation

In accord with the aggregate theory, partnership income "passes through" the partnership and is distributed to the partners under the **conduit theory**. When partners get income from the firm they have to pay tax on it, but the partnership pays no tax (it files an information return with the IRS). This is perceived to be a significant advantage of the partnership form because—often—the total tax bill owing to the government is reduced compared to what would be owing if the firm were a corporation that paid taxes on its profits and then distributed income to shareholders who have to pay taxes on that income (dividends).

> **conduit theory**
>
> In tax, the idea that the money-making business is itself not subject to income tax, but rather acts only as a mechanism by which the owners earn taxable income.

Liability of Partners

Tort Liability

The general rule is this: "A partnership is liable for loss or injury, or for a penalty incurred, as a result of a wrongful act or omission, or other actionable conduct, of a partner acting in the ordinary course" of partnership business or with its authority. This is agency law, and certainly the partner who commits the tort is also personally liable, but we are interested in the vicarious liability of the partnership. Criminal liability is generally personal to the miscreant (unless the firm actually directs the illegal acts).

Contract Liability

The general rule—again from agency law—is that contracts entered into by authorized agents (here the partner) binds the principal (here the partnership). Recall that an agent can make contracts on behalf of a principal under three types of authority: express, implied, and apparent. *Express authority* is that explicitly delegated to the agent; *implied authority* is that necessary to the carrying out of the express authority; and *apparent authority* is that which a third party is led to believe has been conferred by the principal on the agent, even though in fact it was not, or it was revoked. When a partner has authority, the partnership is bound by contracts the partner makes on its behalf.[16] *Hodge v. Garrett*, discusses all three types of authority. A new partner has no personal liability to already-existing creditors of the partnership, and only her capital investment in the firm is at risk for the satisfaction of existing partnership debts.[17]

The partnership, then, is liable for its partners' torts and contracts. Moreover—and alarmingly—each partner is personally liable without limit: "All partners are liable jointly and severally for all obligations of the partnership unless otherwise agreed by the claimant or provided by law."[18] This the big downside to the partnership form.

Termination of the Partnership

Dissolution and Dissociation of the Partnership

The rules governing "getting out" of a partnership are different under the Revised Uniform Partnership Act (RUPA) than under the Uniform Partnership Act (UPA).

dissolution

The end of a legal contractual relationship binding two or more people to that relationship.

dissociation

Under the Revised Uniform Partnership Act, the withdrawal of a partner from the firm without causing dissolution.

Dissolution. Under UPA, when a partner is no longer associated with the firm, it is said to "dissolve"—separate into its component parts. After **dissolution** under the UPA, the firm can carry on as a new partnership, or it can wind up and cease operation.

Dissociation. Under RUPA, when a partner is no longer associated with the firm there is a "**dissociation**," but the next step, dissolution, does *not* necessarily happen. (This follows from RUPA's entity theory: there is no conceptual reason for the firm to dissolve upon a member's withdrawal). RUPA lists ten ways a dissociation can occur[19] (for example, a partner wants out, is expelled or dies). RUPA *dissolution* is caused by act of the partners, by operation of law, or by court order, and then the firm does cease to exist except for winding up.

Ease of alienation. Departing partners are, subject to the terms of the partnership agreement—or the relevant partnership law, if there is no agreement—entitled to a return of their capital contributions. (Often the firm purchases life insurance on its members, so upon a partner's death, insurance pays the heirs their capital share—a life insurance buyout.) But no partner can, without the consent of all, sell her interest in the firm to a new person, so the interest is not easily alienable.

Winding Up

winding up

Finishing up the business (of a corporation, partnership, etc.) at hand and closing the books.

If the business is not to be continued upon dissolution, partners are obliged to wind up the business; business continues only for the purpose of **winding up**, after which it is terminated. Winding up entails concluding all unfinished business pending at the date of dissolution and payment of all debts. The partners must then settle accounts among themselves and distribute remaining assets

Liabilities Upon Dissolution

Upon termination, the surplus or liabilities of the firm are split among the former partners according to their agreement or by general partnership law. As to rights of creditors: former partners are—as noted above—personally liable for debts unpaid by the firm upon its termination.

Case

Tests of Partnership Existence

Chaiken v. Employment Security Commission

Delaware Supreme Court case, 1971, analyzing the elements required to show a partnership exists.

Chaiken v. Employment Security Commission

274 A.2d 707 (Del., 1971)

Storey, J.

The Employment Security Commission levied an assessment against Richard K. Chaiken for not filing his unemployment security assessment report. A hearing was held and a determination made by the Commission that Chaiken was the employer of two barbers in his barbershop and that he should be assessed as an employer for his share of unemployment compensation contributions. Chaiken appealed the Commission's decision. * * *

Both in the administrative hearing and in his appeal brief Chaiken argues that he had entered into partnership agreements with each of his barbers and, therefore, was and is not subject to unemployment compensation assessment. The burden is upon the individual assessed to show that he is outside the scope of the statutory sections requiring assessment. (If Chaiken's partnership argument fails he will have to make the report and pay the unemployment contribution.)

Chaiken contends that he and his "partners":

- properly registered the partnership name and names of partners in the appropriate office.
- properly filed federal partnership information returns and paid federal taxes quarterly on an estimated basis, and
- duly executed partnership agreements.

Of the three factors, the last is most important. Agreements of "partnership" were executed between Chaiken and Mr. Strazella, a barber in the shop, and between Chaiken and Mr. Spitzer, similarly situated. The agreements were nearly identical. The first paragraph declared the creation of a partnership and the location of business. The second provided that Chaiken would provide barber chair, supplies, and licenses, while the other partner would provide tools of the trade. The paragraph also declared that upon dissolution of the partnership, ownership of items would revert to the party providing them. The third paragraph declared that the income of the partnership would be divided 30% for Chaiken, 70% for Strazella; 20% for Chaiken and 80% for Spitzer. The fourth paragraph declared that all partnership policy would be decided by Chaiken, whose decision was final. The fifth paragraph forbade assignment of the agreement without permission of Chaiken. The sixth paragraph required Chaiken to hold and distribute all receipts. The final paragraph stated hours of work for Strazella and Spitzer and holidays.

The mere existence of an agreement labeled "partnership" agreement and the characterization of signatories as "partners" does not conclusively prove the existence of a partnership. Rather, the intention of the parties, as explained by the wording of the agreement, is paramount.

A partnership is defined as an association of two or more persons to carry on as co-owners a business for profit. As co-owners of a business, partners have an equal right in the decision making process. But this right may be abrogated by agreement of the parties without destroying the partnership concept, provided other partnership elements are present.

Thus, while paragraph four reserves for Chaiken all right to determine partnership policy, it is not standing alone, fatal to the partnership concept. Co-owners should also contribute valuable consideration for the creation of the business. Under paragraph two, however, Chaiken provides the barber chair (and implicitly the barbershop itself), mirror, licenses, and linen, while the other partners merely provide their tools and labor—nothing more than any barber-employee would furnish. Standing alone, however, mere contribution of work and skill can be valuable consideration for a partnership agreement.

Partnership interests may be assignable, although it is not a violation of partnership law to prohibit assignment in a partnership agreement. Therefore, paragraph five on assignment of partnership interests does not violate the partnership concept. On the other hand, distribution of partnership assets to the partners upon dissolution is only allowed after all partnership liabilities are satisfied. But paragraph two of the agreement, in stating the ground rules for dissolution, makes no declaration that the partnership assets will be utilized to pay partnership expenses before reversion to their original owners. This deficiency militates against a finding in favor of partnership intent since it is assumed Chaiken would have inserted such provision had he thought his lesser partners would accept such liability. Partners do accept such liability, employees do not.

Most importantly, co-owners carry on "a business for profit." The phrase has been interpreted to mean that partners share in the profits and the losses of the business. The intent to divide the profits is an indispensable requisite of partnership. Paragraph three of the agreement declares that each partner shall share in the income of the business. There is no sharing of the profits, and as the agreement is drafted, there are no profits. Merely sharing the gross returns does not establish a partnership. Nor is the sharing of profits prima facie evidence of a partnership where the profits received are in payment of wages.

The failure to share profits, therefore, is fatal to the partnership concept here.

Evaluating Chaiken's agreement in light of the elements implicit in a partnership, no partnership intent can be found. The absence of the important right of decision making or the important duty to share liabilities upon dissolution individually may not be fatal to a partnership. But when both are absent, coupled with the absence of profit sharing, they become strong factors in discrediting the partnership argument.

In addition, the total circumstances of the case taken together indicate the employer-employee relationship between Chaiken and his barbers. The agreement set forth the hours of work and days off—unusual subjects for partnership agreements. The barbers brought into the relationship only the equipment required of all barbershop operators. And each barber had his own individual "partnership" with Chaiken. Furthermore, Chaiken conducted all transactions with suppliers, and purchased licenses, insurance, and the lease for the business property in his own name. Finally, the name "Richard's Barber Shop" continued to be used after the execution of the so-called partnership agreements. [The Commission's decision is affirmed.]

Case Questions

1. Why did the unemployment commission sue Chaiken?
2. Why did Chaiken set up this "partnership"?
3. What factors did the court examine to determine whether there was a partnership here?
4. Which one was the most important?
5. Why would it be unusual in a partnership agreement to set forth the hours of work and days off?

Key Takeaway

A partnership is defined as two or more persons carrying on a business as co-owners for profit. Partnerships can be created expressly, impliedly, or apparently, and partners can make any partnership agreement they want (except they cannot abolish the fiduciary duty owed among the partners); the Uniform Partnership Act (UPA) or the Revised Act (RUPA) fills in any gaps in the agreement as the default.

Capitalization comes from partners, not investors. Unless otherwise agreed, all partners share equally in control and in compensation from profits of the firm.

The UPA and the RUPA differ somewhat in the mechanisms of terminating the partnership. In either case winding up entails finishing the business at hand, paying off creditors, and splitting the remaining surplus or liabilities according to the parties' agreement or, absent any, according to the relevant act (UPA or RUPA).

Exercises

1. Why is there a difference between what happens when a partner leaves the firm under UPA as opposed to RUPA?
2. What is the difference?
3. If the firm terminates, what obligation do former partners have for its obligations?
4. What are the two basic duties that partners owe each other?

5. Why does the partnership itself pay no federal income tax?

6. Why do sole proprietorships and partnerships require no license from the state to exist, but corporations and other limited-liability entities do require such a license?

7. How could a person be an "accidental" partner—a partner when she does not intend to be one?

8. Why do people often want to "make partner"—become a partner in the firm?

9. What does it mean to say that the UPA or the RUPA is the "default" rule for partnership operations?

11.3 Corporations

Learning Objectives

1. Understand some of the history of the corporate form, the definition and characteristics of a corporation, and the types of corporations.
2. Understand how corporations are created, capitalized, and controlled.
3. Know how corporations' owners are compensated and subject to limited liability.
4. Understand how corporations are taxed and terminated.

Introduction to Corporate Law

Historical Background

Like the partnership, the corporation is an ancient concept, recognized in the Code of Hammurabi, and to some degree a fixture in every other major legal system since then. (The word is related to the Latin *corpse*—body: "to incorporate" is to give a body to.) The first corporations were not business enterprises, but associations for religious and governmental ends in which perpetual existence was a practical requirement; the corporation was a creature of the church or state. Some early business corporations were actually more like joint ventures (partnerships for specific purposes) between the Crown and private investors. Much like China's state-owned enterprises, these companies were controlled by the sovereign, and were both global and expansionist in their intent. They were, in fact, the original "imperialists" that Mao Tse-Tung[20] would inveigh against in the phrase "imperialist lackeys." In the first years of the new U.S. republic, some two hundred businesses were incorporated, none of which were anything like the scale of the British East India Company.[21]

The original idea was that people would petition state legislatures or Congress[22] for a special bill allowing them to get the benefit of the corporate form if what they were doing was considered socially useful—create and run roads, canals, water systems, harbor improvements, and the like. If the corporation became abusive or failed in its public purpose, the legislature could "pull the plug," revoke the corporate charter, and the people who formerly had a corporation would become partners (with its accompanying personal liability). But as industrial development accelerated after the U.S. Civil War, states began to allow incorporation merely by adhering to the requirements of a general statute; special enactments by the legislature were (and are) no longer needed.

moral hazard

A situation in which one party gets involved in a risky event knowing that it is protected against the risk and the other party will incur the cost.

With the advent of general-statute incorporation—not in the legislature's domain to grant—it has become unthinkable that a state legislature would revoke a company's corporate charter for misbehavior.[23] Thus, the "**moral hazard**" of insulation from personal liability for bad actors looms: people will take risks if they aren't held personally liable, and sometimes when the risk doesn't pay off, harm is caused, but not to the ones who took the risk.

States competed with each other to offer the least restrictive corporate law regime in order to attract corporate business. Delaware won! In 1899 it enacted the most liberal corporation statute in the country, and today there are thousands of "Delaware corporations" that maintain no presence in Delaware other than an address on file with the secretary of state in Dover and the appointment of a registered agent (often a lawyer) in order for the company to receive service of process if it is sued.

Twenty-four states have adopted all or major portions of the Model Business Corporation Act or the Revised Model Business Corporation Act. Here you can find the text of (the Washington State) Model Business Corporation Act: http://apps.leg.wa.gov/rcw/default.aspx?Cite=23B.

Definition and Types of Corporations

corporation

An association of persons to carry on a business that has: (1) centralized management, (2) limited liability for its owners, (3) ease of alienation (usually), and (4) perpetual existence.

A **corporation** is an association of persons to carry on a business that has: (1) centralized management, (2) limited liability for its owners, (3) ease of alienation (usually), and (4) perpetual existence. Corporations are legal artifices, considered to be "legal persons" by the Supreme Court of the United States, with some legal rights—though not all the legal rights of natural persons. A corporation can be partly owned by another corporation or a partnership; it may also be a non-profit corporation with members instead of shareholders. The form is useful as a way of encouraging investors to contribute money with no liability for corporate criminal acts and limited liability for civil debts and other obligations. A shareholder can—usually—lose no more than the amount invested, no matter what happens to the company itself.

Types of Corporations:

- **For-profit** or **not-for-profit**
- **Publicly held** or **closely held**; the former is a corporation that has many—maybe millions—of owners (shareholders), who live geographically separated, who do not know each other, and most of whom are not employed by the corporation (such as IBM or the American Red Cross). The latter, closely held (also known as a "family corporation," or a "private corporation"), has a handful of owners (who may be members of the same family) most of whom live in the same area, most or many of whom are also employees of the corporation, and whose ability to alienate their interest (sell to outsiders) may be limited.
- Created for various purposes:
  - A business corporation (for profit or non-profit);
  - An educational corporation (like the local school district or a university);
  - A religious corporation (churches, temples, mosques);
  - A municipal corporation (cities, as in "Entering Seattle: Incorporated 1869").

Corporate Creation and Capitalization

Corporate Creation

The corporation is a contract between the state and the corporation; the contract is called a **charter**; the people who work to get a corporation up and running are **promoters**, sometimes known as "incorporators." The promoters sign and deliver the **articles of incorporation** to the appropriate state authority (usually the secretary of state). By state corporation law, the articles most often must include: the corporate name; the names and addresses of all incorporators (they have to sign the articles); the corporation's duration (usually perpetual); the company's purposes (today usually very broadly worded, as "to operate a hardware store or conduct any other lawful business"); the share structure—classes, numbers, and values of shares (how much will it cost to buy the stock); provisions for the regulation of the internal affairs of the corporation, including any provision restricting the transfer of shares; the statutory agent who will accept service of process. (For a non-profit, the requirements around shares would not apply.)

This is mostly just a matter of filling out forms, but note that the name must include one of the following words (or abbreviations): corporation, company, incorporated, or limited (Corp., Co., Inc., or Ltd.) so that the world is informed that the corporation's owners (shareholders) will not be liable for its debts beyond their contribution. Also, the name cannot deceive the public about the corporation's purposes, nor be the same as that of any other company incorporated or authorized to do business in the state.

In consideration for filling out the forms and paying the filing fee, the incorporators get in return a stamped (certified) charter and the wonderful benefit of limited liability: the state has approved the contract authorizing a business whose owners will not be liable for the firm's debts beyond their contribution, with limited exceptions.

As the corporation is the product of a contract between the state and the incorporators, the corporations may be created expressly, impliedly, or apparently (as with any contract).

---

for-profit

A business, the purpose of which is to make money for its owners.

not-for-profit

A business, the purpose of which is to perform some socially-useful function with its money, not to distribute that money to its owners (e.g., the Humane Society).

publicly held

A corporation whose ownership interests (stocks) are traded on public markets and whose many owners are (usually) geographically widespread, do not know each other, and few of whom are employed by the business.

closely held

A corporation whose ownership interests are not publicly traded, which has relatively few owners, all or most of whom know each other (family) and most of whom work for the company.

charter

The articles of incorporation.

promoters

People who work to get a corporation chartered and started in operation.

articles of incorporation

Documents filed with the state to register and establish a corporation.

de jure corporation

A corporation that has fulfilled the requirements to be issued a charter.

de facto corporation

A corporation that has failed to completely fulfill the requirements to be issued a charter, but its promoters have made a good-faith effort, and have come close enough that it will be treated as a corporation.

corporation by estoppel

A person is prohibited from denying the existence of a corporation if others have reasonably relied on representations of its existence to their detriment.

private equity

Capital investment (as to start up a company) from a few individuals or from a company whose business it is to make such investments that are not publicly listed for purchase.

private equity firm

A company whose business it is to invest its clients' money by buying interests in corporations.

corporate bonds

A corporation's evidence of indebtedness and promise to repay investors who have loaned the company money; the bonds are secured by the assets of the firm.

crowdfunding financing

Funding a project or company by raising small amounts of money from many people, usually via the internet; an alternative source of financing.

- Express corporations. If promoters meet the requirements of corporate formation, a **de jure corporation**, the legal entity, is formed.
- Implied corporations—the "de facto" corporation. What if almost all the requirements are met by the incorporators, but not quite all, and they start doing business? If they meet three conditions, a court may decide that the nearly-correct filing along with actually doing business implies the existence of the corporation—called a **de facto corporation**: (1) a statute must exist under which the corporation could have been validly incorporated, (2) the promoters must have made a bona fide attempt to comply with the statute, and (3) corporate powers are used or exercised. The court may require a correct filing.
- Apparent corporations—corporation by estoppel. Where there is a good-faith belief by two parties to a contract that one of the parties is a corporation, and the parties rely on that belief even though in fact there was no corporation, courts may invoke the doctrine of apparent corporation, or—more often phrased—a **corporation by estoppel**. The party dealing with the "corporation" is estopped to deny its existence. (See *Cranson v. IBM*, below.)

Corporate Capitalization

To finance start-up and growth, any business must have a source of funds. Apart from bank and trade loans, the principal sources are plowback, equity financing (including private equity), debt financing, and—recently—crowdfunding.

- Plowback Financing. Rather than paying out earnings to shareholders, the corporation plows those earnings back into the business. Plowback returning the earnings of a firm to the firm's own account (as for building improvements) as opposed to paying them out to shareholders as dividends, is simply reinvesting earnings in the corporation. It is an attractive source of capital because it is subject to managerial control.
- Equity Financing. To raise money to fund a corporation by selling interests in the business (shares) to buyers who become owners. In general, equity is an ownership interest in property or a business. Investors pay money (or other consideration) and in return get a part ownership in the corporation—a share of the corporation's whole mass of shares which, taken together, constitute the capital of the firm. Selling shares—equity financing—is often of critical importance to the corporation in launching the business and its initial operations. Stock gives the investor a bundle of legal rights—ownership, a share in earnings, transferability and, to some extent, the power to exercise control through voting. The firm may offer various kinds of stock (e.g., preferred stock or common stock) giving the stockholder various rights. Smaller corporations or start-ups sometimes cannot (or do not want to) avail themselves of equity financing or debt financing (noted below). Instead, they raise funds through **private equity**, which involves professional private investors who provide funds to a company in exchange for an interest in the company. A **private equity firm** is a group of investors who pool their money together for investment purposes, usually to invest in other companies. A private equity firm might provide venture capital financing for these start-ups to begin operations, expand, or conduct further R&D, but they typically expect a higher rate of return on their investments than would be available conventionally.

- Debt Financing. To raise capital for a firm by borrowing it from investors who then do not become owners. Corporations may sell **corporate bonds** to investors to finance and capitalize (think about the local school district's "school bonds"). A bond is like an IOU—the corporation owes the bond purchaser periodic interest payments as well as a lump sum at the end of the life of the bond (the maturity date). From management's perspective, bonds are good because bondholders have no ownership interest in the corporation, and because they are usually less risky than equity, they are attractive to many investors, thus they are readily marketable. However, bonds are debt which must be paid, or else the bondholders can force the firm into bankruptcy. Also, there is the "cost" of debt to consider. When interest rates are high, corporations must offer high—expensive—interest rates to attract investors.
- **Crowdfunding Financing**. Crowdfunding is raising capital by on-line solicitation. It is open more generally to the public than traditional capitalization schemes, but it is not unregulated. [24]

Corporate Control and Compensation

Corporate Control

The control of the corporation is divided among three groups: shareholders, board of directors, and officers.

Shareholders

Shareholders are the owners of the corporation, but the power to manage is vested in the directors (hence the term "centralized management"); nevertheless, shareholders have certain ownership rights, four of which may be called out here:

1. The right to vote for members of the board of directors. If you are a resident of the City of Laredo, you have the right to vote for the city council—that's the board of directors in a municipal corporation. In a business corporation, the shareholders (subject to reasonable limitations in the charter or bylaws) have a right to vote for the board (they also have the right to vote to oust board members). This—"corporate democracy"—sounds pretty good; it is usually pretty much a fiction.

Most frequently, the CEO effectively chooses who is nominated for board election. That's not unreasonable: the city mayor—the CEO of the city—should be able to nominate department heads whose governing philosophies are the same as the mayor's.

But Carl Icahn, the billionaire corporate mogul, sharply criticizes "corporate democracy":

Many American corporations are dysfunctional because corporate democracy is a myth in the United States. They run like a decaying socialistic state. Our boards and CEOs exist in a symbiotic relationship where the boards nourish the CEO with massive stock options that are re-priced downward if the companies [sic] stock declines - making them forever valuable. They reward the CEO with pay packages and bonuses when the stock is floundering or the CEO is leaving the company. Corporate performance and the shareholders welfare seldom enter the picture. What kind of democracy is this? There is no accountability.

Board meetings are often a complete travesty. I know because I have sat and do sit on a number of boards where I am in the minority. Because of this, today our economy is in a major crisis. . . . We are in this situation because there is no leadership in the executive suite. Why did we get here? Because in corporate America there are no true elections. It is tyranny parading as democracy.[25]

proxy

A substitute; a power of attorney authorizing a person to vote another's corporate stock; the form on which a person grants the proxy such authority.

Moreover, most shareholders do not attend the annual shareholders' meetings which are sometimes held at inconvenient times (more inconvenient than during working hours—like on a holiday[26]) and at inconvenient places. Shareholders most often vote by proxy (if at all)—they give somebody who will attend the meeting (usually a board member) the right to vote their shares—the form to do that (below) and the person who receives the power to vote for the absent shareholder are both a **proxy**. Here is a simple proxy form:

FIGURE 11.4 Sample Proxy Form

I certify that I am the owner of two hundred (200) shares of ABC Co., Inc., and I hereby appoint Joan Smith (board member) as my proxy with full power of substitution and revocation, to attend and represent me at the shareholders annual meeting of to be held on March 2, 20XX. My proxy may vote my shares on any question, resolution, proposition, or any other business that may come before the body upon which I would be entitled to vote if I were present. This proxy shall be considered null and void if I personally attend the above mentioned meeting.

Sheldon Stockholder   Dec 12, 20XX
Shareholder Signature   **Date**

Today, proxy voting is often electronic, through the Internet. And shareholders may make shareholder agreements among themselves to vote together. The power to vote is exercised at regular or special meetings (in person or by proxy).

2. The right to vote on extraordinary corporate transactions, such as charter amendments, changing the name of the corporation, merging with another firm, or terminating operations.

3. The right to inspect corporate books and records, including the articles, bylaws, and corporate resolutions. Shareholders must have a "proper purpose" for their demand, such as to examine the company's dividend policy or ascertain its true financial worth. Improper purposes include uncovering trade secrets for sale to a competitor or compiling mailing lists for personal business or political purposes.

4. The right to bring a **derivative lawsuit** against abusive management on behalf of the corporation.

Directors

The second group who control the corporation are the directors (also known as regents, trustees, or other names). **Directors**, acting as a board, are agents of the corporation and agency good-faith and fiduciary duties apply to them—they have a duty of care and a duty of loyalty (the latter duty encompasses a duty of confidentiality).

Directors may be **inside directors** (employees of the corporation), or **outside directors** (who are not employees and bring outside perspective, talents, and experience to the board). The board's main responsibilities include the following:

- To select and remove (with or without cause) officers, including the CEO, and to set executive pay levels.[27] (We note again that it is often more accurate to say the CEO selects and removes officers.[28])
- To delegate operating authority to the managers or to committees.
- To approve the annual budget. This is the critical mechanism by which anything is accomplished. If the corporation is to update its computer systems or pave the parking lot, money needs to be allocated and approved for the purpose.
- To declare and pay dividends within its sound discretion.
- To supervise the company as a whole.

FIGURE 11.5 Corporate Governance Model

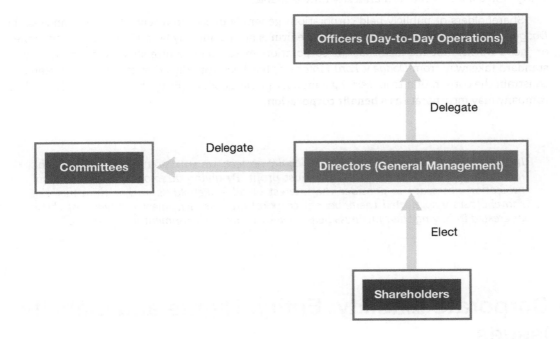

derivative lawsuit

A lawsuit brought against a corporation by its shareholders who claim management is derelict in its duty; the shareholders "derive" the power by virtue of their ownership interest in the firm.

directors

Corporate managers elected by the shareholders who set corporate policy, hire or fire the officers, and who set the officers' compensation.

inside directors

Directors who are also employees of the corporation.

outside directors

Directors who are not employees of the corporation.

Officers

The third group of people who control the corporation are the **officers**. Formerly these people were given titles of president or vice-presidents, but today the usual terminology is "officer." They execute the policies adopted by the board. The officers are the Chief Executive Officer (CEO), Chief Operating Officer, Chief Financial Officer (treasurer), Secretary, and there may be others (Chief Marketing Officer, Chief Information Officer, Chief of Cybersecurity, Chief Sustainability Officer, etc.).

Both officers and directors may be liable for breach of the duties imposed on them, but corporations are permitted to limit or eliminate the personal liability of its directors. For example, Delaware law permits the articles of incorporation to contain a provision eliminating or limiting the personal liability of directors to the corporation, with some limitations.[29]

Directors and officers will not be liable unless they have acted unreasonably, and they have considerable leeway: the **business judgment rule** holds that courts will generally not substitute their own judgment for that of management's, and only the most negligent kinds of actions would ever create personal liability for officers and directors.

Corporate Compensation

The owners of a corporation—the shareholders—have a right to share in the profits of the company. A **dividend** is a divvied-up profit of the corporation; it may be a cash dividend (a check), stock dividend, or—less common—some sort of property.

Dividends are normally payable at the discretion of the directors. Courts will order distribution only if they are expressly mandatory or if the directors abused their discretion by acting fraudulently or in a manner that is manifestly unreasonable.

Shareholders of publicly-held corporations generally expect to receive dividends, and—as in *Dodge v. Ford Motor Co.*—will complain if the firm is not paying any because it is spending money on "good works." But the idea that the corporation "exists to maximize shareholder benefit" (the standard takeaway from *Dodge v. Ford Motor Co.*) has been roundly criticized because it seems to constrain the corporation from serving a broader public good. In thirty-three states as of 2018,[30] a company may incorporate as a **benefit corporation**:

Incorporating as a benefit corporation legally protects an entrepreneur's social goals by mandating considerations other than just profit. By giving directors the secured legal protection necessary to consider the interest of all stakeholders, rather than just the shareholders who elected them, benefit corporations can help meet the needs of those interested in having their business help solve social and environmental challenges.[31]

Corporate Liability: Entity, Rights and Liability Issues

Corporate Liability: The *Entity* Issue

Compared to partnerships there is a big benefit to the corporate form: its owners are not (usually) personally liable for the corporation's obligations beyond their contribution. Shareholders may lose their capital investment, but creditors will not pursue them personally. The corporation is a legal entity in its own right that can provide a "veil" that protects shareholders from personal liability.

FIGURE 11.6 The Protective Veil

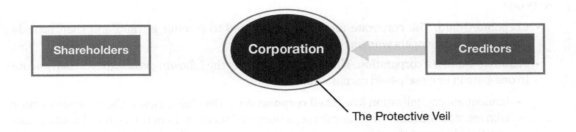

The Protective Veil

The Rights of a Corporate Person

To say that a corporation is a "person" does not automatically describe what its rights are, for the courts have not accorded the corporation every right guaranteed a natural person. Yet the Supreme Court affirmed in (some say "the infamous") *Citizens United v. Federal Election Commission* (2010) that the government may not suppress the First Amendment right of political speech because the speaker is a corporation rather than a natural person. According to the Court, "No sufficient governmental interest justifies limits on the political speech of nonprofit or for-profit corporations."[32] In addition to free speech rights, the corporate person enjoys the following constitutional protections (not an exhaustive list):

- 1st Amendment rights to free exercise of religion.[33]
- 4th Amendment protection against unreasonable warrantless search and seizure.
- 5th Amendment right to due process and protection against double jeopardy

Absence of Rights

But the corporation is not really a person, and it does not have all the constitutional rights of human beings; the corporation does *not* have the following rights:

- Fifth and fourteenth Amendment privilege against self-incrimination. In any legal proceeding, the courts may force a corporation to turn over incriminating documents, even if they also incriminate officers or employees of the corporation.
- Rights under the Privileges and Immunities Clause of the Constitution. States can reasonably discriminate between domestic and foreign (out of state) corporations.

Piercing the Corporate Veil

piercing the corporate veil

A court will disregard the separate entity of the corporation or limited liability company and allow creditors to hold the owners personally liable.

shell corporation

A corporation that is intentionally underfunded so as to work a fraud on creditors; liability is imposed on the owners personally.

Given the importance of the corporate entity as a veil that limits shareholder liability, it is important to note there are exceptions—sometimes the shareholders will be held personally liable. This is known as "**piercing the corporate veil**"; it generally occurs in two instances: (1) when the corporation is used to commit a fraud or an injustice, and (2) when the corporation does not act as if it were one.

- Corporate fraud. The corporate form cannot be used to commit a fraud and then provide "cover" for the managers who directed it to do so.[34]
- Failure to act like a corporation. This category includes the following issues (particularly acute in one-person or closely-held corporations):
  - Inadequate capitalization (the "**shell corporation**"). The classic case is the taxicab operator who incorporates several of his cabs separately and services them through still another corporation. If one of the cabs causes an accident, the corporation is usually "judgment proof" because the corporation will have few assets (practically worthless cab, minimum insurance).
  - Wholly-owned subsidiaries, where one corporation owns a subsidiary, but the subsidiary has the same ownership and management so that it is actually not a separate entity from the parent, but rather a "mere instrumentality" of the parent.
  - Co-mingling of corporate and personal assets. Shareholders write checks for personal expenses on the corporate account or borrow from or loan the firm money, without proper documentation—they don't recognize the corporate entity, so neither do creditors.
  - Failure to follow corporate formalities. Defective incorporation (there is no corporation!), omission of regular meetings, failure to record minutes, or to file annual reports. This includes the situation where corporate promoters enter into contracts on behalf of the as-yet-nonexistent corporation, and, for whatever reason, the corporation does not come into existence—the promoters are personally liable.

FIGURE 11.7 The Protective Veil in Subsidiaries
Can a wholly owned subsidiary serve to shield a parent company against creditors?

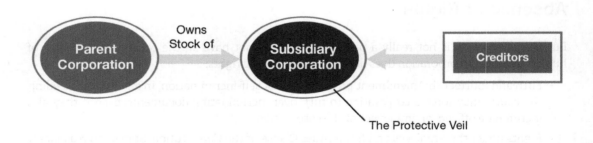

Other Types of Personal Liability

Even when a corporation is formed for a proper purpose and is operated as a corporation, there are instances in which individual shareholders will be personally liable; these include:

- A shareholder agrees to guarantee a corporate obligation (a **pledge of personal assets** as security for the creditor).

- Where a shareholder-manager commits a tort in the scope of corporate business he will remain personally liable; the corporation may also be liable (the master-servant doctrine).

- Promoters are liable for pre-incorporation contracts if the corporation never ratifies them, or if it never comes into existence (because the promoters acted as "agents" for an as-yet non-existent "principal").

pledge of personal assets

A debtor's promise to pay the creditor out of the debtor's own personal property.

Corporate Taxation

The Double Taxation of Corporate Income

The general rule is simple: the corporation, as a legal person, pays federal income tax on its profits, just as a natural person pays tax on his or her "profits" (that is, income after allowable deductions). The wrinkle here is that the shareholder who receives income as dividends pays tax on those. Thus the famous "**double taxation of corporate income**," much disliked by many.[35]

double taxation of corporate income

A corporation pays income taxes on its own income, distributes income to shareholders as dividends, and the shareholders also have to pay income tax on the dividends they receive.

How Double Taxation May Be Avoided

In general, the distasteful double taxation may be avoided by an obvious means: increase corporate expenses until there are no profits. Re-roof the factory, buy new computer equipment, pay corporate employees bonuses. The effect is to disappear the profits so that the firm pays no tax. If bonus as income to employees is the route taken, the employees still have to pay tax on a larger income, but overall they still usually come out ahead as they are not taxed on dividends—there are no dividends, because there is no profit. Thus, it is the case that many closely-held corporations show no profits: they're paid out to employees, but not as dividends (this won't work for publicly-held firms whose owners expect dividends). There is another way to avoid the much-despised double taxation: don't incorporate as a corporation, or failing that, simply lobby Congress to abolish double taxation. That's the point of hybrid business forms, discussed below.

Problems arise, however, where distributions are made to shareholders that are not labelled as dividends, but are considered such by the IRS. This is a "**constructive dividend**" (the law *construes* what happened as the corporation having made an undeclared dividend). For example, the constructive dividend could be a direct payment of money, or paying the shareholder's rent, or paying for the use of an executive jet. But what if the payment is not a legitimate business expense? The executive jet takes the two principal shareholders and their spouses on a trip to Europe, say. Then, if it was not really a business expense, and yet it was value paid out to shareholders and not declared by them as salary, it must have been a dividend, undeclared. In which case—wham!—the corporation has an income tax liability on its constructive profits, and—wham!—the shareholders have an income tax liability on their constructive income. Ouch.

The moral of the story: make sure non-dividend distributions are for legitimate business expenses.

constructive dividend

Distributions made to shareholders that come from firm profits but are not labeled as dividends; the IRS treats them as dividends and imposes tax on both the firm and the shareholders.

Termination of the Corporation

Dissolution is the end of the legal existence of the corporation—it is, basically, "corporate death." It is not the same as liquidation, which is the process of paying the creditors and distributing the assets.

Corporate Dissolution

Corporations can be dissolved voluntarily, involuntarily, or by judicial action.

- Voluntary dissolution. Any corporation may be dissolved with the unanimous written consent of the shareholders.
- Involuntary dissolution. A state may bring an action to dissolve a corporation for failure to file an annual report or pay taxes, fraud in procuring incorporation, exceeding or abusing authority conferred, or failure to maintain a registered agent.
- Judicial liquidation. A shareholder may file suit to have a court dissolve the company if it is being irreparably injured because the directors are deadlocked, or if corporate assets are being misapplied or wasted, or management is acting illegally, oppressively, or fraudulently.

Corporate Liquidation

Corporate liquidation follows dissolution; liquidation is the process of paying the creditors and distributing the assets.

Alienation of Interest and Creditors' Rights

Alienation of Interest. One of the hallmarks of publicly-held corporations is that their owners' interest is readily alienable. If you own stock in Microsoft, you can dispose of it easily: call your broker and sell. If you own stock in a closely-held or family corporation, disposal of the interest may be restricted to a certain group of people or to members of the family. A shareholder who wants out has rights under the Model Business Corporation Act to an appraisal of her interest and a buy-out by other shareholders.

Rights of Creditors. As we have seen, shareholders have—subject to some exceptions—limited liability. If the firm dissolves and goes out of business, creditors can access only corporate assets, not the shareholders'. As an alternative to dissolution, a corporation in financial trouble may look to federal bankruptcy law for relief. A corporation may use liquidation proceedings under Chapter 7 of the Bankruptcy Reform Act or may be reorganized under Chapter 11 of the act.

Cases

Corporate Creation: De Jure and De Facto Corporations

Cranson v. International Business Machines Corp.

234 Md. 477, 200 A.2d 33 (1964)

Cranson v. International Business Machines Corp.

Maryland case, 1964, analyzing the doctrine of "apparent corporation" or "corporation by estoppel."

Horney, J.

On the theory that the Real Estate Service Bureau was [not a] corporation and that Albion C. Cranson, Jr., was a partner in the business conducted by the Bureau and as such was personally liable for its debts, the International Business Machines Corporation brought this action against Cranson for the balance due on electric typewriters purchased by the Bureau. At the same time it moved for summary judgment and supported the motion by affidavit. * * * Cranson asserted in [response] that the Bureau was a *de facto* corporation and that he was not personally liable for its debts.

The agreed statement of facts shows that in April 1961, Cranson was asked to invest in a new business corporation which was about to be created. Toward this purpose, he met with other interested individuals and an attorney and agreed to purchase stock and become an officer and director. Thereafter, upon being advised by the attorney that the corporation had been formed under the laws of Maryland, he paid for and received a stock certificate evidencing ownership of shares in the corporation, and was shown the corporate seal and minutes book. The business of the new venture was conducted as if it were a corporation, through corporate bank accounts, with auditors maintaining corporate books and records, and under a lease entered into by the corporation for the office from which it operated its business. Cranson was elected president and all transactions conducted by him for the corporation, including the dealings with I.B.M., were made as an officer of the corporation. At no time did he assume any personal obligation or pledge his individual credit to I.B.M. Due to an oversight on the part of the attorney, of which Cranson was not aware, the certificate of incorporation, which had been signed and acknowledged prior to May 1, 1961, was not filed until November 24, 1961. Between May 17 and November 8, the Bureau purchased eight typewriters from I.B.M., on account of which partial payments were made, leaving a balance due of $4,333.40 [about $37,000 in 2019 dollars], for which this suit was brought.

[The lower court held I.B.M. could hold Cranson personally liable], but we disagree.

The fundamental question presented by the appeal is whether an officer of a defectively incorporated association may be subjected to personal liability under the circumstances of this case. We think not.

Traditionally, two doctrines have been used by the courts to clothe an officer of a defectively incorporated association with the corporate attribute of limited liability. The first, often referred to as the doctrine of *de facto* corporations, has been applied in those cases where there are elements showing: (1) the existence of law authorizing incorporation; (2) an effort in good faith to incorporate under the existing law; and (3) actual use or exercise of corporate powers. The second, the doctrine of estoppel to deny the corporate existence, is generally employed where the person seeking to hold the officer personally liable has contracted or otherwise dealt with the association in such a manner as to recognize and in effect admit its existence as a corporate body.

* * *

I.B.M. contends that the failure of the Bureau to file its certificate of incorporation debarred *all* corporate existence. But, in spite of the fact that the omission might have prevented the Bureau from being either a corporation *de jure* or *de facto,* * * * we think that I.B.M., having dealt with the Bureau as if it were a corporation and relied on its credit rather than that of Cranson, is estopped to assert that the Bureau was not incorporated at the time the typewriters were purchased. In [Citation], it is stated:

> *The doctrine in relation to estoppel is based upon the ground that it would generally be inequitable to permit the corporate existence of an association to be denied by persons who have represented it to be a corporation, or held it out as a corporation, or by any persons who have recognized it as a corporation by dealing with it as such; and by the overwhelming weight of authority, therefore, a person may be estopped to deny the legal incorporation of an association which is not even a corporation de facto.*

In cases similar to the one at bar, involving a failure to file articles of incorporation, the courts of other jurisdictions have held that where one has recognized the corporate existence of an association, he is estopped to assert the contrary with respect to a claim arising out of such dealings.

Since I.B.M. is estopped to deny the corporate existence of the Bureau, we hold that Cranson was not liable for the balance due on account of the typewriters.

Judgment reversed; the appellee to pay the costs.

Case Questions

1. What is the fundamental question presented by the case?
2. What are the differences between creating a corporation de facto and by estoppel?

Compensation of Corporate Owners: Payment of Dividends

Dodge v. Ford Motor Co.

Michigan case, 1919, analyzing the duty of corporate officers to make money for corporate owners.

Dodge v. Ford Motor Co.

170 N.W. 668 (Mich., 1919)

Ostrander, J.

[Action by plaintiffs John F. Dodge and Horace E. Dodge against defendant Ford Motor Company and its directors. The lower court ordered (as relevant here) that the directors declare a special dividend in the amount of $19,275,385.96 (about $368 million in 2019 dollars). The defendant appealed.]

The case for plaintiffs must rest upon the claim, and the proof in support of it, that the proposed expansion of the business of the corporation, involving the further use of profits as capital, ought to be enjoined because it is inimical to the best interests of the company and its shareholders, and upon the further claim that, in any event, the withholding of the special dividend asked for by plaintiffs is arbitrary action of the directors requiring judicial interference.]

Ostrander, J.

In 1 Morawetz on Corporations (2d Ed.),[36] § 447, it is stated:

> *Profits earned by a corporation may be divided among its shareholders; but it is not a violation of the charter if they are allowed to accumulate and remain invested in the company's business. The managing agents of a corporation are impliedly invested with a discretionary power with regard to the time and manner of distributing its profits. They may apply profits in payment of floating or funded debts, or in development of the company's business; and so long as they do not abuse their discretionary powers, or violate the company's charter, the courts cannot interfere.*
>
> *But it is clear that the agents of a corporation, and even the majority, cannot arbitrarily withhold profits earned by the company, or apply them to any use which is not authorized by the company's charter. . . .*

Mr. Henry Ford is the dominant force in the business of the Ford Motor Company. No plan of operations could be adopted unless he consented, and no board of directors can be elected whom he does not favor. A business, one of the largest in the world, and one of the most profitable, has been built up. It employs many men, at good pay.

"My ambition," said Mr. Ford, "is to employ still more men, to spread the benefits of this industrial system to the greatest possible number, to help them build up their lives and their homes. To do this we are putting the greatest share of our profits back in the business."

With regard to dividends, [during the relevant period] the company paid * * * $1,200,000 [about $29 million in 2019 dollars] in dividends, leaving $58,000,000 [about $10.5 billion in 2019 dollars] to reinvest for the growth of the company. This is Mr. Ford's policy at present, and it is understood that the other stockholders cheerfully accede to this plan.

He had made up his mind in the summer of 1916 that no dividends other than the regular dividends should be paid, "for the present."

"Q. For how long? Had you fixed in your mind any time in the future, when you were going to pay—

"A. No.

"Q. That was indefinite in the future?

"A. That was indefinite, yes, sir."

The record, and especially the testimony of Mr. Ford, convinces that he has to some extent the attitude towards shareholders of one who has dispensed and distributed to them large gains and that they should be content to take what he chooses to give. His testimony creates the impression, also, that he thinks the Ford Motor Company has made too much money, has had too large profits, and that although large profits might be still earned, a sharing of them with the public, by reducing the price of the output of the company, ought to be undertaken. We have no doubt that certain sentiments, philanthropic and altruistic, creditable to Mr. Ford, had large influence in determining the policy to be pursued by the Ford Motor Company—the policy which has been herein referred to. * * *

[Regarding the corporation's refusal to pay a special dividend to its shareholders:] The difference between an incidental humanitarian expenditure of corporate funds for the benefit of the employees, like the building of a hospital for their use and the employment of agencies for the betterment of their condition, and a general purpose and plan to benefit mankind at the expense of others, is obvious. There should be no confusion (of which there is evidence) of the duties which Mr. Ford conceives that he and the stockholders owe to the general public and the duties which in law he and his co-directors owe to protesting, minority stockholders. A business corporation is organized and carried on primarily for the profit of the stockholders. The powers of the directors are to be employed for that end. The discretion of directors is to be exercised in the choice of means to attain that end and does not extend to a change in the end itself, to the reduction of profits or to the non-distribution of profits among stockholders in order to devote them to other purposes. * * * It is not within the lawful powers of a board of directors to shape and conduct the affairs of a corporation for the merely incidental benefit of shareholders and for the primary purpose of benefiting others, and no one will contend that, if the avowed purpose of the defendant directors was to sacrifice the interests of shareholders, it would not be the duty of the courts to interfere.[37] * * *

[The court affirmed the lower court's order that the company declare a dividend and reversed the lower court's decision that halted company expansion. Here is an interesting biography about the Dodge Brothers Company: https://www.allpar.com/corporate/bios/dodge-brothers.html].

Case Questions

1. What basis does the court use to order the payment of dividends?
2. Does the court have a positive view of Mr. Ford?
3. How do you reconcile the quotation from Morawetz on Corporations ("Profits earned by a corporation may be divided among its shareholders; but it is not a violation of the charter if they are allowed to accumulate and remain invested in the company's business") with the court's decision?
4. How does this opinion relate to Milton Friedman's "shareholder theory" discussed in Chapter 2?

Corporate Free Speech: Political Campaigns and Money

Citizens United v. Federal Election Commission

U.S Supreme Court case, 2010, analyzing the free speech rights of corporate persons.

Citizens United v. Federal Election Commission

588 U.S. 310 (U.S. Supreme Court, 2010)

Kennedy, J.

Federal law prohibits corporations and unions from using their general treasury funds to make independent expenditures for speech defined as an "electioneering communication" or for speech expressly advocating the election or defeat of a candidate. 2 U.S.C. §441b. Limits on electioneering communications were upheld in *McConnell v. Federal Election Comm'n*, [citation]. The holding of *McConnell* rested to a large extent on an earlier case, *Austin v. Michigan Chamber of Commerce* [Citation] (1990). *Austin* had held that political speech may be banned based on the speaker's corporate identity.

In this case we are asked to reconsider *Austin* and, in effect, *McConnell*. It has been noted that "*Austin* was a significant departure from ancient First Amendment principles," [Citation]. We agree with that conclusion and hold that stare decisis does not compel the continued acceptance of *Austin*. The Government may regulate corporate political speech through disclaimer and disclosure requirements, but it may not suppress that speech altogether. We turn to the case now before us.

Citizens United is a nonprofit corporation. It has an annual budget of about $12 million. Most of its funds are from donations by individuals; but, in addition, it accepts a small portion of its funds from for-profit corporations.

In January 2008, Citizens United released a film entitled *Hillary: The Movie*. We refer to the film as *Hillary*. It is a 90-minute documentary about then-Senator Hillary Clinton, who was a candidate in the Democratic Party's 2008 Presidential primary elections. *Hillary* mentions Senator Clinton by name and depicts interviews with political commentators and other persons, most of them quite critical of Senator Clinton. * * *

In December 2007, a cable company offered, for a payment of $1.2 million, to make *Hillary* available on a video-on-demand channel called "Elections '08." * * * Citizens United was prepared to pay for the video-on-demand; and to promote the film, it produced two 10-second ads and one 30-second ad for *Hillary*. Each ad includes a short (and, in our view, pejorative) statement about Senator Clinton, followed by the name of the movie and the movie's Website address. Citizens United desired to promote the video-on-demand offering by running advertisements on broadcast and cable television. * * *

It feared, however, that both the film and the ads would be covered by §441b's ban on corporate-funded independent expenditures, thus subjecting the corporation to civil and criminal penalties. In December 2007, Citizens United sought declaratory and injunctive relief against the FEC. It argued that: (1) §441b is unconstitutional as applied to *Hillary*; and (2) [another section's] disclaimer and disclosure requirements are unconstitutional as applied to *Hillary* and to the three ads for the movie.

The District Court denied Citizens United's motion for a preliminary injunction, and then granted the FEC's motion for summary judgment.

* * *

The court held that §441b was facially constitutional under *McConnell*, and that §441b was constitutional as applied to *Hillary* because it was "susceptible of no other interpretation than to inform the electorate that Senator Clinton is unfit for office, that the United States would be a dangerous place in a President Hillary Clinton world, and that viewers should vote against her." [Citation]. The court also rejected Citizens United's challenge to disclaimer and disclosure requirements. It noted that "the Supreme Court has written approvingly of disclosure provisions triggered by political speech even though the speech itself was constitutionally protected under the First Amendment." * * *

The First Amendment provides that "Congress shall make no law...abridging the freedom of speech." * * * The law before us is an outright ban, backed by criminal sanctions. Section 441b makes it a felony for all corporations—including nonprofit advocacy corporations—either to expressly advocate the election or defeat of candidates or to broadcast electioneering communications within 30 days of a primary election and 60 days of a general election. Thus, the following acts would all be felonies under §441b: The Sierra Club runs an ad, within the crucial phase of 60 days before the general election, that exhorts the public to disapprove of a Congressman who favors logging in national forests; the National Rifle Association publishes a book urging the public to vote for the challenger because the incumbent U.S. Senator supports a handgun ban; and the American Civil Liberties Union creates a website telling the public to vote for a Presidential candidate in light of that candidate's defense of free speech. These prohibitions are classic examples of censorship. * * *

Section 441b's prohibition on corporate independent expenditures is thus a ban on speech. As a "restriction on the amount of money a person or group can spend on political communication during a campaign," that statute "necessarily reduces the quantity of expression by restricting the number of issues discussed, the depth of their exploration, and the size of the audience reached." [Citation.]

Speech is an essential mechanism of democracy, for it is the means to hold officials accountable to the people. See [Citation]: ("In a republic where the people are sovereign, the ability of the citizenry to make informed choices among candidates for office is essential.") The right of citizens to inquire, to hear, to speak, and to use information to reach consensus is a precondition to enlightened self-government and a necessary means to protect it. The First Amendment "'has its fullest and most urgent application' to speech uttered during a campaign for political office."

For these reasons, political speech must prevail against laws that would suppress it, whether by design or inadvertence. Laws that burden political speech are "subject to strict scrutiny," which requires the Government to prove that the restriction "furthers a compelling interest and is narrowly tailored to achieve that interest."

This Court has recognized that First Amendment protection extends to corporations, [Citations]. Under the rationale of these precedents, political speech does not lose First Amendment protection "simply because its source is a corporation." [Citation]. The Court has thus rejected the argument that political speech of corporations or other associations should be treated differently under the First Amendment simply because such associations are not "natural persons." * * *

The purpose and effect of this law is to prevent corporations, including small and nonprofit corporations, from presenting both facts and opinions to the public. * * *

When Government seeks to use its full power, including the criminal law, to command where a person may get his or her information or what distrusted source he or she may not hear, it uses censorship to control thought. This is unlawful. The First Amendment confirms the freedom to think for ourselves.

Due consideration leads to this conclusion: *Austin* should be and now is overruled. We return to the principle established in Buckley and Bellotti that the Government may not suppress political speech on the basis of the speaker's corporate identity. No sufficient governmental interest justifies limits on the political speech of nonprofit or for-profit corporations. * * *

Some members of the public might consider *Hillary* to be insightful and instructive; some might find it to be neither high art nor a fair discussion on how to set the Nation's course; still others simply might suspend judgment on these points but decide to think more about issues and candidates. Those choices and assessments, however, are not for the Government to make. "The First Amendment underwrites the freedom to experiment and to create in the realm of thought and speech. Citizens must be free to use new forms, and new forums, for the expression of ideas. The civic discourse belongs to the people, and the Government may not prescribe the means used to conduct it." [Citation.]

The judgment of the District Court is reversed with respect to the constitutionality of 2 U.S.C. §441b's restrictions on corporate independent expenditures. The case is remanded for further proceedings consistent with this opinion.

It is so ordered.

Case Questions

1. What does the case say about disclosure? Corporations have a right of free speech under the First Amendment and may exercise that right through unrestricted contributions of money to political parties and candidates. Can the government condition that right by requiring that the parties and candidates disclose to the public the amount and origin of the contribution? What would justify such a disclosure requirement?

2. Are a corporation's contributions to political parties and candidates tax deductible as a business expense? Should they be?

3. How is the donation of money equivalent to speech? Is this a strict construction of the Constitution to hold that it is?

4. There are fierce critics of this opinion—some have called it the worst U.S. Supreme Court decision since *Dred Scott* (1859, holding that no person of African ancestry could claim citizenship in the United States and thus black people had basically no civil rights). Why is the opinion so criticized?

Piercing the Corporate Veil: Corporate Promoters' Liability

RKO-Stanley Warner Theatres, Inc. v. Graziano

Pennsylvania Supreme Court case, 1976, analyzing corporate promoters' liability.

RKO-Stanley Warner Theatres, Inc. v. Graziano

355 A.2d. 830 (PA, 1976).

Eagen, J.

On April 30, 1970, RKO-Stanley Warner Theatres, Inc. [RKO], as seller, entered into an agreement of sale with Jack Jenofsky and Ralph Graziano, as purchasers. This agreement contemplated the sale of the Kent Theatre, a parcel of improved commercial real estate located at Cumberland and Kensington Avenues in Philadelphia, for a total purchase price of $70,000. Settlement was originally scheduled for September 30, 1970, and, at the request of Jenofsky and Graziano, continued twice, first to October 16, 1970, and then to October 21, 1970. However, Jenofsky and Graziano failed to complete settlement on the last scheduled date.

Subsequently, on November 13, 1970, RKO filed a complaint in equity seeking judicial enforcement of the agreement of sale. Although Jenofsky, in his answer to the complaint, denied personal liability for the performance of the agreement, the chancellor, after a hearing, entered a decree granting the requested relief sought by RKO. * * * This appeal ensued.

At the time of the execution of this agreement, Jenofsky and Graziano were engaged in promoting the formation of a corporation to be known as Kent Enterprises, Inc. Reflecting these efforts, Paragraph 19 of the agreement, added by counsel for Jenofsky and Graziano, recited:

> *It is understood by the parties hereto that it is the intention of the Purchaser to incorporate. Upon condition that such incorporation be completed by closing, all agreements, covenants, and warranties contained herein shall be construed to have been made between Seller and the resultant corporation and all documents shall reflect same.*

In fact, Jenofsky and Graziano did file Articles of Incorporation for Kent Enterprises, Inc., with the State Corporation Bureau on October 9, 1971, twelve days prior to the scheduled settlement date. Jenofsky now contends the inclusion of Paragraph 19 in the agreement and the subsequent filing of incorporation papers, released him from any personal liability resulting from the non-performance of the agreement.

The legal relationship of Jenofsky to Kent Enterprises, Inc., at the date of the execution of the agreement of sale was that of promoter. As such, he is subject to the general rule that a promoter, although he may assume to act on behalf of a projected corporation and not for himself, will be held personally liable on contracts made by him for the benefit of a corporation he intends to organize. This personal liability will continue even after the contemplated corporation is formed and has received the benefits of the contract, unless there is a novation or other agreement to release liability.

The imposition of personal liability upon a promoter where that promoter has contracted on behalf of a corporation is based upon the principle that one who assumes to act for a nonexistent principal is himself liable on the contract in the absence of an agreement to the contrary. * * *

Jenofsky contends the parties, by their inclusion of Paragraph 19 in the agreement, manifested an intention to release him from personal responsibility upon the mere formation of the proposed corporation, provided the incorporation was consummated prior to the scheduled closing date.

However, while Paragraph 19 does make provision for recognition of the resultant corporation as to the closing documents, it makes no mention of any release of personal liability. Indeed, the entire agreement is silent as to the effect the formation of the projected corporation would have upon the personal liability of Jenofsky and Graziano. Because the agreement fails to provide expressly for the release of personal liability, it is, therefore, subject to more than one possible construction.

In [Citation] (1963), we stated that where an agreement is ambiguous and reasonably susceptible of two interpretations, "it must be construed most strongly against those who drew it." * * * Instantly [as regards this immediate case], the chancellor [lower court] determined that the intent of the parties to the agreement was to hold Jenofsky personally responsible until such time as a corporate entity was formed and until such time as that corporate entity adopted the agreement. We believe this construction represents the only rational and prudent interpretation of the parties' intent.

As found by the court below, this agreement was entered into on the financial strength of Jenofsky and Graziano, alone as individuals. Therefore, it would have been illogical for RKO to have consented to the release of their personal liability upon the mere formation of a resultant corporation prior to closing. For it is a well-settled rule that a contract made by a promoter, even though made for and in the name of a proposed corporation, in the absence of a subsequent adoption (either expressly or impliedly) by the corporation, will not be binding upon the corporation. If, as Jenofsky contends, the intent was to release personal responsibility upon the mere incorporation prior to closing, the effect of the agreement would have been to create the possibility that RKO, in the event of non-performance, would be able to hold no party accountable: there being no guarantee that the resultant corporation would ratify the agreement. Without express language in the agreement indicating that such was the intention of the parties, we may not attribute this intention to them.

Therefore, we hold that the intent of the parties in entering into this agreement was to have Jenofsky and Graziano personally liable until such time as the intended corporation was formed and ratified the agreement. [And there is no evidence that Kent Enterprises ratified the agreement. The decree is affirmed.]

Case Questions

1. The plaintiff here was the seller, whose complaint was that the buyer refused to buy as per their contract. How could a court force a person to buy a parcel of real estate?
2. Why are promoters (often) personally liable on contracts they make on behalf of the corporation?
3. Does a promoter's personal liability continue even after the corporation is formed? Can he or she look to the corporation for indemnity after the corporation is formed?
4. In what instance(s) is a contract made by a promoter not binding on a corporation?
5. In whose favor does a court construe an ambiguous agreement?

Key Takeaway

For most of history (and the concept of a corporation goes back millennia) incorporation required a special law adopted by the government. Since the late 1800s, anybody who wants a corporation can apply to the state for a corporate charter—the privilege to operate a business in corporate form—without any significant legislative oversight. Corporations can be for-profit or non-profit; they are the mechanism by which most big businesses, educational institutions, religious organizations, and municipal governments are operated. To create a corporation its promoters make an appropriate filing with the state—although in some cases a defective filing (less than de jure) will create corporations de facto or by estoppel—and pay the filing fee, and in return they get a certified copy of the charter, the contract between the corporation and the state.

There are three main sources of corporate capitalization: plowback financing (reinvesting the profits in the corporation); equity financing (the corporation sells shares of its capital stock to shareholders who become owners), selling publicly, to private venture firms or by crowdfunding; and debt financing (the corporation borrows money from investors—bondholders—who become creditors).

The corporation is controlled by: (1) shareholders, who vote for the board of directors (although often such "corporate democracy" is something of a sham); (2) directors, who make the major policy and budget decisions; and (3) the officers, appointed by the directors (in fact, often the CEO "appoints" the officers), who run the day-to-day affairs. Officers and directors have both good-faith and fiduciary duties to the corporation.

The owners of the corporation (shareholders) are, within the sound discretion of the board, entitled to share in the profits of the company by way of dividends. The benefit corporation allows directors to make charitable uses of profits without fear they will be sued for being too stingy.

As entities, the corporation is (generally) liable for its own obligations—its owners are not personally liable beyond their capital contribution. This is a huge attraction to the corporate form.

As entities, corporations have some legal rights of a natural person: protections of due process and equal protection, Fourth Amendment protection against unreasonable search and seizure, and First Amendment protection of free religious practice, speech and expression. However, corporations do not have the privilege against self-incrimination guaranteed for natural persons by the Fifth and Fourteenth Amendments.

Shareholders are not always free from civil liability. Courts will pierce the corporate veil and hold a corporation liable when the corporation is used to perpetrate fraud or when it fails to act as a corporation; shareholders are of course personally liable if they have pledged personal assets to secure a corporate loan, or if they have committed a tort. Promoters are liable for pre-incorporation contracts unless there is a novation releasing them.

The corporation, as a legal person, pays taxes on its income. And, when that income is distributed to shareholders as dividends, the shareholders pay tax on it as income; the money is taxed twice. This double taxation may be avoided by increasing corporate expenses, but if this expenditure is construed by the IRS to be income to the shareholders, it will be considered a "constructive dividend" and both the corporation and the recipient shareholder will be taxed on it.

Dissolution is the end of the legal existence of a corporation. It is usually followed by liquidation, which is the process of paying debts and distributing assets. There are several methods by which a corporation may be dissolved: voluntary dissolution, which is an elective decision to dissolve the entity; involuntary dissolution occurs upon the happening of statute-specific events such as a failure to pay taxes; or judicial dissolution by shareholder or creditor lawsuit. In publicly-held corporations it is usually easy to alienate (sell) one's interest in the corporation on the market; in closely-held corporations it is not so easy, but corporate law provides a mechanism for the closely-held shareholder to get out with capital-return compensation. Creditors (usually) can only access the assets of the corporation when it quits business, not the shareholders' personal assets.

Exercises

1. What is "moral hazard" and why is it more of a problem for corporations than partnerships?
2. Corporations may be classified in what categories?
3. Aside from limited liability for their owners, corporations have other attractions for business; what are they?
4. What are the main sources of corporate finance?
5. Explain why many "start-ups" might use private equity rather than issue debt or offer stock to the public.

6. What is a corporate bond? What are some advantages to the corporation in issuing bonds? What are some disadvantages to the corporation in using bonds?

7. Why does the government need to approve the creation of a corporation?

8. What rights do shareholders generally have in the corporation?

9. Why might it be said that "corporate democracy" is a sham?

10. What role do directors play in the corporation? Officers?

11. How are the owners of a corporation compensated?

12. Why was the "benefit corporation" invented?

13. Should corporations have rights like those of natural persons? Should any of these rights be curtailed?

14. What is an example of "speaking the corporate mind"?

15. What sense does it make to say that a corporation has free exercise of religious rights? Do corporations go to church?

16. What is the effect on our democratic system of allowing corporations nearly unfettered right to make political campaign contributions in the name of "free speech"?

17. What does this mean: "Follow the money"?

18. What is "the corporate veil"?

19. What is the double taxation of corporate income? How can the owners of a corporation avoid double taxation?

20. What is a "constructive dividend" and why is it undesirable?

21. What are the main types of dissolution?

22. What is the difference between dissolution and liquidation?

23. What are the rights of a stockholder to move for dissolution?

24. How does a closely-held corporation shareholder alienate her interest?

25. A corporation is a legal entity; how does that affect shareholders' liability for the firm's obligation if it cannot pay its debts?

11.4 Hybrid Business Forms and Limited Partnerships

Learning Objectives

1. Understand why hybrid business forms have been invented.
2. Know the main types of hybrid business forms: limited partnerships, Sub-S corporations, limited liability companies, and others.
3. Understand briefly how these business forms are created, capitalized, controlled, etc.

We have examined sole proprietorships, partnerships, corporations, and now—ta ta!—we take on hybrid business forms. These hybrid organizations share characteristics of partnerships and corporations.

Why Hybrid Business Forms Have Been Invented

The rationale for the invention of these hybrid business forms are two: investors seek (1) risk reduction (the benefit of limited liability), and (2) tax reduction via the partnership-like "pass through" (that income is not taxed to the firm as an entity, but only to the owners). Here we take up the most common hybrid types in the order of their invention: limited partnerships, sub-S corporations, limited liability companies, and a couple of others (briefly). All these forms are entities, and note that all of them require a filing with the state; only sole proprietorships and partnerships require no such filing.

Limited Partnerships

Governing Law and Definition

Governing Law

The **limited partnership** is the oldest hybrid form; it is attractive because of its treatment of taxation and its imposition of limited liability on its limited partners.

The Uniform Limited Partnership Act (ULPA)—drafted in 1916—was, like the UPA, a codification of common-law concepts. The Revised Uniform Limited Partnership Act (RULPA), was adopted by the National Conference of Commissioners on Uniform Laws in 1976 and further amended in 1985 and in 2001. All states except Louisiana have adopted some form of the ULPA.

> **limited partnership**
>
> A partnership authorized by statute that affords its limited partners (investors) insulation from personal liability as in a corporation, and the single taxation of a partnership; the general partners of the limited partnership, however, are personally liable.

Definition

A limited partnership (LP) is defined as "a partnership formed by two or more persons under the laws of a State and having one or more general partners and one or more limited partners."[38] The form tends to be attractive in business situations that focus on a single or limited-term project, such as making a movie or developing real estate; it is also widely used by private equity firms.

Creation and Capitalization

Creation

The act requires that the firm's promoters file a certificate of limited partnership with the secretary of state; if they do not, or if the certificate is substantially defective, a general partnership is created. The certificate must be signed by all general partners. It must include the name of the limited partnership (which must include the words *limited partnership* so the world knows there are owners of the firm who are not liable beyond their contribution), and the names and business addresses of the general partners; the general partner may be, and often is, a corporation. Having a general partner be a corporation achieves the goal of limited liability for everyone, but it is somewhat of a "clunky" arrangement. That problem is obviated in the limited liability company, discussed below.

Here is an example of a limited partnership operating agreement: http://www.wyopa.com/Articles of limited partnership.htm.

Capitalization

Capital typically comes mostly from the limited partners, who may themselves be partnerships or corporations. The business is an investment device: limited partners (investors) hope the managers of the firm (the general partners) will take their contributions and give them a positive return on it. The contributions may be money, services, or property, or promises to make such contributions in the future.

Control and Compensation

Control

Control is *not* shared by both classes of partners. General partners run the firm; they may be natural persons, partnerships, or corporations. General partners owe fiduciary duties to other general partners, the firm, and the limited partners; limited partners who do not exercise control do not owe fiduciary duties.

Limited partners traditionally were not allowed to get very involved in running the business, else they became general partners, but under 2001 amendments (even) this check on moral hazard has been abolished.

FIGURE 11.8 Limited Partnerships under ULPA-1985:

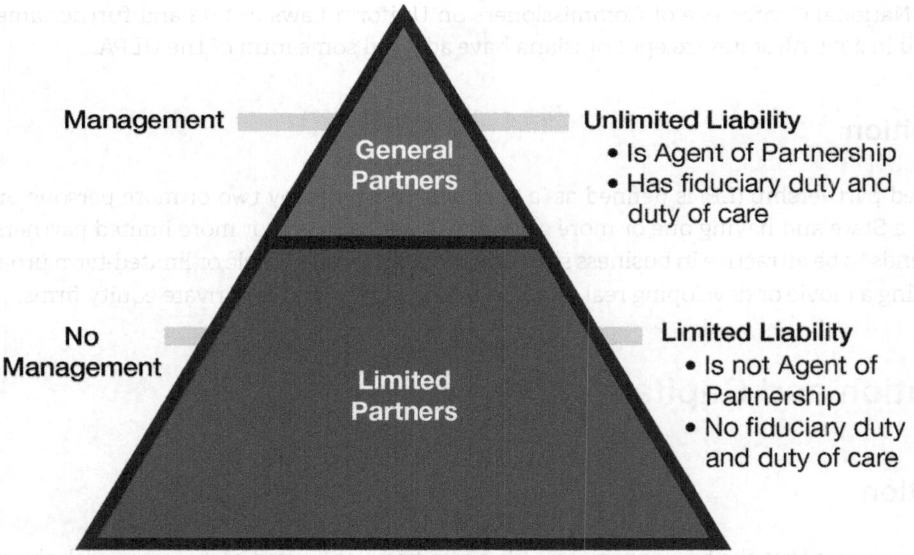

Limited partners may assign their interest (usually that's done as security for a loan); they have the right to inspect books and records; unless the partnership agreement provides otherwise (it usually does), the admission of additional limited partners requires the written consent of all.

Compensation

We noted in discussing partnerships that the partners are not entitled to "compensation," that is, payment for their work; they are entitled to a share of the profits. For limited partnerships, the rule is a bit different. General partners are paid for their work; limited partners get a share of the profits as per the agreement.

Liability

Liability is not shared.

General partners. The general partners are liable as in a general partnership, and they have the same fiduciary duty and duty of care as partners in a general partnership. However, even the general partner is also afforded limited liability under ULPA-2001.

Limited partners are only liable up to the amount of their capital contribution, provided (traditionally) that the limited partner does not participate in control of the firm; but traditions fade. Under the 2001 revisions, "even if the limited partner participates in the management and control of the limited partnership," she is not personally liable. (ULPA-2001, Section 303).

Taxation

The main tax advantage of a limited partnership is that it is a flow-through entity; all profits and losses flow directly to the individual limited partners. Pass-through ("conduit") taxation is usually very important to investors.

Termination

The limited partnership's termination involves the same three steps as in a general partnership: (1) dissolution, (2) winding up, and (3) termination. If an LP is established to make a movie, the firm dissolves when the movie is finished, business is wound up, and profits are distributed.

Sub-S Corporations

The **sub-S corporation** or the S corporation gets its name from the IRS Code, Chapter 1, Subchapter S. It was authorized by Congress in 1958 to help small corporations and to stem the economic and cultural influence of the relatively few, but increasingly powerful, huge multinational corporations. According to the website of an S corporation champion, "a half century later, S corporations are the most popular corporate structure in America. The IRS estimates that there were 4.6 million S corporation owners in the United States in 2014—about twice the number of C [standard business] corporations."[39]

sub-S corporation

A type of small corporation authorized by Congress allowing the IRS to tax it like a partnership.

Creation and Capitalization

Creation

The S corporation is a regular corporation, created upon application to the appropriate secretary of state's office, and operated according to its bylaws and shareholders' agreements. There are, however, some limits on how the business is set up, among them the following:

- It must be incorporated in the United States.
- It cannot have more than one hundred shareholders (a married couple counts as one shareholder).
- The only shareholders are individuals, estates, certain exempt organizations, or certain trusts.
- Only U.S. citizens and resident aliens may be shareholders.
- The corporation has only one class of stock.
- With some exceptions, it cannot be a bank, thrift institution, or insurance company.
- All shareholders must consent to the S corporation election.

Capitalization

It is capitalized as is a regular corporation.

Liability

The owners of the S corporation have limited liability.

Taxation

Taxation is the crux of the matter. The S corporation generally pays no corporate income tax; its shareholders include on their personal income statements, and pay tax on, their share of the corporation's separately-stated items of income, deduction, and loss. That is, the S corporation avoids the distasteful double taxation of corporate income.

Termination

The Sub-S corporation terminates as does a C corporation. Interest in the firm is readily alienable, and shareholders have no lingering liability for the firm's obligations (beyond their capital contribution).

Limited Liability Companies

The **limited liability company** (LLC) gained sweeping popularity in the late twentieth century because it combines the best aspects of partnership and the best aspects of corporations: it allows all its owners (members) insulation from personal liability and it provides pass-through (conduit) taxation. The first efforts to form LLCs were thwarted by IRS rulings that the business form was too much like a corporation to escape corporate tax complications.

Tinkering by promoters of the LLC concept and flexibility by the IRS solved those problems in interesting and creative ways, and today all states have statutes allowing the creation of LLCs. The statutes are not entirely uniform, but the LLC is the entity of choice for many business owners.

Corporations are, like partnerships, an association of persons to carry out a business, but (this was touched on in Section 3) they have four special characteristics: (1) continuity of life, (2) centralized management, (3) limited liability, and (4) free transferability of interests. Under IRS rulings, if the LLC is *not* to be considered a corporation for tax purposes, it must lack at least one-half of these four characteristics of a corporation. The LLC, then, must lack two of these corporate characteristics (otherwise it will be considered a corporation). But limited liability is essential and centralized management is necessary for passive investors who don't want to be involved in decision making, so pass-through taxation usually hinges on whether an LLC has continuity of life and free transferability of accounts—it is extremely important that the LLC promoters avoid the corporate characteristics of continuity of life and free transferability of interests. We will see how the LLC can finesse these issues.

> **limited liability company**
>
> A business form authorized by state statutes in the late 20th century. It is taxed like a partnership while granting its owners limited liability.

Creation and Capitalization of the LLC

Creation

As per the statute, promoters file a "certificate of organization" with the secretary of state; the name must indicate that it is a limited liability company. The members' operating agreement spells out how the business will be run. The typical LLC has relatively few members (six or seven, say), all of whom usually are engaged in running the firm.

Capitalization

Capitalization is like a partnership: members contribute capital to the firm according to their agreement.

Control and Compensation of the LLC

Control

The LLC operating agreement may provide for either a member-managed LLC or a manager-managed (centralized) LLC. Members can make their own rules without the structural requirements (e.g., voting rights, notice, quorum, approval of major decisions) imposed under state corporate law. If the firm has a centralized manager system, it gets a check in its "corporate-like" box, so it will need to make sure there are enough noncorporate-like attributes to make up for this one. If it looks too much like a corporation, it will be taxed like one.

One significant benefit of the LLC as compared with the corporation is that no annual meetings are required, and no minutes need to be kept. Often, owners of small corporations ignore these formalities to their peril, but with the LLC there are no worries about such record keeping.

Compensation

Distributions are allocated among members of an LLC according to the operating agreement; managing partners may be paid for their services. Absent an agreement, distributions are allocated among members in proportion to the values of contributions made by them or required to be made by them.

Liability

Again, the great accomplishment of the LLC is to achieve limited liability for all its members: no general partner has personal liability exposure.

Taxation

Assuming the LLC is properly formed so that it is not too much like a corporation, it will—upon its members' election—be treated like a partnership for tax purposes. This is considered a big advantage: the LLC is a pass-through business form; it pays no tax itself.

Termination

Dissolution. Under most statutes' default position, if a member dies, becomes insane or bankrupt, retires, resigns, or is expelled, the LLC will dissolve *unless* within ninety days the rest of the members unanimously agree to continue. And by this means the firm does *not* have continuity of life. (Again, too many corporate-like attributes and the firm becomes a corporation).

Winding up. If dissolution leads to winding up, things progress as in a general partnership: the business at hand is finished, accounts are rendered, bills paid, assets liquidated, and the remaining assets are distributed.

Ease of alienation. Again, the problem here is that if a member's interest in the LLC is as freely transferable as a shareholder's interest in a corporation (an owner can transfer all attributes of his interest without the others' consent), the LLC will probably be said to have a checkmark in the "corporate-like" box: too many of those and the firm will not be allowed pass-through taxation. Thus, the trick for the LLC promoters is to limit free transferability enough to pass the test of not being a corporation, but not limit so much as to make it really difficult to divest oneself of the interest (then it's not a very liquid or desirable investment). Perhaps it is sufficient to say here that the LLC is cleverly set up so that alienability is precisely not *entirely* easy, but easy enough not to be a problem.[40] The point is that people keep pushing the boundaries to see how close their LLC can come to corporation-like status without being called a corporation.

Statutes for LLCs allow other business entities to convert to this form upon application.

Other Hybrid Forms

Other hybrid forms—after limited partnerships, Sub-S corporations, and LLCs include these:

- Limited liability partnerships. The success of the limited liability company attracted the attention of professionals like accountants, lawyers, and doctors who sought insulation from personal liability for the mistakes or malpractice of their partners. Their wish was granted with the adoption in all states of statutes authorizing the creation of the limited liability partnership in the early 1990s.

- Limited liability limited partnerships. The "triple LP" is the latest invention. This form completely eliminates the automatic personal liability of the general partner for partnership obligations inherent in the limited partnership, and, under most statutes, also eliminates the "control rule" liability exposure for all limited partners. It is noteworthy that California law does not allow an LLLP to be formed in California.

Cases

Limited Partnerships: Limited Partners' Liability for Managing Limited Partnership

Frigidaire Sales Corp. v. Union Properties, Inc.

562 P.2d 244 (Wash., 1977)

Frigidaire Sales Corp. v. Union Properties, Inc.

Washington State case, 1977, analyzes the liability of owner-operators of limited partnerships.

Hamilton, J.

Plaintiff [Frigidaire] entered into a contract with Commercial Investors (Commercial), a limited partnership. Defendants, Leonard Mannon and Raleigh Baxter, were limited partners of Commercial. Defendants were also officers, directors, and shareholders of Union Properties, Inc., the only general partner of Commercial. Defendants controlled Union Properties, and through their control of Union Properties they exercised the day-to-day control and management of Commercial. Commercial breached the contract, and Plaintiff brought suit against Union Properties and Defendants. The trial court concluded that Defendants did not incur general liability for Commercial's obligations by reason of their control of Commercial, and the Court of Appeals affirmed.

[Plaintiff] does not contend that Defendants acted improperly by setting up the limited partnership with a corporation as the sole general partner. * * *

Plaintiff's sole contention is that Defendants should incur general liability for the limited partnership's obligations under [state law], because they exercised the day-to-day control and management of Commercial. Defendants, on the other hand, argue that Commercial was controlled by Union Properties, a separate legal entity, and not by Defendants in their individual capacities. [State law then read: "A limited partner shall not become liable as a general partner unless, in addition to the exercise of his rights and powers as limited partner, he takes part in the control of the business."]

* * * The pattern of operation of Union Properties was to investigate and conceive of real estate investment opportunities and, when it found such opportunities, to cause the creation of limited partnerships with Union Properties acting as the general partner. Commercial was only one of several limited partnerships so conceived and created. Defendants did not form Union Properties for the sole purpose of operating Commercial. Hence, their acts on behalf of Union Properties were not performed merely for the benefit of Commercial. * * *

[P]etitioner was never led to believe that Defendants were acting in any capacity other than in their corporate capacities. The parties stipulated at the trial that Defendants never acted in any direct, personal capacity. When the shareholders of a corporation, who are also the corporation's officers and directors, conscientiously keep the affairs of the corporation separate from their personal affairs, and no fraud or manifest injustice is perpetrated upon third persons who deal with the corporation, the corporation's separate entity should be respected. [Citations]

For us to find that Defendants incurred general liability for the limited partnership's obligations under [state law] would require us to apply a literal interpretation of the statute and totally ignore the corporate entity of Union Properties, when Plaintiff knew it was dealing with that corporate entity. There can be no doubt that Defendants, in fact, controlled the corporation. However, they did so only in their capacities as agents for their principal, the corporate general partner. Although the corporation was a separate entity, it could act only through its board of directors, officers, and agents. [Citations.] Plaintiff entered into the contract with Commercial. Defendants signed the contract in their capacities as president and secretary-treasurer of Union Properties, the general partner of Commercial. In the eyes of the law it was Union Properties, as a separate corporate entity, which entered into the contract with Plaintiff and controlled the limited partnership.

Further, because Defendants scrupulously separated their actions on behalf of the corporation from their personal actions, Plaintiff never mistakenly assumed that Defendants were general partners with general liability. [Citations.] Plaintiff knew Union Properties was the sole general partner and did not rely on Defendants' control by assuming that they were also general partners. If Plaintiff had not wished to rely on the solvency of Union Properties as the only general partner, it could have insisted that Defendants personally guarantee contractual performance. Because Plaintiff entered into the contract knowing that Union Properties was the only party with general liability, and because in the eyes of the law it was Union Properties, a separate entity, which controlled the limited partnership, there is no reason for us to find that Defendants incurred general liability for their acts done as officers of the corporate general partner.

The decision of the Court of Appeals is affirmed.

Case Questions

1. Frigidaire entered into a contract with Commercial Investors, a limited partnership. The general partner in the limited partnership was Union Properties, Inc., a corporation. Who were the limited partners in the limited partnership? Who were the controlling principals of the corporate general partner?

2. Why is it common for the general partner in a limited partnership to be a corporation?

3. Why does the court reiterate that the plaintiff knew it was dealing with a limited partnership that had a corporate general partner?

4. What could the plaintiff have done in this case to protect itself?

5. Why was it significant that Union Properties was the general partner is several limited partnerships, of which Commercial Investors, LP, was only one?

6. The court ruled in favor of the defendants, but is this setup kind of a scam? What is the "moral hazard" problem lurking in this case?

Liability Issues in LLCs

Puleo v. Topel

Illinois Court of Appeals case, 2006, analyzing liability issues in limited liability companies.

Puleo v. Topel

856 N.E.2d 1152 (Ill. App., 2006)

Quinn, J.

Plaintiffs Philip Puleo [and others] * * * appeal the order of the circuit court dismissing their claims against defendant Michael Topel.

The record shows that effective May 30, 2002, Thinktank, a limited liability company (LLC) primarily involved in web design and web marketing, was involuntarily dissolved by the Illinois Secretary of State * * * due to Thinktank's failure to file its 2001 annual report as required by the Illinois Limited Liability Company Act (the Act) [Citation].

[In December 2002], plaintiffs, independent contractors hired by Topel, filed a complaint against Topel and Thinktank in which they alleged breach of contract, unjust enrichment, and claims under the account stated theory. Those claims stemmed from plaintiffs' contention that Topel, who plaintiffs alleged was the sole manager and owner of Thinktank, knew or should have known of Thinktank's involuntary dissolution, but nonetheless continued to conduct business as Thinktank from May 30, 2002, through the end of August 2002. They further contended that on or about August 30, 2002, Topel informed Thinktank employees and independent contractors, including plaintiffs, that the company was ceasing operations and that their services were no longer needed. Thinktank then failed to pay plaintiffs for work they had performed. * * *

On September 2, 2003, the circuit granted plaintiffs' motion for judgment on the pleadings against Thinktank. Thereafter, on October 16, 2003, plaintiffs filed a separate motion for summary judgment against Topel [personally]. Relying on [Citation], plaintiffs contended that Topel, as a principal of Thinktank, an LLC, had a legal status similar to a shareholder or director of a corporation, who courts have found liable for a dissolved corporation's debts. Thus, plaintiffs argued that Topel was personally liable for Thinktank's debts. * * *

The circuit court denied plaintiffs' motion for summary judgment against Topel. * * * In doing so, the circuit court acknowledged that Topel continued to do business as Thinktank after its dissolution and that the contractual obligations at issue were incurred after the dissolution. [The trial court dismissed all of plaintiffs' claims.] * * *

Plaintiffs now appeal that order * * * [contending] that * * * the circuit court erred in dismissing their claims against Topel. In making that argument, plaintiffs acknowledge that the issue as to whether a member or manager of an LLC may be held personally liable for obligations incurred by an involuntarily dissolved LLC appears to be one of first impression under the Act. That said, plaintiffs assert that it has long been the law in Illinois that an officer or director of a dissolved corporation has no authority to exercise corporate powers and thus is personally liable for any debts he incurs on behalf of the corporation after its dissolution. [Citations] Plaintiffs reason that Topel, as managing member of Thinktank, similarly should be held liable for debts the company incurred after its dissolution.

We first look to the provisions of the Act, as they provided the trial court its basis for its ruling. * * *

(a) Except as otherwise provided in subsection (d) of this Section, the debts, obligations, and liabilities of a limited liability company, whether arising in contract, tort, or otherwise, are solely the debts, obligations, and liabilities of the company. A member or manager is not personally liable for a debt, obligation, or liability of the company solely by reason of being or acting as a member or manager. . . .

(c) The failure of a limited liability company to observe the usual company formalities or requirements relating to the exercise of its company powers or management of its business is not a ground for imposing personal liability on the members or managers for liabilities of the company.

(d) All or specified members of a limited liability company are liable in their capacity as members for all or specified debts, obligations, or liabilities of the company if:

(1) a provision to that effect is contained in the articles of organization; and

(2) a member so liable has consented in writing to the adoption of the provision or to be bound by the provision.

[Another relevant section provides]:

(a) A limited liability company is bound by a member or manager's act after dissolution that:

(1) is appropriate for winding up the company's business; or

(2) would have bound the company before dissolution, if the other party to the transaction did not have notice of the dissolution.

(b) A member or manager who, with knowledge of the dissolution, subjects a limited liability company to liability by an act that is not appropriate for winding up the company's business is liable to the company for any damage caused to the company arising from the liability.

[The statute] clearly indicates that a member or manager of an LLC is not personally liable for debts the company incurs unless each of the provisions in subsection (d) is met. In this case, plaintiffs cannot establish either of the provisions in subsection (d). They have not provided this court with Thinktank's articles of organization, much less a provision establishing Topel's personal liability, nor have they provided this court with Topel's written adoption of such a provision. As such, under the express language of the Act, plaintiffs cannot establish Topel's personal liability for debts that Thinktank incurred after its dissolution. * * * *

In 1998, * * * the legislature amended [the LLC statute] * * * and in doing so removed language which explicitly provided that a member or manager of an LLC could be held personally liable for his or her own actions or for the actions of the LLC to the same extent as a shareholder or director of a corporation could be held personally liable [which would include post-dissolution acts undertaken without authority]. * * *

Nonetheless, plaintiffs ask this court to disregard the 1998 amendment and to imply a provision into the Act similar to * * * the Business Corporation Act. We cannot do so. * * * When the legislature amended section [the relevant section] it clearly removed the provision that allowed a member or manager of an LLC to be held personally liable in the same manner as provided in section 3.20 of the Business Corporation Act. Thus, the Act does not provide for a member or manager's personal liability to a third party for an LLC's debts and liabilities, and no rule of construction authorizes this court to declare that the legislature did not mean what the plain language of the statute imports.

We, therefore, find that the circuit court did not err in concluding that the Act did not permit it to find Topel personally liable to plaintiffs for Thinktank's debts and liabilities. We agree with plaintiff that the circuit court's ruling does not provide an equitable result. However, the circuit court, like this court, was bound by the statutory language.

Accordingly, we affirm the judgment of the circuit court of Cook County.

Case Questions

1. Is it possible the defendant did not know his LLC had been involuntarily dissolved because it failed to file its required annual report? Should he have known it was dissolved?

2. If Topel's business had been a corporation, he would not have had insulation from liability for post-dissolution contracts—he would have been liable. Is the result here equitable? Is it fraud?

3. Seven months after the LLC's existence was terminated by the state, the defendant hired a number of employees, did not pay them, and then avoided liability under the LLC shield. How else could the court have ruled here? It is possible that the legislature's intent was simply to eliminate compulsory "piercing" under corporate law principles and to leave the question of LLC piercing to the courts. If so was the court's decision correct? The current LLC act language is similar to the Model Business Corporation Act, which surely permits piercing.

Key Takeaway

These are several hybrid business forms that have been developed to achieve the greatly desired benefits of *both* limited liability (as in a corporation) and pass-through taxation (as in a partnership). A limited partnership is a creature of statute: it requires filing a certificate with the state because it confers on some of its members the marvel of limited liability. It is an investment device composed of one or more general partners and one or more limited partners. The general partner is liable as a partner in a general partnership; the limited partners' liability is limited to the loss of their investment, unless (traditionally) they exercise so much control of the firm as to become general partners. The general partner is paid, and the general and limited partners split profit as per the agreement or, if none, in the proportion as they made capital contributions. The firm is usually taxed like a general partnership: it is a conduit for the partners' income. The firm is dissolved upon the end of its term, upon an event specified in the agreement, or in several other circumstances, but it may have indefinite existence. Winding up is finishing the business at hand and distributing assets.

Other hybrid forms include Sub-S corporations, LLCs, and derivatives of LLCs (limited liability partnerships and limited liability limited partnerships). All of these require compliance with the relevant state statutes in order to achieve limited liability.

Exercises

1. Why does the fact that the LP provides limited liability for some of its members mean that a state certificate must be filed?
2. What liability has the general partner? The limited partner?
3. How easy is it for the limited partner to dispose of (sell) her partnership interest?

11.5 Summary and Exercises

Summary

There are four types of business forms: sole proprietorships, partnerships, corporations, and hybrid forms.

A sole proprietorship is an identity with its owner. It is easy to create—no formalities are required; capitalization is limited because only one person has a real interest in the business. Control is with the owner, who is compensated from profits. Liability is personal and unlimited, and taxation is pass-through or conduit. Termination is simple (stop doing business) but sole proprietorships are not easy to alienate and the owner remains liable on all debts.

Partnerships are ancient business forms now governed by the Uniform Partnership Act or the Revised Uniform Partnership Act, which are the default rules–partners may draw up a partnership agreement as they see fit. Under the UPA a partnership is not an entity, it is an aggregate; the RUPA makes partnerships more entity-like, but partners remain liable as guarantors of the firms obligations. Partnerships may be created expressly, impliedly, or apparently (by estoppel); the partners contribute capital to the firm (and are usually entitled to a return of their capital upon withdrawal). Unless the partnership agreement provides differently, control and profits (and losses) are equally shared. Partners are personally liable without limit as guarantors of the firm's obligations. The firm is a conduit or pass-through for taxes. When a partner withdraws, the firm dissolves (under UPA) or a dissociation occurs (under RUPA); it may then liquidate (UPA) or dissolve and liquidate (RUPA). Again, partners remain liable as guarantors for outstanding debts; a withdrawing partner usually has a right to return of (some or all) of his/her capital contribution, but has no right to sell or assign any significant controlling rights, so alienation of the interest is not necessarily easy.

Corporations, known anciently, are creatures of the state; they are legal entities (persons) and as such have some, but not all, of the rights of natural persons, notably, free-speech rights. Creation is by contract with the state via the corporate charter (most often a fill-in-the-forms affair) which, when completed, gives birth to the corporation, though it is possible that corporations can be implied (de facto) or apparent (by estoppel); promoters are free to organize the firm as they see fit, but if the corporate documents do not address a situation, model corporation acts are the default. Capitalization is from: (1) plowback, (2) equity financing (selling stock), or (3) debt financing (borrowing money from investors who receive bonds as evidence of the debt). The corporation is controlled by: (1) shareholders, who vote for directors and who have other rights as owners (but usually the candidates for directors are chosen by the CEO), (2) directors who hire and fire the CEO and set the firm's budget, and (3) officers who run the day-to-day affairs of the firm. Officers and directors are corporate fiduciaries. Corporate owners (shareholders) are compensated from the firm's profits in the form of dividends. The corporation, as a legal entity, is responsible for its own debts: shareholders may lose their capital contribution, but—absent "piercing the corporate veil" or other irregularities in formation or maintenance—are not personally liable. The corporation pays tax on its profits, and when profits are distributed as dividends, the shareholders pay tax on the dividends ("double taxation"). Corporations may terminate voluntarily (shareholder approval) or involuntarily (the state "pulls the plug"); owners' interests in publicly-held firms is generally easy—just sell the stock—but in closely-held firms there may be restrictions on alienation. In any event, the owners are not (absent irregularities) liable for the firm's debts beyond their capital contribution.

Hybrid business organization forms have been created to obtain the business-organization "holy grail" of limited liability and pass-through (conduit) taxation. The limited partnership (a creature of state statute) is governed by its certificate; it has limited and general partners. The former are usually passive investors (compensated from profits) whose liability is limited; the latter (variously compensated) has control and liability as in a partnership, for which reason the general partner is often a corporation. Taxation is pass-through. The limited partnership—often formed for a specific business purpose (e.g., to make a movie) terminates by dissolution, and business is then wound up and assets distributed.

Sub-S corporations are usually smaller corporations that Congress has seen fit to allow to be taxed like a partnership: the firm itself pays no tax.

Limited liability companies (LLCs)—the most recent invention—are the entity of choice for most small business owners because in their governing documents (the certificate of organization) approved by the state, they finesse the double-taxation problem: they do not have (quite) all the attributes of a corporation. Of course they retain the owners' limited liability, but other corporate-like features (centralized management, free alienability of interest) may be limited.

Professionals can also form LLCs with the Professional Limited Liability Partnerships, and limited partnerships can elect to become Limited Liability Limited Partnerships which go so far as to eliminate the personal liability of the limited partnership's general partner.

Comparison of Business Organization Forms

Type of Business Form	Formation and Owner-ship Rules	Funding	Management	Liability	Taxes	Dissolution
Limited partnership	Formal filing of articles of partnership; unlimited number of general and limited partners	General and limited partners contribute capital	General partner	General partner personally liable; limited partners to extent of contribution[41]	Flow-through as in partnership	Death or termination of general partner, unless otherwise agreed
S corporation	Formal filing of articles of incorporation; up to 100 shareholders allowed but only one class of stock	Equity (sell stock) or debt funding (issue bonds); members share profits and losses	Board of directors, officers	Owners not personally liable absent piercing corporate veil	Flow-through as in partnership	Only if limited duration or shareholders vote to dissolve
Limited liability company	Formal filing of articles of organization; unlimited "members"	Members make capital contributions, share profits and losses	Member managed or manager managed	Limited liability	Flow-through as in partnership	Upon death or bankruptcy, unless otherwise agreed
Limited liability partnership (LLP)	Formal filing of articles of LLP	Members make capital contributions, share profits and losses	All partners or delegated to managing partner	Varies, but liability is generally on partnership; nonacting partners have limited liability	Flow-through as in partnership	Upon death or bankruptcy, unless otherwise agreed
Limited liability limited partnership (LLLP)	Formal filing of articles of LLP; choosing LLLP form	Same as above	Same as above	Liability on general partner abolished: all members have limited liability	Flow-through as in partnership	Same as above

Exercises

1. Able, Baker, and Carr own, as partners, a warehouse. The income from the warehouse during the current year is $300,000, two-thirds of which goes to Able. Who must file a tax return listing this as income, the partnership or Able? Who pays the tax, the partnership or Able?

2. The Havana Club operated in Salt Lake City under a lease running to defendant Dale Bowen, who owned the equipment, furnishings, and inventory. He did not himself work in operating the club. He made an oral agreement with Frances Cutler, who had been working for him as a bartender, that she take over the management of the club. She was to have the authority and the responsibility for the entire active management and operation: to purchase the supplies, pay the bills, keep the books, hire and fire employees, and do whatever else was necessary to run the business. As compensation, the arrangement was for a down-the-middle split; each was to receive $300 per week plus one half of the net profits. This went on for

four years until the city took over the building for a redevelopment project. The city offered Bowen $30,000 as compensation for loss of business while a new location was found for the club. Failing to find a suitable location, the parties decided to terminate the business. Bowen then contended he was entitled to the entire $30,000 as the owner, Cutler being an employee only. She sued to recover half as a partner. What was the result? Decide and discuss.

3. Raul, a business student, decided to lease and operate an ice cream stand during his summer vacation. Because he could not afford rent payments, his lessor agreed to take 30 percent of the profits as rent and provide the stand and the parcel of real estate on which it stood. Are the two partners?

4. Able, Baker, and Carr formed the ABC Partnership in 2001. In 2002 Able gave her three sons, Duncan, Eldon, and Frederick, a gift of her 41 percent interest in the partnership to provide money to pay for their college expenses. The sons reported income from the partnership on their individual tax returns, and the partnership reported the payment to them on its information return. The sons were listed as partners on unaudited balance sheets in 2003, and the 2004 income statement listed them as partners. The sons never requested information about the management of the firm, never attended any meetings or voted, and never attempted to withdraw the firm's money or even speak with the other partners about the firm. Two of the sons didn't know where the firm was located, but they all once received "management fees" totaling $3,000, without any showing of what the "fees" were for. In 2005, the partnership incurred liability for pension-fund contributions to an employee, and a trustee for the fund asserted that Able's sons were personally liable under federal law for the money owing because they were partners. The sons moved for summary judgment denying liability. How should the court rule?

5. The Volkmans wanted to build a house and contracted David McNamee for construction advice. He told them that he was doing business with Phillip Carroll. Later the Volkmans got a letter from McNamee on stationery that read "DP Associates," which they assumed was derived from the first names of David and Phillip. At the DP Associates office McNamee introduced Mr. Volkman to Carroll, who said to Volkman, "I hope we'll be working together." At one point during the signing process a question arose and McNamee said, "I will ask Phil." He returned with the answer to the question. After the contract was signed but before construction began, Mr. Volkman visited the DP Associates office where the two men chatted; Carroll said to him, "I am happy that we will be working with you." The Volkmans never saw Carroll on the construction site and knew of no other construction supervised by Carroll. They understood they were purchasing Carroll's services and construction expertise through DP Associates. During construction, Mr. Volkman visited the DP offices several times and saw Carroll there. During one visit, Mr. Volkman expressed concerns about delays and expressed the same to Carroll, who replied, "Don't worry. David will take care of it." But David did not, and the Volkmans sued DP Associates, McNamee, and Carroll. Carroll asserted he could not be liable because he and McNamee were not partners. The trial court dismissed Carroll on summary judgment; the Volkmans appealed. How should the court rule on appeal?

6. Diane and Rachel operate a restaurant at the county fair every year to raise money for the local 4-H Club. They decide together what to serve, what hours to operate, and generally how to run the business. Do they have a partnership?

7. Anne and Barbara form a partnership. Their agreement specifies that Anne will receive two-thirds of the profit and Barbara will get one-third. The firm suffers a loss of $3,000 the first year. How are the losses divided?

8. Two lawyers, Glenwood and Higgins, formed a partnership. Glenwood failed to file Client's paperwork on time in a case, with adverse financial consequences to Client. Is Higgins liable for Glenwood's malpractice?

9. When Client in Exercise 8 visited the firm's offices to demand compensation from Glenwood, the two got into an argument. Glenwood became very agitated; in an apparent state of rage, he threw a law book at Client, breaking her nose. Is Higgins liable?

10. Assume Glenwood from Exercise 8 entered into a contract on behalf of the firm to buy five computer games. Is Higgins liable?

11. Grosberg and Goldman operated the Chatham Fox Hills Shopping Center as partners. They agreed that Goldman would deposit the tenants' rental checks in an account in Grosberg's name at First Bank. Without Grosberg's knowledge or permission, Goldman opened an

account in both their names at Second Bank, into which Goldman deposited checks payable to the firm or the partners. He endorsed each check by signing the name of the partnership or the partners. Subsequently, Goldman embezzled over $100,000 of the funds. Second Bank did not know Grosberg and Goldman were partners. Grosberg then sued Second Bank for converting the funds by accepting checks on which Grosberg's or the partnership's endorsement was forged. Is Second Bank liable? Discuss.

12. Pearson Collings, a partner in a criminal defense consulting firm, used the firm's phones and computers to operate a side business cleaning carpets. The partnership received no compensation for the use of its equipment. What claim would the other partners have against Collings?

13. Follis, Graham, and Hawthorne have a general partnership, each agreeing to split losses 20 percent, 20 percent, and 60 percent, respectively. While on partnership business, Follis negligently crashes into a victim, causing $100,000 in damages. Follis declares bankruptcy, and the firm's assets are inadequate to pay the damages. Graham says she is liable for only $20,000 of the obligation, as per the agreement. Is she correct?

14. Ingersoll and Jackson are partners; Kelly, after much negotiation, agreed to join the firm effective February 1. But on January 15, Kelly changed his mind. Meanwhile, however, the other two had already arranged for the local newspaper to run a notice that Kelly was joining the firm. The notice ran on February 1. Kelly did nothing in response. On February 2, Creditor, having seen the newspaper notice, extended credit to the firm. When the firm did not pay, Creditor sought to have Kelly held liable as a partner. Is Kelly liable?

15. Two young business school graduates, Key and Peele, form a consulting firm. In deciding between the partnership and corporation form of organization, they are especially concerned about personal liability for giving bad advice to their clients; that is, in the event they are sued, they want to prevent plaintiffs from taking their personal assets to satisfy judgments against the firm. Which form of organization would you recommend? Why?

16. Assume that Key and Peele in Exercise 15 must negotiate a large loan from a local bank in order to finance their firm. A friend advises them that they should incorporate in order to avoid personal liability for the loan. Is this good advice? Why?

17. Assume that Key and Peele decide to form a corporation. Before the incorporation process is complete, Key enters into a contract on behalf of the corporation to purchase office furniture and equipment for $20,000. After the incorporation process has been completed, the corporation formally accepts the contract made by Key. Is Key personally liable on the contract before corporate acceptance? After corporate acceptance? Why?

18. Assume that Key and Peele have incorporated their business. One afternoon, an old college friend visits Peele at the office. Peele and his friend decide to go out for dinner to discuss old times. Peele, being short of cash, takes money from a petty cash box to pay for dinner. (He first obtains permission from Key, who has done the same thing many times in the past.) Over dinner, Peele learns that his friend is now an IRS agent and is investigating Peele's corporation. What problems does Peele face in the investigation? Why?

19. Assume that Key and Peele prepare articles of incorporation but forget to send the articles to the appropriate state office. A few months after they begin to operate their consulting business as a corporation, Key visits a client. After her meeting, in driving out of a parking lot, Key inadvertently backs her car over the client, causing serious bodily harm. Is Peele liable for the accident? Why?

20. Alice is the president and only shareholder of a corporation. The IRS is investigating Alice and demands that she produce her corporate records. Alice refuses, pleading the Fifth Amendment privilege against self-incrimination. May the IRS force Alice to turn over her corporate records? Why?

21. What are the pros and cons of selling bonds as opposed to stock?

22. What financing options are available to promoters other than equity and debt financing?

23. The CEO of First Bank, without prior notice to the board, announced a merger proposal during a two-hour meeting of the directors. Under the proposal, the bank was to be sold to an acquirer at $55 per share. (At the time, the stock traded at $38 per share.) After the CEO discussed the proposal for twenty minutes, with no documentation to support the adequacy of the price, the board voted in favor of the proposal. Senior management approved the proposal, and it was eventually approved by the stockholders, with 70 percent in favor and 7 percent opposed. A group of stockholders later filed a class action, claiming that the direc-

tors were personally liable for the amount by which the fair value of the shares exceeded $55—an amount allegedly in excess of $100 million. Are the directors personally liable? Why or why not?

24. Preston Corporation sold all of its assets to Adam Corporation in exchange for Adam stock. Preston then distributed the stock to its shareholders, without paying a debt of $150,000 owed to a major supplier, Corey. Corey, upon discovery that Preston is now an empty shell, attempts to recover the debt from Adam. What is the result? Why?

25. Would the result in Exercise 24 be different if Corey had a products-liability claim against Preston? Why? What measures might you suggest to Adam to prevent potential losses from such claims?

26. Yolanda and Zachary decided to restructure their small bookstore as a limited partnership, called "Y to Z's Books, LP." Under their new arrangement, Yolanda contributed a new infusion of $300; she was named the general partner. Zachary contributed $300 also, and he was named the limited partner: Yolanda was to manage the store on Monday, Wednesday, and Friday, and Zachary to manage it on Tuesday, Thursday, and Saturday. Y to Z's Books, LP failed to pay $800 owing to Vendor. Moreover, within a few weeks, Y to Z's Books became insolvent. Who is liable for the damages to Vendor?

27. What result would be obtained in Exercise 26 if Yolanda and Zachary had formed a limited liability company?

28. Suppose Yolanda and Zachary had formed a limited liability partnership. What result would be obtained then?

29. Jacobsen and Kelly agreed to form an LLC. They filled out the appropriate paperwork and mailed it with their check to the secretary of state's office. However, they made a mistake: instead of sending it to "Boston, MA"—Boston, Massachusetts—they sent it to "Boston, WA"—Boston, Washington. There is a town in Washington State called "Little Boston" that is part of an isolated Indian reservation. The paperwork got to Little Boston but then was much delayed. After two weeks, Jacobsen and Kelly figured the secretary of state in Boston, MA, was simply slow to respond. They began to use their checks, business cards, and invoices labeled "Jacobsen and Kelly, LLC." They made a contract to construct a wind turbine for Pablo; Kelly did the work but used guy wires that were too small to support the turbine. During a modest wind a week after the turbine's erection, it crashed into Pablo's house. The total damages exceeded $35,000. Pablo discovered Jacobsen and Kelly's LLC was defectively created and sought judgment against them personally. May Pablo proceed against them both personally?

30. Holden was the manager and a member of Frost LLLP, an investment firm. In that capacity, he embezzled $30,000 from one of the firm's clients, Backus. Backus sued the firm and Holden personally, but the latter claimed he was shielded from liability by the firm. Is Holden correct?

Self-Test Questions

1. The basic law of partnership is currently found in:

   a. common law

   b. constitutional law

   c. statutory law

   d. none of the above

2. Existence of a partnership may be established by:

   a. co-ownership of a business for profit

   b. estoppel

   c. a formal agreement

   d. all of the above

3. Which is false?

   a. An oral agreement to form a partnership is valid.

   b. Most partnerships have no fixed terms and are thus not subject to the Statute of Frauds.

   c. Strict statutory rules govern partnership agreements.

   d. A partnership may be formed by estoppel.

4. Partnerships:

   a. are not taxable entities

   b. may buy, sell, or hold real property in the partnership name

   c. may file for bankruptcy

   d. have all of the above characteristics

5. Partnerships:

   a. are free to select any name not used by another partnership

   b. must include the partners' names in the partnership name

   c. can be formed by two corporations

   d. cannot be formed by two partnerships

6. Under UPA, a partner is generally entitled to a formal accounting of partnership affairs:

   a. whenever it is just and reasonable

   b. if a partner is wrongfully excluded from the business by copartners

   c. if the right exists in the partnership agreement

   d. all of the above

7. Donner, Inc., a partner in CDE Partnership, applies to Bank to secure a loan and assigns to Bank its partnership interest. After the assignment, which is true?

   a. Bank steps into Donner's shoes as a partner.

   b. Bank does not become a partner but has the right to participate in the management of the firm to protect its security interest until the loan is paid.

   c. Bank is entitled to Donner's share of the firm's profits.

   d. Bank is liable for Donner's share of the firm's losses.

   e. None of these is true.

8. Which of these requires unanimous consent of the partners in a general partnership?

   a. the assignment of a partnership interest

   b. the acquisition of a partnership debt

   c. agreement to be responsible for the tort of one copartner

   d. admission of a new partner

   e. agreement that the partnership should stand as a surety for a third party's obligation

9. That partnerships are entities under RUPA means they have to pay federal income tax in their own name.

   a. true

   b. false

10. That partnerships are entities under RUPA means the partners are not personally liable for the firm's debts beyond their capital contributions.

    a. true

    b. false

11. In comparing partnerships with corporations, the major factor favoring the corporate form is:

    a. ease of formation

    b. flexible financing

    c. limited liability

    d. control of the business by investors

12. A corporation with no part of its income distributable to its members, directors, or officers is called:

    a. a publicly held corporation

b. a closely held corporation

c. a professional corporation

d. a nonprofit corporation

13. A corporation in which stock is widely held or available through a national or regional stock exchange is called:

a. a publicly held corporation

b. a closely held corporation

c. a public corporation

d. none of the above

14. Essential to the formation of a de facto corporation is:

a. a statute under which the corporation could have been validly incorporated

b. promoters who make a bona fide attempt to comply with the corporation statute

c. the use or exercise of corporate powers

d. all of the above

15. Even when incorporators miss important steps, it is possible to create

a. a corporation by estoppel

b. a de jure corporation

c. an S corporation

d. an LLC

16. A "B corporation" is different from the regular C business corporation; how is it?

a. it can only have 20 or fewer shareholders.

b. it imposes personal liability on directors.

c. it may quite freely devote profits to things other than dividends.

d. it affords pass-through taxation.

17. The principle that mistakes made by directors on the basis of good-faith judgment can be forgiven:

a. is called the business judgment rule

b. depends on whether the director has exercised due care

c. involves both of the above

d. involves neither of the above

18. A director of a corporation owes:

a. a duty of loyalty

b. a duty of care

c. both a duty of loyalty and a duty of care

d. none of the above

19. A limited partnership:

a. comes into existence when a certificate of partnership is filed.

b. always provides limited liability to an investor.

c. gives limited partners a say in the daily operation of the firm.

d. is not likely to be the business form of choice if a limited liability limited partnership option is available.

e. two of these (specify).

20. Reference to "moral hazard" in conjunction with hybrid business forms gets to what concern?

a. that general partners in a limited partnership will run the firm for their benefit, not the limited partners' benefit.

b. that the members of a limited liability company or limited liability partnership will engage in activities that expose themselves to potential liability.

    c. that the trend toward limited liability gives bad actors little incentive to behave ethically because the losses caused by their behavior are mostly not borne by them.

    d. that too few modern professional partnerships will see any need for malpractice insurance.

21. One of the advantages to the LLC form over the sub-S form is:

    a. in the sub-S form, corporate profits are effectively taxed twice.

    b. the sub-S form does not provide "full-shield" insulation of liability for its members.

    c. the LLC cannot have a "manager-manager" form of control, whereas that is common for sub-S corporations.

    d. the LLC form requires fewer formalities in its operation (minutes, annual meetings, etc.).

Self-Test Answers

1. c
2. d
3. c
4. d
5. c
6. d
7. c
8. b
9. a
10. b
11. c
12. d
13. a
14. d
15. a
16. c
17. a
18. c
19. e
20. c
21. d

Endnotes

1. UPA 102(11)

2. A joint venture—sometimes known as a joint adventure, co-adventure, joint enterprise, joint undertaking, syndicate, group, or pool—is an association of persons to carry on a particular task until completed. In essence, a joint venture is a "temporary partnership." In the United States, the use of joint ventures began with the railroads in the late 1800s. Throughout the middle part of the twentieth century joint ventures were common in the manufacturing sector. By the late 1980s, they increasingly appeared in both manufacturing and service industries as businesses looked for new, competitive strategies. They are aggressively promoted on the Internet: "Joint Ventures are in, and if you're not utilizing this strategic weapon, chances are your competition is, or will soon be, using this to their advantage...possibly against you!" (Scott Allen, "Joint Venturing 101," About.com Entrepreneurs, http://entrepreneurs.about.com/od/beyond-startup/a/jointventures.htm). As a risk-avoiding device, the joint venture allows two or more firms to pool their differing expertise so that neither needs to "learn the ropes" from the beginning; neither needs the entire capital to start the enterprise. Partnership rules generally apply, although the relationship of the joint venturers is closer to that of special than general agency as discussed in the Agency chapter. Joint venturers are fiduciaries toward one another.

3. See http://uniformlaws.org/Act.aspx?title=Partnership Act (1997) (Last% 20Amended 2013) for text of the Act and states that have adopted it.

4. RUPA 307(a)

5. RUPA, Section 307(c).

6. RUPA, Section 203. But RUPA is no different from UPA in practical effect. The latter provides that "property originally brought into the partnership stock or subsequently acquired by purchase…on account of the partnership, is partnership property."[10] Under either law, a partner may bring onto the partnership premises her own property, not acquired in the name of the partnership or with its credit, and it remains her separate property. Under neither law can a partner unilaterally dispose of partnership property, however labeled, for the obvious reason that one cannot dispose of another's property or property rights without permission. And keep in mind that partnership law is the default: partners are free to make up partnership agreements as they like, subject to some limitations. They are free to set up property ownership rules as they like.

7. While no agreement is necessary as long as the tests of a partnership are met, the parties involved ought to have an agreement to govern their relationship and the business. It should contain: (1) the name of the firm; (2) the nature, scope, and location of the business; (3) the capital contributions of each partner; (4) how profits and losses are shared; (6) management responsibilities; (7) scope of partners' authority to bind the firm; (8) details on withdrawal from the partnership; (9) continuation of the firm upon a partner's death and the formula for paying a partnership interest to his/her heirs; and (10) method of dissolution.

8. RUPA, Section 101(10).

9. Partners may not abrogate (do away with) the requirement that in most situations they are all fiduciaries of each other. That is, they owe the other partners and the partnership a duty to act in the partnership and partners' best interest, not in their own.

10. The "Official Comment" to UPA 301 observes: "a partner [is] a general managerial agent having both actual and apparent authority in scope with the firm's ordinary business."

11. RUPA 404.

12. *Hishon v. King & Spalding*, 467 U.S. 69 (1984).

13. It is often very important to know whether certain property—real, personal, intellectual—is the property of one partner or of the partnership. Partnership property consists of all property originally advanced or contributed to the partnership or subsequently acquired by purchase or contribution. Unless a contrary intention can be shown, "Property acquired by a partnership is property of the partnership and not of the partners individually." RUPA, Section 203; UPA, Sections 8(1) and 25.

14. It may be a misnomer to describe an involuntary assignment as a "right"; it might better be thought of as a consequence of the right to own property. In any event, if a partner is sued in his personal capacity and a judgment is rendered against him, the question arises: may the judgment creditor seize partnership property? Section 28 of UPA and RUPA Section 504 permit a judgment creditor to obtain a charging order, which charges the partner's interest in the partnership with obligation to satisfy the judgment. The court may appoint a receiver to ensure that partnership proceeds are paid to the judgment creditor. But the creditor is not entitled to specific partnership property. The partner may always pay off the debt and redeem his interest in the partnership. If the partner does not pay off the debt, the holder of the charging order may acquire legal ownership of the partner's interest. That confers upon the judgment creditor an important power: he may, if the partnership is one at will, dissolve the partnership and claim the partner's share of the assets. For that reason, the copartners might wish to redeem the interest—pay off the creditor—in order to preserve the partnership. As with the voluntary assignment, the assignee of an involuntary assignment does not become a partner. If a partner becomes a judgment debtor on non-partnership obligations, the judgment creditor can in effect garnish the partner's take-home pay; the creditor gets a charging order (signed by a judge) allowing the creditor to attach distributions made by the firm to the judgment-debtor partner. This is an involuntary assignment of partnership interest.

15. RUPA Section 401(i)

16. New under RUPA was the ability of partnerships, partners, or even non-partners to issue and file "statements" with the secretary of state's office that announce to the world the establishment or denial of authority. The goal here is to control the reach of apparent authority. There are several kinds of statements authorized, such as "statements of denial" (the world is informed that the person named has no authority), "statements of dissolution" (that the person is no longer a partner), and so on. Since RUPA is mostly intended to provide the rules for the small, unsophisticated partnership, it is questionable whether these arcane "statements" are very often employed, or very useful.

17. RUPA Section 306(b); Sections 17 and 41(7) of UPA are in accord.

18. RUPA Section 306; UPA Sec. 13. Under UPA, contract liability is joint only, not also several. This means the partners must be sued in a joint action brought against them all. A partner who is not named cannot later be sued by a creditor in a separate proceeding, though the ones who were named could see a proportionate contribution from the ones who were not.

19. RUPA Section 601.

20. Mao Tse Tung (1893–1976), commonly called Chairman Mao, was the Chinese Communist revolutionary who founded the People's Republic of China (what used to be called "Red China") in 1949.

21. The East India Company was incorporated in England in 1600. Its original purpose was to trade silk, cotton, spices, and other basic commodities, but two hundred years later, under the leadership of its remarkable (and probably sociopathic) leader, Robert Clive, the company basically controlled the subcontinent. It had a private army of 260,000 men and it succeeded in plunder and looting (the word "loot" is from an East Indian language) an enormous territory. The company literally carried away the riches of India to London. William Dalrymple, "The East India Company: the Original Corporate Raiders." *The Guardian*, March 4, 2015, at https://www.the-guardian.com/world/2015/mar/04/east-india-company-original-corporate-raiders.

22. Most corporations are created by the states, but the federal government can also issue corporate charters, e.g., the Federal Deposit Insurance Corporation—the FDIC—was created in 1934 to promote confidence in the U.S. banking system: https://www.fdic.gov/about/learn/symbol/ Congress has chartered several corporations, savings and loan institutions, deposit insurance companies, hydro-electric generation complexes, but most business corporations are state-chartered.

23. https://www.huffingtonpost.com/ralph-nader/corporate-charters_b_2759596.html

24. https://www.sec.gov/news/pressrelease/2015-249.html

25. Carl Icahn, Corporate Democracy is a Myth, Icahn Rept., June 18, 2008. At http://www.icahnreport.com/report/2008/06/corporate-democ.html.

26. Michael Becket, How the Stock Market Works: A Beginners Guide to Investment (2017), at p. 238.

27. In many cases (in "poorly governed firms") "CEOs have managed to capture the pay process so that they set their own pay, constrained somewhat by the availability of cash or by a fear of drawing shareholders' attention." Marianne Bertrand, Sendhil Mullainathan, "Do CEOs Set Their Own Pay? Ones Without Principals [sic] Do," Nat'l Bureau of Economic Research Working Paper 7604 (2000). http://www.nber.org/papers/w7604. CEO pay in the United States is often enormous, scandalously and outrageously enormous; see, e.g., Who Decides How Much a CEO Makes, John W. Schoen, *MSNBC* (2013), http://www.nbcnews.com/id/11414878/ns/business-answer_desk/t/who-decides-how-much-ceo-makes/. The Dodd-Frank Wall Street Reform and Consumer Protection Act of 2010 made significant changes to compensation, allowing shareholders a "say on pay," or the ability to vote on compensation (in theory). And this: "This spring [2018] the Securities and Exchange Commission (SEC) began releasing data that exposes the unthinkably high ratio of CEO pay to that of their employees—4,987-to-one in one case. Then corporate critics shouted in near unison to pay no attention to those figures behind the curtain: They are misleading, ginned up merely to inflame class hatred, and sure to be a real downer for workplace morale. But despite the complaints of the defenders of the status quo, the SEC figures accurately portray just how unequal U.S. corporate compensation has become." John Miller, "Pay No Attention to the Inequality Behind the Curtain!: Corporate Critics Cry 'Foul!' when SEC Releases CEO Pay Data," *Dollars and Sense*, May/June 2018. http://www.dollarsandsense.org/archives/2018/0718miller.html

28. In 1978, one week before he was scheduled to unveil the 1979 Mustang to trade journalists in person, Lee Iacocca, president of the Ford Motor Company, was summarily fired by unanimous vote of the board of directors, although his departure was billed as a resignation. Iacocca was reported to have asked company chairman Henry Ford II, "What did I do wrong?" To which Ford was said to have replied, "I just don't like you." Friction Triggers Iacocca Ouster, *Michigan Daily*, July 15, 1978.

29. Del. Code Ann., Title 8, Section 102(b)(7) (2011).

30. http://www.socentlawtracker.org/#/bcorps.

31. Doug Bend and Alex King, Why Consider a Benefit Corporation?, Forbes.Com (May 30, 2014), https://www.forbes.com/sites/theyec/2014/05/30/why-consider-a-benefit-corporation/#7f9ad61165e9

32. Citizens United v. Federal Election Commission, 558 U.S. 310 (2010).

33. *Burwell v. Hobby Lobby Stores, Inc.*, 573 U.S. _____ (2014). Closely-held corporations whose religious owners believe that contraceptives are morally wrong cannot be required to pay for insurance coverage of contraception. The case does not address whether publicly-held corporations have freedom of religion.

34. The Felsenthal Company burned to the ground. Its president, one of the company's largest creditors and virtually its sole owner, instigated the fire. The corporation sued the insurance company to recover the amount for which it was insured. The Illinois Supreme Court heard the case: "The general rule of law is that the willful burning of property by a stockholder in a corporation is not a defense against the collection of the insurance by the corporation, and . . . the corporation cannot be prevented from collecting the insurance because its agents willfully set fire to the property without the participation or authority of the corporation or of all of the stockholders of the corporation." But because the fire was caused by the beneficial owner of "practically all" the stock, who also "has the absolute management of [the corporation's] affairs and its property, and is its president," the court refused to allow the company to recover the insurance money; allowing the company to recover would reward fraud.

35. In late 2017 debate raged in Congress and in the media about proposed tax changes, including lowering the nominal corporate income-tax rate. The Republican bill passed both houses and President Trump signed it on December 22, 2017. Some tax rates were lowered; the deficit ballooned. See: https://www.forbes.com/sites/samanthasharf/2018/01/09/what-in-the-final-tax-bill-could-impact-your-housing-costs/#3dd502292c08 and http://thehill.com/policy/finance/382319-gop-tax-law-will-add-19-trillion-to-debt-cbo.

36. This is a citation to a hornbook—a primer, here, about corporations.

37. Henry Ford's motivation for plowing all that money into his company was not entirely eleemosynary (charitable). In 1904 Mr. Ford had given the Detroit machinists, John and Horace Dodge, 25% of the stock of the infant Ford Motor Company in return for their agreement to manufacture precision engine and chassis parts for the Ford Model T. But the Dodge brothers thought they could build a better car; in 1910 they took the million dollars a year in dividends Ford was paying them (about $28 million in 2018 dollars) and started their own automobile company, Dodge Brothers Motor Vehicles. Henry Ford didn't like the competition, funded by his dividends, so he stopped paying dividends. John and Horace Dodge both died in 1920 and their huge manufacturing facility in Hamtramck was taken over by Walter Chrysler in 1926. David Lewis, *The Public Image of Henry Ford* (1976).

38. ULPA, Section 102(11)

39. http://s-corp.org/our-history/

40. Some states' LLC statutes have as the default rule that the remaining members must unanimously consent to allow an assignee or a transferee of a membership interest to participate in managing the LLC. Since this prevents a member from transferring all attributes of the interest (the right to participate in management isn't transferred or assigned), the LLC formed under the default provision will not have "free transferability of interest." But if the LLC agreement allows majority consent for the transfer of all attributes, that also would satisfy the requirement that there not be free transferability of interests. Then we get into the question of how to define "majority": by number of members or by value of their membership? And what if only the managing partners need to consent? Or if there are two classes of membership and the transfer of interests in one class requires the consent of the other?

41. Under ULPA-2001, the general partner has limited liability.

CHAPTER 12
Government Regulation: Environmental Law

Chapter Learning Objectives

After reading this chapter, you should understand:

1. What the "Tragedy of the Commons" is, and its relevance to the regulation of market activities.
2. What "negative externalities" are in terms of "pollution" of the environment.
3. The origins of the environmental movement in the United States.
4. The major pieces of federal legislation affecting our environment.
5. How states regulate environmental issues.
6. How legislatures, the executive branch, the judiciary, administrative agencies, and direct democracy shape the current reality and future of environmental law and regulation.

This chapter is the first of several dealing with government regulation.

You cannot do whatever you want with your land. No society could operate with landowners having total freedom with what they own: there are always constraints. In traditional societies (like Native American) respect for the land is an essential part of religion, and to waste or abuse it is sacrilege. Western culture has seen land as a resource to exploit, but the use of land is still restrained by law. Here, we take up some of the types of land-use and environmental regulation.

12.1 Introduction to Land Use Regulation and Environmental Law

Learning Objectives

1. Understand how strictly "human centered" ethics underlies most of our economic policies and practices.
2. Explain how the economic system is part of a larger natural ecosystem.
3. Explain how the "Tragedy of the Commons" is a metaphor for human interactions that affect economic and environmental well-being.
4. Describe what a "negative externality" is, and how one person or firm's "freedom" can adversely affect another's.
5. Contrast the concepts of "command and control" laws with "market-friendly" regulations.

Business and the Natural Environment

In business schools, we tend to overlook the fact that our economic system is part of a much larger system: our planet Earth and all the resources available to us. As individuals, firms, and nation-states, we all benefit from "natural resources," but we have been using them at an unsustainable rate, and in ways that have created unintended harms to ourselves and other species. Our economic thinking has largely been "homo-centric," or human-centered. That's natural enough, but with an ever-increasing population, greater per capita consumption, an inefficient "take-make-waste" approach to production and consumption, and over-reliance on fossil fuels, we have helped create some unprecedented challenges to social and political systems. Our laws could unify social, environmental, and economic needs, or fall short. As you read through this chapter, consider whether our social, political, and (especially) legal institutions are creating space for the thriving of people, business, and the planet itself.

The Tragedy of the Commons

The difficulty of crafting laws that sustain a beneficial environment is well illustrated by "the Tragedy of the Commons." Good rules that would keep production and consumption within mutually agreed upon boundaries are difficult to negotiate and enforce. Garrett Hardin's classic 1968 article on this "tragedy" sets the framework here.[1] Hardin (1915–2003) was primarily concerned, as was Thomas Malthus (1766–1834), with the ever-growing human population on Earth. Because of the huge impact of human activities on the planet, many are calling these times the "Anthropocene Era." (By contrast, the era of the dinosaurs was the Mesozoic Era.) Hardin asks us to imagine a group of property owners who all raise cattle, and all of them adjoin a large, lovely pasture that is not owned by any one of them, and so is "common" property. Prior to the Enclosure Acts in England, common areas were abundant, and people were able to hunt and harvest freely on common lands. But population growth resulted in a shrinking set of common lands.

negative externalities

Negative externalities arise when an economic activity imposes a cost to a third party not involved in the economic activity. The freedom to dump waste in a river, for example, may well impose costs on people downstream who would use the river for recreation, fishing, swimming, or drinking water.

In Hardin's example, it is entirely rational for each herdsman to put one additional head of cattle on the common meadow, in order to feed on the grasses that grow there. But this will eventually stress the regenerative capacities of the meadow, and overgrazing will kill the grasses that feed the cattle. As Hardin says, "Freedom in the commons brings ruin to all." He advises mutual coercion, mutually agreed upon. Such advice is sensible, but contrary to our personal impulses (it limits freedom!) and difficult to do well, especially in a populous, diverse national economy where some interests are given more weight politically. Our environmental laws (taken up below) are meant to limit our freedom to pollute air, water, and soil, where such freedom often brings **negative externalities** that degrade natural resources and also affect human health and well-being.[2]

We can look at clean air, clean water, and common lands that are not degraded as public goods. If there are no mutually agreed upon and well-enforced rules, individuals and firms are allowed to degrade those public goods, and can even profit by imposing costs on others. When a "pro-business" governor took office in Michigan in 1991, he promised to cut bureaucratic waste, make government more efficient, and work with business to clean up the environment. But the environment was not cleaned up. An extensive study by the Environmental Working Group in 1999 concluded that major industrial polluters in Michigan were violating the federal Clean Water Act and routinely getting away with it. The largest polluters were almost never fined, inspection rates were "abysmal," and violations of the clean water laws continued largely unabated, according to U.S. Environmental Protection Agency (EPA) Clean Water Act enforcement records.[3] After leaving the Governor's office, John Engler went to Washington to be CEO of the National Association of Manufacturers for six years, then President of the Business Roundtable, an influential business organization. (The Roundtable's views on the need to cut bureaucratic "red tape" can be found online.)[4]

Business, the "Free Market," and Negative Externalities

In an economy where perfect or near-perfect competition exists, there would be no monopolies, no government subsidies, an ample supply of public goods, perfect information for both buyers and sellers, and no "negative externalities." (You can see an example of negative externalities in the *Boomer* case, in Section 2). The neighbors of Atlantic Cement's factory did not want the soot, noise, dust, and vibration they experienced. Their increased visits to doctors for emphysema or other ailments, the diminution of their property values, the need to repaint their houses every six years instead of every twelve (and so on) were costs that were imposed on them by Atlantic's production of cement.

In the capitalist system, we like to think that a business transaction is a win-win: the buyer gets what she wants, the seller gets paid, and both parties are usually happy with the outcome (unless there's been a breach of warranty, a hidden defect in the product, a failure of delivery, or the buyer defaults on payment, etc.). In most transactions, that is, buyer and seller get exactly what they bargain for, at a price mutually agreed upon, and neither lawyers nor the court system are needed. But all too often, the market price often does not account for the costs imposed on "third parties" who experience the negative externalities. The involuntary costs experienced by Atlantic's neighbors—the "social costs"—were excluded from the market price, which only included the production and distribution costs of making and selling the cement.

Sometimes, it is the public (the tax revenues) that pays for negative externalities. The Gold King mine in southwest Colorado operated for many years until the company went out of business. The government took over maintenance and supervision of the mine, which had extensive contaminated water on site. Contractors hired by the EPA accidentally destroyed the plug holding water trapped inside the mine, which caused an overflow of the pond, spilling three million gallons of mine waste water and tailings, including heavy metals such as cadmium and lead. Those metals, and other toxic elements such as arsenic, beryllium, zinc, iron, and copper, spilled into Cement Creek, and ran into a tributary of the Animas River in Colorado. The EPA was criticized for not warning Colorado and New Mexico about the operation until the day after the wastewater spilled, because the EPA employee "in charge of Gold King Mine knew of blowout risk."[5]

Entirely lost in most accounts of this disaster is (1) that the mine owners made plenty of money, closed up, and were not held accountable for the mess they left behind, and (2) that tens of thousands of inactive mines around the Western United States still leak toxic metals-laced acidic mining waste into streams and rivers. Certainly, it is rational (like Hardin's herdsman) to maximize income in the short term, and if you can go out of business and leave the cleanup tab for the public to pay, it is "efficient" for you. System-wide, however, it is anything but efficient to have tens of thousands of inactive mines still leaking toxic metals-laced waste into streams and rivers. Negative externalities abound that cost enormous amounts to remedy, and yet the EPA winds up being vilified by "free market" advocates who point to "yet another government failure." Any environmental restraints (mutual coercion, mutually agreed upon) break down in a politically charged atmosphere where government "red tape" is denounced and deregulation is routinely offered as the answer to what ails the economy.

Command-and-Control versus Market-Oriented Regulation

Society has two broad levers to minimize pollution and other damage to the natural environment. It can use traditional regulatory approaches, sometimes referred to as command-and-control approaches through certain laws and regulations. These set specific standards and often require inspections and fines for non-compliance. The law can also employ policies that rely on market forces to correct for producer and consumer behavior, such as allowing environmentally proactive firms the opportunity to sell to other firms the former's "unused" pollution rights. You may enjoy watching a short video that captures the "six Ps" of possible government actions to aid the natural environment: prescriptive regulation, property rights, penalties, payments, persuasion, and provision.

The 6 Ps of Environmental Policy Instruments

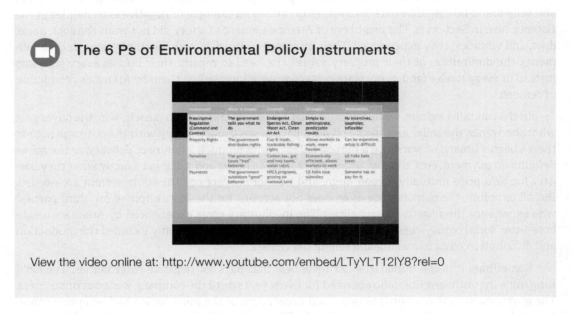

View the video online at: http://www.youtube.com/embed/LTyYLT12lY8?rel=0

Most businesses do not want government regulation (because compliance costs time and money), and political actors in the U.S. tend to avoid becoming too unpopular with business interests.

Key Takeaway

All of our economic activities have taken place within the natural systems of Planet Earth, with all of its natural resources. We have used those resources in ways that are not sustainable, but limiting production and consumption is inherently difficult, as Hardin's "Tragedy of the Commons" makes clear. Mutual coercion, mutually agreed upon is far more difficult, especially in a national or global context, than recognizing "freedom" as a primary social and economic value. But freedom often brings with it "negative externalities," imposing costs on others without their consent. Correcting this via the legal system is difficult, but government and law remain vital to ensuring that people and firms are accountable for damages to others, and to the environment. Government has various options in this regard, including providing information, education, prescriptive regulation and market-based incentives.

Exercises

1. How "efficient" are the industrial and technological systems currently in place in the United States? What do we mean by "efficient"? Take a quick look at the first few pages of Paul Hawken's "Natural Capitalism."[6]
2. What kind of "testing" does the U.S. government do on chemicals, pesticides, fungicides, and other chemicals, and how are they deemed "safe" (or not) for use in our environment? Which agencies decide? Is any chemical ever "banned" for lack of safety? What percentage?

3. What kinds of regulatory reform does the Business Roundtable propose?

4. We say clean air, for example, is a "free good." If it is free, why is it—in many places—so uncommon?

12.2 Regulation of Land Use

Learning Objectives

1. Understand how tort law imposes duties on property owners.
2. Understand how contract may affect property owners' rights and restrictions.
3. Understand how public zoning laws and "eminent domain" can limit a landowner's right to use land as she or he sees fit.

Land use regulations fall into three broad categories: (1) duties imposed on landowners through tort law, (2) private regulation by agreement (contract), and (3) public regulation of land through zoning laws and through the powers of eminent domain and zoning.

Private Regulation of Land Use by Tort Law

As noted in Chapter 7, tort law is used to regulate private property land use in two ways: (1) the owner may become liable for certain activities carried out on the real estate that affect others beyond the real estate; (2) the owner may be liable to persons who, upon entering the real estate, are injured.

The two most common torts in the first category are nuisance and trespass. A common-law **nuisance** is an interference with the use and enjoyment of one's land. Examples of nuisances are excessive noise (especially late at night), polluting activities, and emissions of noxious odors. But the activity must produce substantial harm, not minor injury that quickly subsides, and it must produce those effects on the reasonable person, not on someone who is peculiarly allergic to the complained-of activity.

In *Boomer v. Atlantic Cement Co.*, below, the issue presented was whether an ongoing, substantially harmful nuisance could be permanently enjoined by the court. Usually nuisance does not involve **trespass**. A trespass is the wrongful physical invasion of, or entry upon, land possessed by another. Loud noise blaring out of speakers from your neighbor's house, even at midnight, might be a nuisance but could not be a trespass, because noise is not a physical invasion. But spraying pesticides on your beetle-infested roses could constitute a trespass on your neighbor's property if some of the pesticide drifts across the boundary.

nuisance

At common law, a thing or activity that substantially interferes with the use and enjoyment of an owner's property.

trespass

The intentional invasion of another's real property interests, whether below the surface or in the airspace above, without the consent of the owner of the land.

invitee

Someone who enters onto real property at the invitation of the owner in order to do business with the owner.

licensee

Someone who enters onto the land of an owner who has given express or implied consent to do so.

The second category involves injury to persons who enter onto the real property of others. Traditionally, liability for injury has depended on the status of the person who enters onto the property. If the person is an intruder without permission—a trespasser—the landowner owes him no duty of care unless he knows of the intruder's presence, in which case the owner must exercise reasonable care in his activities and warn of hidden dangers on his land of which he is aware. As noted in Chapter 7, the duties owed by property owners to others will vary, depending on the varieties of state law, and whether the "other" is an **invitee**, **licensee**, or trespasser.

Private Regulation of Land Use by Agreement: Easements

A basic principle of English common law is that someone who has title to real property in "fee simple" has the entire "bundle of rights" that come with complete ownership. But common law, the basis for most U.S. property law, also says that these rights can be parceled out to others. A "surface owner" of rights, for example, can deed away her "mineral rights"—for a price, of course—such that oil, gas, and mining companies have the rights to all subsurface matter, along with the right to use the surface of the land to the necessary equipment for extraction. A business that is not extracting minerals—an oil or gas pipeline company, for example—will ordinarily approach a landowner to get an easement under the surface; the easement will likely specify that drilling could not take place within certain distances of the owner's structures (house, stables, and other buildings), and provide some means of compensation to the landowners for any surface impacts.

Sometimes the owner of such an easement is called a "lessee," as the easement may be for a term of years, instead of a permanent easement. Texas courts have long held that the mineral estate is the dominant estate, and that the mineral owner, or the owner's lessee, has an implied easement to use the surface in a manner that is reasonably necessary to develop the minerals. But there are some limitations to the mineral owner's use of the surface. The "judicial accommodation doctrine" requires the mineral owner to accommodate existing surface uses such as ranching or agricultural operations as is "reasonably practicable." In some states (or in counties empowered under state law to do so), there may be legislative "setback" requirements for fracking, or regulations that limit the discretion of companies to situate their operations on any part of the surface they would like.

If a pipeline company seeks an easement to construct pipelines underneath the owner's property, and the owner refuses, the company may seek a state's help to invoke the power of eminent domain. State law often provides this condemnation authority to pipeline companies if they are acting as common carriers transporting oil or natural gas or their products, to or for the public. As in *Kelo v. New London*, in the section below, the question of "public purpose" is relevant; does forcing a landowner to grant an easement to an oil pipeline qualify as a "public purpose" under the Court's "takings" decisions? Currently, it does.

conservation easements

Legal agreements between a landowner and a land trust or government agency that permanently limits uses of the land in order to protect its conservation values.

Conservation easements are voluntary legal agreements between a landowner and a land trust or government agency that permanently, legally, limits uses of the land in order to protect its conservation values. Landowners retain many of their rights, including the right to own and use the land, sell it, and pass it on to their heirs. Conservation easements "run with the land," meaning that they would limit the use of the land into the future, in "perpetuity" (i.e., forever). A conservation easement's purposes could include any one or more of the following: maintain water quality, maintain wildlife habitat and migration corridors, ensure that lands are managed in accordance with sustainable or durable use practices, limit building on certain portions of the property in order to protect scenic vistas, or other conservation aims. Nearly all of the states have enacted laws specifically authorizing the creation of conservation easements as valid interests in land. These laws are generally modeled after the Uniform Conservation Easement Act adopted by the National Conference of Commissioners on Uniform State Laws in 1981.[7]

Public Regulation of Land Use: Eminent Domain, Takings, and Zoning Regulations

Eminent Domain

The government may take private property for public purposes, its power to do so is known as eminent domain. The power of eminent domain is subject to constitutional limitations, under the Fifth Amendment, the property must be put to public use, and the owner is entitled to "just compensation" for his loss. Guidance for federal and state courts is limited to the language of the Fifth Amendment to the U.S. Constitution, which says: "[N]or shall private property be taken for public use, without just compensation." These requirements are sometimes difficult to meet.

Public use. The requirement of public use normally means that the property will be useful to the public once the state has taken possession—for example, private property might be condemned to construct a highway. Although not allowed in most circumstances, the government could even condemn someone's property in order to turn around and sell it to another individual, if a legitimate public purpose could be shown.

For example, a state survey in the mid-1960s showed that the government owned 49 percent of Hawaii's land. Another 47 percent was controlled by seventy-two private landowners. Because this concentration of land ownership (which dated back to feudal times) resulted in a critical shortage of residential land, the Hawaiian legislature enacted a law allowing the government to take land from large private estates and resell it in smaller parcels to homeowners. In 1984, the U.S. Supreme Court upheld the law, deciding that the land was being taken for a public use because the purpose was "to attack certain perceived evils of concentrated property ownership."[8]

Although the use must be public, the courts will not inquire into the necessity of the use or whether other property might have been better suited. It is up to government authorities to determine whether and where to build a road, not the courts. The outer limits of public use were amply illustrated in the Supreme Court's 2002 decision of **Kelo v. New London**[9] (2005), in which Mrs. Kelo's house was condemned so that the city of New London, Connecticut, could create a marina and industrial park to lease to Pfizer Corporation. The city's motives were to create a higher tax base for property taxes. The Court, following precedent, refused to invalidate the city's taking on constitutional grounds. Reaction from states was swift: many states passed new laws restricting the bases for state and municipal governments to use powers of eminent domain, and many of these laws also provided additional compensation to property owners whose land was taken.

> **Kelo v. New London**
>
> U.S. Supreme Court case, 2005, interpreting the 5th Amendment's "taking" clause (as to what is a "public use").

Just compensation. The owner is ordinarily entitled to the fair-market value of land condemned under eminent domain. This value is determined by calculating the most profitable use of the land at the time of the taking, even though it was being put to a different use. The owner will have a difficult time collecting lost profits; for instance, a grocery store will not usually be entitled to collect for the profits it might have made during the next several years, in part because it can presumably move elsewhere and continue to make profits, and in part because calculating future profits is inherently speculative.[10]

Taking. Takings cases fall into one of three categories–physical occupations, exactions or conditions on development, and permit denials. The level of judicial scrutiny varies among each of these categories, depending upon the level of intrusiveness on the part of the government. In general, the more closely the government action resembles "confiscation" rather than simply a restriction on use, the closer the court will look at the governmental purpose behind the alleged taking and its corresponding impact on the property.

The most difficult question in most modern cases is whether the government has in fact "taken" the property. This is easy to answer when the government acquires title to the property through condemnation proceedings. But often, a government action is challenged when a law or regulation inhibits the use of private land or denies a permit to a property owner wanting to develop the land. Suppose a town promulgates a setback ordinance, requiring owners along city sidewalks to build no closer to the sidewalk than twenty feet. If the owner of a small store had only twenty-five feet of land from the sidewalk line, the ordinance would effectively prevent him from housing his enterprise, and the ordinance could be a taking. A theory of "inverse condemnation" has developed, in which the private property owner claims that the government has effectively condemned the property, though not through the traditional mechanism of a condemnation proceeding.

Lucas v. S.C. Coastal Council

U.S. Supreme Court case, 1992, finding that South Carolina's limitations on beachfront buildings amounted to a compensable "taking" under the 5th Amendment.

In regards to takings, regulations, and just compensation, the Court has determined that "takings" must be total, or deprive the owner of substantially all value, in order to be compensated. The concept that there can be a regulatory taking—that a land use regulation can be so restrictive as to constitute a taking of private property—was first set forth in 1922 in *Pennsylvania Coal v. Mahon.* The often-quoted conclusion of Justice Holmes in this case was, "while property may be regulated to a certain extent, if regulation goes too far it will be recognized as a taking." The Supreme Court's approach **Lucas v. S.C. Coastal Council** illustrates this.

In 1986, Mr. Lucas bought two residential lots on the Atlantic Ocean at Isle of Palms, a South Carolina barrier island. He planned to build single-family beachfront homes on the lots. In 1988, the state legislature enacted a law which set up the South Carolina Coastal Commission, a state agency charged with creating meaningful rules and limits on construction activities along the coast. Erosion of the barrier islands had become a growing problem, and the commission believed that having no construction on beach areas would increase natural protections from flooding and erosion. Accordingly, the rules that were imposed after Lucas bought the two lots barred him from erecting permanent habitable structures on his land.

Lucas claimed a "total taking" of his land, though by regulation, not eminent domain. The lots retained some value, of course; campers might happily pay to put up tents or temporary structures on the beachfront lots, but Lucas had far more profitable uses in mind. He sued and won a large monetary judgment. The state appealed on behalf of the South Carolina Coastal Commission, but because the state had not challenged the "total taking" finding of the trial court, the Supreme Court agreed with Lucas that the state should pay him what he paid for the lots, or allow him to build as he wished.[11]

Very few "regulatory takings" would be total, and property rights advocates were quick to propose that any law or regulation that reduced someone's property value should be compensated by the government whose law or regulation was the cause of the diminished value. Some states have passed laws requiring state government regulatory takings to be compensated, and the Court has had occasion to reconsider the *Lucas* case in the context of Wisconsin riverside lot owners whose development plans were frustrated by state regulations. For now, the Court has given governments considerable leeway as long as there is a demonstrated public interest behind the laws and regulations. But as private property is often regarded as a bedrock principle of U.S. capitalism and political correctness, challenges to government law and regulation for the environment will persist; if the Endangered Species Act requires a property owner to set aside a fourth of her land to protect an endangered species, hasn't one-fourth of the owner's value been taken away by the government? (See Section 5 on the Endangered Species Act.)

Zoning

In the growing cities of the early 20th century—utterly transformed by the automobile—it became apparent that residential, commercial, and industrial land uses were incompatible. Conservation of the natural environment was not relevant here (the natural environment was gone); **zoning** was developed to create areas within municipalities where similar uses would predominate. Predictably, zoning was challenged as a "taking," since it could prevent a residential property from getting a higher price on sale if it were used for commercial or industrial purposes. In *Village of Euclid v. Ambler Realty Co.* (U.S. 1926), the Supreme Court considered whether the Village of Euclid, a town in New York, had violated the Fifth Amendment's takings clause in a zoning plan. The Court said:

> *Until recent years, urban life was comparatively simple; but with the great increase and concentration of population, problems have developed, and constantly are developing, which require and will continue to require additional restrictions in respect of the use and occupation of private lands in urban communities. Such regulations are sustained, under the complex conditions of our day, for reasons analogous to those which justify traffic regulations, which, before the advent of automobiles and rapid transit street railways, would have been condemned as fatally arbitrary and unreasonable.*[12]

Though originally limited to residential, commercial, and industrial uses, today's zoning ordinances are complex sets of regulations. A typical municipality might have the following zones: residential with a host of subcategories (such as for single-family and multiple-family dwellings), office, commercial, industrial, agricultural, and public lands. Zones may be exclusive, in which case office buildings would not be permitted in commercial zones, or they may be cumulative, so that a more restricted use would be allowed in a less restrictive zone. Zoning regulations do more than specify the type of use: they often also dictate minimum requirements for parking, open usable space, setbacks, lot sizes, and the like, and maximum requirements for height, length of side lots, and so on.

Nonconforming Uses. When a zoning ordinance is enacted, it will almost always affect existing property owners, many of whom will be using their land in ways no longer permitted under the ordinance. To avoid the charge that they have thereby "taken" the property, most ordinances permit previous nonconforming uses to continue, though some ordinances limit the nonconforming uses to a specified time after becoming effective. But this permission to continue a **nonconforming use** is narrow; it extends only to the specific use to which the property was put before the ordinance was enacted. A manufacturer of dresses that suddenly finds itself in an area zoned residential may continue to use its sewing machines, but it could not develop a sideline in woodworking

Variances. Sometimes an owner may desire to use his property in ways not permitted under an existing zoning scheme and will ask the zoning board for a **variance**—authority to make a nonconforming use. The board is not free to grant a variance at its whim. The courts apply three general tests to determine the validity of a variance: (1) The land must be unable to yield a reasonable return on the uses allowed by the zoning regulation; (2) The hardship must be unique to the property, not to property generally in the area; (3) If granted, the variance must not change the essential character of the neighborhood.

zoning

Regulation of land use by government to promote compatible uses (e.g., residential, industrial, rural); certain land uses are permitted or prohibited in the zone.

nonconforming use

A land use inconsistent with applicable zoning regulations, but allowed (often because the use pre-dated the zoning).

variance

In zoning law, permission granted to a landowner by the zoning authority to make a nonconforming use.

Case

Regulation of Land Uses: Nuisances

Boomer v. Atlantic Cement Company

26 N.Y.2d 219 (NY, 1970)

Bergan, J.

Defendant operates a large cement plant near Albany. These are actions for injunction and damages by neighboring landowners alleging injury to property from dirt, smoke and vibration emanating from the plant. A nuisance has been found [by the trial court], temporary damages have been allowed; but an injunction has been denied.

The public concern with air pollution arising from many sources in industry and in transportation is currently accorded ever wider recognition accompanied by a growing sense of responsibility in State and Federal Governments to control it. Cement plants are obvious sources of air pollution in the neighborhoods where they operate.

But there is now before the court private litigation in which individual property owners have sought specific relief from a single plant operation. The threshold question raised on this appeal is whether the court should resolve the litigation between the parties now before it as equitably as seems possible; or whether, seeking promotion of the general public welfare, it should channel private litigation into broad public objectives.

A court performs its essential function when it decides the rights of parties before it. * * * It is a rare exercise of judicial power to use a decision in private litigation as a purposeful mechanism to achieve direct public objectives greatly beyond the rights and interests before the court.

Effective control of air pollution is a problem presently far from solution, even with the full public and financial powers of government. In large measure adequate technical procedures are yet to be developed and some that appear possible may be economically impracticable.

It seems apparent that the amelioration of air pollution will depend on technical research in great depth; on a carefully balanced consideration of the economic impact of close regulation; and of the actual effect on public health. It is likely to require massive public expenditure and to demand more than any local community can accomplish and to depend on regional and interstate controls.

* * * A court should not try to do this on its own as a by-product of private litigation and it seems manifest that the judicial establishment is neither equipped nor prepared to lay down and implement an effective policy for the elimination of air pollution. This is an area beyond the circumference of one private lawsuit. It is a direct responsibility for government and should not be undertaken as an incident to solving a dispute between property owners and a single cement plant—one of many—in the Hudson River valley.

The cement making operations of defendant have been found by the court at Special Term to have damaged the nearby properties of plaintiffs in these two actions. That court, as it has been noted, accordingly found defendant maintained a nuisance and this has been affirmed at the Appellate Division. The total damage to plaintiffs' properties is, however, relatively small in comparison with the value of defendant's operation and with the consequences of the injunction which plaintiffs seek.

The ground for the denial of injunction, notwithstanding the finding both that there is a nuisance and that plaintiffs have been damaged substantially, is the large disparity in economic consequences of the nuisance and of the injunction. * * * A doctrine which has been consistently reaffirmed in several leading cases in this court is that where a nuisance has been found and where there has been any substantial damage shown by the party complaining, an injunction will be granted.

The rule in New York has been that such a nuisance will be enjoined although marked disparity be shown in economic consequence between the effect of the injunction and the effect of the nuisance. * * *

There are cases where injunction has been denied. *McCann v. Chasm Power Co.* [Citation, 1914) is one of them. There, however, the damage shown by plaintiffs was not only unsubstantial, it was non-existent. Plaintiffs owned a rocky bank of the stream in which defendant had raised the level of the water. This had no economic or other adverse consequence to plaintiffs, and thus injunctive relief was denied. * * *

Although the court at Special Term and the Appellate Division held that injunction should be denied, it was found that plaintiffs had been damaged in various specific amounts up to the time of the trial and damages to the respective plaintiffs were awarded for those amounts. The effect of this was, injunction having been denied, plaintiffs could maintain successive actions at law for damages thereafter as further damage was incurred.

The court at Special Term also found the amount of permanent damage attributable to each plaintiff, for the guidance of the parties in the event both sides stipulated to the payment and acceptance of such permanent damage as a settlement of all the controversies among the parties. The total of permanent damages to all plaintiffs thus found was $185,000 [about $1.3 million in 2018 dollars]. This basis of adjustment has not resulted in any stipulation by the parties. This result at Special Term and at the Appellate Division is a departure from a rule that has become settled; but to follow the rule literally in these cases would be to close down the plant at once. This court is fully agreed to avoid that immediately drastic remedy; the difference in view is how best to avoid it. (In a footnote, the majority opinion notes that the cement company's investment in the plant is over $45,000,000 [about $322 million in 2018 dollars], and that there are over 300 people employed there.)

One alternative is to grant the injunction but postpone its effect to a specified future date to give opportunity for technical advances to permit defendant to eliminate the nuisance; another is to grant the injunction conditioned on the payment of permanent damages to plaintiffs which would compensate them for the total economic loss to their property present and future caused by defendant's operations. For reasons which will be developed, this court chooses the latter alternative.

If the injunction were to be granted unless within a short period—e.g., 18 months—the nuisance be abated by improved methods, there would be no assurance that any significant technical improvement would occur.

The parties could settle this private litigation at any time if defendant paid enough money and the imminent threat of closing the plant would build up the pressure on defendant. If there were no improved techniques found, there would inevitably be applications to the court at Special Term for extensions of time to perform on showing of good faith efforts to find such techniques.

Moreover, techniques to eliminate dust and other annoying by-products of cement making are unlikely to be developed by any research the defendant can undertake within any short period, but will depend on the total resources of the cement industry Nationwide and throughout the world. The problem is universal wherever cement is made.

For obvious reasons the rate of the research is beyond control of defendant. If at the end of 18 months the whole industry has not found a technical solution a court would be hard put to close down this one cement plant if due regard be given to equitable principles.

On the other hand, to grant the injunction unless defendant pays plaintiffs such permanent damages as may be fixed by the court seems to do justice between the contending parties. All of the attributions of economic loss to the properties on which plaintiffs' complaints are based will have been redressed.

The nuisance complained of by these plaintiffs may have other public or private consequences, but these particular parties are the only ones who have sought remedies and the judgment proposed will fully redress them. The limitation of relief granted is a limitation only within the four corners of these actions and does not foreclose public health or other public agencies from seeking proper relief in a proper court.

It seems reasonable to think that the risk of being required to pay permanent damages to injured property owners by cement plant owners would itself be a reasonable effective spur to research for improved techniques to minimize nuisance.

This should be placed beyond debate by a provision of the judgment that the payment by defendant and the acceptance by plaintiffs of permanent damages found by the court shall be in compensation for a servitude on the land. * * *

The orders should be reversed, without costs, and the cases remanded to Supreme Court, Albany County to grant an injunction which shall be vacated upon payment by defendant of such amounts of permanent damage to the respective plaintiffs as shall for this purpose be determined by the court.

Jasen, J.

(Dissenting).

It has long been the rule in this State, as the majority acknowledges, that a nuisance which results in substantial continuing damage to neighbors must be enjoined. [Citations.] To now change the rule to permit the cement company to continue polluting the air indefinitely upon the payment of permanent damages is, in my opinion, compounding the magnitude of a very serious problem in our State and Nation today.

Case Questions

1. How are the effects the plaintiffs complain of "negative externalities"? Does the price of cement reflect the full "social costs"?
2. How well are the social costs integrated into the price of Atlantic's cement after the appellate court's judgment?
3. Would you have voted with the dissent? Why, or why not? Isn't society better off with more jobs and production? How can it make sense to shut down a factory that is employing so many people in the community?
4. What does the court mean in this part: "It is a rare exercise of judicial power to use a decision in private litigation as a purposeful mechanism to achieve direct public objectives greatly beyond the rights and interests before the court."

Key Takeaway

Land use regulation can mean: (1) restrictions on the use of land through tort law, (2) private regulation—by agreement, or (3) regulation through powers of eminent domain or zoning.

Exercises

1. Give one example of the exercise of eminent domain. In order to exercise its power under eminent domain, must the government actually take eventual ownership of the property that is "taken"?

2. Felix Unger is an adult, trespassing for the first time on Alan Spillborghs's property. Alan has been digging a deep grave in his back yard for his beloved Saint Bernard, Maximilian, who has just died. Alan stops working on the grave when it gets dark, intending to return to the task in the morning. He seldom sees trespassers cutting through his backyard. Felix, in the dark, after visiting the local pub, decides to take a shortcut through Alan's yard, falls into the grave, and breaks his leg. What is the standard of care for Alan toward Felix or other infrequent trespassers?

12.3 Growth of the Environmental Movement

Learning Objectives

1. Understand what pre-modern environmental concerns were about.

2. Understand how modern environmentalism became a wide-spread matter of interest and concern.

Pre-Modern Environmentalism

In the 1300s, London had a population of only 65,000 people and it was filthy. Smoke from thousands of coal-burning fireplaces choked people, sometimes to death. Contaminants in drinking water from lack of proper sewage treatment caused horrible disease: people used outhouses or just dumped body wastes from buckets into cesspools or into the gutter in the middle of the street. When heavy rains fell, the sewage washed into the River Thames through open troughs or gutters. Here is **Johnathan Swift's** (1667–1745) poem, "A Description of a City Shower," (1710) (the title is a scatological rhyming play on the words "city shower"):

> Now from all parts the swelling gutters flow,
>
> And bear trophies with them as they go;
>
> Filth of all hues and odors seem to tell
>
> What street they sailed from, by their sight and smell.
>
> They, as each torrent drives, with rapid force
>
> From Smithfield, or St. Pulchre's, shape their course,
>
> And in huge confluent join at Snow-hill ridge,
>
> Fall from the conduit prone to Holborn-bridge
>
> Sweepings from butchers' stall, dung, guts, and blood,

Johnathan Swift

1667–1745, Anglo-Irish author.

Drown'd puppies, stinking fish, all drenched in mud,

Dead cats and turnip-tops come tumbling down the flood.

(Smithfield was an industrial area; St. Pulchre's was a charnel house, a place for disposition of the bodies or bones of the dead.)

By 1900, London had some 6 million people and an extensive sewer system, directing waste into the River Thames south of the city, and then into the Atlantic Ocean. In modern times, the disposal of human waste must be organized on a large scale. The London sewer system was begun in the 1860s; parts of it are still in use. See https://www.ancestry.com/historicalinsights/london-sewer-system.

The Industrial Age: The Conservation Movement

By the late 19th century it was apparent that America's robust capitalism had not only laid railroad track from ocean to ocean, but was also exploiting and despoiling the once seemingly inexhaustible landscape. The frontier that had so strongly shaped American identity was closing. It is no surprise that environmentalists—there were such, even 120 years ago—like John Muir (1838–1914) advocated preserving the most magnificent untrammeled landscapes; it is interesting that the biggest U.S. corporations promoted creation of national parks (an entirely American invention). Jay Cooke, the promoter of the Northern Pacific Railroad, financed expeditions to Yellowstone, and he—and other railroad magnates—also sponsored national park legislation. Certainly Mr. Cooke's interest was not entirely conservationist: the railroads made a lot of money transporting vacationers to the parks (at least until the 1960s when the automobile took over).

The Emerging Understanding of Ecosystems: *Silent Spring*

It should seem obvious that infinite growth on a finite planet is impossible, but—as is said—it's hard to make people understand something when their income depends on not understanding it. And when we have around us evidence of an enormously productive economic system which seems to benefit many, yet disregards the needs of many who have very little, it is difficult for people to see any alternative to current forms of capitalism. Yet, alternatives other than socialism or communism do exist. From the environmental or "ecosystems" perspective, the capitalist political economy in the United States has consistently placed the freedom to make money above values of equality, community, and even "efficiency" of the entire system over time.[13] This awareness grew exponentially during the 1960s and 1970s, in part because of one scientist who spoke truth to power.

In 1962, **Rachel Carson** (1907–1964) published her hugely influential book, ***Silent Spring***. It was not her first best seller: she had written several very popular books about marine biology (*The Sea Around Us; The Edge of the Sea; Under the Sea-Wind*). This new piece by the shy and mild-mannered marine biologist (she worked for the U.S. Fish and Wildlife Service) has come to be recognized as one of the most influential books of the 20th century—it was a moral call to arms. She revealed, with scrupulous documentation, that DDT—Dichlorodiphenyltrichloroethane—sprayed indiscriminately to kill insects on farms and along city streets, was entering the food chain, and poisoning every animal that touched or ingested it, from ants to humans. She compared DDT to the chilling cold-war prospect of nuclear fallout: "We are rightly appalled by the genetic effects of radiation," she wrote. "How then, can we be indifferent to the same effect in chemicals that we disseminate widely in our environment?"[14]

Rachel Carson was vilified by the chemical industry; she was accused of being a Communist, of being a crazy spinster with cats; they said the book was a hoax; they put out many articles attempting to discredit her. But she had a champion in President Kennedy, who established a presidential committee to investigate insecticides; its report in 1963 substantiated Ms. Carson's claims. Her basic point was this: we should be aware of the effects, short-term and long-term, of our actions on the environment. Her book did not start the environmental movement, but it stimulated a new awareness of environmental "unintended consequences." In 1970 President Nixon signed the National Environmental Policy Act (NEPA), which requires just such awareness of the effects of our actions on the environment.

But degradation of the environment continues. In October 2002 then-Governor Gary Locke of Washington State established a Governor's Sustainable Washington Advisory Panel. The panel's final report admonished as follows:

> *If our present behavior continues unabated, we—and our children and grandchildren who come after us—will live in a state that is likely to offer little of the quality of life that has made Washington so attractive. Indeed, we have already lost much of what was enjoyed by Washingtonians just a few generations ago. It is critical that we take responsibility for the consequences of our actions and attempt to reverse current patterns. Our solutions must be thoughtful and far-reaching, affecting the fundamental choices and actions of our government, our businesses, our communities and our families. This is the essential challenge of our generation.*[15]

The generation that could and should have addressed the problem—or at least put on the brakes—instead became enamored of SUVs and McMansions. But laws to protect the environment are, of course, still on the books, awaiting the national mindset necessary to make them effective, and we turn to them next.

Key Takeaway

From early awareness of environmental problems to the current concerns over chemicals, pesticides, plastics, and greenhouse gases warming the climate, the environmental movement has begun to challenge the long-prevailing assumption that the Earth is just a resource to be used for human pleasure and profit. We can no longer be blind to the consequences of human activities on the planet, or on the people and species that inhabit it.

Rachel Carson

1907–1964, American marine biologist and environmentalist, wrote *Silent Spring*, published in 1962.

Silent Spring

Book by Rachel Carson, published in 1962, detailing environmental contamination by the insecticide DDT.

Exercises

1. Look up "persistent organic pollutants" using your favorite search engine. What are they? Do you recognize any of them? Why were they allowed to be used in the first place?
2. Can "conservation" in the U.S. be done without having "public lands"? What is the value of "public lands," whether in national parks, national monuments, or wilderness areas? Should taxpayers support such "commons," or would there be better "conservation" if all land were privately owned?
3. How much is "enough" in terms of what we consume, individually and as a society? If every person consumed as much as the "average American," what would be the state of our natural environment?

12.4 Federal Environmental Laws

Learning Objectives

1. Understand why common-law pollution (or environmental laws) are inadequate to the task of environmental protection.
2. Describe the major federal laws that govern business activities that may adversely affect air and water quality.
3. Describe the major federal laws that govern waste disposal and chemical hazards, including pesticides.

This section discusses why federal environmental legislation is needed, touches on the National Environmental Policy Act, and takes up pollution. Air, water, and solid waste pollution are the "classic" types of pollution; more recently we see problems with noise and radiation pollution. And all this pollution contributes to species extinction, the topic of the Endangered Species Act.

The Problem with Common-Law Environmental Protection

In one sense, environmental law is very old, as we have seen. Medieval England had smoke control laws that established the seasons when soft coal could be burned, and urban sewage in many large cities was reasonably well disposed of by the mid-19th century: a person could complain if her neighbor dumped untreated human waste on the ground—that would be a nuisance. Nuisance laws give private individuals a limited control over polluting activities of adjacent landowners.

But there are several problems with expecting the common law to protect the environment.

• First, a major shortcoming of common-law pollution control is its "retro" style: it generally cannot prevent the happening of a harm, but usually only provides compensation to injured parties after the harm. Yes, you might successfully complain about a big polluter, but only after the harm has already been caused; before that, you don't (usually) have standing—there is no prophylactic. Courts in common law causes of action cannot enjoin harms already done, though they may enjoin future harms from ongoing nuisances.

- Second, as seen in the *Atlantic Cement* case (above)—courts are reluctant to shut down entire businesses because they pollute. Such draconian regulation is more properly the legislature's job.

- Third, where many individual polluters—maybe dozens or thousands (as on major US rivers)—contribute to the pollution, it is very difficult to find appropriate defendants: whom do you sue? Thousands of defendants?

The common law, in short, generally looks backward to harms already done; it won't do the job of stopping future harms. A comprehensive set of U.S. laws directed toward general protection of the environment is largely a product of the past fifty years, with most of the legislative activity stemming from the late 1960s and '70s, when people began to perceive that the environment was systematically deteriorating from assaults by rapid population growth, greatly increased automobile use, vast proliferation of factories that generate waste products, and a sharp rise in the production of toxic materials. Two of the most significant developments in environmental law came in 1970, when the National Environmental Policy Act took effect and the Environmental Protection Agency was established.

National Environmental Policy Act

Signed into law by President Nixon on January 1, 1970, the **National Environmental Policy Act** (NEPA) declared that it shall be the policy of the federal government, in cooperation with state and local governments,

> to create and maintain conditions under which man and nature can exist in productive harmony, and fulfill the social, economic, and other requirements of present and future generations of Americans....The Congress recognizes that each person should enjoy a healthful environment and that each person has a responsibility to contribute to the preservation and enhancement of the environment. [16]

National Environmental Policy Act

Federal statute, 1970, requiring (in appropriate cases) disclosure of environmental consequences of development.

At about the same time that NEPA was adopted, sixteen states also adopted "little NEPAs," state environmental policy acts (SEPAs).[17] What is said here about NEPA also applies, in general, to SEPA (except the word "federal" or "national" would be replaced by the word "state").

The basic idea behind NEPA is not to set any policy (such as how much sulfur can be emitted from a smokestack), but to *fully disclose* the environmental impacts of a proposed project. The act is *not* the National Environmental *Protection* Act; it is a procedural statute. Using the NEPA process, permitting agencies evaluate the environmental and related social and economic effects of proposed actions. Agencies must also provide opportunities for public review and comment on those evaluations. The most significant aspect of NEPA is the mechanism by which full disclosure is accomplished (the "action-forcing requirement"): project promoters must prepare an **environmental impact statement** (EIS) whenever undertaking action that significantly affects environmental quality and that requires a federal permit.

environmental impact statement

A statement mandated by the National Environmental Policy Act that is required of most federal agencies and includes an assessment of whether the agency's actions will significantly affect environmental quality.

The EIS is written by trained professionals whose job it is to write them; the EIS is not a whitewash job hired up by the project's promoters. The EIS must: (1) detail the environmental impact of the proposed action, (2) list any unavoidable adverse impacts should the action be taken, (3) consider alternatives to the proposed action, (4) compare short-term and long-term consequences, and (5) describe irreversible commitments of resources. Unless the impact statement is prepared, the project can be enjoined (prohibited by an injunction issued by a court) from proceeding. NEPA's scope is broader than it may appear; it does not only apply to projects undertaken by the government itself:

> [T]here is "Federal action" within the meaning of the statute not only when an agency proposes to build a facility itself, but also whenever an agency makes a decision which permits action by other parties which will affect the quality of the environment. NEPA's impact statement procedure has been held to apply where . . . the federal agency took action affecting the environment in the sense that the agency made a decision which permitted some other party—private or governmental—to take action affecting the environment. NEPA's impact statement procedure has been held to apply where a federal agency approves a lease of land to private parties, grants licenses and permits to private parties, or approves and funds state highway projects.[18]

Title II of NEPA established the President's Council on Environmental Quality (CEQ) to oversee NEPA implementation. The duties of CEQ include: ensuring that federal agencies meet their obligations under NEPA, overseeing federal agency implementation of the environmental impact assessment process, and issuing regulations and other guidance to federal agencies regarding NEPA compliance. Over a year and a half into President Trump's administration, the Council was not functioning; his nominee, who had called carbon dioxide the "gas of life" and was a climate change skeptic, withdrew from the process. An immediate replacement, also a climate change skeptic, was nominated in her place, but 16 months past President Trump's inauguration, there was no functioning CEQ.

Again, sixteen states have their own environmental policy acts (SEPAs), often using the same or similar language.

Environmental Protection Agency

Environmental Protection Agency

A federal administrative agency established in 1970 to monitor industry's environmental practices, promulgate environmental regulations, and police the standards.

The **Environmental Protection Agency** (EPA) has been in the forefront of the news since its creation in 1970. Charged with monitoring environmental practices of industry, assisting the government and private business to halt environmental deterioration, promulgating regulations consistent with federal environmental policy, and policing industry for violations of the various federal environmental statutes and regulations, the EPA has had a pervasive influence on American business. *Business Week* noted the following in 1977: "Cars rolling off Detroit's assembly line now have antipollution devices as standard equipment. The dense black smokestack emissions that used to symbolize industrial prosperity are rare, and illegal, sights. Plants that once blithely ran discharge water out of a pipe and into a river must apply for permits that are almost impossible to get unless the plants install expensive water treatment equipment. All told, the EPA has made a sizable dent in man-made environmental filth."[19] But the agency is a lightning rod for political bickering, and one cannot forebear to mention that while politicians bicker, the environment continues to deteriorate. It remains to be seen, years into the Donald Trump administration, whether a credible director of the EPA will ever materialize.

The EPA is especially responsible to regulate water and air pollution and in overseeing the disposition of toxic wastes and chemicals. To these problems we now turn.

Water Pollution

Clean Water Act

Part of the federal clean-water regime imposes responsibilities on the states. Although legislation governing the nation's public waterways goes way back,[20] the centerpiece of water pollution enforcement is the **Clean Water Act of 1972** (technically, the Federal Water Pollution Control Act Amendments of 1972), as amended in 1977, and by the Water Quality Act of 1987. The Clean Water Act is designed to restore and maintain the "chemical, physical, and biological integrity of the Nation's waters."[21] It operates on the states, requiring them to designate the uses of every significant body of water within their borders (e.g., for drinking water, recreation, commercial fishing), and to set water quality standards to reduce pollution to levels appropriate for each use.

Congress only has power under the Constitution's Commerce Clause to regulate interstate commerce, and so the Clean Water Act is applicable only to "navigable waters" of the United States. This has led to disputes over whether the act can apply, say, to an abandoned gravel pit that has no visible connection to navigable waterways, even if the gravel pit provides habitat for migratory birds. In 2001, in *Solid Waste Agency of Northern Cook County v. Army Corps of Engineers*, the U.S. Supreme Court said no.[22] The protection of *intra*state waters is left to the states.

> **Clean Water Act of 1972**
>
> Federal statute, 1972, establishing national water-quality standards.

Private Industry

The Clean Water Act also governs private industry and imposes standards on the discharge of pollutants into waterways and publicly-owned sewage systems. The act created an effluent permit system known as the National Pollutant Discharge Elimination System. To discharge any pollutants into navigable waters from a "point source" like a pipe, ditch, ship, or container, a company must obtain a certification that it meets specified standards, which are continually being tightened. For example, until 1983, industry had to use the "best practicable technology" currently available, but after July 1, 1984, it had to use the "best available technology" economically achievable. Companies must limit certain kinds of "conventional pollutants" (such as suspended solids and acidity) by "best conventional control technology."

Other EPA Water Initiatives

Federal law governs, and the EPA regulates, a number of other water control measures. Ocean dumping, for example, is the subject of the **Marine Protection, Research, and Sanctuaries Act** of 1972, which gives the EPA jurisdiction over wastes discharged into the oceans. The EPA also oversees state and local plans for restoring general water quality to acceptable levels in the face of a host of non-point-source pollution. The Clean Water Act controls municipal sewage systems, which must ensure that wastewater is chemically treated before being discharged from the sewage system.

> **Marine Protection, Research, and Sanctuaries Act**
>
> Federal statute, 1972, gives the EPA jurisdiction over wastes discharged into the oceans.

Drinking water. Obviously, of critical importance to the nation's health is the supply of drinking water. To ensure its purity, Congress enacted the Safe Drinking Water Act of 1974, with amendments passed in 1986 and 1996. This act aims to protect water at its sources: rivers, lakes, reservoirs, springs, and groundwater wells.[23] (The act does not regulate private wells that serve fewer than twenty-five individuals.) This law has two strategies for combating pollution of drinking water. It establishes national standards for drinking water derived from both surface reservoirs and underground aquifers.

wetlands

Distinct ecosystems inundated by water, permanently or seasonally and providing, water purification and storage, carbon processing, stabilization of shorelines, and support of plants and animals.

Wetlands protection. One of your authors, who at the time was serving in local government, was told by an enraged elderly constituent at a meeting on wetlands protection that "Ever'body knows 'wetlands' are just damn *swamps*—do ya hear me?—*swamps*: breeding grounds for mosquitoes and disease!" Well, no. Wetlands are vitally important parts of the ecological system, providing habitat for plants and animals of all sorts, and clean-water recharge "services"—**wetlands** loss is a major problem. That said, there is no comprehensive federal wetlands protection law. The Clean Water Act gives the EPA and the U.S. Army Corps of Engineers authority to protect waters, marshlands, and other wetlands against degradation caused by dredging and fills, but laws and regulations have developed "piecemeal over the years, and often utilize laws originally intended for other purposes."[24] Farmers sometimes want to fill "inconveniently located" wetlands to grow crops; developers find wetlands inconvenient impediments to housing construction. There are various federal and state programs to promote wetland protection other than those mentioned above. For an overview, look here: http://www.lakeandwetland.com/federal-laws-for-wetlands/.

Air Pollution

Clean Air Act of 1970

Federal statute establishing nationwide air-quality standards.

The centerpiece of the legislative effort to clean the atmosphere is the **Clean Air Act of 1970** (amended in 1975, 1977, and 1990). Under this act, the EPA has set two levels of National Ambient Air Quality Standards (NAAQS). The primary standards limit the ambient (i.e., circulating) pollution that affects human health; secondary standards limit pollution that affects animals, plants, and property. The heart of the Clean Air Act is the requirement that, subject to EPA approval, the states must implement EPA standards through state implementation plans (SIPs) applicable to appropriate industrial sources in the state. The act was amended in 1977 and 1990 primarily to set new goals (dates) for achieving attainment of NAAQS since many areas of the country had failed to meet the deadlines.

Beyond the NAAQS, the EPA has established several specific standards to control different types of air pollution. One major type is pollution that mobile sources, mainly automobiles, emit. The EPA requires cars to be equipped with catalytic converters, to use unleaded gasoline to eliminate the most noxious fumes, and to keep them from escaping into the atmosphere. To minimize pollution from stationary sources, the EPA also imposes uniform standards on new industrial plants and those that have been substantially modernized. And, to safeguard against emissions from older plants, states must promulgate and enforce SIPs.

The Clean Air Act is even more protective of air quality in certain parts of the nation, such as designated wilderness areas and national parks. For these areas, the EPA has set standards to prevent significant deterioration in order to keep the air as pristine and clear as it was centuries ago.

The EPA also worries about chemicals so toxic that the tiniest quantities could prove fatal or extremely hazardous to health. To control emission of substances like asbestos, beryllium, mercury, vinyl chloride, benzene, and arsenic, the EPA has established or proposed various National Emissions Standards for Hazardous Air Pollutants.

Concern over acid rain and other types of air pollution prompted Congress to add almost eight hundred pages of amendments to the Clean Air Act in 1990. (The original act was fifty pages long.) As a result of these amendments, the act was modernized in a manner that parallels other environmental laws. For instance, the amendments established a permit system that is modeled after the Clean Water Act. The amendments require felony convictions for willful violations, similar to penalties incorporated into other statutes.

The amendments include certain defenses for industry. For example, companies are protected from allegations that they are violating the law by showing that they were acting in accordance with a permit. In addition to this "permit shield," the law also excuses workers who unintentionally violate the law while following their employers' instructions.

Solid Waste and Soil Pollution

Solid Waste Disposal Act

Every year, the United States generates approximately 230 million tons of "trash"(more technically, "municipal solid waste" or MSW)—about 4.6 pounds per person per day. Less than one-quarter of it is recycled; the rest is incinerated or buried in landfills. But many of the country's landfills have been closed, either because they were full or because they were contaminating groundwater. Once groundwater is contaminated, it is extremely expensive and difficult to clean it up. In the 1965 **Solid Waste Disposal Act**, Congress sought to regulate the discharge of garbage by encouraging waste management and recycling; federal grants were available for research and training, but the major regulatory effort was expected to come from the states and municipalities.

> **Solid Waste Disposal Act**
>
> Federal statute, 1965, to address solid waste disposal problems.

But shocking news prompted Congress to get tough in 1976. The plight of homeowners near Love Canal in upstate New York became a major national story as the discovery of massive underground leaks of toxic chemicals buried during the previous quarter century led to evacuation of hundreds of homes. Next came the revelation that Kepone, an exceedingly toxic pesticide, had been dumped into the James River in Virginia, causing a major human health hazard and severe damage to fisheries in the James and downstream in the Chesapeake Bay. The rarely discussed industrial dumping of hazardous wastes now became an open controversy, and Congress responded in 1976 with the Resource Conservation and Recovery Act (RCRA) and the Toxic Substances Control Act (TSCA) and in 1980 with the Comprehensive Environmental Response, Compensation, and Liability Act (CERCLA).

Resource Conservation and Recovery Act (1976)

No longer can hazardous substances simply be dumped at a convenient landfill. The **Resource Conservation and Recovery Act** (RCRA) expresses a "cradle-to-grave" philosophy: hazardous wastes must be regulated at every stage—they can't just be dumped on the ground. The act gives the EPA power to govern their creation, storage, transport, treatment, and disposal. Any person or company that generates hazardous waste must obtain a permit (known as a "manifest") either to store it on its own site or ship it to an EPA-approved treatment, storage, or disposal facility. Owners and operators of such sites must show that they can pay for damage growing out of their operations, and even after the sites are closed to further dumping, they must set aside funds to monitor and maintain the sites safely.

> **Resource Conservation and Recovery Act**
>
> Federal statute, 1976, giving the EPA regulatory authority over hazardous waste.

This philosophy can be severe in application. In 1986, the Supreme Court ruled that bankruptcy is not a sufficient reason for a company to abandon toxic waste dumps if state regulations reasonably require protection in the interest of public health or safety. The practical effect of the ruling is that trustees of the bankrupt company must first devote assets to cleaning up a dump site, and only from remaining assets may they satisfy creditors.[25] Another severity is RCRA's imposition of criminal liability, including fines of up to $25,000 a day and one-year prison sentences, which can be extended beyond owners to individual employees, as discussed in *U.S. v. Johnson & Towers, Inc., et al.*, below.

Toxic Substances Control Act (1976)

Chemical substances that decades ago promised to improve the quality of life not infrequently later come to show their negative side—they have serious adverse side effects.[26][27] For example, asbestos, in use for half a century as a marvel of insulation and building material, causes cancer and asbestosis, a debilitating lung disease, in workers who breathed in fibers decades ago. The result was crippling disease and death; more than thirty thousand asbestos-related lawsuits were filed nationwide in the '80s and '90s. Other substances, such as polychlorinated biphenyls (PCBs) and dioxin, have caused similar personal tragedies. Together, the devastating effects of chemicals led to enactment of the **Toxic Substances Control Act** (TSCA), designed to control the manufacture, processing, commercial distribution, use, and disposal of chemicals that pose unreasonable health or environmental risks. (The TSCA does not apply to pesticides, tobacco, nuclear materials, firearms and ammunition, food, food additives, drugs, and cosmetics—which are regulated by other federal laws.)

The TSCA gives the EPA authority to screen for health and environmental risks by requiring companies to notify the EPA ninety days before manufacturing or importing new chemicals. The EPA may demand that the companies test the substances before marketing them and may regulate them in a number of ways, such as requiring the manufacturer to label its products, to keep records on its manufacturing and disposal processes, and to document all significant adverse reactions in people exposed to the chemicals. The EPA also has authority to ban certain especially hazardous substances, and it has banned the further production of PCBs and many uses of asbestos.

Both industry groups and consumer groups have attacked the TSCA. Industry groups criticize the act because the enforcement mechanism requires mountainous paperwork and leads to widespread delay. Consumer groups complain because the EPA has been slow to act against numerous chemical substances. The debate continues.

Comprehensive Environmental Response, Compensation, and Liability Act ("Superfund") (1980)

The CERCLA, also known as the **Superfund Act** (1980), gives the EPA emergency powers to respond to public health or environmental dangers from faulty hazardous waste disposal. Currently, there are over a thousand major Superfund sites to be cleaned up, and many more smaller sites where hazardous waste has not been properly disposed of. The EPA can direct immediate removal of wastes presenting imminent danger (e.g., from train wrecks, oil spills, leaking barrels, and fires). Injuries can be sudden and devastating; in 1979, for example, when a freight train derailed in Florida, ninety thousand pounds of chlorine gas escaped from a punctured tank car, leaving 8 motorists dead and 183 others injured, and forcing 3,500 residents within a 7-mile radius to be evacuated. The EPA may also carry out "planned removals" when the danger is substantial, even if immediate removal is not necessary.

The EPA prods owners who can be located to voluntarily clean up sites they have abandoned. If the owners refuse, the EPA and the states will undertake the task, drawing on a federal trust fund financed mainly by taxes on the manufacture or import of certain chemicals and petroleum (the balance of the fund comes from general revenues). States must finance 10 percent of the cost of cleaning up private sites and 50 percent of the cost of cleaning up public facilities. The EPA and the states can then assess unwilling owners' punitive damages up to triple the cleanup costs, filing a "superfund" lawsuit if necessary.

Cleanup requirements are especially controversial when applied to landowners who innocently purchased contaminated property. To deal with this problem, Congress enacted the Superfund Amendment and Reauthorization Act in 1986, which protects innocent landowners who—at the time of purchase—made an "appropriate inquiry" into the prior uses of the property. The act also requires companies to publicly disclose information about hazardous chemicals they use.

Other Types of Environmental Regulation

Noise Regulation

Under the **Noise Regulation Act** of 1972, Congress has attempted to combat a growing menace to U.S. workers, residents, and consumers. People who live close to airports and major highways, workers who use certain kinds of machinery (e.g., air compressors, rock drills, bulldozers), and consumers who use certain products, such as power mowers, leaf blowers, and air conditioners, often suffer from a variety of noise-related ailments. The Noise Regulation Act delegates to the EPA power to limit "noise emissions" from these major sources of noise. Under the act, manufacturers may not sell new products that fail to conform to the noise standards the EPA sets, and users are forbidden from dismantling noise control devices installed on these products. Moreover, manufacturers must label noisy products properly. Private suits may be filed against violators, and the act also permits fines of up to $25,000 per day and a year in jail for those who seek to avoid its terms.

> **Noise Regulation Act**
>
> Federal statute, 1972, delegates to the EPA power to limit noise emissions for major noise-making sources.

Radiation Control

The terrifying effects of a nuclear disaster became frighteningly clear when the Soviet Union's nuclear power plant at Chernobyl exploded in early 1986, discharging vast quantities of radiation into the world's airstream and affecting people thousands of miles away. In the United States, the most notorious nuclear accident occurred at the Three Mile Island nuclear utility in Pennsylvania in 1979, crippling the facility for years because of the extreme danger and long life of the radiation.

Primary responsibility for overseeing nuclear safety rests with the Nuclear Regulatory Commission, but many other agencies and several federal laws (including the Clean Air Act; the Federal Water Pollution Control Act; the Safe Drinking Water Act; the Uranium Mill Tailings Radiation Control Act; the Marine Protection, Research, and Sanctuaries Act; the Nuclear Waste Policy Act of 1982; the CERCLA; and the Ocean Dumping Act) govern the use of nuclear materials and the storage of radioactive wastes (some of which will remain severely dangerous for thousands of years). Through many of these laws, the EPA has been assigned the responsibility of setting radiation guidelines, assessing new technology, monitoring radiation in the environment, setting limits on release of radiation from nuclear utilities, developing guidance for use of X-rays in medicine, and helping to plan for radiation emergencies. The federal Energy Department is responsible for disposing of nuclear waste. The job is not going well: https://www.scientificamerican.com/article/hanford-nuclear-cleanup-problems/.

Endangered Species Act

Congress passed the **Endangered Species Act** (ESA) in 1973 to recognize that our rich natural heritage is of "esthetic, ecological, educational, recreational, and scientific value to our Nation and its people." Its concern was that many of our nation's native plants and animals were in danger of becoming extinct, and its purpose is to protect imperiled species and the ecosystems upon which they depend. The ESA is administered by the U.S. Fish and Wildlife Service (Service) and the Commerce Department's National Marine Fisheries Service (NMFS). The Service has primary responsibility for terrestrial and freshwater organisms, while the responsibilities of NMFS are mainly marine wildlife such as whales and anadromous fish (born in fresh water but spending most of its life in the sea then returning to fresh water to spawn. Salmon, smelt, shad, striped bass, and sturgeon are common examples of anadromous fish).

> **Endangered Species Act**
>
> Federal statute, 1973, requiring preservation of species threatened with extinction.

Under the ESA, species may be listed as either endangered or threatened. "Endangered" means a species is in danger of extinction throughout all, or a significant portion, of its range. "Threatened" means a species is likely to become endangered within the foreseeable future. All species of plants and animals, except pest insects, are eligible for listing as endangered or threatened.

The ESA regulates all "taking" of endangered species by private parties. Take is broadly defined under the statute to include harass, harm, pursue, hunt, shoot, wound, kill, trap, capture, or collect. The agencies that implement the ESA have in turn promulgated regulations that define harm to include destruction of the habitat for a listed species where it will "actually kill or injure" a member of a listed species.

As a litigation tool for conservationists, the ESA proved to be fairly effective, at least initially. Opponents of dams (who prefer rivers to run "free" for ecological reasons) objected to and delayed for years a TVA (Tennessee Valley Authority) project that would imperil a small fish, the "snail darter." The "Delhi Sands Fly," an insect but not a "pest insect," was the imperiled species that held up (temporarily) a real estate development near Sacramento, California. Habitat concerns for the threatened "spotted owl" held up lumbering operations in the Olympic Peninsula, and was a flashpoint of contention between the timber industry and the Clinton Administration. One of the authors, while traveling near Sequim, Washington (in the heart of lumbermen's country) spotted a bumper sticker that read, "I Love Spotted Owls. Baked, Fried, or Fricasseed."

Many have argued that the ESA, as an exercise of Congress' power to regulate interstate commerce, is unconstitutional. About a third of all listed species are only found in one county, let alone one state. Thus, federal power to limit economic activity that may threaten a species' habitat in one county would arguably be over-reach, as the one species would not "affect interstate commerce." See, for example, *People for the Ethical Treatment of Property Owners (PETPO) v. U.S. Fish and Wildlife Service (USFWS)*, where the federal district court granted property owners relief, but the 10th Circuit reversed and remanded, holding for the USFWS.[28] Congress created a loophole in 1978 by creating the "god squad," a federal committee that could exempt selected species from protection when it is economically inconvenient to humans for that species to exist.[29] As it is, man-made extinctions continue apace:

We're currently experiencing the worst spate of species die-offs since the loss of the dinosaurs 65 million years ago. Although extinction is a natural phenomenon, it occurs at a natural "background" rate of about one to five species per year. Scientists estimate we're now losing species at 1,000 to 10,000 times the background rate, with literally dozens going extinct every day. It could be a scary future indeed, with as many as 30 to 50 percent of all species possibly heading toward extinction by mid-century.[30]

State Environmental Protections

Under federalism, states also have police powers over health, education, safety, the general welfare, and the environment. Most states have some set of environmental protections, some of which can be stricter than federal standards. California, for example, has long had stricter air pollution standards than the federal Clean Air Act standards (automakers in Detroit referred to their two kinds of cars as "federal cars" and "California cars). California's laws on disposal of hazardous waste predated federal law. Florida's environmental agencies, as another example, have banned the sale of certain species of snakes because people would not know what to do with their pet snakes after they got too big. Pet owners would drive to the Florida Everglades and abandon their pet snakes there. The snakes are not supposed to live in Florida wetlands and swamps, as they disrupt the natural balance of that fragile ecosystem by threatening certain species. There is no federal law that would protect these snakes (but see Endangered Species Act, below), so there is no preemption of Florida's protective legislation.

> This is some snake. At full maturity, a Burmese python routinely reaches lengths of 12 feet or more. Twenty-footers weighing 250 pounds are not unheard-of. The pythons are prodigious breeders, with voracious appetites to match. They are believed to have eaten their way through the Everglades, bringing about startling changes in the ecosystem. Some mammals native to those marshes, like foxes and rabbits, seem to have disappeared, researchers say. Other species—among them raccoons, deer, opossums and bobcats—are close to being wiped out. Pythons that migrated from the mainland to Key Largo have put indigenous wood rats in mortal peril.[31]

In general, state "EPAs" (or their equivalent) are empowered to enforce federal environmental laws such as the Clean Air Act and the Clean Water Act. The EPA can approve state implementation plans that are equivalent to, or more stringent than, federal standards. It can also withdraw authorization for state programs that fail to meet federal requirements.

Case

Criminal Liability for Polluting under Federal Resource Conservation and Recovery Act (RCRA)

U.S. v. Johnson & Towers, Inc., Jack W. Hopkins, and Peter Angel

741 F.2d 662 (1984) Third Circuit[32]

> **U.S. v. Johnson & Towers, Inc., Jack W. Hopkins, and Peter Angel**
>
> Third Federal Circuit Court case, 1984, analyzing criminal liability for violation of the Resource Conservation and Recovery Act.

Sloviter, J.

In a question of first impression regarding the statutory definition of "person," the district court concluded that the Act's criminal penalty provision imposing fines and imprisonment for illegal waste discharge could not apply to the individual defendants. We will reverse.

The criminal prosecution in this case arose from the disposal of chemicals at a plant owned by Johnson & Towers in Mount Laurel, New Jersey. In its operations the company, which repairs and overhauls large motor vehicles, uses degreasers and other industrial chemicals that contain chemicals such as methylene chloride and trichlorethylene, classified as "hazardous wastes" under the Resource Conservation and Recovery Act (RCRA), [Citation] (1982) and "pollutants" under the Clean Water Act [Citation] (1982).

The indictment named as defendants Johnson & Towers and two of its employees, Jack Hopkins, a foreman, and Peter Angel, the service manager in the trucking department. According to the indictment, over a three-day period federal agents saw workers pump waste from a tank into the trench, and on the third day observed toxic chemicals flowing into the creek.

The counts under RCRA charged that the defendants "did knowingly treat, store, and dispose of, and did cause to be treated, stored and disposed of hazardous wastes without having obtained a permit . . . in that the defendants discharged, deposited, injected, dumped, spilled, leaked and placed degreasers . . . into the trench. . . ." The indictment alleged that both Angel and Hopkins "managed, supervised and directed a substantial portion of Johnson & Towers' operations . . . including those related to the treatment, storage and disposal of the hazardous wastes and pollutants" and that the chemicals were discharged by "the defendants and others at their direction."

Johnson & Towers pled guilty to the RCRA counts. Hopkins and Angel pled not guilty, and then moved to dismiss counts 2, 3, and 4. The court concluded that the RCRA criminal provision applies only to "owners and operators," i.e., those obligated under the statute to obtain a permit. Since neither Hopkins nor Angel was an "owner" or "operator," the district court granted the motion to dismiss the RCRA charges, and the government appealed to this court. * * *

The single issue in this appeal is whether the individual defendants are subject to prosecution under RCRA's criminal provision, which applies to any person who

- (2) knowingly treats, stores, or disposes of any hazardous waste identified or listed under this subchapter either

  - without having obtained a permit under section 6925 of this title . . . or

  - in knowing violation of any material condition or requirement of such permit.

The parties offer contrary interpretations of section 6928(d)(2)(A). Defendants consider it an administrative enforcement mechanism, applying only to those whose owners or operators come within section 6925 and fail to comply; the government reads it as penalizing anyone who handles hazardous waste without a permit or in violation of a permit. Neither party has cited another case, nor have we found one, considering the application of this criminal provision to an individual other than an owner or operator.

As in any statutory analysis, we are obliged first to look to the language and then, if needed, attempt to divine Congress' specific intent with respect to the issue.

First, "person" is defined in the statute as "an individual, trust, firm, joint stock company, corporation (including a government corporation), partnership, association, State, municipality, commission, political subdivision of a State, or any interstate body." [Citation] (1982). Had Congress meant * * * to take aim more narrowly, it could have used more narrow language. Since it did not, we attribute to "any person" the definition given the term in that section.

Second, under the plain language of the statute the only explicit basis for exoneration is the existence of a permit covering the action. Nothing in the language of the statute suggests that we should infer another provision exonerating persons who knowingly treat, store or dispose of hazardous waste but are not owners or operators.

Finally, though the result may appear harsh, it is well established that criminal penalties attached to regulatory statutes intended to protect public health, in contrast to statutes based on common law crimes, are to be construed to effectuate the regulatory purpose. * * *

The original statute made knowing disposal (but not treatment or storage) of such waste without a permit a misdemeanor. Amendments in 1978 and 1980 expanded the criminal provision to cover treatment and storage and made violation of section 6928 a felony. The fact that Congress amended the statute twice to broaden the scope of its substantive provisions and enhance the penalty is a strong indication of Congress' increasing concern about the seriousness of the prohibited conduct.

We conclude that in RCRA, no less than in the Food and Drugs Act, Congress endeavored to control hazards that, "in the circumstances of modern industrialism, are largely beyond self-protection." [Citation]. It would undercut the purposes of the legislation to limit the class of potential defendants to owners and operators when others also bear responsibility for handling regulated materials. The phrase "without having obtained a permit *under section 6925*" (emphasis added) merely references the section under which the permit is required and exempts from prosecution under section 6928(d)(2)(A) anyone who has obtained a permit; we conclude that it has no other limiting effect. Therefore we reject the district court's construction limiting the substantive criminal provision by confining "any person" in section 6928(d)(2)(A) to owners and operators of facilities that store, treat or dispose of hazardous waste, as an unduly narrow view of both the statutory language and the congressional intent.

Case Questions

1. The district court (trial court) accepted the individual defendants' argument as to why they should not be criminally liable. What was that argument?
2. On what reasoning did the appellate court reject that argument?
3. If employees of a company that is violating the RCRA refused to carry out disposal of hazardous substances in violation of the RCRA, they would presumably lose their jobs. What is the moral justification for applying criminal penalties to such employees (like Hopkins and Angel)?
4. The court here is required—apparently as a case of first impression—to interpret the meaning of the statute in question. You may recall from Chapter 4 that one of the functions of the judiciary is to interpret the meaning of statutory language. What was the interpretation in dispute, and how did the court resolve it?

Key Takeaway

Laws limiting the use of one's property have been around for centuries; common-law restraints (the law of trespass and nuisance) exist as causes of action against those who would use their property to adversely affect the life or health of others or the value of their neighbors' property, but the common law is—for various reasons—inadequate for protecting the environment. Since the 1960s, extensive federal laws governing the environment have been enacted. These include laws governing air, water, chemicals, pesticides, solid waste, and nuclear activities. Some laws include criminal penalties for noncompliance. States also have some authority to regulate activities that degrade the environment

Exercises

1. Who is responsible for funding CERCLA? That is, what is the source of funds for cleanups of hazardous waste?
2. Why is it necessary to have criminal penalties for noncompliance with environmental laws?
3. Why are federal environmental laws necessary? Why not let the states exclusively govern in the area of environmental protection?
4. What types of pollution have been regulated by the federal government?
5. Check out light pollution: http://darksky.org/light-pollution/, and see why it is a big deal.
6. If a species, like say, gorillas, grew in population as enormously as the human population has grown in the last 200 years, and if that species caused, as humans have, enormous pollution and damage to the Earth's environment (and indeed its capacity to sustain life), what would humans do about it?
7. If we know, as we do, that our economic system is fundamentally unsustainable, why do we continue to laud "growth" and disdain the mere status quo?

12.5 Current Trends in Environmental Law and Regulation

1. Understand how elections affect environmental policies.

Given the importance of natural systems to the survival of humanity (not to mention the survival of other living things on the planet), and to any kind of economic sustainability, it is remarkable how much the environment continues to deteriorate. Humans are causing it. At one time human actions affecting the environment may have been excusable—we didn't know any better. But now we know, and yet the degradation continues. It certainly continues in the United States, a democracy where 62% of people in a Gallup poll say "government is doing too little on the environment."[33]

When we examined how the law is made (Chapter 4), we looked at the five law-making entities. We will briefly review here those entities, and see how they are responding to the environmental crisis.[34] Environmental protection (or its absence) is an important issue for states, nation-states, and international bodies, because environmental issues transcend state and national borders.

Legislative Action Affecting the Environment

The first law-making entity set out in the U.S. Constitution is the legislative branch—Congress. If Congress adopts a law protecting the environment, Congress can amend or repeal the law. As an example, look again at the Endangered Species Act. This legislation is remarkable in that it recognizes the intrinsic value of non-human species and interests. But there is a big problem: it specifies that "cost" is not a factor to be determined by the U.S. Fish and Wildlife Service (the agency that determines what species should be protected). Thus, while Congress (so far) continues to fund ESA efforts, many critics think the money is wasted: human interests, particularly economic ones, are being needlessly set aside.

In one month alone—July 2018—two-dozen pieces of legislation, policy initiatives, and amendments designed to weaken the ESA were introduced, voted on in Congress, or proposed by the Trump administration. The proposals included reducing the role of science in determining which species are endangered, stripping protections from the gray wolf in Wyoming and along the western Great Lakes, delaying a plan to keep the sage grouse (inhabiting millions of oil rich acres in the west) from being listed as endangered for at least 10 years, and removing the American burying beetle from the endangered list. The burying beetle is an orange-flecked insect that has long been the bane of oil companies that would like to drill where it lives.

Without question, protecting threatened and endangered species is costly, not only to government but also to individuals and business firms. Could it be arrogant for humans to decide that they, above all other life forms, can determine what species survive and which become extinct? Of course not all of the proposed legislation and regulation has been enacted as of this writing; the point is to observe how elections have consequences for the environment, whether voters intend those specific consequences or not.

Executive Action Affecting the Environment

Proposing legislation. In the United States the president, can—and does—propose legislation for Congress to enact. That's very important, especially when the White House and Congress are both of one part. As just noted, legislation proposed by the Trump administration to amend the ESA may be well received by a Senate with a GOP majority.

Executive orders. Congress creates administrative agencies and delegates to them authority to make "law" (regulations), but at the same time they are carrying out a function constitutionally assigned to the executive—they are making up the law (quasi-legislative function) and, simultaneously, carrying it out (quasi-executive functions). Insofar as these government functionaries are agents of the president, the president can tell them what to do by issuing executive orders. So it is that President Trump, early in his administration, issued executive orders directing the EPA to begin rewriting Obama administration regulations limiting greenhouse-gas emissions from existing electric utilities; those regulations mostly affected utilities that burn coal. A second order would change a 2015 rule issued under the 1972 Clean Water Act giving the federal government jurisdiction over not only major water bodies, but the rivers, streams, and wetlands that feed into them.[35]

Agency heads. And, as is clear from Chapter 4 Section 2, the president has the power to appoint (with the Senate's consent) top administrators to various executive agencies such as the EPA. If those appointees are not sympathetic to the apparent mission of the agency, the agency doesn't do much, or it undoes what had been done before. And so it is with environmental protection.

In 2017, President Trump appointed Scott Pruitt as EPA director. The purpose of the EPA is environmental protection; that's right in the name of the agency. Mr. Pruitt (who had to resign in June, 2018 for egregious ethical lapses) apparently followed Mr. Trump's wishes—he oversaw reductions in pollution fines, in agency budget and staff; he reduced to a snail's pace some work on toxins and other health-hazards, and instituted regulatory slowdowns and rollbacks to reduce environmental constraints[36] so the EPA could be "business friendly; he focused especially on undoing Obama-era policies. Secretary Pruitt was proud of his record in that regard, with a program he called "Back to Basics."[37]

And Mr. Trump appointed Ryan Zinke as secretary of the Department of Interior, which oversees federal public lands. In the 19th century the federal government seized land from whomever was in the West before (Native Americans, Mexicans), and took upon itself the task of regulating, managing, and overseeing it. Mr. Zinke has overseen a concerted effort to roll back protective federal rules on how these vast land holdings can be used; he directed very significant reductions in the size of two natural monuments in Utah (Bears Ears and Grand Staircase Escalante).

Nominations of federal court judges. The president nominates people to serve as federal court judges; if confirmed, the judge has lifetime tenure. It matters who the president nominates—is the person philosophically "pro-environment" or "anti-environment"?

This much is clear: presidential authority—proposing and encouraging pieces of legislation, issuing executive orders, staffing high-level agency directors, and nominating judges—can and does influence whether the environment is protected or whether economic purposes prevail.

Judicial Action Affecting the Environment

The judiciary affects environmental policy, too. Five things might be noted here: (1) issues of standing, (2) "SLAPP suits," (3) "the delegation doctrine," (4) "the Chevron Doctrine" (that courts should defer to agencies' expertise), and (5) the power of the judiciary to interpret what the law means.

Standing. In the discussion of administrative agencies (Chapter 4) we touched on the issue of standing: who, if anyone, is allowed to bring legal action in administrative agencies or in court. One salient point: you have to "be aggrieved in fact" to have standing, you have to show you have suffered some kind of harm. When it comes to protecting the environment, it is clear that non-human interests need individuals or groups to speak for them. But who is qualified to do so, if it is "only" nature that is harmed and not the person speaking on behalf of nature? Several federal environmental laws (including the Clean Water Act, the Clean Air Act, and the Endangered Species Act) give citizens the right to sue violators; citizens act as "private attorneys general" to help enforce these anti-pollution and resource-protection laws. In the past 25 years, numerous "citizen attorneys general" have brought numerous suits, often resulting in injunctions and fines payable to the U.S. treasury. But "the ability of Congress to confer standing using citizen suit provisions has come under fierce attack in the courts."[38] With the retirement of Justice Kennedy, President Trump has the opportunity to appoint a Supreme Court justice who may well close courthouse doors to many environmental claims by deciding the claimants lack standing—they themselves have suffered no actual harm, "only" nature has. (Bolivia, Ecuador, New Zealand, and India have granted legal personhood to rivers, glaciers, and other environmental entities.[39])

SLAPP Suits. Another arena for judicial involvement here involves so-called "SLAPP suits": "strategic litigation against public participation" lawsuits. In short—business interests that don't like being criticized for environmental degradation (oil companies, developers) sue their critics; the plaintiffs usually don't expect to win, they want to intimidate, censor, and silence critics by burdening them with legal defense fees until they give up. When they are then criticized for abusing their corporate wealth by hiring lawyers to trample on environmental activists' rights, the corporations point to their own Constitutional rights, noting that when environmentalists say untrue and hurtful things about them, it is defamation, not protected by the First Amendment. For intentionally false claims by activists, corporations can also claim the tort of interference with business relations. Several states have adopted anti-SLAPP statutes in the interest of protecting free speech; such statutes provide for speedy hearings of the claims and the possibility of the defendant recovering legal fees and punitive damages. But the Supreme Court could certainly decide that states cannot effectively deny corporation's right to seek legal redress for alleged grievances in this way, and a whole avenue of potential environmental protection would be curtailed.

The delegation doctrine. A third possible judicial involvement in changing environmental law involves the "delegation doctrine." Congress has power to adopt laws that regulate interstate commerce based on the commerce clause. When it creates an administrative agency, it delegates some of that law-making power to the agency—to agents, to act on Congress's behalf. The U.S. Supreme Court has generally upheld Congress's power to delegate its authority to agents. Were the Court to reverse years of precedent, it could decide that agencies cannot be delegated broad authority to regulate. For example, the delegation doctrine could be revived to hold that the EPA does not have authority to call carbon dioxide a "pollutant" because Congress exceeded its Constitutional power when it assigned broadly-worded authority to the agency. Such a decision would greatly reduce the scope of agency action, because Congress itself would have to issue the detailed regulations, a task which currently seems beyond its capabilities.

The Chevron Doctrine: deference to agency expertise. A fourth area of judicial involvement concerns the "Chevron doctrine." In 1984 the Supreme Court (in *Chevron v. Natural Resources Defense Council*[40]) decided that the judiciary should, in general, defer to the expertise of administrative agencies. You will recall from Chapter 4 that agencies are created so that experts (in agriculture, oil drilling, nuclear waste disposal, clean water regulation, etc.) can help the agency make scientifically sound regulations. If "pro-business" interests can persuade the Court that the experts aren't worth deferring to (consider claims of "fake science" around climate change and other issues), Congress would have to step up and make its own determinations; political interest groups would presumably care more about their earnings than about the environment, environmental NGOs notwithstanding. Some "pro-business" activists would like to curtail the Chevron doctrine so scientific experts can be disregarded by courts. President Trump's nominated Brett Kavanaugh to become an Associate Justice on the Supreme Court, and as a Circuit Court judge, Kavanaugh favored re-examining the Chevron doctrine.

Finally, as we have seen in Chapter 4, the courts must interpret the meaning of legislation. Opponents of the National Environmental Policy Act could argue to the courts that proper interpretation of the statute means the environmental impact statement need only discuss environmental effects in the immediate area of the proposed development, not the broader environmental effects that have been considered under the law for the last few decades. Unless Congress made the point clear that those broad effects should be considered, NEPA would become much less protective in providing "full disclosure" of environmental impacts.

Agency Action Affecting the Environment

We discussed administrative agencies and noted they are sometimes referred to as "the fourth branch of government." An agency headed by somebody who believes environmental protection is an impediment to American capitalism and growth will do what Mr. Pruitt did—reduce government regulation. Mr. Zinke at the U.S. Department of the Interior would like to open up the Arctic National Wildlife Refuge for oil exploration. Other agency heads appointed by those who see environmental laws and regulations as an obstacle to "growth and development" will continue to enforce them lightly, or not at all.

Direct-Democracy Action Affecting the Environment

The fifth law-making entity we took up (Chapter 4) was direct democracy—the initiative and referendum process—if activists can get enough signatures on a petition, a matter of law-making can go directly to the people for a vote. In 2018, for example, environmentalists and others were able to put a carbon tax proposal on the ballot in Washington State, but the measure was defeated.

There are two problems for the environment here. First, obviously, is that if environmentalists can petition to get protective laws on the books, "pro-business" interests can petition to get less-protective laws on the books. And the "pro-business" interests have enormous amounts of money to pay signature gatherers and to mount extensive campaigns to promote their cause. In the case of Washington State's proposed carbon tax, a group of oil and gas companies pumped tens of millions of dollars into the campaign to defeat the measure, far more than the money raised in its support.

The frank corruption of direct democracy by big business was taken up in more detail in Chapter 4. There we quoted Professor Blaine Gavin (political scientist at Gonzaga University): "Interest groups recognize there's another way to make law [besides legislation], and big powerful interests know how to conduct good advertising campaigns."[41]

Key Takeaway

The "environment," upon which we depend for our livelihoods and lives, cannot protect itself (except in geological time-spans) against the getting and spending and wasting of modern economies. Humans are causing environmental degradation.

In the United States, following the 2016 presidential election, it is instructive to see how the levers of power are pulled as affecting the environment.

Congress can repeal or weaken environmental statutes. The president recommends legislation; he or she can issue executive orders directing agencies' activities; the president nominates agency heads and judicial candidates. The judiciary is involved with issues of "standing" (who can represent "nature"), SLAPP suits (big business can use the legal system to intimidate its critics into silence), the delegation doctrine (can Congress even give agencies regulatory power at all), the "Chevron Doctrine" (are agencies decisions to be granted deference by the courts), and in interpreting the meaning of legislation. Agency staff members take direction from their superiors, nominated by the president and confirmed by the Senate. And, by working through the direct-democracy lawmaking function, big business—with big money—can make itself heard.

Exercises

1. Suppose a group of high school students truly believed that in 30 years, a warming climate would drastically affect their quality of life. If they sued the U.S. government for failing to curb greenhouse gas emissions, should the trial court decide that they have "standing" to sue? Why or why not?

2. What we do today enormously affects future unborn generations. Why shouldn't future generations have standing? Should rivers and environmental entities have standing? Who would object to that?

3. Use the internet to find an example of a SLAPP lawsuit, and/or explore whether SLAPP suits are a barrier to "equal justice under law"? (the inscription on the Supreme Court in Washington, DC).

4. What species are threatened or endangered in your region? How well are the laws protecting those species? Can you make an argument as to why all species should be protected, even dung beetles?

5. Dismissing those who simply deny there is an "environmental crisis" at all, what is the objection, by reasonably well-educated people, to government action to protect the environment?

6. What does this mean: "Nature bats last"?

12.6 Summary and Exercises

Summary

Property law and tort law regulate land use by imposing liability for: (1) activities by the landowner that affect those off the land, and (2) injuries caused to people who enter it. The two most important theories relating to the former are nuisance and trespass. With respect to trespass, the common law distinguishes among trespassers, licensees, and invitees, with differing degrees of duty depending on the status of the person coming onto the land. Some states are moving away from the perplexing and rigid rules of the past and simply require owners to maintain their property in a reasonably safe condition.

Land use may also be regulated by private agreement through the restrictive covenant, an agreement that "runs with the land" and that will be binding on any subsequent owner.

Land use is also regulated by the government's power under eminent domain to take private land for public purposes (upon payment of just compensation), through zoning laws, and through environmental statutes, including the National Environmental Policy Act and laws governing air, water, treatment of hazardous wastes, chemicals, and endangered species.

The environmental movement began in earnest in the U.S in the 1960s, marked by Rachel Carson's *Silent Spring*, Earth Day (1970), and a number of landmark federal laws (Clean Air Act, NEPA, Clean Water Act, Endangered Species Act).

Citizen access to the courts to see that agencies are enforcing environmental laws may be limited by the Court's "standing" doctrine, and citizens and NGOs that sue corporations to seek injunctions or damages may be hit with SLAPP suits that discourage such actions. Companies can also challenge agency actions in the courts, and may be successful in supporting politicians that would put business interests and economic growth ahead of environmental conservation and protection.

Exercises

1. Jake McGee lives in a subdivision built onto a "brownfield" formerly owned and used in the manufacture of refrigerants. The developer, though it knew this, did not disclose the presence or degree of contamination from the company's practices. Jake, his family, and many neighbors are suffering from an unusual number of health problems, but the developer/firm refuses to disclose what it knows, and the company no longer exists. Why does the law allow this to happen, and are there any changes that you would recommend?

2. Emily Lookabye is deeply concerned over the fate of the grey wolf in Idaho and Wyoming. While once it was re-introduced into Yellowstone, the current administration is seeking to de-list it, lowering the protections afforded by the Endangered Species Act. She and her friends have watched many videos about the grey wolf, have read a great deal, and want to sue the Fish and Wildlife Service, bringing an action in federal district court to enjoin the FWS from de-listing the grey wolf from the "threatened" list. Will the federal court recognize that she has "standing"? What if she is a wildlife photographer who makes frequent visits to Yellowstone National Park? Is her standing any stronger?

3. The oceans are a commons, at least beyond territorial limits set by the Law of the Sea. Who could make rules for the ocean that would restrain "over-fishing"? What is the current status of whales in terms of sustaining their populations? Which species of whales, if any, are endangered or threatened? What would you recommend be done?

4. Which of the following are "command, and, control" regulations? Corporate Average Fuel Economy standards, a gasoline tax, subsidies for the oil and gas industry, Clean Air Act limits on the emission of sulphur dioxide from industrial facilities.

5. Use your favorite internet search engine to look up "Natural Capitalism." How does it compare to what you think of as capitalism? The authors contend that our legal system is taxing the wrong things (labor) instead of taxing our use of natural resources? Why do they say this, and do you think they are right? If so, why don't our policies shift toward their model?

6. We allow attorneys to represent corporations. Why don't we allow attorneys to represent the interests of, say, orcas (whales) that are being driven to extinction in Washington State's Puget Sound? Why don't we allow attorneys to represent the mountains, streams, and fish that are being destroyed and poisoned by open-pit mining that removes mountain tops and dumps the waste into mountain streams? https://earthjustice.org/features/campaigns/what-is-mountaintop-removal-mining.

Self-Test Questions

Answer true or false.

1. The common law is adequate to address environmental degradation.

2. Because pollution is a national, not local, problem, the states may not adopt environmental regulations, only the federal government can.

3. A defendant's conduct must be unreasonable if the plaintiff is to prevail in a nuisance suit.

4. Pauline's Pickle Factory emits horribly powerful smells of vinegar which waft onto Plaintiff's property and into his house. Plaintiff may win if he sues Pauline for trespass.

5. An environmental impact statement is required only if the federal or state government itself is proposing a project significantly affecting the human environment.

6. NEPA sets standards for pollution and allows the EPA to levy fines against violators.

7. States cannot have stricter environmental standards than those set by the relevant federal agencies.

8. Under the Clean Air Act, standards for allowable pollution are permanently set, subject to Congress's revision of the statute.

9. The EPA may impose civil fines.

10. The EPA may impose criminal fines and defendants who are convicted of violating some environmental laws may be imprisoned.

11. Private citizens can use tort law to address environmental damages.

12. The Clean Water Act does not address wetlands, only "navigable waters."

13. Run-off from contaminated land is not within the purview of the Clean Water Act, only discharge from point sources (pipes) is.

14. An "attractive nuisance" is something that most people would be drawn to out of curiosity or interest; if it causes them harm, they will bear any damages themselves ("assumption of the risk").

Self-Test Answers

1. F
2. F
3. F
4. F
5. F
6. F
7. F
8. F
9. T
10. T
11. T
12. F
13. F
14. F

Endnotes

1. http://science.sciencemag.org/content/162/3859/1243.full

2. Theo Coburn, Diane Dumanoski, and John Peterson Meyers, *Our Stolen Future* (1997), http://www.ourstolenfuture.com/basics/chapters.htm

3. Pollution Pays: Michigan Report Jan. 31, 2000 https://www.ewg.org/research/pollution-pays/michigan-report#.WwtZ9akh00o

4. https://www.businessroundtable.org/media/multimedia/american-innovation-american-competitiveness

5. https://www.denverpost.com/2017/06/12/gold-king-mine-inspector-general-clears-epa/

6. Paul Hawken, Natural Capitalism, *Mother Jones*, March/April 1997. https://www.motherjones.com/politics/1997/03/natural-capitalism/

7. There are federal and state tax benefits for a landowner who sells or donates an easement for conservation purposes.

8. See *Hawaii Housing Authority v. Midkiff*, 467 U.S. 229 (1984).

9. 545 U.S. 469 (2005)

10. However, the government would have to pay the costs of relocating the grocery store, moving the fixtures, inventory, setting up the computerized inventory system, arranging installation of utilities, and so on.

11. *Lucas v. South Carolina Coastal Council*, U.S. Supreme Court case interpreting the 5th Amendment's "taking clause," defining what is a "taking" that requires compensation.

12. *Village of Euclid v. Ambler Realty Co.*, 272 U.S. 365 (1926)

13. See James O'Toole, *The Executive's Compass: Business and the Good Society* (1995), in which the author demonstrates that four basic values have animated U.S. public policy for centuries: freedom, equality, efficiency, and community. Environmentalists identify most strongly with values of community, and the oppositional value of efficiency is closely associated with shorter term profit-seeking interests.

14. Carson, *Silent Spring*, 36–37. Boston: Houghton Mifflin, 1962.

15. Governor's Sustainable Washington Advisory Panel. http://www.cascadiaconsulting.com/uploads/pdf/attachment_5_wa_action_plan.pdf. In late July, 2018, Puget Sound-area newspapers were full of the sad news that a baby orca whale had died, and its mother, apparently grieving, pushed the dead body of the infant around Puget Sound for weeks. The calf was probably killed by pollution, lack of salmon for food (due to pollution and habitat destruction). https://abcnews.go.com/International/wireStory/endangered-puget-sound-orca-dies-birth-56814177

16. 42 United States Code, Section 4321 et seq.

17. California, Connecticut, Georgia, Hawaii, Maryland, Massachusetts, Montana, New Jersey, New York, North Carolina, South Dakota, Virginia, Washington, Wisconsin. See https://ballotpedia.org/State_environmental_policy_acts for a more detailed discussion of the differences among these acts.

18. *Scientists' Institute for Public Information, Inc. v. Atomic Energy Commission*, 481 F.2d 1079 (1973).

19. "The Tricks of the Trade-off," *Business Week*, April 4, 1977, 72.

20. The first federal water pollution statute was the Rivers and Harbors Act of 1899.

21. 33 United States Code, Section 1251.

22. *Solid Waste Agency of Northern Cook County v. Army Corps of Engineers*, 531 U.S. 159 (2001).

23. The EPA dropped the ball in Flint, Michigan, resulting in many thousands of people—children most vulnerably—being subject to drinking-water lead poisoning. See https://www.nytimes.com/2016/01/21/us/flint-michigan-lead-water-crisis.html

24. Watershedds [sic], North Carolina State University at http://www.water.ncsu.edu/watershedss/info/wetlands/protect.html

25. *Midlantic National Bank v. New Jersey*, 474 U.S. 494 (1986).

26. With one notable exception, technological advances are *always* first presented to us as helpful and benign (General Electric used to advertise that "Progress is our most important product." The promoters of "progress" want us to buy their products. But all technology has malign as well as benign aspects: it is quite apparent that automobiles, airplanes, and social media (to name just three) have very serious adverse unintended consequences. The technology that was not introduced as benign progress? Nuclear energy. It was introduced in 1945 with a bomb blast over Hiroshima, Japan.

27. Technological advances are always (with one exception) presented to us as helpful and benign because their proponents want to sell the technology (General Electric used to advertise, "Progress is our most important product"). Only later do we realize that automobiles, airplanes, and social media—to take just three—have very serious unintended consequences. The one technology that was not presented as helpful and benign? Nuclear energy. It was presented to the world in 1945 over the Japanese city of Hiroshima.

28. Utah Prairie Dog Litigation, http://publiclands.utah.gov/current-projects/petpo-v-usfws-utah-prairie-dog-litigation/ See also the 10th Circuit ruling, at https://www.ca10.uscourts.gov/opinions/14/14-4151.pdf

29. https://scienceandsocietybu.wordpress.com/2013/06/01/case-12-the-god-squad/

30. Center for Biological Diversity, https://www.biologicaldiversity.org/programs/biodiversity/elements_of_biodiversity]/extinction_crisis/

31. Clyde Haberman, "The Snake That's Eating Florida," *New York Times*, April 5, 2015 (with video): https://www.nytimes.com/2015/04/06/us/the-burmese-python-snake-thats-eating-florida.html

32. The Third Federal Circuit Court of Appeals has jurisdiction over federal district (trial courts) in Delaware, New Jersey, and parts of Pennsylvania; it is headquartered in Philadelphia. Because many corporations are (nominally) "residents" of Delaware, the court deals with many important corporate-law cases.

33. Frank Newport, "American's Want Government to Do More on Environment," *Gallup*, March 29, 2018. https://news.gallup.com/poll/232007/americans-want-government-more-environment.aspx

34. See Wendell Berry, "The Idea of a Local Economy" in "In the Presence of Fear, Three Essays for a Changed World," 11 (2001): "The so-called environmental crisis is now pretty well established as a fact of our age."

35. Juliet Eilperin and Steven Mufson, "Trump to Roll Back Obama's Climate, Water Rules through Executive Action," The Washington Post, February 20, 2017. https://www.washingtonpost.com/news/energy-environment/wp/2017/02/20/trump-to-roll-back-obamas-climate-water-rules-through-executive-action/?noredirect=on&utm_term=.eac4528f1c6b

36. In an interview with the Christian Broadcasting Network, Mr. Pruitt said his Christian convictions led him to conclude that America should use gas and coal freely because natural resources exist purely for man's benefit. https://www.vox.com/identities/2018/2/23/17044912/scott-pruitt-bible-oil-friendly-policies-evangelicals-environment

37. Margaret Talbot, "Scott Pruitt's Dirty Politics: How the Environmental Protection Agency Became the Fossil Fuel Industry's Best Friend," *The New Yorker*, April 2, 2018. https://www.newyorker.com/magazine/2018/04/02/scott-pruitts-dirty-politics

38. http://www.gelpi.org/gelpi/research_archive/standing/

39. Sangeeth Yogendran, "Natural Entities Now Legally People: Enough to Save Them?", *Eurasia Review*, May 18, 2017. http://www.eurasiareview.com/08052017-natural-entities-now-legally-people-enough-to-save-them-analysis/.

40. 467 U.S. 837 (1984)

41. Jim Camden, Spin Control: Money Pours into Initiative Campaigns, *Spokesman Review*, September 5, 2010, http://www.spokesman.com/blogs/spincontrol/2010/sep/05/money-pours-initiative-campaigns/

CHAPTER 13
Government Regulation: Employment Law

In this chapter, we will examine both the federal laws that govern the relationship between the employer and the employee who belongs, or wants to belong, to a union, and also to the broader state and federal laws that govern employer-employee relationships outside of unions. There are a number of laws dealing with employment discrimination; and beyond discrimination, the law also governs other issues, such as the extent to which an employer may terminate the relationship itself.

Even before statutes governing collective bargaining (labor unions) and various state and federal discrimination laws, the common law set boundaries for employer-employee relationships. We will examine the basic rule that evolved prior to the twentieth century—"employment at will" (that in the absence of a contractual agreement otherwise, an employee is free to leave employment at any time and for any reason; similarly, an employer is free to fire employees at any time and for any reason). But as we go through the key statutes on employment law and employment discrimination, bear in mind that these statutes stand as an important set of exceptions to the basic common-law rule of **employment at will**.

employment at will

The common-law doctrine that allows employers to discharge an employee at any time and for any reason. Courts have created exceptions for "bad reasons."

13.1 Employment at Will

The Common-Law Employment at Will Doctrine

employment-at-will doctrine

The common-law rule that an employee without a contract can be fired for any reason or for no reason (but not a bad reason); an at-will employee has no job security.

At common law, an employee without a contract guaranteed a job for a specific period is an employee at will and can be fired at any time and for any reason, or for no reason at all. After all, the employee without a contract can also quit work at will. The various federal statutes we examine in this chapter have made inroads on the **employment-at-will doctrine**. Yes, an employer can discharge an at-will employee for any reason, or no reason, but not for a *bad* reason. Employers cannot discharge employees for reasons now prohibited by Title VII (prohibiting employment discrimination), among other statutes, or for exercising their employment-law rights.

But beyond the prohibition against discharging at-will employees for exercising their rights, the courts and legislatures in more than forty states have made big changes in the at-will doctrine. They have done so under three theories: tort, contract, and duty of good faith and fair dealing. We will first consider the tort of wrongful discharge.

Courts have created a major exception to the employment-at-will rule by allowing the tort of wrongful discharge. *Wrongful discharge* means firing a worker for a bad reason—touched on previously. What is a bad reason? A bad reason for discharging an employee can be: (1) for refusing to violate a law, (2) for exercising a legal right, (3) for performing a legal duty, and (4) in a way that violates public policy.

Exceptions to the Common-Law Rule

The employment at will doctrine promotes serious insecurity for employees; there are several exceptions—when an employer cannot dismiss an employee at will.

Discharging an Employee for Refusing to Violate a Law

Some employers will not want employees to testify truthfully at trial. In one case, a nurse refused a doctor's order to administer a certain anesthetic when she believed it was wrong for that particular patient; the doctor, angry at the nurse for refusing to obey him, then administered the anesthetic himself. The patient soon stopped breathing, the doctor and others could not resuscitate him soon enough, and he suffered permanent brain damage. When the patient's family sued the hospital, the hospital told the nurse she would be in trouble if she testified. She did testify according to her oath in the court of law (i.e., truthfully), and after several months of harassment, was finally fired on a pretext. The hospital was held liable for the tort of wrongful discharge. As a general rule, you should not fire an employee for refusing to break the law.

Discharging an Employee for Exercising a Legal Right

Suppose Bob Berkowitz files a claim for workers' compensation for an accident at Pacific Gas & Electric, where he works and where the accident that injured him took place. He is fired for doing so, because the employer does not want to have its workers' comp premiums increased. In this case, the right exercised by Berkowitz is supported by public policy: he has a legal right to file the claim, and if he can establish that his discharge was caused by his filing the claim, he will prove the tort of wrongful discharge.

Discharging an Employee for Performing a Legal Duty

Courts have long held that an employee may not be fired for serving on a jury. This is so even though courts do recognize that many employers have difficulty replacing employees called for jury duty. Jury duty is an important civic obligation, and employers are not permitted to undermine it.

Discharging an Employee in a Way That Violates Public Policy

This is probably the most controversial basis for a tort of wrongful discharge. There is an inherent vagueness in the phrase "basic social rights, duties, or responsibilities." This is similar to the exception in contract law—the courts will not enforce contract provisions that violate public policy. (For the most part, public policy is found in statutes and in cases.) But what constitutes public policy is an important decision for state courts. In *Wagenseller v. Scottsdale Memorial Hospital*[1] (set out in Chapter 15 Section 2) for example, a nurse who refused to "play along" with her coworkers on a rafting trip was discharged. The group of coworkers had socialized at night, drinking alcohol; when the partying was near its peak, the plaintiff refused to be part of a group that bared their buttocks to the tune of "Moon River" (a composition by Henry Mancini that was popular in the 1970s). The court, at great length, considered that "mooning" was a misdemeanor under Arizona law and that therefore her employer could not discharge her for refusing to violate a state law.

Other courts have gone so far as to include professional oaths and codes as part of public policy. In *Rocky Mountain Hospital and Medical Services v. Diane Mariani*, the Colorado Supreme Court determined that an at-will CPA could not be fired for refusing to "cook the books" as her employer insisted she do (that is, plug in numbers and results that did not reflect the true situation, using processes that were not in accord with her training).[2]

The court noted that the stated purpose of the licensing and registration of certified public accountants was to "provide for the maintenance of high standards of professional conduct by those so licensed and registered as certified public accountants." Further, the relevant CPA standard proclaimed that "A certificate holder shall not in the performance of professional services knowingly misrepresent facts, nor subordinate his judgment to others." The fact that Mariani's employer asked her to knowingly misrepresent facts was a sufficient basis in public policy to make her discharge wrongful.

Contract Modification of Employment at Will

Contract law can modify employment at will. Oral promises made in the hiring process may be enforceable even though the promises are not approved by top management. Employee handbooks may create implied contracts that specify personnel processes and statements that the employees can be fired only for a "just cause" or only after various warnings, notice, hearing, or other procedures.

Good Faith and Fair Dealing Standard

A few states, among them Massachusetts and California, have modified the at-will doctrine in a far-reaching way by holding that every employer has entered into an implied covenant of good faith and fair dealing with its employees. That means, the courts in these states say, that it is "bad faith" and therefore unlawful to discharge employees to avoid paying commissions or pensions due them. Under this implied covenant of fair dealing, any discharge without good cause—such as incompetence, corruption, or habitual tardiness—is actionable. This is not the law in most states, however.

Key Takeaway

Although employment at will is still the law, numerous exceptions have been established by judicial decision. Employers can be liable for the tort of wrongful discharge if they discharge an employee for refusing to violate a law, for exercising a legal right or performing a legal duty, or in a way that violates basic public policy.

Exercises

1. Richard Mudd, an employee of Compuserve, is called for jury duty in Wayne County, Michigan. His immediate supervisor, Harvey Lorie, lets him know that he "must" avoid jury duty at all costs. Mudd tells the judge of his circumstances and his need to be at work, but the judge refuses to let Mudd avoid jury duty. Mudd spends the next two weeks at trial. He sends regular e-mails and texts to Lorie during this time, but on the fourth day gets a text message from Lorie that says, "Don't bother to come back." When he does return, Lorie tells him he is fired. Does Mudd have a cause of action for the tort of wrongful discharge?

2. Olga Monge was a schoolteacher in her native Costa Rica. She moved to New Hampshire and attended college in the evenings to earn U.S. teaching credentials. At night, she worked at the Beebe Rubber Company after caring for her husband and three children during the day. When she applied for a better job at the plant, the foreman offered to promote her if she would be "nice" and go out on a date with him. She refused, and he assigned her to a lower-wage job, took away her overtime, made her clean the washrooms, and generally ridiculed her. She finally collapsed at work, and he fired her. Does Monge have any cause of action?

13.2 Labor-Management Relations

Learning Objectives

1. Understand a bit of the history of U.S. labor law: how unions were resisted for many years in the United States, the common-law principles used by employers and courts to do that, and how political and economic changes resulted in legalization of labor unions.
2. Understand how and why labor-union representation has declined in the United States since the 1980s.
3. Know the four major federal labor laws in the United States.
4. Understand the organization and functioning of the National Labor Relations Board.
5. Know what an "unfair labor practice" is under modern law.

A Brief History of American Labor Law

Here, we briefly examine the history of American labor law (labor-union law), followed by a short examination of the laws themselves.

Over one hundred years, American labor law has developed out of four basic statutes into an immense body of cases and precedents that regulate the formation and governance of labor unions, and the relationships among employers, unions, and union members. Like antitrust law, labor law is a complex subject that has spawned many specialized practitioners. Though specialized, it is a subject that no employer of any size can ignore, for labor law—despite more than four decades of decline in unionization—still has a pervasive influence on how business is conducted throughout the United States.

Legal rights for laborers in the United States came about through physical and political struggles. The legislation described in this chapter began only after many years of labor-management strife, including judicial opposition to unions, and violent and deadly confrontations between pro-union workers and management.

Labor and the Common Law in the 19th Century

Labor unions appeared in modern form in the United States in the 1790s in Boston, New York, and Philadelphia. Early in the nineteenth century, employers began to seek injunctions against union organizing and other activities. Two doctrines were employed: (1) *common-law conspiracy*, and (2) *common-law restraint of trade*. The first doctrine held that workers who joined together were acting criminally as conspirators, regardless of the means chosen or the objectives sought.

The second doctrine—common-law restraint of trade—was also a favorite theory used by the courts to enjoin unionizing and other joint employee activities. Workers who banded together to seek better wages or working conditions were, according to this theory, engaged in concerted activity that restrained trade in their labor. This theory made sense when conventional wisdom held that an employer was entitled to buy labor as cheaply as possible—the price would obviously rise if workers were allowed to bargain jointly rather than if they were required to offer their services individually on the open market.

In 1806, the union of Philadelphia Journeymen Cordwainers was convicted of, and bankrupted by, charges of criminal conspiracy[3] after a strike for higher wages, setting a precedent by which the U.S. government would use the judiciary to combat unions for years to come. Andrew Jackson became a strikebreaker in 1834 when he sent troops to the construction sites of the Chesapeake and Ohio Canal. In 1877, a general strike halted the movement of U.S. railroads; in the following days, strike riots spread across the United States. The next week, federal troops were called out to force an end to the nationwide strike. At the Battle of the Viaduct in Chicago, federal troops (recently returned from massacring Native Americans) killed thirty workers and wounded over one hundred. Numerous other violent confrontations marked the post–Civil War period in America, including the violent rail strikes of 1877, when President Rutherford B. Hayes sent troops to prevent obstruction of the mails. President Grover Cleveland used soldiers to break the Pullman strike of 1894. Not until the anthracite coal strikes in Pennsylvania in 1902 did the U.S. government become a mediator between labor and management rather than an enforcer for industry.

U.S. Labor Law in the 20th Century

The Early 20th Century Labor Movement

By 1912, labor had organized widely; it played a pivotal role in electing Woodrow Wilson and giving him a Democratic Congress, which responded in 1914 with the Clayton Act's "labor exemption." Section 6 of the Clayton Act effectively reversed judicial determinations that labor unions' activities were a violation of antitrust laws; it provides that labor unions are not "illegal combinations or conspiracies in restraint of trade, under the antitrust laws." Section 20 forbids courts from issuing injunctions in cases involving strikes, boycotts, and other concerted union activities (which were declared to be lawful) as long as they arose out of disputes between employer and employees over the terms of employment.

But even the Clayton Act proved of little lasting value to the unions. In 1921, the Supreme Court again struck out against a secondary boycott[4] that crippled the significance of the Clayton Act's provisions. In that case, a machinists' union staged a boycott against an employer (by whom the members were not employed) in order to pressure the employer into permitting one of its factories to be unionized. The Court ruled that the Clayton Act exemptions applied only in cases involving an employer and its own employees.[5] Without the ability to boycott under those circumstances, and with the threat of antitrust prosecutions or treble-damage actions, labor would be hard-pressed to unionize many companies. More antiunion decisions followed; while management reaped the benefits, and workers toiled and chafed.

Railway Labor Act

U.S. statute, 1926, imposing a good-faith bargaining duty on railroads with employees' representatives. The first successful federal labor-law legislation.

In 1926, Congress enacted the **Railway Labor Act**. This statute imposed a duty on railroads to bargain in good faith with their employees' elected representatives. The act also established the National Mediation Board to mediate disputes that were not resolved in contract negotiations. The stage was set for more comprehensive national labor laws. These would come with the Great Depression when over 1/3 of the U.S. workforce was unemployed.

The Depression and the New Deal

The first labor law of the Great Depression was the **Norris-La Guardia Act** of 1932. It dealt with the propensity of federal courts to issue preliminary injunctions, often ex parte (i.e., after hearing only the plaintiff's argument), against union activities. Even though the permanent injunction might later have been denied, the effect of the vaguely worded preliminary injunction would have been sufficient to destroy the attempt to unionize. The Norris–La Guardia Act forbids federal courts from temporarily or permanently enjoining certain union activities, such as peaceful picketing and strikes. The act is applicable toward any "labor dispute," defined as embracing "any controversy concerning terms or conditions of employment, or concerning the association or representation of persons in negotiating, fixing, maintaining, changing, or seeking to arrange terms or conditions of employment, regardless of whether or not the disputants stand in the proximate relation of employer and employee." This language thus permitted the secondary boycott that had been held as a violation of the antitrust laws in the 1921 case of *Duplex Printing Press v. Deering*.[6] The act also bars the courts from enforcing so-called **yellow-dog contracts**—agreements that employees made with their employer not to join unions.

But these laws did not impress many industrial tycoons. Henry Ford was an obstinate anti-unionist, who hated unions, and Ford employees' efforts to unionize were met with planned violence by Henry Ford's "goons" (thugs, really, hired to break up the union movement). In 1937, the United Auto Workers' (UAW) planned a union rally and caravan along Miller Road in Dearborn, Michigan (site of the Big Ford plant); Henry Ford's internal security forces were waiting to ambush them, but perhaps had not counted on newspaper cameras catching the action:

> The [Ford security forces] attacked as a pack of mad dogs rabid for revenge, flying into a rampage and beating frenzy. According to newspaper accounts, these few men of the UAW, alone and defenseless, were attacked by as many as three dozen Ford thugs with fists, punches, kicks, and clubs. It was the beginning of the end of Fordism, and rise of the union in the Ford factories.[7]

In 1935, the New Deal Congress finally enacted a comprehensive labor statute. The **National Labor Relations Act** (NLRA), often called the **Wagner Act** after its sponsor, Senator Robert F. Wagner (1887–1953) declared in Section 7 that workers in interstate commerce "have the right to self-organization, to form, join or assist labor organizations, to bargain collectively through representatives of their own choosing, and to engage in concerted activities for the purpose of collective bargaining or other mutual aid or protection." Section 8 sets out five key **unfair labor practices**, which can be committed by employers and, where relevant, by unions too:

- Interference with the rights guaranteed by Section 7.
- Interference with the organization of unions, or domination by the employer of union administration (this section thus outlaws "company unions"—sham unions run by the employer).
- Discrimination against employees who belong to unions.
- Discharging or otherwise discriminating against employees who seek relief under the act.
- Refusing to bargain collectively, in good faith, with union representatives. The NLRB requires employers and unions to bargain over "terms and condition of employment." Wages, hours, and working conditions—whether workers must wear uniforms, when the lunch hour begins, the type of safety equipment on hand—are well-understood terms and conditions of employment. But the statutory phrase is vague, and the cases abound with debates over whether a term insisted on by union or management is within the statutory phrase.

Norris-La Guardia Act

U.S. statute, 1932, restricting federal courts from enjoining peaceful labor-union activities and making "yellow-dog" contracts unenforceable.

yellow-dog contract

An anti-union tactic by employers, whereby employees are required in their employment contract not to join unions, and if they do, they can be fired.

National Labor Relations Act

Federal statute, 1935, establishing the right of employees to join unions and mandating that employers recognize and bargain with the unions.

Wagner Act

Federal statute, 1935, requiring that employers recognize unionization efforts, and that they bargain with unions in good faith regarding wages, hours, and working conditions.

unfair labor practices

Acts that violate the National Labor Relations Act (1935), such as failing to bargain in good faith

U.S. Labor from the New Deal to Ronald Reagan

Many U.S. labor historians see the first phase of the labor movement in terms of the struggles in the private sector that led to the labor legislation of the New Deal, described previously. The second phase of the movement, post–World War II, saw less violent confrontation and more peaceful resolution of labor issues in collective bargaining.

Laws adopted in the late 1940s and 1950s include these two:

Taft-Hartley Act

Federal statute, 1947, establishing that unions could be penalized for "unfair labor practices" just as management could under the Wagner Act of '35, and establishing a federal mediation service for labor disputes, among other things.

Landrum-Griffin Act

Federal statute, 1959, regulating internal union procedures, among other things.

- **Taft-Hartley Act**, 1947. The Wagner Act did not attempt to restrict union activities in any way. For a dozen years, opponents of unions sought some means of curtailing the breadth of opportunity opened up to unions by the Wagner Act. After failing to obtain relief in the Supreme Court, they took their case to Congress and finally succeeded after World War II. In 1947, for the first time in 17 years, Congress had Republican majorities in both houses. Congress responded to critics of "big labor" with the Taft-Hartley Act, passed over President Truman's veto. Taft-Hartley—known formally as the Labor-Management Relations Act—did not repeal the protections given employees and unions under the NLRA. Instead, it balanced union power with a declaration of rights of employers. In particular, Taft-Hartley lists six unfair labor practices of unions, including secondary boycotts, strikes aimed at coercing an employer to fire an employee who refuses to join a union, and so-called jurisdictional strikes over which union should be entitled to do specified jobs at the work site. The act guarantees both employers and unions the right to present their views on unionization and collective bargaining. Like employers, unions became obligated to bargain in good faith. The act outlaws the closed shop (where a worker must belong to a union before being hired), gives federal courts the power to enforce collective bargaining agreements, and permits private parties to sue for damages arising out of a secondary boycott. The act also created the Federal Mediation and Conciliation Service to cope with strikes that create national emergencies, and it declared strikes by federal employees to be unlawful. It was this provision that President Reagan invoked in 1981 to fire air traffic controllers who walked off the job for higher pay.

- **Landrum-Griffin Act**, 1959. Congressional hearings in the 1950s brought to light union corruption and abuses and led in 1959 to the last of the major federal labor statutes, the Landrum-Griffin Act (Labor-Management Reporting and Disclosure Act). It established a series of controls on internal union procedures, including the method of electing union officers and the financial controls necessary to avoid the problems of corruption that had been encountered. Landrum-Griffin also restricted union picketing under various circumstances, narrowed the loopholes in Taft-Hartley's prohibitions against secondary boycotts, and banned "hot cargo" agreements.

In 1981, President Reagan stared down the Air Traffic Controllers' union and fired many of its employees (they had been on an illegal strike). It was quite a blow, and signaled to employers that they might deal roughly with unions with little consequence. *The New York Times* observed thirty years later:

> *More than any other labor dispute of the past three decades, Reagan's confrontation with the Professional Air Traffic Controllers Organization, or Patco, undermined the bargaining power of American workers and their labor unions. It also polarized our politics in ways that prevent us from addressing the root of our economic troubles: the continuing stagnation of incomes despite rising corporate profits and worker productivity.*[8]

Labor Law in the 21st Century

Notwithstanding Labor's apparent success in the 20th century, **right-to-work laws** (that say nobody ever has to join a union as a condition of employment) mostly in Southern states, and globalization have weakened unions in the private sector. Right-to-work states provided a haven for certain kinds of manufacturing operations that wanted no part of bargaining with unions. Globalization meant that companies could (realistically) threaten to relocate outside the United States entirely. Unions in the public sector of the United States began to grow stronger relative to unions in the private sector: governments could not relocate as companies could, and over the last half century, there has been a gradual but significant decline in private sector unionism and growth in public sector unionism.

Republicans elected with Tea Party support in 2010, most notably Scott Walker of Wisconsin, launched major efforts against public sector unions, especially teachers' unions. Meanwhile, research shows that declining union membership and increasing income inequality are closely linked.[9]

Thirty-five years after the air traffic controllers' firing, President-Elect Donald Trump announced plans to curb the power of union workers in the federal government.[10]

Only about 9% of non-agricultural workers are members of unions in 2019. This represents a steady decline in union membership since its heyday in the 1950s. There are a number of reasons:

- Automation, including robots, continues to displace workers.
- American businesses—in order to stay competitive with foreign labor—have moved jobs to states that have weak unions or, again, have set up shop in foreign countries where unions are weak or illegal.
- Unions have achieved many of the basic goals they had one hundred years ago. The eight-hour day is now pretty much standard, and the minimum wage, paltry as it is, is—with various federal welfare programs—sufficient to keep most people from starvation (though 25% of children in the U.S. have "food insecurity"—they don't know for sure they will have enough to eat tomorrow[11]).
- After President Ronald Reagan denounced the Air Traffic Controllers' union in 1981 (following an illegal strike) and the union was decertified, it became much more politically palatable for management to "cut the fat" from their organizations and resist unionization.[12]
- Labor unions tend to be out-gunned in the campaign finance merry-go-round: capital (businesses) have more money to influence politics than labor does.

There is much talk recently about the inequality of income distribution in the United States. The rich control a very significantly disproportionate share of wealth—in 2015, the distribution is nearly the same as it was in 1929. Some commentators see the decline of labor unions as part of the reason. The following chart plots middle-class income and union membership rates.

FIGURE 13.1 Union Membership and Middle Class Share of Income

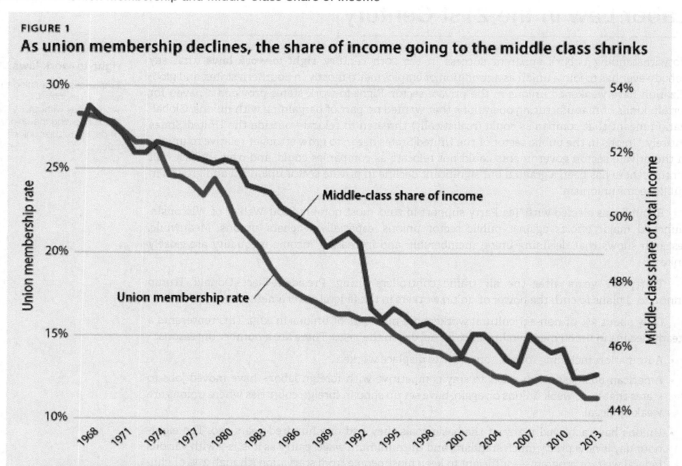

FIGURE 1

As union membership declines, the share of income going to the middle class shrinks

Source: Center for American Progress Action Fund analysis based on union membership rates from updated Barry T. Hirsch, David A. MacPherson, and Wayne G. Vroman, "Estimates of Union Density by State," *Monthly Labor Review* 124 (7) (2001): 51–55, available at http://unionstats.gsu.edu/MonthlyLaborReviewArticle.htm. Middle-class share of total income is from Bureau of the Census, Table H-2. *Share of Aggregate Income Recieved by Each Fifth and Top 5 Percent of Households* (2013), available at http://www.census.gov/hhes/www/income/data/historical/household.

Source: This material [article] was published by the Center for American Progress Action at https://www.americanprogressaction.org/issues/labor/news/2014/09/18/97477/new-census-data-once-again-illustrate-importance-of-unions-to-the-middle-class/. Reproduced with permission.

Although union membership has decreased significantly, the basic laws remain on the books. If workers feel strongly enough that they are not getting a fair share of the economy's productivity, unions may well rise again.

The threat that they might is probably not lost on employers (for example, Walmart announced in early 2015 that it would raise its minimum wage to $9.00 per hour, 24% higher than the federal minimum[13]). Employees frustrated by the appearance that labor law has been turned against labor are finding that social media can help organize their peers without formal union representation (witness teachers' strikes in, for example California, Colorado, Oklahoma, Arizona, and Kentucky).[14]

Enforcing Labor Law: The National Labor Relations Board's Organization and Functions

Assuming workers are unionized, the National Labor Relations Board (NLRB) enforces U.S. labor law. The NLRB consists of five board members, appointed by the president and confirmed by the

Senate, who serve for five-year, staggered terms. The president designates one of the members as chair. The president also appoints the general counsel, who is in charge of the board's investigatory and prosecutorial functions, and who represents the NLRB when it goes (or is taken) to court. The general counsel also oversees the thirty-three regional offices scattered throughout the country, each of which is headed by a regional director.

The NLRB serves two primary functions: (1) it may, as appropriate, oversee union elections to make sure employees can freely select the appropriate union to represent them, and (2) it investigates allegations of unfair labor practices and provides remedies as required. Parties—whether employer or union—may appeal to the federal court of appeals if they feel a ruling by the NLRB is improper.

A union gets voted in as the employees' bargaining representative after it wins an election. The election must be fair, and the employer cannot interfere with the employees' free choice. If it does interfere, the NLRB may declare the action an unfair labor practice and set aside the election results. These elections can be high-stakes affairs, and both sides hire specialized advisers (most often lawyers) who can guide the thrust and parry of the antagonists.

The results of all the electioneering are worth noting. In the 1980s, some 20 percent of the total U.S. workforce was unionized. As of 2019, the union membership rate was 10.5 percent, and more union members were public employees than private sector employees.

Key Takeaway

Common-law doctrines were used in the early history of the labor movement to enjoin unionizing and other joint employee activities. These were deemed to be restraints of trade that violated antitrust laws. In addition, common-law conspiracy charges provided criminal enforcement against joint employee actions and agreements. Politically, the labor movement gained some traction in 1912 and got an antitrust-law exemption in the Clayton Act. But it was not until the Great Depression and the New Deal that the right of collective bargaining was recognized by federal statute in the National Labor Relations Act. Subsequent legislation (Taft-Hartley and Landrum-Griffin) added limits to union activities and controls over unions in their internal functions.

In the 21st century, the percentage of employees who are unionized continues to decline (except among government workers). Some have suggested that this phenomena and the hollowing-out of the middle class are related. In any event, the laws remain on the books. Given the proper conditions, unions may rise again.

Exercises

1. Why were early labor-union advocates sometimes put in jail or prison?
2. What did the Norris-LaGuardia Act of 1932 do to address the problem (in labor-union advocates' eyes) presented in question #1, above?
3. How did the Taft-Hartley Act of 1947 "balance the scales" more in favor of management?
4. Why has the percentage of union members declined since the 1950s?
5. Who pays when public-employee union members succeed in getting good pay and benefit packages? What effect would higher pay for government workers have on private-employee compensation? (Hint: how do you attract good employees?)
6. What is the fundamental conservative political objection to labor unions?

13.3 Federal Employment Discrimination Laws

Learning Objectives

1. Know the various federal discrimination laws and their applications.
2. Distinguish between disparate impact and disparate treatment cases.
3. Understand the concept of affirmative action and its limits in employment law.

employment discrimination

Treating employees or job applicants unequally on the basis of race, color, national origin, religion, sex (gender), age, or disability; prohibited by federal statutes and many state statutes.

As we look at federal **employment discrimination** laws, bear in mind that most states also have laws that prohibit discriminatory practices in employment. Until the 1960s, Congress had legislated only a little in how businesses hired, promoted, and fired employees; the exception was in collective bargaining law. A business could refuse to hire members of racial minorities, exclude women from promotions, or pay men more than women for the same work. But with the rise of the civil rights movement in the early 1960s, Congress (and many states) began to legislate away the employer's power to discriminate. The most important statutes are Title VII of the Civil Rights Act of 1964, the Equal Pay Act of 1963, the Age Discrimination in Employment Act of 1967, and the Americans with Disabilities Act of 1990.

Title VII of the Civil Rights Act of 1964

Title VII

The section of the federal Civil Rights Act of 1964 that addresses employment discrimination.

The basic federal anti-discrimination law in employment is **Title VII** ("title" means "section") of the federal Civil Rights Act of 1964. The key section prohibited discrimination that is based on race, but Congress also included sex, religion, national origin, and color as prohibited bases for hiring, promotion, layoff, and discharge decisions. To put the Civil Rights Act in its proper context, a short history of racial discrimination in the United States follows.

Backgound

The passage of the Civil Rights Act of 1964 was the culmination of a long history that dated back to slavery, the founding of the U.S. legal system, the Civil War, and many historical and political developments over the ninety-nine years from the end of the Civil War to the passage of the act. The years prior to 1964 had seen a remarkable rise of civil disobedience, led by many in the civil rights movement, but most prominently by Dr. Martin Luther King Jr. Peaceful civil disobedience was sometimes met with violence, and television cameras were there to record most of it.

Birmingham protests, 1963

Martin Luther King, Jr. and the civil rights protests in Birmingham, met with police violence.

View the video online at: http://www.youtube.com/embed/KFcCQDkVOjM?rel=0

While the Civil War had addressed slavery and the secession of Southern states, the Thirteenth, Fourteenth, and Fifteenth Amendments, ratified just after the war, provided for equal protection under the law, guaranteed citizenship, and protected the right to vote for African Americans. The amendments also allowed Congress to enforce these provisions by enacting appropriate, specific legislation.

But, during the Reconstruction Era, many of the Southern states resisted the laws that were passed in Washington to bolster civil rights. To a significant extent, decisions rendered by the U.S. Supreme Court in this era—such as *Plessy v. Ferguson*, condoning "separate but equal" facilities for different races—greatly restricted the utility of the new Constitutional provisions. The states effectively controlled the public treatment of African Americans, and a period of neglect (or flat-out abuse—the "**Jim Crow**" laws) set in that lasted until after World War II. The state laws essentially mandated segregated facilities for blacks (restaurants, hotels, schools, water fountains, public bathrooms), facilities that were usually inferior.

Along with these so-called Jim Crow laws in the South, the Ku Klux Klan was very strong, and lynchings (hangings without any sort of public due process) by the Klan and others were designed to limit the civil and economic rights of the former slaves and their descendants. The hatred of blacks from that era by many whites in America has only gradually weakened since 1964. Even as the civil rights bill was being debated in Congress in 1964, some Young Americans for Freedom in the right wing of the GOP would clandestinely chant "Be a man, join the Klan" and sing "We will hang Earl Warren from a sour apple tree," to the tune of "Battle Hymn of the Republic." This was in anger over Chief Justice Warren's presiding over **Brown v. Board of Education**, which reversed *Plessy v. Ferguson*, and determined that segregated schools could not, in fact, be separate but equal.

But just a few years earlier, the public service and heroism of many black military units and individuals in World War II had created a perceptual shift in U.S. society; men of many races who had served together in the war against the Axis powers (fascism in Europe and the Japanese emperor's rule in the Pacific) began to understand their common humanity. Major migrations of blacks from the South to industrial cities of the North also gave impetus to the civil rights movement.

Bills introduced in Congress regarding employment policy brought the issue of civil rights to the attention of representatives and senators. In 1945, 1947, and 1949, the House of Representatives voted to abolish the poll tax (a method used in many states to confine voting rights to those who could pay a tax, and often, blacks could not). The Senate did not go along, but these bills signaled a growing interest in protecting civil rights through federal action. The executive branch of gov-

Jim Crow

State laws in the South that perpetuated discrimination against blacks from about 1880–1954.

Brown v. Board of Education of Topeka

U.S. Supreme Court case, 1954, holding that the 14th Amendment's Equal Protection clause forbids racial segregation in public schools (overruling *Plessy v. Ferguson*).

ernment, by presidential order, likewise became active by ending discrimination in the nation's military forces, in federal employment, and in work done under government contract.

The Supreme Court gave impetus to the civil rights movement in its landmark reversal of the "separate but equal" doctrine in the *Brown v. Board of Education* decision. In its 1954 decision, the Court said, "To separate black children from others of similar age and qualifications solely because of their race generates a feeling of inferiority as to their status in the community that may affect their hearts and minds in a way never to be undone. . . . We conclude that in the field of public education the doctrine of separate but equal has no place. Separate educational facilities are inherently unequal."

This decision meant that white and black children could not be forced to attend separate public schools. By itself, however, this decision did not create immediate gains, either in public school desegregation or in the desegregation of other public facilities. There were memorable standoffs between federal agents and state officials in Little Rock, Arkansas; the Democratic governor of Arkansas personally blocked young black students from entering Little Rock's Central High School, and it was only President Eisenhower's order to have federal marshals accompany the students that forced integration. The year was 1957.

But resistance to public school integration was widespread, and other public facilities were not governed by the *Brown* ruling. Restaurants, hotels, and other public facilities were still largely segregated. Segregation kept blacks from using public city buses, park facilities, and restrooms on an equal basis with whites. Along with inferior schools, workplace practices throughout the South and also in many Northern cities sharply limited African Americans' ability to advance economically. Civil disobedience began to grow.

The bus protests in Montgomery, Alabama, were particularly effective. Planned by civil rights leaders, Rosa Parks' refusal to give up her seat to a white person and sit at the back of the public bus led to a boycott of the Montgomery bus system by blacks and, later, a boycott of white businesses in Montgomery. There were months of confrontation and some violence; finally, the city agreed to end its long-standing rules on segregated seating on buses.

There were also protests at lunch counters and other protests on public buses, where groups of Northern protesters—Freedom Riders—sometimes met with violence. In 1962, James Meredith's attempt to enroll as the first African American at the University of Mississippi generated extreme hostility; two people were killed and 375 were injured as the state resisted Meredith's admission. The murders of civil rights workers Medgar Evers and William L. Moore added to the inflamed sentiments, and whites in Birmingham, Alabama, killed four young black girls who were attending Sunday school when their church was bombed.

These events were all covered by the nation's news media, whose photos—and television was particularly important here—showed beatings and the use of fire hoses and police dogs on peaceful protesters. Social tensions were reaching a postwar high by 1964. According to the government, there were nearly one thousand civil rights demonstrations in 209 cities in a three-month period beginning in May 1963. Representatives and senators could not ignore the impact of social protest, but the complicated political history of the Civil Rights Act of 1964 also tells us that the legislative result was anything but a foregone conclusion.[15]

Basic Provisions of Title VII of the Civil Rights Act of 1964

In Title VII of the Civil Rights Act of 1964, Congress for the first time outlawed discrimination in employment based on race, religion, sex, or national origin. Title VII declares: "It shall be an unlawful employment practice for an employer to fail or refuse to hire or to discharge any individual, or otherwise to discriminate against any individual with respect to his compensation, terms, conditions, or privileges of employment, because of such individual's race, color, religion, sex, or national origin." Title VII applies to: (1) employers with fifteen or more employees whose business affects interstate commerce, (2) all employment agencies, (3) labor unions with fifteen or more members,

(4) state and local governments and their agencies, and (5) most federal government employment. Notably, the act only applies to employees, not independent contractors. If you want plumbing services, under federal law you could refuse to hire a female plumber—she is not your employee.

In 1984, the Supreme Court held that Title VII applies to partnerships as well as corporations when ruling that it is illegal to discriminatorily refuse to promote a female lawyer to partnership status in a law firm. This applies, by implication, to other fields, such as accounting.[16] The remedy for unlawful discrimination is back pay and hiring, reinstatement, or promotion, and tort-like damages for mental distress.

Title VII established the **Equal Employment Opportunity Commission** (EEOC) to investigate violations of the act. A victim of discrimination who wishes to file suit must first file a complaint with the EEOC to permit that agency to attempt conciliation of the dispute. The EEOC has filed a number of lawsuits to prove statistically that a company has systematically discriminated on one of the forbidden bases. The EEOC receives perennial criticism for its extreme slowness in filing suits and for failure to handle the huge backlog of complaints with which it has had to wrestle. Rather obviously (and one cannot but think, intentionally) it is grossly underfunded by Congress.

> **Equal Employment Opportunity Commission**
>
> The federal agency that administers and enforces civil rights laws against workplace discrimination, established in 1965.

Interpretation and Implementation of Title VII

The courts have come to recognize two major types of Title VII cases:

1. Cases of **disparate treatment**

   In this type of lawsuit, the plaintiff asserts that because of race, sex, religion, or national origin, he or she has been treated less favorably than others within the organization. To prevail in a disparate treatment suit, the plaintiff must show that the company *intended* to discriminate because of one of the factors the law forbids to be considered. Thus, in *McDonnell Douglas Corp. v. Green*, the Supreme Court held that the plaintiff had shown that the company intended to discriminate by refusing to rehire him because of his race.[17] In general, there are two types of disparate treatment cases: (1) pattern-and-practice cases, in which the employee asserts that the employer systematically discriminates on the grounds of race, religion, sex, or national origin; and (2) reprisal or retaliation cases, in which the employee must show that the employer discriminated against him or her because that employee asserted his or her Title VII rights.

2. Cases of **disparate impact**

   In this second type of Title VII case, the employee need not show that the employer intended to discriminate but only that the effect, or impact, of the employer's action was discriminatory. Usually, this impact will be upon an entire class of employees. The plaintiff must demonstrate that the reason for the employer's conduct (such as refusal to promote) was not job related. Disparate impact cases often arise out of practices that appear to be neutral or nondiscriminatory on the surface, such as educational requirements and tests administered to help the employer choose the most qualified candidate. In the seminal case of *Griggs v. Duke Power Co.*, the Supreme Court held that under Title VII, an employer is not free to use any test it pleases; the test must bear a genuine relationship to job performance.[18] *Griggs* stands for the proposition that Title VII "prohibits employment practices that have discriminatory effects as well as those that are intended to discriminate."

> **disparate treatment**
>
> A form of employment discrimination that results when an employer intentionally discriminates against employees who are members of protected classes.

> **disparate impact**
>
> A form of employment discrimination resulting from employer practices that appear to be neutral but that have a discriminatory impact on protected classes.

Discrimination Based on Religion

An employer who systematically refuses to hire Catholics, Jews, Buddhists, or members of any other religious group engages in unlawful disparate treatment under Title VII. But refusal to deal with someone because of his or her religion is not the only type of violation under the law. Title VII defines religion as including religious observances and practices as well as belief, and requires the employer to "reasonably accommodate to an employee's or prospective employee's religious observance or practice" unless the employer can demonstrate that a reasonable accommodation would work an "undue hardship on the conduct of the employer's business." Thus, a company that refused to allow a Sikh to wear a turban on the job would violate Title VII.

But the company need not make an accommodation that would impose more than a minimal cost. For example, an employee in an airline maintenance department, open twenty-four hours a day, wished to avoid working on his Sabbath. The employee belonged to a union, and under the collective bargaining agreement, a rotation system determined by seniority would have put the worker into a work shift that fell on his Sabbath. The Supreme Court held that the employer was not required to pay premium wages to someone whom the seniority system assigned to work on that day, and could discharge the employee if he refused the assignment.[19]

Title VII permits religious organizations to give preference in employment to individuals of the same religion. Obviously, a synagogue looking for a spiritual leader would hire a rabbi and not a priest.

Sex Discrimination

Application of Title VII to Sex Discrimination

Pregnancy Act of 1978

Federal law (1978) defining as sex discrimination employers' discrimination against women on account of their pregnancy.

sexual harassment

Demands for sexual favors in return for job promotions or other benefits, or language or conduct so sexually offensive that it creates a hostile work environment, disadvantaging the employee on the basis of sex.

A refusal to hire or promote a woman simply because she is female is a clear violation of Title VII. Under the **Pregnancy Act of 1978**, Congress declared that discrimination because of pregnancy is also a form of sex discrimination. Equal pay for equal or comparable work has also been an issue in sex (or gender) discrimination. *Barbano v. Madison County*, presents a straightforward case of sex discrimination. In that case, notice how the plaintiff has the initial burden of proving discriminatory intent and how the burden then shifts to the defendant to show a plausible, nondiscriminatory reason for its hiring decision.

The late 1970s brought another problem of sex discrimination to the fore—**sexual harassment**. There is much fear and ignorance about sexual harassment among both employers and employees. Many men think they cannot compliment a woman on her appearance without risking at least a warning by the human resources department. Many employers have spent significant time and money trying to train employees about sexual harassment, so as to avoid lawsuits. Put simply, sexual harassment involves unwelcome sexual advances, requests for sexual favors, and other verbal or physical conduct of a sexual nature that creates a hostile work environment or requires the employee to tolerate such conduct in order to keep his or her job or be promotable.

There are two major categories of sexual harassment: (1) quid pro quo and (2) hostile work environment.

Quid pro quo comes from the Latin phrase "one thing in return for another." If any part of a job is made conditional on sexual activity, there is quid pro quo sexual harassment. Here, one person's power over another is essential; a coworker, for example, is not usually in a position to make sexual demands on someone at his same level, unless he has special influence with a supervisor who has power to hire, fire, promote, or change work assignments. A supervisor, on the other hand, typically has those powers or the power to influence those kinds of changes. For example, when the male foreman says to the female line worker, "I can get you off of the night shift if you'll sleep with me," there is quid pro quo sexual harassment. In 2017 and 2018 titans of the American business, entertainment, and political world lost their jobs because of complaints against them for sexual harassment, quid pro quo.[20]

In *Harris v. Forklift Systems, Inc.*[21] and in *Meritor v. Vinson*,[22] the Supreme Court considered hostile work environment. Hostile work environment claims are more frequent than quid pro quo claims and so are more worrisome to management. An employee has a valid claim of sexual harassment if sexual talk, imagery, or behavior becomes so pervasive that it interferes with the employee's ability to work to her best capacity. On occasion, courts have found that offensive jokes, if sufficiently frequent and pervasive in the workplace, can create a hostile work environment. Likewise, comments about body parts or public displays of pornographic pictures can also create a hostile work environment. In short, the plaintiff can be detrimentally offended and hindered in the workplace even if there are no measurable psychological injuries.

In the landmark hostile work environment case of *Meritor v. Vinson*, the Supreme Court held that Title VII's ban on sexual harassment encompasses more than the trading of sexual favors for employment benefits. Unlawful sexual harassment also includes the creation of a hostile or offensive working environment, subjecting both the offending employee and the company to damage suits even if the victim was in no danger of being fired or of losing a promotion or raise.

In recalling *Harris v. Forklift Systems* (Chapter 1 Section 6), the "reasonable person" standard is declared by the court as follows: "So long as the environment would reasonably be perceived, and is perceived, as hostile or abusive there is no need for it also to be psychologically injurious." Following the *Harris* decision, in 2002, the 8th Circuit Court in *Duncan v. General Motors Corporation* determined that the jury verdict in favor of the plaintiff (for over 1 million dollars) should be reversed because the court believed the sexual harassment she suffered was not severe or pervasive enough to unreasonably interfere with her work. The Supreme Court declined to review the case.

Sex discrimination in terms of wages and benefits is common enough that a number of sizeable class actions have been brought. A class action is generally initiated by one or more people who believe that they, along with a group of other people, have been wronged in similar ways. Class actions for sexual harassment have been successful in the past. On June 11, 1998, the EEOC reached a $34 million settlement with Mitsubishi over allegations of widespread sexual harassment at the Normal, Illinois, auto plant. The settlement involved about five hundred women who split the $34 million, although only seven received the maximum $300,000 allowed by law. The others received amounts ranging from $8,000 to $225,000.

Class actions involve specific plaintiffs (called class plaintiffs or class representatives) who are named in the class action lawsuit to assert the claims of the unnamed or absent members of the class; thus, all those with a common complaint need not file their own separate lawsuit. From the point of view of plaintiffs who may have lost only a few thousand dollars annually as a result of the discrimination, a class action is advantageous—almost no lawyer would take a complicated civil case that had a potential gain of only a few thousand dollars. But, if there are thousands of plaintiffs with very similar claims, the judgment could be well into the millions. Defendants can win the procedural battle by convincing a court that the proposed class of plaintiffs does not present common questions of law or of fact.

In the Walmart class action decided by the Supreme Court in 2011,[23] three named plaintiffs (Dukes, Arana, and Kwapnoski) represented a proposed class of 1.5 million current or former Walmart employees. The plaintiffs' attorneys asked the trial court in 2001 to certify as a class all women employed at any Walmart domestic retail store at any time since December 1998. As the case progressed through the judicial system, the class grew in size. If the class were certified, and discrimination proven, Walmart could have been liable for over $1 billion in back pay. So Walmart argued that as plaintiffs, the cases of the 1.5 million women did not present common questions of law or of fact—that is, that the claims were different enough that the Court should not allow a single class action lawsuit to present such differing kinds of claims. Initially, a federal judge disagreed, finding the class sufficiently coherent for purposes of federal civil procedure. The U.S. Court of Appeals for the Ninth Circuit upheld the trial judge on two occasions.

But the U.S. Supreme Court agreed with Walmart. In the majority opinion, Justice Scalia discussed the commonality condition for class actions.

> *Quite obviously, the mere claim by employees of the same company that they have suffered a Title VII injury, or even a disparate impact Title VII injury, gives no cause to believe that all their claims can productively be litigated at once. Their claims must depend upon a common contention—for example, the assertion of discriminatory bias on the part of the same supervisor. That common contention, moreover, must be of such a nature that it is capable of classwide resolution—which means that determination of its truth or falsity will resolve an issue that is central to the validity of each one of the claims in one stroke.*[24]

Finding that there was no common contention, the Supreme Court reversed the lower courts. Many commentators, and four dissenting Justices, believed that the majority opinion has created an unnecessarily high hurdle for class action plaintiffs in Title VII cases.

An additional barrier to class actions for employment discrimination claims has been created by Supreme Court decisions that enforce arbitration clauses in employment contracts. These clauses specifically forbid employees from using any dispute resolution other than individual arbitration with the employer. In general, the use of arbitration has become a convenient way for the courts to limit the number of cases it hears. Some have argued, with considerable force, that the use of arbitration has begun to erode the rights of employees, franchisees, and many others to their "day in court."[25]

Defenses in Sexual Harassment Cases

In 1977, the U.S. Supreme Court issued two decisions that provide an affirmative defense in some sexual harassment cases. In *Faragher v. City of Boca Raton*[26] and in *Burlington Industries, Inc. v. Ellerth*,[27] female employees sued for sexual harassment. In each case, they proved that their supervisors had engaged in unconsented-to touching as well as verbal sexual harassment. In both cases, the plaintiff quit her job and, after going through the EEOC process, got a right-to-sue letter and sued for sexual harassment. In *Faragher*, the employer had never disseminated the policy against sexual harassment to its employees. But in the second case, *Burlington Industries*, the employer had a policy that was made known to employees. Moreover, a complaints system had been established that was not used by the female employee.

Both opinions rejected the notion of strict or automatic liability for employers when agents (employees) engage in sexual harassment. But the employer can have a valid defense to liability if it can prove: (1) that it exercised reasonable care to prevent and correct any sexual harassment behaviors, and (2) that the plaintiff employee unreasonably failed to take advantage of any preventive or corrective opportunities provided by the employer or to otherwise avoid harm. As with all affirmative defenses, the employer has the burden of proving this defense.

Discrimination Based on Race, Color, and National Origin

Title VII was primarily enacted to prohibit employment discrimination based on race, color, and national origin. Race refers to broad categories such as black, Caucasian, Asian, and Native American. Color simply refers to the color of a person's skin, and national origin refers to the country of the person's ancestry.

Exceptions to Title VII

There are several exceptions to Title VII—that is, situations in which an employer has a legitimate defense to discrimination in employment. Here we call out the following: merit, seniority, bona-fide occupational qualification, independent contractors (perhaps better called an exemption rather than a defense[28]) defenses to sexual harassment, and affirmative action.

Merit

Employers are allowed to select on merit and promote on merit without offending title VII's requirements. Merit decisions are usually based on work, educational experience, and ability tests. All requirements, however, must be job related. For example, the ability to lift heavy cartons of sixty pounds or more is appropriate for certain warehouse jobs but is not appropriate for all office workers. The ability to do routine maintenance (electrical, plumbing, construction) is an appropriate requirement for maintenance work but not for a teaching position. Requiring someone to have a high school degree, as in *Griggs vs. Duke Power Co.*, is not appropriate as a qualification for common labor.

Seniority

Employers may also maintain seniority systems that reward workers who have been with the company for a long time. Higher wages, benefits, and choice of working hours or vacation schedules are examples of rewards that provide employees with incentives to stay with the company. If they are not the result of intentional discrimination, they are lawful. Where an employer is dealing with a union, it is typical to see seniority systems in place.

Bona Fide Occupational Qualification (BFOQ)

For certain kinds of jobs, employers may impose **bona fide occupational qualifications (BFOQs)**. Under the express terms of Title VII, however, a bona fide (good faith) occupational qualification of race or color is never allowed. In the area of religion, as noted earlier, a group of a certain religious faith that is searching for a new spiritual leader can certainly limit its search to those of the same religion. With regard to sex (gender), allowing women to be locker room attendants only in a women's gym is a valid BFOQ, or casting men only in a movie about, say, life in a Korean-war era prisoner of war camp would make such discrimination against women a BFOQ. One important test that the courts employ in evaluating an employer's BFOQ claims is the "essence of the business" test.

> **bona fide occupational qualifications (BFOQs)**
>
> Employers may require that employees be of a certain religion, sex, or national origin where that requirement is made in good faith and goes to the essence of the business. Race and color cannot be BFOQs.

In an early case, *Diaz v. Pan American World Airways, Inc.*, the airline maintained a policy of exclusively hiring females for its flight attendant positions, because, the airline said, most of its passengers are men and they want to be "waited on" by young women .[29] The essence of the business test was established with the court's finding that "discrimination based on sex is valid only when the essence of the business operation would be undermined by not hiring members of one sex exclusively." Although the court acknowledged that females might be better suited to fulfill the required duties of the position, this was not enough to fulfill the essence of the business test:

> *The primary function of an airline is to transport passengers safely from one point to another. While a pleasant environment, enhanced by the obvious cosmetic effect that female stewardesses provide as well as...their apparent ability to perform the non-mechanical functions of the job in a more effective manner than most men, may all be important, they are tangential to the essence of the business involved. No one has suggested that having male stewards will so seriously affect the operation of an airline as to jeopardize or even minimize its ability to provide safe transportation from one place to another.[30]*

The reason that airlines now use the gender-neutral term *flight attendant* is a direct result of Title VII. In the 1990s, Hooters had some difficulty convincing the EEOC and certain male plaintiffs that only women could be hired as waitstaff in its restaurants. With regard to national origin, directors of movies and theatrical productions would be within their Title VII BFOQ rights to restrict the roles of fictional Asians to those actors whose national origin was Asian, but could also permissibly hire Caucasian actors made up in "yellow face."

Independent Contractors

One potentially troublesome area here (noted above) involves independent contractors. Title VII generally does not apply to them: if they really are independent contractors, they have no claim for discrimination because the law only protects *employees*. For example, suppose a well-known national magazine wanted to hire a freelance writer for a particular project. Could the magazine legally refuse to hire a writer because she was a woman, or because he was Catholic? Yes. Could the magazine refuse to hire a black plumber for a repair job in its employee lounge? Yes, at least as far as federal employment anti-discrimination laws go. An *employee* is, so to say, "trapped" in the job and cannot usually quit easily. Harassment and discrimination are types of abuse of power. Independent contractors are, usually, not likely to be as powerless as employees: they can move on to another job. "The price of freedom is protecting yourself against the lechery, bigotry, and general idiocies of [your] clients; the benefit is not being bossed around."[31]

Affirmative Action

affirmative action

Actions by an employer, either court-ordered or voluntary, that are designed to make up for past discrimination by hiring or promoting previously disadvantaged classes of workers.

Affirmative action is mentioned in the statutory language of Title VII, as courts have the power to order affirmative action as a remedy for the effects of past discrimination. In addition to court-ordered affirmative action, employers may voluntarily use an affirmative action plan to remedy the effects of past practices or to achieve diversity within the workforce to reflect the diversity in their community. In *Johnson v. Santa Clara County Transportation Agency*,[32] the agency had an affirmative action plan. A woman was promoted from within to the position of dispatcher, even though a male candidate had a slightly higher score on a test that was designed to measure aptitude for the job. The man brought a lawsuit alleging sex discrimination. The Court found that voluntary affirmative action was not reverse discrimination in this case, but employers should be careful in hiring and firing and layoff decisions versus promotion decisions. It is in the area of promotions that affirmative action is more likely to be upheld.

In government contracts, President Lyndon Johnson's Executive Order 11246 prohibits private discrimination by federal contractors. This is important: millions of U.S. workers are employed by companies that do business with the federal government. Because of this executive order, many companies that do business with the government have adopted voluntary affirmative action programs. In 1995, the Supreme Court limited the extent to which the government could require contractors to establish affirmative action programs. The Court said that such programs are permissible only if they serve a "compelling national interest" and are "narrowly tailored" so that they minimize the harm to white males. To make a requirement for contractors, the government must show that the programs are needed to remedy past discrimination, that the programs have time limits, and that nondiscriminatory alternatives are not available.[33]

The Age Discrimination in Employment Act

The **Age Discrimination in Employment Act** (ADEA) of 1967 (amended in 1978 and again in 1986) prohibits discrimination based on age, and recourse to this law has been growing at a faster rate than any other federal antibias employment law. In particular, the act protects workers over forty years of age and prohibits forced retirement in most jobs because of age. Until 1987, federal law had permitted mandatory retirement at age seventy, but the 1986 amendments that took effect in 1987 abolished the age ceiling except for a few jobs, such as firefighters, police officers, airline pilots, and executives with annual pensions exceeding $44,000 (mind you, annual *pensions*, not salary).[34] Like Title VII, the law has a BFOQ exception—for example, employers may set reasonable age limitations on certain high-stress jobs requiring peak physical condition.

Critics claim the U.S. Supreme Court in *Gross v. FBL Financial Services* (below) eviscerated the ADEA by holding that the Act only applies if age was *the* factor that led the employer to discriminate against the 40+-year-old person, not if it was *one* of the factors. The "senior citizen" lobbying group AARP is attempting to get Congress to re-write the Act to make clear that if age is any factor in discrimination, it is illegal.[35]

Age Discrimination in Employment Act

Federal law (1967) generally prohibiting most discrimination against employees on account of their being 40 years old or older.

Disabilities: Discrimination against the Handicapped

The 1990 **Americans with Disabilities Act** (ADA) prohibits employers from discriminating on the basis of disability. A disabled person is someone with a physical or mental impairment that substantially limits a major life activity or someone who is regarded as having such an impairment. This definition includes people with mental illness, epilepsy, visual impairment, dyslexia, and AIDS. It also covers anyone who has recovered from alcoholism or drug addiction. It specifically does not cover people with sexual disorders, pyromania, kleptomania, exhibitionism, or compulsive gambling.

Americans with Disabilities Act

Federal law (1990) prohibiting employers from discriminating against employees on account of disabilities.

Employers cannot disqualify an employee or job applicant because of disability as long as he or she can perform the essential functions of the job, with reasonable accommodation. Reasonable accommodation might include installing ramps for a wheelchair, establishing more flexible working hours, creating or modifying job assignments, and the like.

Reasonable accommodation means that there is no undue hardship for the employer. The law does not offer uniform standards for identifying what may be an undue hardship other than the imposition on the employer of a "significant difficulty or expense." Cases will differ: the resources and situation of each particular employer relative to the cost or difficulty of providing the accommodation will be considered; relative cost, rather than some definite dollar amount, will be the issue.

As with other areas of employment discrimination, job interviewers cannot ask questions about an applicant's disabilities before making a job offer; the interviewer may only ask whether the applicant can perform the work. Requirements for a medical exam are a violation of the ADA unless the exam is job related and required of all applicants for similar jobs. Employers may, however, use drug testing, although public employers are to some extent limited by the Fourth Amendment requirements of reasonableness.

The ADA's definition of disability is very broad. However, the Supreme Court has issued several important decisions that narrow the definition of what constitutes a disability under the act.

Two kinds of narrowing decisions stand out: one deals with "correctable conditions," and the other deals with repetitive stress injuries. In 1999, the Supreme Court reviewed a case that raised an issue of whether severe nearsightedness (which can be corrected with lenses) qualifies as a disability under the ADA.[36] The Supreme Court ruled that disability under the ADA will be measured according to how a person functions with corrective drugs or devices and not how the person functions without them. In *Orr v. Wal-Mart Stores, Inc.*, a federal appellate court held that a pharmacist who suffered from diabetes did not have a cause of action against Wal-Mart under the ADA as long as the condition could be corrected by insulin.[37]

The other narrowing decision deals with repetitive stress injuries. For example, carpal tunnel syndrome—or any other repetitive stress injury—could constitute a disability under the ADA. By compressing a nerve in the wrist through repetitive use, carpal tunnel syndrome causes pain and weakness in the hand. In 2002, the Supreme Court determined that while an employee with carpal tunnel syndrome could not perform all the manual tasks assigned to her, her condition did not constitute a disability under the ADA because it did not "extensively limit" her major life activities. Check out the U.S. Department of Labor's website: http://www.dol.gov/dol/topic/disability/ada.htm.

Equal Pay Act

Equal Pay Act of 1963

Federal law generally requiring that men and women be paid the same for the same work.

The **Equal Pay Act of 1963** protects both men and women from pay discrimination based on sex. The act covers all levels of private sector employees and state and local government employees but not federal workers. The act prohibits disparity in pay for jobs that require equal skill and equal effort. Equal skill means equal experience, and equal effort means comparable mental and/or physical exertion. The act prohibits disparity in pay for jobs that require equal responsibility, such as equal supervision and accountability, or similar working conditions.

In making their determinations, courts will look at the stated requirements of a job as well as the actual requirements of the job. If two jobs are judged to be equal and similar, the employer cannot pay disparate wages to members of different sexes. Along with the EEOC enforcement, employees can also bring private causes of action against an employer for violating this act. There are four criteria that can be used as defenses in justifying differentials in wages: seniority, merit, quantity or quality of product, and any factor other than sex. The employer will bear the burden of proving any of these defenses.

A defense based on merit will require that there is some clearly measurable standard that justifies the differential. In terms of quantity or quality of product, there may be a commission structure, piecework structure, or quality-control-based payment system that will be permitted. Factors "other than sex" do not include so-called market forces. In *Glenn v. General Motors Corp.*, the U.S. Court of Appeals for the Eleventh Circuit rejected General Motor's argument that it was justified in paying three women less than their male counterparts on the basis of "the market force theory" that women will work for less than a man.[38]

Here is a chart from the U.S. Department of Labor showing the disparity between men and women's full-time pay:

FIGURE 13.2 Median Weekly Earnings of Full-Time Male and Female Employees, 2016 Annual Earnings

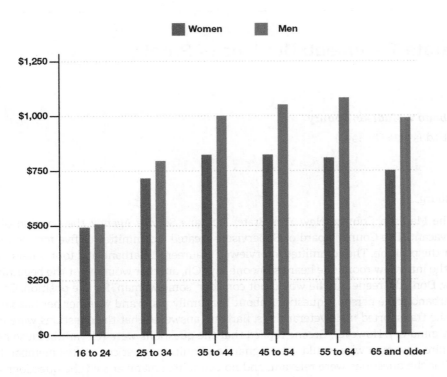

Source: https://www.bls.gov/opub/ted/2017/womens-and-mens-earnings-by-age-in-2016.htm

The main circumstance causing the disparity appears to be that marriage and child-bearing take an income toll on women that they do not on men. Never-married women earn about the same as men.[39]

Sexual Orientation and Gender Orientation

Sixteen states have laws prohibiting employment discrimination against gays or lesbians (sexual orientation) and gender orientation (transgender people). Three states have such laws prohibiting employment discrimination against sexual orientation, but not including gender orientation.[40] In July 2014, President Obama signed an executive order making it illegal for federal contractors (businesses that contract with the federal government, like Boeing or a military backpack manufacturer) to discriminately fire or harass their employees based on their sexual orientation or gender identities, and it explicitly bans discrimination against transgender employees of the federal government. The part targeting federal contractors affects 24,000 companies employing roughly 28 million workers, or about one-fifth of the nation's workforce. It is expected that more states will bar discrimination on account of these factors.

In April 2019 the Supreme Court agreed to decide if sexual orientation or gender identity should get federal job protection nationwide.[41]

Cases

Disparate Treatment: Burdens of Proof

Barbano v. Madison County

Second circuit federal appeals court case (New York) analyzing the defendant-employer's burden of showing it did not engage in sexual discrimination.

Barbano v. Madison County

922 F.2d 139 (2d Cir. 1990)

Feinburg, J.

At the Madison County (New York State) Veterans Service Agency, the position of director became vacant. The County Board of Supervisors created a committee of five men to hold interviews for the position. The committee interviewed Maureen E. Barbano and four others. When she entered the interview room, she heard someone say, "Oh, another woman." At the beginning of the interview, Donald Greene said he would not consider "some woman" for the position. Greene also asked Barbano some personal questions about her family plans and whether her husband would mind if she transported male veterans. Ms. Barbano answered that the questions were irrelevant and discriminatory. However, Greene replied that the questions were relevant because he did not want to hire a woman who would get pregnant and quit. Another committee member, Newbold, agreed that the questions were relevant, and no committee member said the questions were not relevant.

None of the interviewers rebuked Greene or objected to the questions, and none of them told Barbano that she need not answer them. Barbano did state that if she decided to have a family she would take no more time off than medically necessary. Greene once again asked whether Barbano's husband would object to her "running around the country with men" and said he would not want his wife to do it. Barbano said she was not his wife. The interview concluded after Barbano asked some questions about insurance.

After interviewing several other candidates, the board hired a man. Barbano sued the county for sex discrimination in violation of Title VII, and the district court held in her favor. She was awarded $55,000 in back pay (about $117,000 in 2015 dollars), prejudgment interest, and attorney's fees. Madison County appealed the judgment of Federal District Judge McAvoy; Barbano cross-appealed, asking for additional damages.

The court found that Barbano had established a prima facie case of discrimination under Title VII, thus bringing into issue the appellants' purported reasons for not hiring her. [A prima facie case of discrimination is where the plaintiff has sufficient evidence to prove discrimination; then the employer has the burden to show discrimination was not the reason for the action complained of, and if the employer cannot, the employee victim will likely win.]

The appellants provided four reasons why they chose Wagner over Barbano, which the district court rejected either as unsupported by the record or as a pretext for discrimination in light of Barbano's interview. The district court then found that because of Barbano's education and experience in social services, the appellants had failed to prove that absent the discrimination, they still would not have hired Barbano. Accordingly, the court awarded Barbano back pay, prejudgment interest, and attorney's fees. Subsequently, the court denied Barbano's request for front pay and a mandatory injunction ordering her appointment as director upon the next vacancy. This appeal and cross-appeal followed.

Appellants argue that the district court erred in finding that Greene's statements during the interview showed that the Board discriminated in making the hiring decision, and that there was no direct evidence of discrimination by the Board, making it improper to require that appellants prove that they would not have hired Barbano absent the discrimination. Barbano in turn challenges the adequacy of the relief awarded to her by the district court.

Having found that Barbano carried her burden of proving discrimination, the district court then placed the burden on appellants to prove by a preponderance of the evidence that, absent the discrimination, they would not have hired Barbano for the position. Appellants argue that this burden is only placed on an employer if the plaintiff proves discrimination by direct evidence, and since Barbano's evidence of discrimination was merely circumstantial, the district court erred by placing the burden of proof on them. Appellants, however, misapprehend the nature of Barbano's proof and thus the governing legal standard.

The burden is properly placed on the defendant "once the plaintiff establishes by direct evidence that an illegitimate factor played a motivating or substantial role in an employment decision." [Citation.] Thus, the key inquiry on this aspect of the case is whether the evidence is direct, that is, whether it shows that the impermissible criterion played some part in the decision-making process. If plaintiff provides such evidence, the fact-finder must then determine whether the evidence shows that the impermissible criterion played a motivating or substantial part in the hiring decision. [Citation.]

As we found above, the evidence shows that Barbano's gender was clearly a factor in the hiring decision. That the discrimination played a substantial role in that decision is shown by the importance of the recommendation to the Board. As Rafte testified, the Board utilizes a committee system, and so the Board "usually accepts" a committee's recommendation, as it did here when it unanimously voted to appoint Wagner [another candidate]. Had the Board distanced itself from Barbano's allegations of discrimination and attempted to ensure that it was not relying upon illegitimate criteria in adopting the Committee's recommendation, the evidence that discrimination played a substantial role in the Board's decision would be significantly weakened. The Board showed no inclination to take such actions, however, and in adopting the discriminatory recommendation allowed illegitimate criteria to play a substantial role in the hiring decision.

The district court thus properly required appellants to show that the Board would not have hired Barbano in the absence of discrimination. "The employer has not yet been shown to be a violator, but neither is it entitled to the . . . presumption of good faith concerning its employment decisions. At this point the employer may be required to convince the fact-finder that, despite the smoke, there is no fire." [Citation.]

[The court reviewed the reasons the employer gave for choosing another candidate—a man—instead of Barbano.] * * *

To be sure, both candidates were qualified for the Director's position, and it is not our job—nor was it the district court's—to decide which one was preferable. However, there is nothing to indicate that [the lower court judge] misconceived his function in this phase of the case, which was to decide whether appellants failed to prove by a preponderance of the evidence that they would not have hired Barbano even if they had not discriminated against her. The judge found that defendants had not met that burden. We must decide whether that finding was clearly erroneous, and we cannot say that it was.

Case Questions

1. Madison County contended that Barbano needed to provide "direct evidence" of discrimination that had played a motivating or substantial part in the decision. What would such evidence look like? Is it likely that most plaintiffs who are discriminated against because of their gender would be able to get "direct evidence" that gender was a motivating or substantial factor?

2. The "clearly erroneous" standard is applied here, as it is in many cases where appellate courts review trial court determinations. State the test, and say why the appellate court believed that the trial judge's ruling was not "clearly erroneous."

3. Re-read this bit: Madison County needs "to show that the Board would not have hired Barbano in the absence of discrimination." That is, the defendant (at the trial court), Madison County, needs to show that without regard to the fact that the plaintiff was a woman, she wouldn't have been hired; she wouldn't have been hired anyway. Once discrimination is shown to be "a factor," the burden of proof shifts from the plaintiff to the defendant. Does this rule (about shifting the burden of proof) favor the employee who claims discrimination, or the employer who is defending itself?

Title VII and Hostile Work Environment

Duncan v. General Motors Corporation

Federal 8th Circuit court of appeals case analyzing "hostile work environment" for sex discrimination in employment.

Duncan v. General Motors Corporation

300 F.3d 928 (8th Cir. 2002)

Hansen, J.

The Junior College District of St. Louis (the College) arranged for Diana Duncan to provide in-house technical training at General Motors Corporation's (GMC) manufacturing facility in Wentzville, Missouri. Throughout her tenure at GMC, Duncan was subjected to unwelcome attention by a GMC employee, James Booth, which culminated in Duncan's resignation. Duncan subsequently filed this suit under Title VII of the Civil Rights Act and the Missouri Human Rights Act * * * alleging that she was sexually harassed and constructively discharged. A jury found in favor of Duncan and awarded her $4,600 [about $7600 in 2019 dollars] in back pay, $700,000 [about $1.2 million in 2019 dollars] in emotional distress damages on her sexual harassment claim, and $300,000 [about $498,000 in 2019 dollars] in emotional distress damages on her constructive discharge claim. GMC appeals from the district court's denial of its post trial motion for judgment as a matter of law, and the district court's award of attorneys' fees attendant to the post trial motion. We reverse.

Diana Duncan worked as a technical training clerk in the high-tech area at GMC as part of the College's Center for Business, Industry, and Labor program from August 1994 until May 1997. Duncan provided in-house training support to GMC employees.

Duncan first learned about the College's position at GMC from Booth, a United Auto Workers Union technology training coordinator for GMC. Booth frequented the country club where Duncan worked as a waitress and a bartender. Booth asked Duncan if she knew anyone who had computer and typing skills and who might be interested in a position at GMC. Duncan expressed interest in the job. Booth brought the pre-employment forms to Duncan at the country club, and he forwarded her completed forms to Jerry Reese, the manager of operations, manufacturing, and training for the College. * * * Duncan began work at GMC in August 1994. Two weeks after Duncan began working at GMC, Booth requested an off-site meeting with her at a local restaurant. Booth explained to Duncan that he was in love with a married coworker and that his own marriage was troubled.

Booth then propositioned Duncan by asking her if she would have a relationship with him. Duncan rebuffed his advance and left the restaurant. The next day Duncan mentioned the incident to the paint department supervisor Joe Rolen, who had no authority over Booth. Duncan did not report Booth's conduct to either Reese (her supervisor) at the College or Ish (Booth's management counterpart) at GMC. However, she did confront Booth, and he apologized for his behavior. He made no further such "propositions." Duncan stated that Booth's manner toward her after she declined his advance became hostile, and he became more critical of her work. For example, whenever she made a typographical error, he told her that she was incompetent and that he should hire a "Kelly Services" person to replace her. Duncan admitted that Booth's criticisms were often directed at other employees as well, including male coworkers.

Duncan testified to numerous incidents of Booth's inappropriate behavior. Booth directed Duncan to create a training document for him on his computer because it was the only computer with the necessary software. The screen saver that Booth had selected to use on his computer was a picture of a naked woman. Duncan testified to four or five occasions when Booth would unnecessarily touch her hand when she handed him the telephone. In addition, Booth had a planter in his office that was shaped like a slouched man wearing a sombrero. The planter had a hole in the front of the man's pants that allowed for a cactus to protrude. The planter was in plain view to anyone entering Booth's office. Booth also kept a child's pacifier that was shaped like a penis in his office that he occasionally showed to his coworkers and specifically to Duncan on two occasions.

In 1995, Duncan requested a pay increase and told Booth that she would like to be considered for an illustrator's position. Booth said that she would have to prove her artistic ability by drawing his planter. Duncan objected, particularly because previous applicants for the position were required to draw automotive parts and not his planter. Ultimately, Duncan learned that she was not qualified for the position because she did not possess a college degree.

Additionally in 1995, Booth and a College employee created a "recruitment" poster that was posted on a bulletin board in the high-tech area. The poster portrayed Duncan as the president and CEO of the Man Hater's Club of America. It listed the club's membership qualifications as: "Must always be in control of: (1) Checking, Savings, all loose change, etc.; (2) (Ugh) Sex; (3) Raising children our way!; (4) Men must always do household chores; (5) Consider T.V. Dinners a gourmet meal." * * *

On May 5, 1997, Booth asked Duncan to type a draft of the beliefs of the "He-Men Women Hater's Club." The beliefs included the following:

- Constitutional Amendment, the 19th, giving women [the] right to vote should be repealed.
- Real He-Men indulge in a lifestyle of cursing, using tools, handling guns, driving trucks, hunting and of course, drinking beer.
- Women really do have coodies [sic] and they can spread.
- Women [are] the cause of 99.9 per cent of stress in men.
- Sperm has a right to live.
- All great chiefs of the world are men.
- Prostitution should be legalized.

Duncan refused to type the beliefs and resigned two days later.

Duncan testified that she complained to anyone who would listen to her about Booth's behavior, beginning with paint department supervisor Joe Rolen after Booth propositioned her in 1994. Duncan testified that between 1994 and 1997 she complained several times to Reese at the College about Booth's behavior, which would improve at least in the short term after she spoke with Reese.

Duncan filed a charge of sex discrimination with the Equal Employment Opportunity Commission (EEOC) on October 30, 1997. The EEOC issued Duncan a right to sue notice on April 17, 1998. Alleging sexual harassment and constructive discharge, Duncan filed suit against the College and GMC under both Title VII of the Civil Rights Act and the Missouri Human Rights Act. Duncan settled with the College prior to trial. After the jury found in Duncan's favor on both counts against GMC, GMC filed a post-trial motion for judgment as a matter of law or, alternatively, for a new trial. The district court denied the motion. The district court also awarded Duncan attorneys' fees in conjunction with GMC's post-trial motion. GMC appeals.

GMC argues that it was entitled to judgment as a matter of law on Duncan's hostile work environment claim because she failed to prove a prima facie case. We agree. * * *

It is undisputed that Duncan satisfies the first two elements of her prima facie case: she is a member of a protected group and Booth's attention was unwelcome. We also conclude that the harassment was based on sex....Although there is some evidence in the record that indicates some of Booth's behavior, and the resulting offensive and disagreeable atmosphere, was directed at both male and female employees, GMC points to ten incidents when Booth's behavior was directed at Duncan alone. GMC concedes that five of these ten incidents could arguably be based on sex: (1) Booth's proposition for a "relationship"; (2) Booth's touching of Duncan's hand; (3) Booth's request that Duncan sketch his planter; (4) the Man Hater's Club poster; and (5) Booth's request that Duncan type the He-Men Women Haters beliefs. "A plaintiff in this kind of case need not show * * * that only women were subjected to harassment, so long as she shows that women were the primary target of such harassment." We conclude that a jury could reasonably find that Duncan and her gender were the overriding themes of these incidents. The evidence is sufficient to support the jury finding that the harassment was based on sex.

We agree, however, with GMC's assertion that the alleged harassment was not so severe or pervasive as to alter a term, condition, or privilege of Duncan's employment. * * * To clear the high threshold of actionable harm, Duncan has to show that "the workplace is permeated with discriminatory intimidation, ridicule, and insult." *Harris v. Forklift Systems, Inc.* (U.S. 1993). "Conduct that is not severe or pervasive enough to create an objectively hostile or abusive work environment—an environment that a reasonable person would find hostile or abusive—is beyond Title VII's purview." Thus, the fourth part of a hostile environment claim includes both objective and subjective components: an environment that a reasonable person would find hostile and one that the victim actually perceived as abusive. [Citing *Harris.*] In determining whether the conduct is sufficiently severe or pervasive, we look to the totality of the circumstances, including the "frequency of the discriminatory conduct; its severity; whether it is physically threatening or humiliating, or a mere offensive utterance; and whether it unreasonably interferes with an employee's work performance." * * * These standards are designed to "filter out complaints attacking the ordinary tribulations of the workplace, such as the sporadic use of abusive language, gender-related jokes, and occasional teasing." [*Citing Faragher v. City of Boca Raton*, U.S. 1998.]

The evidence presented at trial illustrates that Duncan was upset and embarrassed by the posting of the derogatory poster and was disturbed by Booth's advances and his boorish behavior; but, as a matter of law, she has failed to show that these occurrences in the aggregate were so severe and extreme that a reasonable person would find that the terms or conditions of Duncan's employment had been altered. * * * Numerous cases have rejected hostile work environment claims premised upon facts equally or more egregious than the conduct at issue here. See, e.g., *Shepherd v. Comptroller of Pub. Accounts*, (5th Cir.) (holding that several incidents over a two-year period, including the comment "your elbows are the same color as your nipples," another comment that plaintiff had big thighs, repeated touching of plaintiff's arm, and attempts to look down the plaintiff's dress, were insufficient to support hostile work environment claim); *Adusumilli v. City of Chicago* (7th Cir. 1998) (holding conduct insufficient to support hostile environment claim when employee teased plaintiff, made sexual jokes aimed at her, told her not to wave at police officers "because people would think she was a prostitute," commented about low-necked tops, leered at her breasts, and touched her arm, fingers, or buttocks on four occasions); *Black v. Zaring Homes, Inc.*, (6th Cir.) (reversing jury verdict and holding behavior merely offensive and insufficient to support hostile environment claim when employee reached across plaintiff, stating "nothing I like more in the morning than sticky buns" while staring at her suggestively; suggested to plaintiff that parcel of land be named "Hootersville," "Titsville," or "Twin Peaks"; and asked "weren't you there Saturday night dancing on the tables?" while discussing property near a biker bar); *Weiss v. Coca-Cola Bottling Co.*, (7th Cir. 1993) (holding no sexual harassment when plaintiff's supervisor asked plaintiff for dates, asked about her personal life, called her a "dumb blonde," put his hand on her shoulder several times, placed "I love you" signs at her work station, and attempted to kiss her twice at work and once in a bar).

Booth's actions were boorish, chauvinistic, and decidedly immature, but we cannot say they created an objectively hostile work environment permeated with sexual harassment. Construing the evidence in the light most favorable to Duncan, she presented evidence of four categories of harassing conduct based on her sex: a single request for a relationship, which was not repeated when she rebuffed it, four or five isolated incidents of Booth briefly touching her hand, a request to draw a planter, and teasing in the form of a poster and beliefs for an imaginary club. It is apparent that these incidents made Duncan uncomfortable, but they do not meet the standard necessary for actionable sexual harassment. It is worth noting that Duncan fails to even address this component of her prima facie case in her brief. We conclude as a matter of law that she did not show a sexually harassing hostile environment sufficiently severe or pervasive so as to alter the conditions of her employment, a failure that dooms Duncan's hostile work environment claim. Reversed.

[There was a heated dissent in this case, ripping apart the majority's ruling. To read it, go here: http://caselaw.findlaw.com/us-8th-circuit/1435580.html, and begin reading at III, starting with the second paragraph. The United States Supreme Court declined to take the case.]

Case Questions

1. Is the majority opinion persuasive? How would you have ruled, and why?
2. "Numerous cases have rejected hostile work environment claims premised upon facts equally or more egregious than the conduct at issue here." By what standard or criteria does the majority opinion conclude that Duncan's experiences were no worse than those mentioned in the other cases?
3. Should the majority on the appeals court substitute its judgment for that of the jury?

Age Discrimination: Burden of Proof

Gross v. FBL Financial Services

557 U.S. 167 (U.S., 2009)

Gross v. FBL Financial Services

U.S. Supreme Court case, 2009, analyzing the burden of proof in age discrimination cases.

[Authors' note: In *McDonnell Douglas* (1973), the Supreme Court held that under Title VII, if a plaintiff shows by *indirect* evidence[42] that illegal discrimination was *a* (notice emphasis here) motivating factor in mixed-motive employment decision (that is, the facts are that the employer had both legitimate and illegitimate reasons for the decision), then the burden of proof shifts to the defendant employer to show that the same decision would have been made even without any discrimination. (That's discussed in *Barbano*, above). Example: Male Plaintiff, an older man, wears "loud" clothing and is fired. He says he was discriminated against on account of his age; indirect evidence supports the assertion, but the employer says even if this employee were younger, it still would have fired him because the employer doesn't like loud clothing on employees. Now the burden shifts to the employer: the employer must show by a preponderance of the evidence that it would have fired him even if he weren't old, and if the employer <u>does</u> show that, the plaintiff sort of loses (he is not entitled to reinstatement and back pay, but maybe instead lesser remedies). You recall the line from *Barbano*, above:

> *Having found that Barbano carried her burden of proving discrimination, the district court then placed the burden on appellants to prove by a preponderance of the evidence that, absent the discrimination, they would not have hired Barbano for the position.*

Plaintiff Jack Gross began working for respondent FBL Financial Services, Inc. (FBL), in 1971. As of 2001, Gross held the position of claims administration director. But in 2003, when he was 54 years old, Gross was reassigned (at his same pay rate) and his job was given to a younger associate. Gross considered the reassignment a demotion.

In 2004, Gross filed suit in District Court claiming his demotion violated the Age Discrimination in Employment Act (ADEA), showing by indirect evidence that his demotion was based partly on his age; FBL said it was because of corporate restructuring and Gross's new position was better suited to his skills.

The jury returned a verdict for Gross for about $50,000, and FBL appealed, claiming the court had instructed the jury incorrectly. The 8th Circuit reversed, agreeing with FBL, holding that Gross should have been required to prove that age was the determining factor in his demotion, without switching the burden to the defendant employer at all.

The issue here was whether a plaintiff's presentation of indirect evidence of age discrimination is enough to trigger the burden-shifting to the employer to show it would have made the same decision without regard to the plaintiff's age.]

Thomas, J.

* * * Before reaching this question, however, we must first determine whether the burden of persuasion ever shifts to the party defending an alleged mixed-motives discrimination claim brought under the ADEA. We hold that it does not.

Petitioner relies on this Court's decisions construing Title VII for his interpretation of the ADEA. Because Title VII is materially different with respect to the relevant burden of persuasion, however, these decisions do not control our construction of the ADEA.

Price Waterhouse * * * determined that once a "plaintiff in a Title VII case proves that [the plaintiff's membership in a protected class] played a motivating part in an employment decision, the defendant may avoid a finding of liability only by proving by a preponderance of the evidence that it would have made the same decision even if it had not taken that factor into account." But as we explained in *Desert Palace, Inc. v. Costa* (2003), Congress has since amended Title VII by explicitly authorizing [such burden-shifting].

This Court has never held that this burden-shifting framework applies to ADEA claims. And, we decline to do so now. When conducting statutory interpretation, we "must be careful not to apply rules applicable under one statute to a different statute without careful and critical examination" [Citation]. Unlike Title VII, the ADEA's text does not provide that a plaintiff may establish discrimination by showing that age was simply one of the motivating factors. Moreover, Congress neglected to add such a provision to the ADEA when it amended Title VII, even though it contemporaneously amended the ADEA in several ways.

We cannot ignore Congress' decision to amend Title VII's relevant provisions but not make similar changes to the ADEA. When Congress amends one statutory provision but not another, it is presumed to have acted intentionally. * * * As a result, the Court's interpretation of the ADEA is not governed by Title VII decisions such as *Desert Palace* and *Price Waterhouse*.

The ADEA provides, in relevant part, that "[i]t shall be unlawful for an employer … to fail or refuse to hire or to discharge any individual or otherwise discriminate against any individual with respect to his compensation, terms, conditions, or privileges of employment, *because of* such individual's age." [Citation to a section of the ADEA] (emphasis added).

* * * The ordinary meaning of the ADEA's requirement that an employer took adverse action "because of" age is that age was the "reason" that the employer decided to act. * * *

It follows, then, that under [the ADEA], the plaintiff retains the burden of persuasion to establish that age was the "but-for" cause of the employer's adverse action. Where the statutory text is "silent on the allocation of the burden of persuasion," we "begin with the ordinary default rule that plaintiffs bear the risk of failing to prove their claims." [Citation.]

Hence, the burden of persuasion necessary to establish employer liability is the same in alleged mixed-motives cases as in any other ADEA action. A plaintiff must prove by a preponderance of the evidence (which may be direct or circumstantial), that age was the "but-for" cause of the challenged employer decision.

The burden of persuasion does not shift to the employer to show that it would have taken the action regardless of age, even when a plaintiff has produced some evidence that age was one motivating factor in that decision. Accordingly, we vacate the judgment of the Court of Appeals and remand the case for further proceedings consistent with this opinion.

It is so ordered.

Case Questions

1. What a picky lot of stuff, huh? But wait, does this case make it harder or easier for plaintiffs to prove they were discriminated against on account of age? And who cares? Well, "six out of 10 older workers have seen or experienced age discrimination in the workplace, and 90% of those say it is common. Yet only 3% of those who have experienced age discrimination reported it to their employer or a government agency."[43] What if your mother or father got fired because she or he was, say, 50? How would that affect your family?

2. What is a "mixed motive" discrimination claim?

3. What is a "but for" test? In tort, it means that although the defendant herself was negligent (ran a stop sign), but for the plaintiff's own negligence (speeding, say) the collision would not have occurred and now—ta ta—the plaintiff can collect nothing. Does but-for thinking work in the context of figuring out an employer's mental intention?

4. As Justice Thomas writes about it, does the "but-for" cause mean the "sole cause"? Must plaintiffs now eliminate any other possible cause of discrimination than age in an ADEA case?

5. Based on this opinion, if the employer provides a nondiscriminatory reason for the change in the employee's status (such as "corporate restructuring" or "better alignment of skills"), does the employer bear any burden of showing that those are not just words but that, for example, the restructuring really does make sense or that the "skills" really do line up better in the new arrangement?

6. If the plaintiff was retained at the same salary as before, how could he have a "discrimination" complaint, since he still made the same amount of money?

7. What is the practical effect of this decision? Will plaintiffs with age-discrimination cases find it harder to win after Gross?

8. Here the Supreme Court is interpreting the meaning of Congress's ADEA. You recall from Chapter 4 that interpretation of legislation is one of the ways courts make law. The courts' job in doing so is to give effect to Congress's intention when it adopted the law. How does Justice Thomas figure out what Congress's intention was?

9. The case was decided by a 5–4 majority. A dissent was filed by Justice Stevens, and a separate dissent by Justice Breyer, joined by Justices Ginsburg and Souter. You can access those at http://www.law.cornell.edu/supct/pdf/08-441P.ZD1. Check it out.

Key Takeaway

Starting with employment at will as a common-law doctrine, we see many modifications by statute, particularly after 1960. Title VII of the Civil Rights Act of 1964 is the most significant, for it prohibits employers engaged in interstate commerce from discriminating on the basis of race, color, sex, religion, or national origin.

Sex discrimination, especially sexual harassment, has been a particularly fertile source of litigation. There are many defenses to Title VII claims: the employer may have a merit system or a seniority system in place, or there may be bona fide occupational qualifications in religion, gender, or national origin. In addition to Title VII, federal statutes limiting employment discrimination are the ADEA, the ADA, and the Equal Pay Act. In the last five years, several states have banned discrimination against gays, lesbians, and trans-gendered people, and under a 2014 Executive Order, federal contractors are prohibited from such discrimination.

FIGURE 13.3 A Checklist of Employment Law
Employers have a complex set of state and federal laws to observe in hiring, firing, promotion, pensions, labor standards, and workers' compensation for on-the-job injuries.

> ✔ Employment discrimination laws
>   Title VII, Civil Rights Act of 1964
>   Civil Rights Act of 1866
>   Equal Pay Act of 1963
>   Age Discrimination Act of 1967
>   Pregnancy Discrimination Act of 1978
>   Rehabilitation Act of 1973
>   Americans with Disabilities Act of 1990
>
> ✔ Common law of employment at will
> ✔ Contract law
> ✔ Tort law
> ✔ Agency law
> ✔ Worker Adjustment and Retraining Notification Act
> ✔ Polygraph Protection Act
> ✔ Occupational Safety and Health Act
> ✔ Employee Retirement Income Security Act
> ✔ Fair Labor Standards Act
> ✔ Workers' Compensation laws

Exercises

1. Go to the EEOC website. Describe the process by which an employee or ex-employee who wants to make a Title VII claim obtains a right-to-sue letter from the EEOC.

2. Again, looking at the EEOC website, find the statistical analysis of Title VII claims brought to the EEOC. What kind of discrimination is most frequent?

3. According to the EEOC website, what is "retaliation"? How frequent are retaliation claims relative to other kinds of claims?

4. Greg Connolly is a member of the Church of God and believes that premarital sex and abortion are sinful. He works as a pharmacist for Wal-Mart, and at many times during the week, he is the only pharmacist available to fill prescriptions. One product sold at his Wal-Mart is the morning-after pill (RU 468). Based on his religious beliefs, he tells his employer that he will refuse to fill prescriptions for the morning-after pill. Must Wal-Mart make a reasonable accommodation to his religious beliefs?

5. An employer cannot legally discriminate on account of religion. Can an employer opposed to, say, Jews, Muslims, Hindus, Catholics—you name it—direct its employees to decline service to members of these groups? Is the employer's religious freedom abridged if the answer is yes? Can a bakery refuse to bake a cake for a gay wedding on religious grounds?

13.4 Other Employment-Related Laws

Besides the well-know federal Civil Rights Act and other anti-discrimination acts mentioned above, there are other federal laws protecting certain employee rights.

Federal Plant-Closing Act

Because programs to support dislocated workers depend heavily on the giving of advance notice, a national debate on the issue in the late 1980s culminated in 1988 in Congress's enactment of the **Worker Adjustment and Retraining Notification (WARN) Act**, the formal name of the federal plant-closing act. Under this law (with some exceptions), businesses with 100 or more employees must give employees or their local bargaining units, along with the local city or county government, at least sixty days' notice whenever: (1) at least 50 employees in a single plant or office facility will lose their jobs or face long-term layoffs or a reduction of more than half their working hours as the result of a shutdown, and (2) a shutdown will require long-term layoffs of 500 employees or at least a third of the workforce. An employer who violates the act is liable to employees for back pay that they would have received during the notice period and may be liable to other fines and penalties.

Worker Adjustment and Retraining Notification (WARN) Act

Federal statute, 1988, requiring large employers to give notice to the public in advance of plant closing.

Employee Polygraph Protection Act

Studies calling into question the reliability of various forms of lie detectors led Congress in 1988 to legislate against their use by private businesses. The **Employee Polygraph Protection Act** forbids private employers from using lie detectors (including such devices as voice stress analyzers) for any reason. Neither employees nor applicants for jobs may be required or even asked to submit to them. (The act has some exceptions for public employers, defense and intelligence businesses, private companies in the security business, and manufacturers of controlled substances.)

Employee Polygraph Protection Act

Federal statute, 1988, forbidding the use of lie detectors by private businesses (with some exceptions).

Occupational Safety and Health Act

In a heavily industrialized society, workplace safety is a major concern. Hundreds of studies for more than a century have documented the gruesome toll taken by hazardous working conditions in mines, on railroads, and in factories from tools, machines, treacherous surroundings, and toxic chemicals and other substances. Studies in the late 1960s showed that more than 14,000 workers were killed and 2.2 million were disabled annually—at a cost of more than $8 billion (about $53 billion in 2014 dollars) and a loss of more than 250 million worker days. Congress responded in 1970 with the **Occupational Safety and Health Act**, the primary aim of which is "to assure so far as possible every working man and woman in the Nation safe and healthful working conditions."

Occupational Safety and Health Act

Federal statute, 1970, to promote safe workplaces.

Occupational Safety and Health Administration (OSHA)

The federal administrative agency (a division of the federal Department of Labor) responsible for developing and enforcing rules to promote safe workplaces.

The act imposes on each employer a general duty to furnish a place of employment free from recognized hazards likely to cause death or serious physical harm to employees. It also gives the secretary of labor the power to establish national health and safety standards. The standard-making power has been delegated to the **Occupational Safety and Health Administration (OSHA)**, an agency within the U.S. Department of Labor. The agency has the authority to inspect workplaces covered by the act whenever it receives complaints from employees or reports about fatal or multiple injuries. The agency may assess penalties and proceed administratively to enforce its standards. Criminal provisions of the act are enforced by the Justice Department.

Employee Retirement Income Security Act

Employee Retirement Income Security Act

Federal statute, 1974, establishing standards for private pension funds.

The **Employee Retirement Income Security Act** (ERISA), 1974, is a federal law that sets minimum standards for pension plans in private industry. ERISA does not require any employer to establish a pension plan. It only requires that those who do establish plans must meet certain minimum standards. The law generally does not specify how much money a participant must be paid as a benefit. ERISA requires plans to regularly provide participants with information about the plan, including information about plan features and funding; sets minimum standards for participation, vesting, benefit accrual and funding; requires accountability of plan fiduciaries; and gives participants the right to sue for benefits and breaches of fiduciary duty. ERISA also guarantees payment of certain benefits through the Pension Benefit Guaranty Corporation, a federally chartered corporation, if a defined plan is terminated. The Department of Labor's (DOL) Employee Benefits Security Administration (EBSA) enforces ERISA.

Fair Labor Standards Act

Fair Labor Standards Act

Federal statute, 1938, creating a national minimum wage, setting maximum work hours, and prohibiting child labor (among other things).

In the midst of the Depression, Congress enacted at President Roosevelt's urging a national minimum wage law, the **Fair Labor Standards Act** of 1938 (FLSA). The act prohibits most forms of child labor and established a scale of minimum wages for the regular workweek and a higher scale for overtime. (The original hourly minimum was twenty-five cents, although the administrator of the Wage and Hour Division of the U.S. Department of Labor, a position created by the act, could raise the minimum rate industry by industry.) The act originally was limited to certain types of work: that which was performed in transporting goods in interstate commerce or in producing goods for shipment in interstate commerce.

Employers quickly learned that they could limit the minimum wage by, for example, separating the interstate and intrastate components of their production. Within the next quarter century, the scope of the FLSA was considerably broadened, so that it now covers all workers in businesses that do a particular dollar-volume of goods that move in interstate commerce, regardless of whether a particular employee actually works in the interstate component of the business. It now covers between 80 and 90 percent of all persons privately employed outside of agriculture, and a lesser but substantial percentage of agricultural workers and state and local government employees. Violations of the act are investigated by the administrator of the Wage and Hour Division, who has authority to negotiate back pay on the employee's behalf. If no settlement is reached, the Labor Department may sue on the employee's behalf, or the employee, armed with a notice of the administrator's calculations of back wages due, may sue in federal or state court for back pay. Under the FLSA, a successful employee will receive double the amount of back wages due.

The federal minimum wage is, as of July 2015, $7.25 per hour. It is a shamefully low wage rate and amounts to $14,500 per year (40 hours a week for 50 weeks); you could not live on $14,500 per year. As Congress has been remarkably unresponsive, state and local governments have stepped in. In May 2015, Los Angeles became the largest city in the U.S. to raise the minimum wage. "San Francisco, Chicago, Seattle, and Oakland, Calif., have already approved increases, and dozens more are considering doing the same. In 2014, a number of Republican-leaning states like Alaska and South Dakota raised their state-level minimum wage by ballot initiative."[44]

FIGURE 13.4 Real Value of the Federal Minimum Wage in Constant 2013 Dollars

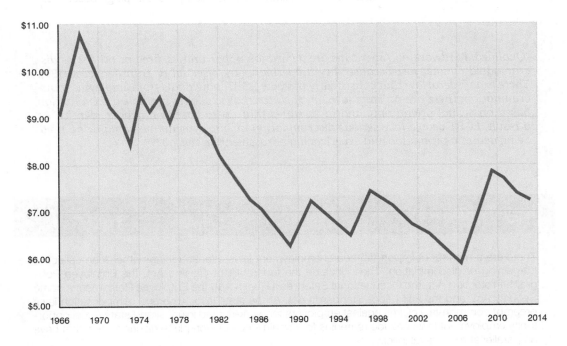

Source: National Employment Law Project at http://campaign.nelp.org/page/-/rtmw/uploads/Minimum-Wage-2013-new.png, used with permission.

Workers' Compensation Laws

Since the beginning of the twentieth century, work-related injuries or illnesses have been covered under state **workers' compensation laws** that provide a set amount of weekly compensation for disabilities caused by accidents and illnesses suffered on the job. The compensation plans also pay hospital and medical expenses necessary to treat workers who are injured by, or become ill from, their work, and it provides pensions for employees who cannot work, or for family members of employees who are killed in industrial accidents. In assuring workers of compensation, the plans eliminate the hazards and uncertainties of lawsuits by eliminating the need to prove fault. Employers fund the compensation plans by paying into statewide plans or purchasing insurance.

workers' compensation laws

State laws to provide income for employees injured in the scope of employment.

Other State Laws

Although it may appear that most employment law is federal, employment discrimination is largely governed by state law because Congress has so declared it. The Civil Rights Act of 1964 tells federal courts to defer to state agencies to enforce anti-discrimination provisions of parallel state statutes with remedies similar to those of the federal law. Moreover, many states have gone beyond federal law in banning certain forms of discrimination. Thus, well before enactment of the Americans with Disabilities Act, more than forty states prohibited such discrimination in private employment. More than a dozen states ban employment discrimination based on marital status, a category not covered by federal law. Two states have laws that protect those that may be considered "overweight."

In late June 2015, the United States Supreme Court declared that same-sex couples have a constitutional right to marry, but that ruling does not guarantee gays and lesbian people won't be discriminated against in employment. In March 2015, the Human Rights Campaign observed:

> "Qualified, hardworking Americans are denied job opportunities, fired or otherwise discriminated against just because they are lesbian, gay, bisexual or transgender (LGBT). There is no federal law that consistently protects LGBT individuals from employment discrimination; there are no state laws in 29 states that explicitly prohibit discrimination based on sexual orientation, and in 32 states that do so based on gender identity. As a result, LGBT people face serious discrimination in employment, including being fired, being denied a promotion and experiencing harassment on the job."[45]

Key Takeaway

There are a number of important federal employment laws affecting things other than collective bargaining or discrimination. These include the federal Plant-Closing Act, the Employee Polygraph Protection Act, the Occupational Safety and Health Act, the Employee Retirement Income Security Act, and the Fair Labor Standards Act. At the state level, workers' compensation laws preempt common-law claims against employers for work-related injuries, and state equal opportunity employment laws provide remedies for certain kinds of workplace discrimination that have no parallel at the federal level.

Exercises

1. United Artists is a corporation doing business in Texas. United Pension Fund is a defined-contribution employee pension benefit plan sponsored by United Artists for employees. Each employee has his or her own individual pension account, but plan assets are pooled for investment purposes. The plan is administered by the board of trustees. From 1977 to 1986, seven of the trustees made a series of loans to themselves from the plan. These trustees did not: (1) require the borrowers to submit a written application for the loans, (2) assess the prospective borrower's ability to repay loans, (3) specify a period in which the loans were to be repaid, or (4) call the loans when they remained unpaid. The trustees also charged less than fair-market-value interest for the loans. The secretary of labor sued the trustees, alleging that they had breached their fiduciary duty in violation of ERISA. Who won?[46]

2. Arrow Automotive Industries remanufactures and distributes automobile and truck parts. Its operating plants produce identical product lines. The company is planning to open a new facility in Santa Maria, California. The employees at the Arrow plant in Hudson, Massachusetts, are represented by a union, the United Automobile, Aerospace, and Agricultural Implement Workers of America. The Hudson plant has a history of unprofitable operations. The union called a strike when the existing collective bargaining agreement expired and a new agreement could not be reached. After several months, the board of directors of the company voted to close the striking plant. The closing would give Arrow a 24 percent increase in gross profits and free capital and equipment for the new Santa Maria plant. In addition, the existing customers of the Hudson plant could be serviced by the Spartanburg, South Carolina, plant, which is currently being underutilized. What would have to be done if the plant-closing act applied to the situation?[47]

13.5 Summary and Exercises

Summary

For the past fifty years, Title VII of the Civil Rights Act of 1964 has prohibited employment discrimination based on race, religion, sex, or national origin. Any employment decision, including hiring, promotion, and discharge, based on one of these factors is unlawful and subjects the employer to making an award of back pay, promotion, or reinstatement. The Equal Employment Opportunity Commission (EEOC) may file suit, as may the employee—after the commission screens the complaint.

Two major types of discrimination suits are those for disparate treatment (in which the employer intended to discriminate) and disparate impact (in which, regardless of intent, the impact of a particular non-job-related practice has a discriminatory effect). In matters of religion, the employer is bound not only to refrain from discrimination based on an employee's religious beliefs or preferences but also to accommodate the employee's religious practices to the extent that the accommodation does not impose an undue hardship on the business.

Sex discrimination, besides refusal to hire a person solely on the basis of sex, includes discrimination based on pregnancy. Sexual harassment is a form of sex discrimination, and it includes the creation of a hostile or offensive working environment. A separate statute, the Equal Pay Act, mandates equal pay for men and women assigned to the same job.

One major exception to Title VII permits hiring people of a particular religion, sex, or nationality if that feature is a bona fide occupational qualification. There is no bona fide occupational qualification (BFOQ) exception for race, nor is a public stereotype a legitimate basis for a BFOQ. Also notable is the independent contractor exception: the act only applies to employees.

Affirmative action plans, permitting or requiring employers to hire on the basis of race, to make up for past discrimination or to bring up the level of minority workers, have been approved, even though the plans may seem to conflict with Title VII. But affirmative action plans have not been permitted to overcome bona fide seniority or merit systems.

The Age Discrimination in Employment Act protects workers over forty from discharge solely on the basis of age. Amendments to the law have abolished the age ceiling for retirement, so that most people working for employers covered by the law cannot be forced to retire.

The Americans with Disabilities Act of 1990 prohibits discrimination based on disability and applies to most jobs in the private sector.

At common law, an employer was free to fire an employee for any reason or for no reason at all. In recent years, the employment-at-will doctrine has been significantly eroded. Many state courts have found against employers on the basis of implied contracts, tortious violation of public policy, or violations of an implied covenant of good faith and fair dealing.

After a century of labor-union agitation, Congress passed in 1935 the major federal legislation affecting labor-management relations. The National Labor Relations Act (the Wagner Act) basically does two things: (1) it provides that employees have a right to join unions and management must recognize and bargain with the union in good faith, and (2) it established the National Labor Relations Board with the power to hear complaints that management—and with the Taft-Hartley Act amendments of 1947, unions too—have committed. The Board may fashion appropriate remedies if it finds an Unfair Labor Practices ULP has been committed. The percent of employees who are unionized has declined very significantly in the last fifty years (except in the government sector), but basic laws allowing unionization remain effective if employees can find the interest, will, and organization to make use of them.

Beyond antidiscrimination law, several other statutes have an impact on the employment relationship. These include the Plant-Closing Act, the Employee Polygraph Protection Act, the Occupational Safety and Health Act, the Employee Retirement Income Security Act, and the Fair Labor Standards Act.

Exercises

1. Rainbow Airlines, a new air carrier headquartered in Chicago with routes from Rome to Canberra, extensively studied the psychology of passengers and determined that more than 93 percent of its passengers felt most comfortable with female flight attendants between the ages of twenty-one and thirty-four. To increase its profitability, the company issued a policy of hiring only such people for jobs in the air but opened all ground jobs to anyone who could otherwise qualify. The policy made no racial distinction, and, in fact, nearly 30 percent of the flight attendants hired were black. What violations of federal law has Rainbow committed, if any?

2. Tex Olafson worked for five years as a messenger for Pressure Sell Advertising Agency, a company without a unionized workforce. On his fifth anniversary with the company, Tex was called in to the president's office, was given a 10 percent raise, and was complimented on his diligence. The following week, a new head of the messenger department was hired. He wanted to appoint his nephew to a messenger job but discovered that a company-wide hiring freeze prevented him from adding another employee to the messenger ranks. So he fired Tex and hired his nephew. What remedy, if any, does Tex have? What additional facts might change the result?

3. Ernest lost both his legs in combat in Iraq. He has applied for a job with Excelsior Products in the company's quality control lab. The job requires inspectors to randomly check products coming off the assembly line for defects. Historically, all inspectors have stood two-hour shifts. Ernest proposes to sit in his wheelchair. The company refuses to hire him because it says he will be less efficient. Ernest's previous employment record shows him to be a diligent, serious worker. Does Ernest have a legal right to be hired? What additional facts might you want to know in deciding?

4. Charlie Goodfellow works for Yum-burger and has always commanded respect at the local franchise for being the fastest server. One day, he undergoes a profound religious experience, converts to Sikhism, and changes his name to Sanjay Singh. The tenets of his religion require him to wear a beard and a turban. He lets his beard grow, puts on a turban, and his fellow workers tease him. When a regional vice president sees that Sanjay is not wearing the prescribed Yum-Burger uniform, he fires him. What rights of Sanjay, if any, has Yum-burger violated? What remedies are available to him?

5. Employees are required to undergo security checks before leaving the Amazon.com warehouse after work, and it takes about 25 minutes a day. The FLSA exempts employers from FLSA liability for claims based on "activities which are preliminary to or postliminary to" the performance of the principal activities that an employee is employed to perform. Is security screening "preliminary or postliminary" to the employees' usual work, and thus not compensable? (*Integrity Staffing Solutions, Inc., v. Busk*, U.S., 2014).

6. Acme industries designates a group of 100 employees as "independent contractors," although their duties are the same as its regular employees. It pays them less, provides no benefits, and it refuses to hire women. What remedy is available to them?

7. Beta Company had an opening for a job and considered two candidates: Alice Able and Betty Baker. Able was just out of college, 25 years old. She was obviously technologically savvy, confident, and had high expectations, but Beta thought she was likely overindulged, impatient, and self-absorbed. So the company decided to hire Baker, who was 42. Neither had directly relevant work experience. Does Able have a remedy for age discrimination? (*General Dynamics v. Cline*, U.S. 2004.)

8. Eleanor Employee, a hard-working single mother of two, worked for ten years at Mid-American Manufacturing as an at-will employee, at which time her supervisor told her the business was being relocated to Mexico. Does Eleanor have any job-saving protection under the employment-at-will doctrine?

9. Why have courts come up with exceptions to the employment-at-will doctrine?

10. Why did Congress adopt the WARN Act?

Self-Test Questions

1. Affirmative action in employment:

   a. is a requirement of Title VII of the Civil Rights Act of 1964

   b. is prohibited by Title VII of the Civil Rights Act of 1964

   c. is a federal statute enacted by Congress

   d. depends on the circumstances of each case for validity

2. The Age Discrimination in Employment Act protects:

   a. all workers of any age

   b. all workers up to age seventy

   c. most workers over forty

   d. no workers over seventy

3. Federal laws barring discrimination against the handicapped and disabled:

   a. apply to all disabilities

   b. apply to most disabilities in private employment

   c. apply to all disabilities in public employment

   d. apply to most disabilities in public employment

4. Under Title VII, a bona fide occupational qualification exception may never apply to cases involving:

   a. racial discrimination

   b. religious discrimination

   c. sex discrimination

   d. age discrimination

5. The employment-at-will doctrine derives from:

   a. Title VII of the Civil Rights Act of 1964

   b. employment contracts

   c. the common law

   d. liberty of contract under the Constitution

Self-Test Answers

1. d

2. c

3. b

4. a

5. c

Endnotes

1. *Wagenseller v. Scottsdale Memorial Hospital*, 147 Ariz. 370; 710 P.2d 1025 (1085).

2. *Rocky Mountain Hospital and Medical Services v. Diane Mariani*, 916 P.2d 519 (Colo. 1996).

3. The theory was that striking employees were committing crimes: trespassing, intentional interference with business relations, and they were doing it collectively—together—as a conspiracy. Striking employees who refused to disband their strikes could be convicted of a crime and sent to prison.

4. A boycott of a firm with which a union does not have a dispute, intended to induce that firm to cease doing business with the employer with which the union does have a dispute. A neutral firm is dragged into the fray.

5. *Duplex Printing Press Co. v. Deering*, 254 U.S. 443 (1921).

6. https://supreme.justia.com/cases/federal/us/254/443/.

7. Mike Marino, "The Battle of the Overpass: Henry Ford, the UAW, and the Power of the Press," *People's World*, September 3, 2014. http://www.peoplesworld.org/article/battle-of-the-overpass-henry-ford-the-uaw-and-the-power-of-the-press/

8. Joseph A. McCartin (opinion piece), The Strike That Busted Unions, *New York Times*, August 2, 2011. https://www.nytimes.com/2011/08/03/opinion/reagan-vs-patco-the-strike-that-busted-unions.html

9. Bruce Western and Jake Rosenfeld, "Unions, Norms, and the Rise in U.S. Wage Inequality." The study noted that from 1973 to 2007, union membership in the private sector dropped to 8 percent from 34 percent among men and to 6 percent from 16 percent among women. During that time, wage inequality in the private sector increased by more than 40 percent. See https://economix.blogs.nytimes.com/2011/08/04/labors-decline-and-wage-inequality/

10. http://www.chicagotribune.com/news/nationworld/politics/ct-trump-federal-workers-20161121-story.html

11. http://www.feedingamerica.org/hunger-in-america/our-research/map-the-meal-gap/child-food-insecurity-executive-summary.html

12. In an opinion piece in the *New York Times*, Jane McAlevey wrote: "Workers who have managed to win National Labor Relations Board elections are up against seriously rigged rules that strongly favor management. They face highly motivated, well-resourced "union avoidance firms" that deploy any means possible to prevent workers from organizing. This same billionaire class, including some of the very same funders behind the Federalist Society's list of judges handed to their populist front—the president—first perfected warfare against workplace democracy, i.e., unions. Billionaires unleashed these methods and machinery against American democracy in the midterms of 2010 and 2014, culminating in the 2016 national election" Jane McAlevey, "What Union Organizers Can Teach Democrats," *The New York Times*, October 10, 2018. https://www.nytimes.com/2018/10/10/opinion/unions-democrats-organizers-midterms.html?rref=collection/sectioncollection/opinion

13. Hiroko Tabuchi, "Walmart Raising Wage to at Least $9," *The New York Times*, February 19, 2015. http://www.nytimes.com/2015/02/20/business/walmart-raising-wage-to-at-least-9-dollars.html?_r=0.

14. https://www.usatoday.com/story/news/education/2019/01/26/teacher-strike-denver-oakland-west-virginia-virginia/2680582002/

15. See CongressLink, "Major Features of the Civil Rights Act of 1964," at http://www.congresslink.org/print_basics_histmats_civilrights64text.htm.

16. *Hishon v. King & Spalding*, 467 U.S. 69 (1984).

17. *McDonnell Douglas Corp. v. Green*, 411 U.S. 792 (1973).

18. *Griggs v. Duke Power Co.*, 401 U.S. 424 (1971).

19. *Trans World Airlines v. Hardison*, 432 U.S. 63 (1977).

20. Among them: Harvey Weinstein - Film Producer; Mark Halperin - MSNBC Senior Political Analyst; Matt Lauer - NBC television journalist and co-host of "The Today Show"; Matt Zimmerman - NBC Senior Vice President of Booking, News, and Entertainment; Charlie Rose - CBS television journalist; Mike Oreskes - NPR News Executive; David Sweeney - NPR Chief News Editor; Louis C.K. - Comedian who lost his ties to HBO and FX, has had his new movie canceled; Netflix special Kevin Spacey - Actor who is being cut from an upcoming film and was fired from the House of Cards Netflix series; Garrison Keillor - Minnesota Public Radio.

21. *Harris v. Forklift Systems, Inc.*, 510 U.S. 17 (1993).

22. *Meritor v. Vinson*, 477 U.S. 57 (1986).

23. 564 U.S. 338 (2011)

24. 564 U.S. ___ (2011).

25. Economic Policy Institute, 2015, "The Arbitration Epidemic." http://www.epi.org/publication/the-arbitration-epidemic/.

26. *Faragher v. City of Boca Raton*, 524 U.S. 775 (1998).

27. *Burlington Industries v. Ellerth*, 524 U.S. 742 (1988).

28. An exception arises where the law does apply, but not in this fact situation; an exemption arises where the law doesn't apply to begin with.

29. *Diaz v. Pan American World Airways, Inc.*, 442 F.2d 385 (5th Cir. 1971).

30. *Diaz v. Pan American World Airways, Inc.*, 442 F.2d 385 (5th Cir. 1971).

31. Wendy Kaminer, "Sexual Harassment and the Independent Contractor," *The Atlantic*, August 24, 2010. http://www.theatlantic.com/national/archive/2010/08/sexual-harassment-and-the-independent-contractor/61976/.

32. *Johnson v. Santa Clara County Transportation Agency*, 480 U.S. 616 (1987).

33. *Adarand Constructors, Inc. v. Pena*, 515 U.S. 200 (1995).

34. Here is the citation to this Department of Labor regulation in the Code of Federal Regulations: 29 CFR 1625.12.

35. https://blog.aarp.org/2012/06/21/fighting-age-discrimination-draws-bipartisan-support-and-you-can-help/

36. *Sutton v. United Airlines, Inc.*, 527 U.S. 471 (1999).

37. *Orr v. Wal-Mart Stores, Inc.*, 297 F.3d 720 (8th Cir. 2002).

38. *Glenn v. General Motors Corp.*, 841 F.2d 1567 (1988).

39. Claire Cain Miller, "The Gender Pay Gap Is Largely Because of Motherhood," *The New York Times*, May 13, 2017. Available at https://www.nytimes.com/2017/05/13/upshot/the-gender-pay-gap-is-largely-because-of-motherhood.html .

40. https://www.aclu.org/map/non-discrimination-laws-state-state-information-map.

41. https://www.usatoday.com/story/news/politics/2019/04/22/lgbt-supreme-court-gay-rights-job-discrimination-cases-heard/2474611002/

42. Evidence that only creates an inference or that does not directly lead to a conclusion of fact is known as indirect evidence.

43. EEOC Age Discrimination Report Challenges Employers To Embrace Older Workers. https://www.forbes.com/sites/ashleaebeling/2018/06/27/eeoc-age-discrimination-report-challenges-employers-to-embrace-older-workers/#1019fabb5538

44. Jennifer Medina and Noam Scheiber, "Los Angeles Lifts Its Minimum Wage to $15 Per Hour," *The New York Times*, May 19, 2015. Available at http://www.nytimes.com/2015/05/20/us/los-angeles-expected-to-raise-minimum-wage-to-15-an-hour.html?_r=0.

45. https://www.gillibrand.senate.gov/news/press/release/schumer-gillibrand-co-sponsoring-legislation-to-end-workplace-discrimination-based-on-sexual-orientation-and-gender-identity

46. *Mc Laughlin v. Rowley*, 69 F.Supp. 1333 (N.D. Tex. 1988).

47. *Arrow Automotive Industries, Inc. v. NLRB*, 853 F.2d 233 (4th Cir. 1989).

CHAPTER 14
Government Regulation of the Market

We observe here and elsewhere in this text that totally "free" markets are rare; historically, constraints have been placed in many societies on the sale of many things, such as sex (prostitution), the sale of votes, physician-assisted suicide, and restrictions on sales of alcohol, tobacco, and drugs. Moreover, the sales of other, legal, products and services no longer have the customary restraint of local producers doing business with local customers. Before businesses became national, and then global, there were better checks and balances between consumers and producers based on face-to-face relationships and local reputation. With the separation of production from consumption the effect of local reputation is much diminished, and bringing lawsuits against large business entities is difficult and time-consuming. A basic question is whether the common law and state statutes can provide sufficient regulation of "the market" to ensure that it is competitive, fair, and that unwanted side effects of economic activity are lessened. In short, this chapter addresses the question of why federal and state protections are needed to keep markets competitive (antitrust law), protect consumers, provide remedies for defective products, regulate insurance and banking, and ensure that securities markets are relatively open and fair.

14.1 Why Government Regulation of the Market Is Necessary

A Truly Unregulated Market Is Societally Unacceptable

laissez-faire

An 18th century economic policy that opposed any government intervention in business affairs and translates as "leave alone."

A truly unregulated market has never existed and is socially unacceptable. In a completely **laissez-faire** society, drugs of all kinds would be for sale, along with weapons of mass destruction and child pornography; children themselves would be bought and sold; contracts could not be enforced, adulterated foodstuffs could be sold without consequence, property would not be protected; there would be no Social Security, and no minimum wage.

In 1999 the British political-economist Professor John Gray wrote:

> *The truth is that free markets are creatures of state power, and persist only so long as the state is able to prevent human needs for security and the control of economic risk from finding political expression. . . . The natural counterpart of a free market economy is a politics of insecurity. In the normal course of democratic life the free market is always short-lived. Its social costs are such that it cannot for long be legitimated in any democracy.*[1] *The* raison d'etre *[the most important reason or purpose for something's existence] of governments everywhere is their ability to protect citizens from insecurity.*[2]

Since the late 1970s, many commentators have come to believe that government is not providing adequate security for its citizens. In 2006 the author and "radical" environmentalist Derrick Jensen wrote:

> *Surely by now there can be few who still believe the purpose of government is to protect us from the activities of corporations. At last most of us understand that the opposite is true: that the primary purpose of government is to protect those who run the economy from the outrage of injured citizens.*[3]

Prof. Gray's point is that left to themselves, people buy and sell, but they do it under self-created regulation. Medieval guilds, or labor unions as we would call them, are an example of formal regulation, but in traditional societies regulation of the market—of the economy—is mostly habitual, customary, and traditional (and significantly reputational). Feudalism, wherever it appeared, organized society and provided mechanisms for security. People do not like insecurity; it is antithetical to the development of a stable, fulfilling society and to healthy personal development; it is intolerable. If broad sectors of society freely vote in a democratic state, Gray asserts, they will vote for regulated markets. That's what happened in the U.S. beginning in the late 19th century. When the railroads destroyed the intimacy of face-to-face relations in commercial transactions (by separating production from consumption), Americans voted for government regulation of business: regulation was "voted in" during the Progressive Era (1890–1918)—think Theodore Roosevelt—and again during the era of the New Deal (1932-1970). But "progressive" government may come and go. Indeed, Derrick Jensen believes that government has abdicated its role in protecting citizens and has, instead, been doing the work of corporate interests, sowing and nurturing insecurity, inequality, and environmental degradation.

Companies and industries typically chafe at regulations and restrictions. They are singularly (thought not exclusively) driven to maximize profits, while the public's attention to regulation is diluted and fitful. Eventually, the more focused business interests—at the lobbying table year after year—will often succeed in convincing the government to relax or abandon its regulation. The cycle of regulation and de-regulation is visible in many areas of the economy, and was evident in Chapter 12's look at environmental law and regulation.

In regulating financial markets, there has been a similar expansion rather than contraction of regulation on banks, securities markets, and labor markets. Strict rules set in place during the Great Depression and the administration of Franklin D. Roosevelt were relaxed gradually, especially during the 1990s. But financial markets are not very good at self-regulation—there was another financial crash in 2008, and its effects are still with us as this book is written. There followed a brief clamor for re-regulation—new laws (e.g., the Dodd-Frank Wall Street Reform and Consumer Finance Protection Act, passed by Congress in 2010) were signed into law by President Obama. Then, renewed pressure from the financial sector convinced Congress to relax some of the new regulations. And so it goes. Or at least that's how it's gone since the progressive era in the late 1800s. Some commentators—Gray and Jensen among them—think our current economic and political system is unsustainable and that there will be another crash from which there is no ready recovery because of environmental degradation.

However it waxes and wanes, government regulation is an inescapable feature of our economy and our national culture. In this chapter we examine regulation of business behavior among businesses themselves (mostly anti-trust law), regulation of the business-customer relationship (consumer protection and product liability), and regulation of banks and financial instruments (mostly security regulation).

Methods of Regulation

There are four main methods by which the market—the economy—is regulated.

- Registration or licensing to approve and permit an activity: practicing law, medicine, plumbing, drivers' licensing, construction and operation of elevators, registration of general or specialized contractors.
- Inspection processes: restaurants, meat-packing plants, electrical inspections to ensure legal compliance.
- Statutes, regulations, or standards of expectation: inter- or intra-business competition, food labeling, automobile safety regulations, street designs, waste-disposal regulations, regulation of competition; and this may include self-regulation—the adoption of voluntary standards.[4]
- De-registration or de-licensing (as for mining operations, nursing homes, licensed professionals).

And we might mention one other method by which the market is regulated: socialism, wherein the government directly owns and runs the business. "Socialism" was once a dirty word in America; today, recognizing the market failures of capitalism more people are looking at it with greater favor: https://www.npr.org/2015/11/21/456676215/why-do-young-people-like-socialism-more-than-older-people.

Many U.S. systems for water and electrical distribution, garbage and sewage disposal operations, airports, bridges, bus systems, tunnels, roads, and in some areas, internet service providers, are owned and operated by a government. The U.S. Postal Service is socialized mail distribution. Theoretically, at least, if the service is unsatisfactory, the public can "vote the bums out." As we briefly examine a range of government regulations of the market it can be useful to think about which of the methods of regulation are employed to achieve the regulation.

Key Takeaway

A completely unregulated market has never existed anywhere and would not be tolerable: unrestrained, market players will usually focus on money-making without considering the public good. In the U.S., when traditional restraints imposed by face-to-face commercial interaction faded with the coming of the railroads, with the rise of a truly national economy, and with urbanism, market players' abuses became politically unacceptable. But regulation has waxed and waned over the past 150 years, and we are currently in a period where "less regulation" has become the political norm. Still, regulations of some sort will always be with us.

Exercises

1. Here is a quotation (March 2018) from a former Facebook executive, speaking about concerns that Facebook's privacy policies are too lax:

   The people whose job it is to protect the user are always fighting an uphill battle against the people whose job is to make money for the company.[5]

   How is this relevant to our discussion of government market regulation?

2. What does it mean to say that in pre-modern times (before the railroads), "traditional market constraints were imposed by face-to-face commercial interaction"? How does a face-to-face relationship in a small town impose restraints on market abuses?

3. Before the railroads, most employers only had a handful of employees, people the employer knew on a first-name basis. How does the rise of huge employers with thousands of employees affect the employer-employee relationship, and why is that relevant to a discussion about government regulation?

4. What is the relationship between on-line anonymity (lack of face-to-face interaction) and Internet vitriol, abuse, lies, scam, and denigration?

5. What do efforts by some politicians to engage in "voter suppression" and the Senate's refusal in 2016 to consider President Obama's nominee for Supreme Court justice (it waited until President Trump was elected to approve his nominee) have to do with crafting today's "political norm" of less regulation?

14.2 Regulation of the Business-to-Business Relationship: Antitrust

Learning Objectives

1. Understand why government regulation of business began in the 1880s.
2. Understand Federal regulation of business behavior, including:

   • Antitrust: Sherman Antitrust Act, 1890

Why Government Regulation of Business-to-Business Competition Began in the 1880s

The first significant United States uprising of the laboring class (Karl Marx's "proletariat") protesting the abuses of capitalism started in the summer of 1877 in Martinsburg, West Virginia. Striking railroad workers, protesting repeated pay cuts, refused to allow any trains to roll. First, the police were overwhelmed by (or were sympathetic to) the mob; the governor called out the militia, but it sided with the mob. Finally, the United States Army was called in, and it had to be supported by 10,000 Civil War veterans who were called out of ten years' retirement from the Army to put down their fellow Americans. The rebellion spread to Baltimore, Buffalo, Chicago, St. Louis, Omaha, and St. Paul. Figure 14.1 shows the National Guard firing on protesters in Baltimore. And it wasn't just railroad workers—miners struck, mill-hands struck, and 20,000 workmen demonstrated in Chicago. In Pittsburgh the strikers besieged the state militia in a roundhouse and destroyed more than $5 million of property ($139 million in 2018 dollars). The popular uprising was crushed by a huge military force.

FIGURE 14.1 The Railroad Strike of 1877
Maryland National Guard's Sixth Regiment fighting its way west along main downtown commercial thoroughfare Baltimore Street through Baltimore, Maryland, 20 July 1877.

Source: Unknown - Harper's Weekly, Journal of Civilization, Vol XXL, No. 1076, New York. Public domain. https://en.wikipedia.org/wiki/Great_Railroad_Strike_of_1877#/media/File:Harpers_8_11_1877_6th_Regiment_Fighting_Baltimore.jpg

Something had to be done. In 1887 Congress adopted the Interstate Commerce Act (ICA), the first modern federal regulatory regime; it gave the federal government power to regulate the railroads, the steaming instrumentality of modernism.

The ICA required "just and reasonable rates," prohibited various unfair practices, and created a five-member Interstate Commerce Commission charged with the responsibility of executing its provisions.[6] The Commission later regulated bridges, terminals, ferries, oil pipelines, trucking and bus transportation. In the spirit of deregulation, the agency's authority was diminished in the 1970s and 1980s; it was abolished in 1995 and its remaining regulatory functions were farmed out to other agencies.

Federal Regulation of Business-to-Business Competition

The ICC regulated the railroads for the public good (though the regulation also served the interests of the railroads in reducing competitive pressures). But the railroads were not the only manifestation of capitalism that abused and infuriated the public. Other aspects of the new industrial economy needed attention, too. Particularly galling were monopolistic tendencies in the oil industry (John D. Rockefeller's Standard Oil Company was infamously monopolistic), but in the 1880s and 1990s combinations, contractual relationships, and—as President Benjamin Harrison said in 1888—"dangerous conspiracies" deformed other industries: cotton, envelopes, paving pitch, linseed oil, lead, sugar, whiskey, telephone, steel, blackboards, and tobacco. Consumers howled in true outrage at the price gouging, lack of competition (and concomitant poor quality of the goods and services), the accumulation of vast wealth for a few (the era is often called "The Gilded Age"—today the same effect is called "the one percent"), gross inequality of wealth, the disappearance of "the little guy"—the traditionally important small-business owner—and the rise of very large companies promoted consumption and growth above all other values.

The Sherman Antitrust Act, 1890

Senator John Sherman[7] wrote early drafts of the act named after him that was adopted in 1890. In the U.S., laws to promote competition are called "antitrust" laws (a trust is a business organization whereby competing companies effectively manipulate the supply or price of their product to reduce competition). In Europe and elsewhere, such laws are known as "competition laws."

Sherman Antitrust Act

Federal statute, adopted in 1890, regulating monopolistic practices and unreasonable restraints of trade.

Section 1 of the **Sherman Antitrust Act** declares

> *Every contract, combination in the form of trust or otherwise, or conspiracy, in restraint of trade or commerce among the several states, or with foreign nations, is declared to be illegal [and a felony].*

This is the Acts' famous "3-Cs": contracts, combinations, and conspiracies. At common law, contracts that unreasonably restrained trade had been illegal for four hundred years (a traditional restraint on the market), and to some extent what the Sherman Act did was codify (put into the statute books) long-standing common-law doctrine. In 1911 the Supreme Court said so clearly; only *unreasonable* restraints of trade were prohibited by the Act. Rephrased, contracts in restraint of trade are okay if they are reasonable.

This is known as "the **Rule of Reason**." and it makes sense. Justice Louis Brandeis noted in 1918 in an early price-fixing case, "Every agreement concerning trade, every regulation of trade restrains. To bind, to restrain, is of their very essence."[8] When a manufacturing company contracts to buy raw materials, trade in those goods is restrained: no one else will have access to them. But to interpret the Sherman Act to include such a contract is an absurdity. Common sense says that "every" cannot really mean *every* restraint. The buyer of a hardware store, for example, will have a non-compete clause in the purchase and sale agreement: the buyer does not want the seller taking the buyer's money from the sale and opening a new store a few blocks away from buyer's newly-purchased place—the seller's old customers would most likely follow seller to the new store. Yes, the non-compete clause is a contract in restraint of trade, but it is reasonable.

However, some restraints of trade are so harmful they cannot ever be reasonable. Courts have determined that price fixing and territorial division of markets, among other actions, are **per se illegal** (by themselves illegal) and no showing of reasonableness is needed.

Section 2 of the Sherman Act provides that "Every person who shall monopolize, or attempt to monopolize, or combine or conspire with any other person or persons, to monopolize any part of the trade or commerce among the several states, or with foreign nations, shall be deemed guilty of a [felony]." Section 1 requires some concerted action among two or more persons (corporate persons, usually) that unreasonably restrains trade. Section 2 does not require a combination between two or more people: a single company acting on its own can monopolize or attempt to monopolize.

Notice, too, that it is monopolization and attempts to monopolize that are illegal, not monopolies as such. As noted above, there are a lot of "natural monopolies" (like electrical companies, water companies) where competition would not make sense (there will not be two or three entire electrical distribution grids set up by two or three different companies for customers to choose from). In the case of natural monopolies the government has rate-setting approval: the firms must submit their rate schedules and otherwise make reports to the relevant government agency showing that their prices and services are acceptable.

The Clayton Antitrust Act, 1914

The **Clayton Act** was enacted in 1914 to plug what many in Congress saw as loopholes in the Sherman Act. Passage of the Clayton Act was closely linked to that of the Federal Trade Commission (FTC) Act. Unlike the Sherman Act, the Clayton Act is not a criminal statute; it merely declares certain defined practices as unlawful and leaves it to the government or to private litigants to seek to enjoin those practices. But unlike the FTC Act, the Clayton Act does spell out four undesirable practices.[9] Also, violations of the Sherman Act require an *actual* adverse impact on competition, whereas violations of the Clayton Act require merely a *probable* adverse impact. Thus, the enforcement of the Clayton Act involves a prediction that the defendant must rebut in order to avoid an adverse judgment.

The Federal Trade Commission Act, 1914

The **Federal Trade Commission Act** is a civil statute, like the Clayton Act. Unlike the Clayton Act, its prohibitions are broadly worded. Its centerpiece is Section 5, which forbids "unfair methods of competition in commerce, and unfair or deceptive acts or practices in commerce." It is up to the Commission established under the act to determine if something is "unfair" or "deceptive." The Commission's rulings on contested cases may stand as its own precedent, but the FTC is very political and its precedents are often short-lived.

The agency has about 1,200 employees divided among three bureaus:

- Bureau of cConsumer Protection. FTC lawyers enforce federal consumer affairs laws and rules promulgated by the FTC.

Rule of Reason

An interpretation of the Sherman Act allowing contracts in restraint of trade if they are reasonable.

per se illegal

A contract or restraint of trade so obviously harmful to public welfare (e.g., price fixing) that no proof of its unreasonableness is necessary; it is automatically illegal.

Clayton Act

Federal antitrust statute, 1914, refining antitrust law following adoption of the Sherman Antitrust Act twenty four years earlier.

Federal Trade Commission Act

Federal statute, 1914 (and companion to the Clayton Act) creating an administrative agency to address antitrust and unfair methods of competition.

- Bureau of Competition. Is charged with prevention of anticompetitive business practices, enforcing antitrust laws, and examining proposed mergers for anti-competitive effect. Referrals are made to the Department of Justice for criminal prosecution of antitrust laws.
- Bureau of Economics. Provides expertise on the economic effect of FTC operations and regulations.

FIGURE 14.2 Distribution of Goods or Services

Restraints of trade can occur either horizontally or vertically. Here is a typical distribution of goods or services showing, in tan, vertical relationships, and in reddish-brown horizontal relationships.

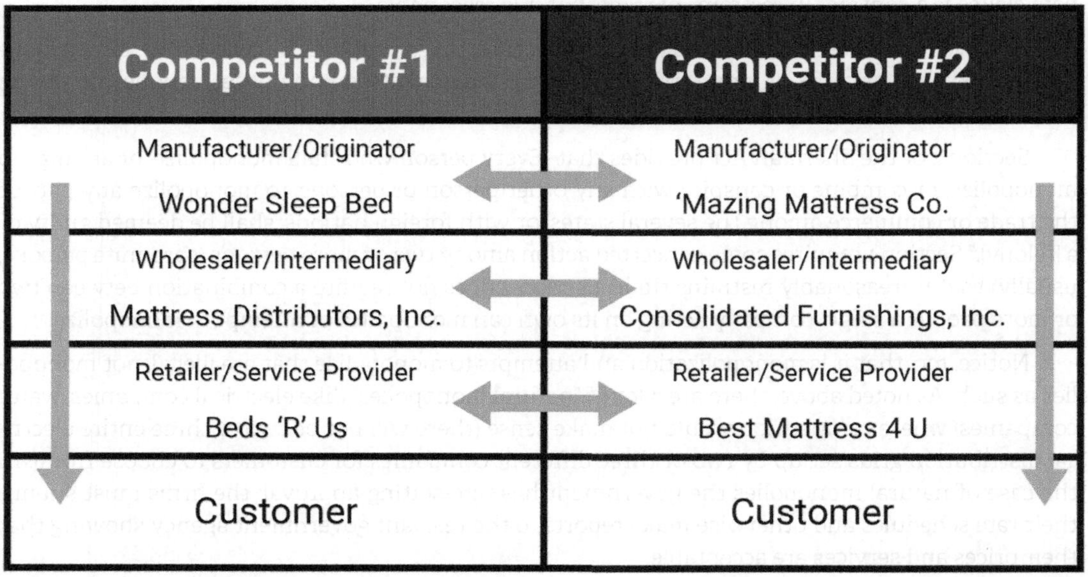

Competitor #1	Competitor #2
Manufacturer/Originator Wonder Sleep Bed	Manufacturer/Originator 'Mazing Mattress Co.
Wholesaler/Intermediary Mattress Distributors, Inc.	Wholesaler/Intermediary Consolidated Furnishings, Inc.
Retailer/Service Provider Beds 'R' Us	Retailer/Service Provider Best Mattress 4 U
Customer	Customer

Applying Antitrust Law: Restraints of Trade, Horizontal and Vertical

Horizontal Restraints

horizontal restraints of trade

In antitrust law, unreasonable restraints of trade among competitors.

Horizontal restraints of trade lessen competition among *competitors*. The classic horizontal restraint (relevant antitrust acts noted) include:

1. **Monopolization**. The government must prove the alleged monopolist (the defendant) can control the price of the product. (Sherman Act)

2. **Price Fixing**. Competitors get together to fix prices. It is per se illegal no matter where the prices are fixed, high or low. Beds 'R' Us and Best Mattress 4 U get together to set the price of mattresses. (Sherman Act)

3. **Group Boycotts** and Refusals to Deal. Wonder and 'Mazing agree not to sell any mattresses to Big-Mart because the retailer discounts the mattresses, undercutting mom-and-pop mattress stores. (Sherman Act; FTCA)

4. **Horizontal territorial divisions**. Pepsi takes Adams County as its territory, and agrees not to sell soda in Baker County; Coke gets Baker County. (Sherman Act)

5. **Mergers and consolidations**. Mergers that significantly reduce competition are illegal as monopolization—as if Ford and General Motors merged. (But not if one or both of the affected firms are failing companies, or if they are small companies hoping to compete better against market giants.) (Clayton Act)

Vertical Restraints

Vertical restraints of trade lessen competition along the *distribution chain*. The classic vertical restraints of trade—illegal if they are unreasonable—include:

---

monopolization

In business, complete control of a line of commerce which prevents other people or companies having any share or influence.

Price Fixing

Competitors get together to fix prices.

group boycotts

Two or more competitors in a relevant market refuse to conduct business with a specific individual or company unless it agrees to stop doing business with a competitor of the firms conducting the boycott.

Horizontal territorial divisions

Competitors divide up geographic territory, each agreeing not to compete with the other in the assigned territory.

vertical restraints of trade

In antitrust law, unreasonable restraints of trade along the distribution chain (e.g., manufacturer to wholesaler).

- **Resale price maintenance**. The manufacturer dictates to the retailer the price at which the goods must be sold. Okay if reasonable. (Sherman Act; FTCA)
- **Sole distributorships**. The manufacturer selects a distributor or retailer as the sole or exclusive outlet for its product. Okay if reasonable. (Sherman Act; FTCA)
- **Monopsony.** The buyer, not the seller, has the ability to control the price. Up until the late 1970s Sears, Roebuck—the famously middle-class department store—had such buying power (for washing machines, power tools, furniture) that when it selected a supplier it could dictate the price.[10] Walmart has been accused of the same thing.[11] (Sherman Act)
- **Tying arrangements.** The manufacturer/seller requires the buyer to take some additional (unwanted by the buyer) product. For example, in a famous early case IBM insisted that customers who wanted to buy its data-sorting machines also had to buy its paperboard-stock punch-cards (data was punched onto the cards and then fed into the machine for tabulation). IBM said its reason for the product tying was to make sure the machines worked (inferior cards would gum up the tabulator) and to protect its reputation and good will. The U.S. Supreme Court held this was a violation of the Clayton Act because anybody who had the right specifications could make the punch cards.[12] (Clayton Act).
- **Vertical territorial restrictions**. Can McDonald's, say, refuse to grant a franchise to somebody in Middletown because there is already one McDonald's store in town? Yes, but only if there are some other fast-food places: there must be adequate interbrand (different brands) competition to offset the reduced intrabrand (within one brand) competition. (Sherman Act)
- **Interlocking directorates**. A member of Company X's board of directors also serves on Company Y's board. This is illegal if the companies compete with each other. (Clayton Act)

Exceptions

As with all law, common law or statutory, there are exemptions and exceptions in antitrust. Not every concerted action that restrains trade is illegal. For various reasons, over the years certain industries and organized groups have been exempted from the operation of U.S. antitrust laws. These include organized labor (the whole point is for employees to join together with the ability to threaten their employer with a restraint of trade—labor-union strike), insurance companies, and baseball. (And notice that mere conscious parallelism—where a leading firm in the market sets its prices and other copy that—is not illegal.[13])

Enforcement of Antitrust Laws

It is beyond the scope of this book to detail enforcement, but note that there are four methods available:

1. The U.S. Department of Justice may bring civil actions to enjoin violations of any section of the Sherman and Clayton Acts and may institute criminal prosecutions for violations of the Sherman Act.
2. The FTC hears cases under the Administrative Procedure Act, as described in Chapter 4. The commission's decisions may be appealed to the U.S. courts of appeals. The FTC may also promulgate "trade regulation rules," which define fair practices in specific industries.
3. In the Antitrust Improvements Act of 1976, Congress authorized state attorneys general to file antitrust suits in federal court for damages on behalf of their citizens.
4. Private individuals and companies may file suits for damages or injunctions if they have been directly injured by a violation of the Sherman or Clayton Acts. Private individuals or companies may not sue under the FTC Act, no matter how unfair or deceptive the behavior complained of; only the FTC may do so. There are fewer private cases filed during Republican administrations than during Democratic administrations—antitrust is very political.

Sanctions and Penalties

Criminal violations of the Sherman Act can result in up to ten years in prison and a $1 million fine; the defendant may suffer forfeiture of property; injunctions obtained by the Justice Department can be a complex set of instructions, listing in some detail the practices that a defendant is to avoid and even the way in which it will be required to conduct its business thereafter. The federal courts also have the power to break up a company convicted of monopolizing or to order divestiture when the violation consists of unlawful mergers and acquisitions.

The crux of the private suit is its unique damage award: any successful plaintiff is entitled to collect *three times* the amount of damages actually suffered—treble damages, as they are known—and to be paid the cost of her attorneys. These fees can be huge: defendants have had to pay out millions of dollars for attorneys' fees alone in single cases. The theory of treble damages is that they will serve as an incentive to private parties to police industry for antitrust violations, thus saving the federal government the immense expense of maintaining an adequate staff for that job.

Notice here that if a company is convicted of a criminal antitrust violation—it is found guilty or it pleads guilty—it is liable "beyond a reasonable doubt," the standard for finding criminal culpability. If on a set of facts a defendant is liable beyond a reasonable doubt, it is also necessarily "probably liable," the standard for finding civil liability. A civil plaintiff need only show a copy of the criminal conviction to win and get treble damages. Therefore it is not uncommon for defendants to plead "No Contest." They don't admit criminal liability and run into treble damages, but they can still be subject to criminal penalties.

State Antitrust Laws

Federal law reaches activities that affect interstate commerce, and the federal antitrust laws are based on Congress's constitutional power to "regulate commerce among the several states." But anticompetitive activity can occur within one state, and so the states have antitrust laws as well. Some state laws track the language of federal acts. Most of them are basically similar to the federal model; some are more expansive in terms of quantity and quality of prohibitive acts.[14]

Case

Horizontal Restraint of Trade

National Society of Professional Engineers v. United States

435 U.S. 679 (1978)

National Society of Professional Engineers v. United States

U.S. Supreme Court case, 1978, analyzing whether rules of professional conduct can be unreasonable restraints of trade in antitrust law.

[The National Society of Professional Engineers adopted in 1964 a "Code of Ethics" that prohibited members from engaging in competitive bidding for projects (like bridges, office buildings, airports). Only after a client had selected an engineering firm would there be any discussion of cost; the selection, therefore, would be based on experience and reputation, and not on the cost of the project. The government claimed the no-competitive-bid code violated Section 1 of the Sherman Act. The Society appealed adverse lower-court rulings.]

Stevens, J.

* * * In this case we are presented with an agreement among competitors to refuse to discuss prices with potential customers until after negotiations have resulted in the initial selection of an engineer. While this is not price fixing as such, no elaborate industry analysis is required to demonstrate the anticompetitive character of such an agreement. It operates as an absolute ban on competitive bidding, applying with equal force to both complicated and simple projects and to both inexperienced and sophisticated customers. As the District Court found, the ban "impedes the ordinary give and take of the market place," and substantially deprives the customer of "the ability to utilize and compare prices in selecting engineering services." On its face, this agreement restrains trade within the meaning of § 1 of the Sherman Act.

The Society's affirmative defense confirms rather than refutes the anticompetitive purpose and effect of its agreement. The Society argues that the restraint is justified because bidding on engineering services is inherently imprecise, would lead to deceptively low bids, and would thereby tempt individual engineers to do inferior work with consequent risk to public safety and health. The logic of this argument rests on the assumption that the agreement will tend to maintain the price level; if it had no such effect, it would not serve its intended purpose. The Society nonetheless invokes the Rule of Reason, arguing that its restraint on price competition ultimately inures to the public benefit by preventing the production of inferior work and by insuring ethical behavior. As the preceding discussion of the Rule of Reason reveals, this Court has never accepted such an argument.

It may be, as petitioner argues, that competition tends to force prices down and that an inexpensive item may be inferior to one that is more costly. There is some risk, therefore, that competition will cause some suppliers to market a defective product. Similarly, competitive bidding for engineering projects may be inherently imprecise and incapable of taking into account all the variables which will be involved in the actual performance of the project. Based on these considerations, a purchaser might conclude that his interest in quality—which may embrace the safety of the end product—outweighs the advantages of achieving cost savings by pitting one competitor against another. Or, an individual vendor might independently refrain from price negotiation until he has satisfied himself that he fully understands the scope of his customers' needs. These decisions might be reasonable; indeed, petitioner has provided ample documentation for that thesis. But these are not reasons that satisfy the Rule; nor are such individual decisions subject to antitrust attack.

* * * Petitioner's ban on competitive bidding prevents all customers from making price comparisons in the initial selection of an engineer, and imposes the Society's views of the costs and benefits of competition on the entire marketplace. It is this restraint that must be justified under the Rule of Reason, and petitioner's attempt to do so on the basis of the potential threat that competition poses to the public safety and the ethics of its profession is nothing less than a frontal assault on the basic policy of the Sherman Act.

The Sherman Act reflects a legislative judgment that ultimately competition will produce not only lower prices, but also better goods and services. "The heart of our national economic policy long has been faith in the value of competition." [Citation.] The assumption that competition is the best method of allocating resources in a free market recognizes that all elements of a bargain—quality, service, safety, and durability—and not just the immediate cost, are favorably affected by the free opportunity to select among alternative offers. Even assuming occasional exceptions to the presumed consequences of competition, the statutory policy precludes inquiry into the question whether competition is good or bad.

The fact that engineers are often involved in large-scale projects significantly affecting the public safety does not alter our analysis. Exceptions to the Sherman Act for potentially dangerous goods and services would be tantamount to a repeal of the statute. In our complex economy the number of items that may cause serious harm is almost endless—automobiles, drugs, foods, aircraft components, heavy equipment, and countless others, cause serious harm if defectively made. The judiciary cannot indirectly protect the public against this harm by conferring monopoly advantages on the manufacturers.

The judgment of the Court of Appeals is affirmed.

Case Questions

1. What kinds of harms are likely if there is unrestrained competitive bidding among engineering firms?
2. By what other means (i.e., *not* including deliberate nondisclosure of price information up to the time of contracting) could the National Society of Professional Engineers protect the public from harm?
3. Four years after this opinion, *The Wall Street Journal* headlined as follows:

> *It was the smallest of mistakes. A detail in a joint, incorrectly designed, weakened a walkway suspended over the lobby of the Hyatt Regency Hotel in Kansas City. The walkway collapsed during a crowded dance party last July [1981], killing 113 people and injuring 186 more. . . . The inspection uncovered weak floor supports. . . . The reasons for flawed buildings are as varied as their design. If there is a common denominator, however, it's money. . . . To control costs, architects are pressured to use the lightest, most economical materials available. . . . Cutthroat competition exacerbates the problem, providing designers with ample incentive to cut corners in their quest for the low bid.*[15]

Key Takeaway

The preservation of competition is historically an important public policy in the United States. Antitrust laws (laws to promote competition) were adopted in the 19th and 20th centuries in response to clear abuses by companies that sought to claim easier profits by avoiding competition through the exercise of monopoly power, price fixing, or territorial agreements. The Department of Justice and the Federal Trade Commission have substantial criminal and civil penalties to wield in their enforcement of antitrust law, and state laws prohibit basically similar anti-competitive activity that does not involve interstate commerce.

Exercises

1. Dairy Queen requires its franchisees to use paper cups, fast-food packaging, and ingredients as dictated by the parent company. Obviously this is a restraint of trade—a franchisee cannot go out and purchase paper cups on the market where they might be cheaper. Is this restraint of trade reasonable?
2. What are horizontal restraints of trade? Give two examples.
3. What are vertical restraints of trade? Give two examples.
4. Why are many more horizontal restraints *per se* illegal than are vertical restraints, which tend to fall into the Rule of Reason?
5. What's different in the second decade of the 21st century—today—that makes rigorous antitrust enforcement, as happened in the early 20th century, seem unlikely?
6. Why are there now serious calls for government regulation of social media?

14.3 Regulation of the Business-to-Customer Relationship: Consumer Protection

Learning Objectives

1. Understand why and how the federal government regulates the market and marketing relationships businesses may have with their customers, or potential customers.
2. Know that state governments also promote consumer protection through legislation and state administrative agencies.

Unfair and Deceptive Trade Practices: The Federal Trade Commission Act of 1914 and 1938

Introduction to the FTC's Consumer Protection Function

We discussed the FTC as it was created in 1914 in conjunction with the Clayton Antitrust Act. At that time it was charged by Congress to declare illegal "unfair methods of competition," which was understood by the courts to mean that the Commission had antitrust authority. In 1938 Congress added a bit to the Commission's power, to make illegal not only "unfair methods of competition, but also "unfair or deceptive acts or practices in commerce." Henceforth, the FTC would not just be a second agency enforcing antitrust (after the Justice Department); it would be the guardian of consumers, too (subject, as always, to politics): it regulates misleading advertising and other deceptive acts.

The common law won't suffice here, although sometimes common-law litigation—successful or not—can serve a quasi-regulatory function by forcing defendants to change their practices to avoid adverse judgments or bad publicity. Also, some deceptive practices within the FTC's purview could be remedied using the common law. A tire manufacturer who advertises that its "special tire" is "new" when it is actually a retread has committed common-law misrepresentation, and the buyer could sue for rescission of the contract or for damages. But having a few buyers sue for misrepresentation does not stop the determined fraudster. Moreover, such lawsuits are expensive to bring, and the damages awarded are usually small; thus, common-law actions alone cannot adequately address deliberately fraudulent practices.

Through Section 5, however, the FTC can seek far-reaching remedies against fraudulent business practices; it is not limited to proving damages to individual customers case by case. As can its state counterparts, the FTC can address business actions in interstate commerce that are either: (1) deceptive acts and practices, or (2) unfair trade practices.

Deceptive Acts and Practices: Regulation of Advertising

The First Amendment prohibits most government interference with free speech, but there is never any public interest in false advertising; thus, false or deceptive advertising can be regulated in a way that is consistent with the First Amendment.

- Failure to disclose pertinent facts. You find a glowing review about a resort on a blog. If you knew the blogger had been given a couple of days' free stay at the resort that might influence your thoughts on the validity of the endorsement. The FTC requires disclosure.

- False or misleading descriptions of products. Certain words are considered mere "puffery" (*greatest*, *best*). Other words with more precise connotations can cause trouble if they are misused. One example is the word *new*. If a product is more than six months old, it is not new and may not lawfully be advertised as such. Labeling of certain products is strictly regulated by specific statutes. Under the Food, Drug, and Cosmetic Act, artificial colors and flavors must be disclosed. Other specific federal statutes include the Wool Products Labeling Act, the Textile Fiber Products Identification Act, the Fur Products Labeling Act, and the Flammable Fabrics Act; these acts are enforced by the FTC. Under the Fair Packaging and Labeling Act (1966) the FTC issues regulations for proper labeling of most of consumer products. In particular, the statute is designed to help standardize quantity descriptions ("small," "medium," and "large") and enable shoppers to compare the value of competing goods in the stores.

- Misleading Price and Savings Claims. "Buy one, get another for half price." "Suggested retail price: $25. Our price: $5.95." "Yours for only $95. You save $50." Unless the ads are strictly true, they are violations of Section 5 of the FTC Act. The FTC has issued a series of *Guides against Deceptive Pricing* that set forth principles the commission uses to judge the merits of price claims.[16]

- Bait and Switch. The retailer "baits" the prospective customer by dangling an alluring offer, but the offer either disappears or is disparaged once the customer arrives.

- "Free" Offers. These need to be objectively free. If it is conditioned on buying another product ("Buy one tube and get another tube free") it is false advertising.

- Product Comparisons and Disparagement. Saying defamatory things about a competitor's product is a common-law tort, actionable under state law. It is also actionable under Section 5 of the FTC Act. The FTC brands as disparagement the making of specific untrue statements o about a competitor's product. An indirect form of disparagement—"comparative misrepresentation"—is making false claims of superiority of one's own product. Again, the common-law puffing rule would permit the manufacturer of an over-the-counter pain reliever to make the general statement "Our pill is the best!" But the claim that a pill "works three times as fast as the leading competitor's" violates Section 5 if the claim is not true.

- Endorsements. It is not a deception for a celebrity to endorse a product without disclosing that she is being paid to do so. But the person giving the testimonial must in fact use the product; if she does not, the endorsement is deceptive.[17]

- Pictorial and Television Advertising. Pictorial representations create special problems because the picture can belie the caption or the announcer's words. The ways of deceiving by creating false inferences through pictures are limited only by our imaginations. White-coated "doctors," seals of the British monarchy, and plush offices can connote various things about a product, even if the advertisement never says that the man in the white coat is a doctor, that the product is related to the British crown, or that the company has its operations in the building depicted.

Unfair Trade Practices

Some trade practices not only have deceptive elements but also operate unfairly in ways beyond mere deception. In general, three types of unfair practices will be challenged:

- Failing to substantiate material representations in advertisements before publishing them or putting them on the air,
- Failing to disclose certain material information necessary for consumers to make rational comparisons of price and quality of products, and
- Taking unconscionable advantage of certain consumers or exploiting their weakness.[18]
- Breach of contract: sometimes, a company's willful breach of contract can be an unfair trade practice, thus violating Section 5 of the FTC Act. Example: a pest exterminating company guaranteed "lifetime" protection against termites; the customer renewed the service each year by paying an unchanging annual fee. Five years in, the company notified 207,000 customers that of an inflation-related fee increase. The FTC challenged the fee hike, and its challenge was sustained on appeal. The eleventh circuit approved the FTC's three-part test for determining unfairness: (1) the injury "must be substantial," (2) "it must not be outweighed by countervailing benefits to consumers," and (3) "it must be an injury that consumers themselves could not reasonably have avoided." In the termite case, all three parts were met: consumers were forced to pay substantially higher fees, they received no extra benefits, and they could not have anticipated or prevented the price hike, since the contract specifically precluded such hikes.[19]

FIGURE 14.3 Unfair and Deceptive Practices Laws

Other FTC Initiatives

The rise of social media and mobile communications is a new field for scammers. FTC initiatives now include a "Mobile Technology Unit" to help it keep apace of current developments such as cramming, mobile tracking in stores, and issues involving privacy and security. In January 2014, the "Commission reached a settlement with mobile platform provider Apple, Inc., for allegedly billing consumers for millions of dollars of charges incurred by children in mobile apps without their parents' consent." In July 2014, the agency sued T-Mobile for cramming bogus charges on consumers' bills. In March 2018 the FTC announced it was focusing on Facebook's case:

> *The FTC is firmly and fully committed to using all of its tools to protect the privacy of consumers. Foremost among these tools is enforcement action against companies that fail to honor their privacy promises, including to comply with Privacy Shield, or that engage in unfair acts that cause substantial injury to consumers in violation of the FTC Act. Today, the FTC is confirming that it has an open non-public investigation into these practices.*"[20]

And the FTC continues, as it has for years, to go after phony diet and weight-loss products and cigarettes. The FTC has waged a kind of war against the latter since 1967.[21]

Remedies

The Federal Trade Commission (FTC) has several available remedies. These include:

- Cease and desist orders (injunctions) against unfair and deceptive acts and practices. For instance, the FTC can order a company to remove or modify a deceptive trade name;

- Corrective advertising: a firm may be ordered to substantiate its advertising, disclose correct facts, and—but rarely, because it is so painful for the affected firm—it may order a company to admit that what it previously advertised was false. Or, if a company fails to disclose facts about a product, the commission may order the company to affirmatively disclose the facts in future advertising. In the *J. B. Williams* case (below), the court upheld the commission's order that the company tell consumers in future advertising that the condition Geritol is supposed to treat—iron-poor blood—is only rarely the cause of symptoms of tiredness that Geritol would help cure.

The FTC has often exercised its power to order affirmative disclosures during the past quarter century, but its power to correct advertising deceptions is even broader. In *Warner Lambert Co. v. Federal Trade Commission,* Warner Lambert had challenged the commission's power to order a company to *correct* in future advertisements its former misleading and deceptive statements; the product was Listerine, the claims for it were many, and the corrective advertising requirement only applied if the company chose to continue advertising Listerine.[22] The court also approved the FTC's formula for determining how much the company must spend: an amount equal to the average annual expenditure on advertising the mouthwash during the ten years preceding the case.

In addition to its injunctive powers, the FTC may seek civil penalties of $10,000 for violations of final cease and desist orders, and if the violation is a continuing one—e.g., an advertising campaign that lasts for weeks or months—each day is considered a separate violation. The commission may also sue for up to $10,000 per violation, as just described, for violations of its trade regulation rules (TRRs). Under the FTC Improvement Act of 1975, the commission is authorized to seek injunctions and collect monetary damages on behalf of injured consumers in cases involving violations of TRRs. It may also seek restitution for consumers in cases involving cease and desist orders if the party continuing to commit the unfair or deceptive practice should have known that it would be dishonest or fraudulent to continue doing so. As for *private* parties, though they have rights under the antitrust statutes, they have no right themselves to sue under Section 5 of the FTC Act.

Other Federal Consumer Protection Agencies and Initiatives

Various federal agencies and federal laws address aspects of consumer protection.

Food and Drug Administration

Federal agency, 1906; it regulates food, drugs, and medical devices.

National Highway Traffic Safety Administration

Federal agency, 1970, regulating to promote motor vehicle and highway safety.

Consumer Product Safety Commission

Federal agency, 1972, to set safety standards for consumer products.

Consumer Financial Protection Bureau

Federal agency, 2010, to regulate consumer financial transactions.

Fair Debt Collection Practices Act

Federal statute, 1977; it regulates professional debt-collection practices.

Magnuson-Moss Act

Federal statute, 1975, regulating product warranties in the sale of goods.

phantom warranty

A warranty that seems good, until the buyer wants to realize (make use of) the warranty, at which point it becomes apparent it provides no real protection at all.

1. **Food and Drug Administration**. The oldest consumer-protection agency, the FDA was created in 1906. It regulates the labeling, safety and purity of food (including dietary supplements), drugs (prescription and non-prescription), biologics (vaccines, blood and blood products, tissue and tissue products), medical devices, electronic products that give off radiation (microwaves, x-ray and laser equipment, sunlamps), cosmetics, veterinary products (food, drugs, and devices), and tobacco products.[23]

2. **National Highway Traffic Safety Administration**, 1970. NHTSA ("NIT-suh" to automakers in Detroit and elsewhere) is "dedicated to achieving the highest standards of excellence in motor vehicle and highway safety. It "works daily to help prevent crashes and their attendant costs, both human and financial."[24][25]

3. **Consumer Product Safety Commission**. This agency was created in 1972 with the passage of the Consumer Product Safety Act. The act gives CPSC the power to develop safety standards for consumer goods and pursue recalls for products that present unreasonable or substantial risks of injury or death to consumers. It has jurisdiction over more than 15,000 products (not including what the FDA regulates, and not including firearms, motor vehicles, pesticides, aircraft, and boats, which are regulated by various other agencies). In 2014, the CPSA was amended to protect whistleblowers who raise concerns about consumer product safety. The CPSC has a colorful, accessible website, including news of products that have been recalled because they are dangerous for consumers: http://www.cpsc.gov/en/.

4. **Consumer Financial Protection Bureau**. Created in 2010 following the disclosure of scandalous behavior by financial institutions that helped precipitate the "Great Recession," Congress established the CFPB to protect consumers by creating and enforcing federal consumer financial law and regulation. Among other things, the Bureau:

   - Writes rules, supervises companies, and enforces financial protection laws,
   - Restricts unfair, deceptive, or abusive acts or practices in regard to consumer financial transactions,
   - Takes consumer complaints,
   - Promotes financial education,
   - Researches consumer behavior,
   - Monitors financial markets for new risks to consumers,
   - Enforces prohibitions against discrimination and other unfair treatment in consumer finance.[26]

   The CFPA has been subject to bitter political attack by those who consider it an example of a "runaway agency" and who want to curtail its actions. "Wall Street," said Sen. Dick Durbin (D-Ill) hates the CFPB "like the devil hates holy water."[27][28] One commentator observed that many of the businesses whose activities have been brought up short by the CFPA "have their talons deeply into the torsos of our elected representatives in Congress, so it's unsurprising that they would grouse about the agency's activities."[29]

5. **Joint Federal Agency Regulation**. The FTC, the Consumer Finance Protection Bureau, the Justice Department (among others), variously enforce federal laws, including:

   - The Equal Credit Opportunity Act: forbids most discrimination in granting credit;[30]
   - The Fair Credit Reporting Act: protects consumers from the willful and/or negligent inclusion of inaccurate information in their credit reports; regulates the collection, dissemination, and use of consumer information, including consumer credit information;
   - The Fair and Accurate Credit Transaction Act: amends the FCRA; adds provisions to improve the accuracy of consumers' credit records; consumers get one free credit report a year; has provisions to prevent and mitigate identity theft.[31]
   - The Truth in Lending Act: lenders must express the cost of consumer credit as an Annual Percentage Rate instead of as self-defined "interest," and requires a three-day cooling-off

period to allow borrows to reconsider if they want their home to stand as security for a loan;[32]

- **The Fair Credit Billing Act:** provides a mechanism for debtors of open-end credit accounts (credit cards, mostly) to challenge and get corrected incorrect credit bills.[33] (Before the act people whose bills were wrong basically argued fruitlessly and indefinitely with a computer.)

- **The Fair Debt Collection Practices Act**: adopted in 1977, regulates the most egregiously abusive debt-collection practices by debt-collection businesses (not private persons who want to collect their own debt.[34]

- The **Magnuson-Moss Act**, 1975: abolished "phantom warranties" in contracts for the sale of goods. A **phantom warranty** typically disclaimed all implied warranties but provided a superficially attractive express warranty: "Your new piano is fully warranted for three years!" And then adds, in small print on the back, "For warranty service, ship your piano to our factory, at your expense . . . ." Of course, that's highly deceptive and is no kind of warranty at all. Under the act, if a warranty is given (no seller is compelled to give one), it must be in writing; it must disclose, fully and conspicuously the terms of the warranty as required by rules of the Federal Trade Commission. In short, meaningless and unreasonable express warranties are invalid, and violation of the rules gives rise to (surprisingly) effective remedies. Here you can read the FTC's "Understanding the Magnuson-Moss" Act: https://www.ftc.gov/tips-advice/business-center/guidance/businesspersons-guide-federal-warranty-law#Magnuson-Moss.

6. **The United States Postal Service** maintains a robust anti-fraud division. Mail fraud is defined by the Post Office as "a scheme to get money or something of value from you by offering a product, service, or investment opportunity that does not live up to its claims. Prosecutors must prove the claims were intentionally misrepresented and that the mail was used to carry out the scheme." Noted by the agency are "free" vacations, government look-alike mail, chain letters, solicitations disguised as invoices, work-at-home offers, and many others. Check it out: http://about.usps.com/publications/pub300a/pub300a_tech_toc.htm.

State Consumer Protection

Little FTC Acts

Even when consumers have no direct remedy under federal law for unfair or deceptive acts and practices, they may have recourse under state laws modeled on the FTC Act, known as little FTC acts. All states have some sort of consumer protection acts, and these acts are often more generous to consumers than the federal unfair trade rules; they permit consumers—and in several states, even aggrieved businesses—to sue when injured by any one of a host of "immoral, unethical, oppressive, or unscrupulous" commercial acts. Often, a successful plaintiff can recover treble damages and attorneys' fees.

The acts are helpful to consumers because common-law fraud is difficult to prove. Common-law fraud elements are rigorous and unyielding: an intentional misrepresentation of material facts, reliance by the recipient, causation, and damages. Many of these elements are omitted from consumer fraud statutes. While most statutes require some aspect of willfulness, some do not. In fact, many states relax or even eliminate the element of reliance, and some states do not even require a showing of causation or injury.

Lemon Laws

Every U.S. state has adopted a "**lemon law**" to help new vehicle owners (and some states extend limited protection to used-vehicle owners) who have substantial continuing problems with warranty repairs on cars, light trucks, and motor homes. Some laws allow owners to submit their dispute to an arbitrator, who may provide appropriate remedies, including that the seller buy back the vehicle.[35]

Nongovernmental Organizations

Businesses recognize that consumers want and will pay for reliable consumer information; businesses also realize that their firms' reputations—and indeed, confidence in capitalism—depends on consumer confidence. Accordingly, there are a large number of nongovernmental organizations (NGOs) involved in testing and reporting on goods and services sold in the U.S. and in countries around the world.

TABLE 14.1 U.S. NGOs

Organization	URL	Focus
Alliance for Justice	https://www.afj.org/	Progressive NGOs monitor federal judiciary appointments
Better Business Bureau	https://www.bbb.org/	NGO to enhance marketplace trust.
Consumer Action	http://www.consumer-action.org/	Empowers underrepresented consumers nationwide to assert their rights in the marketplace and financially prosper.
Consumer Federation of California	https://consumercal.org/	Monitors consumer interest through research, advocacy, and education.
Consumers Union/ Consumer Reports Advocacy	https://advocacy.consumerreports.org/	Tests products and engages in investigative journalism and consumer advocacy.
Consumer Watchdog	https://www.consumerwatchdog.org/	NGO with taxpayer and consumer interests, focus on insurance, health care, political reform, privacy, and energy.
FlyersRights.org	https://flyersrights.org/	NGO to supports legislation protecting the rights and comfort of airline passengers.
Public Citizen	https://www.citizen.org/	Progressive consumer-rights NGO favoring corporate accountability.
Consumer Federation of America	https://consumerfed.org/	Promotes consumer interests through research, education and advocacy.
Center for Science in the Public Interest	https://cspinet.org/	Watchdog and consumer group for safer and healthier foods.
National Consumers League	https://www.nclnet.org/	Provides government and business with the consumer's perspective on privacy, child labor, medication information.
U.S. Public Interest Research Group	https://uspirg.org/sites/pirg/files/cpn/USN-121418-A1/index3.html	Federation of NGOs engaging grassroots organizing to effect liberal political change.

Less reliable, but interesting, are online reviews of goods and services posted by consumers.

Case

False and Misleading Representations

J.B. Williams Co. v. FTC
381 F.2d 884 (6th Cir., 1967)

J.B. Williams Co. v. FTC

6th Federal Circuit Court case analyzing the authority of the FTC to regulate television advertising.

Celebrezze, J.

The question presented by this appeal is whether Petitioners' advertising of a product, Geritol, for the relief of iron deficiency anemia, is false and misleading so as to violate Sections 5 and 12 of the Federal Trade Commission Act.

The J. B. Williams Company, Inc. is a New York corporation engaged in the sale and distribution of two products known as Geritol liquid and Geritol tablets. Geritol liquid was first marketed in August, 1950; Geritol tablets in February, 1952. Geritol is sold throughout the United States and advertisements for Geritol have appeared in newspapers and on television in all the States of the United States.

Parkson Advertising Agency, Inc. has been the advertising agency for Williams since 1957. Most of the advertising money for Geritol is spent on television advertising. * * *

The Commission's Order requires that not only must the Geritol advertisements be expressly limited to those persons whose symptoms are due to an existing deficiency of one or more of the vitamins contained in the preparation, or due to an existing deficiency of iron, but also the Geritol advertisements must affirmatively disclose the negative fact that a great majority of persons who experience these symptoms do not experience them because they have a vitamin or iron deficiency; that for the great majority of people experiencing these symptoms, Geritol will be of no benefit. Closely related to this requirement is the further requirement of the Order that the Geritol advertisements refrain from representing that the symptoms are generally reliable indications of iron deficiency. * * *

The main thrust of the Commission's Order is that the Geritol advertising must affirmatively disclose the negative fact that a great majority of persons who experience these symptoms do not experience them because there is a vitamin or iron deficiency. * * *

While the advertising does not make the affirmative representation that the majority of people who are tired and rundown are so because of iron deficiency anemia and the product Geritol will be an effective cure, there is substantial evidence to support the finding of the Commission that most tired people are not so because of iron deficiency anemia, and the failure to disclose this fact is false and misleading because the advertisement creates the impression that the tired feeling is caused by something which Geritol can cure.

Here the advertisements emphasize the fact that if you are often tired and run-down you will feel stronger fast by taking Geritol. The Commission, in looking at the overall impression created by the advertisements on the general public, could reasonably find these advertisements were false and misleading. The finding that the advertisements link common, non-specific symptoms with iron deficiency anemia, and thereby create a false impression because most people with these symptoms are not suffering from iron deficiency anemia, is both reasonable and supported by substantial evidence. The Commission is not bound to the literal meaning of the words, nor must the Commission take a random sample to determine the meaning and impact of the advertisements.

Petitioners argue vigorously that the Commission does not have the legal power to require them to state the negative fact that "in the great majority of persons who experience such symptoms, these symptoms are not caused by a deficiency of one or more of the vitamins contained in the preparation or by iron deficiency or iron deficiency anemia"; and "for such persons the preparation will be of no benefit."

We believe the evidence is clear that Geritol is of no benefit in the treatment of tiredness except in those cases where tiredness has been caused by a deficiency of the ingredients contained in Geritol. The fact that the great majority of people who experience tiredness symptoms do not suffer from any deficiency of the ingredients in Geritol is a "material fact" under the meaning of that term as used in Section 15 of the Federal Trade Commission Act and Petitioners' failure to reveal this fact in this day when the consumer is influenced by mass advertising utilizing highly developed arts of persuasion, renders it difficult for the typical consumer to know whether the product will in fact meet his needs unless he is told what the product will or will not do. * * *

The Commission forbids the Petitioners' representation that the presence of iron deficiency anemia can be self-diagnosed or can be determined without a medical test. The danger to be remedied here has been fully and adequately taken care of in the other requirements of the Order. We can find no Congressional policy against self-medication on a trial and error basis where the consumer is fully informed and the product is safe as Geritol is conceded to be. In fact, Congressional policy is to encourage such self-help. In effect the Commission's Order 1(f) tends to place Geritol in the prescription drug field. We do not consider it within the power of the Federal Trade Commission to remove Geritol from the area of proprietary drugs and place it in the area of prescription drugs. This requirement of the Order will not be enforced. We also find this Order is not unduly vague and fairly apprises the Petitioners of what is required of them.

Petition denied and, except for 1(f) of the Commission's Order, enforcement of the Order will be granted.

 Geritol: "Keep Women in Line," 1960 Ad

View the video online at: http://www.youtube.com/embed/pni9ZePXR-w?rel=0

Case Questions

1. Did the defendant actually make statements that were false? If so, what were they? Or, rather than being clearly false, were the statements deceptive? If so, how so?

2. Whether or not you feel that you have "tired blood" or "iron-poor blood," you may be amused by a Geritol ad from 1960 (See video). Do the disclaimers at the start of the ad that "the majority of tired people don't feel that way because of iron-poor blood" sound like corrective advertising? Is the ad still deceptive in some way? If so, how? If not, why not?

Key Takeaway

In a modern market economy consumers are not readily able to protect themselves against businesses' anticompetitive collusion, monopolization, or unfair and deceptive trade and sales practices. Beginning in the late 19th century, Congress has enacted a number of laws to regulate the interstate market and curb its abusive tendencies. These include the Sherman and Clayton Acts (prohibiting unreasonable restraints of trade), and the Federal Trade Commission Act (prohibiting restraints of trade and unfair or deceptive sales practices); these laws address horizontal and vertical restraints of trade affecting interstate commerce. States have "little FTC" acts that address anticompetitive or unfair practices intrastate, and "Lemon Laws" that address, mostly, unfair sales practices related to automobile sales.

Exercises

1. To protect its state's businesses against ruinous price wars, the state of Calhio passed a law permitting manufacturers to set a "suggested resale price" on all goods that they make and sell direct to retailers. Retailers are forbidden to undercut the resale price by more than 10 percent. A retailer who violates the law may be sued by the manufacturer for treble damages: three times the difference between the suggested resale price and the actual selling price. But out-of-state retailers are bound by no such law and are regularly discounting the goods between 35 and 40 percent. As the general manager of a large discount store located within a few miles of a city across the state line, you wish to offer the public a price of only 60 percent of the suggested retail price on items covered by the law in order to compete with the out-of-state retailers to which your customers have easy access. May you lower your price in order to compete? How would you defend yourself if sued by a manufacturer whose goods you discounted in violation of the law?

2. Elmer has invented a new battery-operated car. The battery, which Elmer has patented, functions for five hundred miles before needing to be recharged. The car, which he has named The Elmer, is a sensation when announced, and his factory can barely keep up with the orders. Worried about the impact, all the other car manufacturers ask Elmer for a license to use the battery in their cars. Elmer refuses because he wants the car market all to himself. Banks are eager to lend him the money to expand his production, and within three years he has gained a 5 percent share of the national market for automobiles. During these years, Elmer has kept the price of The Elmer high, to pay for his large costs in tooling up a factory. But then it dawns on him that he can expand his market much more rapidly if he drops his price, so he prices the car to yield the smallest profit margin of any car being sold in the country. Its retail price is far lower than that of any other domestic car on the market. Business begins to boom. Within three more years, he has garnered an additional 30 percent of the market, and he announces at a press conference that he confidently expects to have the market "all to myself" within the next five years. Fighting for their lives now, the Big Three auto manufacturers consult their lawyers about suing Elmer for monopolizing. Do they have a case? What is Elmer's defense?

3. Why are on-line consumer reviews of goods and services not very reliable—not a good source for consumer education?

14.4 Regulation of the Business-to-Customer Relationship: Products Liability

You should understand the following after studying this section:

1. Why products-liability law underwent a revolution in the twentieth century.
2. The modern causes of action for products-liability claims and their limitations.
3. Why products-liability reform is a contentious legal and political issue.

Introduction to and History of Products Liability

In the previous section we examined some aspects of consumer protection. That involves—for the most part—government-mandated disclosures, regulations regarding advertising, and standards for safe products. Here, we focus specifically on remedies available when a defective product causes personal injury or other damages to its user. Products liability describes a type of claim, not a separate theory of liability.

caveat emptor

The theory that the buyer alone is responsible for checking the quality and suitability of goods before a purchase is made.

The theory of **caveat emptor**—let the buyer beware—that pretty much governed consumer law from the earliest days until the early twentieth century made some sense. A horse-drawn buggy is a fairly simple device and its workings are apparent—a person of average experience in the 1870s could know whether it was constructed well and made of the proper woods. Most foodstuffs 150 years ago were grown at home and "put up" in the home kitchen or bought in bulk from a local grocer, subject to direct inspection and sampling; people made home remedies for coughs and colds and often made many of their own clothes. Houses and furnishings were built of wood, stone, glass, and plaster—familiar substances. Everyday entertainment was storytelling, a book, magazines, or a piano. The state of technology was such that the things consumed were, for the most part, comprehensible and—very important—mostly locally made, which meant that the consumer who suffered damages from a defective product could confront the product's maker directly. Local reputation is a powerful influence on behavior.

Today's products and foodstuffs are—thanks to government regulation—much safer and more wholesome than those marketed 120 years ago, when commercially-produced food was not infrequently adulterated, boilers exploded, appliances mangled and killed. But one does not have to look very far to find terrible problems today. The news carries stories about Toyota Avalon automobiles with defective steering; tens of thousands of people every year suffer injury from contact lenses; mini-blind cords choke children; bureaus—furniture in bedrooms—fall over on babies; and portable baby recliners kill them. Table saws cut off 4,000 fingers a year.[36] How does a customer who finds a decomposing mouse in her beer bottle, or his thumb on the shop floor, get any remedy over a distant manufacturer-seller? The three current product-liability theories are taken up next.

The Products-Liability Causes of Action

There are three main products-liability theories or causes of action: (1) breach of warranty, (2) negligence, and (3) strict product liability.

Breach of Warranty

Breach of warranty is a contract issue (it "sounds" in contract). What's the difference, then, between breach of contract for the sale of goods, and breach of product warranty involving goods? Here it is: If the plaintiff/buyer accepts an offer to buy goods—say a carjack—and (1) it does not arrive, or (2) it arrives but is obviously not right and so it is rejected, or (3) it is accepted (legally speaking) and then found not as represented and acceptance is revoked, the plaintiff has a cause of action for breach of contract. A buyer's claim for breach of warranty, though, only arises after the buyer has finally accepted the goods and suffers damages using them (sometimes non-buyers can claim breach of warranty, too, as we see below). A warranty is a promise or guarantee of quality or performance. Article 2 of the U.C.C. governs warranties for the sale of goods (2-312 through 2-318).

Types of Warranties

There are two types of warranties: express and implied.

- **Express warranties** are "any affirmation of fact or promise made by the seller to the buyer which relates to the goods and becomes part of the basis of the bargain."[37] Samples or models create express warranties, too.
- Implied warranties come along without any expression—automatically (unless disclaimed). There are three types of implied warranties:
  - **Implied warranty of merchantability**: made only by a merchant, the merchant warrants that the goods are suitable for the purpose for which such goods are used, are adequately packaged, and properly labeled. Foodstuffs must meet the consumer's reasonable expectation as to quality (2-314).
  - **Implied warranty of fitness for a particular purpose**: made by any seller who knows or has reason to know that the buyer is relying on the seller's skill or judgment to select a product that is suitable for the particular purpose the buyer has in mind (2-315). For example, you explain to the seller that you want a sleeping bag for a climbing expedition in the Rocky Mountains; you buy the sleeping bag the seller suggests, but it will not keep you warm at below-freezing temperatures. This is a breach of the implied warranty of fitness for a particular purpose. It's fine as a generic sleeping bag (no breach of merchantability, if the seller were a merchant) but not fine for the purpose on point.
  - **Implied warranty of title**: made by any seller, that the seller is conveying good title, that the goods are not stolen or subject to any creditors' claims (2-312).

Problems with Warranty Theory

Warranty theory is—as noted above—based on *contract*. The theory presents several difficulties for the claimant (plaintiff) who has suffered damages; we call out three:

Express warranties

Any manifestation of the nature or quality of goods that becomes a basis of the bargain.

Implied warranty of merchantability

Merchant-seller's implied warranty that goods are suitable for the goods' normal uses.

Implied warranty of fitness for a particular purpose.

A seller's implied warranty that the goods will be suitable for the buyer's expressed need.

Implied warranty of title

A seller's implied warranty that the seller is conveying good title to the buyer.

privity of contract

The common-law doctrine that a contract cannot confer rights or impose obligations upon any person who is not a party to the contract.

Vertical privity

Refers to the legal relationship that exists between parties in a product's chain of distribution.

Horizontal privity

Determines to whose benefit the warranty "flows"—who can sue for its breach.

- Privity. Generally speaking, you can't sue somebody for breach of contract unless you made a contract with that person. This is called privity of contract—the face-to-face relationship between contracting parties. There are two types of **privity**.

  - **Vertical privity** refers to remote sellers within the chain of distribution with whom the purchaser has no contract: manufacturers and wholesalers (the purchaser has a contract with the retail seller). Vertical privity is pretty much a dead duck in warranty actions.

  - **Horizontal privity** refers to non-contracting parties who suffer damages by defective goods. You take foodstuffs to a potluck not at your house; the guests did not buy the food, but they may have a cause of action for breach of warranty without concern about lack of privity. Horizontal privity has effectively been eliminated in warranty actions (but sometimes the issue still bites).

- Exclusion or disclaimer of warranties. Parties are generally free to enter into such contracts as they see fit, so the UCC permits sellers to exclude or disclaim warranties if they want. If a seller doesn't want to give an *express warranty*, she should just not do it. But sometimes sellers want to "front" an attractive warranty in bold print, and then limit it to mere vapor in the fine print (a "phantom warranty"). As we noted in Section 14.3, the federal Magnuson-Moss Warranty Act of 1975 limits such deceptive warranty practices for consumer purchases by dictating that express warranties meet certain minimum standards. As to *implied* warranties, they can be limited or excluded if the limitation or exclusion is clear and conspicuous; most often all implied warranties are excluded by language such as "as is."

- Contributory and comparative negligence, and assumption of the risk. Although warranty is contract talk, the defendant may still raise the tort-like defenses that the plaintiff herself contributed to her losses by her own carelessness, or that she recognized the danger but assumed the risk. Obviously if a sky diver buys a parachute and then discovers a few holes in it, his family would not likely prevail in court when they sued to recover for his death because the parachute failed to function after he jumped at 5,000 feet. He assumed the risk.

Negligence

Negligence is a second theory raised in the typical products-liability case. It is a tort theory (as compared to breach of warranty, a contract theory), and it does have this advantage over warranty theory—privity is never relevant. A pedestrian is struck in an intersection by a car whose brakes were defectively manufactured. Under no circumstances would breach of warranty be a useful cause of action for the pedestrian—there is no privity at all. Negligence is considered in detail in Chapter 7, "Introduction to Tort Law"; it basically means lack of due care.

Typical Product-Liability Negligence Claims

There are three typical product-liability negligence claims:

- Negligent design. The question is whether the designer used reasonable care in designing a product reasonably safe for its foreseeable use. The concern over reasonableness and standards of care are elements of negligence theory. Defective-design cases can pose severe problems for manufacturing and safety engineers. More safety means more cost. Designs altered to improve safety may impair functionality and make the product less desirable to consumers.

- Negligent manufacturing. The design was okay, but quality control in manufacturing was inadequate; the steel belts on the tire were not fused to the tire rubber with enough heat to make them stick.

- Negligence labeling. Whether a warning should have been affixed is often a question of what is reasonably foreseeable, and the failure to affix a warning will be treated as negligence. The manufacturer of a weed killer with poisonous ingredients is certainly acting negligently when it fails to warn the consumer that the contents are potentially lethal. See the *Laaperi* case (below) for an analysis of negligence labeling.

Problems with Negligence

Negligence is a familiar concept in law, and as was discussed in the torts chapter, it carries with it some well-developed defenses. Here we may call out two: (1) common-law defenses, and (2) preemption.

Common-Law Defenses against Claims of Negligence

Among the problems confronting a plaintiff with a claim of negligence in products-liability suits (again, these concepts are discussed in the torts chapter) are the following:

- Proving negligence at all—just because a product is defective does not necessarily prove the manufacturer breached a duty of care.
- Proximate cause—even if there was some negligence, the plaintiff must prove her damages flowed proximately from that negligence.
- Contributory and comparative negligence—the plaintiff's own actions contributed to the damages, including misuse or abuse of the product (using a lawnmower to trim a hedge), and assumption of the risk (using a dust-producing woodworking tool without proper face-mask protection).
- Subsequent alteration of the product—generally the manufacturer will not be liable if the product has been changed.

Preemption

Here's the problem of **preemption** (or "pre-emption"): suppose there is a federal standard concerning the product, and the defendant manufacturer meets it, but the standard is not really very protective. (It is not uncommon, of course, for federal standard makers of all types to be significantly influenced by lobbyists for the industries being regulated by the standards.) "We built the machine to federal standards; we can't be liable. Our compliance with the federal safety standard is an affirmative defense." Preemption is typically raised as a defense in suits about (1) cigarettes, (2) FDA-approved medical devices, (3) motor-boat propellers, (4) pesticides, and (5) motor vehicles. This is a complex area of law. Sometimes courts find preemption and the consumer loses; sometimes the courts don't find preemption and the case goes forward. According to one lawyer who works in this field, there has been "increasing pressure on both the regulatory and congressional fronts to preempt state laws."[38] That is, the usual defendants (manufacturers) push Congress and the regulatory agencies to state explicitly in the law that the federal standards preempt and defeat state law.

> **preemption**
>
> he theory that a federal law supersedes any inconsistent state law or regulation.

Strict Product Liability in Tort

Why the Doctrine of Strict Product Liability Has Been Developed

We have observed that breach of warranty and negligence both have shortcomings for product-liability claimants. To overcome the obstacles, judges have gone beyond the commercial statutes (UCC) and the ancient concepts of negligence, and have fashioned a common-law tort theory of *strict* products liability. If a person suffers harm using a product that was, in retrospect, dangerously defective, *someone* has to pay the damages. It should be the seller under this theory, the seller because can buy liability insurance to protect itself, and charge the cost of the insurance off as a cost of business—factor it into the price of the product.

The Essential Elements of Strict Product Liablity

The formulation most courts use is abstracted (summarized) in Section 402A of the Restatement of Torts (Second):

(1) One who sells any product in a defective condition unreasonably dangerous to the user or consumer or to his property is subject to liability for physical harm thereby caused to the ultimate user or consumer, or to his property, if

> *(a) the seller is engaged in the business of selling such a product, and*

> *(b) it is expected to and does reach the user or consumer without substantial change in the condition in which it is sold.*

(2) This rule applies even though

> *(a) the seller has exercised all possible care in the preparation and sale of his product, and*

> *(b) the user or consumer has not bought the product from or entered into any contractual relation with the seller.*

Section 402A of the Restatement avoids some UCC Article 2 warranty booby traps. Limitations and exclusions in warranties will not apply to a suit based on strict liability (because warranty is not in issue). Privity is not a requirement; the language of the Restatement says it applies to "the user or consumer," but courts have found that bystanders in various situations are entitled to bring actions under the section (see *Embs v. Pepsi-Cola*, below). The damages, though, are limited to physical harm and property loss. Many courts have held that a person who suffers *economic* loss (lost income from suffering an injury, for example) must resort to warranty law.

The offending product must be somehow defective, and because of the defect, not merely dangerous, but unreasonably so. The seller is not necessarily a "merchant"—the movie theater that sells popcorn isn't a "merchant" in popcorn, but if the popcorn contains a nail, the theater may be liable as a seller.

The crux of strict product liability is that the seller is liable even though "the seller has exercised all possible care in the preparation and sale of the product." It does not matter how reasonably the seller acted or how exemplary is a manufacturer's quality control system—what matters is whether the product was defective and the user injured as a result. Suppose an automated bottle factory manufactures 1,000 bottles per hour under exacting standards, with a rigorous and costly quality-control program designed to weed out any bottles showing even an infinitesimal amount of stress. The plant is "state of the art," and its computerized quality-control operation is the best in the world. It regularly detects the one out of every 10,000 bottles that analysis has shown will be defective. Despite this intense effort, it proves impossible to weed out every defective bottle; one out of one million, say, will still escape detection. Assume that a bottle, filled with soda, finds its way into a consumer's home, explodes when handled, sends glass shards into his eye, and blinds him. Under negligence, the bottler has no liability; under strict liability, the bottler will be liable to the consumer.

Problems with Strict Product Liability

Notwithstanding that strict liability eschews many of the problems with warranty and negligence, the claimant here still faces some difficulties.

- Disclaimers are not allowed in consumer cases, but "strict liability" notwithstanding, they have been allowed in some non-consumer cases involving "sophisticated" commercial business enterprises.

- Assumption of the risk, abuse, or misuse of the product is a defense.

- Lack of proximate cause (as in standard tort law).

- Limited remedy: the Restatement says recovery under strict liability is limited to "physical harm thereby caused to the ultimate user or consumer, or to his property," but not other losses, and not economic losses (such as loss of income from time off work because of an injury).

Product-Liability Reform

With the development of product-liability law since the early 20th century, there naturally has arisen an increase in product-liability cases and damages awards, much to the distaste of the usual defendants—especially big manufacturers. They claim that the law heaps costs upon them and puts U.S. companies at a competitive disadvantage in international business. Business and professional groups beat the drums for tort reform as a means to guarantee "fairness" in the courts, as well as spur U.S. economic competitiveness in a global marketplace, while plaintiffs' attorneys and consumer advocates claim that businesses simply want to externalize costs by denying recovery to the consumer-victims of greed and carelessness.

Each side vilifies the other in very unseemly language—pro-business advocates (the usual defendants) call consumer-oriented states "judicial hell-holes" and complain of "well-orchestrated campaigns by [plaintiffs'] tort-lawyer lobbyists and allies to undo years of tort reform at the state level,"[39] while pro-plaintiff interests claim that there is "scant evidence" of any tort-law abuse.[40] It would be more amusing if it were not so shrill and partisan. Perhaps the most one can say with any certainty is that peoples' perceptions of reality are highly colored by their self-interests. In any event, there have been reforms (or, as the detractors say, "deforms").

- Statutes of repose: These statutes establish a time period, usually from six to twelve years from the product's manufacture, after which the manufacturer is not liable for damages.

- State-of-the-art defense: A manufacturer is not liable if the product was "state of the art" when it was manufactured, notwithstanding later technological improvements that could have improved it.

- Comparative fault: In states that have enacted so-called comparative fault statutes, the plaintiff's damages are pegged to the percentage of responsibility for the injury that the plaintiff is found to have borne.

- Federal reform: As noted in the section on consumer protection, the federal Consumer Product Safety Act (1972) has encouraged manufacturers to adopt safer product standards by regulation. It should be noted that manufacturers' lobbyists are not unknown to influence these standards. The Consumer Product Safety Council (responsible for the regulations) is castigated by manufactures as being too aggressive, and by consumer advocates for being woefully timid.

Cases

Strict Liability and Bystanders

Embs v. Pepsi-Cola Bottling Co. of Lexington

528 S.W. 2d 703 (Ky, 1975)

Embs v. Pepsi-Cola Bottling Co. of Lexington

Kentucky Supreme Court case, 1975, analyzing application of strict product liability.

Jukowsky, J.

On the afternoon of July 25, 1970 plaintiff-appellant entered the self-service retail store operated by the defendant-appellee, Stamper's Cash Market, Inc., for the purpose of "buying soft drinks for the kids." She went to an upright soft drink cooler, removed five bottles and placed them in a carton. Unnoticed by her, a carton of Seven-Up was sitting on the floor at the edge of the produce counter about one foot from where she was standing. As she turned away from the cooler she heard an explosion that sounded "like a shotgun." When she looked down she saw a gash in her leg, pop on her leg, green pieces of a bottle on the floor and the Seven-Up carton in the midst of the debris. She did not kick or otherwise come into contact with the carton of Seven-Up prior to the explosion. Her son, who was with her, recognized the green pieces of glass as part of a Seven-Up bottle.

She was immediately taken to the hospital by Mrs. Stamper, a managing agent of the store. Mrs. Stamper told her that a Seven-Up bottle had exploded and that several bottles had exploded that week. Before leaving the store Mrs. Stamper instructed one of her children to clean up the mess. Apparently, all of the physical evidence went out with the trash. The location of the Seven-Up carton immediately before the explosion was not a place where such items were ordinarily kept. * * *

When she rested her case, the defendants-appellees moved for a directed verdict in their favor. The trial court granted the motion on the grounds that the doctrine of strict product liability in tort does not extend beyond users and consumers and that the evidence was insufficient to permit an inference by a reasonably prudent man that the bottle was defective or if it was, when it became so.

In [Citation] we adopted the view of strict product liability in tort expressed in Section 402 A of the American Law Institute's Restatement of Torts 2d.

[The court sets out Section 402A of the Restatement, Second, of Torts, as presented in the text above "One who sells any product in a defective condition". . . , etc.]

Comment f on that section makes it abundantly clear that this rule applies to any person engaged in the business of supplying products for use or consumption, including any manufacturer of such a product and any wholesale or retail dealer or distributor.

Comment c points out that on whatever theory, the justification for the rule has been said to be that the seller, by marketing his product for use and consumption, has undertaken and assumed a special responsibility toward any member of the consuming public who may be injured by it; that the public has the right to, and does expect, that reputable sellers will stand behind their goods; that public policy demands that the burden of accidental injuries caused by products intended for consumption be placed upon those who market them, and be treated as a cost of production against which liability insurance can be obtained; and that the consumer of such products is entitled to the maximum of protection at the hands of someone, and the proper persons to afford it are those who market the products.

The caveat to the section provides that the Institute expresses no opinion as to whether the rule may not apply to harm to persons other than users or consumers. Comment on caveat o states the Institute expresses neither approval nor disapproval of expansion of the rule to permit recovery by casual bystanders and others who may come in contact with the product, and admits there may be no essential reason why such plaintiffs should not be brought within the scope of protection afforded, other than they do not have the same reasons for expecting such protection as the consumer who buys a marketed product, and that the social pressure which has been largely responsible for the development of the rule has been a consumer's pressure, and there is not the same demand for the protection of casual strangers. * * *

The caveat articulates the essential point: Once strict liability is accepted, bystander recovery is fait accompli.

Our expressed public policy will be furthered if we minimize the risk of personal injury and property damage by charging the costs of injuries against the manufacturer who can procure liability insurance and distribute its expense among the public as a cost of doing business; and since the risk of harm from defective products exists for mere bystanders and passersby as well as for the purchaser or user, there is no substantial reason for protecting one class of persons and not the other. The same policy requires us to maximize protection for the injured third party and promote the public interest in discouraging the marketing of products having defects that are a menace to the public by imposing strict liability upon retailers and wholesalers in the distributive chain responsible for marketing the defective product which injures the bystander. The imposition of strict liability places no unreasonable burden upon sellers because they can adjust the cost of insurance protection among themselves in the course of their continuing business relationship.

We must not shirk from extending the rule to the manufacturer for fear that the retailer or middleman will be impaled on the sword of liability without regard to fault. Their liability was already established under Section 402A of the Restatement of Torts 2d. As a matter of public policy the retailer or middleman as well as the manufacturer should be liable since the loss for injuries resulting from defective products should be placed on those members of the marketing chain best able to pay the loss, who can then distribute such risk among themselves by means of insurance and indemnity agreements. [Citation] * * *

The result which we reach does not give the bystander a "free ride." When products and consumers are considered in the aggregate, bystanders, as a class, purchase most of the same products to which they are exposed as bystanders. Thus, as a class, they indirectly subsidize the liability of the manufacturer, middleman, and retailer, and in this sense do pay for the insurance policy tied to the product. * * *

For the sake of clarity we restate the extension of the rule. The protections of Section 402A of the Restatement of Torts 2d extend to bystanders whose injury from the defective product is reasonably foreseeable. * * * The judgment is reversed and the cause is remanded to the Clark Circuit Court for further proceedings consistent herewith.

Case Questions

- Why didn't the plaintiff here use breach of warranty as a theory of recovery?
- Among the entities in the vertical distribution chain—manufacturer, wholesaler, retailer—who is liable under this doctrine?
- The court offers a rationale for the doctrine of strict products liability. What is it?
- Restatement, Section 402A, by its terms extends protection "to the ultimate user or consumer," but Mrs. Embs (plaintiff-appellant) was not a "user or consumer," she was a passer-by. What rationale did the court give for expanding the protection here?
- What is the controlling rule of law developed in this case?

Failure to Warn

Laaperi v. Sears Roebuck, Inc.

787 F.2d 726 (1st Cir. Fed. Ct. App., Mass 1986)

Campbell, J.

In March 1976, plaintiff Albin Laaperi purchased a smoke detector from Sears. The detector, manufactured by the Pittway Corporation, was designed to be powered by AC (electrical) current. Laaperi installed the detector himself in one of the two upstairs bedrooms in his home. Early in the morning of December 27, 1976, a fire broke out in the Laaperi home. The three boys in one of the upstairs bedrooms were killed in the blaze. Laaperi's 13-year-old daughter Janet, who was sleeping in the other upstairs bedroom, received burns over 12 percent of her body and was hospitalized for three weeks.

The uncontroverted testimony at trial was that the smoke detector did not sound an alarm on the night of the fire. The cause of the fire was later found to be a short circuit in an electrical cord that was located in a cedar closet in the boys' bedroom. The Laaperi home had two separate electrical circuits in the upstairs bedrooms: one which provided electricity to the outlets and one which powered the lighting fixtures. The smoke detector had been connected to the outlet circuit, which was the circuit that shorted and cut off. Because the circuit was shorted, the AC-operated smoke detector received no power on the night of the fire. Therefore, although the detector itself was in no sense defective (indeed, after the fire the charred detector was tested and found to be operable), no alarm sounded.

Laaperi brought this diversity action against defendants Sears and Pittway [manufacturer of the smoke detector], asserting negligent design, negligent manufacture, breach of warranty, and negligent failure to warn of inherent dangers. The parties agreed that the applicable law is that of Massachusetts. Before the claims went to the jury, verdicts were directed in favor of defendants on all theories of liability other than failure to warn. * * *

Laaperi's claim under the failure to warn theory was that he was unaware of the danger that the very short circuit which might ignite a fire in his home could, at the same time, incapacitate the smoke detector. He contended that had he been warned of this danger, he would have purchased a battery-powered smoke detector as a back-up or taken some other precaution, such as wiring the detector to a circuit of its own, in order to better protect his family in the event of an electrical fire.

The jury returned verdicts in favor of Laaperi in all four actions on the failure to warn claim. The jury assessed damages in the amount of $350,000 [$1.7 million in 2019 dollars] for each of the three actions brought on behalf of the deceased sons [about, or about $4.7 million, total, in 2019 dollars], and $750,000 [about $3.2 million in 2019 dollars] in the action brought on behalf of Janet Laaperi. The defendants' motions for directed verdict and judgment notwithstanding the verdict were denied, and defendants appealed.

Defendants ask us to declare that the risk that an electrical fire could incapacitate an AC-powered smoke detector is so obvious that the average consumer would not benefit from a warning. This is not a trivial argument; in earlier—some might say sounder—days, we might have accepted it. * * * Our sense of the current state of the tort law in Massachusetts and most other jurisdictions, however, leads us to conclude that, today, the matter before us poses a jury question; that "obviousness" in a situation such as this would be treated by the Massachusetts courts as presenting a question of fact, not of law. To be sure, it would be obvious to anyone that an electrical outage would cause this smoke detector to fail. But the average purchaser might not comprehend the specific danger that a fire-causing electrical problem can simultaneously knock out the circuit into which a smoke detector is wired, causing the detector to fail at the very moment it is needed. Thus, while the failure of a detector to function as the result of an electrical malfunction due, say, to a broken power line or a neighborhood power outage would, we think, be obvious as a matter of law, the failure that occurred here, being associated with the very risk—fire—for which the device was purchased, was not, or so a jury could find. * * *

[The court determined that the compensation for Janet Laaperi was excessive—she suffered "relatively minor injuries, involving no continuing disability."]

The judgments in favor of Albin Laaperi in his capacity as administrator of the estates of his three sons are affirmed. In the action on behalf of Janet Laaperi, the verdict of the jury is set aside, the judgment of the district court vacated, and the cause remanded to that court for a new trial limited to the issue of damages.

Exercises

1. Why is this case in federal court? (There is no federal question).

2. Why does the court discuss its "sense of the current state of the tort law in Massachusetts" and how this case "would be treated by the Massachusetts courts," as if it were not in the state at all but, somehow outside?

3. What rule of law in play here as to the defendants' liability?

4. This is a horrific situation—three boys died in a house fire. Speaking dispassionately—if not heartlessly—though, did the fire actually cost Mr. Laaperi $1.6 million (in 2019 dollars)? Does it make sense that he should become a millionaire as a result? Who ends up paying this amount? (The lawyers' fees probably took about half.)

5. Is it likely that smoke-alarm manufacturers and sellers changed their installation instructions as a result of this case?

Key Takeaway

Product liability law developed extensively in the 20th century as a result of: (1) the separation of consumption from production, and (2) because of the increasing complexity and dangerousness of the products modernly consumed.

The three causes of action for product liability are: (1) breach of warranty, (2) negligence, and (3) strict tort product liability. The first two involve various problems of proof (privity, exclusion of warranties) that hobble the attempt to recover for damages suffered by plaintiffs; the third cause of action eliminates many of these problems. Federal law has addressed one problem—"phantom warranties" are prohibited in the Magnuson-Moss Act (1975).

However, the product-liability revolution imposes significant burdens on the typical defendants; they are not without power to influence the law through various tort reforms which have had some success at the state level.

Exercises

1. What are the two main types of warranties and the important subtypes?

2. Who can make each type of warranty?

3. How are implied warranties excluded?

4. What general problems does a plaintiff have in bringing a products-liability warranty case?

5. What is the problem of lack of privity, and how does modern law deal with it?

6. What two types of products-liability cases are most often brought under negligence?

7. How could it be said that merely because a person suffers injury as the result of a defective product, proof of negligence is not necessarily made?

8. What is "preemption" and how is it used as a sword to defeat products-liability plaintiffs?

14.5 Regulation of the Bank-to-Customer and Insurance Company-to-Consumer Relationship

Why Banks and Insurance Companies Are Regulated

When bank customers make a deposit, banks keep some of that money on hand to cover withdrawals (this is the "reserve requirement" set by the federal government). But they invest most of it, loaning it out at higher rates than they pay depositors. They loan it out to anybody who meets their creditworthiness tests. There is some risk involved (although bankers have historically tended to be more risk-averse than venture capitalists). When the bank's investments go bad, depositors will rush to get their part of the cash reserve out before the bank runs out of cash on hand; that's a "run on the bank."[41] And then some people lose faith in the banks, won't deposit money in them, and the banks cannot help capitalize entrepreneurs or loan money to people to build new houses. When that happens, the economy wobbles, or—as in 1929–30—crashes entirely. (Many would say that a crash was only narrowly averted in 2008, with government aid.) Some regulation is necessary to keep banks from folding.

Insurance is similar in some ways—insurance companies take the insured's money, keep some on hand for paying immediate claims, and invest most. Insurance is a private contract, but it is a great concern for public policy that insurance companies remain solvent to pay claims—it would be very damaging to the economy and to faith in the economic system if insurance companies failed or misled people as to their insurance coverage. Who steps in when an insurance carrier fails? The government? Is the agent who sold the policy liable? Who is morally responsible to pay the insured whose carrier has gone belly up? We address these concerns in this section.

Regulation of Banks

Federal Regulation: Banking Act of 1933, Dodd-Frank Act of 2010

Congress created a central bank in 1913 with the adoption of the Federal Reserve Act, but as relates to consumer or customer protection, the major piece was the Banking Act of 1933. Then, to maintain faith in banks across the nation, Congress created the **Federal Deposit Insurance Corporation** (FDIC), an independent agency created by Congress to promote confidence in the financial system by:

- Insuring deposits (deposits are now insured up to $250,000).
- Examining and supervising financial institutions for safety, soundness, and consumer protection.
- Making large and complex financial institutions experiencing problems able to remain solvent without government help.
- Managing receiverships (failing banks are placed by court order under the control of an independent person known as a receiver).[42]

Dodd-Frank Wall Street Reform and Consumer Protection Act of 2010

In 2010, Congress passed the **Dodd-Frank Wall Street Reform and Consumer Protection Act**, which is the largest amendment to financial regulation in the United States since the Great Depression. This amendment was enacted in response to the post-2008 economic recession for the following purposes:

- Promote the financial stability of the United States by improving accountability and transparency in the financial system,
- End "too big to fail" institutions,
- Protect the American taxpayer by ending bailouts, and
- Protect consumers from abusive financial services practices.

The institutions most affected by the regulatory changes include those involved in monitoring the financial system, such as the Federal Deposit Insurance Corporation (FDIC) and the SEC. The act created the **Consumer Financial Protection Bureau**—vocally disliked by many Republicans,[43] as noted above. Here you can find a readable summary of Dodd-Frank and what its critics have done and want to do to change it: https://www.thebalance.com/dodd-frank-wall-street-reform-act-3305688.

And there are lots of other important federal banking laws.[44]

State Regulation of Banks

Other aspects of the bank-customer relationship are regulated by state law under the state-adopted Uniform Commercial Code:

- Article 3: Negotiable Instruments, https://www.law.cornell.edu/ucc/3/
- Article 4: Bank Deposits, https://www.law.cornell.edu/ucc/4/
- Article 4A: Funds Transfer, https://www.law.cornell.edu/ucc/4A/
- Article 5: Letters of Credit, https://www.law.cornell.edu/ucc/5/
- Article 8: Investment Securities, https://www.law.cornell.edu/ucc/8/
- Article 9: Secured Transactions, https://www.law.cornell.edu/ucc/9/

Federal Deposit Insurance Corporation

A federal agency (1933) to promote confidence in the U.S. banking system by, among other things, guaranteeing the security of bank customers' deposits; abbreviated FDIC.

Dodd-Frank Wall Street Reform and Consumer Protection Act

Federal law (2010) to promote stability in the U.S. financial system by promoting corporate accounting transparency and ending federal bailouts.

Consumer Financial Protection Bureau

Federal agency, 2010, to protect consumers against fraudulent, misleading, and deceptive financial products.

Article 4, for example, details customer-related rules for stopping payments on checks, on how long after a check is written it is still good, who is responsible for payments over forged signatures, and so on. Article 9 sets rules for secured transactions in personal property. You borrow money from Bank—get credit—to buy a car; Bank can take your car if you don't make the payments.

Regulation of Insurance Companies

Historically, insurance was regulated exclusively by state governments, beginning with New Hampshire in 1851. That tradition was reaffirmed by Congress in 1945 with the McCarran-Ferguson Act, which exempts insurance from most federal regulation. However, in 1999 Congress did adopt the Financial Modernization Act, which sets out minimum standards that state insurance laws must meet. State insurance regulation is supervised by elected or appointed state insurance commissioners; the regulation typically addresses the following issues (among others):

- Company licensing. Failure to comply with regulatory requirements may result in fines and suspension of license to do business.
- Producer licensing. Agents and brokers must pass competency tests and be licensed.
- Product regulation. Insurance policies must be reasonable and fair, and not misleading.
- Financial regulation. Insurance companies' accounting methods and financial statement presentations are audited by the state insurance division.
- Market regulation. Agent sales practices, complaints about rates, claims handling, and other market-related aspects of the insurance product are regulated.
- Consumer services. The state will investigate consumer complaints.

Here you can find the National Association of Insurance Company's brief on state insurance regulation: http://www.naic.org/documents/consumer_state_reg_brief.pdf .

Key Takeaway

Banking and insurance involve mostly private contracts, but because they retain in hand only a small part of their customers' money (deposits for banks, or premiums for insurance companies) and invest the rest, necessarily somewhat speculatively, they are a matter of public interest, and thus subject to government regulation. Federal regulation of banks began in earnest in the 1930s—the FDIC now guarantees depositors' accounts to $250,000; further federal regulation followed the "Great Recession" after 2008 to stabilize the industry and to protect consumers from abusive banking practices.

Insurance is mostly regulated by state insurance commissions. The regulation is meant to assure the solvency of insurance companies and police the production and sale of insurance products so as to avoid misrepresentative practices.

Exercises

1. Why are banks and insurance companies regulated by the government—what do they have in common?
2. Why is banking regulation such a contentious political issue?
3. Why is the Consumer Financial Protection Bureau much disliked by many conservatives?
4. Why are many conservatives so opposed to and unhappy with "Obamacare," when—it might be pointed out—it brings the U.S. into the large majority of nations providing some sem-

blance of universal healthcare for its citizens? What would be the conservative alternative to the Affordable Care Act?

14.6 Regulation of Securities

Learning Objectives

1. Recognize that the definition of *security* encompasses a broad range of financial instruments.
2. Know why the offering and exchange of securities needs to be regulated at the federal level.
3. Understand the basic functions of the Securities Acts of 1933 and 1934, and what companies are affected by them; understand the role of the Securities and Exchange Commission and the penalties for violations of the securities laws.
4. Explore state securities regulation.

Introduction: What Is a "Security"?

If I offer to sell you a textbook, and you pay me $20 for it, you actually get something of use and value. You can read it, you can keep it for reference, you could resell it, or you can use it as a doorstop.

But what if you give me the $20, and I give you two pieces of paper—two stock certificates (or access to electronic certificates). Now, what do you have? Nothing of value, *except* insofar as I or my agents take your money and make it work to start a company. The two papers themselves are worthless; the value lies in the property or ongoing enterprise they represent.

This disparity between the tangible property—the stock certificate, for example—and the intangible interest it represents gives rise to several reasons for regulation.

- First, there is need for a mechanism to inform the buyer accurately what it is she is buying.
- Second, laws are necessary to prevent and provide remedies for deceptive and manipulative acts designed to defraud buyers and sellers.
- Third, the evolution of securities trading on a massive scale has led to the development of numerous types of specialists and professionals; in dealing with specialists, average buyers can easily be at a severe disadvantage, so the law tries to ensure that specialists and professionals do not take unfair advantage of their customers.

The point is, unless people have faith in the integrity of the securities market, they won't buy securities; if they don't buy securities, the capital in "capitalism" will be greatly diminished—there won't be money to start new businesses.

Federal law and cases have broadly defined a **security**, but the crux of it is this: a security or investment contract exists if a "person invests money in a common enterprise and is led to expect profits solely (or primarily) from the efforts of the promoter or a third party."[45] Under this federal test, based on the 1946 case of *SEC v. Howey*, courts have liberally interpreted "investment contracts" and "certificates of interest or participation in any profit-sharing agreement" to be securities interests in such property as real estate condominiums and cooperatives, commodity option contracts, and farm animals. The most common types of securities are bonds (the issuer borrows money from

security

Under federal law, an investment made by a person in an enterprise with others where the buyer looks primarily to the seller for the success of the investment.

investors and promises to pay them back over time) and stocks (the issuer sells shares of itself to the public who then become part owners of the issuer).

The Securities and Exchange Commission

To administer the security-regulation regime, Congress created a federal administrative agency, the **Securities and Exchange Commission**, in 1934.

The SEC is an independent regulatory agency composed of five members who have staggered five-year terms. Every June 5th, the term of one of the commissioners expires. The president cannot remove commissioners during their terms of office, but does have the power to designate the chairman from among the sitting members. The SEC is bipartisan: not more than three commissioners may be from the same political party.

The SEC's basic mission is to ensure that the sellers of securities make a *full disclosure* to potential security buyers so that they can make informed decisions. But whether a particular security offering is worthwhile or worthless is a decision for the public, not for the SEC, which has no legal authority to pass on the merits of an offering or to bar the sale of securities if proper disclosures are made.

The agency investigates complaints or other possible violations of the law in securities transactions and brings enforcement proceedings when it believes that violations have occurred. It is empowered to conduct information inquiries, interview witnesses, examine brokerage records, and review trading data. If its requests are refused, it can issue subpoenas and seek compliance in federal court. Its usual leads come from complaints of investors and the general public, but it has authority to conduct surprise inspections of the books and records of brokers and dealers. Another source of leads is price fluctuations that seem to have been caused by manipulation rather than regular market forces.

Among the violations the commission searches out are: (1) unregistered sale of securities subject to the registration requirement of the Securities Act of 1933, (2) fraudulent acts and practices, (3) manipulation of market prices, (4) carrying on a securities business while insolvent, (5) misappropriation of customers' funds by brokers and dealers, and (6) other unfair dealings by brokers and dealers.

When the commission believes that a violation has occurred, it can take one of three courses:

- refer the case to the Justice Department for criminal prosecution in cases of fraud or other willful violation of law.
- seek a civil injunction in federal court against further violations; the court may impose civil penalties (the maximum penalty is $100,000 for each violation by a natural person and $500,000 for each violation by an entity other than a natural person). Alternatively, the defendant is liable for the gain that resulted from violating securities law if the gain exceeds the statutory penalty. The court is also authorized to bar an individual who has committed securities fraud from serving as an officer or a director of a company registered under the securities law.
- proceed administratively—that is, hold its own hearing before an administrative law judge (ALJ). If after internal appeal, the commissioners accept the findings of the ALJ, they can issue cease and desist orders (injunctions); suspend or expel members of exchanges; deny, suspend, or revoke the registrations of broker-dealers; censure individuals for misconduct; and bar censured individuals (temporarily or permanently) from employment with a registered firm, and impose civil fines.

The Major Securities Laws

The most significant federal securities laws are the Securities Act of 1933, the Securities Exchange Act of 1934, the Foreign Corrupt Practices Act of 1977. We take them up briefly here.

Securities Act of 1933: "Going Public"

The **Securities Act of 1933** is the fundamental "truth in securities" law. Its two basic objectives, written in its preamble, are "to provide full and fair disclosure of the character of securities sold in interstate and foreign commerce and through the mails, and to prevent frauds in the sale thereof."

> **Securities Act of 1933**
>
> Federal statute regulating the issuance of securities for sale in interstate commerce.

How Full Disclosure of New Offerings is Accomplished: Registration and Prospectus

Registration. The primary means for realizing these goals is the requirement of registration of a new securities offering ("**initial public offering**," or "IPO.") Before securities subject to the act can be offered to the public, the issuer must file a registration statement and prospectus with the SEC;[46] the registry has special forms for different types of issuing companies, but in general registration forms call for:

- a description of the company's properties and business;
- a description of the security to be offered for sale;
- information about the management of the company; and
- financial statements certified by independent accountants.[47]

> **initial public offering (IPO)**
>
> The first time a firm offers its securities for sale on the public market.

If the registration is materially incomplete or inaccurate, the commission may suspend or refuse the effectiveness of the registration statement and prohibit any sales until the deficiencies are corrected. Even after the securities have gone on sale, the agency has the power to issue a stop order that halts trading in the stock.

Prospectus. If the SEC approves the registration statement (which, again, is not to be construed as any comment on the offering's merits), the issuer must then provide any prospective purchaser a **prospectus**, basically a (laborious) bit of explanatory sales literature, a brochure (what is this security, who's behind it, what are potential problems) information that a prudent buyer would want to have. (Of course, while the purchaser must receive the prospectus before buying the security—well, you can lead a horse to water, but you can't make him drink.)

> **prospectus**
>
> A type of sales brochure required to accompany an offering for the sale of securities; the purpose is to provide the potential investor with full disclosure of the risks of the investment.

Penalties

The Act of 1933 (Sec. 24) provides for fines not to exceed $10,000 and a prison term not to exceed five years, or both, for anyone who "willfully, in a registration statement filed under this title, makes any untrue statement of a material fact or omits to state any material fact required to be stated therein or necessary to make the statements therein not misleading." Anyone injured by false declarations in registration statements, prospectuses, or oral communications concerning the sale of the security—as well as anyone injured by the unlawful failure of an issuer to register—may file a civil suit to recover the net consideration paid for the security or for damages if the security has been sold.

Securities Exchange Act of 1934: "Being Public"

The Securities Act of 1933 is limited, as we have just seen, to new securities issues—that is the primary market. The trading that takes place in the secondary market is far more significant, however. In a normal year, trading in outstanding stock totals some twenty times the value of new stock issues. The question is, how does a person who is thinking about buying stock, in say, General Motors, know whether the seller's price is reasonable?

To regulate the secondary market, Congress enacted the **Securities Exchange Act of 1934** (SEA '34). This law extended the disclosure rationale to securities actively listed and registered for public trading on the national securities exchanges (if the company has at least $10 million in assets and five hundred or more shareholders).

Major Provisions of the SEA '34

Section 10(b) of the Securities Exchange Act of 1934 prohibits any person from using the mails or facilities of interstate commerce "to use or employ, in connection with the purchase or sale of any security ... any manipulative or deceptive device or contrivance in contravention of such rules and regulations as the Commission may prescribe as necessary or appropriate in the public interest or for the protection of investors." **Rule 10b-5**, developed by the SEC in 1942, gives substance to Congress's general grant of authority; it is a sweeping prohibition of misrepresentation in securities sales:

> *It shall be unlawful for any person, directly or indirectly, by the use of any means or instrumentality of interstate commerce, or of the mails, or of any facility of any national securities exchange,*
> 1. *to employ any device, scheme, or artifice to defraud,*
> 2. *to make any untrue statement of a material fact or to omit to state a material fact necessary in order to make the statements made, in the light of circumstances under which they were made, not misleading, or*
> 3. *to engage in any act, practice, or course of business which operates or would operate as a fraud or deceit upon any person, in connection with the purchase or sale of any security.*

Rule 10b-5 applies to any person who purchases or sells any security. It is not limited to securities registered under the 1934 Securities Exchange Act. It is not limited to publicly-held companies. It applies to any security issued by any company, including the smallest closely-held company (if it trades in interstate commerce). In substance, it is an antifraud rule, enforcement of which seems, on its face, to be limited to action by the SEC. But over the years, the courts have permitted people injured by violators to file private damage suits. This sweeping rule has at times been referred to as the "federal law of corporations" or the "catch everybody" rule.

Using its authority to promote transparency in the sale and exchange of securities and to instill confidence in the integrity of the securities market, the SEC has developed various requirements:

Securities Exchange Act of 1934

Federal statute regulating the exchange of securities in interstate markets.

Section 10(b)

That section of the Securities Exchange Act of 1934 that gives the SEC power to declare deceptive or manipulative acts in securities transactions illegal.

Rule 10b-5

A rule (or regulation) developed by the SEC that prohibits deceptive practices in the sale or exchange of securities.

- **Registration, Periodic Filings, and Press Releases.** Any company seeking listing and registration of its stock for public trading on a national exchange—or over the counter, if the company meets the size test—has several obligations:

  - a registration application must be submitted to both the exchange and the SEC, akin to that filed by companies under the Securities Act of 1933.
  - annual and other periodic reports are to be filed to update information in the original filing,[48] including "interim reports" whenever there is a material change in the business that investors need to know about.
  - proxy solicitation: whenever management, or a dissident minority, seeks votes of holders of registered securities for any corporate purpose (a proxy solicitation), disclosures must be made to the stockholders to permit them to vote yes or no knowledgeably.
  - registration of the exchanges (the markets), brokers and dealers (sellers), and transfer agents (people who keep track of the individuals and entities that own a firm's securities), must be registered; disclosure documents are updated regularly, and false, misleading, or omitted material may be grounds for discipline and sanctions.

- **Insider Trading.** **Corporate insiders**—directors, officers, or important shareholders can have a substantial trading advantage if they are privy to important confidential information. Learning bad news (such as financial loss or cancellation of key contracts) in advance of all other stockholders will permit the privileged few to sell shares before the price falls. Conversely, discovering good news (a major oil find or unexpected profits) in advance gives the insider a decided incentive to purchase shares before the price rises. The Act of '34 (Sections 16(b) and 10(b)) prohibits this kind of trading by insiders. It is also illegal in many situations for an insider to give a non-insider the same kind of good news or bad news tip. That is, "tippees" can be liable along with "tippers," particularly if the tippee has reason to know that the tipper is breaching a fiduciary duty to a company she works for. Liability for insider trading includes a possible fine of $1 million and a ten-year prison term, but Congress, the SEC, and the courts have carved out various exceptions and limitations to the scope of liability for insider trading. For an overview of insider trading, go to http://www.sec.gov/answers/insider.htm.

It is presumed that corporate insiders will trade with inside information. They may do so, but only if the information has been out in the market long enough to no longer be "inside," or if they forfeit the profit on the deal (called the "short-swing profit rule").[49]

Penalties

Generally, private investors may sue in federal court for violations of the statute that led to financial injury. Violations of any provision and the making of false statements in any of the required disclosures subject the defendant to a maximum fine of $5 million and a maximum twenty-year prison sentence; a corporate violator may pay up to $25 million. Any issuer omitting to file requisite documents and reports is liable to pay a fine of $100 for each day the failure continues.

insider trading

The trading of a public company's stock, bonds, or other securities by individuals with access to nonpublic information about the company.

corporate insiders

A director or senior officer of a company, or any person or entity that beneficially owns more than 10% of a company's voting shares.

Other Federal Securities Laws

The Foreign Corrupt Practices Act, 1977

Investigations by the SEC and the Watergate Special Prosecutor in the mid-1970s turned up evidence that hundreds of companies had used corporate funds to bribe foreign officials to induce them to enter into contracts with, or grant licenses to, U.S. companies. Companies paying bribes routinely hid the payments in various accounts because revealing the bribes would defeat the secret purpose of the bribe, and could be expected to stir up immense criticism from competitors, NGOs, and political groups. As a result, one of many statutes enacted in the aftermath of Watergate, the **Foreign Corrupt Practices Act** (FCPA) of 1977 was incorporated into the 1934 Act. Business gained through bribery puts a premium on stealth, influence, and money, rather than goods and services that compete on their own price and merit. The SEC's legal interest in the matter, however, is not premised on the morality of bribery, but rather on the falsity of the financial statements that were being filed, statements that seldom spoke the truth about the money being used to bribe.

The FCPA has two parts:

1. Anti-bribery. No issuer (i.e., any U.S. business enterprise), or "any officer, director, employee, or agent" of an issuer may use either the mails or interstate commerce corruptly to offer, pay, or promise to pay anything of value to foreign officials, foreign political parties, or candidates if the purpose is to gain business by inducing the foreign official to influence an act of the government to render a decision favorable to the U.S. corporation. That is, bribery is illegal. Note that there are exceptions. Payments may be made to expedite routine governmental actions, such as obtaining a visa or getting perishable goods promptly put through customs. And payments are allowed if they are lawful under the written law of a foreign country.

2. Mandatory accounting. More important than the foreign-bribery provisions, the act includes accounting provisions. A competent auditor should be able to open a firm's books and see whether there are irregularities that could conceal bribery, among other things; under the FCPA a firm must show that its books and records comply with GAAP (generally acceptable accounting practices); if they do not, the SEC may issue penalties. In 2015 the SEC fined Goodyear Tire more than $16 million for violations of the FCPA's accounting provisions.[50] Many firms not within the SEC's jurisdiction have adopted the GAAP standards to ensure accounting transparency and promote confidence in their financial affairs.

Sarbanes-Oxley Act, 2002

Following the scandals perpetrated by accounting firms (they "cooked the books" for their corporate clients) at the turn of the 21st century, Congress adopted the **Sarbanes-Oxley Act** in 2002 (referred to generally as "SOX.") The Act mandated a number of reforms to enhance corporate responsibility, enhance financial disclosures and combat corporate and accounting fraud, and created the Public Company Accounting Oversight Board, also known as the PCAOB, to oversee the activities of the auditing profession.

Dodd-Frank Wall Street Reform and Consumer Protection Act, 2010

We touched on the 2010 **Dodd-Frank Wall Street Reform and Consumer Protection Act** earlier as it related to bank regulation. It also imposed new rules affecting the SEC regarding securities regulation. Importantly, the amendment expanded the number of investment advisors who are required to be registered with the SEC. "Registration" means the advisor has to fill out forms attesting to her training, professional history, and the like, and she has to swear it's true. False or incomplete registration statements, or omissions of relevance, give rise to liability. Numerous investment advisors, as well as hedge funds and private equity firms, are now subject to registration requirements.[51]

State Security Regulation

The states responded to the crises of confidence in corporate financing—people got burned investing in stock—before the federal government did: Kansas was the first in 1911. The state security regulations are usually referred to as "**blue sky laws**" (a Kansas legislator purportedly said that "unscrupulous promoters would sell stock in a company designed to extract blue from the sky"). State definitions of a "security" vary somewhat from the federal "Howey test," but they operate on the same idea: the buyer of a security needs the benefit of full disclosure.

Specific provisions vary state-by-state. Generally speaking, however, they require the following:

- All securities sold in-state must either be registered or exempt from registration; and
- All broker-dealers and their agents must be registered or be exempt from registration.

Again, the point about registration is, if the registration filing is false or misleading or omits important items, civil, administrative, and criminal liability may flow.

Case

Tippee Liability

> **Salman v. U.S.**
>
> 580 U.S. ___ (2016)

[*Authors' note.* Insider trading is illegal, as noted above. Insiders are also forbidden from tipping inside information to others for trading. The tippee who receives such information, with knowledge that the tipper breached a duty not to disclose the information, may also be liable if the facts show that the tipper disclosed information for personal advantage. In *SEC v. Dirks* (1984) the Court held that the jury may infer a "personal advantage" where the tipper gets something of value in exchange, or makes a gift of confidential information to a relative or friend.]

Bassam Salman was convicted of insider trading based on information he received from his brother in law, Michael Kara. Michael received the information from his brother, Maher Kara (a former Citibank investment broker). Maher Kara testified that he gave inside information to his

Dodd-Frank Wall Street Reform and Consumer Protection Act

Federal law (2010) to promote accountability in the financial system, to end government bailouts of companies, and to protect consumers from abusive financial services products and practices.

blue sky laws

State laws regulating intrastate sales of securities, as the federal securities acts of 1933 and '34 regulate interstate sales.

Salman v. U.S.

U.S. Supreme Court case, 2016, analyzing the reach of the federal prohibition against insider trading.

brother Michael to benefit Michael, and Michael testified that he shared the information with Mr. Salman, who knew it was from Maher.

Mr. Salman was convicted of being a tippee, sentenced to three years in prison and ordered to pay $730,000 in restitution; he appealed his conviction to the 9th Circuit Court (California). While that appeal was pending, the 2nd Circuit (New York)—in a different insider trading case (*Newman*)—interpreted *Dirks* to mean that there is no inference of personal benefit to the tipper from a gift of confidential information unless two conditions are met: (1) there is a "close personal relationship between the tipper and tippee," and (2) the gift "generates an exchange that is objective, consequential, and represents at least a potential gain of a pecuniary or similarly valuable nature." When the 2nd Circuit's opinion came out, the 9th Circuit (deciding Mr. Salman's case) declined to follow it, holding instead that the breach of fiduciary duty could be inferred if only element (1) above was found—that there was a close personal relationship between the tipper and tippee. No showing of some value having been received in exchange was required.

The Supreme Court took *Salman* to resolve the differences between the two courts of appeal: which one properly interpreted *Dirks*?

1. Choice #1: The tippee is liable if he gets inside information from a close friend or relative *and* the tipper gets something valuable in return.

2. Choice #2: The tippee is liable if he gets inside information from a close friend or relative, even if the tipper gets nothing of value in return.

Alito, J.

* * * Maher testified that he shared inside information with Michael to benefit him and with the expectation that his brother would trade on it. While Maher explained that he disclosed the information in large part to appease Michael (who pestered him incessantly for it), he also testified that he tipped his brother to "help him" and to "fulfill whatever needs he had." For instance, Michael once called Maher and told him that "he needed a favor." Maher offered his brother money but Michael asked for information instead.

Salman contends that a gift of confidential information to a friend or family member alone is insufficient to establish the personal benefit required for tippee liability, claiming that a tipper does not personally benefit unless the tipper's goal in disclosing information is to obtain money, property, or something of tangible value. * * * He claims that our insider-trading precedents, and the cases those precedents cite, involve situations in which the insider exploited confidential information for the insider's own "tangible monetary profit."

Under the Government's view, a tipper personally benefits whenever the tipper discloses confidential trading information for a noncorporate purpose. Accordingly, a gift to a friend, a family member, or anyone else would support the factual inference that the tipper exploited the trading value of inside information for personal purposes and thus personally benefited from the disclosure. * * *

We adhere to *Dirks*, which easily resolves the narrow issue presented here. *Dirks* specifies that when a tipper gives inside information to "a trading relative or friend," the jury can infer that the tipper meant to provide the equivalent of a cash gift. In such situations, the tipper benefits personally, because giving a gift of trading information is the same thing as trading by the tipper followed by a gift of the proceeds. Here, by disclosing confidential information as a gift to his brother with the expectation that he would trade on it, Maher breached his duty of trust and confidence to Citigroup and its clients—a duty Salman acquired, and breached himself, by trading on the information with full knowledge that it had been improperly disclosed. To the extent the Second Circuit held that the tipper must also receive something of a "pecuniary or similarly valuable nature" in exchange for a gift to family or friends, we agree with the Ninth Circuit that this requirement is inconsistent with *Dirks*.

Salman's jury was properly instructed that a personal benefit includes "the benefit one would obtain from simply making a gift of confidential information to a trading relative."

It is so ordered. [The decision was unanimous.]

Case Questions

1. What is insider trading?
2. Why is insider trading illegal?
3. Why would an "insider" give trading tips to a tippee?
4. What was the difference in the opinions of the two circuit courts of appeal, and how did the Supreme Court resolve the difference?

Key Takeaway

A security arises where a buyer invests in a proposal with other investors and looks primarily to some third party (the issuer or offeror) for the success of the venture—the investor actually gets nothing tangible for the investment, only a promise by the offeror to take the investor's money and make more money with it. Because the investor has little control over the success of the venture, and because investors who feel they have been abused will lose faith in the market, the federal government has regulated the sale of securities since the mid-1930s. The main idea is "full disclosure" by the issuer about the offering made to the buyer; that is accomplished by registration and by providing a prospectus to the buyer (Act of 1933) and by periodic reporting by the issuer of things that would affect its securities' value (Act of 1934). There are significant penalties for selling before registration or for misrepresentative statements or omissions in the required filings, activities—among others—supervised by the Securities Exchange Commission (SEC).

State security regulation laws—called "blue sky laws" are similar in defining a security and in regulation by requiring full disclosure through registration.

Exercises

1. Howey sold customers actual strips of land on which were growing orange trees; Howey tended to the trees, watered them, pruned them, harvested the fruit, and gave the customers a percentage of the profit. Was Howey selling securities?[52]

2. Defendant solicited buyer-investors to raise earthworms, in order to help him reach his quota of selling earthworms to fishermen in a promotional newsletter. The newsletter promised that defendant's growing instructions would enable them to have a profitable farm with little effort, because earthworms double in quantity every sixty days, and that defendant would buy back all bait-size worms at a set price per pound. Plaintiffs were promised that they need not worry about the market because defendant would handle marketing. Was defendant selling securities?[53]

3. Why does the government get involved with securities regulation at all? Why not just say, "Buyer beware"?

14.7 Summary and Exercises

Summary

The completely unregulated market is socially unacceptable and historically almost non-existent; total freedom in markets does not create the greatest societal good.

In the U.S., government regulation of the market began in the late 19th century with the adoption of the Sherman and Clayton Antitrust Acts (1890 and 1914) to stop the most abusive concerted actions or monopolistic practices that undermine fair and efficient markets; the laws address both horizontal and vertical anti-competitive activities. Section 5 of the Federal Trade Commission Act (also 1914) gives the FTC antitrust power to prohibit "unfair methods of competition and unfair or deceptive acts or practices in commerce."

Under the "unfair or deceptive" part of its power, the FTC engages in consumer protection; it has held that these acts, among others, are proscribed: failure to disclose pertinent facts, false or misleading description of products, misleading price and savings claims, bait-and-switch advertisements, free-offer claims, false product comparisons and disparagements, and endorsements by those who do not use the product or who have no reasonable basis for making the claims. Among the unfair trade practices that the FTC has sought to deter are certain types of contests and sweepstakes, high-pressure door-to-door and mail-order selling, and certain types of negative-option plans.

The FTC has a number of remedial tools: cease and desist orders tailored to the particular deception or unfair act (including affirmative disclosure in advertising and corrections in future advertising), civil monetary penalties, and injunctions, damages, and restitution on behalf of injured consumers. Private parties have no right to sue under Section 5, but they can sue for certain kinds of false advertising under the federal trademark laws.

In addition to the Federal Trade Commission, several other federal agencies are involved in consumer protection regulation, including the FDA and the CFPA. State attorneys general also have consumer-protection enforcement power through "little FTC acts," "lemon laws," and others.

Product-liability law developed extensively in the 20th century, changing the old rule "let the buyer beware" to a more modern one, "let the seller beware." The causes of action are: (1) warranty, a contract concept with problems of privity and with "phantom warranties" (addressed by the federal Magnuson-Moss Act, 1975) and other defenses; (2) negligence, a tort concept with problems of showing negligence and other defenses; and (3) strict product liability, a tort concept that obviates many of the problems by imposing liability without fault on any seller of a dangerously-defective product. The expansion of product liability law has given rise to a reaction—the clamor for state-level liability reform.

Banks and insurance companies are regulated because the depositor or insured has no control over what investments the bank or insurance company makes with the money they get. Most insurance regulation is done by the states.

The SEC administers securities laws to prevent fraudulent practices in the sales of securities. The definition of *security* is intentionally broad to protect the public from fraudulent investments that otherwise would escape regulation.

The Securities Act of 1933 requires that offerors register their new securities offerings with the Securities and Exchange Commission—they must make a full disclosure about the risks and benefits of the investment. The Securities Exchange Act of 1934 similarly requires periodic disclosures about existing securities that are sold in interstate commerce—investors should have faith that they can understand what they are investing in. The Foreign Corrupt Practices Act proscribes some kinds of bribing by American firms of foreigners to get business done, but it is more significant because it has effectively dictated that most U.S. companies present their financial statements in a uniform way, subject to the application of generally-accepted accounting practices. Sarbanes-Oxley (2002) created new federal oversight of corporate financial behavior.

States also regulate securities via blue sky laws for intra-state sales of securities, similarly requiring full disclosure, as does federal law.

Exercises

1. Vanessa Cosmetics takes out full-page advertisements in the local newspaper stating that "this Sunday only" the Vanessa Makeup Kit will be "reduced to only $25." In fact, the regular price has been $25.50. Does this constitute deceptive advertising? Why?

2. Lilliputian Department Stores advertises a "special" on an electric carrot slicer, priced "this week only at $10." When customers come to the store, they find the carrot slicer in frayed boxes, and the advertised special is clearly inferior to a higher-grade carrot slicer priced at $25. When customers ask about the difference, the store clerk tells them, "You wouldn't want to buy the cheaper one; it wears out much too fast." What grounds, if any, exist to charge Lilliputian with violations of the FTC Act?

3. A toothpaste manufacturer advertises that special tests demonstrate that use of its toothpaste results in fewer cavities than a "regular toothpaste." In fact, the "regular" toothpaste was not marketed but was merely the advertiser's brand stripped of its fluoride. Various studies over the years have demonstrated, however, that fluoride in toothpaste will reduce the number of cavities a user will get. Is this advertisement deceptive under Section 5 of the FTC Act?

4. McDonald's advertises a sweepstakes through a mailing that says prizes are to be reserved for 15,610 "lucky winners." The mailing further states, "You may be [a winner] but you will never know if you don't claim your prize. All prizes not claimed will never be given away, so hurry." The mailing does not give the odds of winning. The FTC sues to enjoin the mailing as deceptive. What is the result?

5. In 1960—before any widespread electronic communication—people did their banking locally. Suppose, in that year, First Bank acquired all six of the other local banks in Middletown. Would you say First Bank had a monopoly—that it could control the price of banking? Today, in 2019, people can sit at their desks in Middletown and bank anywhere in the country over the Internet. If First Bank in 2019 acquired all six of the other local banks, could it control the price of banking? Why has the geographic market changed? Are there some businesses that remain really local?

6. To demonstrate its product's beard-moistening power, Colgate-Palmolive aired a TV ad showing Rapid Shave spread on sandpaper; 15 seconds later, a razor blade is shown "shaving" the sand off the sandpaper: "If it'll soften the sand off sandpaper, think how it will soften your beard!" The FTC complained that the ad was misleading; Colgate responded that Rapid Shave *would* moisten sand off the backing paper. However, it really took 90 minutes (not 15 seconds), and what the viewer saw was not really sandpaper, but rather a piece of Plexiglas to which sand had been applied (because on TV sandpaper would appear as a piece of plain, colored paper). Nevertheless, Colgate argued, there was no false representation of the substantive product, just a demonstration for the brief TV ad. Was the ad misleading?

7. National Widget Company is the dominant manufacturer of widgets in the United States, with 72 percent of the market for low-priced widgets and 89 percent of the market for high-priced widgets. Dozens of companies compete with National in the manufacture and sale of compatible peripheral equipment for use with National's widgets, including countertops, holders, sprockets and gear assemblies, instruction booklets, computer software, and several hundred replacement parts. Revenues from these peripherals run upwards of $100 million annually. Beginning with the 2019 model year, National Widget sprang a surprise—a completely-redesigned widget that made most of the peripheral equipment obsolete. Moreover, National set the price for its peripherals below that which would make economic sense for competitors to invest in new plants to tool up for producing redesigned peripherals. Five of the largest peripheral-equipment competitors sued National under Section 2 of the Sherman Act. One of these, American Widget Peripherals, Inc., had an additional complaint: on making inquiries in early 2018, American was assured by National's general manager that it would not be redesigning any widgets until late 2020 at the earliest. On the basis of that statement, American invested $50 million in a new plant to manufacture the now obsolescent peripheral equipment, and as a result, it will probably be forced into bankruptcy. What is the result? Why?

8. In 1958—the year prior to the merger—Alcoa was the leading producer of aluminum conductor, with 27.8% of the market; in bare aluminum conductor, it also led the industry with 32.5%. Alcoa and Kaiser controlled 50% of the aluminum conductor market and, with its three leading competitors, more than 76%. Only nine concerns (including Rome with 1.3%)

accounted for 95.7% of the output of aluminum conductor, Alcoa was third with 11.6%, and Rome was eighth with 4.7%. Five companies controlled 65.4% and four smaller ones, including Rome, added another 22.8%. The Justice Department sued Alcoa-Rome for violation of Section 7 of the Clayton Act. What is the government's argument? What is the result?

9. Quality Graphics has been buying up the stock of companies that manufacture billboards. Quality now owns or controls 23 of the 129 companies that make billboards, and its sales account for 3.2 percent of the total national market of $72 million. In Texas, Quality has acquired 27 percent of the billboard market, and in the Dallas–Ft. Worth area alone, about 25 percent. Billboard advertising accounts for only 0.001 percent of total national advertising sales; the majority goes to newspaper, magazine, television, and radio advertising. What claims could the Justice Department assert in a suit against Quality? What is Quality's defense? What is the result?

10. In 2018, Panda Bears Incorporated, a small manufacturer, began to sell its patented panda bear robot dolls (they walk, smile, eat bamboo shoots, and poop) to retail toy shops. The public took an immediate fancy to panda bears, and the company found it difficult to meet the demand. Retail shops sold out even before their orders arrived. In order to allocate the limited supply fairly while it tooled up to increase production runs, the company announced to its distributors that it would not sell to any retailers that did not also purchase its trademarked Panda Bear's Bambino Bamboo Shoots. It also announced that it would refuse to supply any retailer that sold the robots for less than $99.95. Finally, it said that it would refuse to sell to retailers unless they agreed to use the company's repair services exclusively when customers brought bears back to repair malfunctions in their delicate, patented computerized nervous system. By the following year, with demand still rising, inferior competitive panda robots and bamboo shoots began to appear. Some retailers began to lower the Panda Bear price to meet the competition. The company refused to resupply them. Panda Bears Incorporated also decreed that it would refuse to sell to retailers who carried any other type of bamboo shoot. What antitrust violations, if any, has Panda Bear Incorporated committed? What additional information might be useful in helping you to decide?

11. Icebox Ike, a well-known tackle for a professional football team, was recently signed to a multimillion-dollar contract to appear in a series of nationally-televised advertisements touting the pleasures of going to the ballet and showing him in the audience watching a ballet. In fact, Icebox has never been to a ballet, although he has told his friends that he "truly believes" ballet is a "wonderful thing." The FTC opens an investigation to determine whether there are grounds to take legal action against Icebox and the ballet company ads. What advice can you give Icebox Ike? What remedies can the FTC seek?

12. An encyclopedia company offers a complete set of encyclopedias to "selected" customers: their only obligation is to pay for a ten-year updating service. In fact, the price of the updating service includes the cost of the encyclopedias. The FTC sues, charging deception under Section 5 of the FTC Act. The encyclopedia company defends itself on the ground that no one could possibly have been misled because everyone must have understood that no company could afford to give away a twenty-volume set of books for free. What is the result? [And yes, printed encyclopedias are still published and sold—they are more credible than the 'Net.]

13. Twenty-five local supermarket chains banded together as Topco Associates Incorporated to sell groceries under a private label to compete with the giant chains, which had the economic clout to sell private-label merchandise unavailable to the smaller chains. Topco acted as a purchasing agent for the members. By the late 1960s, Topco's members were doing a booming business: $1.3 billion [$9.3 billion in 2018 dollars] in retail sales, with market share ranging from 1.5 percent to 16 percent in the markets that members served. Topco-brand groceries accounted for no more than 10 percent of any store's total merchandise. Under Topco's rules, members were assigned exclusive territories in which to sell Topco-brand goods. A member chain with stores located in another member's exclusive territory could not sell Topco-brand goods in those stores. Topco argued that the market division was necessary to give each chain the economic incentive to advertise and develop brand consciousness and thus to be able to compete more effectively against the large nonmember supermarkets' private labels. If other stores in the locality could also carry the Topco brand, then it would not be a truly "private" label and there would be no reason to tout it; it would be like any national brand foodstuff, and Topco members did not have the funds to advertise the brand nationally. Which, if any, antitrust laws has Topco violated? Why?

14. Anne operated a clothing store called Anne's Rags, Inc. and owned all of the stock in the company. After several years in the clothing business, Anne sold her stock to Louise, who personally managed the business. Is the sale governed by the antifraud provisions of federal securities law? Why?

15. While waiting tables at a campus-area restaurant, you overhear a conversation between two corporate executives who indicate that their company has developed a new product that will revolutionize the computer industry. The product is to be announced in three weeks. If you purchase stock in the company before the announcement, will you be liable under federal securities law? Why?

16. Eric was hired as a management consultant by a major corporation to conduct a study, which took him three months to complete. While working on the study, Eric learned that someone working in research and development for the company had recently made an important discovery. Before the discovery was announced publicly, Eric purchased stock in the company. Did he violate federal securities law? Why?

17. While working for the company, Eric also learned that it was planning a takeover of another corporation. Before announcement of a tender offer, Eric purchased stock in the target company. Did he violate securities law? Why?

18. The commercial lending department of First Bank made a substantial loan to Alpha Company after obtaining a favorable confidential earnings report from Alpha. Over lunch, Heidi, the loan officer who handled the loan, mentioned the earnings report to a friend who worked in the bank's trust department. The friend proceeded to purchase stock in Alpha for several of the bank's trusts. Discuss the legal implications.

19. In Exercise 18, assume that after work one day, Heidi told her friend in the trust department that Alpha was Beta's takeover target. The friend proceeded to purchase additional stock in Alpha for a bank trust he administered. Discuss the legal implications.

20. It is claimed by some that Facebook vacuums up people's personal information to such an extent that it becomes intolerably intrusive and violates peoples' privacy, but Facebook users give permission for Facebook to do that when they sign up. What is the solution to this problem—that is, peoples' interest in privacy vs. Facebook's interest in gathering data on its users that is marketable to advertisers and others?

21. Ralph's Hardware updated its accounting system and agreed to purchase a computer system from a manufacturer, Bits and Bytes (BB). During contract negotiations, BB's sales representative promised that the system was "A-1" and "perfect." However, the written contract, which the parties later signed, disclaimed all warranties, express and implied. After installation, the computer produced only random numbers and letters, rather than the desired accounting information. Is BB is liable for breaching an express warranty? Why?

22. Kate owned a small grocery store. One day, John went to the store and purchased a can of chip dip that was, unknown to Kate or John, adulterated. John became seriously ill after eating the dip and sued Kate for damages on the grounds that she breached an implied warranty of merchantability. Kate is not liable; why?

23. Carrie visited a neighborhood store to purchase some ham, which a salesperson cut by machine in the store. The next day, she made a ham sandwich. In eating the sandwich, Carrie bit into a piece of cartilage in the ham. As a result, Carrie lost a tooth, had to undergo root canal treatments, and must now wear a full-coverage crown to replace the tooth. Is the store liable for the damage? Why?

24. A bank repossessed a boat and sold it to Carlos. During the negotiations, Carlos stated that he wanted to use the boat for charter service in Florida. The bank officers handling the sale made no representations concerning the boat during negotiations. Carlos later discovered that the boat was defective and sued the bank for breach of warranty. Is the bank liable? Why?

25. Tom Anderson, the produce manager at the Thriftway Market in Pasco, Washington, removed a box of bananas from the top of a stack of produce. When he reached for a bunch of radishes that had been under the bananas, a six-inch spider—*Heteropoda venatoria*, commonly called a banana spider—leaped from some wet burlap onto his left hand and bit him. Nine months later he died of heart failure. His wife brought an action against Associated Grocers, parent company of Thriftway Market, on theories of: (1) strict products liability under Restatement, Section 402(a); (2) breach of the implied warranty of merchantability; and (3) negligence. The trial court ruled against the plaintiff on all three theories. Was that a correct ruling? Explain

Self-Test Questions

1. Section 5 of the Federal Trade Commission Act is enforceable by:

   a. a consumer in federal court

   b. a consumer in state court

   c. the FTC in an administrative proceeding

   d. the FTC suing in federal court

2. The FTC:

   a. is an independent federal agency

   b. is an arm of the Justice Department

   c. supersedes Congress in defining deceptive trade practices

   d. speaks for the president on consumer matters

3. A company falsely stated that its competitor's product "is known to cause serious computer crashes." Which of the following statements is not true?

   a. The competitor may sue the company under state law.

   b. The competitor may sue the company for violating the FTC Act.

   c. The competitor may sue the company for violating federal trademark acts.

   d. The FTC may sue the company for violating the FTC Act.

4. The FTC may order a company that violated Section 5 of the FTC Act by false advertising:

   a. to go out of business

   b. to close down the division of the company that paid for false advertising

   c. to issue corrective advertising

   d. to buy back from its customers all the products sold by the advertising

5. The ingredients in a nationally-advertised cupcake must be disclosed on the package under:

   a. state common law

   b. a trade regulation rule promulgated by the FTC

   c. the federal Food, Drug, and Cosmetic Act

   d. an executive order of the president

6. Which is not a reason government regulation of the market is necessary in a modern market economy?

   a. the things we consume today are complex and potentially dangerous;

   b. the separation of production from consumption has reduced the effect of reputation in selling to the public;

   c. people are not able to protect themselves very well against professional con artists and grifters;

   d. modern transportation and communication makes collusion among competitors relatively easy.

   e. people are less well educated about consumer affairs than they were 130 years ago.

7. A merger that lessens competition in any line of commerce is prohibited by:

   a. Section 1 of the Sherman Act

   b. Section 2 of the Sherman Act

   c. Section 7 of the Clayton Act

   d. none of the above

8. Which of the following statements is true?

   a. horizontal mergers are always unlawful.

   b. a conglomerate merger between companies with unrelated products is always lawful.

    c. a vertical merger violates Section 2 of the Sherman Act.

    d. a horizontal merger that unduly increases the concentration of firms in a particular market is always unlawful.

9. The issuance of corporate securities is governed by:

    a. federal common law

    b. state law

    c. only by the FTC, a federal administrative agency

    d. the federal Securities Exchange Act of 1934

    e. none of these

10. The law that prohibits the payment of a bribe to foreign officials to gain business is called:

    a. the Insider Trading Act

    b. the federal Whistle Blower's Protection Act

    c. the blue sky law

    d. the Foreign Sales to Aliens Act

    e. none of these

11. The primary means for regulating interstate stock offerings that inadequately disclose risks is:

    a. the registration requirements of the 1933 Securities Act

    b. SEC prohibition of risky stock offerings

    c. the accounting provisions of the Foreign Corrupt Practices Act

    d. state "blue sky" laws

    e. none of these.

12. To enforce its prohibition under insider trading, the SEC prohibits all corporate insiders from trading at any time or way in the stocks of their companies.

    a. true

    b. false

13. Rule 10b-5 refers to what?

    a. the part of the Securities Exchange Act of 1934 that makes illegal fraudulent acts and practices in the sale or exchange of securities.

    b. part of the regulations the SEC has promulgated under the power given to it by Congress to make illegal fraudulent and deceptive acts.

    c. the regulation requiring consumer information on foodstuffs packaging.

    d. the generic name given to state securities regulation laws.

    e. none of these

14. The purpose of the Dodd-Frank Act is to:

    a. promote financial stability

    b. end "too big to fail"

    c. end bailouts

    d. protect against abusive financial service providers

    e. all of the above

15. In a products-liability case

    a. only tort theories are typically asserted.

    b. both tort and contract theories are typically asserted.

16. An implied warranty of merchantability

    a. is created in writing

    b. cannot be disclaimed by the seller

    c. is created by law, not by the parties

    d. can be disclaimed only in writing.

Self-Test Answers

1. c
2. a
3. b
4. c
5. c
6. e
7. c
8. d
9. e
10. e
11. a
12. b
13. b
14. e
15. b
16. c

Endnotes

1. John Gray, False Dawn: The Delusions of Global Capitalism, 17 (1999).

2. Id., at 21.

3. Derrick Jensen is an environmentalist and author. He was described by Amy Goodwin, host of Democracy Now ("a daily, global, independent news show") as the "poet-philosopher of the ecological movement" (https://www.democracynow.org/2010/11/26/author_and_activist_derrick_jensen_the). The quotation is from his book Endgame, Volume 1: The Problem of Civilization, at 6 (2006).

4. See, e.g., The International Organization for Standardization's "ISO 14000 family—Environmental Management": "The ISO 14000 family of standards provides practical tools for companies and organizations of all kinds looking to manage their environmental responsibilities. ISO 14001:2015 and its supporting standards such as ISO 14006:2011 focus on environmental systems to achieve this. The other standards in the family focus on specific approaches such as audits, communications, labeling and life cycle analysis, as well as environmental challenges such as climate change. https://www.iso.org/iso-14001-environmental-management.html

5. Nicole Perlroth, et al., "Alex Stemos, Facebook Data Security Chief, To Leave Amid Outcry," The New York Times, March 19, 2018; available at https://nytimes.com/2018/03/19/technology/facebook-alex-stamos.html?rref+collection%Fissuecollection/todays-new-york-times.

6. U.S. National Archives & Records Administration, Interstate Commerce Act. http://www.ourdocuments.gov/doc.php?doc=49

7. John Sherman (1823-1900) served in the U.S. House from 1854–1861; he was in the Senate from 1861–77, served as secretary of the Treasury from 1877–81, senator again from 1881–97, and secretary of state from 1897–98. (His brother, Maj. General William T. Sherman, lead the Civil War scorched-earth "March to the Sea" from Atlanta to the port of Savannah in November and December of 1864.)

8. Chicago Board of Trade v. United States, 246 U.S. 231 (1918).

9. Clayton's four proscribed behaviors are these: 1. Discrimination in prices charged different purchasers of the same commodities. Standard oil charged low prices where it had competition, drove the competition out, and then charged high prices where it had no competition. That's price discrimination. 2. Conditioning the sale of one commodity on the purchaser's refraining from using or dealing in commodities of the seller's competitors. Tying or tie-in contracts are illegal unless reasonable. 3. Acquiring the stock of a competing corporation, unless reasonable. Membership by a single person on more than one corporate board of directors if the companies are or were competitors.

10. Donald R. Katz, The Big Store: Inside the Crisis and Revolution at Sears, 53 (1987).

11. See, i.e., Paul Ziobro and Serena Ng, Wal-Mart Ratchets Up Pressure on Suppliers to Cut Prices, The Wall Street Journal, March 15, 2015. https://www.wsj.com/articles/wal-mart-ratchets-up-pressure-on-suppliers-to-cut-prices-1427845404.

12. U.S. v IBM, 298 U.S. 131 (1936).

13. In the 1950s and '60s, GM set prices for its automobiles, and other manufacturers copied the price structure. Here there is no conspiracy.

14. See, e.g., https://www.girardgibbs.com/antitrust/state-laws/california-cartwright-act/.

15. Heywood Klein and Hal Lancaster, "Major Flaws Persist in Big Buildings, Often Due to Pressure to Cut Costs," The Wall Street Journal, February 12, 1982. This bridge collapse remains the worst such disaster in modern U.S. history.

16. The FTC guide deals with (1) comparison of the sale price to a former price; (2) product comparisons; (3) false statements of "suggested retail price" to make buyers think they're getting a deal; (4) bargain based on the purchase of something else ("Buy one, get one free") needs to be literally accurate; (5) false claims to explain a "sale" price ("limited offer," "giant clearance sale"—must be true.

17. Here is the relevant federal regulation, https://bit.ly/2NoAra1.

18. Here are some examples: · Targeting vulnerable consumers—seniors and non-English speakers—with false claims in telemarketing or intense pressure tactics. · Door-to-Door, Direct Mail, and Unsolicited Merchandise. The FTC has promulgated a TRR requiring a three-day cooling-off period within which any door-to-door sales contract can be cancelled; contracts must state the buyer's right to the cooling-off period. Also, any unsolicited mailing and subsequent dunning to be an unfair trade practice under Section 5 of the FTC Act. Unsolicited products are treated as gifts; the recipient is under no obligation to return it or pay for it. Negative Option plans. Customers agree, when "joining," to accept and pay for all items unless they specifically indicate, before the goods arrive, that they want to reject them; if they do nothing, they must pay. Difficulties arise when the negative-option notice arrives late in the mail or when a member quits and continues to receive the monthly notices. Internet users will recognize this negative option as the "opt out" process, where you are "in" unless you notice what's going on and specifically opt out. Under FTC TRRs, among other things, a subscriber is entitled to ten days in which to notify sellers that she has rejected the particular item about to be sent. If a customer has cancelled her membership, the seller must take back and pay the former member's mailing expenses for any merchandise mailed after cancellation. The former member may treat any shipments beyond one after cancellation as unsolicited merchandise and keep it without having to pay for it or return it.

19. Orkin Exterminating Co. v. FTC, 849 F.2d 1354 (11th Cir. 1988), cert. denied, 488 U.S. 1041 (1989).

20. Tom Pahl, Acting Director of the Federal Trade Commission's Bureau of Consumer Protection, March 26, 2018. https://www.ftc.gov/news-events/press-releases/2018/03/statement-acting-director-ftcs-bureau-consumer-protection.

21. Its March 2016 "Cigarette Report" is available here (it reviews the year 2014): https://www.ftc.gov/system/files/documents/reports/federal-trade-commission-cigarette-report-2014-federal-trade-commission-smokeless-tobacco-report/ftc_smokeless_tobacco_report_2014.pdf

22. *Warner Lambert Co. v. Federal Trade Commission*, 562 F.2d 749 (D.C. Cir. 1977), cert. denied, 435 U.S. 950 (1978).

23. http://www.fda.gov/AboutFDA/Transparency/Basics/ucm194879.htm.

24. http://www.nhtsa.gov/About. And NHTSA has historically been very successful in reducing the number of deaths and injuries on U.S. roads: "In 2013, more than 32,000 people died on U.S. roads, roughly 90 fatalities a day, according to the CDC. The U.S. has seen a 31% reduction in its motor vehicle death rate per capita over the past 13 years. But compared with 19 other wealthy countries, which have declined an average of 56% during the same period, the U.S. has the slowest decrease. Road death rates in countries such as Spain and Denmark have dropped 75.1% and 63.5%, respectively." Aria Hangyu Chen, "U.S. Has Highest Car Crash Death Rate, Despite Progress, CDC says," *CNN* July 7, 2016, at https://www.cnn.com/2016/07/07/health/us-highest-crash-death-rate/index.html .

25. http://www.nhtsa.gov/About. And NHTSA has historically been very successful in reducing the number of deaths and injuries on U.S. roads: "In 2013, more than 32,000 people died on U.S. roads, roughly 90 fatalities a day, according to the CDC. The U.S. has seen a 31% reduction in its motor vehicle death rate per capita over the past 13 years. But compared with 19 other wealthy countries, which have declined an average of 56% during the same period, the U.S. has the slowest decrease. Road death rates in countries such as Spain and Denmark have dropped 75.1% and 63.5%, respectively." Aria Hangyu Chen, "U.S. Has Highest Car Crash Death Rate, Despite Progress, CDC says," CNN July 7, 2016, at https://www.cnn.com/2016/07/07/health/us-highest-crash-death-rate/index.html .

26. http://www.consumerfinance.gov/

27. Mallory Shelbourne, "Durbin: Wall St. Hates Consumer Bureau 'Like the Devil hates Holy Water.'" *The Hill*, http://thehill.com/homenews/senate/361840-durbin-republicans-hate-cfpb-like-the-devil-hates-holy-water .

28. Mallory Shelbourne, "Durbin: Wall St. Hates Consumer Bureau 'Like the Devil hates Holy Water.'" The Hill, http://thehill.com/homenews/senate/361840-durbin-republicans-hate-cfpb-like-the-devil-hates-holy-water .

29. Michael Hiltzik, "Consumer Protection: Why do Republicans Hate the CFPB So Much?" *L.A. Times*, July 23, 2015. http://www.latimes.com/business/hiltzik/la-fi-mh-cfpb-republicans-20150723-column.html

30. Here you can find the Department of Justice's 2016 Report on ECOA enforcement: https://www.justice.gov/crt/page/file/996791/download.

31. https://www.ftc.gov/enforcement/statutes/fair-accurate-credit-transactions-act-2003.

32. https://www.debt.org/credit/your-consumer-rights/truth-lending-act/.

33. https://www.aprfinder.com/fair-credit-billing-act-overview.

34. https://www.fair-debt-collection.com/debt-collector-help/fair-debt-act.html. https://thompsonlawoffice.net/debt-collection-videos/

35. Here you can find Washington State's lemon law, as per the state attorney general's office: http://www.atg.wa.gov/lemon-law-0. And here is a case demonstrating a customer's use of the lemon law (NY, 2018): https://bit.ly/2Nl2yHg

36. https://www.motherjones.com/politics/2013/05/table-saw-sawstop-safety-finger-cut/

37. U.C.C. 2-313

38. C. Richard Newsome and Andrew F. Knopf, "Federal Preemption: Products Lawyers Beware," Florida Justice Association Journal, July 27, 2007, accessed March 1, 2011, http://www.newsomelaw.com/resources/articles/federal-preemption-products-lawyers-beware.↑

39. American Tort Reform Association, http://www.atra.org.↑

40. http://www.shragerlaw.com/html/legal_rights.html.

41. Here is President Franklin Roosevelt explaining why he ordered a "bank holiday" in March, 1933, and announcing various legal reforms. https://www.fdic.gov/about/history/fdr_fireside_chat_banking_situation_03-12-33.mp3 .

42. https://www.fdic.gov/about/strategic/strategic/mission.html.

43. See also Alan Pyke, "5 Numbers to Know as Dodd-Frank Wall Street Reform Celebrates Its 5th Birthday," *ThinkProgress*, July 21, 2015. At https://thinkprogress.org/5-numbers-to-know-as-dodd-frank-wall-street-reform-celebrates-its-5th-birthday-e145f4360b7c/

44. https://www.fdic.gov/regulations/laws/important/.

45. *Securities and Exchange Commission v. W. J. Howey Co.*, 328 U.S. 293 (1946)

46. There are some exceptions to the registration requirement: (1) private offerings to a limited number of persons or institutions who have access to the kind of information registration would disclose and who do not propose to redistribute the securities; (2) offerings restricted to the residents of the state in which the issuing company is organized and doing business; (3) securities of municipal, state, federal and other government instrumentalities, of charitable institutions, of banks, and of carriers subject to the Interstate Commerce Act; (4) offerings not in excess of certain specified amounts made in compliance with regulations of the Commission, and (5) offerings of "small business investment companies" made in accordance with rules and regulations of the Commission.

47. https://www.sec.gov/answers/about-lawsshtml.html

48. Here is Apple Corporation's "Current Report" "Pursuant to Section 13 OR 15(d) of the Securities Exchange Act of 1934," July 22, 2014: http://investor.apple.com/secfiling.cfm?filingID=1193125-14-275598&CIK=320193&bd=-7#720#1280#1#n .

49. The short-swing rule prohibits officers and insiders from making short-term profits; it is a prophylactic against insider trading.

50. U.S Securities and Exchange Commission, "SEC Charges Goodyear with FCPA Violations," February 24, 2015: Goodyear agreed to pay more than $16 million to settle the SEC's charges. According to the SEC's order instituting a settled administrative proceeding, Goodyear failed to prevent or detect more than $3.2 million in bribes during a four-year period due to inadequate FCPA compliance controls at its subsidiaries in sub-Saharan Africa. Bribes were generally paid in cash to employees of private companies or government-owned entities as well as other local authorities such as police or city council officials to land tire sales. The improper payments were falsely recorded as legitimate business expenses in the books and records of the subsidiaries, which were consolidated into Goodyear's books and records. https://www.sec.gov/news/pressrelease/2015-38.html#.VO3_ZVoll4U

51. For more information on the Dodd-Frank Wall Street Reform and Consumer Protection Act (Pub.L. 111-203, H.R. 4173), see Thomas, "Major Actions," Bill Summary & Status 111th Congress (2009–2010) H.R.4173, http://thomas.loc.gov/cgi-bin/bdquery/z?d111:HR04173:@@@L&summ2=m&#major actions.

52. *SEC v Howey*, 328 U.S. 293 (1946).

53. 604 F.2d 639 (1979)

CHAPTER 15

Government Regulation: The Social Safety Net

Chapter Learning Objectives

After reading this chapter you should understand:

1. Why there is a "social safety net."
2. Some degree of wage and hour protection is provided by the government for employees.
3. Pensions, including Social Security and private pension plans, are provided or regulated by the government.
4. Health insurance is provided for people who don't get it through their employers, including Medicare, Medicaid, and Obamacare.
5. Health insurance is provided for people who are employed through workers' compensation.
6. Parental leave laws.
7. The purpose of bankruptcy relief laws.
8. How the problems of homelessness and hunger in the U.S. are addressed.

At the least, the purpose of government is to provide security for its people. We are familiar with "national security" and "homeland security," but these usually imply security against violent disruptions of the peace. People need more than just security against violence. People need the security afforded by a steady stream of livable income, and if they don't have it, to some extent the government must provide it, or else there will be riots in the streets. The government regulates the minimum wage, provides some health insurance opportunities, and protects—to some extent—honest debtors who do not have adequate income to pay their bills. These are elements of the social safety net which we take up here.

15.1 Why There Is a Social Safety Net

Learning Objective

1. Understand why the government provides a "social safety net"—laws that, to some extent, keep Americans from starving, disease, and other gross insecurities.

Maybe you've heard this saying: "The federal government is basically an insurance company with an army." As is regularly observed in this text, security is a fundamental human need and insurance and armies can both provide security, albeit differently.

You are of course familiar with "national security," and "homeland security," and obviously you have heard of "Social Security," but what does "social security" mean? Franklin Roosevelt expressed the problem when he signed the Social Security Act in 1935:

The civilization of the past hundred years, with its startling industrial changes, has tended more and more to make life insecure. Young people have come to wonder what would be their lot when they came to old age. The man with a job has wondered how long the job would last.[1]

In 1941, President Roosevelt envisioned "a world founded upon four essential freedoms": freedom of speech and expression, freedom of religion, freedom from want, and freedom from fear. Capitalism is very good at generating wealth; it is not very good, by itself, at fairly distributing it. Most people have enough to get by, but little to spare. Many would be devastated by an interruption in their income stream—"one paycheck away from homelessness," as is said. Common things interrupt the stream of income that most of us need to live: workplace injury, a serious illness, unemployment, disability, old age. What became of down-and-out people and their families a hundred years ago? Often it was "the poor house" or the "poor farm"[2] (funded by the county and by residents' labor).

FIGURE 15.1 A "Poor Farm"
A poor farm in Wabaunsee County, Kansas, around 1901.

Source: Internet Archive Book Images [No restrictions], via Wikimedia Commons

Many poor people simply died from disease, malnourishment, despair, and desolation.

We think we are more enlightened today, but the social safety net is supported only by popular will, and it is fickle; here is a funny video of President Franklin Roosevelt, campaigning for his second term in 1936, on the point: https://www.youtube.com/watch?v=S3RHnKYNvx8. (and here is a better-quality snippet of the same speech: https://www.youtube.com/watch?v=Pb-7Dpp-LPk). See if you think Mr. Roosevelt's take on the social safety net is still good.

A final note by way of introduction: What is taken up here, for the most part, is a quick look at laws adopted by the legislature, to address—more or less—the insecurities inherent in a capitalistic system. For the sake of brevity, we will seldom mention the penalties for violating the law, but please know that there are penalties, and in some cases the penalties are serious. Big money can be at stake for businesspeople who are not aware of the law.

Key Takeaway

It is not acceptable in a rich, modern country to have people literally starve to death on the streets, or—at least absolutely—to be unable to survive on full-time income. Nor is it acceptable that when people become old that they suffer the indignity of gross poverty, or that people who become ill or who suffer injury should receive no care: we expect that, to some extent, they should and will receive some care. And people also need protection when they honestly incur debt but cannot repay it. These protections against the vicissitudes (hardships) of life are the "social safety net." We expect, to some extent, the government will provide a social safety net.

Exercises

1. What would happen if there were no "social safety net" at all? What is the point of the story about the French aristocrat just before the French revolution (1789) who, hearing that the masses were starving, said, "If they have no bread, let them eat cake"?
2. What happened to poor people—people who didn't have enough money to buy decent food, clothing, or shelter—before aspects of the modern "welfare state" were adopted?
3. If the problem that a lot of people in the U.S. have is that, frankly, they don't have enough money to live with dignity, why not increase the taxes on multimillionaires to fund more robust social safety net programs?

15.2 Income Security

Learning Objectives

1. Understand that there are federal and state laws (statutory and common law) addressing, to some extent, the universal need for an adequate stream of income.
2. Know the reason for, abuses of, and exceptions to, the employment-at-will doctrine.
3. Know that the government mandates a minimum wage, maximum hours, and family leave, and outlaws most child labor.
4. Understand there is protection against income interruption from unemployment, old age, and inadequate or defective pension plans.

Most of us need a steady stream of income to clothe, feed, and shelter ourselves, and to make ourselves presentable to society so that we may obtain employment. Society recognizes that this stream may be interrupted by common events—unemployment, injury, disease, old age—and to some extent the social safety net addresses these concerns.

Wage and Hour Laws: The Fair Labor Standards Act (FLSA) of 1938

Employment at Will

As noted in Chapter 13, the common law employment-at- will doctrine still survives in the U.S.: absent a contract, an employee can be fired for any reason or no reason. And, certainly, at common law the employer is free to pay whatever the employee is willing to work for; this is fair in a way, as the employee can always quit and find a better job.

The employment-at-will doctrine is loaded with insecurity for employees; it is unheard of in Europe, where employment is considered a right, and not a privilege. The doctrine is harsh, but has been modified in the U.S. in the last 40 years and has exceptions. An employer *cannot* discharge an at-will employee without cause if:

- The parties have modified the at-will contract either expressly or impliedly after the employee got hired;
- The employer has implied in the company personnel handbook or by company policy that employees will not be dismissed except for cause; or
- The employer acted in bad faith (for example, an employer fired a salesman to deprive him of his sales commission[3]);
- The dismissal contravenes public policy. Here are examples of at-will employees whose dismissal was held to be in violation of public policy: a woman was fired because she took time off for jury duty; a woman was fired because she refused to have sex with her boss; an armored-truck driver was fired when—in violation of company rules—he left his vehicle unattended to help a woman who was being assaulted by a bank robber; an employee was sacked for complaining to the Environmental Protection Agency that his employer was illegally dumping contaminated water into a river when such retaliation is expressly forbidden by statute. These dismissals are unacceptable as in violation of public policy.

The upshot is, the scary insecurity of employment at will has been ameliorated (made less awful) by judicial and legislative enactments.

The Fair Labor Standards Act

Background

But exceptions aside, an at-will employee *can* generally be fired for no reason, because—after all—the employee can always find a better job. *Except*, during the late 19th and early 20th centuries it became apparent that the new swarms of urban laborers—many of them off the farm or immigrants—often could *not* find better jobs, and that even those with jobs had no bargaining power against their employer. (You may recall that an "unconscionable contract" is one marked by great inequality of bargaining power.)

The deformations of the free market became more and more obvious in the filthy, bustling cities of the late 19th century: sweat shops, subsistence wages, dangerous working conditions, grotesque inequality of income, no medical care, and no provision for retirement. Legislators at the state and federal level responded and they adopted ameliorative legislation (*i.e.*, legislation to make the working person's life better, more tolerable). But the Supreme Court, wielding the club of "substantive due process"[4] under the Fifth and Fourteenth Amendments, would have none of it. In 1918, in the infamous *Hammer v. Dagenhart case*,[5] it held that the Keating-Owen Act, the first federal child labor law, was unconstitutional: if an employer wants to hire a child to work fifteen hours a day, six days a week, in some fetid mill, and if the child's parents are willing to accept that arrangement, then the federal government has no constitutional authority to interfere. When Congress responded by instead adopting a tax on child-labor-produced goods, the Court struck that down too, observing that now Congress was trying to accomplish indirectly what it could not do directly (prohibit child labor).[6]

Then in *Adkins v. Children's Hospital* the Court took aim and sunk the (Congressionally-adopted) Washington D.C. minimum wage (1923):

> *It has been said that legislation of the kind now under review is required in the interest of social justice, for whose ends freedom of contract may lawfully be subjected to restraint. The liberty of the individual to do as he pleases, even in innocent matters, is not absolute. It must frequently yield to the common good. . . . But, nevertheless there are limits to that power, and when these have been passed, it becomes the plain duty of the courts in the proper exercise of their authority to so declare. To sustain the individual freedom of action contemplated by the Constitution is not to strike down the common good but to exalt it; for surely the good of society as a whole cannot be better served than by the preservation against arbitrary restraining of the liberties of its constituent members.[7]*

With the D.C. minimum wage gone, people wondered what other ameliorative legislation the Court would throw out—all manner of state laws regulating wages, hours, and working conditions were called into question. And, indeed, the Court continued like a man-eating tiger: in 1925 out went Arizona's minimum wage;[8] in 1927 Arkansas' legislation on the topic suffered the same fate.[9] In 1936 the Court struck again,[10] knocking out the New York state minimum wage. Fed up, Justice Harlan Stone dissented:

> *In the years that have intervened since the Adkins case we have had opportunity to learn that a wage is not always the result of free bargaining between employers and employees. . . . It is not for the courts to resolve doubts whether the remedy by wage regulation is as efficacious as many believe, or is better than some other, or is better even than the blind operation of uncontrolled economic forces. The legislature must be free to choose unless government is to be rendered impotent. . . . There is grim irony in speaking of the freedom of contract of those who, because of their economic necessities, give their services for less than is needful to keep body and soul together. . . . [11]*

But, as is said, even the members of the Supreme Court read the newspaper, and the popular pressure for reform could not be resisted forever. In *West Coast Hotel v. Parrish* (1937, excerpted below) the Court did an about-face: it overruled *Adkins* and accepted Washington state's minimum wage.

With *West Coast Hotel* in his pocket, so to say,[12] an elated President Roosevelt urged Congress to adopt a *federal* minimum wage. In his January 1938 State of the Union address he said:

> *The people of this country, by an overwhelming vote, are in favor of having Congress—this Congress—put a floor below which individual wages shall not fall, and a ceiling beyond which the hours of individual labor shall not rise. . . . Wage and hour legislation, therefore, is a problem which is definitely before this Congress for action. It is an essential part of economic recovery. It has the support of an overwhelming majority of our people in every walk of life.*

Basic Provisions of the Act

Fair Labor Standards Act

Federal statute, 1938, creating a national minimum wage, setting maximum work hours, prohibiting child labor (among other things).

Congress responded to President Roosevelt's call and to laboring peoples' plight—much exacerbated by the Great Depression—by passing the **Fair Labor Standards Act** in 1938.[13] It applies to all persons employed in "an enterprise engaged in commerce"—any activity directly or indirectly affecting interstate commerce. The act addressed several problems:

- Minimum wage. The act establishes a federal minimum wage for the regular workweek and a higher scale for overtime; it requires record-keeping and youth employment standards. It applies to all *non-managerial* workers in any business that hits the Department of Labor's dollar-volume of goods or services and that affects interstate commerce (with some exceptions, notably for agricultural workers and tipped employees), including federal, state, and local workers. There is no provision requiring holiday, severance, or sick pay. The act is enforced by the state and federal departments of labor; the department and the employee may sue for back pay and statutory damages. The federal minimum wage is, as of May 2018, $7.25 per hour. It is a shamefully low wage rate; it amounts to $14,500 per year (40 hours a week for 50 weeks). You could not live on $14,500 per year. As Congress has been remarkably unresponsive, state and local governments have stepped in. Twenty-nine states have a higher minimum wage than the federal limit, and 41 localities have adopted minimum wages higher than their state's.[14]

FIGURE 15.2 Real Value of the Federal Minimum Wage in Constant 2016 Dollars

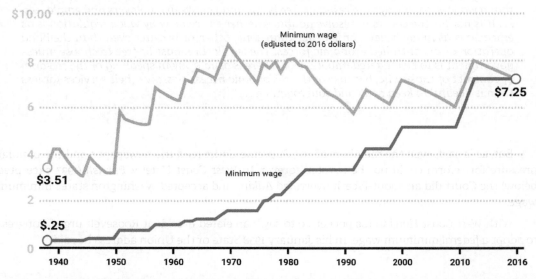

Source: 5 Facts About the Minimum Wage. Pew Research Center, Washington, D.C. (January 3, 2017) http://www.pewresearch.org/fact-tank/2017/01/04/5-facts-about-the-minimum-wage/ft_17-01-03_minwage_1938_2016/.

The Family and Medical Leave Act

Federal statute, 1993, requiring some employers to give employees unpaid leave for some family medical issues.

- Maximum hours. Wage earners (not salaried personnel) must be paid overtime if they work more than 40 hours per week (with some exceptions). Attending meetings or taking employer-required training counts as "hours worked," but commuting to work does not count.[15]

- Child labor. Child labor is generally prohibited by the FLSA. Children (<18 years) may work delivering newspapers, for their parents, and in some agricultural or entertainment activities. They cannot work in hazardous jobs or jobs that jeopardize their educational opportunities. Here is the DOL's website on child labor: https://www.dol.gov/general/topic/youthlabor.

- Family Leave. **The Family and Medical Leave Act** (FMLA), (1993) augments the FLSA; it mandates that covered employers with 50 or more employees grant up to a total of 12 workweeks per year of *unpaid*, job-protected leave for:

  - the birth of a child and to care for the newborn child within one year of birth;

- the placement with the employee of a child for adoption or foster care and to care for the newly-placed child within one year of placement;

- to care for the employee's spouse, child, or parent who has a serious health condition;

- a serious health condition that makes the employee unable to perform the essential functions of his or her job;

- any qualifying exigency arising out of the fact that the employee's spouse, son, daughter, or parent is a military member on "covered active duty;" or

- twenty-six workweeks of leave during a single 12-month period to care for a covered service member with a serious injury or illness if the eligible employee is the service member's spouse, son, daughter, parent, or next of kin (military caregiver leave).[16]

- Nursing mothers. Under 2010 amendments to the FLSA, employers are required to provide "reasonable break time for an employee to express breast milk for her nursing child for 1 year after the child's birth each time such employee has need to express the milk." Employers are also required to provide "a place, other than a bathroom, that is shielded from view and free from intrusion from coworkers and the public, which may be used by an employee to express breast milk."[17]

Enforcement of the FLSA

The Act is enforced by the federal Department of Labor's Wage and Hour Division (WHD). Employees who feel their employer is violating the law are encouraged to contact the WHD. The states also have fair labor standards and, generally, when state and federal rules differ, the rules that are *more* protective will apply.[18]

Job Loss: Federal and State Unemployment Compensation

Losing a job stops most people's income. Two salient federal laws—there are many others—address some aspects of job loss.

- **Federal Unemployment Tax Act (FUTA).** 1935, taxes employers to fund the federal Unemployment Insurance Fund. It provides insurance for most workers who lose their jobs through no fault of their own. Each state has an account with the Fund. The benefits and eligibility requirements vary from state to state (ranging from $742 per week with a 30-week duration in Massachusetts to $235 per week for 26 weeks in Mississippi[19]). Recipients are expected to be looking for work while they receive the benefit, and the states provide the unemployed with some assistance in finding a job.

- **Worker Adjustment and Retraining Notification (WARN) Act**, 1988, requires, in most cases, that employers with 100 or more full-time employees provide employees with a written notice 60 days before a mass layoff or plant closing so that they can, as the DOL puts it, have "sufficient time to seek other employment or retraining opportunities before losing their jobs." Also, the employer is required to give similar notice to specified state and local governments. If a WARN employer fails to give notice as required the employer is liable to "each affected employee for an amount equal to back pay and benefits for the period of violation up to 60 days" and to the "unit of local government for a penalty of $500 for each day of violation."[20]

Federal Unemployment Tax Act

Federal statute, 1935, creating a system of unemployment compensation.

Worker Adjustment and Retraining Notification (WARN) Act

Federal statute, 1988, requiring large employers to give notice to the public in advance of a plant closing.

Old Age and Disability Compensation

The Federal Pension: Social Security

Nothing is certain, as Ben Franklin wrote, but death and taxes. For most people though, there is another certainty—getting old. When people get old they usually cannot work the way they could when they were young—it isn't a very good idea to have a 65-year-old doing roofing (no matter how secure the fall protection—about which, see below).

In 1935 the poverty rate among senior citizens was over 50%. How humiliating and discouraging it was for millions of people who had worked hard all their lives to come to old age and find little or no security: no income, no health care, no recourse except to impose on family (and the poor farm).

Social Security Act of 1935

Federal statute creating the U.S. Social Security Administration and setting up public pensions for retirees.

The **Social Security Act of 1935** created a fund to provide income to retired and disabled workers and their families. It is a pension—the recipient gets a check in the mail every month from the government (or now an electronic deposit). The main source of income for the fund is a tax (half paid by the employer, half by the employee) of 12.4% of the employee's income up to $128,700 (in 2018). After that, there is no further tax on employees' income. The Social Security Administration collected $960 billion in 2016; it paid out some $911 billion:

Social Security distribution of benefits in 2016

Category	$ Billions	Portion of Total Social Security Benefits
Retired workers and their families	$651	71%
Survivors of deceased workers	$117	13%
Disabled workers and their families	$143	16%

Source: https://www.justfacts.com/socialsecurity.asp

Because most of the Social Security Administration's income is from payroll taxes, it will never run out of money (as long as there are people working), but the amount of the benefit received may decrease (because of an aging population) after 2033. The fixes are technically simple, but politically difficult. Yes, students, when you get old there will still be Social Security for you. Here is a very accessible discussion of Social Security: https://www.justfacts.com/socialsecurity.asp.

In 2012, the elderly—thanks to Social Security—were not the largest population group in poverty anymore, children were, and are:[21]

FIGURE 15.3 Poverty Rates for Children and Elderly

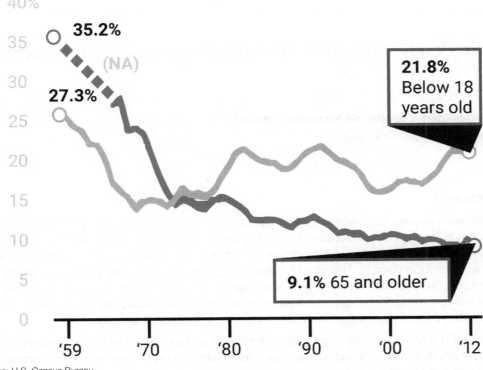

35.2%

(NA)

27.3%

21.8%
Below 18
years old

9.1% 65 and older

'59   '70   '80   '90   '00   '12

Source: U.S. Census Bureau

Regulation of Private Pension Plans

In the early 1970s Congress learned that some private, employer-provided pension plans failed to deliver. Sometimes employees could not carry their pensions with them when they changed jobs (lack of "portability"); sometimes the employee-contribution was imprudently invested in risky investments by the employer, and when the employee came to apply for the benefit, there was no money; sometimes the employee's right to a pension would not vest for a long, long time, so that if the employee quit—even after, say, 30 years—there was no pension available. Sometimes the employer went bankrupt.

Congress responded to these problems in 1974 by adopting the **Employee Retirement Income Security Act** (ERISA). ERISA does not mandate that employers provide any pension program; it sets minimum standards for benefits the employer chooses to provide. ERISA does the following:

- requires that employers make detailed reports as to plan income and outlays;
- limits what investments the employer can make with retirement funds;
- establishes minimum funding requirements;
- dictates that the employer has a fiduciary responsibility to the participants;
- sets vesting limits.

ERISA also created the **Pension Benefit Guaranty Corporation** (PBGC) which, among other things, requires that employers contribute to an insurance fund administered by the PBGC so that employees of out-of-business or bankrupt employers still get some pension benefits.

Issues regarding discrimination against older or disabled employees are taken up in the chapter on employment law (Chapter 13).

Employee Retirement Income Security Act

Federal statute, 1974, establishing standards for private pension plans.

Pension Benefit Guaranty Corporation

Federal insurance corporation, 1974, to insure private pension funds.

Cases

Public Policy Exception for Dismissing At-Will Employees

> **Wagenseller v. Scottsdale Memorial Hospital**
>
> 710 P.2d 1025 (Arizona, 1985)

Feldman, J.

Catherine Wagenseller began her employment at Scottsdale Memorial Hospital as a staff nurse in March 1975, having been personally recruited by the manager of the emergency department, Kay Smith. Wagenseller was an "at-will" employee—one hired without and specific contractual term, a Smith was her supervisor. In August 1978, Wagenseller was assigned to the position of ambulance charge nurse, and approximately one year later was promoted to the position of paramedic coordinator, a newly-approved management position in the emergency department. Three months later, on November 1, 1979, Wagenseller was terminated.

Most of the events surrounding Wagenseller's work at the Hospital and her subsequent termination are not disputed, although the parties differ in their interpretation of the inferences to be drawn from, and the significance of, these events. For more than four years, Smith and Wagenseller maintained a friendly, professional, working relationship. In May 1979, they joined a group consisting largely of personnel from other hospitals for an eight-day camping and rafting trip down the Colorado River. According to Wagenseller, "an uncomfortable feeling" developed between her and Smith as the trip progressed—a feeling that Wagenseller ascribed to "the behavior that Kay Smith was displaying." Wagenseller states that this included public urination, defecation and bathing, heavy drinking, and "grouping up" with other rafters. Wagenseller did not participate in any of these activities. She also refused to join in the group's staging of a parody of the song "Moon River," which allegedly concluded with members of the group "mooning" the audience. Smith and others allegedly performed the "Moon River" skit twice at the Hospital following the group's return from the river, but Wagenseller declined to participate there as well.

Wagenseller contends that her refusal to engage in these activities caused her relationship with Smith to deteriorate and was the proximate cause of her termination. She claims that following the river trip Smith began harassing her, using abusive language, and embarrassing her in the company of other staff. Other emergency department staff reported a similar marked change in Smith's behavior toward Wagenseller after the trip, although Smith denied it.

Up to the time of the river trip, Wagenseller had received consistently favorable job performance evaluations. Two months before the trip, Smith completed an annual evaluation report in which she rated Wagenseller's performance as "exceed[ing] results expected," the second highest of five possible ratings. In August and October 1979, Wagenseller met first with Smith and then with Smith's successor, Jeannie Steindorff, to discuss some problems regarding her duties as paramedic coordinator and her attitude toward the job. On November 1, 1979, following an exit interview at which Wagenseller was asked to resign and refused, she was terminated.

She appealed her dismissal in letters to her supervisor and to the Hospital administrative and personnel department, answering the Hospital's stated reasons for her termination, claiming violations of the disciplinary procedure contained in the Hospital's personnel policy manual, and requesting reinstatement and other remedies. When this appeal was denied, Wagenseller brought suit against the Hospital, its personnel administrators, and her supervisor, Kay Smith.

Wagenseller, an "at-will" employee, contends that she was fired for reasons which contravene public policy and without legitimate cause related to job performance. She claims that her termination was wrongful, and that damages are recoverable under both tort and contract theories. The Hospital argues that an "at-will" employee may be fired for cause, without cause, or for "bad" cause. We hold that in the absence of contractual provision, such an employee may be fired for good cause or for no cause, but not for "bad" cause.

[The court traced the history of the at-will employment doctrine and observed that its foundation is unsound.]* * *

However unsound its foundation, the at-will doctrine was adopted by the New York courts in [Citation, 1895], and soon became the generally-accepted American rule. In 1932, this court first adopted the rule for Arizona: "The general rule in regard to contracts for personal services, ... where no time limit is provided, is that they are terminable at pleasure by either party, or at most upon reasonable notice." *Dover Copper Mining Co. v. Doenges.* Thus, an employer was free to fire an employee hired for an indefinite term "for good cause, for no cause, or even for cause morally wrong, without being thereby guilty of legal wrong." [Citations.]

In recent years there has been apparent dissatisfaction with the absolutist formulation of the common law at-will rule. The Illinois Supreme Court is representative of courts that have acknowledged a need for a less mechanical application of the rule:

> With the rise of large corporations conducting specialized operations and employing relatively immobile workers who often have no other place to market their skills, recognition that the employer and employee do not stand on equal footing is realistic. In addition, unchecked employer power, like unchecked employee power, has been seen to present a distinct threat to the public policy carefully considered and adopted by society as a whole. As a result, it is now recognized that a proper balance must be maintained among the employer's interest in operating a business efficiently and profitably, the employee's interest in earning a livelihood, and society's interest in seeing its public policies carried out.

The trend has been to modify the at-will rule by creating exceptions to its operation. Three general exceptions have developed. The most widely accepted approach is the "public policy" exception, which permits recovery upon a finding that the employer's conduct undermined some important public policy. * * * The leading case recognizing a public policy exception to the at-will doctrine is *Palmateer v. International Harvester Co.*, which holds that an employee stated a cause of action for wrongful discharge when he claimed he was fired for supplying information to police investigating alleged criminal violations by a co-employee. Addressing the issue of what constitutes "clearly mandated public policy," the court stated:

> There is no precise definition of the term. In general, it can be said that public policy concerns what is right and just and what affects the citizens of the State collectively. It is to be found in the State's constitution and statutes and, when they are silent, in its judicial decisions. Although there is no precise line of demarcation dividing matters that are the subject of public policies from matters purely personal, a survey of cases in other States involving retaliatory discharges shows that a matter must strike at the heart of a citizen's social rights, duties, and responsibilities before the tort will be allowed.

It is difficult to justify this court's further adherence to a rule which permits an employer to fire someone for "cause morally wrong." So far as we can tell, no court faced with a termination that violated a "clear mandate of public policy" has refused to adopt the public policy exception.

Certainly, a court would be hard-pressed to find a rationale to hold that an employer could with impunity fire an employee who refused to commit perjury. Why should the law imply an agreement which would give the employer such power? It may be argued, of course, that our economic system functions best if employers are given wide latitude in dealing with employees. We assume that it is in the public interest that employers continue to have that freedom. We also believe, however, that the interests of the economic system will be fully served if employers may fire for good cause or without cause. The interests of society as a whole will be promoted if employers are forbidden to fire for cause which is "morally wrong."

We therefore adopt the public policy exception to the at-will termination rule. We hold that an employer may fire for good cause or for no cause. He may not fire for bad cause — that which violates public policy. To the extent that it is contrary to the foregoing, we overrule *Dover Copper Mining Co. v. Doenges*, supra.

We turn then to the questions of where "public policy" may be found and how it may be recognized and articulated. * * * [Discussion follows about how a court can determine what "public policy" is.] Although we do not limit our recognition of the public policy exception to cases involving a violation of a criminal statute, we do believe that our duty will seldom be clearer than when such a violation is involved.

In the case before us, Wagenseller refused to participate in activities which arguably would have violated our indecent exposure statute, A.R.S. § 13-1402. She claims that she was fired because of this refusal. The statute provides:

Indecent exposure; classifications A. A person commits indecent exposure if he or she exposes his or her genitals or anus or she exposes the areola or nipple of her breast or breasts and another person is present, and the defendant is reckless about whether such other person, as a reasonable person, would be offended or alarmed by the act. B. Indecent exposure is a class 1 misdemeanor. Indecent exposure to a person under the age of fifteen years is a class 6 felony.

We thus uphold this state's public policy by holding that termination for refusal to commit an act which might violate A.R.S. § 13-1402 may provide the basis of a claim for wrongful discharge. The relevant inquiry here is not whether the alleged "mooning" incidents were either felonies or misdemeanors or constituted purely technical violations of the statute, but whether they contravened the important public policy interests embodied in the law. The law enacted by the legislature establishes a clear policy that public exposure of one's anus or genitals is contrary to public standards of morality. We are compelled to conclude that termination of employment for refusal to participate in public exposure of one's buttocks is a termination contrary to the policy of this state, even if, for instance, the employer might have grounds to believe that all of the onlookers were voyeurs and would not be offended. In this situation, there might be no crime, but there would be a violation of public policy to compel the employee to do an act ordinarily proscribed by the law.

Summary. The trial court granted summary judgment against Wagenseller on the count alleging the tort of wrongful discharge in violation of public policy. We adopt the "public policy" exception to the at-will termination rule and hold that the trial court erred in granting judgment against plaintiff on this theory. On remand plaintiff will be entitled to a jury trial if she can make a prima facie showing that her termination was caused by her refusal to perform some act contrary to public policy, or her performance of some act which, as a matter of public policy, she had a right to do. The obverse, however, is that mere dispute over an issue involving a question of public policy is not equivalent to establishing causation as a matter of law and will not automatically entitle plaintiff to judgment. In the face of conflicting evidence or inferences as to the actual reason for termination, the question of causation will be a question of fact.* * *

Case Questions

1. If the behavior that Wagenseller had refused to participate in had been limited to heavy drinking and "grouping up" with other rafters, would that have made a difference in this case?
2. Why would this apparently competent woman be fired for refusing to "moon" an audience of colleagues at a retreat?
3. What is the point of the "public policy" exception?
4. Certainly it would not work if every employee could decide for herself what constituted a "violation of public policy"; where does the court here say public policy comes from?

Supreme Court Validates Wage and Hour Legislation

West Coast Hotel v. Parrish

300 U.S. 379 (1937)

West Coast Hotel v. Parrish

U.S. Supreme Court case, 1937, validating the state minimum wage, and overruling precedent to the contrary.

Hughes, C. J.

The defendant conducts a hotel. The plaintiff, Elsie Parrish, was employed as a chambermaid and (with her husband) brought this suit to recover the difference between the wages paid her and the minimum wage fixed pursuant to the state law. The minimum wage was $14.50 per week of 48 hours [thirty cents per hour, or about $5.40 in 2019 dollars]. The defendant challenged the act as repugnant to the due process clause of the Fourteenth Amendment of the Constitution of the United States. The Supreme Court of the state, reversing the trial court, sustained the statute and directed judgment for the plaintiffs. *Parrish v. West Coast Hotel* Co., 55 P. 2d 1083. The case is here on appeal.

The defendant relies upon the decision of this Court in *Adkins v. Children's Hospital*, 261 U.S. 525 (1923), which held invalid the District of Columbia Minimum Wage Act which was attacked under the due process clause of the Fifth Amendment.

The Supreme Court of Washington has upheld the minimum wage statute of that state. It has decided that the statute is a reasonable exercise of the police power of the state. The state court has refused to regard the decision in the *Adkins* case as determinative and has pointed to our decisions both before and since that case as justifying its position. We are of the opinion that this ruling of the state court demands on our part a re-examination of the *Adkins* case. The importance of the question, in which many states having similar laws are concerned, the close division by which the decision in the Adkins case was reached, and the economic conditions which have supervened, and in the light of which the reasonableness of the exercise of the protective power of the state must be considered, make it not only appropriate, but we think imperative, that in deciding the present case the subject should receive fresh consideration.

The constitutional provision invoked [by the defendant Hotel] is the due process clause of the Fourteenth Amendment governing the states. The violation alleged by those attacking minimum wage regulation is deprivation of [the employer's] freedom of contract. What is this freedom? The Constitution does not speak of freedom of contract. It speaks of liberty and prohibits the deprivation of liberty without due process of law. In prohibiting that deprivation, the Constitution does not recognize an absolute and uncontrollable liberty [of an employer]. Liberty safeguarded is liberty in a social organization which requires the protection of law against the evils which menace the health, safety, morals, and welfare of the people. Liberty under the Constitution is thus necessarily subject to the restraints of due process, and regulation which is reasonable in relation to its subject and is adopted in the interests of the community is due process.

The point that has been strongly stressed that adult employees should be deemed competent to make their own contracts was decisively met nearly forty years ago in *Holden v. Hardy*, where we pointed out the inequality in the footing of the parties:

> *[Employers] and their operatives do not stand upon an equality, and their interests are, to a certain extent, conflicting. The former naturally desire to obtain as much labor as possible from their employees, while the latter are often induced by the fear of discharge to conform to regulations which their judgment, fairly exercised, would pronounce to be detrimental to their health or strength. In other words, the proprietors lay down the rules, and the laborers are practically constrained to obey them. In such cases self-interest is often an unsafe guide, and the legislature may properly interpose its authority.*

And we added that the fact "that both parties are of full age, and competent to contract, does not necessarily deprive the state of the power to interfere, where the parties do not stand upon an equality, or where the public heath demands that one party to the contract shall be protected against himself. The state still retains an interest in his welfare, however reckless he may be. The whole is no greater than the sum of all the parts, and when the individual health, safety, and welfare are sacrificed or neglected, the state must suffer."

With full recognition of the earnestness and vigor which characterize the prevailing opinion in *Adkins*, we find it impossible to reconcile that ruling with these well-considered declarations.

What can be closer to the public interest than the health of women and their protection from unscrupulous and overreaching employers? And if the protection of women is a legitimate end of the exercise of state power, how can it be said that the requirement of the payment of a minimum wage fairly fixed in order to meet the very necessities of existence is not an admissible means to that end? The Legislature of the state was clearly entitled to consider the situation of women in employment, the fact that they are in the class receiving the least pay, that their bargaining power is relatively weak, and that they are the ready victims of those who would take advantage of their necessitous circumstances.

The Legislature was entitled to adopt measures to reduce the evils of the "sweating system," the exploiting of workers at wages so low as to be insufficient to meet the bare cost of living, thus making their very helplessness the occasion of a most injurious competition. The Legislature had the right to consider that its minimum wage requirements would be an important aid in carrying out its policy of protection. The adoption of similar requirements by many states evidences a deep-seated conviction both as to the presence of the evil and as to the means adapted to check it. Legislative response to that conviction cannot be regarded as arbitrary or capricious and that is all we have to decide. Even if the wisdom of the policy be regarded as debatable and its effects uncertain, still the Legislature is entitled to its judgment.

There is an additional and compelling consideration which recent economic experience has brought into a strong light. The exploitation of a class of workers who are in an unequal position with respect to bargaining power and are thus relatively defenseless against the denial of a living wage is not only detrimental to their health and well-being, but casts a direct burden for their support upon the community. What these workers lose in wages the taxpayers are called upon to pay. The bare cost of living must be met.

We think that the views thus expressed are sound and that the decision in the *Adkins* case was a departure from the true application of the principles governing the regulation by the state of the relation of employer and employed.

Our conclusion is that the case of *Adkins v. Children's Hospital* should be, and it is, overruled. The judgment of the Supreme Court of the state of Washington is affirmed.

Affirmed.

[Four justices dissented at length.]

Case Questions

1. What theory was used in previous cases (Adkins among them) to declare unconstitutional the attempt by the government to dictate to employers that a minimum wage be paid to employees?

2. Most of the discussion in this case referring to situations in which the court *upheld* government regulation in situations is omitted here, but why would the Court make reference to those cases?

3. The Supreme Court here validated a state minimum wage law. Why would a *national* minimum wage be necessary if the states can set their own?

4. Why does the Court discuss "the public interest than the health of women and their protection from unscrupulous and overreaching employers" but not the interest that *men* have in such protection?

5. Here in 1937, the Court did a clean 180 degree turn, flatly overruling its previous decision in *Adkins v. Children's Hospital* (1923). What happened in the intervening 14 years that made the Court change its mind? How did it explain the about-face?

6. Mrs. Parrish was a "chambermaid." What is a "chambermaid"?

Key Takeaway

In the urbanizing economy of the late 19th and early 20th centuries it became obvious that most workers and their families had little or no bargaining power as against employers. After forty years of resistance, the Supreme Court in 1936 at last agreed that the government *did* have authority to comprehensively regulate the employer-employee relationship. Congress adopted the Fair Labor Standards Act in 1938. It set a federal minimum wage, maximum hours, prohibited child labor, and in later amendments addressed family leave and nursing mothers.

Certainly, a further government response to the insecurity of the workplace was the adoption in 1935 of the National Labor Relations Act. This landmark legislation—taken up in more detail in Chapter 13 Section 2—provided that employees have the right to join a union for mutual benefit and protection, and that the employer has a legal duty to bargain with the union in good faith on matters regarding wages, hours, and working conditions.

Exercises

1. What is the "employment-at-will doctrine," and why are there exceptions to it?

2. Why was the plight of working people often worse in, say, 1910, than it had been in 1810?

3. What is "substantive due process" that was employed by the U.S. Supreme Court to invalidate state and federal legislation designed to ameliorate the plight of working people?

4. What are the salient features of the Fair Labor Standards Act?

5. Why is a law mandating that employers provide unpaid leave not very useful to the employees who need it the most?

6. Empire Company Inc.'s boss says to Ellie Employee: "Yes, you can take some time to express milk for your baby—go on and use the women's room." Why is that a violation of the FLSA (as amended)?

15.3 Health Insurance

Learning Objectives

1. Recognize that the government provides some health and medical insurance for people who cannot access it through their employers.
2. Know that there are government programs to prevent members of the public from suffering illness and accident by mandating that products meet some minimal safety standards—the prophylactic to prevent problems in the first place.
3. Understand that almost all employees are provided with no-fault workplace insurance through the federal/state workers' compensation program.
4. Know that the federal Occupational Safety and Health Administration (OSHA) promotes safe workplaces to prevent work-related injuries and diseases (the prophylactic for on-the-job incidents).
5. Note that the government requires that (some) employers provide family leave time for employees.

Major Federal Insurance for Non-Work-Related Injuries and Illnesses

The Major Federal Programs

Besides losing their jobs directly people incur job loss from both work-related accidents and illnesses, and—of course—from non-work-related accidents and illnesses. Today most residents of the United States can reasonably expect a modicum, at least, of government-provided health insurance. The major federal programs for non-work related health insurance are here briefly described.

- Medicare. This is a national health insurance program for some 40 million[22] Americans 65 and older, who have worked and who have made payments into the system through payroll taxes. **Medicare** also provides insurance to some younger people with disabilities recognized by the Social Security Administration.

- Medicaid. About 42 million people[23] with limited income get help with medical costs through Medicaid. The federal government pays part of the costs and mandates that the state-run **Medicaid** program provide some benefits, but the states' goals and benefits differ. "Mandatory benefits include services like inpatient and outpatient hospital services, physician services, laboratory and x-ray services, and home health services, among others. Optional benefits include services like prescription drugs, case management, physical therapy, and occupational therapy. See a list of mandatory and optional benefits for Medicaid programs.[24]

- **Children's Health Insurance Program** (CHIP, formerly Children's Medicaid). The federal program provides matching funds for states to offer children's health insurance to low-income families not eligible for Medicaid. It serves about 4.7 million children.[25]

- Department of Defense **TRICARE**. DoD's program provides civilian health insurance and benefits to about 8.4 million[26] U.S. Armed Forces personnel around the world, their dependents, and military retirees.

- **Veterans Health Administration Program**. "The Veterans Health Administration is America's largest integrated health care system, providing care at 1,240 health care facilities, including 170 medical centers and 1,061 outpatient sites of care of varying complexity (VHA outpatient clinics), serving 9 million enrolled Veterans each year."[27]

- **Indian Health Service**. The IHS provides comprehensive, direct public health and medical services to some 1.4 million[28] American Indians and Native Alaskans.

These six programs provide healthcare services to about one-third of Americans at a cost of over $500 billion. There are two other major sources of non-employer-related health insurance:

- **The Affordable Care Act ("Obamacare"**[29]) was adopted by Congress in 2010 to provide health insurance to people who don't get insurance through an employer, or who leave their employer. People are required by law to obtain either private or government-run health insurance; those too poor to afford the premiums are entitled to government assistance. Employers with more than 50 full-time employees must provide affordable health-insurance coverage to employees and dependents (not spouses, however). Obamacare has been a success, notwithstanding its opponents' virulent criticism: the number of uninsured Americans dropped from 41.8 million in 2010 to 33.0 million in 2014.[30]

- Other federal programs and initiatives. These include Health Savings Accounts (allowing people to put money into health savings accounts that are not subject to federal income tax); Access for Infants and Mothers (providing low-cost healthcare for middle-income pregnant women and newborns); and SNAP (the "Supplemental Nutrition Assistance Program," formerly "Food Stamps," providing food-subsidy programs (registration is at the county level).

One problem confronting hospitals is that they must, by federal law, provide adequate emergency medical or pregnancy-delivery services without regard to the patient's ability to pay. The Emergency Medical Treatment and Active Labor Act (EMTALA), adopted in 1986 (as part of COBRA, the Consolidated Omnibus Budget Reconciliation Act of 1985) was intended to prevent "patient dumping"—hospitals' practice of refusing treatment of, or discharging prematurely, poor, sick people or pregnant women to fend for themselves because they have no money to pay for treatment.[31] If a hospital must treat an indigent patient, somebody, somewhere, has to come up with the money—the hospital is forced to raise rates on those who can pay, which drives up health insurance costs. It would be good if people could be convinced to buy their own health insurance.

Medicare

Federal medical insurance program, 1965, for qualified people 65 or older.

Medicaid

Federal low-income medical insurance program, 1965.

Children's Health Insurance Program

"CHIP" federal program to help provide health insurance to low-family-income children.

TRICARE

Department of Defense's health insurance program for armed services personnel and their families.

Veterans Health Administration Program

The U.S. Veterans Administration's healthcare system for veterans of the armed forces.

Indian Health Service

The federal government's health insurance program for native Americans.

The Affordable Care Act ("Obamacare")

Federal statute, 2010, providing some health insurance for those who have no employer-sponsored insurance.

Preventing Injuries and Illnesses in the First Place

It is always better to prevent a harm from happening than it is to treat the damage afterward. The federal government has several programs to *prevent* injuries and illnesses suffered by Americans. Two are noted here.

- **Consumer Product Safety Commission**. This agency was created in 1972 with the passage of the Consumer Product Safety Act. The act gives CPSC the power to develop safety standards for consumer goods and pursue recalls for products that present unreasonable or substantial risks of injury or death to consumers. It has jurisdiction over more than 15,000 products (not including what the FDA regulates, and not including firearms, motor vehicles, pesticides, aircraft, and boats, which are regulated by various other agencies). In 2014, the CPSA was amended to protect whistleblowers who raise concerns about consumer product safety. The CPSC has a colorful, accessible website, including news of products that have been recalled because they are dangerous for consumers: http://www.cpsc.gov/en/.

- **Center for Disease Control and Prevention**. This federal agency's stated mission: "CDC works 24/7 to protect America from health, safety and security threats, both foreign and in the U.S. Whether diseases start at home or abroad, are chronic or acute, curable or preventable, human error or deliberate attack, CDC fights disease and supports communities and citizens to do the same." The agency deals with infectious diseases, food-borne pathogens, environmental health, health promotion, occupational safety and health, injury prevention, and education. For fiscal year 2018 its budget was $11.1 billion[32] and it has some 15,000 employees (including contractors).[33] Its Injury Center studies injuries and violence and researches the best ways to prevent them, including such topics as

  - Prescription Drug Overdose
  - Older Adult Falls
  - Motor Vehicle Injury
  - Traumatic Brain Injury
  - Child Abuse and Neglect
  - Youth Violence
  - Intimate Partner Violence
  - Sexual Violence
  - Self-Directed Violence

For political reasons (the National Rifle Association has effectively forbidden it[34]) the agency has *not* specifically addressed one of the largest causes of injury and death in the United States, gun violence—about 34,000 people in the U.S. are killed by guns every year (including suicide).[35]

Work-Related Injuries and Illnesses

Background Note

The workplace is often dangerous. At common law, an employee could sue the employer if the latter's negligence caused injury or death, but most employees were in no position to mount a lawsuit against their employer, and there were powerful defenses the employer could raise to defeat recovery ("assumption of the risk" was one). It was an untenable situation: while working and furthering the employer's success, the employee was injured, and then—usually—fired, and then reduced to penury (or dead). The first statewide laws affecting workers' compensation were adopted in the early 20th century and survived a Supreme Court review in 1917 against employer challenges that the laws' imposition of no-fault employer liability took property without due process.[36]

Workers' Compensation Laws

Workers' compensation laws provide a set amount of weekly compensation for disabilities caused by accidents and illnesses suffered on the job. The employer has *strict liability*: if the employee is injured or killed in the scope of employment, the employer is liable—there are (almost) no defenses, but there is a big trade-off: the employee *cannot sue the employer* and the benefit received is limited to an amount set by the state unemployment department (this is no plaintiffs' lawyers' tort free-for-all where juries offer up huge dollar awards). The "in the scope of employment" bit is often a hard-fought factual argument.

> **workers' compensation laws**
>
> State laws to provide income for employees injured in the scope of employment.

Except, sometimes the employee *can* sue (and maybe get big bucks):

- If the on-the-job injury was caused by a third party's negligence (a defective product or a toxic substance not directly the employer's responsibility), the third party may be sued. For example, an employee working on a punch press suffers the loss of two fingers when a foot-pedal off switch is defective—the switch sticks. The manufacturer of the machine may be liable.

- If the injury was the result of the employer's *intentional* or egregious conduct, the employer may be subject to a personal injury lawsuit. An employee, digging for a sub-surface pipe in a water-filled trench, is seriously injured because the employer refused to provide trench side-wall cave-in protection: the employer may be subject to a lawsuit outside the workers' compensation system.

The compensation plans also pay hospital and medical expenses necessary to treat workers who are injured by, or become ill from, their work, and it provides pensions for employees who cannot work, or for family members of employees who are killed in industrial accidents. In assuring workers of compensation, the plans eliminate the hazards and uncertainties of lawsuits by eliminating the need to prove fault. Employers fund the compensation plans by paying into statewide plans or purchasing insurance; the amount employers pay for insurance depends upon how risky the job is: transportation and material moving, farming, fishing, and forestry are the most dangerous jobs.

Federal Workers' Compensation

Some 2.6 million federal employees are covered by the Federal Employees Compensation Act (originally adopted by Congress in 1916). Every civilian employee of the federal government, including employees of the executive, legislative, and judicial branches, is covered by FECA (including federal jurors and Peace Corps volunteers). The federal Office of Workers' Compensation Programs (OWCP) administers the act. In FY 2014–15 the FECA paid out over $3 billion in medical, disability, and survivor benefits. Men and women in the U.S. armed forces are insured by federal programs for service members.

Workers' Comp after Employment Ends

"COBRA" allows *former* employees to retain employer-provided health insurance for a while after the job ends. The Consolidated Omnibus Budget Reconciliation Act of 1985 (**COBRA**) provides that private-industry, state, and local-government employees who have lost their jobs or had hours reduced so that they do not qualify for employer-provided health insurance have a right to continue to receive the coverage and benefits they enjoyed while employed for up to 18 months (longer for disabled workers) after the job ends. However, the former employee has to pay the premiums

> **COBRA**
>
> Federal statute, 1985, allowing former employees some access to their former employer's health insurance program.

and a 2% administration fee. The act generally applies to employers with 20 or more employees. Many states have "mini-COBRAs" with different benefits and requirements, including—in some states—affecting employers with two or more employees;[37] some states[38] also offer assistance to eligible former workers to pay the premiums, as does the federal government itself.[39]

Preventing Workplace Injuries in the First Place

The instrumental new technology of modernity was, without doubt, the railroads. They were first in modern corporate governance and management, first in large-scale monopolization schemes, first in modern accounting, first in modern labor law, first in modern large-scale civil engineering, first in the development of tort law, and first in modern safety appliances.

To stop or slow a train in the 19th century the engineer would give a signal; brakemen would climb to the top of moving cars—in all kinds of weather—and apply brakes by turning a wheel. It was very dangerous work, and if not done correctly, train cars could come uncoupled, or trains could run away, unbraked, down mountain slopes. When a brakeman was killed, the 'roads' defense was "assumption of the risk."

The railroad could hire a brakeman for about $1.50 a day [$34 in today's money—$4.25 per hour]. If that brakeman got hurt or killed, just about their only responsibility was to move the body off the tracks and send it home in a basket. It was cheaper, on the whole, for the railroad to just continue maiming and killing its employees than it was to invest millions of dollars in these new technologies.[40]

But passengers were outraged by the carnage on the railroads—not the workers' carnage, the passengers'. Thomas Nast, the famous 19th century political cartoonist, drew this image of railroad travel in 1871.

FIGURE 15.4 Railroad Travel, circa 1871
Passengers were outraged by the carnage on the railroads—not the workers' carnage, the passengers'. Thomas Nast, the famous 19th century political cartoonist, drew this image of railroad travel in 1871.

OUR CONSTANT TRAVELING COMPANION.

Source: Public domain. https://www.mediastorehouse.com/railroad-accidents-1871-our-constant-traveling/print/12401378.html

Belatedly, Congress adopted the Railway Safety Act in 1893. The **Occupational Safety and Health Act** (1970) is one of its descendants; OSHA created the Occupational Safety and Health Administration whose mission is "assure safe and healthy working conditions for working men and women by setting and enforcing standards and by providing training, outreach, education and assistance."[41] OSHA sets and enforces standards—most commonly by conducting work-place inspections—as a prophylactic to prevent accidents, injuries, and illness.[42] OSHA does not preempt state laws that provide a greater degree of protection or benefit for employees.

Here is an example of enforcement of protection standards on falls, from a March 2018 OSHA news release:

Occupational Safety and Health Act

Federal statute, 1970, establishing an administrative agency with the authority to regulate workplace safety standards.

CONCORD, NH – *The U.S. Department of Labor's Occupational Safety and Health Administration (OSHA) has cited Luis Guallpa—doing business as Guallpa Contracting Corp.—for exposing workers to fall and other hazards at a Nashua work site. The Milford, Massachusetts, roofing contractor faces $299,324 in proposed penalties.*

OSHA inspectors observed six of Guallpa's employees working on a roof without fall protection, and also observed workers using ladders unsafely, and failing to use head protection. The Agency cited the employer for exposing employees to fall hazards of up to 25 feet, for ladder and head protection violations, and for failing to provide effective training. OSHA cited Guallpa for similar hazards in 2014 and 2015.

"Fall protection is required when employees are working at heights of six feet or higher," said Rosemarie Cole, OSHA New Hampshire Area Office Director. "This employer's continued failure to follow safety standards is placing employees at risk of serious injury or death."

The company has 15 business days from receipt of its citations and penalties to comply, request an informal conference with OSHA's area director, or contest the findings before the independent Occupational Safety and Health Review Commission.[43]

FIGURE 15.5 Non-Fatal Workplace Injuries

The federal Department of Labor graphs the number of *non*-fatal workplace injuries (incident rate per thousand employees on the left, and number of cases on the right).

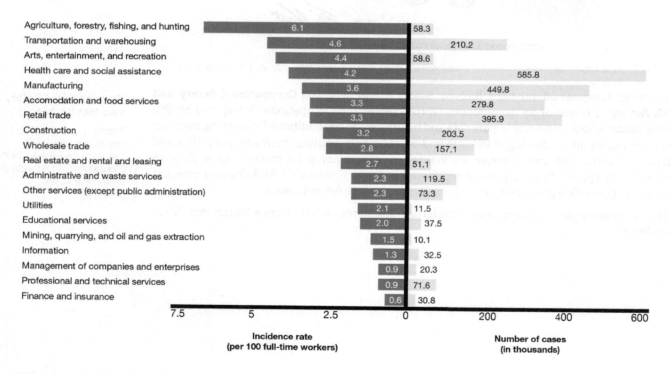

Source: U.S. Bureau of Labor Statistics, U.S. Department of Labor, November 2017, retrieved 8/2/18 at https://www.bls.gov/iif/osch0060.pdf

Other graphs on the DOL cite show incidences of *fatal* injuries—about 4,000 a year. The employer of a roofer—Guallpa Contracting, above—might pay $21.00 per hour in insurance; but a college professor costs the school around $0.50 per hour, and an accountant about $0.17 per hour.[44] The more claims the employer has, the higher the rates (thus it is not uncommon that employers under-report, or discourage employees from making claims).

Case

The Scope of the Occupational Safety and Health Act's Coverage

Head v. Reilly Painting & Contracting, Inc.

Ohio Court of Appeals case, 2015, analyzing the scope of the Occupational Safety adn Health Act's coverage.

Head v. Reilly Painting & Contracting, Inc.

28 NE 3d 126 (Ohio Ct. App., 2015)

Stewart, J.

Decedent William Head ("Head") died from injuries he suffered after falling from the roof of a residential garage while working for defendant Reilly Painting & Contracting, Inc. Sabrina Head, the executor of his estate, filed this intentional tort action against Reilly Painting, Michael Reilly (the owner of Reilly Painting), and Peter Lukas (the job foreman), on grounds that they failed to provide Head with a safety harness in violation of Occupational Safety and Health Administration rules.

In granting summary judgment in defendant's favor, the court found that although Reilly Painting deliberately failed to provide Head with a safety harness, it did not do so with a deliberate intent to cause Head injury because it thought the job was safe: the job site was on a flat roof. The court also rejected common law intentional tort claims against Reilly and Lukas, finding that there was no evidence that the individual defendants knew that Head was substantially certain to be injured while working on the roof. Although there were other legal theories mentioned in the court's summary judgment, these are the only two presented on appeal.

We first consider whether the court erred by granting summary judgment to Reilly Painting, Inc. on the statutory intentional tort claim. The estate maintains that the court erred by finding that it had to offer direct proof of Reilly Painting's subjective intent to injure Head. The estate argues that the evidence showed that Lukas, the job foreman, testified in deposition that he "deliberately" did not require Head to use a safety harness while working on the roof, so reasonable minds could differ on whether Reilly Painting acted with deliberate intent to injure Head.

Because Reilly Painting was Head's employer, the intentional tort claim is governed by [Ohio statute]. That section states that an employer is not liable for injuries suffered by an employee during the course of employment ". . . unless the plaintiff proves that the employer committed the tortious act with the intent to injure another or with the belief that the injury was substantially certain to occur."

The statute defines the term "substantially certain" to mean "that an employer acts with deliberate intent to cause an employee to suffer an injury, a disease, a condition, or death." [Citation.]

It is important to understand [the state statute] in context. This section of the statute was a legislative response to a line of Ohio Supreme Court decisions that had created an exception to the Workers' Compensation Fund as being the sole avenue of recovery for workplace injuries. In *Blankenship v. Cincinnati Milacron Chems., Inc.,* [Citation] (1982), the Supreme Court recognized a cause of action for an employer's intentional tort against its employee, holding that, because intentional tort claims do not arise out of the employment relationship, the workers' compensation laws do not provide immunity from suit. In subsequent decisions, the Supreme Court arguably construed the "substantially certain to occur" intentional tort standard of harm as being coextensive with mere recklessness.

Addressing what it perceived as an unwarranted expansion of the employer/employee intentional tort standard, the General Assembly enacted [the statute in issue here]. As acknowledged by the Ohio Supreme Court, the statute showed that "the General Assembly's intent [was] to permit recovery for employer intentional torts only when an employer acts with *specific intent* to cause an injury. In other words, "absent a deliberate intent to injure another, an employer is not liable for a claim alleging an employer intentional tort, and the injured employee's exclusive remedy is within the workers' compensation system."

The facts are largely uncontested. Head, an experienced laborer working for Reilly Painting, was on the flat roof of a residential garage removing shingles in preparation for installing a new roof. The roof was approximately 11 feet above ground level. Lukas, who was on the ground, asked Head to hand him a broom. Head leaned over to hand the broom to Lukas, but lost his balance and fell to the ground. The fall left him paralyzed, and he later died from complications resulting from injuries suffered in the fall.

In statements made to OSHA investigators following the accident, Reilly Painting admitted that Head was not wearing a safety harness contrary to OSHA regulations, which require safety harnesses for work performed more than six feet above the ground. Reilly Painting had safety harnesses available, but Lukas, the foreman on the job, did not believe they were necessary because the roof was flat and not pitched. OSHA cited Reilly Painting for safety violations.

The court cited our decision in *Schiemann v. Foti Contracting, L.L.C.*, [citation], for the proposition that "under current Ohio law, that without showing evidence of a history of animosity or ill-will between the employer and employee that would support evidence of a subjective intent by the employer to injure the employee, an intentional tort claim will not lie." The facts in *Schiemann* are very similar to those in this case: Schiemann, a stone mason who had been working without a safety harness on an 18-foot high platform, suffered injuries when he fell. Schiemann brought an intentional tort action against his employer on grounds of failing to provide him with a safety harness in violation of OSHA standards for "fall protection." * * * Finding no direct evidence of animosity or ill-will that supported a finding that the employer subjectively intended to injure Schiemann, we noted that the evidence tended to show the contrary—Schiemann admitted that he would not have worn a safety harness if one had been made available to him and that, in any event, there was no evidence of any other person being injured while performing the same type of work, so the employer had no reason to believe that Schiemann, or anyone else for that matter, would be injured while working without a harness.

* * *

In this case, there was no evidence that Reilly Painting acted with deliberate intent to injure Head. Reilly Painting knew that injuries were substantially certain to occur in the event an employee fell from a roof without wearing a safety harness, but that knowledge begs the question of whether Reilly Painting knew that Head would fall. Lukas, the job foreman, testified at deposition that he did not believe there was any need for the safety harness because he felt safe working on a flat roof. Also, there was no indication that Head believed he was in danger without a safety harness.

The estate makes much of Lukas's statement that he made a "deliberate" decision not to use safety harnesses on the job. * * * [But] making a deliberate decision not to use a piece of safety equipment does not by itself show a specific intent to cause an injury. To find otherwise would reinstate the past employer intentional tort paradigm that the legislature so clearly rejected.

There is no evidence that Reilly Painting intended to harm Head.

We next consider whether the court erred by granting summary judgment in favor of Michael Reilly and Peter Lukas on the estate's claims for common law intentional tort [against the two individuals as defendants separate from the employer, Reilly, Inc.]. The estate argues that the statute applies only to *employers* [the corporation] so its intentional tort claims against Reilly and Head are "common law" claims that should be reviewed under the standard set forth in *Fyffe* [Citation] (1991). Reilly and Lukas agree that the statute applies only to employers, but rely on precedent for the

proposition that a fellow employee cannot be sued for a common law workplace intentional tort. *
* *

Under *Fyffe* (the terms of which we modify in this action by an employee against a co-employee), a plaintiff seeking to prevail on a claim of co-employee intentional tort must show: (1) knowledge by the co-employee of the existence of a dangerous process, procedure, instrumentality, or condition within its business operation; (2) knowledge by the co-employee that if the employee is subjected by his employment to such dangerous process, procedure, instrumentality, or condition, then harm to the employee will be a substantial certainty; and (3) that the co-employee, under such circumstances, and with such knowledge, did act to require the employee to continue to perform the dangerous task. * * *

There is no dispute on the first element of the *Fyffe* test—that both Reilly and Lukas were aware of the obvious danger in falling while working on a roof. The dispute centers on the application of the second element: knowledge by either defendant of the substantial certainty of harm to Head.

In the end, there was no evidence to show that either Reilly or Lukas knew that Head would fall because he was not wearing a safety harness. The court's conclusion that the increased risk of injury resulting from not wearing a safety harness did not mean that Head's injury was substantially certain to occur was consistent with our holding in *Magda*, and thus not in error.

Judgment affirmed.

Case Questions

1. If an employer *deliberately* caused injury to the employee, the employee may seek redress outside workers' comp. Why would an injured employee (or the employee's heirs, as here) want redress outside workers' compensation?

2. The boss here *deliberately* let the employee work without fall protection; why didn't that satisfy the "employer deliberately caused the injury" requirement.

3. The common-law "fellow employee" doctrine provided that if an employee's injuries were caused, not by the employer, but by a fellow employee, then the employer could not be liable. Workers' comp laws abolished the "fellow employee" doctrine; workers' comp *is* generally the sole remedy where an employee has suffered damages caused by a co-worker. Except, when could the injured employee (or, as here, his wife) sue a co-worker? Why didn't the lower court allow a suit against the co-workers (the appeals court affirmed)?

4. What was the tug-of-war expressed by the appeals court here between the Ohio judiciary (construing legislation) and the Ohio legislature? Who "won," and why?

Key Takeaway

In "advanced" societies it is generally expected that people should not work full time and yet starve; that people should not work their whole lives and yet still have a penurious old age; they should not suffer illness or bodily injury and have no access to medical treatment.

Addressing income security, the government imposes a minimum wage, and the employment-at-will doctrine is eroding. Addressing old-age poverty, the government has established Social Security and regulates, to some extent, private pension plans. Addressing healthcare, the government has various programs, including Medicare and "Obamacare" to provide some non-work-related insurance. Addressing work-related injuries and illness, the government mandates that most employees be covered by workers' compensation: insurance to pay them if they suffer on-the-job losses.

Exercises

1. Andrew took three months off for family leave upon the illness and then death of his mother, aged 83. His employer refused to pay him during his absence. Is this legal?

2. What are the major exceptions to the employment-at-will doctrine? Who has devised them, and why?

3. In the last fifty years, when did people earning the federal minimum wage have the most buying power? Why isn't the minimum wage pegged to inflation?

4. Which age group in the United States today is most likely to be poor—the old or the young? Why?

5. What health insurance is available to most employees? How is it paid for?

6. What health insurance is available to people who are not employed? How is it paid for?

7. Some members of Congress have been very critical of "Obamacare"; what is the objection, and what do they propose instead?

8. It is always better to prevent harm in the first place than to remedy it after the harm has happened. What are the prophylactics for occupational injuries? For non-occupational injuries?

15.4 Debtors' Protection

Learning Objectives

1. Understand the federal regulation of debt collection.
2. Know about federal bankruptcy law.
3. Understand debtor's prison.
4. Know about state debtors' relief.

Background

When people suffer job loss, disability, or when they are the unfortunate victims of illness, natural or man-made disaster, they often lose the necessary stream of income required to get along, to pay their bills. In a capitalist system we laud people who take risks to capitalize businesses, but sometimes the business doesn't flourish and they can't repay the loans. What then? The poorhouse?

The first thing that usually happens is they get dunned (hounded to pay up) by bill collectors—most often professionals who are hired by the creditor to collect debts and who get paid a percentage of what they collect. It isn't pretty. Here is the Texas Supreme Court describing debt-collection practices in the early 1950s:[45]

Daily telephone calls to both Mr. and Mrs. Duty, which extended to great length; threatening to blacklist them with the Merchants' Retail Credit Association; accusing them of being deadbeats; talking to them in a harsh, insinuating, loud voice; stating to their neighbors and employers that they were deadbeats; asking Mrs. Duty what she was doing with her money; accusing her of spending money in other ways than in payments on the loan transaction; threatening to cause both plaintiffs to lose their jobs unless they made the payments demanded; calling each of the plaintiffs at the respective places of their employment several times daily; threatening to garnishee their wages; berating plaintiffs to their fellow employees; requesting their employers to require them to pay; calling on them at their work; flooding them with a barrage of demand letters, dun cards, special delivery letters, and telegrams both at their homes and their places of work; sending them cards bearing this opening statement: "Dear Customer: We made you a loan because we thought that you were honest."; sending telegrams and special delivery letters to them at approximately midnight, causing them to be awakened from their sleep; calling a neighbor in the disguise of a sick brother of one of the plaintiffs, and on another occasion as a stepson; calling Mr. Duty's mother at her place of employment in Wichita Falls long distance, collect; leaving red cards in their door, with insulting notes on the back and thinly-veiled threats; calling Mr. Duty's brother long distance, collect, in Albuquerque, New Mexico, at his residence at a cost to him in excess of $11 [$109 in 2019 dollars], and haranguing him about the alleged balance owed by plaintiffs.

Some of this is not actionable under tort law, but some of it may be. The tort of intentional infliction of emotional distress is defined as intentionally or recklessly causing another person severe emotional distress through extreme or outrageous acts. This can be a result of either the defendant's *acts* or *words*.[46]

The Fair Debt Collection Practices Act of 1977

In response to abusive debt-collection practices, Congress enacted, as part of the Consumer Credit Protection Act, the **Fair Debt Collection Practices Act** (FDCPA) in 1977.

Debt collection is a big business. Many stores, hospitals, and other organizations attempt on their own to collect unpaid bills, but thousands of merchants, professionals, and small businesses rely on collection agencies to recover accounts receivable. The debt collection business employed over 130,000 people in 2013; in 2016, $67.6 billion in debt was collected and returned to creditors"[47] and the agencies collected billions in fees.

Nearly $70 billion dollars is no trivial sum of money. To collect that money, some pressure must be brought against the debtor. Maybe just a couple of letters will do, but—as noted above—for decades, some of these collectors used harassing tactics: posing as government agents or attorneys, calling at the debtor's workplace, threatening physical harm or loss of property or imprisonment, using abusive language, publishing a deadbeats list, misrepresenting the size of the debt, and telling friends and neighbors about the debt.

The FDCPA now regulates how third-party collection agencies conduct their business. It covers collection of all personal, family, and household debts by collection agencies. It does *not* deal with collection by creditors themselves; the consumer's remedy for abusive debt collection by the creditor is in tort law.

Under the FDCPA, the third-party collector may not

- contact the debtor at unreasonable times of the day, and not at work if the debtor's employer prohibits it. The debtor may write the collector to cease contact, in which case the agency is prohibited from further contact (except to confirm that there will be no further contact). A

Fair Debt Collection Practices Act

Federal statute, 1977, regulating professional debt-collection practices.

written denial that money is owed stops the bill collector for thirty days, and he can resume again only after the debtor is sent proof of the debt.

- file suit in remote places, hoping for default judgments; any suit must be filed in a court where the debtor lives or where the underlying contract was signed.

- use harassing and abusive tactics, including false and misleading representations to the debtor and others (e.g., claiming that the collector is an attorney or that the debtor is about to be sued when that is not true), is prohibited. Unless the debtor has given the creditor her cell phone number, calls to cell phones (but not to landlines) are not allowed.

- use a return address that indicates the letter is from a debt collection agency (so as to avoid embarrassment from a conspicuous name on the envelope that might be read by third parties).

- communicate with third parties about the debt, except when the collector may need to talk to others to trace the debtor's whereabouts (though the collector may not tell them that the inquiry concerns a debt) or when the collector contacts a debtor's attorney, if the debtor has an attorney. The federal statute gives debtors the right to sue the collector for damages for violating the statute and for causing such injuries as job loss or harm to reputation.

Federal Bankruptcy Law

Why are bankruptcy laws necessary? Relief from debt, honestly incurred but unrepayable, is necessary because in a capitalistic system we expect people to take economic risks, to open the restaurant or buy the house on credit; they will be afraid to take such risks if they will be dunned horribly (as above) or if they will lose everything. Without entrepreneurial risk-taking (broadly defined), and some of the cost of immediate gratification bought on credit, to be repaid later (e.g., that trip to Paris on an airplane) capitalism won't work.

Bankruptcy Abuse Prevention and Consumer Protection Act

Federal statute, 2005, amending previous federal law on bankruptcy.

Debt relief and protection from creditors is available under federal bankruptcy law. The Constitution of the United States gives Congress the power to enact "uniform laws on bankruptcy." Until the closing of the West, in about 1890, there was no big need for bankruptcy protection: debtors could simply disappear West; most often they could not be traced or found. But with Social Security numbers and all the recorded disclosures demanded in a modern society, hardly anybody can just disappear (without dying). Current bankruptcy law is based on the Act of 1898, as amended most recently by the **Bankruptcy Abuse Prevention and Consumer Protection Act** (BAPCPA), 2005. The purpose of bankruptcy law is to give the honest debtor a fresh start. Below, we discuss six types of bankruptcy recognized under federal bankruptcy law:

FIGURE 15.6 Six Types of Bankruptcy
Six types of bankruptcy are recognized under federal bankruptcy law (Title 11 of the United States Code); the three most common are Chapters 7, 11, and 13, but debt relief is available in other cases also.

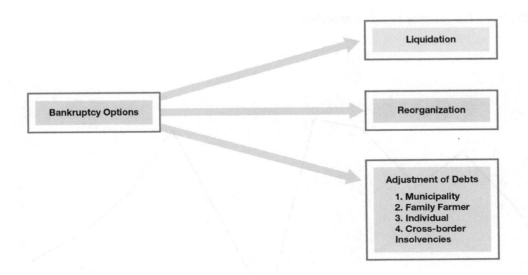

- **Chapter 7**: liquidation, known as "straight bankruptcy": the debtor lists all debts and all assets on the Bankruptcy Petition (the document filed with the bankruptcy court that starts the proceedings); the bankruptcy court sends notice to all listed creditors who then are forbidden from any further direct contact with the debtor (called the stay on proceedings). Under Chapter 7, debtors get to keep most of what is needed for a lower-middle-class lifestyle (called "exempt assets": car, most furniture and clothing, books, household goods, some equity in a house, a small amount in cash); anything extra, non-exempt assets (a sailboat, say, or more than two cars for a married couple), will usually be taken from the debtor by the trustee in bankruptcy (a court employee who represents creditors) and sold to satisfy debts. Most Chapter 7 cases are "no asset"—there is nothing for creditors. Note two things: (1) the stay on proceedings stops debtors from being dunned, and (2) not all debts are dischargeable: in general, taxes owed, liability for intentional torts or drunken driving, and student loans are *not* dischargeable (with some exceptions).

- Chapter 9: municipal bankruptcy, for cities and counties that cannot pay their debts.

- **Chapter 11**: reorganization, used by business debtors, but also by individuals with substantial debts and assets; usually known as "corporate reorganization." The debtor prepares a repayment plan which typically allows companies to operate as going concerns while they follow debt repayment plans; some debt may be shed, other debt rescheduled. Chapter 11 is useful if a firm is worth more as a "going concern" than it would be if liquidated.

- Chapter 12: rehabilitation for family farmers and fishers.

- **Chapter 13**: adjustment of debts for individuals with a regular source of income; enables individuals with such income to present, and have approved by the court, a plan to repay all or part of their debts; also known as wage earner's bankruptcy. In contract to Chapter 7, the debtor surrenders no property, and discharge is available for debts that might not be in straight bankruptcy.

- Chapter 15: ancillary and other international cases. Adopted in 2005, it is a mechanism for dealing with bankruptcy debtors and helps foreign debtors to clear debts. It is the U.S. adoption of the United Nations Commission on International Trade Law (UNCITRAL), which addresses international bankruptcy issues. In 2016, 178 Chapter 15 cases were filed.

Chapter 7

The section of the federal bankruptcy code dealing with liquidation.

Chapter 11

That section of the federal bankruptcy act dealing with "corporate reorganization"—allowing a corporation to pay off most of its debt via a court-approved plan.

Chapter 13

That section of the federal bankruptcy act allowing debtors with regular income to pay off debt according to a court-approved plan.

Here you can see how many non-business bankruptcies were filed between 1994–2015 (notice the decrease after the BAPCPA's adoption in 2005, and the increase following the "great recession" of 2008–10):

FIGURE 15.7 U.S. Non-Business Bankruptcy Filings 1994–2015

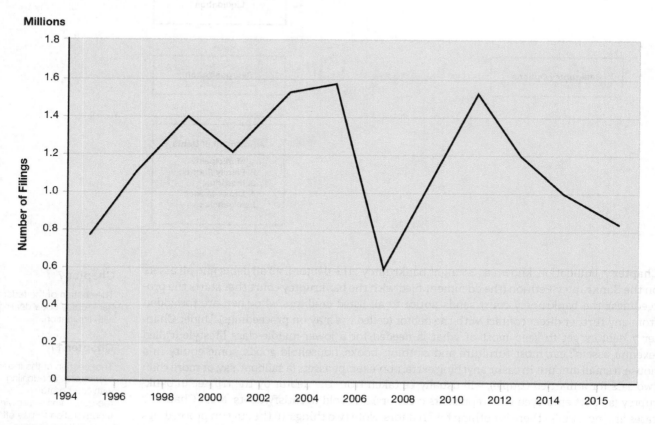

Source: Data from http://www.bankruptcyaction.com/USbankstats.htm

Debtors' Prison

Up until the mid-19th century debtors' prisons were common in the United States. People who couldn't pay their bills were put in jail until they—or their families—could figure out how to pay their way out. The growing use of poorhouses and then the adoption of modern bankruptcy laws in the late 19th century obviated the need for debtors' prison, which, certainly, make people afraid to incur debt (even useful debt) and which made it very difficult for debtors to pay. But it is still possible under some state laws for people to be put in jail for failure to pay their debts.[48]

State Debtors' Relief

There are alternatives for people who do not want (or can't get) debtor's relief under federal law[49] The alternatives are as follows:

- Assignment for benefit of creditors. Under a common-law **assignment for the benefit of creditors**, the debtor transfers some or all of his assets to a trustee—usually someone appointed by the adjustment bureau of a local credit managers' association—who sells the assets and apportions the proceeds in some agreed manner, usually pro rata, to the creditors.

- **Composition among creditors.** A composition is simply an agreement by creditors to accept less than the full amount of the debt and to discharge the debtor from further liability.

- Receivership. A creditor may petition the local state court to appoint a receiver; receivership is a long-established procedure in equity whereby the receiver takes over the debtor's property or business under instructions from the court. The receiver may liquidate the property, continue to operate the business, or preserve the assets without operating the business, until the court finally determines how to dispose of the debtor's property.

assignment for the benefit of creditors

A common-law type of debtor's relief where the debtor's assets are transferred to a trustee to dispose of for the benefit of creditors.

composition among creditors

An agreement among a debtor's creditors whereby each accepts less than the creditor is owed in order that all creditors may get some payment on the debt.

Case

Dischargeability of Student Loans under Chapter 7

In re Zygarewicz

Bankruptcy case (Cal., 2010) analyzing the dischargability under federal bankruptcy law of student loans.

In re Zygarewicz

423 B.R. 909 (BK.E.D.Cal. 2010) [Bankruptcy Court for the Eastern District of California]

McManus, Bankruptcy Judge.

Angela Zygarewicz, a Chapter 7 debtor and the plaintiff in this adversary proceeding, borrowed 16 government-guaranteed student loans totaling $81,429. The loans have been assigned to Educational Credit Management Corporation ("ECMC"). By September 2009, the accrual of interest on these student loans had caused the debt to balloon to more than $146,000. The debtor asks the court to declare that these student loans were discharged in bankruptcy.

The Bankruptcy Code provides financially distressed debtors with a fresh start by discharging most of their pre-petition debts. * * * However, under 11 U.S.C. § 523(a)(8), there is a presumption that educational loans extended by, or with the aid of, a governmental unit or nonprofit institution are non-dischargeable unless the debtor can demonstrate that their repayment would be an undue hardship. See [Citation]. This exception to a bankruptcy discharge ensures that student loans, which are typically extended solely on the basis of the student's future earnings potential, cannot be discharged by recent graduates who then pocket all of the future benefits derived from their education. See [Citation].

The debtor bears the burden of proving by a preponderance of the evidence that she is entitled to a discharge of the student loan. See [Citation]. That is, the debtor must prove that repayment of student loans will cause an undue hardship.

The Bankruptcy Code does not define "the undue hardship." Courts interpreting section 523(a)(8), however, have concluded that undue hardship [and] is something more than "garden-variety hardship." [Citation.] Only cases involving "real and substantial" hardship merit discharges. See [Citation.]

The Ninth Circuit has adopted a three-part test to guide courts in their attempts to determine whether a debtor suffering an undue hardship is required to repay a student loan:

1. First, the debtor must establish "that she cannot maintain, based on current income and expenses, a 'minimal' standard of living for herself and her dependents if forced to repay the loans." * * *

2. Second, the debtor must show "that additional circumstances exist indicating that this state of affairs is likely to persist for a significant portion of the repayment period of the student loans." * * *

3. The third prong requires "that the debtor has made good faith efforts to repay the loans. * * *"[Citation]

Debtor must satisfy all three parts of the test before her student loans can be discharged. Failure to prove any of the three prongs will defeat a debtor's case.

When this bankruptcy case was filed in September 2005, the debtor was a single woman and had no dependents. She is 39 years old.

Schedule I reported that the debtor was unemployed. The debtor's responses to the Statement of Financial Affairs revealed that she had received $5,500 in income during 2005 prior to the filing of the petition. Evidence at trial indicated that after the petition was filed, the debtor found work and earned a total of $9,424 in 2005. In 2004 and 2003, she earned $13,994 and $17,339, respectively.

Despite this modest income, the debtor did not immediately file an adversary proceeding to determine the dischargeability of her student loans. It was almost three years after the entry of her Chapter 7 discharge on January 3, 2006 that the debtor reopened her Chapter 7 case in order to pursue this adversary proceeding.

In her complaint, the debtor admits that after she received a discharge, she found part-time work with a church and later took a full-time job as a speech therapist. During 2006, the debtor earned $20,009 and in 2007 she earned $37,314. Hence, while it is clear the debtor's income was very modest in the time period immediately prior to her bankruptcy petition, her financial situation improved during her bankruptcy case.

The court cannot conclude based on the evidence of the debtor's financial circumstances up to the date of the discharge, that she was unable to maintain a minimal standard of living if she was required to repay her student loans.

However, in January 2007, the debtor was injured in an automobile accident. Her injuries eventually halted the financial progress she had been making and eventually prevented her from working. She now subsists on social security disability payments.

The circumstance creating the debtor's hardship, the automobile accident, occurred after her Chapter 7 petition was filed; indeed, approximately one year after her discharge was entered. The debtor is maintaining that this post-petition, post-discharge circumstance warrants a declaration that her student loans were discharged effective from the petition date.

When must the circumstances creating a debtor's hardship arise: before the bankruptcy case is filed; after the case if filed but prior to the entry of a discharge; or at any time, including after the entry of a discharge?

The court concludes that the circumstances causing a Chapter 7 debtor's financial hardship must arise prior to the entry of the discharge. If the circumstances causing a debtor's hardship arise after the entry of a discharge, those circumstances cannot form the basis of a determination that repayment of a student loan will be an undue hardship. * * *

[T]here is nothing in the Bankruptcy Code requiring that a complaint under section 523(a)(8) [to discharge student loans] be filed at any particular point in a bankruptcy case, whether it is filed under Chapter 7 or 13. [Relevant Federal Rules of Bankruptcy Procedure] permits such dischargeability complaints to be brought at any time, including after the entry of a discharge and the closing of the bankruptcy case. * * *

While a debtor's decision to file an action to determine the dischargeability of a student loan is not temporally constrained, this does not mean that a debtor's financial hardship may arise after a discharge has been entered. * * *

[The] *Coleman* [case, cited by debtor] deals with the ripeness of a dispute concerning the dischargeability of a student loan. [The Ninth Circuit held that it] is ripe for adjudication at any point during the case. The Ninth Circuit did not conclude, however, that a debtor could rely upon post discharge circumstances to establish undue hardship. In fact, the court in *Coleman* made clear that the debtor could take a snapshot of the hardship warranting a discharge of a student loan any time prior to discharge. [*Coleman* was a Chapter 13 case.]

Here, the debtor was injured in an automobile accident on January 17, 2007, almost exactly one year after her January 3, 2006 Chapter 7 discharge. Because the accident had no causal link to the misfortune prompting the debtor to seek bankruptcy relief in the first instance, the accident cannot be relied on to justify the discharge of the student loans because repayment would be an undue hardship.

To hold otherwise would mean that a bankruptcy discharge is a perpetual license to discharge student loans based on events that occur years after the bankruptcy discharge is granted. If a discharged debtor suffers later financial misfortune, that debtor must consider seeking another Chapter 13 discharge subject to the limitations imposed by [the sections of the code stipulating how often a person can petition for bankruptcy]. In the context of a second case, the debtor could then ask that the student loan be declared dischargeable under section 523(a)(8).

In this instance, the debtor is now eligible for a discharge in a Chapter 13 case. * * * She would not be eligible for a Chapter 7 discharge until September 19, 2013.

This is not to say that post-discharge events are irrelevant. The second and third prongs of the Pena test require the court to consider whether the circumstances preventing a debtor from repaying a student loan are likely to persist, and whether the debtor has made good faith efforts to repay the student loan. Post-discharge events are relevant to these determinations because they require the court to look into the debtor's financial future.

Unfortunately for the debtor, it is unnecessary to consider the second and third prongs because she cannot satisfy the first prong.

Case Questions

1. What is the rationale for making the bankruptcy discharge of student loans very difficult?

2. Petitioner argued that she should be able to use a post-discharge event (the auto accident) asa basis for establishing that she could not maintain a "minimal" standard of living, and thus she should get a retroactive discharge of her student loans. What benefit is there to her if she could successfully make the argument, given that she could—as the court noted—file for Chapter 13?

3. The court cites the *Coleman* case; that was a Chapter 13 proceeding. Here were the facts: Debtor had not yet completed her payments under her five-year repayment plan, and no discharge order had yet been entered; one year into the plan, she was laid off work. She had been trying to repay her student loans for several years, and she claimed she would suffer hardship in committing to the five-year repayment plan without any guarantee that her student loan obligations would be discharged, since she was required to commit all of her disposable income to payments under the plan and would likely be forced to pursue undue hardship issue pro se upon completion of the plan." In *Coleman*, the court held that Debtor could, post filing but pre discharge—one year into the five-year plan—bring up the hardship issue. Now, in the case here, after the auto accident, the petitioner "subsists" on Social Security disability payments, and she has almost $150,000 in debt, yet the court prohibited her from claiming a hardship discharge of student loans. Does this result really make sense? Is the court's concern that allowing this post-discharge relief would mean "that a bankruptcy discharge is a perpetual license to discharge student loans based on events that occur years after the bankruptcy discharge is granted" well founded? Suppose it is scheduled to take

thirty years to pay off student loans; in year 4, the student-borrower, now Debtor, declares Chapter 7 bankruptcy, student loans not being discharged; in year 6, the person is rendered disabled. What public policy is offended if the person is allowed to "reopen" the bankruptcy and use the post-bankruptcy event as a basis for claiming a hardship discharge of student loans?

4. The court suggests she file for Chapter 13. What if—because of timing—the petitioner was not eligible for Chapter 13? What would happen?

Key Takeaway

Honest people sometimes find themselves unable to pay their debts. Federal law limits the most abusive debt-collection practices, and we no longer have debtors' prison (at least not directly). Debt relief is afforded under federal bankruptcy law and is available, to some extent, under state law too.

Exercises

1. Why is debt collection an actual job for professionals whose business it is?
2. Why was the Fair Debt Collection Practices Act adopted in 1977?
3. Ingrid Interior, an interior decorator, did not get paid $3,000 indisputably owed her by Carlene Customer for interior design and consultation. Is Ingrid bound to follow the FDCPA?
4. Why is bankruptcy law necessary?
5. What entities are entitled to protection under Chapter 7, Chapter 11, and Chapter 13?
6. Can a person in the United States today be put in jail for failure to pay debts?
7. What alternatives are there to federal bankruptcy?

15.5 Homelessness and Hunger: The Worst Insecurities

Learning Objectives

1. Recognize that homelessness is an aspect of far too many Americans' lives and that governments—federal, state, and local—attempt to address the problem. It is a complex issue.
2. Understand that many people in the United States are "food insecure"—they do not know if they will get a next meal. Governments at all levels attempt, with mixed success, to address the perennial human problem of hunger.
3. Know that some people have suggested a guaranteed income to address problems of poverty in the United States.

Homelessness

Introductory Note

It is difficult to imagine an insecurity more fundamentally unsettling than having no home—no place of your own to live, to have privacy, to be secure with oneself or loved ones. In the United States every year many millions of people suffer **homelessness**. You have seen them on the streets, pushing shopping carts with their few belongings, living under bridges and in tent encampments; they are in nearly every city. Here are some statistics from 2016 (the most recent year for which statistics are available):

> **homelessness**
>
> The condition, caused by poverty, of having no house to live in, no shelter.

- 570,000 people in the U.S. are homeless at any time—today. These people live in the streets, in cars, or in homeless shelters. One-quarter of them are children.
- About 3 million people each year experience homelessness and sleep in shelters, transitional housing, and places not intended for human habitation.
- Another 7 million or so have no home of their own and are doubled-up with others.
- 48,000 people are veterans (about 8% of homeless people), and another 1.4 million are at risk of homelessness.
- 550,000 unaccompanied single youth and young adults under the age of 24 experience homelessness.
- 110,000 LGBTQ youth in the U.S. are homeless
- Half the homeless are older than 50.[50]

In some places homelessness is probably more disturbing than others. The city of Seattle has some 3,000 homeless, "and no place to put them inside."[51] Meanwhile, less than five miles away, in Bellevue, the richest man in the world lives in an amazingly opulent and expensive house (Bill Gates and his wife certainly do fund one of the largest charitable organizations in the world). It doesn't seem right: can't we do better?

Causes of Homelessness

In one way, it's easy to know what causes homelessness: lack of money. People often cannot afford a place to live. Housing is too expensive, a problem exacerbated by "gentrification," and income insufficiency. Women particularly suffer from homelessness as a consequence of domestic violence and divorce. Mental illness and lack of needed services are also a significant factor. Homelessness is a huge issue; here we are concerned with what the government has done to provide some social safety net for the homeless.

Response to Homelessness

It is beyond the scope of this book to get into detail on the response to homelessness—it is a very complex problem. There are dozens of federal programs run by, among others, the federal Health and Human Services Department (https://www.usich.gov/solutions/housing); the Veterans Administration has programs and initiatives (https://www.va.gov/homeless/); as does Housing and Urban Development—the "Section 8 vouchers" are federal grants to help people afford housing—(https://www.hud.gov/topics/housing_choice_voucher_program_section_8). Every state has programs to address homelessness, as do thousands of counties and cities. There are a vast number of nongovernmental organizations attempting to address the problem (e.g., https://destinationhomesv.org/).

The problem is, of course, money. It costs money to help the homeless, and taxes are usually not popular. In Seattle, Amazon threatened to stop construction of a huge new office building if the city did not back down on its proposal to impose a 26-cent "per Seattle employee-hour" head tax on employers that gross at least $20 million per year. It's a "tax on jobs" says the Chamber of Commerce.[52] Indeed it is.

One homeless person in Seattle observed, "I am not homeless, I'm houseless." Seattle was his home, the problem was that digital behemoths—Amazon, Microsoft, and the like—hire thousands of relatively well-paid employees who bid up the cost of housing, drive rents up, and generally make it impossible for not-rich people to call a house a home. Homelessness remains a serious problem.

Food Insecurity

The problem is obvious. In 2015, some 16 million U.S. children lived in food-insecure families:

> After multiple risk factors are considered, children who live in households that are food insecure, even at the lowest levels, are likely to be sick more often, recover from illness more slowly, and be hospitalized more frequently. Lack of adequate healthy food can impair a child's ability to concentrate and perform well in school and is linked to higher levels of behavioral and emotional problems from preschool through adolescence.[53]

The cause—again, of course—is lack of money to buy food. It is difficult for many of us to believe—there are a lot of people in the United States who cannot afford food.

FIGURE 15.8 Adult Food Insecurity
Here, the federal Department of Agriculture graphs the percentage of households reporting *adult* food insecurity (the circumstance, caused by poverty, of having no sure next meal), and how such insecurity manifested itself.

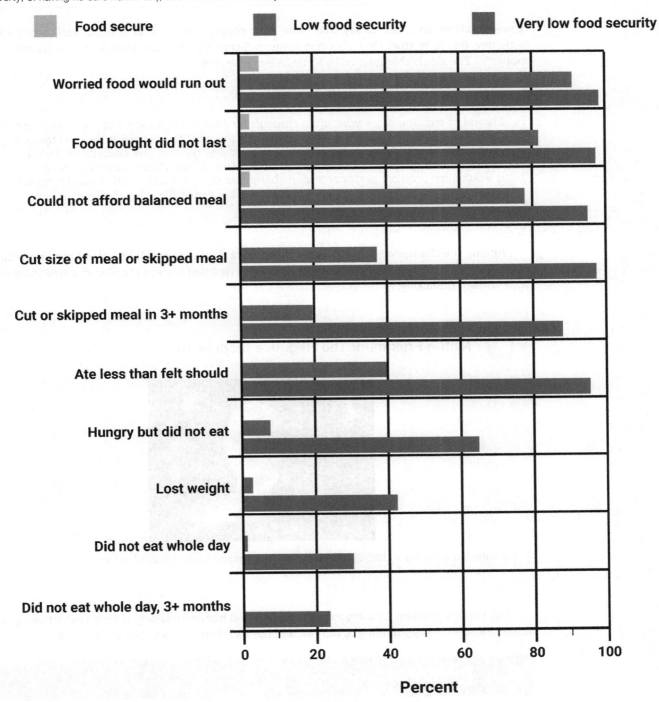

Guaranteed Income

It seems rather simplistic to say that what poor people need to find housing and to buy food is money, but it is true. One idea has been to "scrap the welfare state and give people free money."[54] The idea is championed by some free-marketeers:

> *Instead of treating those who, often through no fault of their own, have fallen on hard times like children who are incapable of making the right choices about the food they eat or the drugs they may or may not choose to take, why not just give them cash? Doing so would not only cut down on the huge administrative costs of America's welfare programs, it would also promote personal responsibility and abolish much of the humiliation and stripped dignity associated with the current welfare system.[55]*

Among the champions of the "negative income tax" was the much-heralded libertarian economist Milton Friedman. Here you can see Professor Friedman discuss the idea in a 1968 interview with William F. Buckley:

 Milton Friedman: The Negative Income Tax

View the video online at: http://www.youtube.com/embed/xtpgkX588nM?rel=0

But here's a problem: to some extent people spend money unwisely. If they spend their guaranteed income on, say, gambling or alcohol, and then are homeless and hungry, what then?

Key Takeaway

To provide some security against ruinous medical bills, the federal government has a number of programs addressing non-work-related illnesses and injuries, including Medicare, Medicaid, CHIP (for children of poor families), Veterans, Indian health services, and "Obamacare." For work-related injuries the federal and state governments coordinate to provide workers' compensation, post-work compensation programs (COBRA) and—to prevent injuries in the first place—OSHA (occupational safety rules).

Debtors are protected against the most egregious debt-collection practices by the Fair Debt Collection Practices Act (it only applies to professional debt collectors). Federal bankruptcy laws provide mechanisms by which individuals and businesses may discharge their debts and make a "fresh start," and there are non-federal debtors' relief laws, both common-law and statutory.

Homelessness is an especially poignant type of insecurity. Governments at the federal and state level address the issue with varying degrees of success, and thousands of nongovernmental organization—charities and churches—work the problem. To some extent, too, governments and NGOs address food insecurity problems.

Exercises

1. Critics of "Obamacare" are determined to undo this federal health insurance program which has provided some degree of security for tens of millions of people. If the program is abolished the United States would be the only "advanced" country in the world that doesn't have a national health insurance program. What is the objection to the program, and what will happen to people who lose their insurance coverage?

2. At common law, an employee who suffered injury on the job could sue the employer if the employer was negligent; the family of an employee who was killed could likewise sue. What was wrong with this state of affairs that gave rise to the demand and implementation of workers' compensation?

3. Linda Kidwell, employed by the CHP, hurt herself at home practicing the standing long jump, a required test protocol of the California Highway Patrol's annually-administered physical fitness test. She filed a workers' compensation claim. Is she entitled to workers' comp benefits? What is required to be so entitled?[56]

4. OSHA's funding was cut by the Donald Trump administration in its first year—40 inspectors who quit through attrition were not replaced. In March 2017, the Trump administration killed an Obama-era OSHA regulation that "required businesses competing for large federal contracts to disclose and correct serious safety and other labor law violations." And, Congress killed a long-standing OSHA regulation that allowed the agency to issue citations and fines for companies that failed to keep proper records of illnesses, injuries, and death that dated back as far as five years. Why would a company not want to keep proper records of such occurrences? Why would Congress want to kill the rule? Why would some government leaders not want businesses competing for federal contracts to disclose serious OSHA violations before the business gets a contract?[57]

5. Why does the Fair Debt Collections Practices Act apply only to *professional* debt collectors?

6. The Constitution provides that Congress can make "uniform laws on bankruptcy." Why would it be a bad idea if the states could make up their own bankruptcy laws?

7. Homelessness and hunger are, basically, the result of people being too poor to afford housing and food. People can get housing assistance and food hand-outs, but what would make such charity unnecessary and why are such alternatives not widespread enough to address the problem?

15.6 Summary and Exercises

Summary

A basic human need, and the fundamental purpose of government, is to provide some degree of security. A traditional rule fostering significant *insecurity* is the common-law doctrine of employment at will. At common law, an employer was free to fire an employee for any reason or for no reason at all. In recent years, the employment-at-will doctrine has been seriously eroded.

Many state courts have found against employers on the basis of implied contracts, tortious violation of public policy, or violations of an implied covenant of good faith and fair dealing.

The Fair Labor Standards Act (1938) sets minimal federal standards for wages, hours worked, and child labor (among others).

Beyond a reasonably secure income, we need security against the inevitable interruptions in such income caused, in a modern economy, by unemployment and by old age or disability. Unemployment compensation is a joint state-federal insurance program for unemployed workers funded by a payroll tax on employers and employees. Social Security is similarly funded to provide federal old-age and disability pensions for elderly and disabled workers; private pensions are subject to regulation by federal law to help ensure their integrity and effectiveness.

Most people require health insurance if they are to receive even modest medical care. The federal government insures millions of people through Medicare, Medicaid, Children's Health Insurance, veterans insurance, Indian Health Insurance, and "ObamaCare."

Workers' compensation provides medical, disability, and pension insurance for many workers who suffer injury or illness in the course of their employment. It is funded by a joint employer-employee payroll tax based on the number of claims made by the employer: the more likely an employee is to get injured, the higher the tax (or insurance premium). Federal employees are also covered by workers' compensation programs, and workers are, in many cases, allowed to continue on their former employer's group-insurance programs (under COBRA, though the former employee must pay the cost). To prevent injuries in the first place, OSHA and its state equivalents set out rules to avoid dangerous conditions in the workplace.

Capitalism requires some degree of individual financial risk taking. If the risk fails, it is not acceptable for people to be mercilessly dunned by their creditors, hence the Fair Debt Collection Practices Act limits the debt-collection practices of professionals. And, if the risk fails it is also not acceptable for debtors to be thrown into hopeless poverty by forcing them to meet their financial obligations if they are insolvent. Federal bankruptcy law provides significant relief for distressed debtors, both through straight bankruptcy (liquidation) and several reorganization and adjustment-of-debts options. State law provides alternatives to bankruptcy.

Of all the insecurities, hunger and homelessness are no doubt the most pressing. They are also difficult and expensive to address. The various governments—federal, state, and local—and nongovernmental organizations have many programs that address these issues. The programs are by no means adequate to meet the need. Some people have suggested just giving poor people money—it would obviate the welfare system as we know it.

Exercises

1. Why does the federal government run a health insurance program for Native Americans ("Indians")?
2. What has been the major objection to "Obamacare" by its dogged critics?
3. In the old days debtors would be put in prison until they could pay their debts. Why is debtors' prison not a very good idea?
4. In bankruptcy, what is the "stay on proceedings" and why is that important to debtors?

5. What is a "negative income tax" and why would libertarians—those wanting a minimum of government—champion such a thing?

6. Eleanor Employee, a hard-working single mother of two, worked for ten years at Mid-American Manufacturing, at which time her supervisor told her the business was being relocated to Mexico. Does Eleanor have any job-saving protection under the employment-at-will doctrine?

7. Why did Congress adopt the WARN Act?

Self-Test Questions

1. Why does a modern economy require some social safety net for citizens?

   a. employers generally do not pay enough for employees to get along.

   b. people, in general, tend to be lacking in foresight, so government must help them financially.

   c. the inevitable vicissitudes of life cause income interruption, illness, and injury for which most people have inadequate resources to address.

   d. two of the above.

   e. none of the above.

2. The employment-at-will doctrine provides for which of these:

   a. In general, employees can keep their jobs as long as they wish, except for misconduct or necessary layoffs because of a decrease in work available.

   b. Employers can fire employees at any time for any reason.

   c. Employers can fire employees for any reason, but not a bad reason.

   d. Employers can only dismiss employees if any employee has violated a legal requirement.

   e. Nepotism is generally considered an unconscionable reason to dismiss an employee.

3. The Fair Labor Standards Act does *not* address which issue:

   a. Minimum wage.

   b. Pregnancy discrimination.

   c. Maximum hours for managerial employees.

   d. Child labor.

   e. Two of the above.

4. Unemployment compensation is paid for by a tax on employers only.

   a. true

   b. false

5. The "WARN Act":

   a. requires that employers give 30 days' advance notice to any employee about to be laid off.

   b. sets up workplace safety rules for warehouses and animal processing plants.

   c. provides that municipalities must inform residents if their water is not up to federal drinking-water standards.

   d. establishes a system of sanitation standards for food workers.

   e. requires employers to give employees and the local government advance notice of mass layoffs.

6. Social Security benefits are funded by:

   a. taxing employers

   b. a federal tax on corporations and other limited-liability business organizations.

   c. co-equal taxes paid by the employer and the employee.

d. a tax of about 8% levied on the active-working employee's income up to $3 million.

e. a tax on employees to establish a fund for that employee to retire on.

7. ERISA regulates what?

a. Credit union savings accounts.

b. Disclosure requirements for sellers of annuities.

c. Interest rate calculations on consumer goods costing more than $3000.

d. Private pension funds.

e. Debt collection practices by private parties collecting their own debts.

8. Aside from "Obamacare," the federal government leaves the states to provide health insurance for most residents.

a. true

b. false

9. The Centers for Disease Control and Prevention may best be described as:

a. a federal initiative to prevent diseases affecting major crops to help farmers use fewer chemicals.

b. a U.S. agency that addresses teen pregnancy.

c. a federal agency that promotes safe toys for infants and children less than 6 years old.

d. the federal agency that works to promote health and safety for residents in the United States.

e. none of these.

10. At common law, an injured employee could sue the employer if the latter's negligence caused the employee disease or injury.

a. true

b. false

11. Which of the following was *not* among the common-law defenses available to an employer when an employee sued claiming the employer's negligence caused the employee injury?

a. contributory negligence.

b. comparative negligence.

c. assumption of the risk.

d. fellow servant (or "fellow employee") rule.

e. all of these were common-law defenses.

12. Federal workers are covered by the same workers' compensation laws as private employee workers.

a. true

b. false

13. Federal unemployment compensation programs are managed by:

a. the Social Security Administration.

b. the Works Progress Administration.

c. state workers' compensation agencies.

d. the National Labor Relations Board

e. the American Employee Protection Board

14. The Fair Debt Collection Practices Act applies to:

a. debt-collection agencies attempting to recover debt discharged in bankruptcy.

b. private individuals collecting their own debt.

c. debt collection practices for creditors enforcing government-insured student loans.

d. professional debt-collection agencies practices.

e. medical debt collectors.

15. The most common bankruptcy is which chapter:

a. chapter 7, straight bankruptcy.

b. chapter 9, secured transactions.

c. chapter 11, corporate reorganization

d. chapter 12, farmers' insolvency

e. chapter 13, "wage earner's plan"

Self-Test Answers

1. c

2. c

3. e (b and c)

4. b

5. e

6. c

7. d

8. b

9. e (because it works to protect Americans all over the world)

10. a

11. b

12. b

13. c

14. d

15. a

Endnotes

1. http://www.presidency.ucsb.edu/ws/?pid=14916.

2. In the U.S., these were county-run working farms where residents were housed; they were expected to labor as much as their health allowed, on the farm itself, or by providing housekeeping for others residents.

3. *Fortune v. National Cash Register*, 364 NE2d 1251 (Mass., 1977).

4. The idea was that if, for example, the government ordered the employer to pay a wage of fifty cents per hour when the employer was willing to pay and the employee was willing to accept twenty-five cents per hour, then the government was "taking" twenty-five cents per hour times all the hours of all the employees—hundreds of thousand of dollars over a year, perhaps. And all this forfeiture by the employer occurred with no trial, no finding of liability for negligence or breach of contract.

5. 247 U.S. 251 (1918).

6. *Baily v Drexel Furniture*, 259 U.S. 20 (1920).

7. 261 U.S. 525 (1923).

8. *Murphy v. Sardell*, 269 U.S. 530

9. *Donham v. West-Nelson Mfg. Co.*, 273 U.S. 657

10. *Moorehead v. New York*, 298 U.S. 587 (1936).

11. 298 U.S. 587 (1936).

12. And there is an interesting bit of history here, too. In the face of an intransigent Court that repeatedly struck down ameliorative legislation, President Roosevelt had an idea. The Constitution sets out a Supreme Court, but it doesn't say how many judges are on it. Roosevelt proposed to get Congress to change the law so that the president could nominate and the Senate approve as many new justices as needed to give the president's judicial philosophy a majority on the bench. Even President Roosevelt's staunch supporters thought this "Court packing plan" was going too far. Before it could be implemented—maybe the threat helped—the Court did its about face and stopped applying substantive due process to strike down federal economic regulations. https://www.history.com/this-day-in-history/roosevelt-announces-court-packing-plan. Here you can listen to President Roosevelt explain his plan: https://fdrlibrary.org/utter-ancesfdr (about the sixth recording down the list).

13. The federal Department of Labor has a user-friendly video explaining workers' rights under the FLSA: https://www.youtube.com/watch?v=SUstGn-mxP9l&feature=youtu.be

14. Albuquerque, New Mexico; Berkeley, California; Bernalillo County, New Mexico; Birmingham, Alabama; Chicago, Illinois; Cook County, Illinois; Cupertino, California; El Cerrito, California; Emeryville, California; Flagstaff, Arizona; Las Cruces, New Mexico; Los Altos, California; Los Angeles County, California; Los Angeles, California; Malibu, California; Milpitas, California; Minneapolis, Minnesota; Montgomery County, Maryland; Mountain View, California; Nassau, Suffolk, and Westchester Counties, New York; New York City, New York; Oakland, California; Palo Alto, California; Pasadena, California; Portland Urban Growth Boundary, Oregon; Portland, Maine; Prince George's County, Maryland; Richmond, California; San Diego, California; San Francisco, California; San Jose, California; San Leandro, California; San Mateo, California; Santa Clara, California; Santa Fe City, New Mexico; Santa Fe County, New Mexico; Santa Monica, California; SeaTac, Washington; Seattle, Washington; Sunnyvale, California; and Tacoma, Washington

15. See: https://www.law.cornell.edu/uscode/text/29/254

16. https://www.dol.gov/whd/fmla/. Probably the FMLA is not of very much use to employees who cannot afford to take unpaid leave—it is not very useful except for fairly well-to-do employees.

17. https://www.dol.gov/whd/regs/compliance/whdfs73.htm

18. Here you can find state wage and hour laws compared: https://www.dol.gov/general/topic/youthlabor

19. http://aboutunemployment.org/faqs/best-and-worst-states-for-unemployment-benefits/

20. https://www.doleta.gov/layoff/pdf/WorkerWARN2003.pdf

21. Drew DeSilver, "Who's Poor in America? 50 years into the 'War on Poverty,' a Data Portrait, *The Pew Research Center*, January 13, 2014. http://www.pewresearch.org/fact-tank/2014/01/13/whos-poor-in-america-50-years-into-the-war-on-poverty-a-data-portrait/

22. Janet M. Corrigan, et al., Leadership by Example: Coordinating Government Roles in Improving Health Care Quality, *Institute of Medicine of the National Academies*, 2013. https://www.nap.edu/read/10537/chapter/4#29

23. Ibid.

24. https://www.medicaid.gov/medicaid/benefits/index.html

25. Note 11, supra.

26. *Ibid.*

27. https://www.va.gov/health/http://www.cpsc.gov/en/

28. Note 11, supra.

29. The term "Obamacare" was invented by Republicans to ridicule, and thus help in their repeated efforts to repeal, President Obama's landmark federal national health insurance program. Campaigning in late 2011 Mr. Obama asked—speaking of the Republicans—"They call it 'ObamaCare? I do care! That's their main agenda? That's their plank? Is making sure 30 million people don't have health insurance?" Julian Pecquet, "President Embraces 'ObamaCare Label," *The Hill*, October 6, 2011. http://the-hill.com/policy/healthcare/185877-president-embraces-obamacare-label

30. Jessica C. Smith and Carla Medalia, U.S. Census, September 2015, "Health Insurance in the United States: 2014." http://www.pnhp.org/news/2015/september/census-bureau-33-million-uninsured-is-good-news

31. Tony Abraham, "Patient Dumping a Symptom of Health System Woes," February 5, 2018. HealthcareDive, https://www.healthcaredive.com/news/patient-dumping-symptom-of-health-system-woes/516018/

32. Assistant Secretary for Financial Resources, Department of Health and Human Services (2017-05-19). "FY 2018 Budget in Brief - CDC". HHS.gov. Retrieved 2018-04-19.

33. Office of the Associate Director for Communication. State of CDC: Budget and Workforce" (XHTML). CDC Impact Story Topics. Centers for Disease Control and Prevention.

34. Julie Barzilay, et al., "Why the CDC Hasn't Launched a Comprehensive Gun Study in 15 years, *ABC News*, June 16, 2016. http://abcnews.go.com/Health/cdc-launched-comprehensive-gun-study-15-years/story?id=39873289 and see also https://www.dallasnews.com/news/news/2016/06/13/the-cdc-isnt-banned-from-studying-gun-violence-its-just-too-scared-to-do-its-job.

35. https://gun-control.procon.org/view.resource.php?resourceID=006094.

36. *New York Central R. Co. v. White*, 243 U.S. 188 (1917)

37. http://www.takecarewageworks.com/doc/COBRA/WW-5163-STATE-CONT-INFO_072111v1_000.pdf

38. https://www.michigan.gov/documents/uia/COBRA_FILE_271421_7.pdf

39. https://www.dol.gov/recovery/

40. John P. Hankey, in "The History of Railroads that Tamed the West" (documentary video): https://binged.it/2Th55YE

41. https://www.osha.gov/about.html

42. Here you can find the complete listing of OSHA regulations: http://www.osha.gov/pls/oshaweb/owasrch.search_form?p_doc_type=STANDARDS&p_toc_level=0&p_keyvalue=.

43. https://www.osha.gov/news/newsreleases/region1/03272018

44. https://www.floridawc.com/workerscompensation/policy/rates/

45. *Duty v. General Finance Corp.*, 273 SW 2d 64 (1954)/

46. See *Fletcher v. Western National Life Insurance Co.*, 10 Cal.App.3d 376 (1970).

47. EY [Ernst & Young, Accounting Firm], "The Impact of Third-Party Debt Collection on the U.S. National and State Economies in 2013," http://www.wacollectors.org/Media/Default/PDFs/_images_21594_impacteconomies2014.pdf

48. Eli Hager, "Debtors' Prisons, Then and Now. Congress Outlawed Them. The Supreme Court Ruled Them Unconstitutional. Yet They Live On." *The Marshall Project*, February 24, 2015. https://www.themarshallproject.org/2015/02/24/debtors-prisons-then-and-now-faq

49. Some people feel they have a moral obligation to pay their debts, pretty much no matter what. Some people don't qualify for bankruptcy protection because they make too much money.

50. Social Solutions, "2016's Shocking Homelessness Statistics," http://www.socialsolutions.com/blog/2016-homelessness-statistics/

51. http://time.com/4598570/seattle-homelessness-sweeps-tent-encampments/

52. Daniel Beekman, "Seattle City Council Releases Plan to Tax Businesses, Fund Homelessness Help," *The Seattle Times*, May 3, 2018. https://www.seattletimes.com/seattle-news/politics/seattle-city-council-releases-plan-to-tax-businesses-fund-homelessness-help/

53. http://pediatrics.aappublications.org/content/early/2015/10/20/peds.2015-3301

54. Matteh Feeney, "Scrap the Welfare System and Give People Free Money," Reason: Free Minds and Free Markets, https://reason.com/archives/2013/11/26/scrap-the-welfare-state-give-people-free/

55. Ibid.

56. *Kidwell v. Workers' Compensation Appeals Board*, 39 Cal. Rptr. 2d 540 (1995).

57. Suzy Khimm, "Number of OSHA Workplace Safety Inspectors Declines under Trump," *NBC News*, January 8, 2018, https://www.nbcnews.com/politics/white-house/exclusive-number-osha-workplace-safety-inspectors-declines-under-trump-n834806. And Kimberly Kindy, Trump Kills Second of Two Obama-era Worker Safety Rules," *The Washington Post*, April 4, 2017, https://www.washingtonpost.com/news/powerpost/wp/2017/04/04/trump-kills-second-of-two-obama-era-worker-safety-rules/?noredirect=on&utm_term=.fc18ed2da9f8 .

Index